The Pioneer History of Illinois containing The Discovery in 1673

John Reynolds

Copyright © BiblioLife, LLC

This book represents a historical reproduction of a work originally published before 1923 that is part of a unique project which provides opportunities for readers, educators and researchers by bringing hard-to-find original publications back into print at reasonable prices. Because this and other works are culturally important, we have made them available as part of our commitment to protecting, preserving and promoting the world's literature. These books are in the "public domain" and were digitized and made available in cooperation with libraries, archives, and open source initiatives around the world dedicated to this important mission.

We believe that when we undertake the difficult task of re-creating these works as attractive, readable and affordable books, we further the goal of sharing these works with a global audience, and preserving a vanishing wealth of human knowledge.

Many historical books were originally published in small fonts, which can make them very difficult to read. Accordingly, in order to improve the reading experience of these books, we have created "enlarged print" versions of our books. Because of font size variation in the original books, some of these may not technically qualify as "large print" books, as that term is generally defined; however, we believe these versions provide an overall improved reading experience for many.

THE PIONEER
HISTORY OF ILLINOIS

CONTAINING

THE DISCOVERY IN 1673,

AND THE

HISTORY OF THE COUNTRY TO THE YEAR 1818,

WHEN THE STATE GOVERNMENT WAS ORGANIZED.

BY

JOHN REYNOLDS,

LATE GOVERNOR, MEMBER OF CONGRESS, STATE SENATOR
AND REPRESENTATIVE, ETC., ETC ;

AUTHOR OF
"JOHN KELLY", "A GLANCE AT THE CRYSTAL PALACE IN THE CITY OF NEW YORK",
"MY OWN TIMES", ETC.

SECOND EDITION,

WITH

PORTRAITS, NOTES, AND A COMPLETE INDEX.

(FIRST EDITION "PUBLISHED BY N. A RANDALL, BELLEVILLE, ILL , 1852.")

CHICAGO:
FERGUS PRINTING COMPANY,
185–193 ILLINOIS STREET.
1887.

PUBLISHERS' ARGUMENT.

THE success which attended our republication of Gov. Reynolds' "My Own Times", and the favorable comments which such rehabilitation received from the press and the public; was a sufficient attestation of two facts: that works of unquestioned historic value and accuracy are demanded and appreciated; and that research that develops additional facts or adds to the intrinsic value of some historic exposition, also receives commendation from the student and the reader, even if such illumination should, by the cold light of reason, dissipate some of the roseate hue of romance.

Therefore the publishers determined upon issuing the present volume, Reynolds' PIONEER HISTORY OF ILLINOIS, and in adding such explanatory notes, comments, and biographical data obtainable as will be not alone requisite to a thorough comprehension of the text, and the individuals therein discoursed upon; but will also add to the valuable information contained in the original volume. This material has long been cited by numerous authorities as a well-spring of historical data, crystalline and sparkling; the very brusqueness of Gov. JOHN REYNOLDS' phraseology—like the emery-wheel of the lapidary—but makes the delineation clearer and crisper, the description more forcible and vivid, and his admirable common-sense renders his deductions the most feasible solutions of a problematic question.

Occasionally, however, the depicting of individuals by the historiographer has to be read *cum grano salis;* as he would allow his imagination to run riot with his pencil in eulogizing those persons for whom he entertained sentiments of admiration; but in the essentials of history, Gov. John Reynolds is eminently reliable, his biographical utterance being merely an expression of his own opinion—a character appended to the picture by "Old Ranger".

As instances of the value added to the original matter by the annotations and *addenda* of the publishers, especial attention is called to the picture and description of the celebrated François Vigo, and, *inter alia*, the list of the first pensioners who received

PUBLISHERS' ARGUMENT.

lands under acts of Congress; while, as examples of how history, written thirty years since, may be augmented in value by subsequent research, these instances are cited.

[From the *Missouri Gazette and Illinois Advertiser*, Saturday, May 25, 1816]
"FIFTY DOLLARS REWARD
will be given to any person who will deliver to me, in Cahokia, a negro boy named Moses, who ran away from me in Cahokia about two months since. He is about 16 years old, well made, and did belong to Messrs McNight & Brady in St Louis, where he has been seen frequently, and is supposed to be harbored there or about there. He had on a hunting-shirt when he left me May 14, 1816 JOHN REYNOLDS "

[From the *Illinois Herald*, Oct 1, 1815]
"NOTICE —I have for sale 22 slaves Among them are several of both sexes, between the years of 10 and 17 years If not shortly sold, I shall wish to hire them in Missouri Territory I have also for sale a full-blooded stud-horse, a very large English bull, and several young ones. October 1, 1815 NINIAN EDWARDS."

Both the above advertisements demonstrate a fact of which Gov. Reynolds says nothing: that both he and Gov. Edwards were adherents of the "peculiar institution", and believers in the doctrine that property in a human being could be held by legal tenure; and that no inconsideration for the feelings of his fellow-creatures was a motor in Gov Reynolds' entity the following advertisement will manifest.

[From the *Illinois Herald*, Kaskaskia, Ill., Dec 16, 1815]
"To the poor people of Illinois and Missouri Territory. To the above class of mankind whose pecuniary circumstances will not admit of feeing a lawyer, I tender my professional services as a lawyer, in all courts I may practise in, without fee or reward JOHN REYNOLDS "

The paradox of a man owning human beings and treating them as chattels, and defending the legal rights of poor free-persons *gratis*, was only one out of many antagonisms created by the ownership of slaves. These three advertisements, exhumed from old newspaper files, testify to the accession of fact gained by patient investigation.

Thus, the publishers consider themselves justified in the completed volume here presented: the intrinsic value of the history is conceded, and their additions are merely cumulative evidence and testimony; and this republication places within the reach of every student or reader this intrinsically and extrinsically valuable work, and the knowledge of one's own country—which is commended as peculiarly desirable—is easily attainable from the writings of a careful, conscientious, and reliable narrator.

INTRODUCTION.

My friends will think it strange that I have written a book, no matter how small or unpretending it may be. Having the control of my time and actions, it was a very pleasant occupation to employ some of my leisure hours to write, in my humble manner, "The Pioneer History of Illinois." Time is rapidly sweeping off from the scene of action the pioneers of our country; and even the recollection of their actions will soon be forgotten, if no attempt is made to perpetuate the history of this worthy and noble race of men.

The pioneers suffered, without a murmur, all the privations and difficulties in the early settlement of the country; and by their energy, bravery, and sound practical sense, the country we now enjoy, with all the comforts and blessings of civilized life, they reclaimed from a wilderness infested with hostile savages and wild beasts

It is a story of these pioneers, French, British, and Americans, in their discovery and early settlement of Illinois, that I now attempt to narrate. Moreover, I know of no work, of this character, that is confined solely to the discovery and early settlement of Illinois, but the present unpretending one, which is now presented to the public. This was some inducement to the task I hope my humble performance may please and interest the reader, as it has done the writer.

Among the many authors I consulted on this subject, I obtained much valuable information from the works of my friend, the talented and Rev. Mr. PECK, of St. Clair County, Ill. Many facts stated in the "Pioneer History," since the year 1800, came under my own personal observation, which may be relied on as true.

This humble attempt at history must speak for itself, and the only recommendation I can give it, is, I think it contains the truth.

JOHN REYNOLDS.

BELLEVILLE, ILL., 1852.

ILLUSTRATIONS.

Gov John Reynolds, - - - -	Frontispiece
Fort Chartres, Plan of - - - - -	46
Gen George Rogers Clark, - - - -	83
Gen John Edgar, - - - - - -	116
Rev John Mason Peck, - - - -	253
Henry Gratiot, - - - - - -	309
Gov Shadrach Bond, - - - - -	323
Gov Ninian Edwards, - - - - -	367
Hon Daniel Pope Cook, - - - -	395
Gov Joseph Duncan, - - - - -	403
Col François Vigo, - - - - -	423

CONTENTS.

CHAPTER I.
The Indians of Illinois, - - - - - 17

CHAPTER II.
The Discovery and Settlement of Illinois, to the first Government of the "Company of the West," in 1718, - - - 25

CHAPTER III
Illinois under the French Government, - - - 46

CHAPTER IV.
Illinois under the British Government, - - - - 74

CHAPTER V.
Illinois under the Government of Virginia, - - 83

CHAPTER VI.
Illinois under the Government of the Northwest Territory, - 145

CHAPTER VII.
The Religion and Morals of Illinois prior to 1818, - 253

CHAPTER VIII
Illinois under the Government of Indiana Territory, - - 276

CHAPTER IX
Illinois under the Government of the Illinois Territory, - 365

Appendix, - - - - - - - - 419

Index, - - - - - - - - 427

THE PIONEER HISTORY OF ILLINOIS

CHAPTER I

The Indians of Illinois.

IT is difficult to give to the history of the Indians of Illinois any thing like authenticity. The information we obtain on this subject is frequently founded on Indian tradition, which is often destitute of truth

The explorers of the country from Canada, in the year 1673, found certain Indians southwest of Lake Michigan, whose generic name was known as *Illinois*, or *Illini*, as Hennepin wrote it Those Indians having that name, and residing on the banks of the river, gave that name to the Illinois River, and to the whole country, down to the mouth of the Ohio

We are informed that *Illini* means, according to the Indian understanding of that word, "real men" or "superior men" The Delaware Indians attach the same meaning to *Lenni*, and indicates, in their language, "real, or superior men."

The writers on this subject state: that almost all the Indians of North America are of the Algonquin race, except the Iroquois We may therefore conclude that the Delaware name of *Lenni*, or *Lenni-Lenape*, is the same as the *Illini*, which gave the name of Illinois If we take Indian tradition for our guide, we may conclude that the Delawares and the Illinois Indians are of the same family. Many of the western tribes call the Delawares their "Grandfathers"

It is an Indian tradition, that the Indians inhabiting the country between Virginia and Canada were of two races—the *Lenni-Lenape* and the *Mengwe* The *Lenni-Lenape* were the Delawares, and the *Mengwe* the Iroquois or Five Nations The tradition states further, that the *Lenni-Lenape* emigrated from the Far-west, to the *Namæ-si-sipu*—Mississippi or Fish River—

and there they found the *Mengwe*, who also came from the West, and inhabited the country toward the sources of the Missisippi. These migrating tribes found a great warlike nation, the Allewige, located in the country between the Mississippi and the Alleghany mountains. This nation gave the name of Alleghany to the river and mountains of that name. The Delawares and Iroquois united and conquered the country from the Allewige This Indian story is fortified by the missionaries Heckewelder and Zeisberger It is a fact, which is better than tradition, that the Iroquois conquered and drove out west the Delawares. The Delawares being relations of the western Indians, and being forced out amongst their cousins, they may have given the name *Illini* to the Indians inhabiting the banks of the Illinois River.

The derivation of the name, Illinois, is not important. The State and country have the name, and the citizens feel proud of it.

The Illinois Indians are of the Miami stock, as well as the Delaware, and in the year 1673, when the whites first visited the West, they occupied the country south of a line from about the lower *rapids* of the Mississippi to Ottawa, and down to the mouth of the Ohio.

The Illinois confederacy embraced five tribes: the Peorias, Cahokias, Tammarais, Mitchagamies, and Kaskaskias. The Mitchagamies at first occupied the shores of Lake Michigan, and gave the name to that Lake. Afterwards, we find them located on the Mississippi near Fort *Chartres*, in the present county of Monroe, Illinois They inhabited this tract of country before the year 1720, as the French Government reserved their lands from the whites from that date. Afterward they became extinct as a nation, and the remnants merged into the Kaskaskia tribe. The Peorias, Cahokias, and Kaskaskias occupied respectively the villages of Peoria, Cahokia, and Kaskaskia, and the country adjacent. The French continued the names of these villages, which they retain to this day. The Tammarais inhabited also the village of Cahokia, and the "country 'round about." They have left no name of any locality indicating their residence in Illinois, except, perhaps, the Twelve-Mile Prairie, in St Clair County In olden times, this prairie was called "*Prairie Tammarais.*" The tribe may have had a village in or near this prairie; but it has been swept off by time, so that their existence is only known in history.

These were the confederated tribes of Illinois Indians, who were gradually driven off by their enemies from the north to the south, until they took refuge amongst the whites, near the villages of Kaskaskia and Cahokia They diminished for more than one hundred years, and left the country at last, being a remnant only of their former greatness

A melancholy reflection forces itself on us: that the nearer the Indians reside to the white population, so much the worse it is for the Indians, and all the attempts heretofore made by the most worthy and pious men to Christianize and civilize the nations have produced an injury rather than a blessing to them. There may be some exceptions to this statement; but they are only exceptions which do not disprove the statement. The policy of the United States to remove the Indians as far as possible from the white population is the only course to preserve their existence. And it is doubtful, even if this humane policy will secure them from annihilation.

The Piankeshaws inhabited the country on both sides of the Wabash toward its mouth, and between the sources of the Kaskaskia and Saline rivers, to the Ohio. They have left no name in the country they occupied.

The Shawnee Indians had a village, in ancient times, on the north bank of the Ohio River, and inhabited the adjacent country. The same site is now occupied by Shawneetown, in Gallatin County, Illinois.

The Miamis inhabited the northeastern section of the present State of Illinois, but their country mostly lay east of that.

The Pottawatomie Indians occupied in modern times a large portion of the northeast section of Illinois They were a branch of the great Chippeway nation, and were also connected with the ancient Miamis. They extended their hunting and fishing almost the whole length of the Illinois River. But toward Chicago was their main residence. Branches of this nation extended to Wisconsin, Michigan, and Indiana. They were the largest nation of the West in modern times, and figured ferociously in the wars against the whites.

The Winnebagoes, or *Puants*, as the French called them, from their unsavory and "ancient fishy smell," inhabited the country west of Green Bay. The old French maps often call this bay *Le Baie des Puants*, for these Indians.

These Indians occupied a section of the northern part of Illinois, on Rock River, but their country, for the most part, lay north and east of that in Illinois. They were a tolerably large nation; but dirty and savage in their habits. If we can say anything of the Indians—that they advanced in civilization —it will be nearer true to say: the Winnebagoes advanced *backward*

There is a tradition amongst the Winnebagoes, and other nations, that the Winnebagoes emigrated from the West, and settled near the lakes. They claim no connexion with the other Indians, nor do I think there is any. Their language is different from any other near them. Almost all the nations in the West have some affinity in their language, except the *Puants*. They speak a gutteral language, and it is very difficult to learn or speak it. An interpreter must be raised with them, to be able to speak or understand their language. They are stout, robust people, and about the copper color of their Indian neighbors. Their cheek bones are higher, and they are generally a degree more uncouth and savage than the other tribes near them. I presume, they are not connected with any of the other tribes in the West.

A small, but energetic tribe of Indians, the Kickapoos, resided on the east side of the State of Illinois, between the Illinois and Wabash Rivers, and including the Sangamon River and the country thereabout. Some lived in villages near the Elk-Heart Grove, and on the Mackinaw River. They claimed relationship with the Pottawatomies, and perhaps the Sauks and Foxes also. This nation was the most bitter enemy the whites ever had. It may be said in truth of this tribe, that they were the "first in a battle, and the last at a treaty with the Americans." They were more civilized, and possessed more energy and talents than the other Indians in their vicinity. They were also more industrious and cleanly. They were better armed for war or the chase. This energy, and their implacable enmity to the United States, caused them to be first and the most efficient in all the Indian battles with the whites in the Northwest. They bore a conspicuous part against Harmar, St Clair, and Wayne; and at Tippecanoe they were first in all the bloody charges of that savage battle. The Kickapoos disliked the United States so much, that they decided that when they left Illinois, that they would not reside within the limits of our Government: but settle in Texas. What will they do now? Texas is annexed, and forms a part of the Union The northern tribes of Indians waged a destructive war against the Illinois Indians for ages, and at last nearly exterminated them. The last hostile attack was made by the Kickapoos, in 1805, against the poor Kaskaskia Indian children These children were gathering strawberries in the prairie above Kaskaskia, in this year, and their relentless enemy captured and carried away a considerable number of them. The Kaskaskias followed the Kickapoos, to recapture the children, a long distance; but failed to overtake them The enemy escaped with the children to their towns, and thus ended this outrage

Power in the hands of frail man—Indian or white—is apt to be abused The Northern Indians destroyed the Illinois tribes, because they had the power; and then the white man destroys the Indian, and occupies his country because the civilized man has the power.

"Man's inhumanity to man makes countless thousands mourn."

The Sauks and Foxes emigrated from the lakes west, and occupied the country on both sides of the Mississippi, of whose residence Rock Island was about the centre These Indians extended their hunting-ground toward Peoria, and to Galena and Wisconsin They are a large, stout, well-made people, and not so dark as the southern Indians. It was a band of these natives, called the British, or Black-Hawk Band, that caused so much trouble and expense to the United States, in the years 1831-2 Not only the expense, but many valuable lives were lost in this war, commonly known as the Black-Hawk War.

The Sauks and Foxes drove back the weaker nation—the Iowas—and occupied the country wherein the State of Iowa is established

In the year 1778, Julien Dubuque, a Canadian and a man of

talent and great enterprise, established a trading-post, near the present city of Dubuque, in Iowa. This trader was in fact a talented man, and was as such recognized by the Indians. All grave and important matters they submitted to his decision. The Indians, in a drunken frolic, caught a horse near the post of Dubuque—two got on the horse and run him throu' the prairie. The horse fell and killed one of the Indians. This homicide caused a bitter quarrel between the families of the two Indians. The family of the deceased insisted on revenge, and that was to be blood. The other side contended it was an accident, and blood should not be shed for it. The parties submitted the case to Dubuque, for his decision. After hearing the statements, Dubuque, in a grave and serious manner, pronounced judgment that it was just and right to have blood for blood—that no man had a right to shed his brother's blood without having blood shed for it. But Dubuque, in a most solemn and severe manner, also pronounced: that two Indians, one of each family, should mount the *same horse*, and run him throu' the prairie, until one or the other Indian be killed. This judgment reached the common-sense of the Indians and quieted the parties; and also raised Dubuque high in the estimation of the nation.

The city of Dubuque is called for this man, whose grave is situated near it. For years after Dubuque's death, the Indians kept a lamp burning at his grave every night, in honor of his memory. He was much esteemed by the whites as well as by the Indians.

It is impossible to ascertain the precise dates of Indian migrations. There are no records kept of the movements of Indians. Not long after the first whites came to the country, in 1673, the Illinois Indians were started south by their enemies, and in 1720 the Mitchagamia band was located on the Mississippi near Fort Chartres. Before the year 1730, the most of the Illinois Indians were forced south from the Illinois River. Kaskaskia was the last place of refuge for the whole of the Illinois confederacy, united into the Kaskaskia band, and from this place the tribe migrated west. About the year 1800, the whole confederated tribes amounted to about one hundred and fifty warriors.

At this time the Kaskaskia tribe had for their chief, Ducoign, who was a cunning man, and had considerable talents. He was a half-breed, and was well qualified to take charge of his nation in their present condition. He boasted of never—he or his nation—shedding white blood This no doubt was true, but the reason was that he and nation depended on the whites for support and protection. He had visited President Washington at Philadelphia, and wore a medal received from his great father, as he called the President. He had two sons, Louis and Jefferson Ducoign, who were drunken, worthless men.

A Peoria Indian, being bribed by the British, stabbed to death, in the streets of Cahokia, the celebrated Pontiac, the greatest Indian warrior, perhaps, that ever existed. This was one main reason the northern Indians were so bitter against those of Illinois.

These Kaskaskia Indians were afraid to venture out far from the white settlements, on account of the hostility of the other Indians. This almost forced them to starvation. Their spirit and national character were destroyed; and they became a degenerate people, always drunk, when they could obtain the liquor. By these means, they diminished, not only in numbers, but also in standing or character, until a few years ago the remnants of them moved to the Southwest.

Although it may seem hard, to force the Indians from their own country to accommodate the white population, yet it is the only wise and humane policy that can be adopted. The two classes of people can not live in peace together. The tide of white population is flowing on, and the Indians must recede from it. It is a heart-rending sight to see the poor natives driven from their own country. Their tears and lamentations on leaving Illinois would pierce a heart of stone.

We must submit to the decrees of Providence. It is quite possible, that these same tribes drove off the peaceable occupants of the country, and then took possession of it by force, as we have done. Moreover, I think Providence will be best pleased in having a greater number of the human family in existence than a few. A white population can sustain more numbers on the same territory than the Indian mode of living will permit. Nevertheless, it is difficult to find good reasons for the expulsion of the Indians from their own country. But, with, or without reason, the Indians must emigrate, leaving Illinois—the finest country on earth, for the peaceable occupation of the white man

There is another etimology of the name of Illinois. It is said, it is derived from *Isle au Noix*, the "Island of Nuts," in English. It is well known, that when the French first discovered the country, they were excited and enchanted with its fertility, climate, products, grapes, etc., etc ; and no doubt it was also blessed with nuts. And as the country was almost surrounded with rivers—the Mississippi, the Ohio, Wabash, Illinois, and Lake Michigan on the northeast—the country, in fact, was nearly an Island; so that it was not so unreasonable that the country should be called *Isle au Noix*. The sound of *Isle-au-noix* in French, is almost similar to that of Illinois.

CHAPTER II.

The Discovery and Settlement of Illinois, to the first Government of the "Company of the West," in 1718.

JAMES MARQUETTE, a Jesuit missionary, first conceived the idea to explore the Mississippi, and suggested it to M. Talon, the intendant of Canada. At length the governor of Canada, M. Talon, assisted Father Marquette in this laudable expedition, and joined with him M. Joliet, a merchant of Quebec.

The first white men that saw the Mississippi were DeSoto and his army in the year 1541 They crossed the Mississippi about the site of the present city of Memphis, Tennessee The next were Marquette and Joliet, Frenchmen from Canada, in the year 1673 The Mississippi lay quiet from the time DeSoto explored the lower Mississippi, until the indefatigable Jesuit, Marquette, entered it at the mouth of the Wisconsin.

In early times, two passions entered deep into the breasts of the people of Europe: one the Christianization of the North American Indians; and the other, a northwest passage to the East Indies and China Both of these popular enterprises sank deep into the heart of Marquette, but particularly the conversion of the Indians to the Christian faith M Joliet was a merchant of Quebec, and no doubt possessed the common mania of that day, for the Indian trade if nothing higher or better.

I am sorry I can not find much material for the history of Marquette He was, so far as I can discover, the Napoleon, the *ne plus ultra* of all the Indian missionaries in the Northwest. He was a Recollect monk and Jesuit, and was fired with all the zeal and enthusiasm of that order of religionists. He followed the footsteps of Layola, his illustrious predecessor, in all religious duties, so far as he had the ability to act. He had abandoned the Old World, and the common comforts and enjoyments of life, for the sole object of Christianizing the Indians in the wilds of America. He gave himself up entirely to the most severe and dangerous services—to uncommon hardships and perils, and almost starvation itself, amongst the wildest savages of North America. All these dangers and perils did he perform and endure, with the greatest pleasure, because his conscience assured him he was doing the will of God. Among all the devout and benevolent Indian missionaries, Marquette, for his true piety, holiness of purpose, and grand enterprises he performed, stands unrivalled in the West. He at last ended his days, as he had lived them, in the actual service of God.

The Jesuits, at this time, were the most energetic order of Christians in Europe. There was no country on the globe but the Jesuits visited and administered to the spiritual wants of the people. Such was the case in the northwest of America. No Indian nation was too far off, or too wild, to deter these Jesuit missionaries from visiting. And Marquette was always first to do good in these missions.

In the year 1669, he had been out west of Green Bay, or *Le Baie du Puants*, as the French sometimes called it, preparing the Indians for his great enterprise West, and obtaining an Indian of the remote region of the Mississippi, for an interpreter.

These preparations being made, he and Joliet left Mackinac, the mission-station of Marquette, on the 13th May, 1673, for Green Bay. Father Marquette had been all thro' this region of country, and had acquired an excellent character amongst all the nations, for his piety and kindness to the Indians.

In two canoes, with five men, Marquette and Joliet left the missionary-station of Green Bay, on the 10th June, 1673, for the far-West. The Indians gave a terrible history of the monsters in the great river—that would swallow them up and their canoes. The Maneto at the Piasa was represented as devouring all passengers. This was to deter Marquette from his voyage, but he had the same fearless courage that Martin Luther possessed, when his friends persuaded him not to make a certain journey in Germany.

The explorers passed over the portage between Fox River and the Wisconsin, and down the latter to the Mississippi. They saw the Mississippi for the first time, June 17th, 1673, and "entered it," Marquette says in his journal, "with a joy I can not express." No doubt the hearts of these enthusiastic

French bounded with joy at the sight of this noble and majestic river.

They floated down the river about one hundred miles, and on the west side they discovered Indians. To use the pious language of Marquette, "they commended themselves to God, and approached the village." They remained with this tribe for six days, and "in full council" Marquette "proclaimed to them the one true God, the Creator." The journal of Marquette reports that "they passed the most beautiful confluence of rivers in the world," where the Missouri, called by the Indians *Peckitanoni*, mingles its muddy waters with the Mississippi. They mention the painted rock*—the Piasa—near the present city of Alton. They saw also the great rock, the grand Tower, in the Mississippi, and came to the mouth of the Ohio, which they mistook for the Wabash River.

It is well-authenticated history, that the hostility of the Iroquois Indians kept the French from any knowledge of the Ohio River for many years after the voyage of Marquette and Joliet to the West, and for a long time, the Ohio River was called the Wabash from the mouth of the Wabash down to the junction of the Ohio with the Mississippi.

After a few days' delay at the junction of the Ohio, Marquette and Joliet passed down the river to the Arkansas Indians, in latitude 33 degrees north. At this point, the party narrowly escaped destruction by the Arkansas Indians.

The pious-hearted Marquette says, "they resolutely presented the peace-pipe to the warriors, and God softened their hearts;" so the explorers escaped unhurt. They descended no further. This party reached somewhere on the river, about the place that DeSoto crossed it in the year 1541.

* I saw what was called the picture sixty years since, long before it was marred by quarrymen or the tooth of time, and I never saw anything that would have impressed my mind that it was intended to represent a bird. I saw daubs of coloring matter that I supposed exuded from the rocks that might, to very impressible people, bear some resemblance to a bird or a dragon, after they were told to look at it in that light, just as we fancy in certain arrangements of the stars we see animals, etc., in the constellations. I did see the marks of the bullets shot by the Indians against the rocks in the vicinity of that so-called picture. Their object in shooting at this place I never could comprehend. I do not think the story had its origin among the Indians or was one of their superstitions, but was introduced to the literary world by John Russell of Bluff Dale, Ill., who wrote a beautiful story about it —J. GILLESPIE, Jan 25, 1883

Marquette, being a little shocked by the warriors of the Arkansas, and also hearing it was a long voyage yet to the ocean, determined to return to the lakes. But after the reconciliation with the Indians, they feasted on corn and dogs This tribe cooked in and eat out of earthen-ware, and were at last kind and loving to their French friends.

On the 17th July, 1673, Marquette and company commenced to ascend the river. At the mouth of the Illinois, the Indians informed the explorers, that to ascend that river it was shorter to the lakes than by the route of the Wisconsin. The party ascended the Illinois, and entered the lake at the present city of Chicago, and in September they reached Green Bay in safety, not, during their voyage, losing a man, or receiving any hurt or injury whatever. Marquette writes that, "no where did we see such grounds, meadows, woods, stags, buffaloes, deer, wildcats, bustards, swans, paroquets, and even beavers, as on the Illinois River."

It is true, as Marquette states, that there are "no grounds" on earth superior in fertility and productiveness, than are found for many miles on each side of the Illinois River.

After the return of Marquette and Joliet to Green Bay, the latter proceeded to Quebec, while our pious Christian quietly returned to his Indian charge, laboring night and day to save the heathen from destruction.

Joliet, on his way to Canada, lost his papers, and nearly his life, by the upsetting of his canoe. By this misfortune the narrative of the discovery of the great Father of Waters was lost Marquette cared not so much for the discovery of the country, as the discovery of Indians, so they might be converted to God from savage paganism. Therefore he kept a very limited journal of their voyage; but it is recognized by all authors as correct and true Thus it is, that we find very little in detail of this discovery of a country, the valley of the Mississippi, which is not equalled for fertility of soil, climate, extent, and beautiful surface, on the globe. This valley extends from the Alleghany to the Rocky Mountains, a distance of nearly three thousand miles, and from the Gulf of Mexico to the sources of the Mississippi, with a climate of the temperate zone, congenial to the culture of almost all the produce of the earth. This valley is without mountains and without swamps, intersected with large navigable rivers, and possessing a surface adapted to the construction of railroads in every direction; so that, in fact, Marquette saw "a terrestial paradise," as the French called it, when he entered this valley, in 1673.

It appears, from the journal of Marquette, that they were astonished at the magnitude of their discoveries—the soil, the products, the rivers, buffaloes, etc.; but if they could have seen thro' the future to this time—1852—they would be still more amazed and astonished. The improvements of the country—the cities on the margins of the rivers they sailed on, and the large steamboats passing their bark canoes, would cause these Frenchmen to believe, that Omnipotent power alone could effect this extraordinary change. Almost the same conclusion will be forced upon all rational men: that the unparalleled growth of the United States is fostered by Divine Providence. Our free institutions, in the hands of Deity, are the foundation of our growth and prosperity. The Constitution of the United States presents to the world the perfection of human wisdom. Our national greatness and grandeur rest upon this glorious instrument It binds us together in patriotic love, from ocean to ocean, and from the tropics to the frozen North, and may God bless it and preserve it *eternal*.

Marquette and Joliet, on their return, made out such a glowing report that it set all Canada on fire, and also swept over France like a tornado The French, always excitable, caught the mania, and became almost crazy to see and settle the West This rage for western enterprise reached LaSalle, and bound him in its folds during the remainder of his life.

Robert de La Salle was a native of the city of Rouen, in Normandy, France; and possessed a liberal education. By some means he lost his patrimony and attached himself to the Jesuits. It is stated by his biographer, that he was a scholar, versed in the arts and sciences, and fitted for any business. The great and dominant trait of his character was an iron will, and a moral and physical courage; that all the evils of life—all the disasters and misfortune that man is heir to—had no effect on him A despondency or retreat found no place in his character. He also possessed, in an eminent degree, an ungovernable ambition.

When a character of this description gets strongly impressed with a great enterprise, he becomes enthusiastic and almost crazy on the subject. Such was the case with LaSalle, in the discovery, and the Indian trade of the far West,

LaSalle arrived in Canada in the year 1670, and had become, to some extent, acquainted with the country, at the time Marquette and Joliet reported their discoveries of the West.

He was strongly impressed with the notions of that day, to find a direct passage to China. He supposed a river might be found to ascend, which would lead a northwest route to the Pacific Ocean. He also urged warmly on Frontenac, the governor-general of Canada, the propriety, and even the necessity for France to establish a line of forts from Canada thro' the Illinois country to the Gulf of Mexico. The governor entered into the views of LaSalle with ardor, and advised him to lay his plans before the Government of France. LaSalle consented, and set sail for France in the year 1675. The minister of the king, the great Colbert, approved his scheme, and entered warmly into the subject. LaSalle was created chevalier, and invested with the Seigniory of Fort Frontenac, on condition that he would rebuild the fort. He returned to Canada and labored on the fort to the close of the year 1677 Again he returned to France, and was received with favor by the court. The king granted him new privileges. His mission having succeeded so well, that he procured his lieutenant, M Tonti, an Italian, and thirty men, and sailed from Rochelle the 14th July, to Quebec, where he arrived the 15th September, 1678. He made little or no stay at Quebec; but proceeded direct to Fort Frontenac. This fort occupied the site of the present town of Kingston, in Upper Canada.

Another character in these discoveries was Louis Hennepin. He was, as Marquette was, a Recollect monk of the Jesuit order; but very unlike the pious and pure-hearted Marquette, in almost everything else. He was full of ambition to be a discoverer—"daring, hardy, energic, vain, and self-exaggerating, almost to madness." He possessed talents and courage, but was ambitious of fame, even at the expense of truth

The religious superiors of Hennepin appointed him to proceed with the expedition of LaSalle, and he was ready at Fort Frontenac, October 1678.

What a contrast between these two dignataries of the church —Marquette and Hennepin. One dedicated himself entirely to the pious and holy works of religion, while the other wore the garb of religion to advance his own fame

Marquette returned to Illinois, and pursued his holy ambition in converting the Indians to Christianity, until the year 1675. On the 18th May of that year, he was with his boatmen on Lake Michigan, and proposed to stop and say mass. Leaving his men with the boat, he went a small distance to pray. He staid some time, and his friends became alarmed at his stay They called to mind something he had hinted, that "he should die there." They found the reverend father dead, in the posture of praying. The death of Marquette occurred at the mouth of a small river emptying into the lake from the east, which is named for him, and there he was buried in the sand. His body would have been exposed to the rise of the waters, but the river retired and left the holy man's grave in peace. Charlevoix was at the place some fifty years after, and discovered that the waters of the river had forced a passage in another direction, and cut through a solid bluff, rather than to disturb this good man's grave. Thus ended the life of Marquette, in glory, while Hennepin enjoys a celebrity of another character.

LaSalle and party, on the 18th November, 1678, embarked on a small vessel of ten tons, from Fort Frontenac to the West, and in four weeks' sailing on Lake Ontario, they landed near the Niagara River. The winter was setting in, and they remained in that neighborhood until the next spring.

Another vessel, the *Griffon*, was built during the winter and and spring of 1679, at the mouth of Tonnawanto Creek, and during this time, LaSalle returned again to Fort Frontenac On his return the vessel carrying his goods was destroyed, and part of his stores lost. This was the first of a series of misfortunes which he suffered.

On the 20th January, 1679, LaSalle arrived at Niagara; and this whole summer was employed by him, in preparing for the West, gathering furs, etc , while Chevalier Tonty was sent on West to prepare the way for LaSalle

On the 7th of August, 1679, the *Griffon* was ready to sail Then, with *Te Deum* and discharge of fire-arms, she set sail upon Lake Erie.

At Green Bay the *Griffon* was loaded with furs, and sent to Niagara, while LaSalle, with fourteen men, started for the Miamis, or St Josephs There the party waited for the return of the *Griffon*. At this point, LaSalle built a fort. The party, on the 3d December, consisting of thirty laborers, and three monks, went up the St Joseph, crossed the portage to *The-an-ke-ki*, now Kankakee, and down to the Illinois River About the last of December, they reached a village of the Illinois Indians, containing five hundred cabins; but no inhabitants. The travelers discovered a large quantity of corn, and being in great need of provisions, took as much of this article as satisfied their wants. This village is supposed to have been near the Rock Fort, LaSalle County, Ill. The party entered Peoria Lake on the 4th January, 1680, and proceeded some distance down the River, where they were well received by the Indians They obtained permission of the Indians to erect a fort at this place.

About the middle of January, the news of the loss of the *Griffon* and cargo reached LaSalle. Other disasters also visited him, so that he called this Fort *Creve Cœur*—in English, broken heart. LaSalle discovered a mutiny amongst his men; and also the Indians were excited to unfriendly feelings against him. But by a bold and daring energy, based on truth and honesty he quieted these troubles around him. Yet his heart was sorely afflicted, as the name of this fort indicated He was far in advance of the settlements of Canada—amongst Indians, whose friendship was precarious and uncertain; and even his own men, on whom he was compelled to rely for support in perils and dangers, were disaffected. Altho' all these calamities surrounded the Chevalier LaSalle, he hesitated not a moment in the pursuit of his daring object, the exploration and the commerce of the Mississippi

They completed the fort and established friendly relations with the Indian tribes far and near.

At this fort, some of LaSalle's own men, more treacherous than the red skins, attempted to poison him, but did not succeed. This great man was richly entitled to the honor of being called "Chevalier", as his fortitude and resolution never for a moment forsook him, in any of the perilous trials.

He organized a party to explore the upper Mississippi; while the reliable lieutenant of LaSalle, the Chevalier Tonty, would remain in the Fort *Creve Cœur*, and the brave Norman himself return to Fort Frontenac.

The exploring party consisted of Louis Hennepin, M. DuGay, or D'Ucan, and six Frenchmen, oarsmen, woodsmen, or otherwise, as occasion might require.

In bark canoes, on the 28th of February, 1680, they left Fort *Creve Cœur* for the Mississippi, and waited at the mouth of the Illinois River for ten days, to permit the floating ice in the Mississippi to pass out. Hennepin, with the consent of LaSalle, called the western side of the Mississippi Louisiana, in honor of the king of France, and the Mississippi, St. Louis River. One of these names remains to this day, while the old Indian name of the Mississippi was not changed by the French explorers

Hennepin and party proceeded up the river to the Great Falls, which he called St. Anthony, in honor of his patron saint of Padua. On a tree near the falls, the Franciscan friar and Jesuit monk, Hennepin, caused the cross and arms of France to be carved.

About the 11th of April, near the mouth of the Wisconsin, Hennepin's party were captured by the Sioux Indians; and detained in captivity for several months, but were released. They explored the river above the falls, up to latitude 44 deg. north, but not to the source, as Hennepin asserts. They met another party of French from Lake Superior, under the command of Sieur de Luth, trading and reconnoitring the country They returned by the route of the Wisconsin to Green Bay, the most western missionary station

The same season, 1680, Hennepin was ambitious to supercede LaSalle in the discovery of the mouth of the Mississippi— descended the Wisconsin and the Mississippi to the mouth of Arkansas, and returned late in the year to the upper Illinois. He then returned to Europe, and got into the hands of the British, who were jealous of the French discoveries in the New World, and the said monk and Jesuit priest published an inaccurate history of his exploration of the Mississippi. His book gave the world an untrue view of the discovery; but "truth is powerful," and did prevail. Altho' Hennepin is suspected of exaggeration, yet he did much, and showed himself a great man And I would ask any one to reflect on the situation of both Hennepin and Marquette, in their discoveries. They made these explorations without means and almost without men, and also without the direct sanction of their Government. I can not conceive how they procured their supply of provisions. I think they must have existed greatly on energy and enthusiasm

The Chevalier LaSalle, it is true, had the authority of his Government *direct;* but I can not find that he had any other support from his king He was crippled all the time by his commercial operations

In March, 1680, LaSalle, preparing himself with a gun and powder, with deer-skins for moccasons, and a sack of parched corn on his back, to eat, he and three men started on foot from Fort *Creve Cœur* to Frontenac This was a dreary and perilous trip Not only had LaSalle to pass over the black swamps in the northern part of the State of Ohio, which impeded General Harrison so much in the winter of 1813 in the war with Great Britain; but the Iroquois Indians were at that time engaged in a war with the French Altho' the journey was dangerous and perilous, he arrived safely at Fort Frontenac in June

LaSalle left M. Tonty in possession of Fort *Creve Cœur* and the country, "with orders to repair Fort St. Louis"

There is some confusion with authors in regard to these forts, and their precise location. There were two forts one called *Creve Cœur*, and the other Rock, or Fort St. Louis *Creve Cœur* was located somewhere, I presume, on the southeast side, eight miles above Peoria, on the lake; and Rock Fort, or Fort St. Louis, at either the Starved Rock, or the Buffalo Rock, in LaSalle County, Illinois. It is difficult to determine at this day, the exact location of either of these forts. The Starved Rock, or the Buffalo Rock either, will answer the description given them in the first exploration of the country I have often been on both these rocks, and think there is not room on the Starved Rock for a fortress Yet, it may have been large enough for the occasion It is easier fortified than the other.

The tradition of the Indians being starved on this rock, was unknown to the pioneers, or else we would have had the name in their journals. The tradition of calling this rock the Starved Rock, is a pretty tale, which may or may not be true. The history of the Buffalo Rock is believed by many that the French and Indians drove the buffaloes on this high ground on the northeast side, and forced them over the rocks at the southwest, where the rocks are perpendicular, and thereby killed them. The buffaloes were butchered, and the meat and skins shipped from that point to the New Orleans market These are the traditions of the names of these two localities in Illinois

Starved Rock and Buffalo Rock are both situated in, or adjacent to, the low lands of the Illinois River, and they and the country generally, exhibit indubitable evidence of a great volume of water, at some remote time, having passed down this valley of the Illinois River The Buffalo Rock rises up, in the midst of the low lands, or Illinois Bottom, to a great height, and is perpendicular on three sides It must have been an island in former days, when this whole valley of the Illinois River was water

At this remote period, the waters of the Niagara River passed down this valley. The outlet of the waters of the lakes was then not at Niagara Since the discovery of the country, the rocks at the falls of Niagara have been worn away by the action of the water flowing over them This outlet of the waters has been of modern 'date to the ancient discharge of the waters thro' the Illinois River. Engineers have leveled the country around the lakes and find that if the chasm at the falls of Niagara was filled up, the waters of the lakes would pursue their ancient course down the Illinois River The waters broke thro' the rocks at Niagara, and turned their course from the Illinois River to Lake Ontario The appearance of greater quantities of water having formerly passed than at present, is visible in many places on the Mississippi.

During the absence of LaSalle, in the summer of 1680, M. Tonty had much trouble with the Indians. The Iroquois waged a bitter war with the prairie Indians, which forced Tonty to join his neighbors of the West. This war brought him into great peril and danger, which at last compelled him to abandon Fort *Creve Cœur*, and seek safety at Mackinac.

After LaSalle enduring much embarrassment at Frontenac,

and on his journey out, he arrived at *Creve Cœur* late in December, or early in January, 1681. But to his great astonishment and disadvantage, found no one in the fort, altho' it was in good repair. This was another calamity to swell the list of misfortunes which he suffered But dejection or despondency found no place in his remarkable composition. He returned with his party to Mackinac, and greeted Tonty with the same feeling and friendship as if he had met his friend at the Hotel de Ville in Paris

LaSalle again visited Fort Frontenac, and made the last preparations for his grand discovery. On the 3d November, 1681, he was at the fort of St. Joseph, as full of courage as ever.

About the middle of December, with twenty-three men, eighteen eastern Indians, ten squaws, and three children, he started by the way of Chicago River, and on the 6th January, 1682, they left the borders of Lake Michigan, traveling on foot, and the baggage on sledges. They passed on to Fort *Creve Cœur*, and found that place in good repair On the 6th February, they were on the Mississippi, and on the 13th they set sail down that river

At the Chickasaw Bluffs they erected a fort, which they called Prudhomme, and on the 6th April they discovered the three outlets of the Mississippi into the Gulf of Mexico.

The following is the description of their doings at the mouth of the Mississippi by LaSalle himself: "We landed on the bank of the most western channel about three leagues from its mouth. On the 7th M. de la Salle went to reconnoitre the shores of the neighboring sea, and M de Tonty examined the great middle channel They found three outlets, beautiful, large, and deep On the 8th we reascended the river a little above its confluence with the sea, to find a dry place beyond the reach of inundations The elevation of the north pole was about twenty-seven degrees Here we prepared a column, and a cross, and to the said column we affixed the arms of France with this inscription:

"LOUIS LE GRAND, ROI DE FRANCE ET NAVAARE, REGNE;
LE NEUVIEME, AVRIL, 1682."

The whole party was paraded under arms, chanted the *Te Deum* and other hymns in praise of God for the great discovery

They shouted *Vive le Roi* and raised the column. LaSalle himself, in a very orderly and solemn manner, took possession for the King of France of all the country watered by the River Colbert, or Mississippi.

The provisions being scarce, Sieur LaSalle was compelled to return north; and became sick at Fort Prudhomme. He sent M Tonty on to the Governor of Canada with the report of his discoveries He himself did not reach the fort at the mouth of St Joseph River, until September At this place, LaSalle sent Father Zenobe with his despatches to the court of France, and he remained amongst the Indians, trading for their furs, and repairing his favorite fort, St Louis, supposed to be on the Buffalo Rock But hearing he had enemies at the government of France, who represented him as a man more ambitious to advance his own interest than that of his government, he, in the autumn of 1683, set sail for France and reached there on the 13th December The overbearing deportment of LaSalle, which was the greatest defect in his character, caused him many enemies, and amongst the rest was M. de la Barre, who had succeeded Count Frontenac in the government of Canada.

The presence of LaSalle put all idle rumors against him to flight at the court of his king The ministers saw him, believed him, and found him to be, what he really was, sincere, energetic, brave, and enthusiastic The king also believed, and the City of Rochelle resounded with the uproar of fitting out a fleet for the New World

On the 24th July, 1684, four vessels sailed from Rochelle, carrying two hundred and eighty persons for the mouth of the Mississippi Amongst these persons were soldiers, artificers, volunteers, and "some young women." They started with high hopes of honors and fortunes, but sad reverses overtook them Not one of the emigrants escaped destruction except six men with Joutel, who reached Illinois in the year 1687, in a most deplorable condition. LaSalle and Beaujeau, the commander of the fleet, did not agree on the voyage to America, but had a bitter quarrel, which was the cause, perhaps, of the failure of the expedition There is nothing so dangerous to an enterprise as quarrels amongst the leaders,—we see in ancient, as well as in modern times, disputes prove fatal to the greatest and best expeditions. M. Joutel was the commander of one hundred soldiers, and was a man of judgment and courage. He was afterward the historian of the expedition.

This fleet, after much delay, storms, and calms, and one vessel being captured by the Spaniards, on the 15th January, 1685, reached the coast of America in latitude 29, 10 degrees north, supposed to be not far from the mouth of the Mississippi. But LaSalle caused the fleet to sail west; so that the mouth of the river was not discovered for years afterward. While in the Gulf of Mexico, a storm visited the fleet and destroyed one of the vessels loaded with provisions, implements, and other necessary articles, which were all lost.

The marine commander Beaujeau considered he had performed his duty in reaching the Gulf of Mexico with the fleet, and decided he would land LaSalle and his colony and return to France. He came to this conclusion, more by the dissention between him and LaSalle than on any other consideration. The colony was landed at Madagorda Bay, now called St Bernard, seven or eight hundred miles by the indentations of the sea, west of the mouth of the Mississippi At this bay, LaSalle made a "lodgement," as he called it, and fortified the place to some extent.

Every hour and every day from LaSalle's landing at the Madagorda Bay until his assassination, he had more perils, difficulties, and calamities to encounter and suffer, until death seemed to be his best friend He never ceased hunting for the "hidden river" for two years. He tried to reach the Mexican colonies and failed, and made an attempt to go to the North, and also failed. In March, 1687, he started to the Illinois country, in company with sixteen men, provided with horses procured from the Indians, to carry their baggage They had proceeded about three hundred miles to Trinity River (some say, the Brazos), where the party encamped to recruit themselves, and to procure supplies by hunting. Jealousies and rankerous feelings took possession of the individuals of the party to such extent that two men of the party murdered Moranget, a nephew of LaSalle, and three days after LaSalle himself was shot dead by Dehaut, one of his own men. This murder occurred on the 20th March, 1687, and soon after, Dehaut and

Leotot, two of the murderers, met the same fate by the hands of their comrades.

The French writers make some very sensible remarks on the character of LaSalle. They say he possessed all the elements of a very great man, one alone excepted, and that was to secure the affection and friendship of his men. It has been astonishing to me, that a man of the abilities of LaSalle could not see this defect in his character, and remedy it. It is strange that a man with his discernment could not see the disaffection of his men. Bonaparte had this element in an eminent degree. His soldiers and officers were always willing to thrust themselves into danger and death to save their general.

Joutel, the best friend of LaSalle, says of him: "He had a capacity and talent to make his enterprise successful, his constancy and courage, and extraordinary knowledge in the arts and sciences, which render him fit for anything, together with an indefatigable body, which made him surmount all difficulties, would have procured a glorious issue to his undertaking, had not all those excellent qualities been counterbalanced by too haughty a behavior, which sometimes made him insupportable, and by a rigidness to those under his command, which at last drew on him an implacable hatred, and was the occasion of his death."

Illinois has been not unmindful of the services of LaSalle, Hennepin, Joliet, and Marquette. Counties are named for LaSalle and Marquette, and towns for Joliet and Hennepin.

Joutel and six men after passing thro' hardships, dangers, and perils of almost every description, found a post of the French on the Arkansas River, sixty miles from the Mississippi. The sight of these countrymen was the next thing to the full view of heaven, to Joutel and party. They took up the line of march north in May, 1687, and on the 24th July, they reached the post of Arkansas, and on the 14th of September, they arrived at the Fort St. Louis, or Rock Fort, on the Illinois River. Joutel remained here until March, 1688, and then went to Canada.

It will be recollected that the Chevalier LaSalle left Tonty in command of the whole Illinois country, which was beginning to be settled by the clergy and the Indian traders. Tonty acquitted himself with honor and benefit to his country. He was compelled in the time (which lasted three years) to join the Illinois Indians in repelling the British and Iroquois, as a war raged then between France and Great Britain, and it reached out into the remote regions of the West

Tonty was the chief and captain-general in conducting the war against the British and the Iroquois, and became, as he deserved, a conspicuous character in the infant settlement of Illinois.

In the year 1686, he heard of his friend LaSalle being in the West Indies, and descended to the mouth of the Mississippi in search of him, but returned without him. On the route he established the post of Arkansas, which name it retains to this day, being one hundred and sixty-six years old And I presume the settlements of Illinois, Peoria, Cahokia, and Kaskaskia may date their existence from the same period, 1686 We have indubitable record evidence that Tonty established the post of Arkansas in 1686, and the conclusion is irresistible that the settlements of Cahokia and Kaskaskia, right under the eye of Tonty, were also commenced at that time or before.

M. Tonty was the commander-in-chief of all the vast region of Illinois, which, at that day, had no defined limits, extending from Canada to the Gulf of Mexico, and east and west from the Mississippi as far as French imagination pleased to stretch it. Tonty was viceroy of this vast country almost the whole time since he first saw it, with LaSalle, in the year 1679, to the year 1700, which is the last we hear of him at the mouth of the Mississippi with Iberville

In the year 1687, he was commanding the Rock Fort, when Joutel was there. Joutel remained at this fort all winter, and it seems his travels in Illinois closed up in the Spring of 1688; he left the Rock Fort in March of that year for Quebec, and then on to Rochelle, being absent four years in America, and experiencing every peril and misery except death itself

The Chevalier Tonty, the Italian, was actively employed for twenty-one years in erecting forts, defending the country from Indian and British depredations, and organizing the first settlement of Illinois. We must therefore conclude that Tonty was a clear-headed, discerning man, of moral and physical courage, and of such energy, with these other qualities, as made him successful in all his enterprises

From the time, 1686, Tonty descended the Mississippi to meet LaSalle, the Illinois country commenced settling. The minds of the people in Canada, and even in France, became enthusiastic in favor of Illinois, which caused emigration to it, and the religious institutions, and particularly the Jesuits, were also much interested to snatch from destruction the Indians that were unconverted. All over the West the French had missionaries, and at every Indian village the holy father was seen employing all his talents and energies to convert the savages to Christianity. It was at the Indian villages, Cahokia and Kaskaskia, that the missionaries first located themselves to instruct the aborigines. And then next came the Indian traders. The traders built store houses and forts in these villages, and the missionaries erected houses of worship, and thereby both classes became stationary, and the excitement to emigrate to Illinois soon made farmers and mechanics join them, and they located in these villages. Many of the traders, and others, married Indian women, and other families came from Canada, so that in a few years both Kaskaskia and Cahokia became places of civilization and residence of a white population. It was about the year 1686 that the Reverend Claude Allouez, a companion of LaSalle, made his first missionary entry into the Indian village of Kaskaskia. He was the first white man that made this village his permanent residence. Some time after, the Reverend Gabriel Marest also visited the place, and dated a letter: "Aux Cascaskias, autrement dit de l'Immaculee Conception de la Sainte Vierge, le 9 Novembre, 1712." About the same time, Father Pinet formed the station of the missionaries in the Tammarais and Cahokia villages of Indians which was first called "Notre Dame de Kahokia."

Peoria arose in the vicinity of the old Fort *Creve Cœur*, but did not improve as the other settlements did at Kaskaskia and Cahokia; but now, in its turn, is far the largest place, and bids fair to be one of the largest cities in Illinois.

The missionaries emigrated to Illinois in numbers, and did all in their power to make the Indians drink of the waters of everlasting life, but the natives refused even to this day to embrace Christianity.

In our opinion, the doctrines of Christianity are too refined, too subtle, and too obtuse, for the comprehension of the illiterate natives. They must have a religion more suited to their capacities, and more to be evidenced by their senses The experiments made by thousands of good men to convert the savages to Christianity have signally failed, the aborigines must have their minds cultivated and enlarged before they can comprehend Christianity.

Father Marest says that "our life is spent in rambling thro' thick woods, in climbing over hills, in paddling the canoes across lakes and rivers to catch a poor savage who flies from us, and whom we can tame neither by teachings or caresses"

Sebastian Rasles, or Raleau, came to Illinois in 1692, and remained here two years He was recalled and stationed in Maine, where he and his Indian flock were murdered by the Pilgrims of New England

The next pioneer who figured in early Illinois history, is Baron la Hontan This adventurer sailed up the River of St Peters, and returned without adding much to the development of the country, or to his credit His journal is considered doubtful authority in all cases where the truth is required.

Gabriel de la Rebourde and Zenobe Membre, were two missionaries in Illinois who collected a troupe of Indians, mostly females about St Louis on the "Great Rock." This was sometime in 1690.

In the year 1711, a missionary station was established at Fort Massacre on the Ohio River and a fort was there built by the French in 1758.

About the year 1700, the inhabitants commenced cultivating the alluvial soil in the American Bottom around the villages of Kaskaskia and Cahokia, and to erect buildings fit for the habitation and comfort of the white man The missionaries built churches at those villages, and attended with apostolic care their flocks.

The government of France decided to establish a colony toward the mouth of the Mississippi, therefore in the year 1699, Iberville, under the direction of France, commenced a settlement at Mobile, and also at Dauphin Island. He left France with two ships on the 11th Oct, 1698, and on the 31st Jan, 1699, arrived in Mobile Bay Iberville was a man of sound judgment, discretion, and prompt action.

These settlements in the South, in early times were considered intimately connected with the Illinois country, and so they always will be esteemed Iberville, after much search on the 2d of March, 1699, found the Hidden River, whose mouth had been so long sought for A vessel was despatched to France with the glad tidings The natives called the river "Malbouche," and the Spaniards "La Palissade," from the trees growing on its banks

After ascending the Mississippi for some distance, Iberville sailed to the Bay of Biloxi and there erected a fort Leaving this place in the command of Bienville, he embarked for France, and in his absence Bienville again returned to the Mississippi, and alarmed an British ship ascending the river, so that the vessel turned down the river, and this place on the Mississippi is to this day called "the English Turn." General Jackson, on the 8th of Jan , 1815, gave the British a much more bloody "turn down," about the same section of the river.

In the year 1700, Iberville returned from France, and built a fort at the mouth of the Great River, and ordered M. le Sueur to proceed up the Mississippi and the St. Peters, in search of a copper mine, which order was fulfilled, and much matter was found similar to copper, but, on being analyzed in France, it turned out to be worthless. Sueur erected a fort on the St Peters, in latitude 44. 13 north, and called it L'Huiller [1702]. The Indians being hostile, the party returned

In 1705, the same party ascended the Missouri River to the Kansas, but soon returned without finding any valuable mines, but commenced a profitable commerce with the Indians.

M. Dutisne, another pioneer, was sent out to explore the country of the Missouris, Osages, and Pawnees. He ascended the Mississippi to the Saline River, some fifteen miles below Ste Genevieve, and crossed the country by land to the above-named Indians. He traveled west over a broken and hilly country to the Osages and finally reached the Pawnees in a fine buffalo region in the prairies, four or five hundred miles from the Mississippi.

The emigration in 1708, and about this time, commenced to flow into Illinois from the South as well as from Canada. The country around Mobile, Biloxi, and Dauphin Island being colonized from France to some extent, emigrants found their way to Illinois and settled in the villages of Cahokia and Kaskaskia This last-named village was honored with the appellation of Old Kaskaskia, and was, in truth, the metropolis of Illinois.

The French government, seeing it was difficult to colonize Louisiana, as the public concerns were then conducted, granted a monopoly of the commerce of the whole country to Crozat, a wealthy merchant of Paris. This grant is dated 14th September, 1712, and conferred on Crozat the absolute property of all mines he might discover. He was associated with Cadillac, the founder of Detroit and governor of Louisiana.

Crozat established a trading company in Illinois. About this time, a considerable commerce was carried on between Illinois and the French in the South. We read of fifteen thousand deerskins, in one year, being sent from Illinois to Dauphin Island. Also flour and buffalo meat were sent to the South. Illinois in the year 1712 commenced assuming the character of a civilized and permanent-settled country. The villages of Kaskaskia and Cahokia were fast changing their Indian character for that of civilized communities. The clergy and the traders, who first located in the country, had with them associated other families and citizens that cultivated the soil and improved the country

There was no organized government in the country, until the Company of the West was established. The small number of the inhabitants, and their destitution of wealth, made a government entirely useless. The leaders of the first French settlements of Illinois were men of talents and, for the most part, of classic education. They were characters of the first order and rank in any society, while the *payans voyageurs* and *coureurs de bois* were innocent, honest, and kind, and obedient to the commands of their leaders. They gave themselves no trouble to think about or to discuss public matters. They were regardless of wealth and also of their time and labor; so that if they were provided with a scanty supply of clothes, corn, and deer's tallow or meat, to eat, they would sing and dance, and were in fact *happy* whether they were in the snows of the Rocky Mountains or in the dancing saloons of Quebec. The community thus constituted in the first settlement of Illinois, needed little, or no government; in fact, they had none until the Company of the West ["*Compagnie d'Occident*"] was established in the country.

The society in Illinois, before any government was organized, was moral, honest, and innocent, and perhaps no more happiness in any other condition could be enjoyed; but so soon as the inhabitants increased, and wealth, altho' not great, was accumulated, then came also a new order of things, which did not add to the happiness of the people.

CHAPTER III.

Illinois under the French Government.

CROZAT surrendered his charter in 1717, and the celebrated Company of the West was organized in Paris for the New World.

John Law, a Scotchman, made all France crazy with his banking scheme. I presume, no nation ever became so wild and inconsiderate as France did on this subject.

The Mississippi or Western Company was established to aid and assist the banking system of this crazy Scotchman.

In 1718, colonies were sent out from France, and in that year New Orleans was laid out. The directory of the Western Company, the same year, sent its agents and officers to Illinois. Sieur Dugué de Boisbriand, the commandant; and Mark Antoine de la Loire des Ursins, the principal secretary, with a small military force, reached Illinois with orders to erect a fort in or near old Kaskaskia.

About sixteen miles above Kaskaskia, in the American Bottom, three miles from the bluff and three-quarters of a mile from the river, a fort was commenced in 1718, and completed in eighteen months, which was called *Fort Chartres*. Fort Chartres, while the French retained the country, was the seat of government of Illinois, and it was also the headquarters of the military forces of Great Britain until the year 1772, when an extraordinary freshet in the river destroyed one side of the fort, so that the British abandoned it and made Kaskaskia the seat of government.

The fort was an irregular quadrangle; the sides of the exterior polygon are 490 feet; the walls are two feet two inches thick, and built of limestone

This fort was enlarged and improved in the year 1756, when war was declared by Great Britain against France. It is strange that such a site would be selected for a fort by a nation famous for two thousand years past in all the science of the military

PLAN OF FORT CHARTRES
ON THE MISSISSIPPI.

Drawn from a survey made in 1820 by Nicholas Hansen of Illinois, and Lewis C. Beck.

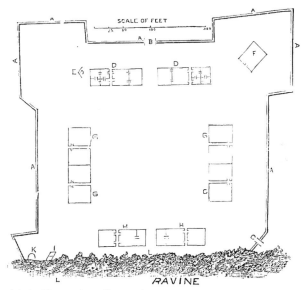

A A A   The exterior wall—1447 feet.
B   The gate or entrance to the fort.
C   A small gate.
D D   The two houses formerly occupied by the commandant and commissary, each 96 feet in length and 30 in breadth.
E   The well.
F   The magazine.
G G G G   Houses formerly occupied as barracks, 135 feet in length, 36 in breadth.
H H   Formerly occupied as a storehouse and guard-house, 90 feet by 24.
I   The remains of small magazine.
K   The remains of a furnace.
L L L   A ravine, which in the spring is filled with water. Between this and the river, which is about half-a-mile, is a thick growth of cotton-wood.

The area of the fort is about four square acres.

art The place in the bluff may be seen to this day where the stone was quarried to erect the fort. A lake intervened between the quarry and the fort, so that the rock must have been boated across the lake and then carted to the building. The site is on alluvial soil which has been washed away; so that the wall of one side has been swept off by the Mississippi, and then again, the river after destroying part of the fort, has left it out of sight

This fort is situated in the southwest corner of Monroe County, Illinois, and is an object of antiquarian curiosity. The trees, undergrowth, and brush are so mixed and interwoven with the old walls, that the place has a much more ancient appearance than the dates will justify. The soil is so fertile that it forced up the large trees in the very houses which were occupied by the British soldiers.

A regular government being established in the country gave a standing and character to Illinois that caused a great emigration from Canada and also from Louisiana to flow into it. The government of the Western Company was mild and equitable. No complaints were made of oppression or misrule against this company

A branch of the Company of the West, called the Company of St Phillips, was organized in Paris, for the express purpose of mining; and Phillip François Renault, a native of Picardy, France, was appointed the principal agent. He sailed from France in the year 1719, with two hundred mechanics, miners, laborers, etc. In the West Indies he purchased five hundred negro slaves to work the mines, and reached Illinois with all the necessary means of prosecuting the business of the company. These were the first negroes introduced into Illinois, and were the ancestors of the French slaves, who existed in the country for many years after.

Renault was a man of sound mind, and much energy. He obtained a large grant of land to enable him to prosecute his mining operations This grant was located a few miles above Fort Chartres, and on it was built the village of St. Phillips; so called in honor of the founder. A chapel and a water-mill were built in this place for the accommodation of the inhabitants. A part of the grant to Renault extended over the hills adjacent to the bottom, the title of which is not, to this day settled. Farmers and mechanics were encouraged to settle on this grant in the bottom, so that the necessary supplies for the mining operations might be obtained from it.

Other grants were made to him, one including the mines in upper Louisiana, and another near Old Peoria, to embrace a copper mine, which was supposed at that day to exist there Renault and his company of mechanics, laborers, etc., were the greatest acquisition Illinois had heretofore received. These people for the most part were more intelligent and efficient than the first inhabitants of the country; and the whole West was much advanced by them.

Exploring companies were sent out on both sides of the river In Jackson, Randolph, and St. Clair Counties, in Illinois, the ancient traces of furnaces, etc., may yet be seen. Silver Creek was so called because they supposed silver ore was found near it

Renault turned his attention finally to the smelting of lead. Pack-horses conveyed it to the river and then in perogues it was transported to New Orleans

In May, 1719, the Company of the West was united by the king to the Company of the Indies under the name of the Royal Company of the Indies. This retarded the operations of Renault and he finally left the country in the year 1744 and returned to France, where he remained.

The Company of the West being vested in fee simple with the right of the public domain, made grants of land to private individuals and to the villages. The French system to dispose of the public land was not very dissimilar to that of the United States, only in this: one government granted the land without a price and the other sold it for a valuable consideration.

The French system required the grants to be adjacent to each other and numbered so that no intervening tracts could exist. The grants were generally made by so many arpents in front and extending at right angles to the requisite quantity. The lines were, not like the lands of the United States, run on the cardinal points, but were run the same course and frequently the same length. Generally, the French grants in Illinois commenced at the river, and extended to the bluff, or from river to river, as they are at Kaskaskia. A French acre, or arpent, is eleven rods and sixty-seven hundredths of a rod, English measure being the square of the arpent. This system contemplated either large enclosures, embracing the lands of many farmers, or the fields cultivated without fencing. It would be too expensive for a farmer having a grant of one arpent, in front $11\,^{67}/_{100}$ rods, and running, perhaps, many miles the other way, as they do in the Cahokia common field, to fence his farm to himself. And in consequence of this system, the French of the villages had, in olden times, their whole common field enclosed together. The fence generally extended near the villages from either the Mississippi to the bluff, or from the Mississippi to the Kaskaskia River, as it was at Kaskaskia. The common field was on one side of this fence, and the stock: cattle, horses, hogs, etc., were formed to range on the other side. This was the ancient manner of enclosing the common fields of Kaskaskia and Cahokia for nearly one hundred years, and the same system was adopted by all the other villages of Illinois. A large gate was erected in the fence, near the village, and a keeper was stationed at it, to permit the farmers and others to enter the field and return at pleasure.

In the fall, when the corn and other crops were gathered, the gate was thrown open, and the stock took possession of the field during the winter.

Grants of land were made for almost all, or entirely so, of the American Bottom, from the upper limits of the common field of St Phillips to the lower line of the Kaskaskia common field, a distance of nearly thirty miles, and the traces of cultivation could be discerned in the greater portion of this tract of country down to the year 1800, and after.

Wind, water, and horse-mills were built in this region of country to manufacture flour for the use of the inhabitants and for exportation to Mobile and New Orleans. The Jesuit missionaries were mostly instrumental in procuring the erection of mills. The remains of water-mills may be seen to this day at various places in the bluffs of the Mississippi opposite to this cultivated tract of country; and the traces of a wind-mill was visible not many years ago in the prairie between Prairie du Rocher and Kaskaskia.

The first grant of land, which is preserved, was made to Charles Danie on the 10th May, 1722, and the next to the missionaries of the Cahokia and Tammarais tribes of Indians, dated 22d June, of the same year.

Soon after the completion of Fort Chartres in the year 1720, a village near the fort was commenced and became the habitation of many families. The site of this village was swept off by the Mississippi; so that not much or any vestage of it remains at this day. This village had its common field, commons for wood and pasture, its church and grave-yard, like the other settlements of Illinois. The common field and commons remain, but scarcely any other traces of the village exist.

About the year 1722, the village, called appropriately by its location, (Prairie du Rocher) Rock Prairie, may date its commencement. It is situated at the base of the perpendicular rocks of the Mississippi Bluff, about four miles below Fort Chartres. It had its church, common field, and commons, together with its priest, catechism, and mass. As it was situated so near the rocks, many of the houses were made of that material. In the outlet of a creek thro' the bluff near this village are the vestages of a water-mill, said to have been erected by the Jesuits in the palmy days of the French settlements in Illinois. This village, like many others in Illinois, is now, like the poet said of Troy, *Illium fuit.*

In olden times, Kaskaskia was to Illinois what Paris is at this day to France. Both were at their respective days the great emporiums of fashion, gaiety, and I must say happiness, also. In the year 1721, the Jesuits erected a monastery and college in Kaskaskia, and a few years afterward it was chartered by the government. Kaskaskia for many years was the largest town west of the Alleghany Mountains. It was a tolerable place before the existence of Pittsburgh, Cincinnati, or New Orleans. In this year, Charlevoix visited the country, and he states that "the inhabitants of Kaskaskia have black cattle and poultry, and are doing well." The Jesuits had erected water and wind-mills near this village. The streams thro' the bluff exhibit the traces of water-mills to this day, and the present flouring-mill of Mr. Riley occupies the same site of a mill of one hundred years anterior date.

Charveloix, in a letter dated, Kaskaskia, 20th Oct., 1721, in relation to Cahokia, says: "We lay last night in a village of the Cahokias and the Tamaroas, two Illinois tribes, which have been united, and together compose no very numerous canton. I passed the night in a missionary's house, with two ecclesiastics from the Seminary of Quebec. M. Taumur, the elder, was absent; but I found the younger, M le Mercier, such as he had been represented to me, rigid to himself, full of charity to others, and displayed in his own person an amiable pattern of virtue"

The common fields of Cahokia and Prairie du Pont were extensive. I presume the arpent land attached to these villages are fifteen miles long, and in places extending from Cahokia Creek to the bluffs. They are five or six miles wide The greater portion of these lands was cultivated, and enclosed in two large fields. A chapel of some character always existed in Cahokia since its foundation. In Prairie du Pont there was none. Each village had granted to it a large common. Prairie du Pont, in English Bridge Prairie, is situated on the south side of the creek of that name, and one mile south of Cahokia. Its first commencement was about the year 1760. In olden times, a water-mill was erected on the creek near the village

Cahokia never was as large as Kaskaskia, and Peoria was not so large as Cahokia in early times. Cahokia was a greater trading-post than Kaskaskia for the northern Indians; while Kaskaskia was more agricultural, and extended its commerce to New Orleans and Mobile instead of the Indians in the North.

In the early settlement of the country, the horned cattle came from Canada, and the horses reached the country from the South and the West. The cattle were a hardy race, not large but of neat formation. The horses were of the Arabian strain. The Spaniards introduced them into their American possessions, and from this race originated the French horses. This blood of horses was brought into Spain from Arabia by the Moors. These French horses were small, but performed better to their size than any others.

Spain, knowing of the improvements and settlements of the French on the east side of the Mississippi, became jealous and were determined to occupy the west side of the river themselves. Some authors say Fort Chartres was erected to guard against the assaults of the Spaniards. At all events, a considerable colony of Spaniards started from Santa Fé in 1720, and marched for the Pawnee villages on the Missouri River. The Missouri Indians resided on the same river, above the mouth of the Kansas. These nations of Indians were at war with each other, and the Missouris were in alliance with the French. The Spaniards made a mistake They halted with the Missouris, thinking they were Pawnees. They divulged to the Missouri nation their object, which was to destroy the Missouris, and asked the Pawnees to assist them. The Missouris concealed the mistake of the Spaniards, but in forty-eight hours two thousand of the Missouri tribe appeared under arms They attacked the Spaniards at night, and all were killed except the priest, who escaped on horseback.

This bold attempt of the Spaniards, crossing a wilderness of eight or nine hundred miles, alarmed the French, and Sieur de Bourgmont was dispatched with a considerable military force to take possession of an island in the Missouri River above the mouth of the Osage, and on it he erected a fort, which was called Fort Orleans Bourgmont set out from the fort on the 3d July, 1724, to take an extensive tour amongst the north-west Indians, and returned on the 5th Nov. of the same year. His object in this expedition was to pacify the Indians, and secure their trade

Soon after this period the Indians destroyed Fort Orleans, and massacred every soul in it. A bitter war with these Indians continued for sixteen years Three forts and settlements of the French in the West were almost entirely destroyed by the Indians The fort at Matagorda Bay in 1690, or thereabouts, was annihilated, as the inhabitants were never after heard of.

The fort at Natches, on the 28th Nov., 1729, was attacked and all killed by the Indians, except a few women and children; and the inhabitants of Fort Orleans, on an island in the Missouri River, were entirely annihilated, as above stated

It is surprising to any one at this day to read the perils, dangers, and deaths which the pioneers of America suffered in the colonizing of the country Examine the history of the early settlements of Virginia and Massachusetts, as well as of Illinois, and it is almost beyond belief—the calamities and loss of life which the first emigrants to the country suffered.

These disasters and sufferings were not visited on the pioneers of Oregon or California

Although the distance by land to California and Oregon from the States may not be as great as from Europe to America, but the overland travel to the Pacific is more difficult than to cross the Atlantic, and the voyage by sea to Oregon and California is much greater. Yet, under these circumstances, the first settlements on the Pacific were a pleasure in comparison to the difficulties in colonizing the Atlantic coast or the West.

About this time, 1722, the valley of the Ohio River was explored by the French The bitter hostility of the Iroquois or Five Nations to the French, prevented, hitherto, the explorers of the Mississippi from visiting the Ohio Valley. The Five Nations having, in the year 1713, an accession from the Tuscarowas from North Carolina, was called the Six Nations, and became hostile to the British. Thus it was that the French were permitted to explore the river of the Iroquois, as the Ohio was then called. And soon after, it was garrisoned by the French troops.

The date of the first settlement of Vincennes, on the Wabash, is not precisely known Its settlement might be dated at 1722, about the time Illinois, of which Vincennes was then considered a part, commenced its permanent and substantial improvement The French established a fort at Massacre, on the Ohio River, as it has been stated

The reason of this fort acquiring its name is a little singular The Indians on the southeast side of the Ohio, the opposite side from the fort, covered themselves with bear-skins, and imitated the bear in their movements on the sandy beach of the river. The French soldiers in the garrison supposed them "true and genuine" bears, and crossed the river to have a bear hunt, but sorely did they suffer for it The Indians threw off the bear-skins, and massacred the soldiers Hence the name of Fort Massacre, pronounced in English Massac A county is called Massac including the fort and missionary station

The Illinois settlements continued to flourish, and no people were more happy It is said that in the Illinois country in 1730, there were about one hundred and forty French families, besides about six hundred converted Indians, and many traders, voyagers, and *coureurs de bois*. The Jesuit college at Kaskaskia, continued to flourish until the war with Great Britain, in 1754, was declared.

It is stated that the upper Wabash was considerably settled, and that a lucrative commerce was carried on between the French colonies of the upper and lower Mississippi.

In the year 1732, the Company of the West (part of the Royal Company of Indies) requested to return their charter to the king, which was accepted; and thereupon the Illinois country became a part of the royal government of Quebec.

Altho' the company did not do much for themselves, they introduced into Illinois and protected the culture of wheat and other crops. The mines of lead in Missouri were opened and worked, and the cultivation of rice, indigo, sugar, tobacco, and silk was commenced in lower Louisiana.

At the dissolution of the company, in 1732, Loubois was appointed royal governor of Louisiana, and Artaguiette, for Illinois. Both these officers had distinguished themselves in the southern wars with the Indians, and were well qualified to take command of their respective provinces.

From this date, 1732, and during the time the country was under the administration of the French government to the year 1754, when war was declared by Great Britain, the Illinois French experienced their most palmy days. In these twenty-two years, the whole county exhibited a scene of flourishing prosperity. With a very few exceptions, the Indian tribes, far and near, were on peaceable terms with the French and gave their trade to them.

A considerable trade was carried on between Illinois and the lower Mississippi and Mobile. In return, all the necessaries not produced in the country, and much of the luxuries of life were received and used by the inhabitants. This country was remote from the old world, and thereby never experienced any of the evils or corrupt influences of a dense and profligate population. The vices and crimes, arising out of a wealthy and vicious community, were unknown in the early history of Illinois.

These settlements in Illinois being so weak and so far removed from any civilized communities, and amidst savage nations of Indians, that the inhabitants were forced to rely on each other for self-preservation. This made them kind and friendly to each other.

These virtues were cherished and cultivated for ages, and transmitted thro' many generations; so that kindness and generosity became a fixed character with the Creole French.

They were ambitious for neither knowledge or wealth, and therefore, possessed not much of either That sleepless, ferocious ambition to acquire wealth and power, which seizes on so many people at this day, never was known amongst the early settlers of Illinois. The French of these twenty-two years had exactly, almost to a mathematical certainty, a competency of worldly gear There is a happy medium between the extremes of poverty and wealth, if mankind could settle on it, that would render them the most happy These people had, at that day, in my opinion, found the philosopher's stone of wealth and happiness. They lived in that fortunate medium, which forced itself on them rather than they on it.

The people, with scarce an exception, at that day had neither the means or disposition to suffer the pains and penalties of drunkenness The French, to a proverb, are a temperate people, as to drink; and, moreover, at the above date, there was not much in the country. The people were then enjoying that high and dignified standing of teetotal temperance which conduced not a little to their happiness

The inhabitants were devout and strong believers in the Roman Catholic Church. They were willing to fight and die for the maintenance of the doctrines of their church They considered the Church of Rome *infallible*, eminating direct from God, and therefore all the dogmas were received and acted on by them without a why or wherefore. They performed their devotions in this church with a confidence that rendered them happy in religious matters

Their spiritual teachers were of sincere piety and religion. It was the duty and it became also the pleasure of these Christian men to administer to the religious wants of the people.

The people being governed by the precepts of the Gospel, enforced by the power and influence of the church, formed a pious and religious community, which was the basis of the happiness of the Illinois people in the primitive times.

This was the golden age of Illinois, and at no subsequent period will the people enjoy the same happiness. Wealth and greatness do not necessarily make a community happy Christian virtues must govern the heart before a people can be prosperous or happy.

The British government became vexed and jealous at the occupation and settlement by the French of the Mississippi Valley. They not only by intrigue soured the minds of the Iroquois and Southern Indians against the French, but were evil enough to encourage the slaves to mutiny and to leave their masters. About the year 1734, the commerce by the Mississippi was almost entirely cut off by the hostility of the Chickasaws and other Indians, caused by British intrigue. There was a great wilderness on the river between Illinois and lower Louisiana, and the hostile Indians occupied it to the great danger of commerce on that section of the river. It therefore became the imperious duty of the government to restore safe intercourse between these two settlements.

In order to accomplish this desirable object, the Chickasaws were to be humbled or destroyed. The governor, Bienville, of Louisiana, with the approbation of the French king, decided on a campaign against the enemies of France—the Chickasaws. All the disposable military force of the Mississippi Valley was brought into requisition, and organized into an army under Bienville. Artaguiette, the governor of Illinois and commanding at Fort Chartres, was ordered to join the campaign with all the military force he could muster in Illinois and Wabash countries, and to meet Bienville and the Southern army on the 10th of May, 1736, on the sources of the Tombigbee and the Yazoo Rivers The Illinois troops, whites and Indians, were to descend the Mississippi to the lower Chickasaw Bluffs, and then march in a northeast direction to the sources of the Tallahatchie River. Bienville was to ascend the Tombigbee to the forks, and then march to the northwest to meet the Illinois army.

Bienville started from New Orleans to Mobile with thirty barges and thirty perogues, and ascended the Tombigbee. The river was so low that he and Artaguiette never met. Bienville had a battle with the Chickasaw enemy, and was unsuccessful He left the Indian country for New Orleans on the 29th of May, 1736, abandoning the Illinois troops to their fate.

In this bloody battle, which was fought by Bienville, near Pontotoc Creek in the county of the same name, State of Mississippi, thirty-two men were killed and sixty-one wounded The slain were left on the field, but the army was withdrawn in tolerable order.

Artaguiette, whose fame extended from Louisiana to Quebec, exerted his influence, and many of the Indian warriors from the Mississippi to Detroit joined his standard The brave and gallant young hero, Chevalier Vincennes who was the hope and pride of the Wabash country, joined, with his forces, the troops under Artaguiette This army consisted of one thousand Indian warriors, all the regulars that were in the country, and whatever militia force that could be collected They left Fort Chartres and landed at the lower Chickasaw Bluffs according to instructions. They marched in a northeast direction, toward the sources of the Tallahatchie, and were on the spot at the time—10th of May, 1736—appointed by Bienville, but found no Southern army, as was promised. The Illinois troops, from the 9th of May until the 20th, camped in sight of the enemy, waiting for Bienville and his army.

The Indian allies became restless, and forced Artaguiette to lead them to battle The plan of the battle was devised with judgment and vigorously executed, but they were too weak to contend against such fearful odds On the 20th of May, the fearless and gallant leaders of the Illinois division of the army marched their forces against the enemy The Chickasaw towns were fortified under the direction of the British and the flag' of that nation waved over the Indian and British enemies of France

The Illinois forces drove the Chickasaws out of two of their fortified towns, and were almost certain of success at the third and last fortified village, when Artaguiette received two wounds, which laid him helpless on the battle-field at the very moment that victory was about to crown his noble efforts But such are the vicissitudes of a battle-field.

When the soldiers, who fought like tigers under Artaguiette, while he was able to command, discovered him down and almost lifeless, they retreated under the command of M Voisin, a youth of only sixteen years—with the Indian enemy at their heels for sixty-five miles. This noble youth, who, in the wilds of America, amidst a victorious and savage enemy, in such a masterly manner, withdrew the remnant of the Illinois army, imitated the most heroic deeds of his chivalric nation.

The Chévalier Vincennes, with that nobleness of character which few possess, remained with his beloved commander, altho' he might have escaped, and was captured by the enemy The Jesuit monk, Senat, also despised life by running to save it, and staid with the noble-hearted and generous Artaguiette.

At first the Chickasaws treated their prisoners with kindness and attention. They supposed that they would be ransomed at a great price, or that they might be made useful, if the fortune of war should turn against them But when the enemy learned the defeat and retreat of Bienville and his army, they changed their treatment of the prisoners to the utmost barbarity and brutality, and at last burned them at the stake with slow and lingering tortures Only one man escaped to tell the sad story of the fate of his countrymen

The French were compelled to observe in America, a most rigid discipline and subordination with their troops The soldiers at Cat Island rebelled and killed the commander. They attempted to escape to Carolina, but failed The Choctaws brought them all back except one, who destroyed himself, rather than suffer a military execution. Two of the ringleaders were broken on the wheel, and one—a Swiss—after the manner of his country, was nailed in a wooden coffin and sawed in two, by two sergeants, with a whip-saw.

These brave French officers, Artaguiette and Vincennes, together with the noble-hearted ecclesiastic, Senat, perished in the service of their country in the vigor of life and usefulness in the present County of Pontotoc, State of Mississippi The lamented Vincennes has his name perpetuated by the ancient and respectable town of Vincennes on the Wabash River in Indiana. Vincennes bids fair to be as honorable on the list of cities, as its namesake was noble, courageous, and generous in the military service of his country.

Bienville discovered that his military fame was clouded, and made, during the following year, another attempt to chastise the Chickasaws

In the year 1739, Bienville erected a fort, called St. Francis, at the river of the same name; and reached there with all the Louisiana militia, regulars, and a few companies of marines, with sixteen hundred Indians.

La Buissoniere was appointed governor of Illinois and commanded at Fort Chartres after the death of Artaguiette. He was ordered to meet the Southern army at Fort St. Francis. The governor, with his lieutenants, M Celeron and M St Laurent, assembled their forces, which were two companies of white men, and some cadets from Canada, with three hundred Indians, and descended the river to Fort St. Francis

The army crossed over to the mouth of Margot Creek, and a fort, called Assumption, was built there This fort was completed about the middle of August, 1740, when the fever raged amongst the troops Only two hundred men were able, with the negroes and Indians, to march against the enemy. This division of the army was commanded by M. Celeron, who made a patched up treaty with the enemy, which Bienville ratified, much to his discredit.

Thus ended these two campaigns against the Chickasaws, without doing much good to the country and at the loss of many valuable lives.

Bienville was superceded by the Marquis de Vaudreuil, governor and commanding general of Louisiana

During these campaigns, the whole of the French colonies increased their numbers and their wealth The Illinois and Wabash countries were much improved and enlarged. The commerce now had a free passage between the upper and lower Mississippi, and the whole valley was in a most thriving and prosperous condition.

For ten years after the close of the Chickasaw war, the valley of the Mississippi enjoyed a prosperous and happy peace.

The Indians, throughout the whole length and breadth of the valley, were at peace with the French, and rendered them their whole traffic. Not an Englishman from the Atlantic colonies, or otherwise, even to this date, 1740, put his foot on the shores of the Mississippi, except the vessel whose turn has given the name of the English Turn to a section of the River below New Orleans. The French had a quiet and peaceable possession of the valley, and occupied it by forts and settlements from Canada to New Orleans.

The country enjoying these blessings, induced many persons of capital and enterprise to come and settle in it.

In the fall of 1745, a destructive storm visited lower Louisiana, and destroyed almost all the crops. But the Illinois and Wabash settlements relieved them. Boats descended in the fall, and returned early in the spring. It is stated that four thousand sacks of flour were sent this fall to the lower Mississippi from Illinois alone. These sacks weighed 100 pounds each and were made of deer-skins.

In the year 1751, La Buissoniere, who had administered the government in the Illinois country for several years, and had the command of Fort Chartres, was succeeded in the command by the Chevalier Makarty. On the 20th August, 1751, Makarty left New Orleans with a small military force, to take command in Illinois. Makarty remained in Illinois in command of Fort Chartres and the country until a short time before the British took possession of the country, by virtue of the treaty of Feb. 10, 1763 At that time M. St. Ange de Belle Rive commanded.

The British, waxing warmer and more hostile to the French occupying the valley of the Mississippi, made preparations to colonize the country on the Ohio River. About this time, the hostile feeling that never dies between the French and British, became stronger and more developed in the western country.

The Indians throughout the Mississippi Valley were on friendly terms with the French, except, perhaps, some few bands of the Cherokees and Chickasaws. There were no Indian wars in Illinois, as was the case around the frontiers of the British colonies

By British excitement, the red skins but very seldom committed depredations on the French. M. Paget with some negroes were killed in his water-mill, situated on the east side of the Kaskaskia River, where Mr. Riley's mill now stands, not far from the village. The head of Paget was cut off and thrown into the hopper of his mill.

A Frenchman will yield to circumstances. He can adapt himself to a civilized or savage life. He is pliant and accommodating, and is willing to permit another person to have some privilege of thinking for himself.

An Englishman is the reverse of the above. He is unwilling to yield to almost unavoidable circumstances. He is far from being pliant or accommodating, and he is not willing to permit any one to have an opinion but himself.

With these different characteristics, it is not strange that the French were on friendly terms with the natives, while the British were disliked by them. Moreover, the French made their settlements in villages, and did not occupy so much of the Indian country as the British colonists did. When a Frenchman was with the Indians, he became almost an Indian. He painted, dressed like them and frequently married with them.

Under all these considerations, it was quite natural, that almost all the Indian population of the Mississippi Valley became warm and efficient allies of the French, in the war with Great Britain, which was declared a few years after.

The British were determined to occupy a part, or all if they were able, of the western country. Governor Spottswood of Virginia, as early as the year 1710, made arrangements to secure part, at any rate, of the valley of the Mississippi, and at no period after that did that government cease making efforts to seize the country and expel the French. They bought part of the West of the Iroquois, and the treaties of cessions were confirmed at various periods, from the year 1684, down to the Lancaster treaty in 1744.

Companies were organized by British authority to settle and occupy the West. The Ohio Company was established in the year 1748, and many others after that date, to secure the valley of the Ohio.

The government of Canada were sensible of the efforts of the British to seize the West, and wrote to France on the 10th May, 1744, that the consequences of the British establishing trading-houses amongst the western Indians would be injurious to the interests of the French colonies. In November, 1748, the governor of Canada superceded the British, by occupying Fort Prudhomme on the Yazoo, where LaSalle had first erected it.

In the summer of 1749, he despatched Louis Celeron with a party of soldiers from Canada, to deposit lead plates in the mounds, and in conspicuous parts of the western country, to notify the British of the French right to the same, but it was disregarded by the voracious British. The storm was gathering and nothing could avert it but for the French to abandon their own country to their ancient enemy.

The valley of the Oyo, as it was sometimes called, was doomed to experience a bloody war.

Christopher Gist, the agent of the Ohio Company, made a tour thro' the West, in 1751, preparatory to the settlement of the country. The French, in opposition to this, repaired the forts, beginning at Presque Isle, and extending to New Orleans.

In 1756, old Fort Chartres, the Gibraltar of the West, was repaired and rebuilt.

In 1752, the French and their Indian allies destroyed a British trading-house and some families, and carried the traders to Canada. This house was situated at *Pickawillany*, or perhaps Piqua, in the present State of Ohio. In this battle, fourteen Indians, called the Twigtwees, in the British service, were killed, and whose tribe, supposed to be the Miami Indians, never ceased reminding the British of the loss of their warriors, and to make reparation for the same. Pennsylvania made a present of £200 to this nation for the loss of their warriors.

The British, in 1752, sent their commissioners to Logstown to treat with the Indians, right or wrong, for the benefit of the Ohio and other Companies. This town was situated on the north bank of the Ohio, 17 ½ miles below Pittsburgh. By means not the most honorable, a treaty confirming the former cessions was made, and thereby the British had an *artificial foothold* in the West. But, in fact, it was their interest, as they considered it, that made them so tenacious for the western country, and not for any just claim they had to it by treaty.

The French were not idle. They prepared cannon and all the munitions of war in their power, from Canada to New Orleans, and had enlisted in the cause almost all the Indians of the waters of the Mississippi. But the British had still vastly the advantage, by the proximity of the hardy and energic warriors of the British colonies—a race that soon after conquered their freedom and independence from the same British.

PIONEER HISTORY OF ILLINOIS. 63

Robert Dinwiddie, governor of Virginia, being disposed to know the situation of the French, and their feelings in the West, sent George Washington, a lad of nineteen years of age, to Logstown on the Alleghany River, and north to Venango and the head of French Creek. Major Washington was in the West late in the fall of 1753, and returned over the mountains in the winter with Gist, his guide.

On Washington's return, in January, 1754, he met seventeen horse-loads of materials, and some families, by autnority of the Ohio Company, going out to erect a fort at the confluence of the Alleghany and Monongahela Rivers—Pittsburgh, at present. But as soon as Dinwiddie received the report of Washington, he ordered two companies to be raised; one by Washington, and the other by Trent, a backwoods-man. The last-named company was ordered to march forth to the forks of the Alleghany and Monongahela Rivers, and assist the Ohio Company to complete the fort, and to retain the same at all hazards. Trent had left the fort for supplies; and Ensign Ward in command, on the 17th April, 1754, saw a sight that caused him to feel a little like Nebuchadnezzar felt, without the tremor. He saw descending the Alleghany River, sixty batteaux and three hundred canoes laden with men and cannon, under command of Contrecœur, and was compelled to surrender to this French and Indian force, which is stated to be a round thousand.

On the 28th May, 1754, Col. Washington, in command of a corps of Virginia militia, found a party of French soldiers on the west side of the mountains, not far from the Laurel Hill, under the command of M. Jumonville. Washington made an attack on them and killed ten with the commander

This skirmish was near Braddock's grave and wherein Washington lost but one American and had only two wounded. M. Villiers, the brother of Jumonville, who was a military officer at Fort Chartres in Illinois, requested and obtained leave to attack Washington to avenge the assassination, as he alleged, of his brother. M Villiers left Fort Chartres, ascended the Ohio River, gathering strength as he proceeded, and on the 3d of July, 1754, Washington surrendered the fort to him, called Fort Necessity. Washington had 70 men killed. Altho' these transactions occurred on the upper Ohio, they were at that day, nevertheless, directly connected with Illinois, and as such they are narrated here.

During these years, 1750 and onward, while the war was being commenced on the western side of the Alleghany mountains, both the French settlements in Illinois and lower Louisiana were not only improving in population, but also in the substantial articles of produce. Rice and indigo were the chief crops in Louisiana, and cotton was introduced into both Louisiana and Illinois about the year 1750. Tobacco was also cultivated at Baton Rogue, Natches, and Illinois.

It is stated that M. Dubreuil invented a cotton-gin, to pick the seeds from the cotton. The invention is not described; but it is stated that the facility of picking the cotton by this invention increased the culture of cotton in Louisiana.

The invention of the cotton-gin is amongst the greatest efforts of human genius. It has become old and common since Whitney's invention; so that it is now looked upon as an invention almost growing with the cotton. There have been so many other discoveries and improvements made since Whitney's day, that his great invention is not regarded as it should be

I well remember the trouble to extricate the seeds from the cotton before the cotton-gin was in use. Cotton was then worth little or nothing; now it clothes millions and millions of people. Whitney deserves to be ranked with the greatest and best benefactors of mankind

At this time the whole coast toward the mouth of the Mississippi was in a state of tolerable cultivation, and mostly protected by levees on the banks

The Jesuits, in 1751, introduced into Louisiana the sugarcane for cultivation. They imported a quantity of cane from St Domingo. M. Dubreuil, I presume, the cotton inventor, a man of capital and enterprise, in 1758, opened a sugar plantation on a large scale He erected the first sugar-mill in Louisiana. His plantation occupied the lower part of New Orleans, known as the "suburb of St. Marigny."

This year, 1752, another Chickasaw war commenced, and terminated almost similar to the other wars against that tribe of Indians The Marquis de Vaudreuil, governor of Louisiana, with seven hundred regular soldiers and Indians almost without stint, commenced the march. The route of invasion was up the Tombigbee, the same that Bienville pursued in 1736. He had cannon and munitions of war in abundance, but failed He left a strong garrison in the heart of the Chickasaw country

I do not see that any Illinois troops were engaged in this campaign. I presume the British on the upper Ohio occupied the attention of the people of Illinois too much for any of the military to be spared South.

Contrecœur, the French commander, fortified the forks of the Alleghany and Monongahela Rivers, and called it Fort Duquesne, in honor of the governor of Canada. This fort occupied a conspicuous situation even in the year 1754, as the City of Pittsburgh does at the present time

About this time, the Marquis de Vaudreuil was transferred to the government of New France or Canada, and M. Kerlerec, a captain in the navy, was appointed governor of Louisiana

Efforts were made to work the mines of lead and copper in Illinois, and miners were sent from Paris for this purpose

As the war was raging between Great Britain and France, and as the quarrel arose about the western country, Great Britain sent to America a large army to invade the West

General Braddock landed from England in 1755, at Alexandria, Virginia, with 1000 regulars, and, April 20, with about 2000 men, regulars and provincials, proceeded west to capture Fort Duquesne. Braddock was defeated and killed, and a great portion of his army destroyed by the French and Indians. In consequence of this signal overthrow of this great British army, the valley of the Mississippi remained quiet for two years.

In 1758, another British army was organized under Gen. Forbes, and at whose approach near Duquesne, Contrecœur and his forces burnt the fort and descended the river to Illinois and Louisiana

Altho' the war raged in Canada and south of the lakes, yet Illinois remained as quiet and as peaceable as if none existed.

From the hostility of the French and Indians to Great Britain, no Briton ever saw the upper Mississippi, until the treaty of Paris, Feb 10, 1763, ceded all New France to Great Britain. The first Britons who visited the country, were the military detachment under the command of Capt Sterling, of the Royal Highlanders, to take possession of the country, in the year 1765, two years after the treaty of cession.

This is the strongest evidence of the hatred entertained by the French and Indians against the British, that no Briton ever saw the Mississippi before the year 1765, altho' it was inhabited by the French from the year 1686—always excepting the English Turn, below New Orleans.

The French settlements in Illinois were at the greatest prosperity at the close of the war, in 1763, and ever since, to this day, the French inhabitants have been declining in Illinois. It is stated that Old Kaskaskia, the Paris of Illinois, in 1763, contained two or three thousand inhabitants, and was a place of business, wealth, and fashion. The Jesuits had a college there, and all other ecclesiastical concerns, suited to the wealth and population of the country. The commerce to New Orleans was regular and profitable. A great portion of the Illinois Egypt, the American Bottom, was in a state of profitable cultivation. Wheat, tobacco, and various other crops were raised, not only for consumption but for exportation. But over this happy prosperity a sad cloud of misfortune extended. The British, whom they so bitterly hated, and for good cause, captured the country by force of arms, from these innocent and inoffending people.

The inhabitants of Illinois saw how the British treated the Acadians, in the year 1755. At the treaty of Aix la Chappelle, Acadia was ceded to Great Britain, but retained in it some French inhabitants. The British were fearful that these Acadians, would join their countrymen—the French of Canada—in the war. This was "the front of their offending." The Navy of Great Britain was ordered to kidnap these unoffending people, and drag them from their own country. Their personal property was destroyed, and themselves landed on the shores of the colonies, without friends or means of support. The public odium of a cold-blooded murder would be a measure of too atrocious a character for even the British government to bear; but they did perform acts of atrocity to the Acadian people, in the dark, that were equally criminal.

These poor people, destitute of everything, even the support of life, until relieved by their countrymen of the West, wandered over the States, "not knowing where to lay their heads," and at last crossed the Alleghany mountains, in the year 1755 Boats were provided for them on the Ohio, and they reached the open arms and hearts of their friends in New Orleans

In the annals of history such an act of outrage and atrocity scarcely can be found It is of the same character as the British government offering, and giving gold for the scalps of women and children in our Revolutionary War. These Acadians were helpless. The British government had them under her protection, and by having the power, and these people being French, they committed this crime which would make a Turk blush. And yet we hear some in the United States talking favorably of the "fatherland." God preserve me from such a fatherland.

These Acadians settled on the banks of the Mississippi, which has given to that part of the river the name of the Acadian Coast, to this day. Their descendants are there yet, and are respectable citizens. It will be seen in the next chapter, that one-third left the country, on account of their hatred to the British.

Cahokia, at the session in 1763, was also a respectable village, as to population and improvements. As has been stated, a large tract of country was under cultivation, which yielded them much for exportation, besides an ample supply for home consumption.

The village of Prairie du Pont was settled by emigrants from the other French villages, in the year 1760, and was a prosperous settlement They had their common field and commons, which were confirmed to them by the government of the United States. This village is situated about one mile south of Cahokia, and extended south from the creek of the same name, for some distance. It is a kind of suburb to Cahokia. The arpent lands of this common field extended from the bluff to the Mississippi, with a few exceptions, and were three or four miles in width. It is stated that this village, in the year 1765, contained fourteen families.

The custom amongst the inhabitants of the Illinois villages, in regard to making and keeping in repair, the fence of this common field was, that each proprietor of land should make and keep in repair the fence passing over his land. And if a tract of land was abandoned by its owner, as was the case sometimes, the land was sold out at the church-door to any one who would make the fence to enclose it. This system was based on the principle that each land proprietor should make the fence in proportion to his land.

These early French had many customs in relation to the common fields that were just and equitable. There was a time fixed, that all should have their crops gathered. After that the fence was not attended to, and the same in the spring, to repair the fence and keep the stock out of the field.

The French, in those days, mostly sowed spring wheat, so that the wheat crop was preserved in the spring, which was the object of being rigid in repairing the fences. Sometimes wheat was sowed late in the fall, and the cattle did not much injure it during the winter.

Indian corn was not so much cultivated as wheat, or used by the inhabitants. A species of Indian or hommy corn was raised for the voyagers, which was an article of commerce. The early French did not use Indian corn-meal for bread to any great extent. They raised some corn for stock, and to fatten hogs. The corn they cultivated was of the flinty, hard grain, and ripened early in the fall.

Their farming implements were neither well made or of the proper kind. The old plow used by the French would be a curiosity at this day. It had not much iron about it. A small piece of iron was on the front part, covering the wood, which in some manner resembled our Cary plows of the present day. They had no coulter, and had a large wooden mould-board. The handles were short and almost perpendicular, the beam was nearly straight, and rested on an axle supported by two small wheels, the wheels were low, and the beam was so fixed, on the axle, with a chain, or rope of raw hide, that the plow could be placed deep or shallow in the ground. The wheel made the plow unsteady.

The French settlers seldom plowed with horses; but used oxen. It is the custom of the French everywhere, to yoke oxen by the horns, and not by the neck. Oxen can draw as much by the horns as by the neck, but it looks more savage.

Sometimes the French worked oxen in carts, but mostly used horses. I presume that a wagon was not seen in Illinois for nearly one hundred years after its first settlement. A French cart, as well as a plow, was rather a curiosity. It was constructed without an atom of iron. When the Americans came to the country, they called these carts "barefooted carts," because they had no iron on the wheels.

In a country where there was no rocks to travel over, these carts answered a valuable purpose. They were mostly used for farming business. The ox-yoke was almost a straight stick of wood, cut at the ends to fit the horns of the ox, and was tied to the horns with a strap of raw hide.

The primitive French had no tanned leather for any purpose whatever. They made harness out of raw hide, which was strong but rough. They had the traces for their horses plaited of small strands of raw hide, so that they were round and neat. These traces were very strong, and such are used to this day in France.

The French houses were generally one story high, and made of wood. Some few were built of stone. There was not a brick house in the country for one hundred or more years from the first settlement. These houses were formed of large posts or timbers; the posts being set three or four feet apart in many of them. In others the posts were closer together, and the intervals filled up with mortar made of common clay and cut straw. The mortar filled up the cracks, so that the wall was even and regular. Over the whole wall, outside and inside, it was generally whitewashed with fine white lime, so that these houses presented a clean, neat appearance. The other class of houses having the posts farther apart, the spaces were filled up with puncheons. The posts were guttered for the puncheons to fit in. These houses were used for stables, barns, etc., etc. Some dwelling-houses and the stables and barns were made of longer posts set in the ground, instead of a sill as was used in the other houses. These posts were of cedar or other durable wood. The small houses attached to the residence were generally set with the posts in the ground. The covering of the houses, stables, etc., was generally of straw, or long grass cut in the prairie. These thatched roofs looked well, and lasted longer than shingles. They were made steep and neat. All the houses, almost, had galleries all around them. The posts of the gallery were generally of cedar or mulberry.

The floors of the galleries, as well as the floors of the houses, were made of puncheons, as sawed boards were scarce. The roofs of the dwelling house were uniform and peculiar. They were made of rafters and lath for sheeting. These roofs had no gable ends perpendicular, but were shingled on the ends as well as the sides. The ends sloped considerably toward the centre of the building, so that the shingles would lie on the lath. No nails were used to fasten the shingles to the lath. Holes were bored in the shingles and pegs put in them. With these pegs the shingles were hung on the lath, and the holes and pegs covered so completely that no one would know at a distance that the shingles were not nailed on. The outside course of shingles was generally nailed, and then one course bound another, until the whole roof was solid and good; never leaking one drop. The shingles were generally made of white oak, and lasted for many years. On the comb of the roof a cross of wood was often placed, that also lasted a long time.

The doors were plain batton work, out of walnut mostly. The windows had generally some glass in them, and the sash opened and shut on hinges, as the French fashion is generally. The houses were mostly raised from the earth a foot or two by a stone wall. The French, in these their happy days, had neat, clean wells, nicely walled with rock; and a windlass fixed to them, so that water was convenient and clean.

The French villages were laid out by common consent on the same plan or system. The blocks were about three hundred feet square, and each block contained four lots. The streets were rather narrow, but always at right angles. Lots in ancient times were enclosed by cedar posts or pickets, planted about two feet in the ground and about five feet above. These pickets were placed touching each other, so that a tight and safe fence was made around each proprietor's lot. The upper ends of the pickets were sharpened, so it was rather difficult to get over the fence. A neat gate was generally made in the fence, opposite to the door of the house, and the whole concern was generally kept clean and neat; so that their residences had the air of cleanliness and comfort.

The *costume* of the French was like all other matters appertaining to them, of that day, singular and peculiar. It seems the masses of the French, in France as well as Illinois, have a strong predeliction for the blue color. Blue handkerchiefs were generally worn on the head by both male and female. It was tastfully tied on the head, and seemed rather to become the male in place of a hat.

Hats in olden times were very little used. The *capot* made of white blanket, was the universal dress for the laboring class of people. A kind of cap was attached behind at the cape, which in cold weather was raised over the head, in the house, or in good weather, was permitted to rest on the shoulders like an ordinary cape. Coarse blue stuff the working men used for pantaloons in summer, and buckskin, or cloth in the winter. The females did not labor so hard as the males, and, therefore, dressed neater and better than the male part of community.

The French generally, and the females of that nation particularly, caught up the French fashions from New Orleans and Paris, and with a singular avidity adopted them to the full extent of their means and talents. The females generally, and the males a good deal, wore the deer-skin moccasons. A nicely made moccason, for a female in the house, is both neat and serviceable.

The men out of doors wore a coarser and stronger article made out of thicker leather, which the Americans call "shoe packs." But both sexes were always provided with something tasty and neat for the church and ballroom. In these places the French took great pleasure. I do not believe there was a more devout people than the primitive French. With sentiments of true piety it afforded them the utmost happiness to attend the church and perform their devotions. After their religious duties were performed, recreation and amusement of an innocent and harmless character were indulged in, on perhaps the afternoon of the same day they attended church.

But it was in the ballroom where these merry and innocent people enjoyed themselves. Dull care was entirely cast aside for the pleasures of the dance. It is astonishing the excitement and animation that is experienced in a French ballroom. The old and young, the rich and poor, all meet together in good feeling, and mingle together with hearts overflowing with the ecstasies of merriment.

The ancient innocent custom was for the young men about the last of the year to disguise themselves in old clothes, as beggars, and go around the village in the several houses, where they knew they would be well received. They enter the houses dancing what they call the *Gionic*, which is a friendly request for them to meet and have a ball to dance away the old year.

The people, young and old, met each one carrying along some refreshment, and then they do, in good earnest, dance away the old year.

About the 6th of January, in each year, which is called *le Jour de Rais*, a party is given, and four beans are baked in a large cake; this cake is distributed amongst the gentlemen, and each one who receives a bean, is proclaimed king. These four kings are to give the next ball. These are called "king balls." These kings select each one a queen, and make her a suitable present. They arrange all things necessary for the dancing party.

In these merry parties, no set supper is indulged in. They go there not to eat, but to be and make merry. They have refreshments of cake and coffee served round at proper intervals. Sometimes bouillon, as the French call it, takes the place of coffee. Toward the close of the party, the old queens select each one a new king, and kisses him to qualify him into office; then each new king chooses his new queen, and goes thro' the ceremony as before. In this manner the king balls are kept up all the carnaval.

In the ballroom much order and decorum are observed. Two aged discreet persons are chosen, who are called provosts, one to select the ladies for the dance, and the other for the gentlemen, so that each one dances in proper turn. It is in this manner that these innocent and merry people spend much of their nights in the winter. The old people regulate all; the time to retire and the time to meet again. By this regulation, much of the excesses of dancing parties are avoided. The young people are not so capable to judge in these matters as the old.

The French, in the early settlement of the country, turned their attention to the Indian trade, and to hunting, in a great measure, for their support. Game was then plenty. Buffalo and other wild animals were found in the prairies between Kaskaskia and Vincennes, that served to supply the inhabitants with animal food. The Indians called the Kaskaskia Raccoon River, for the number of those animals living on it A great many of the inhabitants were expert voyagers and hunters. These hunters and voyagers were a hardy and energetic race of men. No hardships or perils terrified them, and this laborious and difficult service was performed with pleasure, and frequently with songs. Often these innocent and kind-hearted men performed this labor with scanty allowance of food, and at times without anything, for days together, to eat.

These people solved the problem. that an honest and virtuous people need no government. Nothing like a regular court of law ever existed in the country prior to the British occupation of Illinois, in the year 1765.

The governor and commandants of posts, together with the advice of the priests, regulated the police of the country, and gave friendly council, which either settled controversies, or prevented them arising.

The customs of Paris, or more properly, the laws of France, were recognized, and governed in descents of property, and all other things. These people never paid any taxes, and, I think, worked on the public roads very little or none It is true, they were organized into military companies, and mustered. They had militia officers in each village, who, it seems, were commandants in other matters as well as military.

Keeping up a military organization was natural with the French, and their extreme exposed situation was also another reason. They had three wars with Great Britain during their occupation of Illinois, and the British were endeavoring all the time to poison the Indians against them; so that the military services were punctually rendered to the country.

On the 10th February, 1763, a treaty of cession of New France, except a small portion of Louisiana, was made between Great Britain and France, and thereby the Illinois country passed to the government of Great Britain.

CHAPTER IV.

Illinois under the British Government.

ILLINOIS was so remote, and so small a settlement, that the British did not take possession of it until Capt. Stirling, of the Royal Highlanders, as has been already stated, arrived at Fort Chartres, in the year 1765, and took possession of the country

M. Saint Ange de Belle Rive was then commandant at Fort Chartres, and governor of Illinois. Saint Ange retired to St. Louis on the arrival of Capt Stirling.

It is stated that all the population of Illinois, black and white, before the cession, did not exceed three thousand souls, and one-third left it at, and on account of, the cession. Writers say not more than two thousand French, British, and Negroes, remained in the country after the British took possession of it.

The mission of St. Sulpice had a fine plantation near Cahokia, in Prairie du Pont, in the year 1764, and a very good mill for corn and planks. They sold their plantation and mill to a Frenchman, M. Gerardine, who remained under the British government, and they returned to France.

Capt. Stirling brought with him the proclamation of Gen. Gage, who was commander-in-chief of all the British forces in North America This proclamation was dated at New York, 30th Dec , 1764, and was a kind of constitution for the government of Illinois. It granted the right of worship to the Cathoiics and many other salutary regulations.

Capt Stirling died a short time after he arrived in Illinois, and was succeeded first by Major Frazier, and next by Col. Reed—the latter became notorious for his military oppressions. These all gave place to Col. Wilkins, who arrived at Kaskaskia on the 5th Sept , 1768.

Col. Wilkins issued a proclamation authorized by Gen Gage, to establish a court of justice. Col. Wilkins appointed seven judges, who held the first court at Fort Chartres, 6th Dec., 1768. This was the first court of common-law jurisdiction established in the Mississippi Valley. Courts were held once each month.

Pontiac, perhaps one of the greatest Indian chiefs that ever existed in North America, was killed in Cahokia, in the year 1765, by a Peoria Indian. This great man was dreaded by the British, who employed an Indian to assassinate him This nation feared the great Napoleon She did not assassinate him in open day, but confined him on the sickly island of St Helena, so that he dragged out some years of existence, in mental agonies worse than death

Pontiac was a chief of the Ottawa nation and raised near Detroit He had in his veins French blood, and was imbued and trained with the mos tdeadly hostility to the British He declared before the "Great Spirit—the Master of Life," eternal hostility to the British, like Hannibal did against the Romans Both he and Hannibal were fighting in the most holy cause— the defence of their countries—and both were sacrificed, and their respective countries wrested from them by their merciless enemies.

After the French ceded the country to the British, and they making preparations to garrison and occupy it from the Mississippi to the Alleghany Mountains, Pontiac saw at once that the Indians must either defend their country or entirely lose it They knew the mode of the British was different from the French, in colonizing the country. The British drove the natives from their homes, while the French lived in peace with them.

Pontiac (sometimes pronounced Pondiac), whose soul, like that of Patrick Henry, was fired with true patriotism, conceived the grand design to unite all the Indians in one league, from the Carolinas in the south to the northern lakes, and from the Mississippi in the west to the Alleghany Mountains, against the British This was the greatest and most efficient combination of Indians ever made on the continent, and it was not an idle scheme, conceived in the brain and never executed, but in fact, it was executed to the destruction of many British forts, and to the loss of many lives

Pontiac saw and advised his brethren to a sense of their common danger He visited, in a short time, all the tribes within the above limits, containing at this day eight or ten millions of

Americans. He settled and quieted, for the common cause, all the old feuds and differences amongst the various nations, from the north to the south, and from the east to the west He appealed to the passions of the warriors, and stated to them that the French king had authorized him to drive the British out of the country. That the Great Spirit also decided that the Indians should destroy the British enemy The will of the "Master of Life" was given to a Delaware chief in a dream. The Great Spirit said: "Why do you suffer these dogs in red coats, to enter your country, and take the lands I have given to *you?* Drive them from it. Drive them—and when you are in trouble I will help you."

Pontiac had acquired, by his military powers and wise councils with his brethren, a standing amongst the Indians, that Tecumseh, or perhaps any other Indian warrior, never possessed. He had been the master-spirit amongst the Indians, in their wars with the French, against the British, from the Acadian war, in 1747, to the year 1763, when this extraordinary Indian effort was made to force their enemy out of the country. He was a conspicuous Indian leader in the defence of Fort Duquesne, and in the memorable defeat of Braddock, in the year 1755 He had acquired, and richly deserved, the name of emperor, amongst the Indian nations.

The plan of attack was for the Indians to rise and take all the British forts in the West, on the same day, and this was kept a profound secret, except in one instance, where a squaw divulged it

This Indian Bonaparte was well acquainted with the country, as well as with the Indian character He also knew all the leading warriors amongst the various tribes, and with this knowledge he made out the plan of attack of each fort, and the warriors and tribes that should execute it. All these things were done by the force of genius, without education, and even without writing The forts were numerous, and lay at a distance from each other All, except Fort Niagara, were to be captured on the same day—some by open attack, and others by stratagem Fort Niagara was considered by the Indians too strong for their means of attack. The forts, trading-posts, and settlements, which were to be destroyed, were

Detroit, Mackinac, Green Bay, St. Joseph, Ouiatenon or Weas town on the Wabash, Miami, Sandusky, Presque Isle, Le Bœuf, Venango, Ligonier, Pitt, Bedford, and Cumberland. All these forts perished under the hand of Pontiac except three

When Major Rogers was marching his military forces to take possession of Detroit and Mackinac, by orders of Gen. Amherst, in the year 1760, and when the detachment entered the territory of Pontiac, he sent messengers to inform Maj. Rogers that their chief, Pontiac, was master of that country, and that no armed warriors of any nation, should pass thro', or settle in it, without his permission.

Pontiac knew he was not prepared at that time to contend in battle with the British, and made a treaty with Maj Rogers, merely to deceive him, and to gain time to prepare for the general destruction of the British forts and settlements.

It required much sagacity, talents, and courage to plan the attacks against these forts, and to capture them. It must be recollected that the Indians had no cannon, and if they had, they had not science to use them They had no provisions to sustain an army, more than they could obtain from the game in the forest. The leaders had no power by government over the warriors, to enforce order or obedience, longer or different, than the parties pleased. The various tribes and the forts and settlements to be destroyed were a great distance apart To plan this organization and to execute it showed extraordinary talents. Under the circumstances, so adverse and so appalling to ordinary minds, for Pontiac to accomplish all, as he did, raises him high in the temple of fame, as one of the greatest men that lived in any age or any country. If he had a Homer to sing his battles, his name would be transmitted to posterity with as much honor and glory as any of the Greek heroes. The Greeks fought to conquer—Pontiac to defend his country.

Stratagem was frequently resorted to by Pontiac, in order to obtain possession of the commanders of the forts, and then destroy the soldiers and inhabitants At Miami, on the Maumee River, a squaw enticed the captain of the fort off two hundred yards to a man dying, as she represented Thereby the captain was led into an Indian ambuscade and killed The rest of the garrison all perished under the tomahawk of the savages.

A British trader, Alexander Henry, was present at the massacre of the whole fort at Mackinac, and relates a most horrid scene of this butchery, where seventy persons were slain and scalped

The Indians acted with great cunning and sagacity in getting possession of this fort. It was a strong and important garrison It was in the heart of the Indian country, and was much dreaded by them. It was provided with cannon, and impregnable to an Indian enemy without sagacious management

The Indians pretended a great game of ball, called *baggatowa*, to celebrate the birthday of the British king. They bet high and played with great excitement; so that many of the soldiers and officers of the garrison were out of the fort to look on, as the game commenced on a beautiful plain outside of the fort, but in the excitement of the game, the ball, as if by accident, was thrown over the walls of the fort, and vast crowds of Indians entered it in search of the ball. They had weapons concealed, and the garrison was destroyed The French were spared About four hundred warriors were engaged in this massacre.

The posts of Mackinac, St. Joseph, and Presque Isle were captured with the general slaughter of the garrisons. Presque Isle held out for two days, and at last was taken and destroyed.

A squaw divulged the plan to capture Detroit, which put Maj Gladwyn the commander on his guard. This post being the most important; containing vast stores of Indian goods, Pontiac in person conducted the operations against it

His plan was to gain the interior of the fort in friendship, and then kill all within. He pretended to the commander of the fort that the Indians desired to "take their new father, the King of England, by the hand." And that a council was to be held the next morning, but during the night the squaw apprised Gladwyn of the scheme.

The commandant had his garrison prepared and well armed to receive Pontiac and his red warriors, the next morning.

Pontiac, when he entered the fort, enquired "why all this military display;" the commander answered "it was to keep his young men from being idle." About this time, Gladwyn raised the blanket of Pontiac and saw he was armed with a short gun. The Indians had provided themselves with short guns and concealed them under their blankets

The officer ordered them out of the garrison, and on the Indians retiring they yelled and fired their guns, but to no effect. They murdered several persons outside the fort, and besieged the garrison for several months, until it was relieved from Montreal· The fort contained 122 men

Fort Pitt was attacked, and besieged for a long time, until Bouquet with 300 men gave them relief The posts of Detroit, Niagara, and Pitt were successfully defended, and retained by the whites, but the balance fell into the hands of the savages. At the fall of these forts the frontiers of Pennsylvania and Virginia were forced back over the mountains, the Virginians over the Blue Ridge. More than twenty thousand in Virginia fell back on the old settlement. Horrid massacres were the common practices on the frontiers from Carolina to Montreal. The Indians remained active in the war during the summer of 1763, until fall, when the savages were compelled to retire for the want of provisions

Pontiac, failing to take all the forts, was discontented and desponding. He retired to the far West The British, knowing his power amongst the Indians, bribed a savage to murder him in the streets of Cahokia. Thus fell one of the greatest men nature ever formed. His dust is now reposing in peace, near the old and deserted village of Cahokia, "but yesterday the word of Cæsar might have stood against the world, now he lies there, and none so poor as to do him reverence." The northern Indians held Pontiac in the greatest estimation. They knew their loss was irreparable. The murder of Pontiac so enraged them, that they almost exterminated the whole Illinois Indians, whose tribe participated in this horrid murder of their friend and protector, the great Pontiac.

In the year 1765, Col George Croghan, a commissioner, was sent out West to conciliate the Indians, after the cession of the country to the British He descended the Ohio River, and was at the falls of the Ohio on the 1st June, 1765. The party came to the mouth of the Wabash, where they discovered some Indian fortifications. They still descended to an old Shawnee village, the same that retains the name of Shawneetown, in

Gallatin County, on the north bank of the Ohio River. Col. Croghan and party remained there six days, making friendly arrangements with the Wabash Indians.

On the 8th of June, they were attacked by eighty warriors, mostly of the Kickapoo and Mascouten tribes, and many of the whites were killed and more wounded, and all made prisoners.

The party from this point went to Vincennes, by land, where they found eighty or ninety French families. From the Shawnee village, Col Croghan sent messengers to Lord Frazier, who had been sent to Fort Chartres; and also dispatches were forwarded to Saint Ange at the same fort After remaining at Vincennes several days, Col Croghan went up the Wabash 210 miles, to Ouiatenon, the Weas Town, as the Americans called it, and on by the Miami post to Detroit, where they arrived on the 17th August At Ouiatenon there were fourteen families, and at Detroit about eighty houses of all sorts

On the 27th February, 1764, Major Loftus, a British officer, who was stationed at Bayou Manchac, on the Mississippi, was despatched with 400 men to Fort Chartres, to take possession of the fort and country in the name of his government But as he ascended the Mississippi, at a place now known as Loftus Heights, or Fort Adams, the Tunaca Indians killed many of his party, so that the balance returned down the river.

The defeat of Loftus and party delayed the British from the occupation of the country until Capt Stirling assumed the command from the benevolent Saint Ange A short time after Capt Stirling took possession of the country, he died, and Saint Ange considered it his duty to return from St Louis to Fort Chartres, and take command, as he had under the French government

It is stated that the first Anglo-American settlement that was made on the Mississippi, was in the year 1764, by Americans from Roanoak, North Carolina. They settled on the highland north of Iberville Bayou, and thence northwardly toward Baton Rouge.

The remoteness of Illinois from the British colonies—the hatred of the French and Indians to the Long Knives and the Bostonians, and weakness of the settlement, that very few Americans or British, visited the country during the government of the British. Scarcely another man was seen of the British, except the British troops, in any part of Illinois, until the Americans under Col. Clark took it in 1778.

The British, in the year 1769, erected, on the Wabash River, a fort, which was called Sackville. This fort was a short distance below Vincennes, and was a regular stockade fort, with bastions, and a few pieces of cannon, under the command of an officer and soldiers.

In 1756, as has already been stated, Fort Chartres was repaired and improved, by the French, to guard the country against the invasion of the British. It was believed that this fort was the most "convenient and best in North America." In this year (1756), it stood half a mile from the bank of the river. In 1766 it was only eighty yards. The bank of the river next it was continually wearing away. In the year 1770, the river made further encroachments, and in 1772, the river inundated the American Bottom, and washed away one of the side walls of the fort.

At this time, the British garrison abandoned it, and moved the seat of government to Kaskaskia. Fort Chartres has never been occupied since. It is stated in 1820, that "at the southeast angle there is a gate, and the wall is perfect. It is about fifteen feet high, and three feet thick. There is also a large gate eighteen feet wide."

After the year 1772, the British garrison occupied Fort Gage, which stood on the Kaskaskia River bluffs opposite the village; this fort continued the headquarters of the British while they possessed the country.

Fort Gage was built of large square timbers, and was an oblong, measuring 290 by 251 feet.

There were in this fort, in the year 1772, an officer and twenty soldiers. In the village of Kaskaskia, there were two French companies organized, and in good discipline, ready to march at a moment's warning.

At the time the British troops came to take possession of Fort Chartres, two young officers, one French and the other British, had a misunderstanding at the fort. This quarrel arose, as did the war of the Greeks against the Trojans, on account of a lady. These officers fought with small swords, early on a

Sunday morning, near the fort, and in this combat one was killed The other left the fort, and descended the river. I was informed of the above duel nearly fifty years ago, by a very aged Frenchman. He informed me of the details, and said, he was present and saw the combat. This duel was, no doubt, the first fought in Illinois. That barbarous, anti-christian mode of settling controversies has never been much practised in this country. Public opinion, which is the certain corrector, has been always strong against it. And the last Constitution of Illinois, eminating from an enlighted public opinion, has placed a positive *veto* against the practice forever.

When the British took possession of Illinois, many of the first inhabitants, as was before stated, emigrated to Louisiana, which was nothing more than to cross the Mississippi.

On the 3d Nov, 1762, France made a secret treaty with Spain, by which Louisiana was ceded to Spain; but it was not made known before April 21, 1764. About this time, and before the treaty was known, the villages of St Louis and Ste. Genevieve made their appearance on the west side of the Mississippi

The French are always celebrated for giving persons and places nicknames suitable to the occasion. St. Louis was called *Pain Court*—Short Bread; Carondelet, *Vide Pouche*—Empty Pocket; Ste. Genevieve, *Missier*—Misery These names were the only ones for many years by which these places were known and called. It was not until after the cession of Louisiana to the United States, in 1803, that St. Louis, in common parlance was known by any other name than *Pain Court*. The same of Ste. Genevieve; and it was not long since that *Vide Pouche* lost its cognomen, and assumed its present city-name of Carondelet. St. Charles, in Missouri, was known as *Petite Cote*.

In the year 1766, a plantation of the Jesuits, near Old Kaskaskia, containing two hundred and forty arpents of cultivated land, a very good stock of cattle, and a brewery, was sold by the French government to Monsieur Beauvois. This property was taken by the French government when the order of Jesuits was suppressed. Monsieur Beauvois was a wealthy citizen of that day. He had eighty slaves and furnished eighty-six thousand pounds of flour to the king's store; and this was not near all his harvest of one year.

CHAPTER V.

Illinois under the Government of Virginia.

THE first part of the American Revolution was not much perceived in Illinois. The country was so remote from the Atlantic States, and peaceably yielding to British authority, that nothing transpired in Illinois during the first years of the Revolution that can be interesting to narrate The inhabitants continued in their usual avocations, during the first years of the struggle But, in the year 1778, Illinois was visited by a small army of the most valiant and courageous heroes that, perhaps, ever invaded and captured any country.

I do not believe that history presents a parallel of such extraordinary invasion and conquest of a country, of such vast extent and importance, as was the result of Col. Clark's expedition into Illinois, in the year 1778. This invasion was conducted to an honorable and successful termination, without the loss of lives, and almost without means or men.

George Rogers Clark was born in the Old Dominion, Albemarle County, 19th Nov., 1752. In his youth, like Washington, he was employed in surveying land

Col. Clark was in the West, on the upper Ohio, in the year 1773, and was in the neighborhood of the murder of Logan's family in 1774, but not concerned in that bloody transaction. He was a staff-officer in Governor Dunmore's war with the Indians, in the campaign to the Scioto, and reached Kentucky in the next year—1775.

From the year 1774, and after the murder of Logan's family, a murderous Indian war raged throughout all the West. This war extended from the western frontiers of Georgia to Canada. It was not alone the massacre of Logan's family that caused the war. It mainly was attributable to British influence, together with the encroachments of the Americans, on the Indian country The settlements of Virginia, Pennsylvania, and the other Atlantic States, were rapidly extending west.

Boone and others discovered Kentucky, and were locating themselves in it as early as the year 1774

The Revolutionary War was discerned and feared by Dunmore in his campaign to the Scioto. It was believed by Washington, Marshall, and others, that instructions were sent to Dunmore, when he was on his march west of the Ohio River, to treat with the Indians, and leave them as friendly as possible. It may be said that this was the first spark of the Revolutionary War which was discovered in the movements of Dunmore and the last was extinguished by Gen Wayne, also in the West, at the Greenville treaty in the year 1795 The commencement and the termination of the American contest for freedom was in the West, and the Godess of Liberty has raised her standard higher and it shines with more splendor in the valley of the Mississippi than in any other section of the globe.

It was quite reasonable that the British authorities in America should discover symptoms of revolt in the colonies at this time. It was on the 5th Sept., 1774, that the first Continental Congress convened at Philadelphia, and it was on the 16th Dec, of the previous year, that the tea was destroyed in the harbor of Boston In the next year occurred the battle of Lexington and other movements for liberty in the old Bay State. It is not strange, therefore, that Dunmore was easing off from the troops of the colonies and making fair weather with the Indians of the West

For nineteen years this Indian war was prosecuted with the utmost rancor and with bloody vengeance against all the western frontiers of the United States. Old people, now alive, well recollect the indiscriminate slaughter of all classes of people on the frontiers. The Cherokees, the Shawnees, and other hostile Indians, were dreaded around the frontiers, in olden times, as much as the Asiatic cholera is at this day. There was scarcely a family in the West but could mourn the loss of some of its number And many times the evenings were spent in narrating the horrid tales of the slaughter of women and children as well as of their fathers and husbands.

Altho' this frontier life exposed the people to many hardships, dangers, and deaths that were not known in the interior settlements; yet it had its peculiar advantages. This border life produced a most hardy, energetic, and daring race of men whose characters were peculiar to themselves. They were raised in such a dangerous and hazardous condition of the country that every latent spark of talent and energy was elicited and brought into active employment. For many years in the West, danger of the Indians was ever, night and day, pressing on the frontier settlers. Those persons who could not withstand these incessant shocks of Indian warfare retired to the interior of the country and left those on the frontiers who disregarded danger and death.

Together with these dangers and hardships of Indian wars, the frontiers had many other disadvantages and privations to encounter. In all new countries the people have not the necessaries or the ordinary means of comfortable living that they enjoy in an old country. No schools, no churches, no mills, and no courts were the common destitutions of the new settlements, but when the horrors of an Indian war are added, it is then that the people, to sustain themselves against all these united calamities, become the most courageous and energetic of the human family. This mode of life also developes their mental faculties. Their education was not acquired in schools or in colleges but it was forced on them by passing events. The minds of the pioneers were developed and improved by the force of circumstances which they could not control.

This primitive race of men was also the most independent and self-sustaining people on earth. They relied on their own resources, in all emergencies, and by which they generally sustained themselves. They were for the most part at remote distances, out of the reach of relief, and were compelled to rely on themselves for support, and by this mode of life they obtained a character for freedom and independence that people raised under different circumstances can never attain.

In this kind of life, under all these circumstances of a new country, in a bloody war with the Indians, the character of George Rogers Clark was formed. He was the noble and talented representative of this class of men. He possessed a great and comprehensive mind. It was moulded on the gigantic order, not capable of embracing both extended views of policy and various military combinations. His mode of life being in constant hostile array against the Indians, gave him a perfect knowledge of their character, and also, the want of sufficient military force to contend with them, compelled him to resort to stratagem, the *ruse de guerre*, as well as to open daring and bravery. It is not common for commanders to excel in both these modes of warfare. But such was the character of Col. Clark that he excelled in both.

Such are some of the traits of this extraordinary character who, almost without troops and without any support from the government, conquered and retained the Illinois country against the combined forces of the British and their Indian allies.

At this time, in the beginning of the Revolution, two characters, Simon Kenton and Simon Girty, arose in the West whose celebrity was extended throughout the country.

Simon Girty was a native of Pennsylvania and of Irish extraction. He was a spy in the campaign to the Scioto country under Lord Dunmore in 1774 and was a companion of Simon Kenton. In 1755, the home of Simon Girty, who lived with his father, was attacked and burnt by the Indians. His stepfather, some years after, was burnt at the stake, in the presence of his family, the rest of the family were taken prisoners. Simon was adopted by the Seneca Indians and became an expert hunter. He returned and resided in western Pennsylvania. In the Revolution, he joined the Tory side and resided among the hostile Indians. He commanded on many occasions the war parties of the Indians and became a terror to the frontiers. He witnessed the burning of Col. Crawford and made some effort to save his life. He saved the life of Simon Kenton when he was tied to the stake to be burnt; they had shared the same blanket together, in Dunmore's war. He resided at Sandusky at which place he had a store. He entertained, all his life, a bitter hatred to the United States and a corresponding friendship to the British and Indians. He was in Proctor's army in 1813, and was killed by Col. Johnson's men at the Thames. He was intemperate and when intoxicated was savage to friend and foe.

As it was said, Kenton was a ranger and spy in Dunmore's war and came down the Ohio River in a canoe with two other men to the place on the Ohio where Augusta now stands He was tall, robust, and athletic, and a man of great energy of character. He spent one season hunting on the Licking River; he was taken by the Indians and sentenced to be burnt. He was tied to the stake and the fire was burning around him. His old comrade, Simon Girty, saved him from the fury of the Indians Simon Kenton was with Col. Clark in the campaign of 1778 to Kaskaskia and headed a party on the night of the 4th July of that year who entered Fort Gage and captured Lieut.-Governor Rocheblave in his bed.

After the conquest of Kaskaskia, Col. Clark sent Kenton with despatches to the "Falls," and to pass by Vincennes in his route. Kenton lay concealed during the days, for three days, and reconnoitered the village of Vincennes during the nights. He acquitted himself as usual in this service to the satisfaction of his general. He employed a trusty messenger to convey the intelligence of the feelings, numbers, etc., of the people of Vincennes to Col. Clark at Kaskaskia.

Simon Kenton served under General Wayne in the Indian war, which was closed at the treaty of Greenville in 1795. He ended his days in the State of Ohio not long since, full of years, and what is better, his heart full of Christian piety

These two singular characters were a good deal similar, each possessing an extraordinary degree of energy and decision of character. Each one honest in his professions and attachments. They espoused different sides in the Revolutionary contest, but were always friends as to personal feelings.

The enemies of Girty give him a horrid character; and, perhaps, if we were to see the British and Indian history of Kenton's character, some specks might appear not so angelic. The different society they kept might have produced some effect to make one blood-thirsty, while the other, by the influence of correct and proper principles, became humane and merciful.

They both, like the lesser prophets, became conspicuous in a small way, and both, after a very long and active life, are now resting in peace.

Col. Clark was appointed to drill and organize the militia at Harrod's Station, and at Boonsboro', in Kentucky. He was then, and ever afterward, recognized as the main defender of the Western frontiers.

Late in the fall of 1775, he returned to Virginia, and prepared to leave in the early spring for Kentucky, to make the West his permanent residence.

During this year, a great meeting was held at Harrodsburg, to take into consideration the political situation of Kentucky; and at this convention Major Clark, so called at that day, and Gabriel John Jones were appointed delegates to the general assembly of Virginia. These members of the Virginia legislature crossed the mountains at the Cumberland Gap, and suffered much with scald feet in walking to the seat of government of the Ancient Dominion.

When they arrived at the capital, the general assembly had adjourned; but Clark and Jones waited on Governor Patrick Henry, and urged on him the necessity of furnishing the frontier with a supply of powder, and also strongly pressed the necessity of a new county. After much difficulty, a supply of powder was granted to be received at Pittsburg, and on the 7th Dec., 1776, a county was organized, and called Kentucky. The powder being at Pittsburg, Clark and Jones were compelled to pass there, on their route to Kentucky, and conveyed the precious article down the Ohio to the creek called Limestone, where Maysville is now built. There they concealed the powder, and sent adrift their boat, so that the Indians might not discover them or the powder. On their way to Harrodsburg, they heard of Col Todd being in the vicinity with some troops, and Jones, with five of the boatmen, remained with Todd, to return and convey the powder to the settlements, while Clark and the other two men went direct to the station.

Todd and party were defeated near the Blue Licks, on the 25th Dec., by the Indians, who were in ambuscade, on the trail of Clark and Jones. Jones and two others were killed, but Clark and his men reached Harrodsburg in safety, and the powder at last reached the station.

Clark, altho' only 25 years of age, had learned, in the school of Indian danger and peril, so much, that his education was complete in Indian warfare. His mind, naturally strong and vigorous, comprehended at once the condition of the West, and was determined to give it relief.

The British posts of Detroit, Vincennes, and Kaskaskia, were

PIONEER HISTORY OF ILLINOIS. 89

stations for the hostile Indians, where the British government furnished them with all the necessary means to murder the exposed frontier inhabitants, and paid them in gold for the scalps of men, women, and children.

On the first of October, Clark left Harrodsburg for the seat of government of Virginia.

After much delay and caution, the government of Virginia, on the 2d January, 1778, decided to appoint Clark lieut.-colonel, to take command of such forces as could be raised, to conquer the British garrisons in the West.

Altho' the Illinois country was remote from the seat of the Revolutionary War, yet the inhabitants knew of its existence, and were, in their hearts, unfriendly to the British, and warmly attached to the American cause. This being the case, the French people were ready, on all favorable occasions, to engage in any expedition against their ancient enemy—the British.

Thomas Brady, commonly called Mr. Tom, resided in Cahokia in the year 1777, and was a man of sound mind and an enterprising and courageous disposition. In his youthful days he had been much inured to Indian warfare, and had been long in the midst of the dangers and adventures of a Western life. His neighbors, the French of Cahokia and Prairie du Pont, were ready at a moment's warning to enter into any enterprise, military or civil, that was honorable, and had no work attached to it. And, altho' the Illinois French were not ambitious or enterprising in individual capacities, yet no people made better soldiers. They were obedient to orders, never murmured, and possessed the inherent courage of their nation, to face danger and death, in all its horrors, on a battle-field, without the least trepidation.

Thomas Brady organized a band of sixteen volunteers, from the villages of Cahokia and Prairie du Pont, and on the first of October, 1777, set out to capture a British post at St. Joseph, on the southeast side of Lake Michigan. This party marched thro' the prairies from Cahokia to the Cow Pens,—so called at that day—which is the same place that LaSalle first established a post, in 1679, and called it St. Joseph.

Brady and party were successful in capturing the post, containing twenty-one soldiers and a considerable quantity of Indian goods. Only one person was killed. This was a negro slave, who had run off to the Indians from the settlements on the Mississippi. He left the fort when it was attacked, and was shot. The victorious party packed up the merchandise and started for Cahokia, but they moved slow, and were overtaken at the Calumet, a few miles southeast of Chicago. The British traders roused the Indians and the British soldiers into action. Several hundred Indians fell on the party when they were camped for the night on the Calumet. Two men were killed, two wounded, and one made his escape; twelve were made prisoners and sent to Canada. Brady was with the prisoners, but escaped, and returned to Illinois by the way of his native state, Pennsylvania. These prisoners remained in Canada two years. A Mr. Boismenue of Cahokia was one of the party, and was wounded. He remained with the Indians all winter, to heal his wounds, and returned to Cahokia in the spring.

It is stated of Mr. Boismenue, that when he saw these two Cahokias *tomahawked* by the Indians, he supposed it would be his fate next to be served in the same manner, and to avoid the sight of the hatchet sinking into his brains, he was sitting before the fire, and threw a blanket over his head. He was saved; and was afterward the father of a very respectable family, some of whom are yet living in the country.

Mr. Boismenue's desire not to know the time of his death shows the wisdom of Providence in not letting his creatures know that important epoch. Man would be miserable if he knew the time of his decease, were it one hundred years off.

This was rather a wild and hazardous expectation. Seventeen men to take a fort of twenty-one regulars with arms and other means of defence, required masterly skill and bravery. They surprised the fort at night, but could not escape with any of the spoils, which was, no doubt, one great object of the enterprise. But Col. Clark undertook a more noble enterprise, to take all the British garrisons in the West.

Two sets of instructions were given to him by the governor and council of Virginia. One, which was public, was for Col. Clark to raise seven companies for the protection of Kentucky, and to proceed west. These men were enlisted for three months. The second instructions were, that Col. Clark should raise seven companies of men, fifty in each company, and proceed to Kaskaskia to attack the British garrison at that place. That if successful, to take and preserve the cannon and munitions of war found at that post. That boats would be furnished at Pittsburg for the transportation of the troops, and that the expedition must be kept a profound secret That Gen Hand, at Pittsburg, would supply the powder and lead. The inhabitants of the country captured were to take the oath of allegiance, or otherwise be visited with the miseries of war Two men, who were from Kaskaskia, were to be secured at Williamsburg, for fear of their developing the object of the expedition. In their instructions it was particularly enjoined, that humanity should be observed to all persons who might fall into the hands of the Virginia troops. The Gov. Patrick Henry signed these instructions, which were dated the 2d of January, 1778, and none knew anything about them, except Gov Henry, Thomas Jefferson, George Wythe, and George Mason, who were his council, and Col. Clark.

On the 4th of February following, Col. Clark left the capital of Virginia for Pittsburg. It was decided that troops could not be spared on the east of the mountains, as they were so much needed there, but must be raised in the West.

The situation of Col. Clark can be easily imagined. He was acting under immense responsibility His plan was adopted. His instructions were secret, and the whole and sole management of the expedition was confined to his judgment. He had received but twelve hundred pounds of depreciated currency to carry out the expedition, and the country without troops or even credit. But the genius and talent of the leader supplied all deficiencies, and the British posts were captured.

Maj. William B. Smith was ordered from Virginia to go to the Holston country, Tenn., to raise troops, and to join Clark at the appointed time and place

He succeeded in raising four companies, but never joined Clark, having use for them on the other frontiers.

It was unpopular at Pittsburg to enlist men to take them away from the frontiers of Pennsylvania to Kentucky, but the character of Clark, and by his extraordinary exertions, three companies were raised at Pittsburg With these companies, and several adventurers, Col. Clark descended the Ohio to the Falls, and the small island opposite the present City of Louisville was occupied and fortified This island was then called Corn Island. He had ordered Capt Bowman to meet him at this island Bowman had been sent on a southern route from Pittsburg through Kentucky to raise a company of men. Capt. Bowman and a company from Kentucky, under the command of Capt Dillard, met him at the island.

With all the exertions that could be made, Col. Clark could not raise more than four companies for the expedition. These companies were commanded by Captains Montgomery, Bowman, Helm, and Harrod Simon Kenton joined the expedition at this place with many other resolute persons It appears that Captain Montgomery was found at the Falls, being an "Irishman and full of fight." It was on Corn Island when Col Clark announced that his destination was to Kaskaskia in the Illinois country This information was received by this brave band of warriors with enthusiasm and joy But, in fact, the troops under Clark were like all soldiers under great leaders, ready to go anywhere and do anything in their power commanded by their generals.

After the fainthearted were discharged, all the troops mustered into the campaign to Kaskaskia were one hundred and fifty-three men.

Keel-boats being procured, Clark, on the 24th June, 1778, while the sun was eclipsed, started down the river from Corn Island on this hazardous expedition to Kaskaskia

They descended the river to the old Cherokee Fort, or Fort Massacre, below the mouth of the Tennessee River, and forty miles above the mouth of the Ohio, where they found a party of hunters from Kaskaskia commanded by John Duff. Clark learned from these hunters that Lieut.-Governor Rocheblave, a Canadian Frenchman, commanded Fort Gage at Kaskaskia and the country: and that the militia were organized and well disciplined· that spies were out to give information if the Long Knives came into the country This was the Indian name for the Virginians, and the New England people were called Bostonians by the French and Indians of that day

Col. Clark, before he left Corn Island, obtained two items of information, of which he made good use One was, that France had joined the Americans in the war against Great Britain; and the other was, that the French in Illinois were made to believe by the British that the "Long Knives" were cannibals, worse than demons

Clark secured his boats, and engaged John Saunders, one of Duff's hunting-party, to be his guide to Kaskaskia The whole hunting-party were willing to return with Clark, but he took only one of them

Clark's warriors had no wagons, pack-horses, or other means of conveyance of their munition of war or baggage, other than their own robust and hardy selves Col. Clark himself was nature's favorite, in his person as well as mind. He was large and athletic, capable of enduring much; yet formed with such noble symmetry and manly beauty, that he combined much grace and elegance, together with great firmness of character. He was grave and dignified in his deportment; agreeable and affable with his soldiers when relaxed from duty; but in a crisis —when the fate of his campaign was at stake, or the lives of his brave warriors were in danger—his deportment became stern and severe. His appearance, in these perils, indicated, without language, to his men, that every soldier must do his duty.

The country between Fort Massacre and Kaskaskia, at that day, 1778, was a wilderness of one hundred and twenty miles, and contained, much of it, a swampy and difficult road

At one time, poor Saunders, the guide, was bewildered, and the party suspected him of treachery, but soon after, he became himself again and led the party safe to the vicinity of Kaskaskia. Within a short distance of the village, Col Clark concealed his men until dark, and spies were sent out to reconnoitre and report. This was on the 4th of July, 1778. After dark he proceeded to a house on the river—the old ferry-house—three-fourths of a mile above the village He took possession of this house, and there made the following disposition of his troops Two parties were to cross the Kaskaskia River, and the other was to remain on the east side, so as to capture the town and fort at the same time. The fearless Captain Helm commanded the troops to cross the river, and take the village; while Clark himself commanded the other wing to capture the fort. Boats and canoes were procured to cross the river.

About midnight, on the banks of the Kaskaskia River, in the dark, Col. Clark delivered a short address to his troops. He said:

"Soldiers—We are near the enemy for which we have been struggling for years. We are not fighting alone for liberty and independence, but for the defence of our own frontiers from the tomahawk and scalping-knife of the Indians. We are defending the lives of our women and children, altho' a long distance from them. These British garrisons furnish the Indians with powder and lead to desolate the frontiers; and pay gold for human scalps. We must take and destroy these garrisons. The fort before us is one of them, and it must be taken. We can not retreat. We have no provisions, but we must conquer. This is the 4th of July. We must act to honor it, and let it not be said in after-times, that Virginians were defeated on that memorable day. The fort and town, I repeat, must be taken, at all hazards."

After these remarks the troops in silence separated; two parties crossed the river, and the other remained with Col. Clark, to attack the fort. Each party at the two extremes of the village, entered it first, in silence, so not one in the town knew of the Long Knives being in the country, until they heard the most terriffic yelling and hollowing in the streets, that ever before, or since, was heard in Old Kaskaskia The French supposed the whole nation of the Long Knives had broken loose on them at once. Those among the Americans, who could speak French, proclaimed to the terrified inhabitants, that if they remained quiet within their houses, they would not be hurt; but if they came out, or made any resistance, they would be exterminated. The inhabitants were much alarmed. The inhabitants were night to day light. In two hours after the town was first entered the inhabitants surrendered all their guns and means of defence, thinking this was the only means to save their lives

In the daylight the citizens were not the less terrified at the appearance of the Long Knives, than they had been at their noise. The troops had no change of clothes. All their supplies, provisions, and all, they were compelled to pack on their backs from Fort Massacre to Kaskaskia, and could not carry with them their extra clothes, if they had any, and that was doubtful. They had no means or time to shave or dress. They possessed brave hearts under ragged and soiled clothes.

Their appearance and furious noise in the night made the French believe that the Long Knives would almost devour them

Col. Clark took to himself the most perilous enterprise, to take Fort Gage, which was a strong British fortification, defended with cannon and regular soldiers. This would seem, at this day, a similar perilous enterprise to Wayne storming Stony Point. Clark had no cannon or means of assaulting the fort, and therefore must use stratagem He found the garrison unprepared for defence The brave and sagacious Simon Kenton commanded a detachment to enter the fort; they found a light burning in it. An American, a native of Pennsylvania, was there in the fort and conducted Kenton and his small party into the fort by a small back gate. This was a perilous situation for Kenton's men, to be housed up in a British strong fortification, if the gate had been shut on them The noble Pennsylvanian was true to liberty and conducted them to the very bedchamber of the sleeping governor, Rocheblave. The first notice Rocheblave had that he was a prisoner, was Kenton tapping him on the shoulder to awaken him.

Thus the fort and village were both captured without shedding one drop of blood The wife of the governor concealed some papers which were supposed to be public, and ought to be delivered with the garrison to the captors, but the gentlemanly bearing of Col. Clark made him respect female prerogative, and the lady secured the papers in that adroit manner peculiar to female sagacity.

Clark had now possession of the fort and cannon, which commanded Kaskaskia, and could at his ease have coerced the inhabitants into submission, if it became necessary.

The conquest of Fort Gage and Kaskaskia, the capital of Illinois, is one of the most singular and important events recorded in history. It was the extraordinary genius and capacities of Col. Clark that achieved it He had scarcely any men; and all their armor, provisions, camp equipage, etc., were packed on their backs, to the scene of action; and this, too, to take a strong garrison, defended with cannon, British soldiers, etc. This may be taken in after-days as romance, but now it is known to be reality.

It seems Governor Rocheblave was insolent. Clark put him in irons, and sent him, in the care of Capt. Montgomery, to Williamsburg, the capital of Virginia. Clark was stern and severe, when his duty required it.

The next day after the conquest, Col. Clark organized the post, and confined some suspected persons. His actions and appearance among the inhabitants of Kaskaskia were on purpose made to correspond with what the British had informed them, that the Americans were the most savage beasts on earth, and that no mercy could be expected at their hands, were they to conquer the country. Clark withdrew his troops from the village; observed the most rigid discipline; and appeared to be meditating what was the worst mode of torture and death to inflict on the inhabitants of Kaskaskia. This deportment of Clark and troops, together with their uncouth and savage appearance, aroused the people to a sense of their danger and destruction. Father Gibault, the priest, with others of the "grave and reverend seigniors," waited on Col. Clark at his camp, and appealed to him to permit them, the inhabitants, to meet in the church once more before they were destroyed, or remove to a foreign land. Clark still kept up the appearance of annihilation in his deportment. His words were few, and scorched like they had proceeded from a fiery furnace.

When Clark had the people of Old Kaskaskia worked up to the utmost excitement of terror, he addressed them thus:

"Do you mistake us for savages? Do you think Americans will strip women and children, and take the bread out of their mouths? My country disdains to make war on helpless innocence. To prevent the horrors of Indian butchery on our own wives and children, we have taken up arms, and penetrated to this stronghold of Indian and British barbarity, and not for despicable plunder. The king of France has united his powerful arms with those of America, and the contest will soon be ended. The people of Kaskaskia may side with either party. To verify my words, go and tell your people to do as they please, without any danger from me."

When this good news came to the ears of the people, gloom and dejection changed into extravagant joy. The people were nearly frantic, and entered the church to thank God for their happy deliverance. Clark's policy had its desired effect, to make the people his steadfast friends.

Captain Bowman was despatched to capture the post of Cahokia, and several influential persons of Kaskaskia volunteered their services to prepare the minds of the people of Cahokia for the change. The party, mounted on French ponies, proceeded to Cahokia, and seized on it without resistance. This expedition was conducted with the same celerity and secrecy as that to capture Kaskaskia. In fact, there were not many soldiers in the fort at Cahokia; so that a defence was useless.

Col. Clark had it instilled into his army, and he also propagated it: that a large army of Americans, Long Knives, were organized at the Falls, and were ready to take Vincennes and Detroit, and to reinforce the American garrisons at Kaskaskia and Cahokia. These statements were believed by the French and Indians, and had a powerful effect in keeping, not only order and peace in the country, but also, the American domination throughout the West. As Clark and men had done so much, the inhabitants and Indians concluded that another such army could conquer any nation; and the judgment was not so incorrect; but the army must have had another Clark to command them; and that such genius and talents as his are rare at any time and in any country.

Col. Clark soon heard that the British governor at Vincennes had gone to Detroit, and that the fort, old Sackville, was in the hands of the citizens of Vincennes, and none of the redcoat gentry were in it.

Arrangements were readily made for an embassy, headed by the good old priest, Gibault, to go to Vincennes and bring the people over to the American cause. This enterprise was successful. The French of Vincennes declared for the Americans, and Gibault and his party, together with several gentlemen from Vincennes, returned to Kaskaskia, about the first of August, with the joyful intelligence.

The enlistment of the volunteers under Clark was about to expire, and his instructions were vague; so he acted at discretion. His judgment at once advised him that the country should not be abandoned, so he enlisted again many of the same men he had first, together with many of the French. Those troops, who were to be discharged, were sent back to the Falls at Louisville, under the command of Capt. William Linn, with instructions to abandon the station on Corn Island and erect a permanent fort on the main shore. For the command of the post at Vincennes, Col. Clark selected Captain Leonard Helm. He had great confidence in this officer. He knew him to be a brave, talented man, and one who was well acquainted with the Indian character Clark appointed him Indian agent in the department of the Wabash. About the middle of August he went and took possession of his command.

Captain Helm was a very adroit negotiator with the Indians, and brought the whole Wabash Indians, thro' the influence of the Big Door, the chief of the Piankeshaw nation, to the American interest. All the Indians on the Wabash, as far up as Ouiatenon, came down to Vincennes and treated with Capt. Helm. The British interest with the Indians lost ground at last for some time.

Captain Montgomery reached the seat of government of Virginia with the British governor of Illinois, a prisoner of war, and with dispatches from Col. Clark

The whole country spontaneously resounded with the warmest gratulations to Col Clark and his brave little band.

The legislature of Virginia, in 1778, formed the Illinois country into a county of that name. Illinois had the honor to extend her name, in former times, over the territory of the States of Ohio, Indiana, Michigan, and Wisconsin All the settlers on the west side of the Ohio were included in this county, and John Todd, Esq., of Kentucky, was appointed lieut.-colonel and civil commandant of the same.

The governor of Virginia did not send troops to Col. Clark, as they both expected, which forced Clark to receive into his service many of the Illinois French. With the troops he had he garrisoned Kaskaskia and Cahokia, and appointed Williams captain at Kaskaskia, and Bowman at Cahokia. In the fall of the year, Major Bowman organized a respectable force and proceeded from Cahokia north to Rock River. This expedition was intended to influence the Indians to abandon the British interest to join the Americans.

By proper arrangements, Col. Clark had a great number of Indians convened at Cahokia, in the month of September, 1778, and made friendly treaties with them

He was extremely sagacious to discover the secret moving springs of human action, and particularly, he knew well the Indian character.

At Cahokia, Col. Clark waited for the Indians to make the advance to peace and friendship He waited with determined obstinacy until the red-skins threw away the hostile wampum given them by the British before he said anything to them, and cautioned his men not to shake hands with the Indians until peace was made; so that heart and hand could go together.

Before the close of the season, all the Indians, far and near, were friendly to the Americans The country inhabited by the whites was all quiet and peaceable in the hands of Virginia The famous Capt Helm was in peaceable possession of the strong British fort, Sackville, with only two Americans and some French militia, while Clark occupied the whole Illinois country with less than one hundred men.

The "House of Delegates" of the Virginia legislature passed the following complimentary resolution:

"IN THE HOUSE OF DELEGATES,
Monday, the 23d Nov, 1778.

Whereas, authentic information has been received, that Lieutenant-Colonel George Rogers Clark, with a body of Virginia militia, has reduced the British posts in the western part of this Commonwealth on the river Mississippi and its branches, whereby great advantage may accrue to the common cause of America, as well as to this Commonwealth in particular:

Resolved, That the thanks of this House are justly due to the said Col. Clark and the brave officers and men under his command, for their extraordinary resolution and perseverance in so hazardous an enterprise, and for their important services thereby rendered to their country

Attest, E. RANDOLPH, C H D"

Governor Hamilton, hearing at Detroit that the Americans had seized on the country in his absence, was much concerned and chagrined that the country he had in charge was wrested from him by a few ragged militia from the Old Dominion

He collected his forces—thirty regular troops, fifty Canadians, and four hundred Indians—and reached Vincennes on the 15th December, 1778 The people made no defence, but the whole defence of the fort devolved on Capt Helm and one other American, by the name of Henry When Gov Hamilton came within hailing distance, Helm called out with a loud voice, "halt"! This show of defence caused Hamilton to pause. Henry had a cannon well charged and placed in the open gateway, while Helm stood by it with a lighted match Helm exclaimed, "no man shall enter here until I know the terms." Hamilton responded, "you shall have the honors of war" The fort was thereupon surrendered, and the one officer and one private received the honor aforesaid, for their defence of the fort

A portion of Hamilton's forces was dispatched to the frontiers to kill and scalp the inhabitants, while Helm was detained a prisoner of war. The French were disarmed.

Clark was in a most perilous and distressing situation. No supplies of troops or munitions of war reached him from Virginia The country infested with hostile Indians, direct from Detroit, and Hamilton preparing to attack him at Kaskaskia This posture of affairs gave Clark excessive uneasiness, and harassed him day and night To abandon the country to the hostile Indians, he could not think of for a moment; but he had no means of defence However, his courage and judgment never forsook him His talents and resources were always superior to the occasion. He called Major Bowman and his little force from Cahokia down to Kaskaskia. He burnt down some houses in the village near his fort and prepared for a siege. But on mature reflection, he came to the bold and hazardous conclusion, that he would muster all his forces and capture Hamilton; "for," he said, "if I do not take him, he will take me."

This expedition to Vincennes was conducted in the dead of winter, thro a wilderness country, without resources, and without any of the common necessaries for the support of an army.

Clark, with his uncommon sagacity to penetrate the hearts of men, engaged Col. Vigo, who resided at the time in St Louis, upper Louisiana, to go to Vincennes and reconnoitre Fort Sackville, and ascertain the disposition of the people. No choice could have been better. Col. Vigo was an Italian by birth, but in his heart the principles of freedom and love for the American cause sunk deep He was a merchant possessing great wealth, all of which, together with the most of his time, he spent in the cause of the American Revolution. Not a more worthy man lived in the West than Col Vigo. He resided a long time in Indiana, and died there. The State honored his memory by calling a county for him and Congress refunded much of the money he expended in the early settlement of the country.

Col. Vigo, after conferring with Col. Clark at Kaskaskia, with only one man started for Vincennes; but at the Embarras, five miles from his destination, he was taken prisoner by the Indians, and brought before Governor Hamilton. He was suspected of being an American spy, but being extremely popular with the inhabitants and a Spanish subject, Hamilton did not detain or punish him as such The inhabitants threatened to give no more supplies to Hamilton if Vigo was not suffered to depart in peace. Hamilton was reluctant to yield, and on this condition only, that "Vigo was not to do any act during the war injurious to the British interest " He peremptorily refused to sign such an article; but agreed that he would not do any "act on his way to St. Louis!" This was accepted, and Col Vigo was permitted to leave in a perogue down the Wabash and up the Mississippi to St. Louis He kept his pledge with the sanctity of an oath; but he remained at St. Louis only to change his clothes, when he started to see Col. Clark at Kaskaskia.

From Vigo, Clark learned that many of the soldiers were out with the Indians on marauding parties; that Hamilton had eighty regulars in the fort; and that the French were friendly to the Americans. He also learned that there were in the fort three brass field-pieces and some swivels; and that Hamilton intended in the early spring to reconquer the Illinois country.

On receiving this information, Clark still continued his

determination to capture Fort Sackville to prevent Hamilton from taking him He also wrote to Governor Patrick Henry of Virginia, and gave him in detail the condition of the country and his extreme perilous situation He wanted more troops but received none

There was no time left for Clark to delay any longer; or else Hamilton would be on him. A boat was fitted up carrying two four-pound cannons, four swivels, and provisions; and commanded by Capt. John Rogers with forty-six men. This boat was to meet Clark at a point near Vincennes with all convenient speed.

Clark organized two companies of French into his army, and, all told, his whole force amounted to no more than one hundred and seventy men. One company from Cahokia was commanded by Capt. McCarty, and the other company from Kaskaskia was commanded by Capt. Charleville

On the 7th February, 1779, this band of heroes commenced its march from Kaskaskia on the Old Vincennes trace to Fort Sackville. This trace was celebrated in Illinois The Indians laid it out more than one hundred and fifty years ago. It commenced at Detroit, thence to Ouiaton on the Wabash, thence to Vincennes, and thence to Kaskaskia It was the Appian way of Illinois in ancient times It is yet visible in many places between Kaskaskia and Vincennes This expedition of Col. Clark was the most dreary and fatiguing that was performed during the Revolution.

During the march the weather was uncommonly wet. The watercourses were out of their banks, and the larger streams had inundated the bottoms from bluff to bluff, often three or four miles wide. Yet our hardy backwoodsmen, on foot with their knapsacks on their backs filled with parched corn and jerked meat, waded thro mud and water to the forks of the Little Wabash River. The bottom here was three or more miles wide and inundated never under three feet and often four feet

Thro this low land the battalion was forced to march, feeling for the trace. At this place, to cross the river Little Wabash, the party made a canoe, ferried themselves over the stream, and put their baggage on a scaffold to keep it out of the water while they were crossing the river. They crossed this river on the 15th Feb., and proceeded on over the streams, Fox River and others, until on the 18th they heard the morning gun of Fort Sackville at Vincennes.

Before the party reached the Great Wabash, they were nearly exhausted by fatigue and traveling in the cold water. At the Little Wabash, many of the troops were sinking and their spirits exhausted. Clark, always fruitful in resources, called upon an Irishman, a drummer in the battalion, who had a peculiar talent to sing comic songs. When the men wading for hours in the icy water up to their middles and armpits, and were nearly chilled to freezing, this Irishman would sing lively, cheering songs, and thereby rouse the troops to life again. But it was at the Great Wabash where the party experienced all the hardships and sufferings of which human nature is capable of surmounting.

The party reached the Wabash below the mouth of the Embarrass, and were in the most exhausted, destitute, and starving condition. The river was running all over its banks and the lowlands near it; so that it was several miles wide. Colonel Clark had not time or means to make canoes to cross the river. The party was literally starving.

On the 20th of February, the Americans hailed a party of French in a boat from Vincennes and brought them to. From them Col. Clark learned that the people of Vincennes were friendly to the Americans, and that the British garrison had no knowledge of the expedition. This information was cheering; but a sea of cold water, the Wabash bottom, which they had no means of crossing, lay between Clark and Fort Sackville.

Clark and his party experienced the greatest difficulties and perils in crossing Wabash River and the lowlands attached to it. They waded and rafted, and suffered every sort of hardship except death itself. On reaching the high ground below Vincennes, and when they were seated on dry ground, Clark addressed the following note to the citizens of Vincennes:

"*To the Inhabitants of Post Vincennes:*—Gentlemen. Being now within two miles of your village with my army, determined to take your fort tonight, and not being willing to surprise you, I take this method to request such of you as are true citizens, and would enjoy the liberty I bring you, to remain still in your houses. Those, if any there be, that are friends to the king, will instantly repair to the fort and join the hair-buyer general, and fight like men; and such as do not go to the fort, and shall be discovered afterward, they may depend on severe punishment. On the contrary, those that are true friends to liberty shall be treated as friends deserve. And once more I request them to keep out of the streets, for every one I find in arms on my arrival, I shall treat as an enemy.

"G. R. CLARK."

This singular address had the desired effect. It made the people believe that Clark had a large army there from Kentucky, as none, as they supposed, could reach there from Kaskaskia. Clark sent in various names of gentlemen from Kentucky to their friends in Vincennes, which made the citizens believe that half Kentucky was there with him. The colonel, in marching thro the prairie to the town, made a large display of his troops, by marching them back and forward around certain mounds, so that the army made the appearance of a great body of troops. The flags were changed, so that the delusion of many fierce Kentuckians being present was riveted on the garrison, as well as on the citizens of Vincennes.

On the 23d of Feb., 1779, about sunset, the attack was made on Fort Sackville, by Lieut. Bayley and fourteen men. This small party lay concealed behind a bank of earth within thirty yards of the fort and secure from the guns of the garrison. Whenever a port-hole was opened the bullets from the American rifles would whistle in, destroying the men at the guns; so that none would dare to work the cannon. Some were killed at the port-holes, and none others could be got there to defend the works against the Americans.

At nine o'clock, on the 24th, Clark sent into the fort a note. While this was going on, his men ate the first breakfast they had seen for many days. The letter is the following:

"SIR: In order to save yourself from the impending storm which now threatens you, I order you immediately to surrender yourself, with all your garrison, stores, etc. If I am obliged to storm, you may depend upon such treatment alone as is justly due a murderer. Beware of destroying stores of any kind, or any papers or letters that are in your possession, or hurting one house in town; for by heaven if you do there shall be no mercy shown you. G. R. CLARK."

Gov. Hamilton was affected by the above communication, as will appear by the following mild answer:

"Governor Hamilton begs leave to acquaint Col. Clark, that he and his garrison are not to be awed into any action unworty of British subjects."

The attack was renewed. About midnight before, Clark had cut a ditch near the fort, and in it his riflemen had a secure shelter from the guns of the fort. They poured in an incessant fire thro the port-holes, and silenced two pieces of artillery in fifteen minutes. Every gunner who approached the cannon at the port-holes was instantly killed or driven back from the guns horror-stricken.

This terrible and incessant fire for eighteen hours made the garrison believe that they would all be destroyed. To avoid this catastrophe, Gov. Hamilton sent the following communication to Clark:

"Governor Hamilton proposes to Col. Clark a truce for three days, during which time he promises that there shall be no defensive works carried on in the garrison, on *condition* that Col. Clark will observe on his part a like cessation of offensive works; that is, he wishes to confer with Col. Clark as soon as can be, and promises that whatever may pass between them two and another person, mutually agreed on to be present, shall remain secret until matters be finished as he wishes, whatever the result of the conference may be, it may tend to the honor and credit of each party If Col. Clark makes a difficulty of coming into the fort, Lieut.-Gov Hamilton will speak to him by the gate.

"February 24th, 1779. HENRY HAMILTON."

To this address Clark sent the following reply:

"Col. Clark's compliments to Gov. Hamilton, and begs leave to say that he will not agree to any terms other than *Mr. Hamilton surrendering himself and garrison prisoners at discretion.* If Mr Hamilton wants to talk with Col. Clark, he will meet him at the church with Capt. Helm."

A conference was held between Clark and Hamilton. A surrender was demanded by Clark, or otherwise, he threatened a massacre of the leaders in the fort for the gold given for American scalps. Clark was in earnest, and so the garrison believed.

In one hour, Clark dictated the following terms:

"1st. Lieut.-Gov. Hamilton agrees to deliver up to Col. Clark, Fort Sackville and all the stores, etc., etc.

"2d. The garrison are to deliver themselves as prisoners of war, and march out with their arms and accoutrements.

"3d. The garrison to be delivered up tomorrow at ten o'clock.

"4th. Three days are allowed the garrison to settle their accounts with the inhabitants and traders.

"5th. The officers of the garrison are to be allowed their necessary baggage.

"Signed at Post St. Vincennes, this 24th day of February, 1779; agreed to for the following reasons: 1st. Remoteness from succor. 2d. The state and quantity of provisions. 3d. The *unanimity* of the officers and men in its expediency. 4th. The honorable terms allowed; and, lastly, the confidence in a generous enemy.

"HENRY HAMILTON, Lieut.-Gov. and Superin't."

On the 25th February, under this arrangement, the fort was surrendered to Clark, and all the arms and public stores of the fort amounting to fifty thousand dollars or more. Seventy-nine prisoners were sent off on parole to Detroit, and Col. Hamilton and Major Hay with some other officers were sent with a strong guard to the capital of Virginia.

During the attack on the fort the second day, a war-party of Indians, ignorant of the presence of Clark, arrived at Vincennes from an excursion to the frontiers of Kentucky, bringing with them two white prisoners, and camped in the vicinity of the fort. Clark sent out a detachment against them, and in a short time routed the Indians with the loss of nine warriors. The remainder of the Indians, being terrified at the impetuosity of the Long Knives, were well pleased to get off with their lives.

Intelligence was received at Vincennes that a large amount

of merchandise with an escort of soldiers was on the way for Sackville; Clark, with his usual and unaccountable celerity and sagacity, ordered Helm at the head of sixty men to intercept the convoy and take the goods. In a few days' absence, Helm returned with the escort and goods, amounting to ten thousand pounds, without the loss of a single man.

Clark organized a government at the Wabash, and returned to Kaskaskia. It was in contemplation to march a military force to Detroit and take it, but it was not carried out.

Clark had treated with a great portion of the Indians in the northwest, and had captured the general of the hair-buying government, so that the Indians after the conquest of Illinois were never so powerful or so hostile as before. The British Government never after this conquest attempted to regain possession of the country. Thus terminated one of the most remarkable conquests of a country recorded in history. This small army was provided with nothing to sustain them and guide to victory and honor except the extraordinary talents of the commander.

John Todd being appointed the commandant of the county of Illinois, arrived at Kaskaskia early in May, and on the 15th June, 1779, issued a proclamation. He organized courts of justice, and appointed officers, etc., to establish a regular government in the country. On his return thro Kentucky from Virginia, where he had been on public business, he was killed at the battle of the Blue Licks in Kentucky. Another commandant, Timothy Demountbrun, was appointed over the County of Illinois, but what he did or when his official duties expired no one at this day knows.

It is an extraordinary fact, that very few Americans visited Illinois or lived in it before the conquest by Clark. All the intercourse Clark had was with the French, and of them he obtained supplies for his army. Oliver Pollock was a kind of an agent for the Government stationed at New Orleans, to settle and pay drafts sent to him by the officers of the army and others in the West. Clark gave drafts on this agent for the supplies for his army when they were in Illinois, but not many of these orders are paid to this day.

Virginia had not the means to spare to send either men or

money to Clark to sustain his troops. It is true, the government of the Old Dominion gave a large grant of land, which is located on the Ohio River opposite the celebrated Corn Island, to Clark and his men. This tract of land amounts to one hundred and fifty thousand acres.

At the time Clark and his army occupied Illinois, there was very little metallic currency in the country, and bank paper was almost unknown. The currency was more in shaved deer-skins, three pounds for the dollar, than in any other currency. If books were kept in reference to any other currency it was merely nominal, as the exchange of one article for another was the mode of doing business at that day and for many years after.

The cultivation of the soil gradually diminished, and the French population of Illinois declined from the time the British took possession of the country, yet the French who remained, cultivated the common fields and were also engaged as voyagers and *courcurs de bois*, as they were designated.

These early Canadian French were robust, strong men and made excellent boatmen. They were hardy and became accustomed to voyaging; so that on a boat to New Orleans or to the Falls of St. Anthony or to the Rocky Mountains they were at home. A great number, forty, fifty or more would embark on a single barge to New Orleans and return with it heavily freighted with southern products and European merchandise.

About the year 1775, Joseph Trotier, an enterprising trader from Canada, settled in Cahokia. He carried on a large commerce from his village—Cahokia—to New Orleans. On a voyage from New Orleans to Cahokia in one of his large boats heavily laden, a large cotton-wood tree fell across the boat and destroyed it and the cargo. Such an occurrence was not unfrequent during high water with boats ascending the Mississippi.

The current of the Mississippi was so strong that boats were compelled to run close to the shore, where the current is less forcible. The river, when it was high, frequently washed the sands from under acres of the banks with large trees growing on them, and this land, when undermined, would sink at once into the water with a great noise, which may be heard for miles. It was in one of these slides that Trotier's boat was destroyed.

The boatmen had great difficulty in ascending the Mississippi, on account of the strong current. It frequently required them four or five months to ascend the river with a large *batteau* from New Orleans to Kaskaskia, and often on the voyage many of the boatmen were swept off by sickness.

It was not only sickly on a voyage ascending the river in the summer, but it was extreme hard labor to navigate a large vessel against the current of the Mississippi. In the most rapid current the oars would not answer the purpose. In such extraordinary sections of the river a large rope or *cordelle* was used. One end was fastened to the boat and ten, fifteen, or twenty men, according to the necessity of the case, placed at the other end, towed the boat after them. When the party reached a river or creek entering into the Mississippi, they swam over with the *cordelle* and towed on the boat. Canoes or skiffs were sometimes used in crossing these intervening streams. In some currents that were very strong, the upper end of the *cordelle* was fastened to a tree and the other end put round a windlass and thereby the boat was forced up the river against the current.

These *cordelle* ropes were frequently very long, measuring five or six hundred yards, and the size in proportion to the boat which was to be towed.

Every one has witnessed the extraordinary difference in ascending the river between common barges and steamboats. Comfort and even pleasure is enjoyed on a steamer, while excessive labor, tardy progress, and sickness attended the barges in their slow head-way up the river.

In the first settlement of the country, the inhabitants were in great distress for want of salt, but they discovered in the present county of Gallatin, salt-springs, which were much used by the Indians and French of Vincennes. From the first settlement of the Wabash by the French for nearly one hundred years after, much salt was made out of the water of these springs and conveyed to Vincennes. The enterprising and energetic United States Senator Henry Dodge of Iowa and the French before him made salt at the saline below Ste Genevieve. From these works much salt was conveyed to Illinois. Whether Gen Dodge manufactured salt or served in the United States Senate, he always deported himself with that dignity and noble bearing that forms the true character of a western pioneer. Mr. Cabanne of St. Louis, another sample of these noble pioneers, made salt at his works west of St. Louis near the Merrimac River Salt was manufactured here in early Spanish times in Louisiana.

The city of Nashville, Tennessee, is situated at the site of the salt-works known in the early times as the French Lick. Salt was manufactured and conveyed to Illinois Salt-water in modern times has been discovered in many places in Illinois. On Big Muddy River, quantities were manufactured by Conrad Will and others. Judge Biggs made salt in Madison County on Silver Creek; and in Bond County on Shoal Creek salt was also manufactured Gen Edger owned the works and manufactured salt many years at a saline in Monroe County at the Mississippi Bluff.

In Vermilion County salt-water was discovered, and salt manufactured by Mr Vance. This gentleman bored into the rock for salt-water to the depth of four or five hundred feet.

It appears that there is salt-water throughout the State of Illinois, and, in fact, all over the western country salt-water has been discovered either in springs or by digging for it; so that this indispensable article may be found in every section of the country.

The Kannahwa salt-works, the Ohio Saline, situated in Gallatin County; and the Boone's Lick works, Mo.; in modern times furnished great quantities for the West; but the conveyance of sea salt from New Orleans being so cheap, and the article being stronger, not so much is manufactured at these works as formerly. Much salt is now conveyed to Chicago from New York.

In the early settlement of the country, the inhabitants used not much iron. The earth was, for the most part, clear of gravel and rocks, so that the *luxury* of horse-shoeing was not much indulged in. The plows were almost strangers to iron, and the carts entirely so. Iron was not much in use, and none made in the country.

In very early times, very little intoxicating liquor, if any at all, was introduced into the country. Indian traders may have had small quantities; but so small that it was scarcely noticed. In after-times, a liquor from New Orleans, called Taffia, was brought to Illinois. This was manufactured out of sugar or sugar-cane in the West-India Islands, and resembled New-England rum. Some considerable wine was manufactured out of the native grapes. This wine was made by the first settlers but disappeared with the Europeans. The creoles made little or none.

In the middle ages of Illinois, the Monongahela whisky *reigned triumphant*, and was hailed at shooting-matches and horse-races by many as "the poor man's friend", the "kindest and the best." Yet, in truth, the Illinois people were never in early times intemperate.

In the pioneer times of Illinois, the mechanic arts did not flourish. Mason work of that day was good, but of the rest I can say nothing in praise of them. The cooperage of the country amounted to very little more than making well-buckets. The carpenters were unskilful in their profession. They framed houses and covered them with peg shingles; made batton-doors, etc, in a rough fashion. No shoemakers or tanners; but all dressed deer-skins and made moccasons. Almost every inhabitant manufactured his own cart and plow, and made his harness, traces, and all out of raw-hide. Blacksmith's-shops were like iron—scarce. Altho the citizens had cattle, yet scarcely any butter or cheese was ever seen in the country. In fact, neither male or female worked much; but the females assumed their prerogative of doing less than the males. There was neither spinning-wheels nor looms in the land. It must be awarded to the French, and particularly to the ladies, that they expended much labor and showed much taste in making nice gardens. They received not only much profit and comfort of living out of their gardens, but they also enjoyed the pleasure of rearing and seeing the beautiful plants and flowers growing in their gardens, which is so congenial to French taste.

The invading army under Col. Clark was made acquainted with the fertility and advantages of Illinois, which caused many of his men and others to settle in the country.

It was the war with Great Britain in 1812, that gave Illinois a modern notoriety. The troops from Kentucky and the West, seeing the northern section of Illinois, reported the advantages of the country, which caused it to settle. Clark's campaign made the country known and thereby it was settled.

I can not agree with the generality of mankind, that war is a great scourge and curse on mankind. If a war is carried on without its being based on some proper and just principle, it is a curse; but this is not often the case in these modern days.

I consider that the war of the American Revolution was serviceable to the whole human family. The result of this war was the first practical demonstration that man is capable of self-government. The free institutions of America, which are the fruit of the Revolution, will have a tendency to liberate all people who are oppressed by an arbitrary government. In this view, the Revolutionary War was the best and most holy that ever existed; and is a blessing to all mankind.

The wars of the crusades done good to Europe. This is the decision of the best and wisest of men. The revolutionary war of France, altho much blood was shed, yet it was serviceable to the world. It made the people know their rights, power, and importance. And the campaign of Col. Clark not only made known this country to the colonies, but the conquest of Illinois figured strong in our favor in making the treaty of 1783 with Great Britain.

It was during the Revolution, while the colonies were struggling for their independence, and the whole country in arms, one against the other, that a small band of enterprising emigrants from the colonies settled in Illinois in the year 1781 At this early period, and while no one knew in traveling whether he would fall into the hands of a friend or foe, James Moore, Shadrach Bond, Robert Kidd, Larken Rutherford, and James Garrison decided to make Illinois their homes This small party crossed the Alleghany Mountains, descended the Ohio, and stemmed the current of the Mississippi to Kaskaskia. The emigration of these pioneers was also during a bloody Indian war This party was for peace and for the settlement of the country, having with them their women and children; so that they were not armed and prepared for war as a military expedition would be. It is therefore extraordinary that this small party of emigrants could escape all the dangers of the Revolution and Indian hostilities and reach Illinois in safety It would seem that Providence was fostering this infant settlement in Illinois

James Moore was the leader of the party, and was a native of Maryland Kidd and Rutherford had been soldiers under Col. Clark Bond was also a native of Maryland, and raised near Baltimore, until he made the Far-west his home Garrison, Moore, and Rutherford located themselves near the Bellefontaine in the present county of Monroe, while Bond, Kidd, and Garrison settled in the Mississippi Bottom

These American families settling in the Mississippi lowland, gave the name of American Bottom to the alluvial land of the river from Alton to the mouth of the Kaskaskia River This is perhaps the largest and most fertile body of alluvial soil in the United States. Some of it has been cultivated for more than one hundred and fifty years without improvement of the soil, and it yet yields excellent crops Almost all the early French settlements were made in it, and when it is drained of some lakes and ponds it will be the largest tract of land of the same fertility in North America

The river at times not frequent inundates the American Bottom. The first notice history gives us of a great rise of water in the Mississippi was in the year 1770 That year the water encroached on the banks of the river opposite Fort Chartres, erected in 1718 At that time the river was three-fourths of a mile from it, but continued to advance on the fort until the year 1772, when the bottom was inundated and one of the walls of the fort washed down The next extraordinary freshet in the river was in the year 1784, this was a deep inundation of the bottom. The inhabitants of Kaskaskia made a temporary encampment on the high land east of the town and some of them cultivated land on the hills that year. The same of the Cahokia people Many of them retired to the rocky bluff, southeast of Cahokia for relief during the high water and called it *Bon Succour* Others went to St. Louis The next very high water in the American Bottom was in the year 1844 Large steamboats in this flood sailed from bluff to bluff This rise of water did great damage to property in the bottom, and almost destroyed the villages of Cahokia, Prairie du Pont, Prairie du Rocher, and Kaskaskia. These villages have not recovered from the injury of the floods of 1844. The past year, 1851, the bottom was again flooded and much damage done to the real and personal property. This rise of water was not so high as either that of 1784 or 1844. A considerable flood occurred in the bottom in 1826; but not to compare with those mentioned above.

The first site at which Moore made his resting-place was not far southwest of the present town of Waterloo at a spring called to this day Slab Spring.

Bond, Garrison, and Kidd made a settlement in the bottom known at that day as the Block-House Fort.

Not long after the arrival of James Moore, he was employed by Gabriel Cere, a wealthy merchant of St. Louis, to take goods and trade with the Indians in the western part of Tennessee.

Mr. Moore continued in this trade with the southern Indians for many years, and made his general headquarters at the site the city of Nashville occupies at this time, called then the French Licks.

Mr. Moore had a large family whose descendants in Illinois are both numerous and respectable. The same may be said of the other early emigrants, only, perhaps, their offsprings are not so numerous.

Mr. Bond numbered many years before his death. As he advanced in age, his excellent traits of character became more and more known to the people, and the more was his character esteemed He was often elected to the legislature of both Territories of Indiana and the Northwestern Territory. He was in the legislature at Cincinnati, September, 1790. He was a justice of the Court of Common Pleas of St. Clair County for many years together and was always held in high estimation by the people. Judge Bond in his neighborhood possessed a standing for integrity and honesty that could not be surpassed. In his younger days, as most others did, he hunted part of his time and was considered an excellent woodsman. He was not ambitious for wealth and when he acted for the public it was to accommodate them, not himself.

He possessed a strong mind and an excellent heart He had a very limited education; but nature supplied all the omissions of education and made him a most worthy character.

James Garrison was almost a *fac-simile* of Judge Bond except he always successfully refused office. He was an honest, upright citizen and an excellent soldier; as that part of his character was frequently put to the test in the many Indian skirmishes he and others of the emigrants had with the hostile Indians. He lived and died in the American Bottom where he left a posterity of very exemplary citizens.

Robert Kidd continued his residence in the American Bottom until his death. He lived for many years on a mound in the American Bottom near Fort Chartres. He was a good citizen, quiet and domestic. He raised a family of children; some of whom are now alive and are like their father, worthy and respectable Mr. Kidd was a farmer and lived a long life to enjoy the country he assisted to conquer under Col Clark. He died in 1849, at his residence in the Bottom in Monroe County, numbering more than four score years.

Larken Rutherford was also one of Col. Clark's valiant men that aided in the conquest of Illinois. He was large and athletic, bold and fearless. He was in his decline of years a member of the regular Baptist Church, and exercised the same energy and zeal in this avocation as he did with the rifle in storming Fort Sackville in 1779. In the organization and government of the church Mr Rutherford was not a dormant member but up and active in the work, whether the job was difficult or not. He was in his church like he was in the army, ready at any moment for mortal combat. He was honest but rather inclined to a vigorous observance of his duties, and a trouble in the clerical camp if the others did not come to the exact point as he did He was a farmer in the county of St. Clair and resided for many years not far north of the present city of Belleville

About this time, 1781, and from the time Col. Clark first came to the country, which was about four years before, private individuals and families emigrated to Kaskaskia and many of them permanently remained there. Kaskaskia was the metropolis of the country while the French and British possessed it, and it continued the same under the American government until 1819 The seat of government of Illinois soon after this date was established at Vandalia

John Edgar, during the American Revolution, left the naval service of Great Britain in 1776, came to the United Colonies, and arrived at Kaskaskia in 1784 He had command of a vessel on the lakes, but he resigned all for liberty and confided his life to the American cause This was quite natural and honorable to him He was a native of Ireland and a gentleman of liberal education His heart burned for freedom, and he was born and educated with an intense hatred to Great Britain

He was intelligent and felt with a keen sensibility the heartless despotism exercised by Great Britain over his native land He was found in the British service when the colonies raised the standard of freedom and independence. What was he to do? He could not with a clear conscience fight for a country that in his heart he despised, and against a people he admired and loved The decision was easily made and he became a citizen of the United States He emigrated to Kaskaskia with a large stock of goods suitable to the market, and remained there till his death which occurred in 1832 He lived in Kaskaskia for at least half a century and during all that time sustained a very conspicuous and honorable character

He came to the country wealthy, and shared it out among the people with unbounded hospitality He possessed in an eminent degree the kind and benevolent heart of an Irish gentleman, and with his wealth and benevolent disposition it afforded him happiness to make all around him happy He was in his younger days an active business man, and was largely engaged in the land trade In very early times, he erected at great expense, a fine flouring-mill on the same site where M Paget had built one sixty years before This mill was a great benefit to the public and also profitable to the proprietor Before the year 1800, this mill manufactured great quantities of flour for the New-Orleans market which would compare well with the Atlantic flour

Gen Edgar was the owner of a splendid mansion in Kaskaskia, and in it, on all occasions, the traveler and stranger found a hearty welcome. No one ever displayed more real hospitality

than he did in his house. Hospitality was the common custom of the country; but he improved on it. This agreeable dwelling was the fashionable resort for almost half a century, and many yet alive can testify to the comforts and kind treatment they have enjoyed under his hospitable roof.

For many years he was the most wealthy man in Illinois. He held real estate throughout the country, and paid more taxes than any other person at one time in the territory. With all this wealth and influence, he was kind and benevolent to the poor; nor did it ever change his deportment from an American gentleman. He enjoyed the confidence of the public, and was, when in active life, very popular. He was elected from Illinois a member of the legislature of the Northwestern Territory. This General Assembly convened at Chilicothe, Ohio; and was held under the administration of Arthur St. Clair, governor of the Northwestern Territory.

Gen. Edgar acted as justice-of-the-peace and judge of the Court of Common Pleas for a long series of years and gave general satisfaction. He had never made the profession of the law his particular study; but common sense, a good education, and experience in business with perfect honesty made him a very respectable officer. The United States appointed him major-general over the Illinois militia, and he reviewed the general musters with that dignity that became his high station. And when his years were almost numbered, the general assembly of Illinois named in honor of him a county. Edgar County on the east side of the State is one of the first counties in the Wabash Valley.

Gen. Edgar in person was large and portly. In his youth he was active, and was always in both youth and age an accomplished gentleman. He possessed a well-balanced mind, no one trait prevailing over the others except his benevolence. This quality was predominant, which was exhibited in him throughout a long and eventful life. His dust is mixed with his mother-earth at Kaskaskia, where the people will long remember Gen. Edgar with love and gratitude. He had a wife but no children. And altho he was accused of many gallantries with the ladies, yet he died without issue. Gen. Edgar well sustained the honorable character of a pioneer. He possessed many of the qualities that adorn the human race, with very few that are condemned. He died as he lived, "the noblest work of God."

The treaty of peace between the United States and Great Britain made in 1783 had a great effect in advancing the emigration to Illinois.

The acknowledged Independence of the United States by Great Britain gave the whole country, Illinois included, a fixed character and standing at home and abroad. This was a great inducement to emigration.

In fact, the American Revolution is an event so interesting to the whole people that it had a great influence on Illinois as well as on every section of the Union. I shall, therefore, give the outlines of that extraordinary change of government; because it is connected with the "Pioneer History of Illinois."

The founders of the Republic of the United States were raised and lived in adversity. The school of adversity made the colonists a great and energetic people, capable of achieving a revolution that has produced more beneficial effects to mankind than any other recorded in history.

All men are influenced by surrounding circumstances, and can not avoid it. The various colonies along the Atlantic seacoast were planted and reared under very adverse circumstances. They had a long series of hardships and perils to encounter. They were annoyed with almost everything that could injure the human family. Indian wars, sickness, famine, and destruction of almost everything that rendered life comfortable were visited on the first settlements of the colonies. This kind of life for several generations together, gave the people of the colonies a decided character of independence and courage. In fact, they possessed all the qualities of mind and body to enable them to accomplish this memorable revolution.

The very moment the British Parliament infringed on their rights as freemen, they resisted it. It is true, at first they had no idea of freedom and independence of the British crown. They were not, at the commencement, united, and therefore did not know their strength, nor did the parent country know the young lion she was rousing into action. The British Government continued their oppression and illegal measures in parliament, until these colonists, who knew their rights and dared maintain them, would not submit any longer.

The energies and bravery of the colonies were exerted for the mother-country in the French war, so called; which was closed by the treaty of Paris in 1763 In this war the colonies lost twenty-five thousand men and expended their revenues to sustain it until they were reduced to poverty It was these colonies that wrested the western country and Canada from France, and it enabled them also to conquer their own freedom and independence from the mother-country.

The British Government being clear of any embarrassment arising from France in the new world, commenced a different policy with the colonies, and in March, 1764, the next year after the treaty of Paris, commenced the memorable stamp act and similar oppressive measures. The Government of Great Britain decided to raise a revenue from the colonies without them being represented in parliament. This measure violated that fundamental principle, that taxation and representation must go together, and the Americans resisted it with all their energies.

The colonies from the beginning established for themselves in each province a legislative assembly. These assemblies were the great means of achieving the freedom and independence of America; and for ten years these assemblies and the people continued a political warfare with Great Britain, one party contending for despotism and the other for the rights and privileges of other Britons. It was at last recommended by the people and adopted that a general assembly or continental congress of all the colonies should convene at Philadelphia The object of this congress and their constituents was not independence, but to petition the Government of Great Britain for a redress of their grievances. No one in that body thought of independence.

This continental congress, the first ever convened in America, met in Philadelphia on the 5th Sept, 1774. This assembly contained some of the greatest men that ever figured in the actions of men. In it there were a few above fifty members, elected from the different colonies. Peyton Randolph was elected president and Charles Thompson secretary. In this assembly were George Washington, John Adams, Roger Sherman, Patrick Henry, Richard Bland, Benjamin Harrison, Edward Pendleton, John Jay, Silas Deane, John Rutledge, Sam'l Adams, Thomas McKeon, and a host of others of equal merit and notoriety—all known to fame.

This congress was composed of not only great men, but also of moral, pious men. On the 6th September, it was

"*Resolved,* That the Reverend Mr. Duche be desired to open the congress tomorrow morning with prayers at the Carpenter's Hall at nine o'clock."

"WEDNESDAY, September 7, 1774, 9 o'clock a.m.

"Agreeable to the resolve of yesterday, the meeting was opened with prayers by the Rev. Mr. Duche.

"*Voted,* That the thanks of the Congress be given to Mr. Duche by Messrs. Cushing and Ward for the performance of divine service and for the excellent prayer which he composed and delivered on the occasion."

These proceedings prove that this assembly entertained the proper respect for morality and religion, and they also established the fact that they were much pleased with the prayer of Mr. Duche

This congress made a short session. They petitioned the crown for the redress of grievances and made an address to the people of the colonies. They also recommended the meeting of another congress.

The following is the census of the colonies, in Sept., 1774:

	SOULS.
Massachusetts,	400,000
New Hampshire,	150,000
Rhode Island,	95,678
Connecticut,	192,000
New York,	250,000
New Jersey,	130,000
Pennsylvania (including lower counties),	320,000
Virginia,	650 000
N. Carolina,	300,000
S. Carolina,	225,000
Total,	3,025,678

I presume the above census included the colored population as well as white. It may be presumed that the above census is, at least, not low, but, perhaps, enlarged to some extent It appears from the proceedings of this congress that Georgia took no part in the movement

Another continental congress convened at Philadelphia on the 5th of September, 1775, but not a sufficient number of members to do business were in attendance They adjourned to the 13th. To this congress Georgia sent members. This assembly also contained great and wise statesmen. Gen. Washington had been appointed by the previous congress to be "commander-in-chief of all the troops raised" and "to be raised in North America," but the great philosopher and statesman, Thomas Jefferson, was returned in his place Washington was appointed to the command of the army on the 10th May, 1775.

The contention between Great Britain and her colonies was so much widened toward the close of the year 1775, that every discerning man in America saw at once that the case was independence of Great Britain or a slavish subjection to her despotism. This congress was occupied in preparing the country for defence, rather than presenting petitions to the king.

This assembly voted to raise twenty thousand troops for defence and three millions of dollars with which to prosecute the war The nation was preparing for the terrible conflict to be freemen or slaves, and this to be decided by the force of arms.

This congress adjourned, and the most memorable assemblage of men that perhaps ever existed convened at Philadelphia in the year 1776. This year is so intimately connected with liberty that it will be respected and admired so long as liberty and freedom exist on earth Thomas Jefferson, a member from Virginia whose extraordinary fame and character is known all over the earth, drafted the celebrated Declaration of Independence, and on the 4th July, 1776, it passed the congress and was signed by all the members. This declaration with the force of arms made the colonies a free nation.

After a most bitter struggle of seven years, Great Britain acknowledged the independence of the United States and agreed to the treaty of peace, signed at Paris Sept. 3d, 1783.

During the Revolutionary War, a most singular character arose, whose actions were excessively bold and energetic. Paulette Maillet, which is pronounced Mia, was born at Mackinac, in the year 1753, of French parents, and, like Othello, from his tender years he "used his dearest action in the tented field," and he knew little of the world, "except what pertains to feats and broil of battle." He was an Indian trader, and roamed over the country toward the sources of the Mississippi and the Rocky Mountains. He was raised and lived out of the pale of civilization He possessed an extraordinary strong mind and a kind of singular ferocity of courage

He founded, in the year 1778, the new town of Peoria which occupied the site of the present city of that name. The old village was a mile and a-half up the lake from the present city. This new village was often called *Le Ville a Maillet.* The Indian traders and others settled around Maillet and made a village at the outlet of the lake

He heard of the defeat of Thomas Brady of Cahokia by the British and Indians, in the fall of the year 1777, at St Joseph on the east side of Lake Michigan and was determined to avenge it. He had relatives and acquaintances in the expedition conducted by Brady, and some of them were killed, which roused him into a great rage to have satisfaction. The next year, 1778, Maillet called on his legions, who were always ready to serve him, for support to take the British fort at St. Joseph and to revenge the death of his friends This was not made in vain. About three hundred warriors, white, mixed, and red, assembled under his standard. In this corps were many of the most respectable citizens who marched with Maillet for the relief of their countrymen, who were taken prisoners the previous year while under the command of Brady.

The Indians joined the expedition for plunder and friendship for Maillet. They started from Peoria and marched on foot to St. Joseph On the march in the hot prairies, exhausted with fatigue and not much to eat, one of Maillet's men, M Amlin, gave out and was unable to travel Maillet had no time to spare, and no provisions except a scanty supply of dried meat packed on their backs, and if the British garrison knew of their approach their defeat was certain. This great savage warrior coolly and deliberately took his tomahawk and sunk it deep into the brains of the exhausted soldier. This was savage and ferocious; there is some palliation for it but no justification. The object of the expedition would be defeated if the utmost secrecy and celerity were not practised. If the sick man was left he might perish or give notice of the campaign. Maillet may have performed this act to impress his followers with fear and dread of him. He had with him rather a piratical crew, and if severe and decisive measures were not practised on them, the expedition must have failed. It was a bold and decisive stroke that few men would have the nerve to perform.

After this decisive act, Maillet's men marched under his standard with vigor, and they fought the British garrison like tigers. They captured the fort altho defended by British troops and cannon. The party took all the stores of the Indian goods, which amounted to fifty thousand dollars; they permitted the British to retire to Canada in peace. The wounded men of Brady's party were safely returned to Cahokia and thus the expedition of Maillet ended.

Maillet was of a strange composition and had a strong, uncultivated mind, but a great preponderance of courage and savage combativeness. He at last lost his life by this trait of character. In Peoria, in the year 1805, he had an affray with a Frenchman called Senegal. Maillet, still accustomed to use violence to obtain victory, was shot dead by Senegal.

Another singular character arose above the horizon in Illinois in the year 1779. Dominique Ducharme was a Canadian and an Indian trader. He was another of this class of Northwestern traders who possessed great talents, extraordinary energy, and indomitable courage. He lived at intervals in Cahokia and had a brother residing there. Ducharme was habituated to the savage life and had unbounded influence over the Indians from Lake Superior to the Falls of St. Anthony, and down toward the Illinois River. He obtained a supply of Indian goods at Mackinac, and contrary to Spanish regulations, he entered the Missouri River to trade with the natives in the Spanish dominions. He had proceeded up the Missouri some distance, when a party of Spanish soldiers from

St Louis with an officer in a barge overtook them and captured his boat, goods, and all except himself He made his escape with only his gun and his life.

St. Louis was the Spanish post from which the armament proceeded that captured Ducharme's boat and merchandise. This made him swear vengeance against this post. All winter he was active in raising his savage friends for an attack on St. Louis His war-whoop was heard from Lake Superior to the Falls of St Anthony, and down to Rock River, and fifteen hundred warriors responded to the call The British garrison at Mackinac furnished a few regular soldiers and some Canadians to join Ducharme

With these forces Ducharme made arrangements to capture St. Louis on the 26th of May, 1780. He made the assault, and killing as many as appeased his wrath, he withdrew his red warriors and abandoned the massacre. It is said that when Ducharme and his Indians saw many of their old friends dead, their anger turned into sorrow and they withdrew to their wigwams in the North The year of this attack on St. Louis, 1780, was known afterward as "*L'anne au coup!*"

It is astonishing the great influence Ducharme had over the Indians. The British joined in, as Spain and Great Britain were then at war; but the British acted a subordinate part to Ducharme in this matter. It was Ducharme's campaign, not the British.

In the fall of 1780, La Balme, a native of France, organized an expedition from Kaskaskia to capture Detroit He marched from Kaskaskia with twenty or thirty men, at Vincennes they engaged a few more. He moved up the Wabash to the British trading-post, Ke-ki-ong-a, at the head of the Maumee, and destroyed the place. After securing the plunder, he marched to the river Aboite, and while encamped, a party of Miami Indians attacked his troops in the night and killed him and dispersed the balance.

The expedition must have been rather of the privateering order than regular war The celebrated Col. Clark was on the Mississippi, perhaps at Fort Jefferson—now the Iron Banks—at the time when La Balme organized his party to capture Detroit, and if a regular campaign had been on hand Clark would have been its leader

Thomas Hughes from the western part of Pennsylvania, visited Illinois in the year 1783 to settle in the country. He made a tomahawk improvement on Nine-mile Creek in the present county of Randolph. He returned for his family the next year, and on the Ohio River near Fort Massac, where they landed for the night, the Indians attacked the boat, killed Hughes and a sucking child in the arms of its mother, and wounded severely the mother in the shoulder. The rest of the emigrants escaped down the river in the boat to the Iron Banks, not being able to stem the current of the Mississippi to Kaskaskia This defeat interrupted the emigration of this family for many years, but in the year 1797, the surviving children of Hughes, together with the widow and her second husband, Pillars, as she had married again, moved to the country and located in Randolph County where many of their descendants reside at this day The child spoken of above was shot thro the head and its brains scattered over the mother's breast. Such is the barbarity of Indian warfare.

It has been stated that the French population of Illinois commenced to decline from the conquest of the country by the British in the year 1763, and the villages of Fort Chartres and St Philip were at this time, 1783, rapidly declining. After the year 1800, not a French family resided in either of them The other French villages of Illinois are fast verging to the same fate of their extinct neighbors Mr Everett was the only inhabitant of the village of St. Philip in 1803. It is almost impossible to give a satisfactory reason for the decline and fall of these French villages in Illinois.

Both the Government of Great Britain and the United States that had dominion over the country, permitted the French inhabitants a free toleration of their religion and allowed them all the rights and privileges of other citizens And, moreover, grants of land were given to them that were denied to Americans who settled in the country after the year 1788. The French settlers enjoyed the first selections of the lands in the country, and with all these advantages that population has in all the settlements declined, and in some localities none at all exist where once were populous villages The French population will not reside on farms, each family to itself, like the Americans. They always live in villages where they may enjoy their social pleasure. The church also induces them to settle near it in villages. In these villages the inhabitants can not farm to the same advantage as those living on separate plantations. The French also neglected to educate their children. This is another heavy drawback against them. It seems that the creole French do not possess that indomitable energy of character that the Americans so eminently enjoy. The masses of the French are unambitious of wealth or office They are innocent and honest, and care but little for the future if the present is prosperous and happy. They do not trouble themselves with that restless ambition to obtain wealth and power that frequently renders the American population extremely unhappy. This course of conduct and life will, of necessity, make one class of people outreach the other in the race for wealth and worldly advancement. One class of people will be the most efficient and will extend itself throughout the country, while the other race will at least remain stationary or decline in the vicinity of the Americans. Yet it is doubtful which race is the most happy Excessive, restless, ungovernable ambition, such as actuates the American population, does not produce happiness—while the French are less actuated by ambition and have less energy, they enjoy more of the calm of life and indulge more in the social enjoyments which I believe makes them a happier people than the Americans; but not so energetic.

This course of life of the creole French has almost entirely secured them from any infractions of the penal laws of the country Very few or none of the creoles were ever indicted for the crimes the law-books style *malum in sc.* Not one to my knowledge was ever in the penitentiary for a crime I believe the records of the courts in Illinois do not exhibit an indictment against a creole Frenchman for any crime higher than keeping his grocery open on a prohibited day of the week.

In the year 1782, the Spanish authorities at St Louis, Upper Louisiana, fitted out an expedition to capture the same British post, St. Joseph, that both Brady and Maillet had before taken, and the same that LaSalle erected in 1679 It is known that the British Government retained some of the posts in the Northwest after the treaty of 1783 which were within the limits of the United States This fort was one of them It will also be recollected that Spain and Great Britain were at war at the time A company commanded by a Spanish captain with sixty-five men marched from St Louis across the prairies of Illinois and captured the British garrison at St. Joseph

This was a singular expedition—not known whether it was against the British or to seize by force of arms some of the western country which the Spaniards laid claim to, as they had assisted the Americans in the Revolution The court of Spain urged this conquest against the Americans when the Spaniards contended for a part of the western country. The Spanish captain retained possession of the post only for a short time and returned to St Louis

About this time, 1783, Cahokia was the partial residence of many Northwestern Indian traders Julien Dubuque made it his residence before he established himself on the west side of the Mississippi near the present city of Dubuque He purchased of the Indians the lead-mines to which his name was given, situated on the west side of the Mississippi, 22d September, 1788, and on his petition to the Baron de Carondelet at New Orleans on the 10th November, 1790, these mines were granted to him This tract of land extends on the river six leagues and three back

Dubuque's grave is about one mile below the city of Dubuque, and was by the Indians held in great veneration while they remained in the country It was stated by the Indian traders that the Sauk and Fox Indians made it a duty of religion to visit once a year the grave of Dubuque and perform some religious ceremonies over it. Every visit an Indian made to the grave, he cast a small stone on it in honor of the deceased The superstition of the Indians made them believe that Dubuque was not entirely dead; but that he would soon be restored to life and be their guide and friend again

William Arundel, a merchant from Canada and an Indian trader, resided in Cahokia before the year 1783, and had before that time resided in or near Peoria. He was an orderly, moral, correct man and dealt largely in lands He emigrated from Ireland and had received a liberal education His handwriting for a long series of years may be seen in the various offices of St Clair and Randolph counties. He lived to a very old age and died at Kaskaskia in 1816 Thomas Brady and William Arundel were the only two persons who were not French that resided in Cahokia before the year 1788. Thomas Brady lived in Cahokia for many years and was sheriff of St. Clair County under the organization of Gov. St Clair in the year 1790 He had the reputation of an honest, correct citizen, and I believe he deserved it.

Capt McCarty was a citizen of Cahokia and was captain of the French company that joined the standard of Col. Clark in February, 1779, in the Revolution, and endured the fatigues and perils of the campaign to Vincennes thro high water and ice; and almost in a starving condition. He assisted in the conquest of Fort Sackville and Vincennes, and performed his duty there to the satisfaction of Clark

Another McCarty, called English McCarty, built a water-mill on the Cahokia Creek about three-quarters of a mile northeast of the present Illinoistown He expended much money and time on this mill, and did not obtain any great profit in return. It is impossible to establish on such streams as Cahokia Creek mills that will be profitable to the proprietors and serviceable to the public. McCarty's mill was large and did much business at times; but the banks of the creek being so easily washed away, the dam could not be made to stand. The vestages of this mill may yet be seen altho it was built seventy or eighty years since. McCarty obtained an improvement right of four hundred acres of land covering his mill-site which is worth more than ten times as much as his mill ever was. McCarty emigrated to Illinois from Canada and left no heirs in the West to enjoy either the mill or his land.

About this time, a water-mill was built at the Falling Spring, two miles southeast of Prairie du Pont. The French call this spring *L'eau Tomb*—which gushes out of a perpendicular rock of the Mississippi Bluff with a fall of sixty or eighty feet to the bottow below. At times in the spring a great quantity of water rushes out of this channel in the rock and the fall of which may be heard for several miles A mill was constructed at these falls for grinding wheat A kind of trunk or hollow log conducted the water to the wheel of the mill This mill was small and at this day not a trace of it remains to be seen. This spring is rather a curiosity and is now made a fashionable watering-place in the hot days of summer It is a celebrated site of picnic parties, and the young and gay assemble there in the summer to *look love* at each other.

The first water-mill erected in this section of the country was that built on Prairie-du-Pont Creek by the Mission of St. Sulpice. This mill was the nucleus around which the village of Prairie du Pont was formed This mill and settlement must date its commencement about the year 1754. The mill and the plantation of this religious society were in fine repair in 1764, when they sold out to M Gerardine and left the country on account of the British Government

A wind-mill was erected in the prairie, two miles southeast of Cahokia, by the Jesuits in the year 1744, or a short time before. This mill also declined and went to decay about the time that the British took the country and the order of the Jesuits was suppressed. Some of the millstones are yet lying in the prairie where the mill once stood There is an ancient graveyard near this old mill-site

Col. Clark, by order of the executive of Virginia, in the spring of 1780, left Kaskaskia to establish Fort Jefferson at the Iron Banks on the east side of the Ohio River, some distance below the mouth It became necessary for Col Clark to leave Fort Jefferson and return direct to Kentucky. This tour he performed on foot with only one man with him, while the Indians were numerous and extremely hostile in the section of the country thro which he was obliged to travel He lay by in the daytime, generally, and traveled at night. He packed his gun, provisions, and other articles indispensable for his journey, on his back Tennessee and Cumberland Rivers were crossed on rafts When out in the current of these rivers on a raft, he pulled down the stream for a mile or two and then landed. He feared that the Indians seeing him would place themselves at the bank where he would most likely land and destroy him before he could land or see them. By row-. ing down the stream, the enemy could not keep pace with him, he being in the current of the river and they on the shore. Thus he saved his life and reached Kentucky in safety. He was appointed by Virginia, brigadier-general and established his headquarters at the Falls of the Ohio. He remained in this office until the close of the Revolutionary War, and was disbanded by his State, because the country was about that time transferred to the general government, and thereby Virginia ceased to have the particular defence of the country from Indian depredations The whole country, and particularly his native State, awarded to him the greatest honor and thanks for his extraordinary services in the West

On the 2d July, 1783, Benjamin Harrison, governor of Virginia, wrote to General Clark a letter from which I give the following extracts:

"Before I take leave of you, I feel myself called upon, in the most favorable manner, to return to you my thanks and those of my council for the very great and singular service you have rendered your country in wresting so great and valuable territory out of the hands of the British enemy, repelling the attack of their savage allies, and carrying on a successful war in the heart of their own country. This tribute of praise and thanks so justly due, I am happy to communicate to you as the united voice of the executive"

On or before the year 1783, there were in Illinois about forty-five improvements made by Americans that entitled the owners to four hundred acres of land under the act of Congress passed 1791 This act granted four hundred acres of land to all who made improvements in Illinois prior to the year 1788, except in villages

All the American heads of families amounted to seventy-five, and the Americans who resided in the country on or before 1791, who were capable of bearing arms as militia-men, were only sixty-five All the heads of families in the country, French and Americans, who received donations of four hundred acres of land, were two hundred and forty-four All the militia-men amounted to about three hundred

It is very near correct that the heads of families in Illinois being two hundred and forty-four in the year 1788, because each head of a family received a donation of four hundred acres of land, which would induce them to be recognized before the proper officers to obtain their lands. The public documents of the government state the above number, and by estimating each family at an average to have five members, the whole population of Illinois in the year 1788 would be twelve hundred and twenty souls. It might reach to two thousand by counting transient persons and all others.

The Indian depredations were severe on the Americans in these early settlements which compelled the inhabitants to erect stations or block-house forts all over the country for their protection. Many of the sites of these stations are almost forgotten at this time. They were important in war times.

A block-house was erected near Bellefontaine by the first emigrants to that section of Illinois. Another was established in the American Bottom by Bond and his followers at his first residence in the present county of Monroe. Another station was erected by the Flannarys, that was on the main road from Kaskaskia to Cahokia, and known in after-times as Whitesides' Station Another was built by James Piggot and others, that was situated at the foot of the Mississippi Bluff, where the small creek, the Grand Risseau, so called by the French, south of Columbia, runs thro the bluff, and about one and a-half miles west of Columbia in Monroe County. Capt. Nathaniel Hull erected one including his residence, also at the foot of the Mississippi Bluff in Monroe County about twelve miles southwest of Waterloo and above the Narrows

The families of McElmuny and Flannary built a station fort as early as the year 1783, on the Mississippi opposite the Island 22 in the present county of Alexander in township 16, south.

These settlements were composed of hunters who made small improvements Some of them may have been those who met Col Clark in the year 1778 near Fort Massac. These inhabitants left the country long before 1800, and scarcely a trace of their settlements could be discovered at this date. Beshears erected a fort in the American Bottom, south of

Bond's, near section 18 in township 3, south range 11, west Golden erected another in the same neighborhood near section 24 No traces of these stations are visible at this time.

A block-house fort was generally a defence against Indian attacks. The lowest order of these forts was a single house, built strong, and a story and a-half or two stories high. The lower story was provided with port-holes to shoot thro, and also with strong puncheon doors, three or four inches thick, with strong bars to prevent the Indians from entering. The second story projected over the first, three or four feet and had holes in the floor, outside the lower story, to shoot down at the Indians attempting to enter

A higher grade of pioneer fortifications were four large, strong block-houses fashioned as above and erected at the four corners of a square lot of ground as large as the necessities of the people required The intervals between these block-houses were filled up with large timbers placed deep in the ground and extending twelve or fifteen feet above the surface Within these stockades were cabins built for the families to reside in A well of water or spring was generally found to be necessary in these forts In dangerous times, so called, the horses were admitted in the forts during the night for safe-keeping Dogs, cats, etc, as a matter of course, remained with their owners The cattle and milch cows were not often admitted Generally two strong gates were made to these garrisons with bars in proportion to secure the doors against the red-skins Port-holes were cut in the stockade above the head and platforms raised to stand on to shoot.

It was never neglected to clear off the timber near these forts or build them in the prairie; so that the enemy might not conceal himself behind the trees, brush, etc In the mornings it was dangerous at times to open these gates and go out Many times the Indians attacked the milking parties and others first going out of the fort Sentinels were sometimes kept up all night like a regular garrison

Altho this backwoods life made the people friendly as brothers, yet at times the injunction of the Scriptures "to love thy neighbor as thyself" was forgotten It must be recollected that in these forts the party was not select, as the emigrants occupying the forts came from all parts of the Union and some from Europe; so that a mixture of all sorts was frequently crowded together in these garrisons Sometimes the rights of property were not respected. This was often the ground of quarrels. It must also be recollected that no regular courts of law existed in the country in these times The mothers of children could not see, as they said, "their children imposed on," and if they possessed red hair and thin lips, generally a battle of words ensued. Sometimes the unwise and irritable husbands enlisted in these petticoat squabbles At times a rude boy would throw clods of dirt into another boy's victuals and then run to his mother for protection, informing her that "the bad boy was just going to whip him;" and the mother, nine times out of ten, believed her darling child. But the most prolific source of trouble in these forts arose out of the violation of the seventh commandment. The territory within the walls of these garrisons was so limited that Venus had no shady groves or sweet-scented bowers in which to open her court; so that her votaries had no suitable shrine in which to adore that godess. Detection suddenly followed the act and the injured party made the fort resound with fume, froth, and female thunder. For those not particularly concerned these love broils were a source of much amusement. Some would remark: "How he run when he saw his wife coming " Others would say: "The lady looked beautiful." But the grave old ladies and old aunts with spectacles on would raise their eyes in pious detestation of the crime and exclaim: "Oh! the sins of the world! It is no wonder we have an Indian war upon us."

These troubles were generally hushed up after the proper amount of female tears were shed and male sorrows displayed by solemn promises made by the husbands "not to do so any more." Then they "kissed and made friends "

In these forts, like other communities, were frequently excellent, moral, pious people; and sermons were often preached in them that would do honor to Christianity in any country. Family worship was kept by some, while dice, cards, or other games for amusement were indulged in by others in the evenings.

The most danger was from the Indians when the families left the fort for their homes in the neighborhood. They found their houses, yards, and fields out of repair and the grass grown over the yards, so that all wore a dismal appearance; and, perhaps, the blood yet on the floor or yard where a member of the family had been killed by the Indians before they moved into the fort.

Sometimes these garrisons were attacked by the Indians and then was human thunder displayed in all its various forms and shapes The Indians yelling, whooping, and firing into the fort from the outside, while the inside was energy and activity in the highest degree.

The commander, dressed in moccasons and hunting-shirt, with his rifle in hand, gave his orders in such a cool, dignified manner that soon quieted the first uproar of the women and children and placed every soldier at his proper post. Such men as these could not be conquered. Perhaps many of the same men who defended these forts possessed the talents, in peace times, to fill the highest offices in the gift of the people These trials and dangers developed their minds and educated them to grace the highest stations in the country

It is not an idle story that the females in these forts run bullets and did other services in defence of the garrisons in time of Indian attacks

By habit and experience in these times of difficulties with the Indians, all the pioneers, male and female, became accustomed to the use of the rifle in self-defence; and on many occasions saved themselves and families from destruction by these means.

About this time, 1788, a singular tragedy occurred at Peoria An Indian trader, Louis La Vossiere, resided at Peoria and was a singular high-toned Frenchman from France. He was fitted for the ages of chivalry more than for the grovelling times of money-making. The same Paulette Maillet, as he believed, was too well acquainted with his wife, and thereby La Vossiere became diseased of a kind of mania. He was determined to put an end to his existence. That he might do this in an honorable, chivalric manner and with his friends, he decided on having a splendid dinner; and when all were in perfect happiness and being ethereal with wine, to fire a quantity of powder prepared for the purpose in the cellar under the table, and all to go off in a frolic together.

He prepared the dinner, wine, and powder and called in his friends. The feast for a while went on well. The dinner over and the wine going round in floods, when his guests perceived something strange, and just before the powder was fired off they had retired barely far enough away to save their lives, while La Vossiere was killed by the explosion. He left two children who are yet alive. His widow married her paramour, Maillet, whose fate is before narrated.

It is the great misfortune of all new countries that there are no means of educating the children This was the case with Illinois from its earliest settlements by the French and for one hundred years after. The Jesuits at Kaskaskia had some kind of a religious institution of learning established in the year 1720, but the children had no schools at all, or scarcely any, wherein they could receive a common education It is true, the clergy attended particularly to the learning of the children the catechism and other religious teaching, but not much more was given to the youth of that day It was not the custom of the times, and thereby this essential ingredient of man's happiness was almost entirely neglected. There is much excuse for the omission of schools in early times with the Americans, and almost a justification of it.

The people were, almost all of them, poor, and the hostile Indians were always pressing danger and death on the frontier settlers. In many instances the school-houses were guarded and the children on going to and returning from school were in danger all the time. Schools to exist under such circumstances were out of the question Thus it was, the greater portion of the people raised on the frontiers received no book education But this defect, to a great degree, was remedied by the circumstances of the country. As it has already been stated that the dangers, perils, and troubles of various kinds which are experienced by pioneers in settling a new country, and that country in a war with the Indians, will develop and improve the mind. The inhabitants must become active and energetic in self-defence. Reflection and action will both be forced on the people in such situation, and thus they become wise and energetic men They can not make a display in literature, but they possess wisdom and practical commonsense which is far preferable

The frontier inhabitants raised in adversity have more practical sense than those living in the old settlements One race have their minds always in action, while the other indulges in a lifeless monotony.

A mixture of book education and backwoods activity produces the greatest race of men Education by means of schools or otherwise must be extended to all classes of citizens in this Republic, or otherwise it is impossible to maintain a free government.

The system of Sunday-schools is among the greatest discoveries of human wisdom. The great man, R. Raikes, who first put this machinery in operation, should be hailed all over the world as "the poor man's friend, the kindest and the best" The children of the wealthy can always obtain an education; but it is the poor and the humble that this system accommodates and relieves from ignorance and oppression. The benevolent and the charitable have the time and power on the Sabbath to attend in the schools and instruct the children in morality and the Scriptures. Nothing can be so pleasing to the heart of a good man or woman as to instruct the children to pursue that course of life which will make them good and happy On this earth a more dignified and pleasing sight can not be seen than a talented and accomplished lady having her flock of little girls and boys with her going to the Sunday-school. These groups having with them the sacred writing to teach them happiness here on earth and at the close of life the way to heaven will be ready to open to those that are happy here.

Sunday-schools must be regulated by wisdom The proper books and the proper teachers must be provided, or otherwise they will be a curse rather than a blessing to mankind This is the case with all systems of education or teachings To educate the heads of children and leave their hearts uninstructed in morality and honesty, is doing mankind an injury and harm. Science and literature without morality and honesty will be a curse to the human family Sunday-schools will aid in the education of the heart to a great extent

The female children deserve more the attention of the public in their education than the males. It is the mother who first gives their tender offspring the leading bent of mind. The infant around its mother receives its first impressions from her, which may govern it thro life. How difficult it is to discard early impressions If they are good and received from a kind mother they are calculated to make the person happy thro life.

The legislature should do something to advance the cause of Sunday-schools. The teachers might be paid, books and rooms provided for the schools at the public expense. No money could be expended to do as much good, if it were properly applied, as to advance the Sunday-school system.

James Piggot, John Doyle, Robert Whitehead, and Mr Bowen were soldiers in the expedition under Colonel Clark in the year 1778, and soon after the campaign settled in Illinois. Doyle had a family and resided in or near Kaskaskia. He was something of a scholar and taught school. He spoke French and Indian and was frequently employed as an interpreter of those languages into the English. He was unambitious and lived and died without much wealth. He was considered an honest man and was always respected while alive— as he is now, when dead—as one of the brave men who assisted Col Clark in the conquest of Illinois.

Bowen and Whitehead were both correct men Whitehead raised a large family and lived to an advanced age Bowen lived single and received a pension as a Revolutionary soldier.

All these soldiers of the Revolution, Biggs, Piggot, Kidd, Rutherford, Doyle, Whitehead, Bowen, and others who aided in the conquest of Illinois under the celebrated Col. Clark, performed services for their country that entitle them to the gratitude and respect of a people who are now enjoying the harvest of their labors. Under any circumstances a brave soldier of the Revolution is entitled to much honor and gratitude. The conquest of Illinois under the perilous and dangerous circumstances attending it entitles those brave men who achieved it the highest honor that man can bestow on them.

During the Revolution, Mr. Huff and family left the Monongahela country in Western Pennsylvania for Illinois He had married a widow Murdoch, who had three sons with the party. This emigrating party was tolerably strong and had prepared and fortified their boat They started from Red Stone, Old Fort, so called in those days, where the town of Brownsville was built in the year 1786 On the Mississippi near the Grand Tower, while encamped for the night, the Indians attacked the party and killed Mrs. Huff, one of her sons, and some others The survivors retreated in the boat and thus saved themselves. Mrs Huff was mangled in a shocking manner before the eyes of her husband and family. She was cut open and quartered and the Indians drank her blood This was the reason that her son, John Murdoch, who was a very conspicuous character in the early times of Illinois, swore vengeance against all Indians, and could scarcely be restrained from killing them in time of peace as well as in war.

The party came on to the American Bottom and settled there Mr Huff, only a few years after, was killed by the Indians on the road between Prairie du Rocher and Kaskaskia His watch and some other articles were found, many years after, where he had been killed

Toward the close of the Revolutionary war, many American families settled in Kaskaskia. Ichabod and George Camp first resided in Kaskaskia, and afterward made improvements on the high land west of the Kaskaskia River, on a stream called Camp's Creek. They afterward moved to St Louis and resided at what is now called Camp Spring, west of that city They gave the name to that spring

John and Israel Dodge resided in Kaskaskia; so did John Cook and Jacob Judy and their families

Israel Dodge was the father of Hon Henry Dodge,* the pres-

---

* Gov Dodge represented the State of Wisconsin after its admission to the Federal Union, as one of its first senators in congress from 1848-51, at the expiration of the first term he was reelected and served a second term, ending in 1857, when having been continuously in public life for a period of more than fifty years, he retired to a well deserved rest, making his home with his son, Gen A C. Dodge, in Burlington, Iowa, where he departed this life, full of years and honors, June 19, 1867

Gen Augustus C Dodge, son of Gov. Henry Dodge, had a career of no less interest than that of his honored sire. Born in Ste Genevieve, Missouri, in 1812, he received the best tuition the country afforded, which was but spare. He removed

ent senator in congress from the State of Wisconsin. The father had resided at the Iron Banks and was on his way from there by Vincennes to Kentucky, and at Vincennes Henry Dodge was born, in the year 1777. Israel Dodge resided with his family for several years at Kaskaskia, while Henry composed part of his family. The Dodge family left Kaskaskia about the year 1790, and resided in upper Louisiana.

Henry Dodge was raised in a new country, where the opportunities for education were almost entirely denied the children whose fathers had not the means to send them abroad; and the society, sixty or seventy years ago, about Kaskaskia and Ste. Genevieve, where young Dodge was raised, was not celebrated for its morality; but Dodge steered clear of the vices

with his father some years later to the neighborhood of the lead-mines in the territory of Wisconsin, where he remained until 1838, when he settled in what afterward became the State of Iowa, in the City of Burlington. He rendered valuable services in the Black-Hawk War, attaining the rank of brigadier-general. He was the first delegate to represent the territory of Iowa in the United States congress, a position to which he was a second time elected. He was one of Iowa's first United States senators, serving from 1848-55. At the expiration of his term as senator, he was appointed by President Buchanan as minister to the court of Spain. On his return to Burlington from Madrid, he retired to private life and, except serving a few terms as mayor of the city and the filling of a few minor positions of trust, he never again entered the political arena. Gen. Dodge died, universally esteemed and generally regretted by a large circle of personal friends, Nov. 20, 1883.

From 1848-55, the Dodges, father and son, were members at the same time of the United States senate, a coincidence without a parallel in American history, and the untimely death of Gov. Dodge's half-brother, Dr. Lewis Lynn, before the expiration of his term as senator from the State of Missouri, prevented his service in the same senate with the father and son.

A daughter of Gov. Dodge is also well known in Illinois history. Mary Louise Dodge was married to Col. John Dement at Ft. Leavenworth in 1835, and has been truly one of the pioneer mothers of our State. By the death of her distinguished husband on January 17, 1883, she is left to survive most of her family. Her present residence is in Dixon, Lee County, Ill.

Her son, Hon. Henry Dodge Dement, is the present secretary of state of the State of Illinois, a position he has attained by the exercise of those qualifications of integrity, ability, and geniality, which have descended to him from both families of his illustrious ancestry. Mr. Dement has represented his county in the State legislature, and served four years as a senator from his district in the State senate. He also has maintained the fighting reputation of both sides of the house by making a good soldier in the late war, entering the service as a second lieutenant while a mere boy, early in 1861; he was promoted to a first lieutenant shortly afterward; and made an honorable record in one of the veteran regiments of Illinois—the Thirteenth Infantry.
—J. H. G.

and immoralities so much practised at that time. And altho he had not the opportunity to receive much education *inside* of a college, yet he studied men and things *outside,* so that he has acquired a great store of intelligence and information, which enables him to occupy an elevated and conspicuous standing in society. Nature bestowed on him some of her most precious gifts He possesses a strong and solid judgment; but he moves to a conclusion with caution and reaches it with mathematical certainty. His leading traits of character are a strong intellect, great firmness, and much dignity Nature designed him for the profession of arms, and he has embraced the military on all fit and appropriate occasions. In his youth he was much engaged in hunting the wild game and often remained in the woods for weeks and months together. On these occasions his apparel corresponded with his vocation, which would make a strong contrast with his present respectable and dignified appearance in the senate of the United States Such are the blessings of our free institutions, that merit can rise from the humble life of a hunter to the most dignified and elevated stations known to the people.

In former days, he manufactured great quantities of salt at the works below Ste. Genevieve He had several hundred laborers in his service, at times working this saline

In the late war with Great Britain, he was engaged almost the whole time in the defence of the frontiers. He was elected a general of the militia of Missouri before the war of 1812, which enabled him to keep the militia in a proper organization for active operations.

He took command of a battalion of four hundred men, composed of United-States rangers, mounted riflemen, and others, with a squad of friendly Shawnee Indians, and removed a band of the Miami Indians from the Boone's-Lick Settlement on the Missouri River to the Wabash. These Indians were made to unite with their own nation on the Wabash, for safe-keeping out of the influence of the hostile Indians in the north. When they resided on the Missouri and professed to be friendly, it gave rise to suspicion that they harbored and sustained the others who were hostile It was wise and benevolent policy to settle them with their own people on the Wabash; thereby "keeping them out of temptation." Gen. Dodge performed this delicate service with judgment and discretion.

He was appointed United-States marshal in the State of Missouri at the first organization of the State government, and continued to execute the duties of that important station for many years. He was punctual, prompt, and decisive in performing the duties of this office

In 1822, he emigrated from the State of Missouri to the Michigan Territory. He located in that section of the territory north of the State of Illinois which composes the State of Wisconsin at this time In this new country, he operated in the lead business A town is called Dodgeville for him, including his residence.

In the Black-Hawk war, his section of the territory of Wisconsin was very much exposed to the Indian depredations, and he was the main defender and protector of the country, as almost the whole country was a frontier. He organized all the male persons, old and young, that could be raised in the country for the defence of their firesides. After Gen. Stillman's battle on Sycamore Creek, above Dixon's Ferry on Rock River, in 1832, I sent an express at night to Gen. Dodge, who was in the neighborhood, informing him of the facts and that his country in the territory was in imminent danger from the attacks of the Indians. We knew that the hearts of all the Indians, who resided within three hundred miles of the scenes of the Black-Hawk war, were with him in the quarrel and wished him success.

If Black Hawk had succeeded in some skirmishes, and no efficient efforts been made against him, all the tribes around about would unite with his band and harass the frontiers To prevent this outbreak of the Indians, it was necessary to act with despatch and efficiency. Gen. Dodge carried out this policy with great activity and spirit The Indians were prevented from joining Black Hawk, and much injury to the country was thereby avoided.

A bold and decisive battle was fought by Gen. Dodge and fifteen of his men against sixteen Indians These Indians had committed some murders near Hamilton's Fort, in the territory, and Dodge and party pursued them. There was no time to lose, or the Indians would escape. The whites pursued the Indians toward Rock River and overtook them. Dodge and party rushed on them and destroyed every one He had three or four of his men killed and some wounded It was necessary to make this energetic and decisive attack on the Indians to make them sue for peace

In the Black-Hawk war he acquired much reputation ; and at the close of it, was appointed a colonel over a regiment of dragoons At the head of this regiment, he marched, in the year 1833, across the plains to the Rocky Mountains, and made several important treaties with the Indians at the mountains and also on the plains. He returned in the fall with his regiment in good order and health. This regiment of dragoons, after being disciplined and inured to service with Col. Dodge at its head, was an efficient corps and would have sustained the honor of the service in any situation on a battle-field or otherwise.

He was appointed governor of the Wisconsin Territory, and executed the high and responsible duties of that office to the entire satisfaction of both the people of the territory and the general government. He was also superintendent of Indian affairs, which is an office incident to that of the governor.

This territory was, at that time, surrounded with Indians, which made the office of superintendent one of much delicacy, and required sound judgment to execute it; but he performed the duties of this station to the honor of himself and much to the interest of the people Gen Dodge has occupied for many years the high and dignified office of senator in the congress of the United States, and has made an excellent member He has now before him the experience of a long and eventful life, together with a sound and solid judgment, so that he now makes an efficient, substantial, and dignified member of congress He has a large and respectable family One of his sons, A C. Dodge, is in the United-States senate from the State of Iowa

William Musick, James Piggot, Robert Sybold, and some few others were inhabitants of Kaskaskia before the close of the Revolution

Before the year 1778, many American families made improvements in Illinois, by which they obtained a bounty of land from the government

John Montgomery improved that tract of land two or three miles east of Kaskaskia River, Randolph County, on the Vincennes old road, where Stace McDonough has since resided for more than half-a-century Montgomery erected a small water-mill on a spring near his house. The remains of the old dam may be seen to this day, although it must be about seventy years old.

George Lunsford made an improvement, and by it obtained a grant of land Henderson, Harniss, Huff, Chaffin, Sybold, and many other Americans with their families resided in Illinois and made improvements before the year 1783

It will be recollected that Col John Todd[*] of Kentucky

[*] Col. John Todd, the first of the name to emigrate to Illinois, was a son of David Todd and Hannah Owen, who came from Ireland, where they were married, to the town of Pequea, Lancaster County, Pennsylvania, prior to the Revolution David Todd had three sons, John, Robert, and Levi, who were all educated by their uncle, Rev John Todd, who conducted a literary institution of an educational character in that county. The three brothers emigrated together to Fayette County, Kentucky, in 1778, and shortly afterward, Col John Todd was commissioned by Patrick Henry, then governor of Virginia, to be lieutenant-colonel and civil commandant of Illinois County, then just authorized by an act of the Virginia assembly, October, 1778 Afterward he organized the new county government, June 15, 1779, and everything was running smoothly when he had occasion to visit Virginia in reference to land-titles, in the summer of 1782, and on his return, while visiting his family in Kentucky, the Indian invasion from the western side of the Ohio River occurred, and in a battle which was fought with them at Blue Licks, in which Col Todd was a volunteer commander, he was killed, on August 18, 1782

Levi Todd, brother to John Todd, was a lieutenant under George Rogers Clark in the expedition which captured Kaskaskia, in 1778, and he returned with the detachment which took the British commander, M Rocheblave, a prisoner to Virginia He never returned to Illinois, but spent the balance of his life at Lexington, Kentucky, where he filled many important positions of trust and confidence Gen Levi Todd is best known in Illinois by his descendants. His daughter Hannah was married to Rev Robert Stuart, a distinguished Presbyterian divine, and former professor of languages in Transylvania University From this union sprang Hon. John T Stuart, a distinguished member of the Springfield, Ill , bar, the preceptor and afterward the law-partner of Abraham Lincoln

Gen Todd's son, Robert S , was the father of Mrs Ninian W. Edwards, Mrs. Dr. Wm S Wallace, Mrs. C. M Smith, and Mrs Abraham Lincoln, all of whom have lived in this State for many years, and those of the number yet living still reside in Springfield Dr John Todd, brother to these, emigrated to Edwardsville in 1817, and afterward, in 1827, to Springfield. The numerous descendants of Dr Todd and

organized the government of Illinois at Kaskaskia in the year 1778, under the jurisdiction of Virginia, and whatever government the people had, was that established by Col Todd and Capt. Stirling, when the British conquered the country, in the year 1763

The government was very imperfect; but the people needed little or none. Rocheblave was governor when Clark captured the country, and Timothy Demountbrun was the commandant when Col Todd came to Kaskaskia There was a kind of mixture of the civil and British law in the country, administered by courts down to 1790, when Gov. St Clair came to Kaskaskia and set in motion the territorial government under the ordinance or act of congress of 1787 A people, such as those in Illinois were, in sparse settlements, poor and honest, needed very little government. And it is a curse all over the earth that "the people are governed too much" When a people are shackled down with excessive legislation, with charters for corporations, and sometimes with a public debt, they are in a humble and degraded condition, and if no other relief can reach them, they should resort to a revolution for it.

his sisters rank among the best people, socially and intellectually, about the State capital One of them, Robert Todd Lincoln, being at the present time secretary of war —J. H. G.

CHAPTER VI.

Illinois under the Northwest Territory of the Government.

AFTER the close of the war of the Revolution, the people of the United Colonies were much embarrassed and largely in debt. A seven years' war with the most powerful nation on earth was severely felt by all classes of people. The federal government and many of the States earnestly solicited the State of Virginia and other States to cede their western lands to the general government, and thereby a fund could be realized by a sale of these lands to pay the public debt and carry on the government.

Virginia, with that nobleness of character and disinterestedness which has always influenced its councils, on March 1, 1784, ceded to the general government her public domain, that now forms the states of Ohio, Indiana, Illinois, Wisconsin, and Michigan, and also transferred to the United Colonies the government and jurisdiction of the ceded country.

As it has been stated, in the year 1785, an ordinance of the old congress passed to survey and prepare for market some of the public domain. The ordinance required townships of six miles square to be laid off by lines running north and south and east and west on the true meridian. The first of these lines were to commence on the Ohio River at a point north of the western termination of the western boundary of Pennsylvania; thence due north, and another line commencing at the same point running due west. Each township was to be subdivided into thirty-six square miles, and numbered from one to thirty-six, commencing in the northeast corner and numbering west and east to the termination in the southeast corner, at the number 36. One of these sections (16th) was reserved in each township for the use of schools.

Various acts of congress on the subject have passed; so that as low a number as forty acres of land may be entered to accommodate purchasers. This land-system has been adopted over all the public domain in the United States, and has proved to be of general utility This system also gave the first direction of public opinion in favor of schools. In this, as in other things, the provisions of this act of congress were based on wisdom and with a just regard to the claims of posterity

The New Design was the name of the settlement made about four miles south of Bellefontaine, in the present county of Monroe This location of emigrants was established as early as 1782, and then received the name of New Design It is a beautiful country whereon this settlement was made. It is elevated and commands a view of both rivers, the Kaskaskia and Mississippi, and withal, the soil is fertile. It was first a prairie and barrens, but at present the timber has grown up all over the country which is not cultivated

This was the largest settlement made by Americans in Illinois in early times, and was generally the first rendezvous of the emigrants It was the headquarters, together with the Bellefontaine settlement, of the whole American population Before the year 1790, a considerable settlement was formed in the New Design Horse-mills and blacksmith's-shops were established there. Mr. Dougherty erected a band-mill, which answered the pioneers a good purpose in 1795.

John Murdoch, it will be recollected, came to the American Bottom with his brother, Barney, and Mr. Huff, his step-father, in the year 1786, and resided there during life.

Barney Murdoch died in early life and the step-father, Huff, as was before stated, was killed by the Indians, leaving much estate, and thereby John Murdoch inherited for that early time a large property. He came to the country when a mere lad, and his mind and character were formed under the perilous circumstances of a wild and new country. He had, in his younger days, little opportunity of education and therefore his book-learning was limited He could merely read and write and was acquainted with some of the common rules of arithmetic Making a living in the American Bottom was not difficult and he paid not much attention to it His youthful days were spent by him in a kind of poetic action. If ever a gay young man acted poetry, it was John Murdoch, in his limited sphere. He possessed a mind of extraordinary ability and let it loose like Childe Harold: "He vexed with mirth the drowsy ear of night" Nature blessed Murdoch with an active and vigorous intellect But few individuals, in any country, possess the strong mind that nature bestowed on him. But the situation of the country, together with his associations, rendered this gift of nature to him useless and perhaps injurious A great and vigorous mind, when it has a wrong direction, does much more injury than a weak one. This was the case with Prince Henry until his father's death, when he became king of England and then Henry the Fifth was the greatest monarch of his age

John Murdoch was a model of symmetry and masculine beauty, rather above the ordinary size of men, and somewhat corpulent He was as straight as an arrow and of a dark complexion; his eyes were large and black and displayed an uncommon brilliancy; his head was large and forehead uncommonly capacious In all societies, with the young or old, with the wild or religious, he was always the centre of attraction and the commanding spirit of the circle

The manners and customs of early times permitted him to enter into the dissipations of the country. He acquired among the French their language and their accomplishments in the dance. He performed well on the violin and possessed an excellent natural talent for music In his early day, no one could sing with more grace and glee than he could. The necessities of the country learned him the use of the gun and he became an excellent marksman and hunter. Horse-racing at that day was indulged in by almost all classes of citizens, and in that sport he took great delight He was also enamored with the various games of cards, which grew on him and at at last ruined him.

A palliation, not a justification, for gambling with cards may be given in the fact that nearly the whole country, forty or fifty years ago, enjoyed the luxuries of a card-table, and public opinion was somewhat in its favor; but notwithstanding this, this sin will, earlier or later, bring ruin on those who practise it.

As he grew in years, he became more dignified and commanding in person and deportment. There was in his character nothing frivolous or trifling. In all situations, in the woods, the camp, or the legislative halls, he also deported himself with that *hauteur* of character and manly bearing which is becoming a gentleman.

Easy, graceful manners seem to have been born with him; he was polite by instinct and in all his various scenes of pleasure and gayety, he never forgot the good breeding of a gentleman, and always showed respect to religion and to the aged part of community.

John Murdoch was benevolent and kind and possessed no malignity or malice in his heart; he had no gall in his composition, yet firm and warm in his attachments. If he had been raised in different society, and had received a competent education, he would have been a great man. Nature did much for him, and he depended on these natural gifts and did nothing for himself, yea, worse, he contended against these natural gifts.

Like almost all of these characters that nature has done so much for, he did nothing for himself. He was indolent, to an extreme, in everything except in the pursuit of pleasure. He had no business talents; he was raised in wealth, in a country where industry was not known, he grew up in a country where the people lived free and easy; he, like the others, indulged in everything that tended to pleasure and to his amusement.

When he reached the age of manhood, he was frequently called upon to serve the public. He was elected, in 1803, as one of the three members of St Clair County to the territorial legislature, which convened at Vincennes in the same year. This was the first general assembly held under the authority of the Indiana Territory.

In the year 1802, the territory of Indiana was established and Illinois constituted a part of it. This was an important legislature, to organize the new territorial government. Murdoch acquitted himself in the legislature to the satisfaction of the public. He was at that day very young for a legislator; but his mind under the circumstances of the country and his situation in it was considerably developed. He had been thrown on his own resources from his infancy, and had thereby become old in experience tho young in years.

He was very popular with the ladies; his gayety and personal attractions made him a great favorite with them. He acted the gallant as part of a gentlemanly deportment to the fair sex; but he did not extend the power he possessed in that respect beyond a decent propriety

He married a Miss Garrison, who was the step-daughter of Judge Bond, and likewise an amiable and agreeable lady of excellent family. He and family occupied a plantation in the American Bottom until his death.

He had some talent and taste for military life. He was first captain of a company and afterward became a major of a battalion. In this office, on a general muster-day, no officer ever appeared in the field to equal the imposing appearance of Major Murdoch He was a splendid horseman, together with his dashing uniform and manly military display on parade, which made him show off to great advantage. Yet all this good fortune did not spoil him. He was neither vain or overbearing.

He declared an eternal warfare against the whole Indian family, in peace or in war. He had a mother, father, and two step-fathers killed by the Indians Perhaps no other man had the same reason to dislike the Indians, as he had, on account of so many of his parents being killed by them. Ever since he was able to raise a gun, he was, on all proper occasions, out against them.

In the late war of 1812, against Great Britain and her Indian allies, Murdoch was active and zealous to fight the red men. He was field-officer in the campaign under Gov Edwards, in the fall of 1812, to the upper end of Lake Peoria, and acted as major in that expedition. He also acted as major in the campaign of 1813, under Gen Howard.

Murdoch never gave himself the trouble to study military tactics, but depended on his natural resources, which seldom failed him.

He was elected November 10, 1813, from St.Clair County to the legislative assembly, held at Kaskaskia under the territorial government of Illinois. He was a quiet voting member of the assembly, and always had the sound judgment to prevent him from frothy declamation, by which the public good is not advanced; and in every particular he made a good solid member, and his constituents highly approved his conduct In fact, being raised among his constituents, and having good sound sense, with extremely popular manners, he almost made public opinion in his county. Almost everything he did was popular It was his great popularity with the young men of his day that led many of them estray into the paths of pleasure and dissipation They imitated him, but had not the talents to shun the rocks that lay concealed under the waves of dissipation as well as he did, and even he at last was ruined by this course

Murdoch spent much of his spare time in hunting He was a great hunter and marksman, and camped out for weeks to hunt and recreate himself in the woods

Murdoch being past the meridian of life, these follies and foibles of human nature increased on him until his death He died in 1830, regretted by all Monroe County.

John Murdoch was a noble pioneer He had united in him a strong mind, graceful manners, and the self-sustained independence of the perfect backwoodsman

Murdoch had human foibles and frailties One great defect in his character was that he had not the power to resist temptation The gayety and fascination of agreeable society he could not resist He was all life and animation, and indulged in these fascinations, at first, without much injury; but at last, this course of life became second nature to him, so that he could not refrain from it The weak point in man is that he has not the power to withstand temptation

Truth requires it to be stated of Murdoch that he was one of the greatest men that was ever raised in Illinois; he was Nature's nobleman.

The old village of Prairie du Chien, situated on the east bank of the Mississippi, a few miles above the mouth of the Wisconsin River, was built by the French not long after the first discovery of the country, and was occupied by the Indian traders and farmers. It was the outpost of the Indian trade.

This village took its name from a band of the Fox Indians, who resided there and were called the dog band. Prairie du Chien is in English, the prairie of the dogs.

The French inhabitants cultivated the Mississippi Bottom for four miles up and down the river, and nearly a mile wide from the river to the bluff. The present village of Prairie du Chien is about one mile above the old village, and was built in the year 1783, under the British authority The site was purchased of the Fox Indians. In 1807, in the village and vicinity, there were thirty-seven houses, and counting ten persons to each house, there would be three hundred and seventy inhabitants A few houses were erected on the west side of the Mississippi, at Girard's River.

In the year 1812, Dubuque, Antya, and Girard were the principal settlers in Prairie du Chien Brisbois, N Boilvin, and others also resided there At some seasons of the year, there was a great influx of traders at this village, to the number of six or eight hundred white persons and Indians in proportion.

The citizens being so remote from the white population had children with the squaws, so that many of the present generation have some Indian blood in their veins. This is considered no disparagement in that section of the country

It is no disparagement in any country The Indian blood is found in the veins of many of the greatest Americans that figured on the stage of public action John Randolph, whose celebrity is extended over Europe as well as America, had a share of the bow-and-arrow blood in his composition; as also many other great and eminent men in the United States. The only misfortune is that the Indian race is not equal to the European, and far below the North American The compound will not improve the stock The American race of people with the various crosses, and being raised and educated under the influence of free and liberal institutions, present to the world a race superior to any other nation. A great variety of circumstances produce this result.

In the first place, the most talented and energetic people leave Europe and settle in America. The drones are left at home in the old country The various races intermarry, whose offspring is improved by it In the next place, the country of North America is large and presents opportunities and facilities for the pursuit of wealth and power that accommodates all the different views of the citizens and urges them on to action. And our republican institutions, based upon equal principles and their influence Education is diffused and the road to power and wealth and the highest offices are open to merit, so that all these incentives to action develope the intellect and energies of the people until the Americans are a superior race. Our old enemies, the British, and their American friends give us the name of new Anglo-Saxons. Our name, blood, and lineage are American and not Anglo-Saxon. It is true that most of the Americans are descendants of Europeans, but the preponderance of blood is not of the Anglo-Saxon race. There are more of the descendants of the Irish and Germans in the United States than English. In fact, the American race at present is so compounded and improved that we are a stock of our own.

It is stated that in 1814, the farms of Prairie du Chien were in high cultivation. Between two and three hundred barrels of flour may have been manufactured there that season besides a vast quantity of corn.

The first American school-master ever appeared in Illinois was Samuel John Seely, in 1783. This school-teacher entered on his labors in the New Design in the present county of Monroe. I would respectfully recommend to the attention of the directors of the common-school system in Illinois the propriety of doing honor to Mr. Seely and to the subject of education by establishing great anniversary jubilees on the occasion.

The next teacher was Francis Clark, an intemperate man, who appeared in 1785. The next was an Irishman named Halfpenny, who taught school in many sections of Illinois for many years. This preceptor taught almost all the American children in Illinois in his day that received any education at all. He might be styled the school-master general of Illinois at that day.

The next teacher was John Clark, a preacher and a talented man. He was a Scotchman and was well educated. He taught the higher branches of education—mathematics, philosophy, etc.

The Indian depredations prevailed throughout the country so much that the education of the children could not be much attended to before the peace with the Indians in 1795.

The Indians were never hostile to the French population. They might do some injury to their property and at rare invals kill a white man; but there was never a settled determination to wage war against the French, with some exceptions, where the British instigated the savages to the deed But far different it was with the American population. It is difficult to say when Indian depredation on the Americans commenced; but Wayne's treaty, in 1795, put a stop to these hostilities

Wherever the American population was large enough in Illinois for the attention of the Indians, then a bitter marauding warfare commenced.

In 1786, was the first decisive Indian war waged against the Americans in Illinois. James Flannary was killed in 1783, by the Indians, but this was not considered a general war

In 1786, not far northwest of Waterloo, Monroe County, James Andrews, his wife, and daughter, James White, and Samuel McClure were killed by the Indians and two daughters of Andrews were taken prisoners One died with the Indians and the other was ransomed by the French traders This first act of Indian warfare on the Americans in Illinois was bold and decisive Five were killed and two taken prisoners. The daughter of Andrews who was ransomed is still alive and is the mother of a large family.

This slaughter of part of the infant settlement of Illinois produced a great panic among the pioneers and caused them to erect the stations and forts that are heretofore mentioned for their protection A continual murderous warfare was kept up against the first American settlers until 1795. It is astonishing how so small a settlement as was in the country in 1785 could sustain itself against the great numbers of Indians that were in the country at that day. The whites not only fortified to protect themselves, but were compelled to mount guard day and night for their safety When a man was plowing in the field, one other or more were stationed outside to protect him The same with the domestic affairs of a family, guards for protection were indispensable to save their lives from the attack of the hostile Indians.

In 1788, December 10, Benjamin Ogle and James Garretson were fired on by two Indians while they were hauling hay from the Bottom A ball lodged in Ogle's shoulder and remained there. Garretson made his escape in the woods. In stacking the same hay, Samuel Garretson and Mr Reddick were both killed and scalped. Mr. Ogle received a pension for this wound.

The year 1789 was one of continual commissions of murders and depredations by the Indians on this small defenceless settlement The citizens at that day must have had iron wills or otherwise they would have been exterminated by the Indians. We read of repeated an *i* repeated murders of the inhabitants almost daily, and yet the wise conduct and unparalleled bravery of the people saved them from destruction.

Three boys were attacked by six Indians a small distance from the block-house fort in the American Bottom, situated not far from the Fountaine Creek, where it first enters the Bottom David Waddle was struck with a tomahawk in three places—scalped—made his escape and recovered. The other boys run to the fort and were saved. James Turner, John Ferrell, and three others were killed this year at several times by the Indians, and John Dempsey and another were scalped and left for dead, but recovered.

These are only the partial items of the horrid and revolting murders of this year. No individual, male or female, night or day, was safe. This year may be denominated the year of blood in Illinois The settlement of the present county of Monroe must have suffered this year by the Indians a loss of one out of every ten of its population.

The enemy acted with savage ferocity, not only on the inhabitants, but turned that same savage malignity to destroy the animals of the whites. They not only stole horses—which is rather a beggar commerce with the Indians—but destroyed the stock with a wantonness unparalleled in Indian warfare.

We will abandon these horrid murders committed by the Indians for a moment, and turn our attention to the organization of the Northwestern Territory and other matters more pleasant.

It will be recollected that Virginia ceded Illinois to the United States in 1784, and on July 13. 1787, the ordinance, so called and known in the territory, was passed by congress. This territory included five States, as they are at present organized, Illinois being one This act of congress, which calls itself a compact as well as an ordinance, is made the foundation of all territorial governments organized since that day. The great and leading feature in it is the provision against the introduction of slavery in the territory. This ordinance secured all the Northwest from slavery. I think congress has the power to legislate on the subject, as was done in the case before us, but it is unwise and impolitical to act in the case, but permit the people of the territory to use their own judgment on the occasion, whether they have slavery or not.

Arthur St Clair was appointed governor of this territory, and remained in office until the State of Ohio was organized, in 1802.

In contemplating the life and character of Gov. St Clair, a melancholy reflection forces itself on us, as he appears to be a man doomed to misfortune. His motives and impulses were pure and patriotic; yet, in almost every enterprise or business in which he was engaged during a long and eventful life, he failed in almost every instance.

He was born in Edinburgh, in 1734, and was of good family, but unknown to history. He came to America with Admiral Boscowen, in 1755. Having served in Canada as lieutenant under Gen Wolf in 1759 and 1760, he was, after the close of the war, appointed to the command of Fort Ligonier, in Pennsylvania. When he left the British army is not known; but in December, 1775, he was married and held six offices in the State, to wit: clerk of the court, prothonotory of a court, judge of probate, register of wills, recorder of deeds, and surveyor of the largest county in the province. In this same year, 1775, he acted as secretary to the commissioners who held a treaty at Pittsburg with the Indians. He became known and popular; so that without solicitation, he was, in January, 1776, appointed colonel in the continental army with orders to raise a regiment to operate in Canada. He raised the regiment in six weeks, and left Philadelphia with six companies on March 12, and reached Quebec on May 11, to cover the retreat of the troops from that place, while the other four companies remained at Sorel, on the St Lawrence. He was appointed brigadier-general on August 9, 1776, and ordered to join Gen. Washington's army, then retreating thro New Jersey. Gen. St Clair acted well his part in the battles of the Revolution, at Trenton and Princeton.

On Feb. 9, 1777, congress appointed him a major-general, and on June 5, he was ordered to take command of the fort at Ticonderoga. He abandoned this fort, and altho it was done on the consultation of officers, yet the public disapproved of it. A court-martial sustained the movement, and congress, in 1778, confirmed it. But still the wound was not healed in public estimation.

Washington always retained his first confidence in General St. Clair. He acted his part well at the battle and siege of Yorktown, at the capitulation From this point he was sent with six regiments to Gen Greene in South Carolina, with orders to reduce all the British garrisons in North Carolina. These posts were abandoned at his approach, and on December 27, 1781, he joined Gen. Greene at Jacksonburg. After the peace, Gen. St. Clair resided in Pennsylvania, and was elected a member of congress in 1786, and the president of that body in 1787. When the Northwestern Territory was established, in 1787, he was appointed governor of the territory. He did not desire this appointment, but he seems to have acted on the principle recognized by Gen Jackson, "he would neither ask or refuse office." St. Clair observed that "to accept the office of governor was the most imprudent act of my life." He was appointed in 1788, and remained in office to the year 1802, when the State of Ohio was organized.

On July 15, 1788, Gov. St. Clair appeared at Marietta and put the machinery of government into operation as far as possible. Washington County was the first-organized county in the territory. In September, 1788, the governor and United-States judges for the territory—Parsons, Barnum, and Symms —prepared and adopted a code of laws for the Northwestern Territory, which has formed the basis of the statute laws of all the States formed out of this territory. Gov. St. Clair and Winthrop Sargeant, his secretary, in February, 1790, arrived at Kaskaskia and organized the county of St. Clair. The governor also appointed the various officers in the new county necessary to the administration of justice, and partially adjusted the land-titles of the citizens.

The county of St. Clair was called for the governor and was bounded as follows: beginning at the mouth of the Little Mackinaw Creek, where it empties into the Illinois River, and running a direct line to the mouth of a creek which empties into the Ohio not far above Fort Massacre; then down the Ohio to the Mississippi; then up that river and the Illinois to the place of beginning.

St. Clair is the mother of counties in Illinois, and still retains her youthful vigor, looking around with pleasure on her happy offspring. It will be recollected that the Ancient Dominion, in October, 1779, erected Illinois into a county of that name, which retained a kind of obsolete existence down to the year 1790, when the county of St. Clair was carved out of part of it.

Gov. St. Clair appointed William St. Clair clerk of the court and recorder of deeds in St. Clair County, and many others to office the same year.

He had, in the year 1788, organized the second grade of territorial government and caused elections to be held in the several counties which he had established.

Both the branches of the legislature met in Cincinnati, first, on September 16, 1789, and adjourned on the 24th of the same month. Knox County, at that day, included both Vincennes and the Illinois country, and from the Illinois part of Knox County, Shadrach Bond, Sr., was elected to the house of representatives.

At that session an excited struggle was had for the election of a representative to congress from the territory. Public opinion settled down on William H. Harrison and Arthur St. Clair, Jr., the nephew of the governor. Harrison had eleven votes and St. Clair ten. This election came off on Oct. 3, 1799.

Gen. St. Clair died August 31, 1818, on the top of the Alleghany mountains, in Pennsylvania.

Henry Levens and family settled in the New Design in 1797. He landed at Fort Massacre with two teams and wagons; one was an ox team. He put a large skiff on one wagon, for a wagon-body on land and a ferry-boat when they reached the creeks that were swimming, on their march to Kaskaskia. They were twenty-five days in this pilgrimage from the Ohio to Kaskaskia.

He emigrated from the western part of Pennsylvania and was well calculated to brave all the dangers and difficulties incident to the settlement of a new country. He was a very large, stout man, and a stranger to fear. He was not educated to any great extent, and was rather decisive and energetic in his common intercourse with society. He was kind and hospitable to those he esteemed, and to those he disliked he acted the reverse.

He possessed rather a strong mind, but uncultivated, which was formed under circumstances unfavorable to advance the meek, mild, or amiable traits of the human character. He was, withal, kind and hospitable to those, friend or foe, under his roof, his house was the common hotel for dancing and convivial parties. He raised a large family, and as the old and young, male and female, were inclined to gayety and sociability, they indulged in the pleasures of the ballroom and other amusements of a similar character. A greater portion of his sons and some of his daughters played on the violin, and all, young and old, danced.

This family was the centre of attraction, and many are the happy days, and particularly nights, of innocent amusement and recreation, which were enjoyed in pioneer times at the friendly and hospitable mansion of Henry Levens, on Horse Creek.

In 1800, Levens erected a saw-mill and grist-mill on Horse Creek, near his residence, and carried this mill on with energy and advantage to the public. The lumber for nearly all the flat-boats built in early times in Illinois was sawed at this mill. The sons of Levens were like their father, active and resolute men, and as most other pioneers, they, too, were excellent hunters and marksmen. The rifle with the early settlers was literally a staff of life, and almost every one became not only expert with the gun at the shooting-match, but were also excellent hunters. Old Nimrod would have been pleased to have the young Levens in his corps, as they would, in the chase, do honor to their captain.

The Levens family, while they lived together, became more wealthy than the neighboring pioneers. Their stock was raised, winter and summer, without much labor, and the mill and farm yielded considerable income, so that the family had the means of supporting the frolics and amusements they indulged in. The sons also made something by the peltries arising from hunting. The whole family were active and energetic people, but they delighted in sport more than in work The gun, race-horse, and violin were articles of the greatest admiration in the family. They were strictly honest and extremely kind and hospitable, after the manner of their father. The Levens family were an excellent sample of a prominent pioneer family. They were all blessed with good intellectual faculties, and were very active and energetic, and were also large and portly men and resolute to excess. For many years there were four or five grown sons and two daughters in the family before any were married The sons or father never indulged in any great intemperance, nor much gaming, farther than amusement

The sons delighted in the rural sport of foot-racing, wrestling, jumping, etc. Horce-racing, shooting-matches, and dancing in early times were enjoyed by almost the whole community, and the Levens family indulged in these amusements with a particular delight. The males, young and old, were not bashful in a fight, in which they indulged at times to the great discomfiture of their adversaries

In fact, the Levens family possessed a respectable and conspicuous standing in society, which, together with the circumstances already stated, enabled them to enjoy an uninterrupted round of pleasure and of happiness of the character above described.

The aged sire, at last, like Boone, was interrupted by the approach of neighbors, which produced too near him a species of mathematical society, which he disliked, and he sold out his possession on Horse Creek, in 1818, and moved to the frontiers of Missouri. He lived to advanced age and died in that State, the aged patriarch of a large family.

The Indian murders and troubles seemed to increase in 1790. This may have arisen on account of the Indians seeing the Americans flocking to the country and a government being organized in it. The red men on this consideration may have made greater efforts to prevent the settlement of the country, and thereby the natives would occupy the homes of their fathers longer. This year was a sad and sorrowful one with the infant settlements of the Americans in Illinois.

It was mostly the Kickapoos that were so extremely hostile and ferocious against the whites. This nation resided nearest the Americans, and were better armed and more vigorous than the other Indians to commit depredations on the settlements And they committed their savage warfare with a vengeance unequalled in any other country

In the winter of this year, 1789, the Osage Indians crossed the Mississippi and stole some horses from the whites in the American Bottom. The Americans pursued them toward the river, and James Worley, being in advance of the rest of the party, was killed and scalped by the Indians before his companions could rescue him It was not common for the Osages to commit depredations on the whites on this side of the river It was stated that the Indians cut off the head of Worley and threw it in savage triumph toward the whites as they advanced. I presume that when Worley was killed and the whites found that the Indians outnumbered them, that they recaptured the horses and came off about "second best"

William Morrison emigrated from Philadelphia to Kaskaskia in 1790. He was recognized by the act of congress granting land to all those who were enrolled in Illinois for military duty on August 1 of that year He was a native of Bucks County, Pennsylvania, and soon became, after his arrival in Illinois, one of the most influential and conspicuous characters in the country. He was a self-made man, casting his lot in a new wild country and depending on his own resources for fortune and fame, and he accomplished both in an eminent degree. Like most great men, he never underwent the drudgery of a scholastic education Whether his means or other circumstances prevented it, I know not, however, such was the fact that he acquired barely an English education at the schools; but he studied in nature's great academy and became a very eminent man His natural genius and talents were of such high order that he acquired information at every step he made thro a long and eventful life His business and his proper sense of propriety enabled him to frequent the higher circles of society and thereby become one of the eminent. He made one of the most interesting and conspicuous characters in every society wherein he associated. Dignity and polish of manners seemed to be natural with him. He was a polished gentleman without effort. Nothing little or cramped existed in his character. His mind and impulses were fashioned on a large scale. It is seldom united in the same person, the strength of mind and the polish of manners that were blended together in the character of William Morrison. He was not only kind and benevolent in all his relations with society, but also honest and upright. As to a husband, he was everything that would make a wife's heart overflow with love for him, and a kind and indulgent father to his children.

Morrison came to Illinois, ambitious, enterprising, and talented. He located himself in the centre of the great valley of the Mississippi, where his talents and energies had ample scope for operation, and most nobly and honorably did he execute his destiny. By his great activity and sound judgment, he was the head and front of almost all the commercial operations of Illinois and upper Louisiana during a long series of years. He was associated with his uncle, Guy Bryant of Philadelphia, in merchandising, and the firm of Bryant & Morrison was known throughout the West as one of great wealth and honorable standing. Bryant did not himself operate in the West; so that his partner, Morrison, had the control of all the commercial business of this vast region of country. The commercial business of this house extended from Kaskaskia around to Pittsburg, New Orleans, Prairie du Chien, and the Rocky Mountains, and William Morrison was the master spirit that managed and conducted all these vast mercantile transactions to a successful termination. No ordinary talents could combine, control, and execute with success all this complicated machinery. It required the first order of intellect, and such was Nature's gift to this great and noble pioneer.

Kaskaskia was, when he came to Illinois, one of the largest towns west of the Alleghany Mountains, and possessed not only its central position for commerce, but had many other advantages, and he settled himself in it.

By his industry and energy, he became very wealthy. His main store, wholesale and retail, he kept in Kaskaskia, and from it the merchants of St. Louis, Ste. Genevieve, Cape Girardeau, and New Madrid received their goods. About 1800, he established a store in Cahokia and placed in it a clerk—William Atchison This clerk was a singular and eccentric Irishman. He soon, by excessively high prices, acquired by derision the name of Chape Wollie, which he retained while he remained in the store.

Many anecdotes are told on this Irishman. Rev. Benjamin Young, a Methodist circuit rider, at the request of Chape Wollie, preached at his store in Cahokia in 1807, and it turned out that Young had a small congregation. Atchison made excuses for his French neighbors not attending the preaching. "For his part," he said, "he would walk, on Sunday, miles thro *briars* and *hell* to hear such a sermon as that ye prached; but these d——d French love dancing better than praching. An', Misther Young, could ye not stay with us tonight and go to the ball this evening?" The Methodist preacher begged off from Mr. Atchison's civility in going to the dancing-party on Sunday evening.

Mr. Morrison furnished the Indians and Indian traders with great quantities of goods, and on them a great profit was realized.

He accumulated great quantities of land, which descended to his children, yet he was not what is known as a land speculator. He purchased much, but sold little.

About the time his store opened in Cahokia, he encouraged the farmers of the New Design, and, in fact, throughout all the sparse settlements at that time, to cultivate wheat He commenced a commerce in flour He conveyed the wheat to Edgar's mill, near Kaskaskia, and had it there manufactured into flour Flat-boats were built at Levens' mill, on Horse Creek, and on them and other vessels he shipped the flour to New Orleans.

He was generally fortunate in his voyages on the river; but a large boat laden with wheat from Cahokia and bound to Kaskaskia, struck a sawyer in the river above Ste. Genevieve and sunk with the entire loss of the wheat. I think there were more sawyers in the river at that day than at present.

For a long series of years, he carried on a heavy commerce on the Mississippi, between Kaskaskia and New Orleans He shipped to Pittsburg and New Orleans almost all the surplus products of the country, to wit: peltries, furs, lead, flour, horses, etc, and returned with articles for the consumption of the people. His boats were large and of the first class of that day. On these large barges it required forty or fifty boatmen to force them up against the strong current of the Mississippi, and it sometimes occupied four or five months to make the voyage from Kaskaskia to New Orleans and back.

In 1804, a fine young creole Frenchman, La Chappelle of Kaskaskia, had charge of his boat laden with a costly cargo, worth probably fifty thousand dollars, and he died on the voyage up, at Natchez. When the commander, La Chappelle, died, none other on the boat was competent to take command. Many others of the men also died on the voyage, so that the boat was left at Natchez. The cargo was put in a warehouse, but the liquors and wines leaked out of the casks, and other articles also were destroyed, so that the whole cargo was almost entirely lost.

In 1801, he built a fine stone-house in Kaskaskia and furnished it in an elegant manner. This house, at that day, was the best in the country, and in it he lived in a princely style. At his table, with his friends and family, he displayed the hospitality and elegant bearing of a well-bred gentleman.

In the war of 1812, with Great Britain, he obtained the contract for this military district to furnish rations to the troops, and with his talents, energy, and wealth, he performed the responsible duties to the satisfaction of all concerned. Out of this contract he made a large sum of money, altho he abounded in wealth before.

The garrisons to be furnished were situated from Prairie du Chien to the extreme South and throughout the West. They were punctually supplied with rations, altho so remote from the settlements and surrounded by hostile Indians.

He employed Thomas Van Swearengen and John Postlewait, two men well known here at that time, to take charge of beef-cattle along with Harrison's army to the battle of Tippecanoe, in the fall of 1811. Swearengen and Postlewait were bold and daring characters, and withal, men of strong minds. They had no guns or arms at the commencement of the battle, and were sleeping in a wagon. The Indians' bullets soon shattered off the splinters of the wagon into their faces, which compelled them to enter the battle-field. They soon found guns and other weapons, whose owners were already killed in the battle. With these arms, these two men sought the hottest of the conflict and fought with such cool and determined bravery that they excited the admiration of the whole army

Mr. Morrison possessed a public spirit and was ready and willing to enter into public improvements that would advance the interests of the country. He was the main pillar in erecting two bridges across the Kaskaskia River; one adjacent to the town of Kaskaskia and the other at Covington, in Washington County. That at Covington he built himself

He was exemplary in his morals and never indulged in light and frivolous amusements. Gambling and drunkenness he abhorred When the graceful and noble animal, the race-horse, was led out on the turf at Kaskaskia, he frequently attended the races and became much excited in the sport. He at times bet on the race a suit of clothes with a friend, or some such small amount, and cared very little whether he lost or won

His personal appearance was dignified, commanding, and prepossessing. He was of the ordinary size of men, and in his advanced age, rather inclined to be corpulent. Energy and activity were discernable in his walks and movements, as well as in all his conduct. He made it one of his fixed principles to dress richly and with taste and elegance He had a just sense of propriety on this subject. He was always uneasy when in company with a sloven He often said that a man frequently made his fortune by a decent appearance. He was always extremely gallant and polite to the ladies, and often advised his friends to frequent female society. He said intelligent and correct female society was the great lever to govern human actions and to promote morals and religion.

Mr. Morrison possessed a decided and marked character. His predominent traits were a strong mind and great energy. All his impulses were of the noble and elevated order.

Toward the close of his earthly career, he became interested in religious matters, and after due reflection, he joined the Roman-catholic church. He devoted much of his attention to the church before his death, and performed all the duties enjoined upon him with a sincere devotion.

He died in the arms of the church, praising God. His death, altho he was aged, was much regretted by the community, as "one of the great had fallen in Israel." He died in April, 1837, and his remains rest in peace and quiet in the old graveyard at Kaskaskia, where he, in his life, displayed so much energy and activity. How death changes the scene!

In 1798, Robert and James Morrison, brothers of William, arrived in Kaskaskia from Pennsylvania Robert remained an inhabitant of Kaskaskia during life. He held various offices under the territorial governments and performed the duties to the satisfaction of the public. This gentleman was extremely civil and polite to all persons, and particularly to strangers. His house was made the home of many gentlemen of merit whose means were limited. It afforded Mr. Morrison great pleasure to extend to his friends the civilities and hospitalities of his table. He died in Kaskaskia in 1842, much regretted by his family, friends, and the public.

He married in 1806, his second wife, a sprightly and talented lady from Baltimore. This lady, Mrs. Robert Morrison, being of wealthy and respectable family, received an excellent education and was, in fact, a finished and classic scholar. She possessed a strong, original, and sprightly mind. She was endowed with strong perceptions and much originality of thought. Her mind disdained the ancient shackles of any system when its strength was based on its antiquity alone for its support.

Nature gave her rather a romantic turn of mind, and by reason of this disposition, she accompanied her brother, Colonel Donaldson, from Baltimore to the West, in 1805. He was a commissioner to investigate the land-titles at St. Louis, Missouri, and his sister, Mrs. Morrison, after her marriage, made her residence at Kaskaskia in 1806. She, like most others who are endowed by nature with rare gifts, possessed great energy and activity of mind Her delight and home were in the rosy fields of poetry. Her grave deserves to be decorated with flowers. Her versification was decided by critics to be far above medium and many of her pieces to reach the higher order of poetry.

She remodeled in verse the old orthodox Psalms of David, and had the volume presented to the dignitaries of the church in Philadelphia for adoption, instead of the Psalms used in the church. The divines gave the work of Mrs Morrison a critical examination, and barely rejected it, more by its advent from an unknown individual than from a want of merit. Her pen was never idle. She wrote for the scientific publications of Mr. Walsh of Philadelphia, and many of her pieces in prose and verse grace and sustain that celebrated work. Her contributions to periodicals were numerous and highly prized. Many of the political characters of Illinois in early times were greatly benefited and advanced by her energetic and talented productions in the newspaper discussions of that day.

This lady wrote, on many occasions, at the request of her friends, petitions and memorials to congress and to the president that were chaste and classic in their composition and sound and substantial in their appeals made to the general government. For this class of writing this lady was celebrated and much esteemed by her friends.

She entered thoroly into the investigation of the various religious systems. She became a Presbyterian, but on further research and much reflection, she entered the Roman-catholic church and became a very warm and zealous member.

This lady was ardent and enthusiastic in all her pursuits. She was also ambitious of honor and fame and possessed a force of character that was almost irresistible. By her example and influence almost all who came within her circle became Roman catholics and joined that church.

She lived to an advanced age and died in Belleville in 1843, much regretted by her friends and the public generally.

The fruit of the marriage of Mr Morrison with this lady was an interesting family, three of whom are now alive. These three sons were born in Kaskaskia and are at this time conspicuous members of the bar.

Jesse Morrison, who is the youngest of the family, emigrated to the country in 1805. He and his brother, James, formed a commercial partnership and established themselves at St Charles in Missouri. Both these gentlemen raised large and respectable families. Jesse Morrison is now a resident of Galena, Illinois, enjoying, amidst a large number of relatives and friends, the happiness of a well-spent life. He has reached that elevated stand of human nature when all the wild and unruly passions have subsided and the perfection of that nature remains triumphant; so that he, in his old age, tastes some of the bliss laid up beyond the grave for the upright and just

Samuel Morrison, a brother of the above, arrived in Kaskaskia in 1807 He was a moral and excellent youth. He did business for his brother and remained in Kaskaskia until, it was said, a young lady, whose beauty and charms were so irresistible that she wove a web of love around him from which he could not extricate himself till he called in time and distance for relief. He was too young and unsettled to extricate himself from love by marriage. For redress, he embarked in the Rocky-Mountain Company of Emanual Liza and others, and trapped and traded with the Indians on the mountains for three years. He returned home safe and cured of his love monomania.

He returned home in 1811, and some time afterward married. He made his residence at Covington, Washington County, Ill., where he died in 1828. He was universally respected and esteemed, and his death was lamented and regretted by a great portion of the community.

Another brother, Guy Morrison, emigrated to Kaskaskia in 1814, and soon entered into the business of his brother William at Cahokia He was employed in furnishing provisions to the army. He, like the others of the family, possessed a strong mind and great energy, so that he was an efficient agent for his brother in the contract with the United States. He remained in Cahokia eleven years, and became well acquainted with the people and the manner of doing business in Illinois. He married and turned all his energies of mind and body to agriculture. He located himself on a fine farm in the American Bottom, northwest of Collinsville, in 1826, and with his sound judgment and unbounded activity, has acquired an immense fortune. His rents annually and increase arising from his farms are eight or ten thousand bushels of grain His income every year must amount to twelve or fifteen thousand dollars. His lands are well selected and valuable

With all this wealth, he is a plain business man, without ostentation or parade. He resides at this time in Collinsville, in a plain, neat style and is always pleased to receive and entertain his friends in his hospitable mansion. He has no children to inherit his fortune.

A singular lady pioneer emigrated to Cahokia from the lakes about 1770. She was born of French parents of the name of LaFlamme, at St Joseph, on Lake Michigan, in 1734. She first emigrated to Mackinac, and after residing there some time, settled at Chicago with her husband, Sainte Ange, or Pelate, as he was sometimes called, about 1765. Sainte Ange dying, she married M La Compt, a Canadian, in Cahokia, about 1780 From this marriage proceeded one of the largest French families in Illinois. After the death of La Compt, her second husband, she married the celebrated Thomas Brady They had no issue This female pioneer possessed a strong mind, with the courage and energies of a heroine. She was also blessed with an extraordinary constitution She was scarcely ever sick, altho exposed often in traveling and otherwise to the inclemency of the weather and other hardships.

The Indians were her neighbors and friends from her infancy to nearly her death By a wise and proper course with these wild men, and by sage councils to promote their interest, she acquired a great influence over the Pottawatomies, Kickapoos, and other nations bordering on the lakes.

She was familiar not only with the language of the Indians, but also with their character In the early American settlements of the country, from 1781 down to the peace in 1795, this lady prevented many an Indian attack on the white population. The Indians often became hostile to the French during the American Revolution, by the intrigues of the British, as the French had joined Clark in the capture of the British garrisons in the West.

On many occasions this lady was awakened in the dead hours of the night by her Indian friends, from the hostile warriors, informing her of the intended attack, that she might leave Cahokia. Her friends among the Indians could not think of permitting her to be killed. She has started often to meet some hundreds of warriors who were camped near the Quentine Mound, at the foot of the bluff, near the present French Village, or at some other place in the neighborhood. She would cause herself to be conveyed near the Indian camp, perhaps, in the night, and then dismiss her company and proceed on foot to the camp of the Indians. No one knew the Indian character better than she did. A female on foot approaching several hundred armed warriors would produce a sympathy that she followed up with wise councils to the Indians that were irresistible She often remained with them for days and nights, appeasing their anger. She never failed to avert the storm and prevent bloodshed. The inhabitants of the village were often waiting with their arms in their hands, ready for defence, when they would see this extraordinary woman escorting to the village a great band of warriors, changed from war to peace. The Indians were painted black, indicating the sorrow they entertained for their hostile movements against their friends. The Indians were feasted for days in the village They would remain in peace for some time after these reconciliations

Mrs. LaCompt, as she was commonly called after Brady's death, lived to an extreme old age and died in Cahokia in 1843, at the age of one hundred and nine years

I knew this old lady for thirty or more years, and I believe that her health and longevity depended much on her hardy and frugal mode of living She never feared the inclemency of the weather. The health of more people is injured by walking on fine, rich carpets, between the piano and the air-tight stove, than by walking on the ice and snow in the open air.

The increase of the population in Illinois diminished the wild game. The migratory race of fowls in early times were quite numerous near the Mississippi and Illinois River. Swans, geese, brants, cranes, and ducks passed north in the spring and south in the fall, in immense flocks. On their passage they remained a short time in the lowlands of the river, where the hunters killed great numbers. In the fall, cranes were the first that made their appearance. They rose so high in the air that they were scarcely visible These fowls wintered in the swamps south, toward the Gulf of Mexico, and hatched in the summer on the shores of the lakes. They, like the Indians, have almost entirely disappeared on the approach of the white population.

The honey-bee acts on the reverse of the instincts of the fowls. The bees do not much precede the white population. There is nothing the Indians dislike more than to see the bee arrive in the country. They know then that the white man is not far behind. The bees came to Illinois from Kentucky and the Northwest Territory.

The flowers in the prairies sustained great numbers of bees. At one time, in Illinois, the wild honey-bees were very plenty.

In 1790, an enterprising and very conspicuous character, John Rice Jones, arrived in Kaskaskia and located himself there. Mr. Jones was born February 10, 1759, in Merionthshire, Wales. He received a classical education in the old country. He was a regular college graduate; he studied law in Great Britain. He was a good linguist, having become well acquainted with the Greek, Latin, and French, as well as the English. The soundness of his mind enabled him also to become an excellent mathematician, which he preferred to all other science. He was, in fact, an accomplished scholar, and with these advantages, soon became a scientific and profound lawyer, and thro life he was a sound and enlightened expounder of it.

In 1780, Mr. Jones emigrated to the United States and settled in Philadelphia. He opened a law-office in that city and practised his profession there for some time. During this time, he became acquainted with Dr Franklin, Dr Rush, Myers Fisher, and other distinguished characters.

He left Philadelphia and emigrated to Vincennes in 1787, when the Northwest Territory was organized.

Mr. Jones, the next year, 1788, assisted William Briggs to return to his family in the New Design in Illinois from his captivity with the Indians.

In 1790, he settled in Kaskaskia and there practised his profession. He was the first practising lawyer in Illinois and would be a conspicuous member of his profession in any country. He possessed a strong and active mind, rather restless, and excessively energetic. This energy of character enabled him to practise law in important cases at different times of his life throughout the West; Louisville, Ky., Vincennes, Indiana, Kaskaskia, Cahokia, Illinois, and many of the courts in Missouri, after the cession of the country, in 1803, from France to the United States. Mr. Jones being an excellent French scholar, enabled him to do the business of the French population to the advantage of both parties.

He always employed his time in some honorable business and never permitted himself to be idle or engaged in light or frivolous amusements. Like most of his countrymen, he possessed strong passions, and at times, altho he possessed a strong mind, his passions swept over his reason like a tornado. His friendships were ardent and sincere, and his hatred and anger were excessively scathing for the moment. When his feelings of ire were excited, his words burnt his victims like drops of molten lead on the naked skin. He was mild and amiable until some injury or insult, as he supposed, was offered to him, then he burst asunder all restraints and stood out the fearless champion of his right, bidding defiance to all opposition. He possessed a great degree of personal courage.

In the forepart of 1802, he again moved to Vincennes and was appointed a United-States judge of the Indiana Territory. He and Col. Johnson revised the statute laws of Indiana in 1807, and the legislature of that State enacted them with very little alteration. The substance of these acts is still retained in our statute-books, as Illinois at that time comprised a part of Indiana.

In 1810, Judge Jones moved to St. Louis, Missouri, but did not reside there any great time, but settled in Washington County, Missouri, at Petosi.

Here he found Moses Austin, with whom he formed a partnership in the lead business. They erected the first cupola or reverberating furnace ever made in the United States. By this furnace, fifteen or twenty per cent more lead can be extracted from the ore than by the former furnaces.

Judge Jones was a member elected from Washington County, Missouri, to form the first constitution of that State. Jones was a wise and efficient member of that convention, which sat in St Louis in 1819. He was a candidate before the next general assembly of the State for the United-States senate, but Col. Benton was elected.

Judge Jones was elected by the same legislature one of the judges of the supreme court of Missouri, which office he retained during his life. His decisions in the supreme court were always much respected by the bar and the public.

He died in St. Louis, while in office, in 1824, and was nearly sixty-five years of age. On his death-bed he said "he did not desire to live any longer, as he could be of no further use to his family or country, and might be a source of trouble if he lived any longer." He was perfectly resigned to his fate and died with that calm composure that always attends the exit of the "noblest work of God," an honest man

The person of Judge Jones was small, but erect and active. His complexion was dark and his hair and eyes very black. His eye, when excited, was severe and piercing.

Judge Jones lived a life of great activity and was conspicuous and prominent in all the important transactions of the country. In his youth, altho not bred to the military profession, yet he was engaged in the wars against the Indians, both in Indiana and Illinois The death of Judge Jones was regretted by a wide circle of friends and the public generally His integrity, honor, and honesty were always above doubt or suspicion He was exemplary in his moral habits and lived a temperate and orderly man in all things. He left a large and respectable family. His sons have filled, with credit to themselves, many of the most important offices in the country, and one, at this time—Hon G W Jones—is in the senate of the United States from the State of Iowa.

Rice Jones, the eldest son of John Rice Jones, was born in Philadelphia in 1781 When his age permitted, he was placed in the institution in Kentucky, and was a classmate of the late Colonel Richard M Johnson of that State Young Jones was endowed with great intellectual powers and thereby made rapid advances in his education He quitted the school in Kentucky with a reputation for talents and education not inferior to any student that was at the institution.

After finishing his education, he studied medicine in Philadelphia, and graduated from the medical school with a diploma and what is better, with much honor

After practising medicine a short time and disliking that profession, he abandoned it and commenced, in Litchfied, Conn., the study of the law. After some years of intense study, he quitted the institution with increased honor

He located himself in Kaskaskia in 1806, and opened a law-office No young man at that day, and not many since, commenced with prospects of a more brilliant career of life than Rice Jones did. He possessed a strong intellect, but was also endowed with an excessive ambition, together with an ardent and impetuous disposition, and showed the Welsh temper more than his father. He practised his profession some time and his friends needed his talents and energies in their political campaigns.

Party spirit raged in and about Kaskaskia with a violence not equalled at any time since. Many of the prominent politicians were almost crazy on the subject. Young Jones caught the mania and became excessively zealous Altho he was young, yet from his talents and energy he was at the head of one of the parties in that day. He had been elected a member of the legislature of Indiana, held at Vincennes, and was becoming a very conspicuous character in the country. The other party did not like his prominency or standing with the people.

In this excited state of the parties, and Jones at the head of one party, it was not difficult for the parties to quarrel or even fight.

A controversy growing out of politics commenced between him and Shadrach Bond, the first governor elect for the State of Illinois, and a duel between those persons (Jones and Bond) was agreed upon. The parties met on an island in the Mississippi, between Ste. Genevieve and Kaskaskia, and when they had taken their positions and about to fire, Jones' pistol, having a hair trigger, went off by accident. Dunlap, the second of Bond, said it was Jones' fire and Bond might fire at Jones; but Bond, with that greatness of soul that appeared in all his actions, public and private, cried out, "it was an accident."

The parties settled the controversy on the ground on honorable terms; but a bitter quarrel ensued between Jones and Dunlap on the subject This controversy waxed warmer and more malignant, until at last Dunlap shot Jones in the public streets of Kaskaskia. Jones was standing in the street, leaning on the railing of the gallery and talking to a lady, when Dunlap came up behind him and shot him dead with a pistol.

This horrid murder of such a talented and promising young man shocked the community and to some extent quieted the party feuds for a time.

This murder occurred in 1809 Dunlap escaped to Texas and was never punished by the temporal courts.

Thus ended, in his twenty-eighth year, a young man of exceedingly great promise. Judging from the character he acquired at school, and what was known of him at Kaskaskia, it is not improbable that his superior was not in the country before or after his death

The whole community mourned for the death of this fine young man—cut off in his prime by an assassin. It was indeed shocking to the public.

In early times the inhabitants of Illinois were in a small degree tinctured with the absurdity and nonsense of witchcraft and fortune-telling, but in after-days this ignorant superstition has entirely disappeared.

The French at no time were troubled with the apparitions, ghosts, or spirits. Haunted houses were out of fashion with them It is true, they had an imaginary being they called *le loup garreau*—the growling wolf This was hatched up more to scare children than the grown folks. Yet the ancient French in Illinois believed that the negroes in the West-India Islands possessed a supernatural power to do injury to any one that had incurred their displeasure, and had power, also, to look into futurity. This power, the old French ladies believed, came from Africa and was retained with the African negroes It may be said that this belief of fortune-telling was mostly *female*, as the intelligent among them, as they do now, laugh at the nonsense.

The French in Cahokia dreaded to incur the displeasure of certain old colored people, as they could do them injury, even to death, by these African incantations. The great empress of France, Josephine, had her fortune told her in the West Indies, which to some extent influenced her conduct thro life The old sibyl in Martinique said to Josephine. "You will be queen of France." With all the good sense of that celebrated woman, she rather believed the prophecy, yet laughed at it. It was the belief of some people and families that an old woman living on Silver Creek, Ill., had the power of witchcraft to take the milk from her neighbors' cows without seeing or touching them. All this ignorance and nonsense have disappeared from the minds of the people by a proper education. School-houses always destroy witchcraft. The people, in proportion to their ignorance, will be troubled with this superstition.

The Creator gave no power to the demons of darkness to change the laws of nature at their diabolical pleasure, and to vex and harass mankind at their will.

I think it is blasphemy to believe that witches are the vicegerents of God to change his laws at their pleasure.

In Cahokia, about 1790, this superstition got the upper hand of reason, and several poor African slaves were immolated at the shrine of ignorance for this imaginary offence. An African negro, called Moreau,* was hung for this crime on a tree not far southeast of Cahokia. It is stated that he had said, "he poisoned his master, but his mistress was too strong for his necromancy." Another slave, Emanuel, was shot in Cahokia for this crime, and an old woman, Janette, was supposed to have the power to destroy persons and property by her incantations. Many grown people and all the children were terrified at her approach.

All countries have had their *witches*, and I hope Illinois will never again return to such scenes of bloodshed, to appease the demon of ignorance.

In May, 1791, John Dempsey was attacked by the Indians, but escaped. It will be recollected that this same Dempsey was, a few years before, scalped by the Indians and left for dead. This pioneer was determined to stand his ground in Illinois, dead or alive. Eight men, Capt. N. Hull, commanding, James Lemen, Sr, Joseph Ogle, Sr., Benjamin Ogle, J. Ryan, William Bryson, John Porter, and Daniel Raper pursued this party of Indians, who were double the number of whites. The hottest of the battle was fought in the timber northwest of the camp-meeting ground, at the Big Spring, in Monroe Co., and not far east of the road from Waterloo to Whiteside's Station. This was a running fight from tree to tree, the Indians fleeing and the whites pursuing. This bloody conflict was kept

* In "Fergus' Historical Series. No 12, By Edward G. Mason," may be found "Col John Todd's record book," and on page 58 is the order for the execution of "Negro Manuel, a slave," and on page 59 is the order for the detail of a party of militia to "guard Moreau, a slave condemned to execution, up to the town of Kokos," dated "June 15, 1779".—J. H G.

up until dark separated the combatants. Five Indians were killed and not a white man's blood was shed

These trials and dangers in the first settlement of the country made the pioneers an iron race of men, and they were like the army of Oliver Cromwell — they cared very little about the numbers of the enemy opposed to them. This was verified in the case of Capt. Hull and seven men running sixteen Indians and killing five of them

Several emigrants had stopped at Kaskaskia and Jacob Judy among the rest He sold out his property at Kaskaskia and located himself and family on the site where at present stands the old water-mill known at this day as Judy's mill This mill is a small distance west of Whiteside's Station, in Monroe Co. It was erected in 1794, and was at the time the first water-mill in that section of the country It was of great service to the infant settlement, as many of the pioneers can testify at this day.

A few years after, other water-mills and some band-mills of two or four horse-power, as the parties were provided with these animals, were also erected in the same neighborhood. George Valentine built a water-mill on a stream nearly west of Judy's mill.

These mills relieved the people, when the water was high and plenty, from the use of graters, hand-mills, and mortars to manufacture corn-meal

In early times, these various expedients were resorted to by the people to manufacture corn-meal The band-mill was so called because a raw-hide band twisted was put on the large wheel in the place of cogs. It saved the gearing of the mill They are the lowest and cheapest order of horse-mills Pins are put in the arms of the large wheel and around them the band is placed. These pins may be changed into holes made for the purpose, so the band may be made tighter when necessary.

The next is the hand-mill The stones are smaller than those of the horse-mill and propelled by man or woman power. A hole is made in the upper stone and a staff of wood is put in it, and the other end of the staff is put thro a hole in a plank above, so that the whole is free to act One or two persons take hold of this staff and turn the upper stone with as much velocity as possible. An eye is made in the upper stone, thro which the corn is put into the mill with the hand in small quantities to suit the mill, instead of a hopper. This is a hand-mill. A mortar wherein corn is beat into meal is made out of a large round log, three or four feet long. One end is cut or burnt out, so as to hold a peck of corn, more or less, according to circumstances. This mortar is set one end on the ground and the other up, to hold the corn. A sweep is prepared over the mortar, so that the spring of the pole raises the piston and the hands at it force it so hard down on the corn that after much beating, meal is manufactured.

The last and lowest order of inventions to manufacture meal is a grater. A plate of tin is pierced with many holes, so that one side is made very rough. The tin is made oval and then nailed to a board. An ear of corn rubbed hard on this grater, whereby the meal is forced thro the holes and falls down into a vessel prepared to receive it.

These are the contrivances which the pioneers, in early times, were forced to adopt. In the fall of the year, the water-mills generally were idle, for the want of water, and the people were compelled to resort to these shifts for meal.

In my youth, I had a very intimate and personal acquaintance with all these modes of manufacturing corn-meal, and was as happy then as at any time of my life, under different circumstances.

The Irishman, Halfpenny, the school-master general, likewise erected a water-mill on the Fountaine Creek, not far west of the present town of Waterloo. This mill was built about 1795. In 1798, Josiah Ryan built a water-mill on the stream below the mill of the late Gen. James, in Monroe County. These two last-named mills and all traces of them have disappeared from their respective localities. It may be that in the course of time the finest steam-mills that now ornament and benefit the country so much at this day, and even the populous cities themselves, may cease to exist, and the remains of them present as melancholy a spectacle to other ages as the ruins of Palmyra and Balbec do to us at this day. Man and his works are all transient and evanescent. The very continent of North America itself may again be submerged by the ocean, as it once was, and thereby the most promising part of the globe, with all its population and free institutions, may disappear and a dreary waste of water again occupy its place.

There is nothing permanent but the great Supreme Being and His eternal laws which govern the universe

After the close of the Indian wars, the French and Americans associated themselves together more and adopted each others customs and habits to some extent

The Americans became enamored with the French custom of *charivari*, and practised it sometimes right, but more often wrong, according to the rules established by the French

The old French *charivari* was innocent It was, in their hands, a merry rural serenade, sustained by all sorts of loud and discordant noises. The *charivari* party was composed of old and young, and generally conducted by some orderly and aged man. They enlisted into their service all sorts of things that could by any means be forced to make a noise. They used bells, horns, drums, pans, tin kettles, whistles, and all such articles as would make loud, harsh sounds This French organized *charivari* was such a merry, noisy uproar that it would make a monk laugh if he heard it

The proper French custom was that if persons married of the same condition, there was no *charivari;* but when discordant materials were tied together with that delicious silken cord, which is so dazzling to the female eye, then a similar discordant noise attended the celebration For example, when neither of the parties ever before tasted the delicacies of matrimony, there was no ground for a serenade, but when a widower, who had before worshiped at the shrine of Venus, married a lady who was never before bound in wedlock, then, in such cases, the *charivari* was invoked with all its merriment And the same with a widow who had before feasted on the sweet viands of love and married a man whose lot had heretofore been celibacy, in such cases the *charivari* was in order

Generally among the French the married parties were as willing as the others for the sport, and were prepared to extend some civilities to the good-humored crowd Thus frequently the case ended in the best of feeling. But when the married folks were refractory, the *charivari* was kept up for a succession of nights, until they yielded to the custom. As the farce proceeded, if the married parties were *sour*, the serenading crowd had the privilege to hint, in a wild manner, first at the character of the bride and then at that of the bridegroom These hints generally closed the scene in good humor. When the noise was made in the crowd, some one would cry out at the top of his voice, "*charivari! charivari!*" and some other in the party would sing out, "*pour qui?*"—"for whom?" The answer to this question gave rise to hint at the female and her character. At times, the bridegroom also was charged with things he would not like

This was the *dernier resort*. When this or other means produced some kindness or civility, then the whole farce ended in the best of feelings among the French. But with the Americans this *charivari* is sometimes attended with disagreeable consequences. And, in fact, the serenading party is sometimes indicted for a breach of the peace.

In all countries the administration of the laws is extremely important to the people. No matter how free a people may be, if the laws are not properly executed, that people can not prosper and be happy.

To make a people prosperous and happy, the laws must be not only equitable and just, but executed in the same manner, with equity and justice.

In 1790, Governor St. Clair organized the government of the Northwest Territory, and also the judiciary of St. Clair County. He appointed justices of the peace throughout the county; but their jurisdiction was limited to twenty dollars in civil matters, and in criminal cases they had no power whatever, except to act as an examining court. The opinion of the people in olden times was opposed to giving justices much jurisdiction in civil and none in criminal matters The rule of ancient times is relaxing, with experience, and at this day, the justices' courts are the most important tribunals in the country. A jury before a justice of the peace, in former times, was never known.

Gov St. Clair also appointed judges of the court of common-pleas, or quarter-sessions as they were sometimes called They held these offices at the discretion of the governor, but he scarcely ever exercised his power in dismissing any from office.

The practice of dismissing men from office was not much exercised in early times, and it is a discretion that requires a sound judgment and a just sense of propriety to exercise it to the public interest. The old saying of Jefferson is known to all " Is he capable? Is he honest?" It may be proper to change the policy of the republic on account of the great changes in the quantity and quality of the population in these days.

These county-courts held sessions to do business every three months, which gave them the name of quarter-sessions. The governor and judges of the Northwest Territory adopted the common-law of Great Britain and the British statutes in aid thereof, to the fourth year of the reign of James I. of Great Britain

These laws provided for the trial by jury and recognized all such other appendages as are found in the common-law, applicable to our government. The ordinance of 1787 introduced the common-law into the territory and many other salutary regulations. The *habeas corpus* was secured to the people and such other fundamental principles as are generally provided in the various state constitutions

St. Clair County was parcelled off into three judicial districts, and the courts held their sessions in each district; one at Kaskaskia, one at Prairie du Rocher, and one at Cahokia. The judges, sheriff, and clerk had jurisdiction throughout the county, but the citizens could not be sued out of their districts.

I saw a case in the ancient records of Kaskaskia district, where a citizen entered his plea of abatement, in 1790, to the jurisdiction of the court, because he was [not] sued in the district of Prairie du Rocher, where he resided. This plea was made by John Rice Jones, his attorney, and prayed a nonsuit from the court at Kaskaskia.

The writs are dated at these villages: Kaskaskia, Prairie du Rocher, and Cahokia, and run within the respective districts.

In 1790, John Edgar of Kaskaskia, Jean Baptiste Barbeau of Prairie du Rocher, and John de Moulin of Cahokia were the chief-justices of their respective districts, and in whose names the judicial processes of their districts were issued.

William St. Clair and William Biggs were the clerk and the sheriff, whose authority extended throughout the county of St Clair

Grand-juries were organized in each district and returned indictments.

I saw a record proceeding at Prairie du Rocher against a colored man for the murder of a hog At that day no prosecuting attorney attended the court, and I presume the grand-jury found the form of an indictment in some book, for murder, and applied it to the negro and the hog. It was malicious mischief in destroying the hog, which I presume was the offence the grand-jury was investigating. The same equitable justice may have been done under the indictment for murder, as if it were one for malicious mischief and prosecuted by the ablest attorneys in the country.

In those days John Rice Jones was the only attorney practising in these courts, and the next, in 1794, was the celebrated Isaac Darnielle of Cahokia.

Ejectment suits were common, at that day, for particular and valuable tracts of land. I can not perceive that there was any mode pointed out for an appeal from these courts, and in no case was it practised, so far as I can discover. The United-States judges of the Northwest Territory held their sessions at the seat of government at Cincinnati or Chillicothe, which was so remote from Illinois that an appeal to this court was much more impracticable than an appeal at this day is to Washington City. The people, at that day, required not much from the courts and nothing from appeals.

Toward the close of the Indian war, the country south of the New Design commenced its settlement Johnson J Whiteside and others laid off a town, not on paper, but on a site situated on the west bank of the Kaskaskia River, not far south of the northern limits of the present county of Randolph, and called it Washington. This town was commenced in 1795, and occupied a beautiful situation on the high bluff of the river, overlooking, to the west, much of the Horse Prairie. The inhabitants enclosed and cultivated large fields of grain and raised stock to a considerable amount. The houses in this town were log-cabins, but streets and other *town notions* were observed in the building of the place.

In the early settlement of this town, the Going families were conspicuous. The Goings, the old and young William, emigrated from Kentucky in 1794, and erected a station a short distance southwest of the Bellefontaine. In this fort, John Pulliam located himself and family in 1796. Some other families likewise were tenants of this station this year.

Both father and son were blacksmiths, and the younger was a man of considerable talents. The old gentleman was a plain man, except when he became excited with tafia. Then he was a rough customer. At courts and other gatherings he had bells to sell, and he often put a cord thro the staples of the bells, perhaps a dozen, more or less, of all sizes, and then tied the cord around his waist. To make the scene more imposing, he dressed himself with a fox-skin cap, with the tail suspended behind, and other dress of the same outlandish character. Thus equipped, he danced in the crowd, so that his noise would drown thunder. He was not large, but very active and strong. In early times, Judge Symmes, one of the United-States judges of the Northwest Territory, held court at Cahokia and Going tormented the judge with his bell-dance. Many other such wild freaks, Going and others of his day indulged in. The old man died in Washington, on the Kaskaskia River, and is buried, with many more, in the old graveyard, north of the town.

William Going, the son, was of a different order of men. His mind and person were both formed on a large and substantial scale. He received a very limited education and could barely read and write. But nature did much for him, tho he did little for himself. With his natural gifts, he might have been among the first men in any country. As it was, he was leader, in his manner. He possessed a strong natural mind and a bold energy that was on some occasions exerted in a manner of which the community did not approve. His courage and daring bravery were always equal or superior to the emergency. These traits of Going's character no one ever doubted. His person was large and modeled on the stern and rather defiable order. He was neither repulsive or very prepossessing in his appearance; but all who saw him, at once came to the same conclusion that he was a decided, firm, and great man in his sphere. His decision among his comrades was the law and the gospel to them. No one of his friends ever murmured at, or attempted an appeal from, his judgment. He was the great governing spirit in his circle at the races, shooting-matches, and card-tables. His impulses were naturally on the side of honesty and integrity, but bad associations and habits gradually grew on him, which forced the public to think strange of his conduct. He was ardent and sincere in his friendships He had a high sense of honor in his peculiar notions of that virtue. He would suffer martyrdom before he would desert or abandon a comrade in his distress, and would risk his life for a tried friend. The wealth of a nation might be committed to his care, and it would be safe, if he pledged his honor in the case and confidence were placed in him. If he had lived in the days of the crusades to the Holy Land, he would have been a leader of magnitude Talents, courage, energy, and chivalric notions of honor would have placed William Going the leader of many of the bold and daring attacks on Jerusalem. If Going had been with General Wayne in his army, he would have been, in all probability, one of Wayne's men in storming Stony Point. But as it was, his life was wasted away in an obscure corner, where his talents and energies had not the proper theatre in which to act.

He was a blacksmith and gunsmith, but like many others raised at that day in Illinois, he had no ambition for hard labor. He worked in his shop for his pleasure and cared but little for wealth, save a support for himself and family. He possessed a talent for repairing guns and shooting them, having steady nerves and excellent eyesight. With these qualities and much practise with fine rifles, he shot with great exactness. An eye-witness, who is now alive, informed me that he saw Going, in 1807, at his residence on the Kaskaskia River, a short distance below the present town of Fayette, shoot a rifle, with a rest, ninety yards, and put four balls into the same hole, near the centre of the target. The fifth bullet touched the same hole. This is a precision in shooting that is rarely reached. It will be remembered that a great portion of the time of the people at that day was occupied with the gun, either in defending themselves from Indian attacks or in procuring a living for their families.

Altho Going was possessed of a strong mind and great firmness, yet he was not invulnerable against the attacks of beauty. Love made him sever the ties of a former marriage, and he became the victim of a new flame. This second marriage *de facto* remained during life and the parties lived in peace and harmony. He died in Arkansas in 1830.

John Pulliam was also, in early times, a resident of this town By common consent, this place changed its name from Washington to that of Horse-Prairie Town. Under this name it lingered and died.

In 1796, John Pulliam emigrated from Kentucky to New Design, in Illinois. He was a native of Botetourt County, Virginia, and emigrated to Kentucky just after the war of the Revolution He moved to the west of St. Louis in 1797, and remained some years at the Flourisant and Owen's Station He returned to Illinois in 1799, and settled in the Horse-Prairie Town. He cultivated the field near the town for a few years and then made a farm, in 1802, on the Prairie-du-Long Creek, near the mouth of Richland Creek, in the present county of Monroe. He sold his place and made another plantation on the Kaskaskia River, on which he lived and died. His last residence was near the present town of Fayette, where he settled in 1808, and died in 1813

Mr. Pulliam was a man of good mind and more energy and activity than ordinary. He had a large family, whose descendants and connections were very numerous in Illinois Not many pioneer families in Illinois, of whom I am acquainted, are so numerous in their lineal descendants and the connections and ramifications as the Pulliam family, all descending from John Pulliam, the aged patriarch of the family.

John Grosvenor resided in this town in 1799, and for some years. He was a native of Connecticut and was a stone-mason and farmer. He cultivated a large farm adjacent to the town and sold much produce. He was an honest, correct man, moral in all things, except, perhaps, in his young days he permitted the Godess of Love to furnish him with a traveling companion, from Connecticut to Illinois, at whose departure some *one*, at least, in Connecticut felt sorry.

As the country in the Horse Prairie improved, this town declined, until the village ceased to exist and the country flourished.

Another town was staked off at the Bellefontaine, but obstinately refused to grow. French as well as Americans settled in this village It had a shorter life and a more humble one than the Horse-Prairie Town.

In 1793, Illinois received a colony of the most numerous, daring, and enterprising inhabitants that had heretofore settled in it. The Whitesides and their extensive connections emigrated from Kentucky and settled in and around the New Design in this year. Not only the numerous names of Whiteside was in this colony, but also were their connections: Griffin, Gibbons, Enochs, Chance, Musick, Going, and. others This large connection of citizens, being all patriotic, courageous, and determined to defend the country at the risk of their lives, was a great acquisition to Illinois, which was hailed by all as the harbinger of better times

The Whitesides and their early connections were born and raised on the frontiers of North Carolina, and emigrated to Kentucky. They had been inured to Indian hostilities and other hardships incident to frontier life, from their early years to manhood The patriarch and leader, William Whiteside, had been a brave soldier in the Revolutionary war and was in the celebrated battle of King's Mountain To be a soldier in the battle of King's Mountain is an honor of itself His brother, John Whiteside, was also in the war for independence, and acted well his part in that struggle The Whiteside family were of Irish descent and inherited much of the Irish character They were warm-hearted, impulsive, and patriotic. Their friends were always right and their foes always wrong in their estimation. They were capable of entertaining strong and firm attachments and friendships If a Whiteside took you by the hand, you had his heart He would shed his blood freely for his country or for his friend

William Whiteside erected a fort on the road from Cahokia to Kaskaskia, which became celebrated as Whiteside's Station At this station, Whiteside raised a large and efficient family of children.

John Whiteside, his brother, resided at the Bellefontaine for many years, and died there He also had a large family, whose descendants are very numerous and settled in many parts of the West

William Whiteside, soon after he arrived in Illinois, became conspicuous and efficient as a leader in the Indian war. He was the captain of many parties that took signal vengeance on the savage foe for murders they committed on the women and children, as well as on the grown men. One trait of character — bravery — the Whiteside family possessed in an eminent degree, and the patriarch of whom I am speaking was as cool, firm, and decided a man as ever lived. Scarcely any of the family ever knew what fear was

William Whiteside was the captain of a party of eight men, who pursued a large number of Indians and overtook them on Shoal Creek.

In 1793, the Kickapoo Indians stole a number of horses from the American Bottom, not far distant from the present residence of Mr. Miles, and fled toward their towns at the sources of the Sangamon River Many of the citizens assembled to pursue the Indians, but only eight came to the sticking point, William Whiteside, captain, Samuel Judy, John Whiteside, Samuel Whiteside, William Harrington, Wm. L. Whiteside, John Porter, and John Dempsey They pursued the Indian trail near the present City of Belleville, toward the Indian camp on Shoal Creek.

It was a hazardous and dangerous march, eight men in pursuit of a large body of Indians, and going into a country where hundreds of the enemy could be called forth in a few hours Scarcely eight men in any country could be selected, with the same talents and efficiency, to succeed in such a perilous attempt on the enemy, as those composing this almost forlorn hope.

These pioneers had no time to prepare for the march, or the Indians would escape. They had scarcely anything with them to eat Their guns, ammunition, and bravery were almost all they had along. One other essential ingredient they had in an eminent degree, great talents, caution, and experience in the captain and also many of his party. They followed the trail, day and night, with great rapidity. One of the party was generally out before on the trail as a spy, to prevent the whites from rushing into an ambuscade Better to lose one man than all the party

They came up with the Indians on Shoal Creek and found

three of the horses grazing in the prairie. They secured these horses and then made arrangements to attack the Indian camp By order of the captain, altho the party was small, yet it was divided into two parties, and each to attack the camp at the same time, from the opposite sides The captain's gun to fire was the signal to commence the battle. One Indian, the son of the chief, old Pecon, was killed, one mortally wounded, and others slightly.

The Indians, altho many more than the whites, ran off and left their guns and everything but themselves. The old chief surrendered and gave up his gun to Whiteside. The chief, judging from the bold and energetic attack, supposed the whites to be numerous behind But when he discovered the whole were only eight men, he cried with a terrific voice to his braves to return and fight the Americans, and at the same time seized his gun in Whiteside's hands and attempted to wrench it from him Whiteside was an extraordinary stout man and never at a loss in any personal scramble that resembled a fight. Whiteside's men were afraid to shoot the Indian, as they might kill their captain; but he was in no danger from the Indian. Whiteside retained the gun in triumph and the Indian, altho a brave man, was forced to acknowledge the superiority of the white man. Whiteside would not injure or let his men kill an unarmed foe, altho the Indian broke the truce. The Indian escaped to his warriors unhurt, much to the honor of Whiteside. These were the days of chivalry in Illinois.

Whiteside, who was famous for his prudence as well as his courage, said it was unwise to remain in the Indian country a moment longer They started back with the horses they caught and neither eat or slept until they reached Whiteside's Station And the very night they arrived at the station, Pecon and seventy warriors camped in the vicinity of Cahokia, in pursuit of Whiteside and his party.

The wisdom of Whiteside was verified in this case. Suppose the whites had loitered at the Indian camp on Shoal Creek a few hours, these seventy savages would have destroyed a part or all of Whiteside's party before they reached the settlement

Savage malignity and revenge was not appeased by the noble and generous act of Capt Whiteside in saving the life of the old chief, Pecon, but in revenge for the loss of his son, the old warrior and his braves shot, near the station, a young man, Thomas Whiteside, and tomahawked the boy of the captain while he was out at play, so that he died. These murders occurred the next year, 1794, after the son of Pecon was killed. There is no passion in the breast of a savage so strong as that of revenge.

In 1795, a Frenchman in Cahokia informed Capt. Whiteside that a camp of Indians of considerable number was established at the bluff, a short distance south of the present macadamized road from Belleville to St Louis, and that they meditated some injury to him—to kill him, or steal horses, etc. This information aroused the blood of the old warrior, Whiteside, and he called on his tried band of heroes. His passion was not cooled down for the loss of his people, and, moreover, he was acting in self-defence. His small company, Samuel and William L Whiteside, Samuel Judy, Isaac Enochs, Johnson J Whiteside, and others, to the number of fourteen, were assembled, and just before day, the camp was surrounded and all the Indians killed except one. He escaped, not to live, but to die, as the other Indians killed him for his cowardly running off. The Indians numbered more than the whites, but were surprised and killed. This is Indian war. The bones of these Indians were seen at this battle-field for years after.

In this battle, Capt Whiteside was wounded, he supposed, mortally. He fell to the ground, and in this condition, he exhorted his men to fight bravely, never to give an inch of ground and never permit the enemy to touch his body when he was dead, supposing he would die in a short time. His son, Uel, was also wounded in the arm and could not use his gun. He examined his father's wound and discovered that the ball had not passed thro the body, but struck a rib and glanced off toward the spine. On further examination, he found that the bullet had lodged near the skin, and with his butcher-knife he cut it out, saying, "father, you are not dead yet." The old man jumped to his feet, remarking, "boys, I can still fight the Indians." Such desperate feats of courage and military enthusiasm rarely occur in any age or in any country

As Capt Whiteside and party were returning to Whiteside's

Station, they halted at Cahokia to dress the wounds of the captain and his son. A widow lady, an American, had two beautiful and intelligent daughters, and as few Americans resided in the village, the wounded men stopped at this lady's house a few minutes to dress their wounds. William B. Whiteside* was with the party to this lady's residence. He was quite young and very handsome. This accidental meeting made these young people acquainted with each other and at last the two brothers married the two sisters, Misses Rains, and each party raised large families. It is singular that such small circumstances may decide the destiny of a person during life.

The father and son both recovered of their wounds and lived a long time after. The name of Whiteside was a terror to the Indians.

The old warrior, William Whiteside, rested in peace from Indian wars for many years, as this battle was the last, until 1811, when the Indians again commenced depredations. He was elected colonel of St. Clair County and held that office for many years. He never cared much about the parade of military office. He admired more "the hair-breadth 'scape in the imminent deadly breach."

Col. Whiteside, after the peace with the Indians, turned his attention to his farm at 'the station, and improved it. He cul-

---

* I am inclined to think the Governor was indebted to his imagination for this piece of romance. Wm. B. Whiteside, called Bohn, was one of the sons, and Uel the other. I knew Bohn intimately, and the family of Uel. I also knew Mrs. Bohn Whiteside, whose maiden name, according to my recollection, was Arendell. In a sketch of the Whiteside family that I furnished Hon. E. B. Washburne, to be used in an address delivered by him before the Agricultural Society of Whiteside County, in 1877, I fell into the error of taking the Governor's account of this double marriage without due reflection. Afterward, on meeting with Michael Whiteside, since deceased, who lived in this county, he said he did not believe the story, and referred to circumstances that satisfied me that it was not true, and upon reflection I am constrained to believe either that the Governor culled this ornamental story from his imagination or some one injected it into the story. The Governor was in the habit of having fine passages written by his friends. Col. Nathaniel Niles of Belleville has been suspected of writing a very fine passage, touching the return of Reynolds to the hearthstone of his early life and the scenes of his childhood in Tennessee. If this passage in regard to the double marriage is a *canard* or was an interpolation, the Governor should be held responsible, for he knew the history of the Whitesides, as his brother Robert married a daughter of Wm. B. or Bohn Whiteside. This I know.
—JOSEPH GILLESPIE, Jan. 25, 1883.

tivated a fine apple-orchard, which, in days gone by, was quite celebrated, as very few orchards were in the country.

He and his brother, John Whiteside, in 1806, purchased a land-warrant of one hundred acres and located it on a mill-seat on Wood River, where the main road crosses the creek from Edwardsville to Alton. They prepared and hauled much timber to the premises for the mill, but never built it.

Col. Whiteside was a justice-of-the-peace and judge of the court of common-pleas. These offices he executed to please the people, not himself, as the military was his fort and pleasure.

In the war of 1812, Col. Whiteside was active and efficient in organizing the militia of St. Clair County and preparing them for active service. He himself was in the service and attended at Camp Russell in carrying out the military operations in the defence of the frontiers. He died at his residence, the old Station, in 1815. He was universally known throughout the country, and his death cast a gloom over the community.

He had been a regular member of the Baptist church for many years previous to his death. He was an exemplary and moral man and possessed a strong, uncultivated mind His education was limited, but his life, being one of extraordinary events, made him intelligent Reflection and study were forced on him in self-defence. His frontier life, with the Indian war and all its dangers and perils impending over him for many years, developed his mind and made him a grave, reflecting man. His person was stout and active. He, as it was with most of the name, was a stranger to fear He was calm and meditative in times of peril He never permitted any rash impulses to influence him in battle His remains now rest at his old Station, in peace and quiet, from the din and uproar of the battle-field, where his energies and commanding talents have, on many occasions, won the victory for the stars and stripes. He was the leader and pioneer of the Whiteside family and connections in Illinois. They are exceedingly numerous, extending throughout the country. They may look back at him with esteem and respect as the pioneer, Moses, that conducted them thro the wilderness to Illinois, the "promised land"

Joseph Kinney came to the New Design in 1793, and rais d

a crop preparatory to the emigration of his family to Illinois. He resided at the time on Bear-Grass Creek, seven miles from Louisville, Kentucky, and the next year he moved his family to the New Design. He had seven sons and four daughters, and raised them all to years of maturity before any one of them died. This family was a great acquisition to a new country. They descended the Ohio from Louisville to Fort Massac, and then crossed the country from Massac to Kaskaskia. In this early time there was scarcely any road for a wagon, or even for pack-horses, from Massac to Kaskaskia; but the energetic pioneers overcome all obstacles and performed the tour. It was said that William Kinney, the son of Joseph Kinney, and afterward lieutenant-governor of the State of Illinois, drove the first wagon on this road from Massac* to Kaskaskia.

Not only had this family great difficulty in moving to the country, but they also experienced many more disasters and dangers in this new country. One of the greatest misfortunes that the family had to suffer was the want of schools to educate the children. The younger portion of the family were almost entirely deprived of this blessing. Nature had gifted this family with strong minds and great energy, but they had no opportunity of improving their minds in their younger days.

The youngest daughter of Joseph Kinney, when she was married to Rev. Joseph Lemen, in 1809, possessed no book-education, whatever; but her husband, much to his credit, sent her to school, and she learned, after she was married, to read and write. She is now an intelligent lady and the mother of a large and respectable family.

* The French commander who evacuated Fort Duquesne in October, 1758, on the approach of Gen. Forbes, descended the Ohio River, and Monette says: "Made a halt about forty miles from the mouth, and, on a beautiful eminence on the north bank of the river, commenced a fort, and left a detachment of one hundred men, as a garrison. The post was called 'Fort Massac', in honor of the commander, M. Massac, who superintended its construction. This was the last fort erected by the French on the Ohio, and it was occupied by a garrison of French troops until the evacuation of the country, under the stipulations of the treaty of Paris. Such was the origin of Fort Massac, divested of the romance which fable has thrown around its name "—"History of the Valley of the Mississippi." Vol. I, p. 31.—J. H G.

Toward the close of the Indian war, Joseph Kinney settled on Rock-House Creek, a few miles east of the New Design, and erected a mill on this creek. He also made a farm on the premises. This creek being small, and in the fall deficient of water to propel the mill, he built a horse-mill. These mills were a relief to the neighborhood and were hailed, with the others built about the same time, as a great blessing to the public.

Before these mills were constructed, the people were forced to resort to expedients or to go to the horse-mills at Prairie du Rocher or Cahokia to procure their grinding. Trips to the mills at these villages were dangerous, on account of the Indians, and also a considerable distance to travel.

Joseph Kinney possessed a good sound mind and much enterprise. He left the old settlements and located in a new country, for the benefit and advantage of his large family. Scarcely any emigrant that ever settled in Illinois was blessed with such a numerous family as the patriarch, Joseph Kinney, was. He lived at the Rock-House Creek, in the even tenor of his way, for many years, and died there in 1803. He was a strong, athletic man, and enjoyed, as he deserved, an excellent character. He was moral and correct in all his actions, and his death was much lamented by his friends and the community generally.

Mr. Dement married one of his daughters in Kentucky, in 1792, and moved to Illinois. He located himself and family a few miles southeast of the New Design, and made a fine farm on his premises. He was a pious, orderly man. One Sunday morning he was preparing to go to meeting and went to bridle his horse. The horse kicked him so that he died of the injury. His death occurred in 1811.

Andrew Kinney, one of the sons of Joseph Kinney, built a water-mill on a spring branch, southwest of the New Design. This mill occupied the same site where the late Gen. James owned and rebuilt the Kinñey mill. This mill, while in the hands of Andrew Kinney, was one of the first in this section of country that manufactured flour for the St. Louis market. Before the war of 1812, this mill manufactured flour for the foreign markets.

In building this mill, Kinney was much injured by a large piece of timber falling on his breast, which caused him to be confined to his house for years. He became melancholy or depressed of mind. The public considered him laboring under the hypochondria Either by dreams or otherwise, he decided in his own mind that he would die at such a time—naming the day. For months before the time, he still adhered to his notion, and so stated it to his friends and family. On the day he was to die, a large concourse of people assembled at his residence to see what they would see. Kinney went to bed and lay out as if he were to die. *He* supposed he would die The crowd gazed on the scene, but he did not die. He lived for many years after. During this time of his melancholy, he either could not, or supposed he could not, ride on horseback He was conveyed about in a sled, and hunted and killed deers while riding in his sled, with his son driving him. He became a candidate for the office of member of the State convention, in 1818, and either the exercise or the excitement cured him He then rode on horseback and became a sound man in mind and body. He died a few years since, in Missouri, at a respectable old age. Mr. Kinney was an upright, honest man, and always deported himself with great propriety and morality

Robert McMahon was an emigrant from Kentucky and settled in the New Design in 1794 He was venturesome and risked himself and family on a new place in 1795 He located himself a few miles southeast of the New Design, in the prairie now known as the Yankee Prairie Four Indians attacked his house in daylight and killed his wife and four children before his eyes. They laid the dead bodies in a row on the floor of the cabin, and took him and two of his small daughters prisoners. A child in the cradle was found unhurt by the Indians, but dead The cradle was upset, but the people supposed the infant died of hunger. What a shocking sight this must have been to McMahon—to see his family butchered and himself and two daughters in captivity! He presumed the Indians were taking him to their villages to burn him to atone for some loss of their warriors killed in the battles with the whites This murder was committed in December, 1795, and the weather was excessively cold. The party were on foot and the frozen ground was severe on the feet of the daughters of McMahon, but this was nothing to compare with burning at the stake. The Indians were in a great hurry to get off, for fear the whites would follow them. They took from the house whatever light articles they could pack on their backs, and started. Before they left the house, they tied one of McMahon's arms behind his body and left the other loose, to hold on his pack. They packed on him a full load of his own goods and steered their course northeast, with a quick and determined step.

These Indians were brave and determined warriors and used no more rigor with McMahon than was necessary to secure him. After the rage of the murder of the family subsided, the Indians were kind and friendly to the little girls. They cheered them up, by signs, and attended to their wants. They fixed their shoes and made them as comfortable as the nature of the case would permit.

They marched a straight course, crossing Prairie-du-Long Creek not far from the mouth of the creek whereon Gen. Moore had a mill afterward, and they camped the first night on Richland Creek, about one-half mile below the present City of Belleville.

McMahon was secured with tug-ropes and tied down on his back, so he could not turn or stir. His shoes and most of his clothes were taken from him and put under the Indians, to prevent him from getting them if he attempted to escape. They also put on him a belt, finely wrought with porcupine quills and small bells, so that if he stirred, the bells would rattle and give them alarm. The Indians themselves were almost starving, and, of course, McMahon and girls had very little to eat A small pittance of dried meat was all their food.

What a contrast is often seen in the human family! What a striking difference between the condition of these captive girls and the well-dressed and lively little girls of this city! The little captives camped all night on the creek, below Belleville, with four savage warriors, who had, the day before, killed their mother and four sisters or brothers, and had their father in bondage—perhaps to burn him. They were also oppressed with the travel and all day without victuals or rest. They had scarcely a stitch of clothes to preserve them from freezing during the night. What a contrast with the gay and cheerful little girls of Belleville at this time! One party enjoying all the comforts of life, with kind parents to administer to their wants, while the other had no mother, and a father, probably to be burnt, and they themselves in the hands of the murderers of their mother and family, to be, perhaps, also murdered.

An Indian war is horrible, because of its barbarity on the defenceless part of community.

The party pursued their course across Silver Creek, above the present town of Lebanon, on to the sources of Sugar Creek, and there camped the second night. It snowed this night. McMahon meditated his escape, but of it did not inform his girls. He supposed they would cry and try to prevent it, and it would do them no good to see him burnt, and so did not tell them. The Indians tied and secured him as they did the preceding night. But in the night, when all were sound asleep, he slipped off the cords from his arms and body. He covered his clothes, what little he had on, over the belt of bells, so they made no noise, and was about rising quietly to escape, when one of the large Indians, just as he had the cords loose and preparing to rise, raised his head up and looked around, but laid it down again without noticing him.

This was a perilous time for McMahon and children, as, probably, if he had been detected in his attempts to escape, they would have killed both him and his children.

When the Indian laid down his head and again slept, McMahon escaped, without his shoes, hat, or much of his clothes. He was almost naked and barefooted on the snow. He slipped back to the camp and tried to get his shoes or the Indians' moccasons, but could get neither. He thought either way was nearly death—to stay with the Indians or leave them in the wilderness, without shoes, clothes, or anything to eat. He started in the night toward the New Design, as well as he could discover his course. He slept out one night besides the night he left, and came near freezing. He lay beside a log and gathered up some dry leaves with which to cover himself. He thought this world lost to him, as he must freeze that night. His feet and elbows froze to some extent; his elbows being exposed, as his clothes had holes in them. He steered, as well as he could, toward the southwest, but missed the New-Design settlement, and found himself at Prairie du Rocher, the first place he saw a white man.

He was in a horrid and deplorable condition when he reached the settlement. He was without shoes, hat, or much clothes, almost exhausted with hunger, having eaten very little for four days, together with his feet and arms frozen. His clothes, what little he had on, were torn and tattered, and his skin and flesh injured and wounded in many places.

His family lay dead some days before the neighbors knew of the murder, and therefore they were not immediately buried.

A small Spitz dog, who had been much admired and petted by McMahon's family, came frequently to the settlement of the New Design, and would run back and forward toward the residence of McMahon; but no one perceived the object of the dog, which was made manifest after the murder was discovered. The poor dog wanted to give the information, but could not.

Old Mr. Judy was the first that discovered the dead bodies, and reported it to the settlement. He had seen such a horrid sight that he shed tears when he told the sad story of the murder.

The citizens went out and buried the dead and had a religious meeting called on that same evening, at the fort of James Lemen, Sr., as a kind of funeral devotion for the deceased family.

Just as the meeting closed, at nine or ten o'clock in the evening, McMahon entered the house from Prairie du Rocher. All parties were surprised and much affected at the scene. McMahon sat at the fire and his little dog was also there, but did not know his master at first, as he was so changed; but the moment he looked into his master's face, he leaped into his lap with exceedingly great joy. This little incident produced a sensation in the assembly that was very affecting and sorrowful McMahon could not restrain his feelings and burst out into loud lamentations for the murder of his family.

After McMahon became calm from the first gush of sorrow, and his friends informed him that they had buried all his family in one grave, he, with a pious ejaculation, exclaimed. "They were lovely and pleasant in their lives, and in their death they were not separated."

His daughters were ransomed and one of them married a Mr. Gaskill of Madison County, and has raised a large family. McMahon himself, in a few years after the murder of his family, married again and made a fine plantation on a beautiful eminence in the Horse Prairie. He was appointed a justice-of-the-peace and judge of the court of Randolph County, and executed the duties of these offices with punctuality and honesty. He possesed a good standing in community. He moved from Randolph County to St. Clair, and resided on a plantation a mile or two northeast of Lebanon. At last he settled in Madison County, southwest of Troy, and died there after living a long and eventful life.

The Indians, in very early times, cared but little about the Americans emigrating to the country. They supposed they would occupy but a small portion of the territory, which would not do the Indians any injury. The Indian wars raged in Kentucky and Tennessee before much trouble was experienced in Illinois from them.

This was a great inducement to the Ogles, Moores, and Lemens, and many other early settlers, to emigrate to the country. But the Indians saw that a great number of Americans were locating themselves in the country and organizing a government.

In 1790, the red-skins commenced the defence of their country, by attempting to prevent the whites from settling in it. In the whole West, the Indian war, in 1790, and for several years after, was carried on with rancor and bitterness not experienced before. The federal government commenced hostilities on a large scale against the Indians located in the northern section of the present State of Ohio It was thought advisable to carry the war into Africa, and the northern nations of Indians must be subdued before a permanent peace could be established.

With this view, the government ordered Gen. Harmar to march against the Indians in the Northwest. He organized an army of one thousand four hundred and fifty men, three hundred and twenty of whom were federal troops and the balance Kentucky and Pennsylvania militia This army left Fort Washington, which is now occupied by the City of Cincinnati, Sept. 30, 1790, and marched toward the Indian towns on the Maumee·

He separated his army into several divisions and made many charges on small parties of Indians and on deserted villages; but on the whole, he did not sustain the honor of the stars and stripes.

On October 19 and 22, he was partially defeated. The public and the Indians considered Harmar as having failed in his campaign; but the general himself, at least, at the time did not think so. The Indian account of the battles is that Harmar lost five hundred men, killed, and the rest retreated, while the Indians only lost fifteen or twenty warriors. The Shawnees, Pottawatomies, and Miamis were the Indians engaged in these battles against the American army. The government believed that the campaign of Gen. Harmar was a failure, and in consequence, made arrangements for a more powerful prosecution of the war against the Indians.

An act of congress for the protection of the frontiers passed March 3, 1791, and Gov. St. Clair was, on the 4th of the same month, appointed to the command of the Northwestern army. Messengers of peace were sent to the Indians, but the British agents prevented them from accepting the terms offered by the United States.

Before St Clair could get ready, Gen. Charles Scott of Kentucky was ordered on a campaign, in May, 1791, against the Wabash Indians. He destroyed all the towns at and near Ouitenon, or Weastowns, and returned. Gen Wilkinson was also engaged against the Wabash Indians, and both expeditions were successful.

Gen. St Clair and Gen Butler, who was second in command, made the utmost exertions to raise and organize an army to retrieve the honor of the country, which in the other campaign did not shine out with the accustomed brilliancy. The army under St Clair amounted to two thousand three hundred strong, and left Ludlow's Station, near Cincinnati, on September 17, 1791, for the Indian country toward Detroit.

Gen St Clair halted at the Miami and built a fort, called Fort Hamilton. Then the army proceeded forty-four miles and erected Fort Jefferson. This fort was commenced Oct 12, and finished on the 24th When the troops commenced the march, the army did not proceed more than seven miles per

PIONEER HISTORY OF ILLINOIS.   199

day, and at many times sixty or more of the militia deserted at a time

Twenty-nine miles from Fort Jefferson, the army camped on a small stream twelve yards wide, which was a branch of the Wabash River. The regiment of Col Hamtramck, and the colonel himself, were sent back for deserters and other troops, so that on November 3, he had only fourteen hundred men under his command at the disastrous battle   Half-an-hour before sunrise, the Indians, on the 4th, surprised the army and defeated it, killing and wounding eight or nine hundred men In Braddock's defeat of one thousand two hundred men, he lost seven hundred and fourteen, in killed and wounded.   Braddock had eighty-six officers, of whom sixty-three were slain or wounded. In St. Clair's army there were between eighty-six and ninety officers, and sixteen were killed and wounded

The causes of the defeat of St Clair and army have been much canvassed and discussed before military committees of the army and of congress. The defeat has been placed on the grounds of lateness of the season, want of discipline in the army, and a disagreement between the generals, St. Clair and Butler. All these minor causes go to show a want of such great military talents in the general that he must possess to enable him to succeed.

St Clair was honest and upright, and possessed ordinary, good talents as a general, but his health was bad   He could not get on or off a horse without help, and old age was advancing on him, so he was not the energetic and talented man that he was in the Revolution   He was surprised by the Indians, his troops were not trained or disciplined; it was late in the year (and not very late either—November 4), and Col Hamtramck was absent with his regiment   All these were causes a man of talents would have guarded against. He could not stop at the time, but he could have been out sooner, or not at all, that season   If he had fortified his position and waited for the return of Col. Hamtramck, the loss of eight or nine hundred men might have been avoided, and what was also desirable, the honor of himself and army. To be surprised by Indians is an argument against the sagacity of a general

Gen. St Clair, after this battle, retired from the army and

demanded an enquiry into his conduct, which was granted him. He was acquitted by the committees, but the public and the Indians did not discharge him from blame

The next year, Gen. Wayne was appointed to take command of the army to conquer a peace over the Indians in the Northwest. The government disliked to shed blood and to expend the treasure of the country, and therefore they resorted to negotiation for two long years

It seems unreasonable that the government would try peace measures with the Indians when the British agents and officers were urging them up to fight the Americans and they having already whipped two American armies All the peace-talks ever presented to the red men could not have kept them in peace under these circumstances.

Gen. Wayne said he had with him about four thousand messengers of peace to make a treaty with the Indians at the muzzle of the cannon It must be written for the Indians with powder and lead. No other treaties had ever any good effect with savages and scarcely with any other nation.

All this time, two years, the government were coaxing the Indians into peace, Wayne was preparing his army for active service, and on August 19, 1794, he arrived in the vicinity of the enemy. He here erected a strong fort, called Fort Deposit. In it he put all his heavy baggage, etc., and on August 20, gave battle to the Indians, nearly under the guns of the British garrison. He entirely defeated them, and the next year, on Aug. 3, 1795, a general peace was made with the Indians at Greenville. This peace relieved the people of Illinois, as well as throughout the western frontiers, from Indian hostilities

After this memorable epoch, immigration set into Illinois and the settlements commenced to extend themselves from the New Design and the forts in the American Bottom, into other sections of the country.

About 1799 and 1800, a settlement commenced in the Horse Prairie. Samuel and Winder Kinney, Chance Ratcliff, Gibbons, McMahon, and some others settled in the upper end of Horse Prairie. At the time they settled there, the country was almost entirely prairie and barrens, with a few scattering large trees. Now it is covered with young growing timber, except the fields that are cultivated. So soon as the fire is kept out of the prairies they soon grow up with timber.

It is a fact that is known to all the pioneers, that there is, at this day, much more timber in all these old counties than was in them fifty years ago. The timber grows faster than it is used, since the first settlement of the country.

Teter and others afterward also settled in the Horse Prairie; but the settlement almost entirely broke up before 1810, and nearly all the inhabitants left. Levens and some others remained.

The Horse Prairie lies west of the Kaskaskia River and east of Horse Creek, and both the creek and prairie obtained the name by herds of wild horses running, in early times, in and around this prairie. These horses escaped from the French villages and lived in the prairie.

About 1796, the Ogles, Biggs, and some others formed a settlement in the Bottom and on the hills near the Bottom, where the road from the Bellefontaine to Cahokia descends the bluff. The Ogles made a large farm in the Bottom.

George Lunceford and Samuel Judy purchased the sugar-loaf tract of land and made a farm on it. Judy sold out to Lunceford and went, in 1800, to his residence in the present county of Madison, where he died. The sugar-loaf was rather remarkable in the first settlement of the country. A small mound rises on the top of the rocky bluff, which is supposed to resemble a sugar-loaf, that gives the name to this place. It is five or six miles south of Cahokia.

The American Bottom received many immigrants about this time. Many from the New Design moved to the Bottom. Edward and Thomas Todd, the Badgleys, and others left the New Design and settled in the Bottom.

James Gilham, Sr., emigrated from Kentucky to Illinois in 1797, and settled in the American Bottom. He had resided on the frontiers of Kentucky and the Indians had taken two of his sons prisoners. These two boys, Samuel and Clement Gilham, remained with the Kickapoos for several years, and were ransomed in Illinois. The Indian traders purchased the young men from the Indians and it took the family many years' toil and labor to pay the ransom. They paid "Chape-Wollie" Atchison at Cahokia.

Mr. Murdoch and family emigrated from Kentucky and settled in the American Bottom in 1796. He resided near Judge Bond, where he died the next year. He was the father of John Murdoch, the eccentric and quizzical personage, of some celebrity in after-times. The widow Murdoch, in a few years after her husband's death, married George Blair, the first proprietor of the site of Belleville.

The Big Prairie, in the American Bottom, contained a considerable settlement before 1800—more than it ever did since.

James Gilham being the pioneer, a large connection of that family followed him and came to Illinois at an early period. They settled first in the Big Prairie.

The American Bottom, in early times, contained a dense settlement almost from Fort Chartres to Cahokia. At one time, I presume, three-fourths of the American population in Illinois, resided in this bottom. The people residing in the American Bottom gave tone and character to a great extent to the entire population of the country.

The customs and habits of the early settlers of the Bottom were fashioned very much on the French model. They were extremely gay, polite, and merry.

In the American Bottom a support for a man and family arose almost spontaneous. The Indian wars were closed and the people enjoyed a kind of perpetual jubilee for many years. They associated themselves with the French and imitated that people in their amusements and recreations.

When any work of any importance was to be done and it could not be put off any longer, the neighbors assembled together and organized themselves into a kind of working frolic, and the job was performed.

The harvest of wheat was always gathered in this cheerful and jovial manner. No one heard of pay for work in harvest in old times. House-raisings were the same. And if a neighbor got behind with his work from sickness or otherwise, his friends around him assembled together and performed his work without pay or reward, except the pay of an approving conscience, which is better than all the gold of California.

Flax was cultivated in these times, and was often pulled at the time that the wheat was harvested. The girls frequently attended these flax pullings and then animation and brilliancy were infused into the whole atmosphere at the gatherings A proper number of old ladies were mixed with the girls to see that matters were conducted with a proper proportion of gayety and merriment, together with moderation and decorum Other females were in attendance at the cooking-department, while the grown men were out in the wheat-field, with each one a reap-hook or sickle in his hand. The aged men and boys were shocking the wheat and carrying out water.

At noon all came in to dinner Then there was a feast of good feeling with both the young and the old. The whole people, male and female, would wash and fix up for dinner. These personal preparations with the young people were speedily made, so that they would be the sooner in the gay and cheerful society of each other.

When these pioneers mixed together under shade trees at these gatherings, much kind feeling and sociability were enjoyed. The aged sires were proud to see their sons do a man's work in the harvest-field, while the old matrons were excited with intense feeling of pleasure to see their daughters make such a decent appearance and so much admired and esteemed by the people.

Groups of old men were often sitting on the grass, under the shade of a tree, with a bottle of Monongahela or tafia in the centre, and talking over the Indian battles they fought before Wayne's treaty, and what hard fights they had with the British and tories at the Cow-Pens, Guildford Court-House, and King's Mountain These old sires, at times, were excited at these convivial meetings, with liquor and the wars, until they burst all restraint and swore eternal enmity against the British and tories

It did their hearts good to exult over the manner they hung the tories in North Carolina, and at last Providence and Washington conquered the whole concern at Yorktown

It must be recollected that these times were but a few years after the Revolution, and all the transactions of that terrible conflict were fresh in the minds of these old men and perhaps many of them had been engaged in them But it was the young folks at these harvest noons that forgot dull care and enjoyed themselves with a hilarity and social feeling that can not be described. These young people, after they washed and the girls made their toilets, under the shade of a tree, met perhaps at a fine spring of water, in the shade, and talked, laughed, and almost amalgamated together. Then was seen innocent and honest society. Many of this young group had neither shoes or moccasons on their feet, but washed them clean, and the custom and times made it all right.

After the common salutations were closed and the crowd seated on the grass, some one would propose a song. At that day songs were much admired and enjoyed. The singer, as a matter of course, had a bad cold. He "*kotch* his cold," he said, "by running after a wounded deer." However, after the proper solicitation, he commenced to cough and spit and then asked, "What song will I sing?" Half a dozen mouths shouted for "William Riley."

In old times, if a song was not sung loud, it was no singing at all. Often this "William-Riley" song was sung so loud that it could be heard to a considerable distance. He finished, and the common praise was given to the song and singer, and dinner was announced.

A table was erected under a shade, with the sides and bottom planks of a wagon-body, placed on cross-pieces of timber, supported by forks set in the ground. This table was made in proportion to the company. All the dishes, plates, knives, etc, of the neighborhood were collected for the occasion. Benches, stools, boards, and all such articles were prepared, on which to seat the company.

Almost always two very dissimilar things were mixed together at these dinners, grace at the table and on it several bottles of liquor. It was the universal custom, in olden times, to use spiritous liquors at these gatherings. Sometimes these harvest-frolics were closed up at night with a dance. At all events, all went home in fine humor.

I do not believe that any happier people existed anywhere than in the American Bottom for twenty years, from 1790 to 1810. These were the palmy days of the American Bottom, and such a feast and flow of good feelings, generosity, and most of the virtues that adorn human nature, as were experienced in the American Bottom, rarely exist in any country.

About this time, 1796, a small settlement was formed between the Bellefontaine and the Mississippi Bluff. Short, Griffin, Gibbons, Roberts, Valentine, and some others were located in this vicinity. These inhabitants resided here a few years and abandoned the new settlement entirely. A large graveyard in this settlement may be seen to this day.

William Scott, an ancient and respectable pioneer of Illinois, was born of Irish parents, in Botetourt County, Va., in 1745 He emigrated to Woodford County, Kentucky, and remained there for many years. He was energetic and ambitious, like most of the pioneers, to explore new countries. He visited Illinois in 1794, with an intention to reside in it if he liked it; but he returned to Kentucky and entered into a traffic between Frankfort and St. Louis, in the then Spanish country.

He and his partner, Branham, fitted out at Frankfort, on the Kentucky River, a small craft, laden with articles for the St. Louis market. They continued this trade to St. Louis for two years, and when they dissolved the partnership, Mr. Scott found that his partner had injured him to a considerable amount. This was one reason of his leaving Kentucky

Late in the fall of 1797, the family of Mr. Scott and son-in-law, Jarvis, emigrated from Kentucky to Illinois by land and reached the Horse-Prairie Town, on the Kaskaskia River, which was the first white settlement they saw in the country.

Mr. Scott, having remained in Kentucky a short time, joined his family at the New Design the same fall, and about Christmas, they all located themselves on Turkey Hill. This place, with the French and Indians, was conspicuous as a trading-post. The Indians had made this place their camping-ground for ages past, and the traders had met them there with merchandise to exchange for their peltries, furs, etc. Blue-grass grew around this beautiful eminence, and other indications show it to be a place of general and ancient resort of the Indians and Indian traders. Turkey Hill is a commanding and imposing situation. It rises to a considerable height and can be seen from the east at thirty or forty miles distance. Turkey Hill was known to the French by the name of *Cote de Dinde* for more than one hundred years past, and many legends and tales of olden times are told of the Indians of this place.

Tradition says that the Tamarawa Indians had a large town on Turkey Hill a great many years ago, and that the Great Spirit sent an old Indian, a wise, good man, with the seeds of all the good things for the Indians—corn, beans, potatoes, and peas—and this old man showed them how to plant and raise them. That the old man lived with them many years and gave them good advice: never to go to war or to kill any one. For a long time, while this good man lived with them, the Tamarawas did well; but at last the Indians got too proud and did bad; then this good, wise man left them. This tradition may be the reason that the prairie south of Turkey Hill was called Prairie Tamarawas.

At the time Mr Scott settled himself on Turkey Hill, he and the Indians held the country as tenants in common. The Kickapoos were his nearest neighbors. They hunted and resided much of the year near him, but were friendly after Wayne's treaty.

Mr. Scott and family were the first American settlers northeast of Whiteside's Station, in the present county of Monroe, and remained so for several years. He had a large family of sons, which enabled him to sustain himself in his new settlement, which was so much in advance of the white population.

His sons, in 1798, being the next year after their arrival at Turkey Hill, cultivated a crop in the American Bottom, and also some improvement was made on Turkey Hill the same year. After this year, the family made a large improvement on Turkey Hill, where they all resided for many years together in peace and happiness.

At length the sons married and settled in the neighborhood around the venerable patriarch, until he might, with propriety, say: "I have filled my destiny; I have run my race; I see my family and my country happy, and that makes me happy."

Turkey-Hill settlement was the next important colony of the Americans after that of the New Design and the American Bottom. This settlement and Mr. Scott became quite conspicuous and were known throughout the West, until the country became densely populated and the original names disappeared. He was known far and near as Turkey-Hill Scott, and around him, the next year after his location, Hosea Rigg, Samuel Schook, and a few others, settled.

Mr Scott lived a long and eventful life of nearly eighty-three years, and died on Turkey Hill in 1828, regretted and lamented by the community generally. He was a man of excellent moral and honest character. He was a member of the Methodist-Episcopal church for many years, and sustained himself in that high and honorable station, which proved that his heart was impressed with Christian principles. He possessed a sound judgment and much practical experience, and was not ambitious of either wealth or worldly distinction. He purchased, in early times, four military land-warrants, of one hundred acres each, and located them on Turkey Hill. He also was possessed of sufficient worldly gear to make himself and family comfortable and happy.

Toward the close of his life, he turned his attention to books and study; passed off his advanced years in the pleasures of meditation and reflection. He was intelligent and communicative, and when he died, he left no enemies, but a host of friends and acquaintances to mourn his death

Nathaniel Hull was born and raised to almost maturity in the State of Massachusetts. He was, like most of those of the Bay State, educated, and was a plain, good scholar. He emigrated to Illinois about 1780. He and several other young men in the Revolution left their native State and traveled west. Hull descended the Ohio to a point near Ford's Ferry, on that river, and came across by land to Kaskaskia. This place on the Ohio was afterward known as Hull's Landing, and at it, in 1786, the Lemen family and others landed and came across the country to the settlements

At this day the Indians were not hostile as afterward, so that Hull and party escaped thro the wilderness without injury. He located himself in the American Bottom, and in a few years after, he married into the O'Hara family. He settled at the foot of the bluff in the Bottom, and there made a plantation and erected a block-house fort, as has already been narrated. He soon acquired the name of Capt. Hull, which he richly deserved by his talents and energies in defending the country from Indian depredations

The residence of Capt. Hull became, in early times, a common centre of attraction of the people, for information and for the backwoods discussions of the best mode of defence against the Indians. His sage councils were always received with much respect A post-office and small store were established at his block-house He headed many a party in pursuit of the common enemy when any depredation was committed by them

In 1794, he went back to Massachusetts for his brother, Daniel Hull, and moved him and family to the American Bottom

Capt. Hull raised a large and respectable family One of his sons, Daniel Hull, joined the Rocky-Mountain Company of Emanuel Liza and others, and started to the mountains in 1809. He was destroyed there by a white-bear.

Capt Hull was not only a good scholar, but he read, reflected, and made himself a very respectable and intelligent man. He delighted to read the scenes and transactions of the Revolution. He was unambitious for office, but the public prevailed on him to act as justice-of-the-peace and county-court judge for Randolph County He administered justice and equity for many years in these capacities. The whole community was satisfied and pleased with his official acts; but it was in the county-court where his sound judgment and influence did the people the most service He was for many years the main pillar of the Randolph-County court

At all times the county-court, under our system of laws, is an important tribunal. It assesses the taxes and enforces their collection. Bridges, public roads, court-houses, etc, are within the jurisdiction of this ancient county-court. Justice Hull performed well, to the satisfaction of the people, all of these duties

He turned his attention almost exclusively to the improvement and cultivation of his plantation He delighted in his residence. Just before he died, he enjoined it on his friends to bury him on the bluff adjoining his plantation, and, moreover, he requested them to bury him standing on his feet, overlooking his premises. His grave was made and he was buried in the manner he requested, it was handsomely paled in and was an object of inquiry and discussion for many years after his burial He died in 1806. He possessed a character for probity and integrity that was recognized by all His death, in his neighborhood and, in fact, throughout the country, was very much lamented and regretted. Capt. Hull stood as the main

pillar of society in his neighborhood, and was in the same proportion mourned for at his decease But such are the immutable laws of Providence. We may regret death, yet the law is just, because it is the command of God. The great Roman poet said:
"Nor loud lament, nor silent tear deplore
The fate of Ennius when he's no more."

John De Moulin was a native of Switzerland and was a man of science and high classic attainment. He was educated a gentleman and sustained that character thro life. De Moulin emigrated to Canada from Switzerland. He settled in Cahokia in 1798, and became a conspicuous and interesting character.

In 1790, he was the chief-justice of the court of common-pleas of the Cahokia district of St. Clair County. The writs of that day were issued in his name and dated at Cahokia He was also elected colonel of the county and held that office for many years He was, for a long series of years, a justice-of-the-peace and also a judge of probate At this time, in 1790, and for many years after, Col De Moulin was the most popular man in the county.

He was a large trader in lands. His name is found on the ancient records of land titles, almost as much as any other person in the county Being a classic scholar in Europe, he understood well the civil law and was a good lawyer, altho he did not practise in the courts He practised law to great advantage in his own business He studied the titles of the lands in market at that day, and was well versed in the science of land speculation By this commerce he obtained a living and a competency. At one time he was considered a wealthy citizen, but in the decline of his life, he was not so attentive to business and was stationary or declined in wealth

He was colonel of the county and made it his duty, as it was his pleasure, to drill, train, and keep in organization the militia of the county. De Moulin studied military tactics as they were understood and practised in the time of Louis Quatorze.

The French were born a military people and the Americans were harassed by the Indians, so that the whole community, French and Americans, were zealous and anxious to carry out the efforts of the colonel on this subject.

The spirit of military training was more popular in olden times than at present. I think the old custom should be preserved. It should be a part of the education of an American citizen to know well the use of arms, so that he could be a soldier, ready for battle at the shortest notice. For the defence of our free institutions the citizens should be prepared at all times.

It is not the friendship that the monarchies of Europe have for us that makes them respect us, it is our power of defence. Therefore, to be prepared for defence, we should drill and train our citizens. To be always prepared for an effectual defence, will secure us an eternal peace.

Col. De Moulin was large, portly, and an elegant figure of a man. He took great pride in his appearance on parade days, and wore generally a splendid military dress on these occasions. His subaltern officers respected him and obeyed his orders to the letter. He had that natural gift to command without giving offence. The militia of the county, under his command, was well trained and well disciplined and efficient.

He continued a single man during his residence in Illinois, and died without wife, children, or relatives of any degree in the country. He kept house and was slandered in friendship, after the manner Jefferson was, in reference to his female cook of a sable color.

It was rumored that Col. De Moulin had a female acquaintance in Europe, whom he had promised before the church to love and cherish. This was not true, I presume, as no one ever came after his death to examine his estate. His residence in Cahokia was a medium between a bachelor-hall and the staid mansion, governed by a wise and decent matron. He was himself a moral and correct man, and never permitted himself to relax into low or vulgar society. He always deported himself, as he was, a well-bred gentleman.

He made a commencement of a small water-mill on the Mississippi Bluff, not far east of the Falling Spring. He died at this place in 1808. He was universally esteemed and respected. His virtues of benevolence, kindness, and generosity were not questioned, and he lived and died very popular. His death was considered a calamity to the country. He had very few, or rather no, enemies. Altho he speculated in lands, he was honest and correct. His character was much to be admired and very little to be condemned. He possessed a sound, well-balanced mind, not of the higher order, but very respectable.

Nicholas Jarrot was an ancient and respectable pioneer of Illinois. He was a native of Franche Compté in France and was a younger branch of a highly respectable family. He received a liberal education and was, withal, a gentleman of elegant and accomplished manners. His education and his suavity of manners made him an acceptable member of any society wherein he might be

The troubles in France in 1790 caused him to emigrate to the land of the free and the home of the brave. He landed at Baltimore and traveled to New Orleans and perhaps to Havana. At last he reached Cahokia, in 1794, and pitched his tent in this place for his residence during life. He came to Cahokia a poor young man, a stranger and a foreigner, without family connections or friends, but by his talents and energy, in a few years he acquired an immense fortune, and what is better, a very respectable standing.

It was not in the nature of Mr. Jarrot to be idle. His very composition was activity and energy. All the repose or leisure he desired to take was enough to recruit his physical strength, that he might enjoy the luxury of activity and his incessant application to business. His pleasure, his happiness, and his *summum bonum* was an indefatigable industry. His mind was strong, active, and sprightly. It was trained and disciplined by education.

In early times he was elected a major in a battalion of the St. Clair military, and for years he was known, far and near, as Major Jarrot

He was like the honey-bee: as soon as he reached Cahokia, he commenced business He obtained a small supply of Indian goods and became partially an Indian trader. Almost every year he either went himself in his boat or sent it with goods to the Upper Mississippi, to Prairie du Chien, or the Falls of St. Anthony, or in that region of country. He bartered off such articles as the natives needed, for their furs, peltries, etc. He also kept a small retail store of goods, suitable to the market in Cahokia, for many years after his first arrival.

Altho he commenced in an humble manner in these commercial operations, yet to advance his capital was certain. He saw and attended to the business in person, so that he knew every moment what he was doing. In early times the Indian trade was very lucrative. At times two or three hundred per cent was realized on the goods sold to the Indians. This traffic was the first rise that Major Jarrot made to reach the fortune he acquired.

Not long before the war of 1812, with Great Britain, the British traders excited the Indians against the American population and the American traders. Altho Major Jarrot was a Frenchman, yet he was carrying on his commerce under the American flag. It was the custom of the Indian traders to make the village of Prairie du Chien their main depot of goods and carry such articles out to the Indian hunting-grounds as the red-skins needed.

Jarrot took two men and some goods out from the village some distance to a large Indian camp. The Indians expected him and were frantic with rage against him, because he was an American. This was effected by the British traders. The Indians were determined to kill him and take his merchandise. Jarrot and his men were only armed with shot-guns, expecting no enmity from the Indians. The warriors, to a considerable number, armed themselves for murder and proceeded out of the camps to meet Jarrot.

The Indians raised the warwhoop and brandished their spears and tomahawks in the air. It was approaching an alarming crisis. Jarrot and men seemed to be doomed to destruction. The furious savages would not permit a parley; but at last, when the warriors were so near Jarrot that it might be fatal with him, one of his old friends, a Winnebago Indian, stepped before the crowd of warriors and raised a terrific warwhoop, such as the Indians use in a battle where they are sure to be destroyed. It is a kind of death-cry, so called by them. The Indian was armed with all the weapons used by the infuriated savages in mortal conflict.

The warriors saw the danger they were in. One or more of them must be slain by the friend of Jarrot, if they persisted in the attempt to murder him and party. The bravery of the

Winnebago made them reflect, and they desisted from the cowardly act to assassinate the trader.

Jarrot and men were saved by the noble daring of this wild savage. The Indians changed his former name to that of Jarrot, and he was always known by that name afterward. I saw this Indian, who was called Jarrot, at Galena, in 1829.

Maj. Jarrot erected a horse-mill in Cahokia, which was profitable to himself and serviceable to the public. This mill was in operation before and during the war of 1812, and assisted much in providing the supplies for the troops engaged in that war.

In 1810, while Jarrot was at Prairie du Chien, trading with the Indians, altho it was greatly against his interest, reported faithfully to the government the hostile disposition of the Indians toward the United States.

In the war of 1812, he organized a company to proceed to Peoria, and he fortified his boat for the expedition in 1813, and made the voyage to Peoria in safety, altho the Illinois River was lined with the hostile Indians.

In early times, he turned his talents and energies to the commerce in land claims and to the land itself. Various acts of congress granted to the ancient inhabitants of Illinois certain claims to land. These claims were to be adjusted and allowed by the proper officers of the general government. Many of the inhabitants were poor and could not wait for the general government to adjust the claims; also many were uninformed as to the manner of obtaining their rights. This situation of the country enabled Jarrot and others to make advantageous purchases of these land claims.

He acquired an immense fortune in real estate, which, with some debts, descended to his heirs at his death. He owned the best selection of land in the country. At one time he owned the greatest portion of the Wiggins-Ferry Landing, opposite St Louis.

The most unfortunate policy of Major Jarrot was his mania for mills. His talents, energies, wealth, and ambition were all enlisted to build and maintain a water-mill on Cahokia Creek This mill was situated a few miles northeast of Illinoistown, and was not only the cause of his expending great quantities of money to no effect, but at last he lost his life by the exposure, fatigue, and sickness he experienced at this mill During a period of about ten years, he exerted all his energies and means to sustain this mill, and at last he and it both perished in the struggle. He was contending against the elements in the American Bottom like Napoleon did at Moscow. The sandbanks of the creek, the swamps near the mill, and sickness succeeded over him like the cold winter did over Napoleon Bonaparte in Russia. Moreover, this mill caused Major Jarrot much trouble and expense by the dam raising the water and flooding the lowlands near Cahokia Creek, above the mill.

William Robb built another water-mill on the creek, above Jarrot's, and contended that Cahokia Creek was a navigable stream below his mill. Robb built a boat and loaded it with flour. He assembled many of his neighbors and forced his boat thro Jarrot's mill-dam. He did much injury to the dam. Robb was indicted, but the traverse jury did not agree; thus the matter ended.

Maj. Jarrot held the offices of justice-of-the-peace and judge of the county-court of St. Clair for many years. Jarrot's name is often found on the records of the court in ancient times, and his services in the judicial department were always respected by the people; his decisions on the bench were prompt and quick.

Maj. Jarrot erected in Cahokia one of the first and finest brick-houses in the country, and lived in it, enjoying all the comforts of life. The kindness of heart and urbanity of manners which marked his actions attracted many visitors to his mansion, where they were received and entertained by him and his interesting family in a polished and elegant style.

Maj. Jarrot raised a very large and respectable family. His first wife was a Miss Barbeau of Prairie du Rocher, who died soon after the birth of her first child; his next wife was a Miss Beauvais of Ste. Genevieve. This lady possessed a strong mind, together with a mild and amiable disposition; so that she was, thro the earthly career of her husband, a great support and solace to him.

Jarrot was much devoted to his family, and educated and improved them all in his power. In 1823, he died in Cahokia, and his family showed their sorrow and grief not only in their kind feelings and affection for him, but also the irreparable loss they sustained in his death

Jarrot was a strict and zealous Roman-catholic, and performed with sincere devotion all his religious duties enjoined by that church. He and his wife always headed the family in going to and returning from church on the Sabbath.

Being strictly moral, he set his family and others a good example of piety and religion. The remains of this good man are resting in peace in the ancient graveyard of Cahokia; this small territory contains most of the deceased of this village for the last hundred and fifty years.

A small and sparse settlement, mostly of Americans, was made on the east side of the Kaskaskia River as early as 1780, and for some few years thereafter, this colony continued to increase. Hilterbrand, Henry and Elijah Smith, Daniel Hix, Hayden Wells, Teel, and some few others resided on the east side of the Kaskaskia River above Nine-Mile Creek, and made small improvements there John Doyle, John Montgomery, John Dodge, M Arstugus, and only a few others resided in the neighborhood opposite Kaskaskia, on the east side of the river. Jean B Beavois made an improvement at the head of Gravelly Creek, four miles east of Kaskaskia. Thos. Hughes improved on Nine-Mile Creek and was killed emigrating to the country, as before narrated

This colony did not flourish to any great extent. From 1780 to 1795, the Indian war raged and broke up this settlement This colony disappeared and in 1796 and 1797, the first steps were taken toward reestablishing it. In these two years, several families permanently settled on the east side of the Kaskaskia River and remained there Hughes, McDonough, Kelly, Anderson, and Pettitt, with their families, formed a small settlement and occupied about the same neighborhood which the previous colony did. Andrew Dunks arrived soon after and improved on Nine-Mile Creek, in this settlement

This small colony did not increase in numbers for many years, altho they lived happy and improved their farms They had the village of Kaskaskia and the Kaskaskia Indians for their neighbors Gen Edgar's mill in their immediate vicinity was a great inducement to reside there. No schools or religious meetings were enjoyed for many years in this settlement The Indians who were disposed to friendship, begging and stealing, were their most common visitors.

Stace McDonough was the main pillar and leader in this settlement He was born in New Jersey in 1770, and when an infant, his father and mother died, leaving him on the cold charities of the world; he was bound out, but followed the common practice of leaving his boss, and both sides throwing the blame on the other This much can be said against his principal: that McDonough never received any *school-house* education whatever. This fault is set down on the side of his employer.

As soon as he was able, he emigrated West, and when a youth, he was engaged in the military service of the country

McDonough was a soldier in many of the expeditions with the Kentucky troops against the Indians toward Detroit. He was athletic, stout, and courageous, and was, moreover, an excellent marksman With these qualifications, he frequently acted as a spy He possessed a strong natural mind and employed all his energies, mind, and body to the service of his country; and was a conspicuous man in his sphere in the campaign under Gen. Clark, from the Falls to the Wabash, in 1786. Altho he was then only sixteen years old, the experience of many years was realized by him.

McDonough entered the service of the government in 1790, and was entrusted with the command of a number of pack-horses in the campaign of Gen. Harmar In that campaign he was engaged and was always found in the many charges on the Indians, ordered by the general. After returning with the troops, he entered the service under Gen. St. Clair in 1791, and was again engaged in the responsible duties of commanding the convoys of provisions for the army, and was an honest, trustworthy agent of the quartermaster department. Altho he knew not a letter in the book, yet he was intrusted with this important command.

McDonough was in the disastrous defeat of Gen. St. Clair, November 4, 1791, where eight or nine hundred men were slain, and always said the whole catastrophe was the fault of the officers—that the number, strength, and capacity of the Indians were disregarded by the officers in command, and sorely did they pay for it. Butler lost his life and St. Clair his character and standing.

McDonough often informed me that the Indians surprised the army and surrounded it. The militia were without officers and were so panic-stricken that they rushed about from one side of the camp to the other, like a herd of cattle, without the least attempt to fight or defend themselves. They were butchered like so many bullocks in a pen. By a kind of instinct the crowd of men, not soldiers, of St Clair's army made a movement to break thro the hords of savages who were around them, and the Indians could not kill all before some escaped. The regular soldiers often charged on the Indians and drove them a considerable distance; but other savages were assailing the troops in the rear, so that it required another charge back to reach the camp again. McDonough always uniformly stated that the carnage and numbers slain in that battle never were stated in the reports.

McDonough escaped on foot from this defeat and left the main route, where the Indians made such havoc on the straggling men. After he left the road some distance, he found a wounded officer. This man was badly wounded, supposed then to be mortal. He was lying on the ground almost exhausted, and mistook McDonough to be an Indian when he first came up to him. The noble spirit of an American officer still remained in this man, lying almost lifeless on the ground. He drew his pistol and prepared for battle; but soon discovered a friend instead of a savage foe. McDonough said he could not help smiling, altho it was a serious time, at the ridiculous attempt this officer made to fight; but it showed the true courage of an American officer. After much exertion and suffering from hunger, McDonough got this officer and himself safe into camp. Without help, the wounned man must have perished; but he recovered and lived many years afterward.

McDonough was as efficient on the water as on land; being an excellent river pilot. He commanded one of the United-States boats on the Ohio River in 1793, and near the mouth of the Kentucky River, he was shot from the shore by an Indian in the shoulder. Some white man with the Indians hallooed out in English, "to throw that man overboard—he will die in a short time!" This was a severe wound and from which he never recovered altho he lived for many years after. He was about obtaining a pension for this wound when he died. Altho not well, he embarked in the campaign under Gen Wayne He was anxious to see the eagles of his country raised from the dust where the Indians had trampled them. He delighted to serve under Mad Anthony.

McDonough was of Scotch descent and was easily fanned into a flame. Of such soldiers as McDonough, Wayne was the commander. He fought thro the battle under Wayne and hoped the general would order a charge on the British garrison. The Americans were more enraged against the British, who urged the savages on to fight, than against the Indians themselves

The war having closed with honor, McDonough left the service in 1795, and retired to Louisville, Kentucky. He married there, and in 1797, as above stated, settled on the place where he died.

He turned his attention to agriculture and improved a fine plantation a short distance east of Kaskaskia He was always extremely fond of the rifle and spared some of his time to hunt. In early times, a man who hunted none was a rare thing.

During the war of 1812, he had the contract to carry the mail from St. Louis to Shawneetown thro the wilderness country from Kaskaskia to the Ohio River. This mail-route was very important in the war, as that was the route thro which the correspondence was kept up between Illinois and Washington City. It was a dangerous service on account of the hostility of the Indians, but he carried the mails with punctuality.

In the war, he was captain of a mounted company to defend the frontiers He performed this service to the satisfaction of the public. He was thro life a man of great energy and activity. Nature gifted him with a sound, strong mind, and altho he had no A-B-C education yet his long life thro so many scenes and trials made him intelligent and wise. He entertained a high sense of honor and integrity, and no one doubted his patriotism and devotion to his country His mind was well balanced, and he was honest and correct in all transactions. He lived for almost half-a-century on his farm and died there. He was deservedly popular and the public regretted very much his death.

As soon as the West increased its population and raised a surplus produce, the navigation of the Mississippi was all important to ship their surplus to market It is astonishing at this day to look back at the excitement of the Western people for the free navigation of the river to the ocean. The people seemed to be frantic and almost crazy to do anything or join any government to secure the free use of the Mississippi

It must be recollected that Spain owned both sides of the Mississippi at the mouth and did actually prevent the West for a time to export their products to market.

And what is still more astonishing that many leading characters in the West were willing to sever the Union for the sake of the navigation of the river to the Gulf of Mexico. A meeting of the staff-officers who were engaged in a campaign in 1786, from the Falls of the Ohio, Kentucky, to chastise the Wabash Indians, met at Vincennes, October 8 of that year, and agreed to organize a separate and independent government. The object of this organization was mostly to secure the navigation of the Mississippi.

The Spaniards were either to be driven off or joined, as the circumstances might be This board of field-officers determined "to garrison that post (Vincennes), to raise supplies by impressment, and to enlist new troops."

This new government was about to treat with the Indians and had seized a large amount of Spanish property in Vincennes and Illinois. Letters were written to the State of Georgia to induce that State to join in the cause, as the territory of Georgia came in contact with the Spanish frontier

Congress hearing of this movement at Vincennes, prepared troops to suppress this new government. Public opinion and the good-sense of the people put this scheme down, as they did the whiskey insurrection and the South-Carolina treason to dismember the Union in modern times

The officers decided at Vincennes that, as the Spaniards would not permit the Americans to descend the Mississippi, the Spaniards should not ascend the river.

About this time, 1793, Gennet, the minister of the new French Republic, arrived in the United States He landed at Charleston, South Carolina, and made a kind of a triumphal procession from that city to the seat of government. He presumed much on the friendly relations, which were or ought to be in his opinion, between the United States and the French government It will be recollected that France had commenced her glorious revolution for freedom and had established a republic. Gennet was its minister to the Federal government and presented himself, on March 18, 1793, to President Washington. It also must be borne in mind that the federal and republican parties raged with violence and bitterness at this time. The federalists took part with Great Britain against France, while the republicans were for France and opposed to Great Britain. The administration was rather federal.

Gennet, by all the means and arts in his power, attempted to induce the government to take sides with France against Great Britain, but the firmness and wisdom of Washington and his cabinet kept aloof from any "entangling alliances" with Europe. The same wise policy has governed the councils of the Nation to this day Gennet was dissatisfied with the government and appealed to the people. He was a talented man and had just come from a warm political discussion in France and attempted it here. He had not neglected the West and had given commissions out, even in Illinois, to levy troops to sustain the West against the Union. Our government requested the Republic of France to recall him and they did so

The next minister, Adet, who came to the United States in 1796, attempted the same policy but failed more signally than his predecessor.

During this season of excitement and confusion in the West, the Spanish authorities were active and vigilant in carrying on intrigues with many influential citizens of the West to induce them to throw off their allegiance and become an independent republic

The free navigation of the Mississippi was the great cause of dissatisfaction, and it was not healed up until Jay, our minister at the court of Madrid, made a treaty with Spain in 1795, which secured the free navigation of the river to us forever.

The Federal government was vigilant and active in guarding against all these assaults on the Union. The garrison at Fort Massac was repaired and fortified. Troops were stationed there and increased as danger threatened In fact, soldiers had been stationed there almost all the time since the treaty of peace in 1783. Gen Wilkinson, about 1795, made below Massac what was called Contonment Wilkinson. The remains of this fort can be seen at this day.

In 1800, two companies of regular soldiers were stationed in Fort Massac. Capts. Russell and Daniel Bissell were the commanders. One of these companies was, in 1802, ordered to Kaskaskia and occupied the top of the river bluff east of Kaskaskia, where once stood Fort Gage. This company remained there almost three years and until Louisiana was transferred to the United States in 1805 Then it was ordered off to St. Louis, in Upper Louisiana, and never returned. The celebrated Zebulon Pike, who was destroyed in Upper Canada, at Queenstown, was attached to this company as a subaltern officer. He was very young at that day and was an active, energetic youth He was restless and ambitious, and was mostly out of the garrison on some scientific excursion He delighted, while at Kaskaskia, to be on horseback and exploring the country far and near.

Gen Wilkinson, in the West, acted a singular part as well in the transactions with Spain as with Aaron Burr in 1805. He seemed to have been born and to have acted all his life equivocal. Courts of inquiry and the strictest investigations could not reach any solid charge against him; but still the public always believed him to be not entirely free from blame or at least of suspicion. He had fine talents and wrote his own memoirs and even that work leaves him doubtful.

An officer of the United-States army, high in command, should act in that elevated and upright manner that his conduct should be above doubt or uncertainty. He should "be like Cæsar's wife, above suspicion."

In 1794, the celebrated Isaac Darnielle arrived in Cahokia and remained in the West for several years. He was the second professed lawyer that emigrated to Illinois, John Rice Jones being the first. He was a classic scholar and was in his person genteel and agreeable; he possessed the easy and graceful manners of a polished gentleman. He was large and portly and made it a *sine qua non* to be extremely neat in his dress and attentive to his personal appearance He studied all the arts and mysteries of gallantry and thereby made very deep and rather lasting impressions on his female friends Darnielle studied the ladies more than he studied his profession of the law. He was benevolent and kind to all mankind, and particularly to the ladies. Rumor said that he had been educated in Maryland for the ministry, but his gallantry was too strong for the proper observance of the gospel precepts It was also stated that he had occupied the pulpit for some time, but took French leave of his congregation and appeared next in Cahokia He possessed a strong intellect and his faculties had been well disciplined to study His honesty, except in gallantry, was unquestionable. With these advantages it did not take him long to study the law, which he did, and practised it also. He being an agreeable speaker, together with a fine appearance of person, made him conspicuous and popular at the bar.

The courts and juries at that day were not remarkably well versed in the technical learning and therefore Darnielle could figure with ease and safety before these tribunals He was indolent, except in the pursuit of the pleasures of gallantry, and in this pursuit he spared neither time or exertions. When in a phrenzied state of love with a married lady of Cahokia, and she in the same delightful state of madness, they took a snap judgment on the husband and escaped to Peoria, where for many years they lived on love. The husband remained in Cahokia in sullen silence

At one time he and his lady love—not, perhaps, the same that lived with him at Peoria—made their resting-place on the highest pinnacle of the Mississippi Bluff, northwest of the penitentiary at Alton. Altho Cupid selected this spot as the most delicious place of love, yet Col. Easton of St Louis made sober reality out of it by purchasing the preemption right of Darnielle to the land granted to him by act of Congress.

Darnielle became acquainted with the land-titles in Illinois and made a commerce in land He never was wealthy; this was not his ambition He indulged in the land-trade more for occupation than for profit. He never married according to the laws of the country, but to all appearances, he was never without a wife or wives. It was also rumored that he left a married wife in Maryland who was an obstacle to a second marriage in this country.

Darnielle had no malice or bitterness in his composition, but seemed to consider his *summum bonum* to consist in an easy, luxurious life He was moral and correct in his deportment, except as above referred to.

Darnielle never indulged in drinking or gaming, but frequently slept all day and made the evenings extend all night, in the sight and hearing of his terrestial angel. At one time, while in the zenith of his glory, he was the beau ideal of Cahokia. His talents, his gay and graceful manners, together with his *penchant* for this sort of life, authorized him to some extent to be styled the Lord Chesterfield of Cahokia; but in practice he was more the Earl of Rochester than Chesterfield.

While Darnielle retained his youthful vigor, this life passed off very well; but when old age crept on him, his former pursuits were abandoned from necessity and he remained an old man without sincere friends or means for support. He taught school in the western part of Kentucky, where he died, rather humbled and neglected, in 1830, aged sixty years.

If Darnielle had abandoned this one failing, the excess of gallantry, he would have enjoyed the character of one of the most honorable and respectable gentlemen in Illinois.

In 1793, John Hays emigrated to Cahokia and remained there and in the vicinity during life. He was born in the city of New York in 1770, and when quite a youth, entered the Indian trade in the Northwest. He was a clerk to a wealthy house in Canada and was sent first to Mackinac and afterward toward the Lake of the Woods and the sources of the Mississippi. It was toward the headwaters of Red River, of Selkirk's Settlement, that he and two Canadians were caught out in a snow-storm in the prairie, and were compelled to lie under the snow for three days and nights, during the storm. They had a scanty supply of dried meat to eat and thin blankets to cover them. The storm raged with such violence that they were not able to travel in the open prairie and were forced to remain under the snow to preserve their lives. It snowed in the time to a considerable depth No one who has not experienced the hardships in the Indian trade of the Northwest can realize it. The want of water under the snow was that which incommoded them most

He returned safe from this storm, and afterward he made arrangements with Messrs Todd & Hays, who had formed an extensive commercial partnership, to act as the agent and clerk in their business He settled in Cahokia, in the employ of the company of Todd & Hays But Todd dying and the company dissolving, forced Hays out again on his own resources. He turned his attention, as many others did, to the Indian trade At times he also kept a small assortment of goods in Cahokia. His boats, either with himself or agent, generally made a voyage once a year to Prairie du Chien with articles for the Indian trade, and returned sometimes the same fall and sometimes in the spring. With a due regard to economy he made money in this commerce.

He married a lady in Vincennes of excellent family and what is still better, of sound, good sense They lived together in Cahokia and raised a respectable family. He turned his attention to agriculture. He purchased land in the common-field of Cahokia and cultivated it to some considerable advantage. He managed his farm with good-sense and economy, as he did all his other business.

He held the office of postmaster in Cahokia so long that "the memory of man" scarcely "runneth to the contrary." This was no profit to him, but he held the office for the accommodation of his creole neighbors, whose acquaintance with school-houses was extremely limited He was appointed to the office of sheriff of St. Clair County by Gov. St Clair in 1798, and he continued to exercise the duties of this office down to 1818, when the State government was organized I presume this was the longest term of office ever held in Illinois It is the strongest evidence of the punctuality and honesty of the incumbent. Rotation in office was not then practised

In 1822, he was appointed Indian agent of the Pottawatomies and Miamis at Fort Wayne, in the northeast section of the State of Indiana. He remained in this office for several years and received a handsome annual salary. He returned home to Cahokia and enjoyed his old age in peace and happiness with his family and friends. During a long life of industry and economy, he acquired a handsome property, and was in his advanced years very comfortably situated, having all the comforts of life that render the human family happy. He died in old age, much regretted by his family and friends.

Mr. Hays possessed a moral and honest character; his morality throughout life was very exemplary. He was not a member of any Christian church, but observed the precepts contained in the word with due respect and devotion. At his death his fortune descended to three daughters, his only children.

He possessed a common-English education and spoke French fluently, and enjoyed a very respectable character; his memory is well entitled to the respect of posterity.

Another personage of considerable celebrity, John Hay, whose memory is much esteemed by his friends and numerous acquaintances, settled in Cahokia in 1793. This pioneer was born in Detroit, on May 8, 1769 John Hay, his father, was a native of Chester County, Penn, and was the last British governor of Upper Canada The mother of Mr. Hay was a French lady, a native of Detroit, ten years younger than her husband, the governor of Upper Canada.

The subject of this brief sketch, when quite young, was sent to college at the Three Rivers, in Canada, and graduated with the common honors of the institution, receiving a classic education. Particular attention was paid by him to the languages taught at that day—Latin, French, and English. His mother-tongue was French, but he spoke English without any French accent. The high standing of his family in Canada and the amiable and kind heart of himself attracted the attention of the most respectable inhabitants of the province.

Lady Hamilton, whose husband was the highest officer in Canada, wrote to Mr. Hay, when he was at Three-Rivers college, the following letter:

"QUEBEC, March 16th, 1785

"*Sir:*—Your letter of the 11th inst. persuades me that you are diligent and desirous of improving yourself. I have, therefore, for your father's satisfaction, enclosed your letter to him.

"When you next favor me with a letter, let me know to what particular profession your disposition leads, and not only consult your inclination in a point so essential to your future happiness and credit, but take the opinion of some friend as to the talents nature may have supplied you with for making your way thro the world. I shall be happy to serve you, on occasion, should it happen to be in my power, and am, sir, your very obedient and humble servant,

"ANNY HAMILTON.

"Mr. JOHN HAY."

This short letter of Lady Hamilton shows her kind heart—her interest for Mr Hay and also her good-sense

The British government held possession of Detroit and other posts on the lakes long after the treaty of peace in 1783, and the father of Mr Hay continued to be the governor of Upper Canada until his death, in 1785. Mr Hay was only seventeen years old at the death of his father and thereby was turned out into the world on his own resources. His friends procured him a situation as a clerk in a wealthy commercial house in Montreal He remained a few years at the merchants' desk and kept the books under the eye of a lank, lean, hungry-looking Scotchman This nation, the Scotch, engrossed to a great degree the Northwest fur-trade in olden times, and they exercised that talent of cool, calculating shrewdness for money-making, for which they are so celebrated to great advantage. These Scotch traders have made Montreal a very wealthy city

Mr. Hay was fitted out with "an equipment," as it was called, and started for the extreme Northwest An equipment among the Northwest traders means an assortment of goods for the Indian trade. It comprises a proportion of the several articles sold to the Indians—guns, blankets, strouding, flints, powder, bullets, knives, paints, etc He embarked in a bark-canoe with several light-hearted, singing Canadians, for the Assinnaboin country, which is near the base of the Rocky Mountains, in latitude about 45 degrees north. The Northwest Company at that day had the entire trade and control of the country.

When Mr. Hay got out into the wintering-ground and erected his quarters for winter, he forgot to some extent the sage counsels of his Scotch friends in Montreal in relation to prudence, economy, and the profit on the stock, which profit, in their eyes, was the *ne plus ultra* of all human aspirations.

Mr. Hay was then young and full of vigor, and with the clerks in the same region were other young men of the same character, so that these young folks forgot the Scotch lessons on economy they had so plentifully received before they left the counting-desks in Montreal. Gallantry in any country, even in the Northwest, is attended with both loss of time and money.

Mr. Hay did not make a fortune on his outfit, but he saw the world even if it were in the Northwest. In that region he formed an acquaintance with a Mr Todd, a merchant of considerable celebrity This acquaintance ripened into friendship and a commercial partnership They determined to establish their main store in Cahokia and send out in boats or otherwise goods into the Indian country.

Mr. Hay started to the Illinois from the wintering-ground with only one Indian. They traversed the country in a southeast direction to reach the sources of the St Peter's River, and after much difficulty they found the St Peter's, which they descended and the Mississippi until they arrived at Prairie du Chien, where the Indian was dismissed and Mr. Hay came to Cahokia in 1793, as heretofore stated.

He and Todd commenced business with fair prospects of success, when Todd had business at New Orleans and while there he died. His death deranged all the business of the partnership and Mr. Hay never after that attempted merchandising on a large scale.

He had by this time seen some of the world and came to the conclusion that a wandering life was not the most happy, and settled himself down in Cahokia for life. He became acquainted with an amiable and beautiful young creole, born in Cahokia, Miss Margaret Poupart, and in 1797, married her. For several years after he settled in Cahokia he was doing a small business and settling up the concern of Todd & Hay. He purchased a house and lot in the village of Cahokia and commenced housekeeping, and now depended on his talents and exertions for a living Altho his family and relations were wealthy and respectable in Canada, yet he depended on his own labor and industry for support rather than to resort to his friends.

He wrote and did business for the merchants of St Louis, in Upper Louisiana, and the American side also, for support. But his abilities to serve the people in office were made manifest, and Gov St. Clair of the Northwest Territory, on February 15, 1799, bestowed on him four several offices: the clerk of the court of quarter-sessions, clerk of the court of common-pleas, clerk of the orphans' court, and treasurer of the county of St. Clair. These commissions were dated at Cincinnati and signed by the governor and his secretary, William Henry Harrison.

By his proper and honest deportment and his kindness and affiability, he continued in office and in several at a time, from the above date to the hour of his death. He has been, almost all the time, a notary public and justice-of-the-peace, and was often judge of probate and for a series of years, as the records will testify, was the recorder of land-titles in St. Clair County

The commissioners at Kaskaskia to adjust land-titles, having the utmost confidence in his honesty and integrity, entrusted him to take depositions in support of land-claims in the Kaskaskia district. This was a very delicate trust, and he was found, as in all other situations, worthy of that confidence.

All the administration of the governments, commencing with Gov St Clair in 1799, down thro all the territorial and State governments, to his death, have placed confidence in him and have given him office. It is not common that a man can retain as many offices as he did at the same time and enjoy them for almost half-a-century without the people losing confidence in the incumbent. It is evidence of his accommodating disposition and his honesty and capacity in the performance of the duties of these offices.

For many years he filled the office of judge of probate of St. Clair County. This office is an important one. The duties involved very often the most abstruse principles of the law, but he performed them and the duties of the various others to the entire satisfaction of the public.

Out of all these offices he made a bare living. He had a very large family and raised them with great tenderness and affection, so that he expended much of his income to raise and educate them, and he was so kind and indulgent to his children that he could scarcely deny them anything they asked, if it were necessary or not He never was wealthy but always enjoyed a full and plentiful competency. He had not the least talent for speculation, altho the whole country, almost, were engaged in it. He never bought or sold any land, as most of the other gentry of Cahokia did, and his own right to the land the government gave him, he sold at a very reduced price He lived in peace and happiness in Cahokia among his French friends until the county-seat of St. Clair County was moved from Cahokia, in 1814, to Belleville This was a terrible shock to the whole family.

The French, by living together many ages, begin to think they could not exist out of a French village Their social intercourse are so interwoven in their composition that to separate one from another are looked upon with a kind of horror. Thus it was with Mr. Hay and family. They were supported so long on the proceeds of these offices that they became a kind of second-nature to them, and to leave Cahokia, the church, and the ballroom was quite impossible.

The offices had to be kept in Belleville and Mr. Hay attended to them for many years in this place and saw his family at the end of each week. At last this was found to be disagreeable and he sold out in Cahokia and located permanently in Belleville.

In early times, a majority of the country were French inhabitants, and he spoke and wrote the French language as well as the English; so that he was well qualified to accommodate each class of people in performing his public duties.

In 1804, when Gen Harrison took possession of Louisiana, it was becoming the occasion to make a demonstration of our good feeling to our newly-acquired citizens, and that the people of Cahokia and St Clair County should attend at St Louis on the occasion With heart and hand, he headed the cavalcade and made a grand display in the ceremony of taking possession of the country

At the treaty with the Indians, in 1815, at Portage de Sioux in Missouri, he was employed as interpreter and assistant-secretary to the board He was very expert with the pen and was quite serviceable on such occasions. He had many peculiarities and became quite systematic. For many years he went to St. Louis, Missouri, at a stated time in the fall and remained there for a week. In this time he purchased the stationery for his office and other articles and visited his friends. He went and returned to the hour; and toward the close of his life, no matter what was on hand, if the weather permitted, he and his old lady took an evening walk. He and his wife lived together for almost half-a-century, and very few ever enjoyed more of domestic happiness than they did. Their marriage was based on proper principles and their union was sincere. It was founded on mutual and ardent affections.

At mature age, he read, reflected, and became a Catholic. He was raised to respect the church of England more than any other, and was, thro the early part of his life, inclined to that church; but he changed his notions and became zealous and enthusiastic in the faith of the Romish church. He often became excited in conversation on religious subjects and frequently used words in the excitement of the moment, and forgot their unfitness in such cases. These words were similar to those Uncle Tobey used when his feelings were excited to the highest pitch at the sight of his friend about to expire and said: "By G——, he sha'n't die." The angel above did not record it against Uncle Toby, nor will the angel record the utterance of these words against Mr Hay

Morality, virtue, and honesty governed him, and he observed the injunctions imposed on him by these great guides to happiness with scrupulous exactness. It was in his last sickness that he displayed the calm philosopher and the Christian hero. Age had naturally destroyed in him much of the frailties of human nature. The passions had ceased to bewilder his calm reflection

The mind will turn back on the actions of life, and if they are good an approving conscience makes a kind of "heaven on earth below." This seemed to be the case of our friend. It appeared to be his transit from a sinful mortality to a happy immortality. Death reached him in that state of existence when its terrors were not regarded by him. He was anxious and pleased to realize that "undiscovered country from whose bourn no traveler returns." He died in Belleville in 1843, aged seventy-four years. His friends and the public felt real sorrow and grief for his death When he died he had no enemies, but a host of friends who yet converse of him with tender regard Their hearts and affections are with him in the tomb

In the first settlement of the country, wild animals were very plenty, which induced almost the whole community to become hunters. The range was so good and the vegetation in summer grew so luxuriant that a vast number of these wild animals were sustained in Illinois.

The vegetation—particularly the grass—grew much stronger and higher fifty years ago than it does at this time. Corn does not grow as large or yield as much per acre as it did in these olden times. This is the opinion of almost all the pioneers: that the vegetation is not so luxuriant and stout as in former days. This is a fact and to account for it would be difficult. If a tract of land were fenced and thereby the tame animals prevented from pasturing on it, yet it is doubtful if the earth would produce as it did in former days

Fifty years ago the fire in a dry prairie with a strong wind was grand and rather terrific In the fall it is often dry for months together, so that the prairies were very dry toward Christmas and the Indians and others in hunting universally set them on fire. Sometimes the hunters made what they called ring-fires. They set fire to the grass and leaves around a considerable tract of country so as to enclose a number of deer and other animals The fire, as it burns, contracts; so the game is huddled up in the centre and killed, more or less. These dry prairies on fire with a high wind were dangerous to man as well as beast Often deer, raccoons, and the smaller animals were destroyed by the fire It was also "death on the snakes." At many times a prairie miles long and on fire with a strong wind was in a dense flame for hundreds of yards wide at the same time. This flame often arose many feet high and would destroy any animal, man, or other that would be caught in it. The old pioneers will recognize the truth of this description of the prairies on fire

It was this excessively thick and strong vegetation, burning in the fall, that caused the prairies. It is generally the case that the prairies are the most fertile soil. This caused the strongest fire which destroyed the timber. In the poor soil, where the vegetation did not grow rank, these fires did not destroy the timber, and about the water courses timber grew without the disturbance of the fire. The proof of the above is that the prairies, when the fire is kept out of them, soon grow up with trees. Illinois will have in twenty years more timber in it than there is at present.

While the prairie is in a general conflagration, a terrible roaring, something similar to thunder, is heard. With this terrific noise and the flames so high, broad, and dense, a terror is produced easier imagined than described.

Two men were burnt to death in the American Bottom by the prairie burning, a few miles southeast of the ferry opposite St. Louis These unfortunate men took refuge under their cart, but were, nevertheless, destroyed.

In the first settlement of the country, hundreds of acres of timber, in some seasons, were all killed at the same time by fire. These trees would fall down—rot or burn—and a prairie would soon be formed. At that time the small undergrowth was burnt out and in many places nothing but the large trees were standing. In process of time these trees would also disappear and a prairie be formed where they grew.

Not only was the summer range good but the winter also. All along the Ohio River and up the Mississippi to Muddy River and sometimes higher, the cane grew so thick and strong that man or beast could scarcely penetrate it. These were called brakes and were so thick and matted together that deer, buffaloes, horses, and other animals were completely housed and sheltered from the storms Hunters say they have often heard buffaloes in the winter bellowing in these canebrakes as if it were summer in the prairies.

Above the cane region the rushes grew on the sandy margins of the Mississippi and on sandy islands, strong and thick. They are more nutritious and better on which to winter animals than cane. Horses, cattle, deer, buffaloes, etc., will keep as fat on the rushes as if they were put in a cornfield in the fall.

In the fall of 1807, my father put a large gang of horses on Gabont Island, in the Mississippi River above St Louis, and they wintered well.

The region of country adjacent to the Illinois River, as

Father Marquette observed, produced the strongest vegetation in olden times of any other section of Illinois, and the river and the swamps adjacent to it afforded the natives more support than any other part of the West The fowls, in the spring and fall in their migrations, stopped here and the Indians killed many of them Also a great number of musk-rats were caught in the lakes near the river, and it was conceded by all that no river in America produced as many fresh-water fish as the Illinois did. This great supply of provisions for the Indians enabled more of them to subsist in this section of country than in any other in the West. The Indian traders visited this river in great numbers and many made fortunes by the traffic with the natives

Under these circumstances, Peoria was, perhaps, the greatest trading-post in the Mississippi Valley. At Mackinac more wealth was collected on its transit there than at any other point The traders of the North met the merchants from Canada at this post and exchanged the peltries, furs, etc., they collected from the Indians either to pay old debts or for Indian goods At some seasons of the year Mackinac was a very important and interesting place; but when the traders and Indians disappeared the village assumed its former size and inefficiency.

Prairie du Chien possessed something of the character of both Peoria and Mackinac. In it goods were exchanged with the traders for their peltries, etc., as well as sold to the Indians.

At Mackinac and other points where the traders, voyagers, and hordes of Indians met those from Canada, a general jubilee was instituted. Great and grand doings of all sorts of amusements and pleasures of which the French genius and their limited means at that place permitted were carried on at Mackinac during these celebrated festivals. Men who had been in the Northwest trade for years, came to this post to meet, perhaps, their wives, relatives, and friends. Parents came out from Canada to see their absent sons and to give and receive some kind civilities. Or, perhaps, the more substantial article, personal property, was exchanged on the occasion. Old debts and new ones were attended to

Many of the transactions of mankind, either in business, pleasure, or otherwise, were exhibited at these annual fairs in olden times.

At times Mars, the god of war, was invoked to settle some old feud or to gain the triumph at the time in some personal quarrel, and even duels were not neglected at these gatherings. That barbarous practice of dueling, which is the brutal remains of the Roman shows of the gladiators, the Spanish bull-fights, and the English boxing-matches were hailed at these meetings by the code of honor and to some extent adopted

A duel was fought between two Northwest traders, Crawford and Campbell, that was so grossly unjust and inhuman and so much against the laws of both God and man that it had a tendency to arrest this brutal mode of settling disputes for a time

All this Northwest trade was conducted mostly in bark-canoes and on the backs of the stout and hardy Canadians Sometimes a Mackinac boat, so called, and at rare intervals a schooner were employed in the commerce on the lakes. No craft can equal the bark-canoe for its cheapness of construction and for its neatness and utility Its invention by the natives is before Indian antiquities and used by them on the lakes and adjacent rivers so long as they remained in the country. The bark-canoe is made out of strong, light, and elastic wood for the timbers within and covered with strong birch-bark, which gives the craft the name of a bark-canoe. The timbers within are strong in proportion to the size of the canoe, and are tough light, and elastic. They are formed with great neatness and strength, and at the same time with shape to sail with the most facility They are very sharp at the ends and rounding on the bottom; so they may glide thro the water with the greater speed Pitch is used on these canoes to prevent them from leaking, and the voyagers are always provided with the means of sewing up the splits and repairing them in the shortest possible time. When the canoe becomes leaky it is unladen, carried on the shore, sewed up, and repaired in a few hours These canoes are light and portable When the waters of the lakes are rough, they are unloaded and taken on shore, out of the reach of the waves, and at the portages they are easily packed on men's shoulders across from water to water They are propelled by the voyagers using paddles and the patroon at the stern steering it also with a paddle The paddles are made nice and neat, out of strong, elastic wood, and painted with all the taste and elegance of a boatman's genius. These canoes were, on occasion, greased with deer's tallow that they might sail the easier and swifter thro the water.

Races were common and wagers made on them Boat-racing seems to be coeval with boats. It is a cheering and interesting spectacle to see a crew of hardy, stout Canadians dressed in the uniform of the Northwest voyagers, paddling a bark-canoe under the excitement of boat-songs and an animated race There is no excitement more intense and acute than these voyagers experience in a canoe-race They would freely exchange their freedom for life, for success, and almost life itself. They invoke the Virgin and promise masses for victory. These races are topics for French discussion of the canoe-men for years after.

The Mackinac boat is a plain, unpretending vessel, somewhat similar to our skiffs, but larger and coarser made. They are sharp at the ends but flat on the bottom. They are not honored with a deck, but a tarpaulin cloth was generally used to secure the merchandise from the rain From three to six men navigated them One at the steering-oar and the other hands row the boat. They were generally about thirty feet long and the planks of the side three or four feet high. These boats were intended to be carried over the portages. They sustained a heavy burden to their looks.

As to the schooners used on the lakes in French times, whoever saw a fishing-schooner on the shores of old France saw a vessel almost similar to these lake schooners. The French are a greater people on land than on the water in ships. In vessels below a schooner the Canadians did well enough.

These Northwest traders also used the most simple and primitive mode of carrying on commerce, and that was by packing the articles of traffic on men's backs The packs of merchandise were generally weighed and the Canadians packed them over the portages. Often they carried these packs out many leagues from the depots to the Indian camps and the peltries back again. Very little horse-power was used in this commerce

An efficient and enterprising colony of Americans immigrated from Hardy County, Virginia, and settled at the New Design, Illinois, in 1797. This was the largest and most flourishing company of farmers, mechanics, and laborers that ever came to Illinois at or before that day.

A year or so before 1797, David Badgley and Leonard Car came out to explore the country. Daniel Stookey, Abraham Eyeman, Mr. Whetstone, and Abraham Stookey also explored the country before the colony settled in Illinois. These explorers came from the south branch of Potomac, Hardy County, Virginia, on horseback and examined the country thoroly. They remained in the country most of the summer and Rev. David Badgley frequently preached. Mr. Stookey and others crossed the Mississippi at St. Louis in 1796, and gave that French village, the country around it, and the commandant a passing notice.

This exploring party decided on making Illinois their homes for life. They returned to Virginia and reported the facts of their discoveries to their neighbors and friends. This whole colony then mustered up and commenced a long and arduous journey, at that day, for the Far-West

It is said that Solomon Shook and Mr Borer came to Illinois the year before. This colony, all numbered and all told, amounted to about one hundred and fifty-four souls They crossed the mountains in wagons, on pack-horses, and on foot to Morgantown, on the Monongahela River. Here they waited some time for their boats to be finished. At last, in May, they set sail down the rivers to the land of promise—Illinois After a long, tiresome, and exposed voyage down the rivers, they landed at Fort Massac, on the Ohio River. The flat boats or broad horses, as they were sometimes called in derision, were not covered and the families in them were exposed to the inclemency of the weather and the heat of a summer sun

This year, 1797, was uncommonly wet and the streams between the Ohio and Kaskaskia were all out of the banks and swimming It rained almost every day and the roads between Kaskaskia and Massac were literally covered with water and the mud almost impassable This colony fixed up their wagons, horses, and all things for the New Design, Illinois, and left Massac They were detained in this wilderness of mud and water for almost a month—exposed to almost a vertical sun over their heads and positive mud and water under their feet

It must be recollected that at this time not a house stood between Kaskaskia and Massac They rafted the creeks and at last reached civilization and contemplated relief, but wofully were they disappointed They were hailed at Kaskaskia and the New Design with all the good feelings peculiarly incident to the pioneers, but a tempest of the most direful calamity was gathering to burst upon their devoted heads. Almost one-half of this cheerful and flourishing colony died during the first summer and fall of their arrival.

This mortality is almost unprecedented in any country or under any circumstances. A most malignant fever prevailed, which was supposed to be contagious. This prevented the people from paying that kind attention to the sick which they needed Scarcely a physician could be procured

When they reached the New Design, they could not procure houses to receive them and they were huddled together to the great injury of their health In fact, provisions were not plenty. The Indian war had only ceased a year or two before and the inhabitants had not raised much support for themselves or the immigrants At any rate, such was the mortality that even the burying of the dead was scarcely attended to.

The graveyard of 1797 may yet be seen at the New Design, which will cause the observer to shudder at the mortality and consequent distress at that day. Scarcely a family of all these immigrants but had to mourn the loss of one or more of its number, and many of the families were almost entirely extinct, leaving, perhaps, a few helpless children to grieve over the loss of their parents, brothers, and sisters At this time there were no means of relief for this distress in the country, except kind and benevolent hearts The country was healthy after this year and the immigrants who were not swept off soon did well

Scarcely at any time or in any country will be found so many moral, honest, and laborious citizens, to the number of this colony, as the immigration from Hardy County to the New Design The names of Car, Stookey, Eyeman, Shook, Mitchell, Clark, Badgley, Teter, Miller, and others will be recognized as the heads of families of this colony, whose descendants at this day are numerous and respectable.

This colony introduced into the country an orderly and moral influence, which did great service to the previous inhabitants. The emigrants from Virginia attended strictly and honestly to business and not only improved the country, but their example also improved the people. They were the first who raised sheep to any number and manufactured the wool into clothes. They turned their attention to the culture of wheat and raised a surplus for market. They also encouraged the breed of horses and cattle and raised a great number themselves.

The beneficial influence of this colony to improve the country was in a short time perceived by everyone. The people composing it were not proud or overbearing, but on the contrary, they were remarkable for their modest and amiable deportment; so that they taught by example the people, who esteemed and admired them. This colony was extremely moral and correct and their descendants to this day are notorious for their sober and orderly conduct.

It was stated in a former page that John Murdoch came to the country with his father in 1796, and that his father, dying soon after, left the son with his widowed mother. He was born in Kentucky in 1790. He, like most of the youths at that day, acted his own part as he pleased, without the control of his mother. Murdoch run almost wild and attended very little at the school-house. He received a very limited education, but nature had bestowed on him singular parts. He was in his youth an odd kind of boy—more intellect than ordinary children, but always applied it in a singular and quizzical manner.

He was accustomed to play tricks on his step-father, Blair, when he was very young. He often pinned a cloth to the coat-tail of his step-father, and when the prank was discovered, he never showed the least emotion or laughed. He shaved the hair off the manes and tails of his step-father's horses; so as to "have a joke on the old man." As he grew up, these tricks increased on him, until Blair and almost all others were heartily tired of him. From his infancy to manhood, it cost more coaxing, threatening, and labor to make him work than the work he ever did was worth. He was born to a kind of involuntary hatred to work or to do any business that was not of his own selection.

He would labor for days and weeks to accomplish some

prank; such as to carry rails a half-mile to make a fence in the night around a man's door. He would get up out of bed when the family were asleep and ride miles to accomplish tricks, and would be back in bed before morning, and no one would, perhaps, ever detect him. But he obstinately refused to work. In a sly manner at church he often put old decks of cards in the preacher's pockets.

He had not much friendship for an old Baptist preacher in his neighborhood, and when the old man was engaged in the house of devotion, Murdoch slipped to the preacher's horse, which was hitched in the brushwood, took the saddle and bridle off the horse and put them on a large, old mulley ox. The horse ran home, but there stood the old ox, saddled and bridled for the preacher when he went to get his horse. No one could scarcely ever detect him in these tricks.

He possessed in his composition not much malice or malignity; but at the same time, a moderate share only of the disposition that adorns the human race was found in his character. He married and lived only at intervals with his wife. He made a sorry husband, as he did almost everything else he attempted. He entered the military service of the country in the war of 1812, and ranged or staid at home almost at his pleasure. The officers could not do much with him.

At Peoria, in the fall of 1813, he provided himself with two black bottles; one he filled with water and the other he left empty. He had not much credit with the sutlers; but asked for a quart of whisky and had it put into his empty bottle. Murdoch was slow, orderly, and circumspect in putting his whisky under his hunting-shirt. He put the bottle containing the water where the sutler first saw him put the whisky-bottle. In a grave, serious manner he observed to the sutler that he had no money, as he was out from home, and he must charge him with it. The sutler refused and then Murdoch offered him the bottle containing the water and said, he must put the liquor back again into the barrel. The grocer did so and put the neck of the water-bottle into the bung-hole of the barrel and let the water pour in. Thus it was that Murdoch exchanged a bottle of water for a bottle of whisky.

He played another trick in the present county of Madison,

on a landlord near Rattan's Prairie, in the war of 1812. He and several other jovial fellows were in a drinking frolic and had not the means to obtain as much liquor as they wanted. Murdoch had but one bit (twelve and a-half cents) and gave it for a half-pint of whisky. He watched where the landlord put the bit and saw him place it into a teacup which stood high up on a shelf. The master of the house went about his business out of doors, and when he was absent, Murdoch took the same bit out of the teacup and called for another half-pint of liquor. The bit was again put into the same cup and the same process was carried on until evening, when the landlord supposed he had a cup almost full of bits, when lo! and behold! he had barely one bit in the cup and his company, Murdoch and others, were in high glee.

It was the law that the United-States Rangers should find themselves provisions, and they were permitted to go home, fix up, and return with the necessary supplies. Murdoch had been at home and on his return to Camp Russell, near Edwardsville, he caught a ground-hog and put it alive in his saddle-bags. When he got off his horse, which was hitched near the fort, he whispered that "*something* was in his saddle-bags;" making the man believe that it was a bottle of whisky in them. His confiding friend, having more taste for liquor than discretion, slyly alone went to Murdoch's horse and thrust his hand into the saddle-bags for the whisky; but the moment he put his hand in, the ground-hog bit him.

This ranger that got bit thought he would bite someone else. He said nothing about the ground-hog biting him; but told another ranger, in under tone, that he got a first-rate dram out of Murdoch's saddle-bags. The man put his hand into the saddle-bags and the animal caught his hand and held on; so the second bit man roared out for help to get his hand out of the ground-hog's mouth.

Such transactions gave Murdoch great pleasure altho he always appeared serious and scarcely ever laughed or made any outward demonstrations of joy or pleasure on their success.

This singular and curious character was rather silent in company and never indulged in loud or boisterous conversation. His remarks, like his pranks, were severe and satirical. The same talent that caused him to perform these tricks also enabled him to make similar remarks His person was of the ordinary height and erect; but spare and emaciated almost to a skeleton. He seemed to possess no great passions or impulses; but his energies of mind were inclined to such feats as above.

The pranks of his life would fill a volume. His mind possessed some strength in its peculiar manner. It was active, elastic, and sprightly, but was deficient in solid, sober judgment. It ranged in the lower regions of poetry, but never reached the platform of common-sense. If he had been raised and educated under different circumstances, he would have been a character of some celebrity. His natural gifts, without improvement, were an injury to him. By a proper education, these parts would make him rather a shining and brilliant character, but not a solid or judicious one. After the close of the war of 1812, he enlisted in the regular army and died.

For years after the peace was established with the Indians, in 1795, many cases of hardship and suffering were the consequences of that war.

It will be recollected that James Gilham, Sr., emigrated to Illinois at an early day, and at a still earlier one, he emigrated from South Carolina and settled on the frontiers of Kentucky In 1790, he had selected himself a residence in Kentucky and was in the field plowing his corn, with one of his sons, Isaac, then a small boy The boy was with his father, clearing the young corn from the clods and sods which the plow might throw on it, while the rest of the family were in the house Several Kickapoo warriors went to the house and captured Gilham's whole family that were not with him in the field. The field was some distance from the house and he did not immediately discover the disaster These savages captured his wife, one girl, and two sons

What horrid feelings Gilham experienced when he returned from his work as he supposed to his family and dinner; but discovered his house sacked by the Indians, his family captured and either killed or doomed to savage bondage! His grief and anguish must have been excessive; but

"Man was made to mourn."

The Indians made the family, by signs, remain quiet, so as

not to alarm Gilham in the field. They made quick work of it and started for the Kickapoo town, toward the sources of the Sangamon River, Illinois. They cut open the bed-ticks and took such articles out of the house as they could carry away on their backs They were afraid to take any horses, lest the whites would follow their trail and destroy them.

The country where Gilham resided was thinly settled, and before he could get a party to pursue the Indians, they escaped. Mrs. Gilham was so terrified that she was almost bereaved of her mind.

After the Indians had taken the house and the family, the first thing she recollected was her son Samuel, a small boy, saying: "Mamma, we're all prisoners." Gilham and neighbors followed the Indian trail a considerable distance; but could not overtake them He, on his return, suffered misery and mental anguish that is indescribable. Yet hope lingered with him that as the Indians had not killed his people, he would again recover them Hope never entirely abandons anyone in almost any affliction.

The Indians steered clear of the settlements and were extremely cautious in their march. They kept a spy before and one behind on the trail; so that their retreat was guarded as much as possible by their numbers. The party suffered much from hunger. The three white children were in great misery from their hurried march and the want of food. But human nature can endure much and will contrive many expedients before suffering death Mrs. Gilham patched up rags round the feet of her children to save them from the briars and thorns. They traveled over a wilderness without roads A mother's love for her children knows no bounds. Sympathy at last seized on the warriors and they treated the prisoners with all the savage kindness and mercy in their power.

They were out of provisions and one day they halted to hunt for something to save them from starving. The children had a small morsel of dried meat to eat, and the grown ones nothing. Two of the best hunters were sent out and one returned with a poor summer raccoon Mrs. Gilham said the sight of this poor coon caused her more happiness than any other earthly sight she ever saw. She was afraid her children would either perish with hunger or the Indians would kill them to save them from starvation

The party could not hunt near the white settlement for fear of detection, and if they delayed, the whites would overtake them This was the reason of their going so long without food and almost suffering death from hunger.

This coon was not dressed in Parisian style, but most of the hair and fur were taken off and some of the contents of the *extreme inside* were thrown away, while the balance was put in a brass kettle and placed over a fire. The coon was soon boiled into a nondescript dish—mixed together the meat, bones, hide, some hair, some entrails, claws and feet of the animal. As soon as this mess was cool and before, the horn and wooden spoons were in complete operation and the whole assembly of white and red-skins got some relief from absolute starvation.

As they approached the Ohio River, they became more cautious, for fear of meeting the Americans on the river, either waylaying for them or in boats descending the river. They came to the Ohio a small distance above Hawesville, Kentucky, and camped near the river until rafts could be made on which to cross it They were detained more than a day in making rafts Dry logs were, procured and tied together with red-elm bark and the rafts placed near the edge of the water, so that they might be put in the river in a moment and not touch the water before they started over; as they would not be so light, having received some water before. The wily savages were afraid to cross the river in daylight. Mrs Gilham was much terrified at the idea of crossing the river at night The party had three rafts The largest one took Mrs. Gilham and her three children, with two prudent old Indians to paddle it over. The others crossed in the two rafts prepared for them The embarkation was in the night, as silent as if they were in a graveyard, and the rafts were paddled over the Ohio with the same secrecy

These warriors considered it a great triumph to take these four prisoners and conduct them in safety to the Indian towns. In this proportion they exercised all their talents of bravery and sagacity to accomplish it But when they had crossed the Ohio, they considered themselves safe and released their watchfulness and caution to some extent

In the country south of White River, in the present State of Indiana, they hunted, marched slow, and lived well in comparison to the time they ate the coon. They steered clear of the small white settlements around Vincennes and crossed the Wabash below Terre Haute. They marched thro the present counties of Clark, Coles, and Decatur, Illinois, and finally, after a long and hazardous travel from the southwestern frontiers of Kentucky—three or four hundred miles—they reached in safety the Kickapoo town, which was situated on Salt Creek, northeast of the Elk-Heart Grove in Sangamon County.

What a horrid situation the Indian war placed the Gilham family in! Four with the Indians and two in Kentucky in great misery and affliction

Gilham, as soon as he found his family were not killed, but taken prisoners by the Indians, took courage and hoped again to see his wife and children. He sold his improvement in Kentucky, put his son Isaac with a friend, and set out in search of his people After much delay and fatigue of mind and body, he found they were alive among the Indians and made arrangements to purchase them. At last he obtained all his lost family and they lived together many years in happiness. The young son, Clement, could not talk a word of English when he was regained by his father.

In 1815, Ann Gilham, the wife of James Gilham, obtained a grant of land of one hundred and sixty acres from congress, as an honorable testimony of the sufferings and hardships in her captivity with the Indians, as above narrated.

The principal town with the Peoria Indians, in 1680, when the whites first explored the country, was at the outlet of Peoria Lake, on the site of the present City of Peoria and Fort Crevecœur, where LaSalle first erected it in January, 1680, was one mile and a-half east on the lake from this Indian town The site at Crevecœur has been uniformly recognized by the old French inhabitants as the Old Fort, ever since that day down to the present time.

It was quite natural for LaSalle to erect this fort a short distance from this large town of Indians and not directly in the village. And it may be said with equal truth that some continuous settlement has existed at and near Fort Crevecœur ever since its first establishment to the present time, only at two intervals, when the people were either driven off by the Indians or by Capt. Craig, in the war of 1812.

About 1781—during the Revolutionary war—when Major Montgomery visited Peoria and the inhabitants joined him against the British and Indians, the red-skins, under the influence of the British, became hostile for a short time to the people of Peoria, and in consequence of this, the inhabitants left it, but in a short time, friendly feelings were restored and the citizens of Peoria returned to their village The village was abandoned but for a short time, and before the peace in 1783, it was restored to its former or greater size.

In the fall of 1812, in the war with Great Britain, Capt Thos. E Craig fell out with the place and carried off many citizens. He landed these people at Savage's Ferry, on the Mississippi, where the town of Gibraltar was afterward laid out In a few years, the citizens returned to Peoria and some went back the same winter after they were taken away.

The traders, their voyagers, and others in their employment occupied this post more or less ever since its first establishment As it has been said, the Indian trade of that section of country was better than at any other point. This made it the interest of the traders to occupy the place

Peoria never, in ancient times, was as large a village as either Kaskaskia or Cahokia, but it is more ancient than either of them LaSalle, when he first saw the country, was charmed with the beauty of the place and established a fort there. He also knew the resources of the country arising from the Indian trade, which was another and perhaps a greater inducement to erect his grand depot here for the Indian trade than for any other consideration.

In the first settlement of the country, the missionaries settled at this post and had their flocks of the young natives around them Peoria can boast of a higher antiquity than any town in Illinois, and about the same date with St. Joseph, Green Bay, Mackinac, and Detroit

The French cultivated some ground, more or less, at Peoria for more than one hundred years past. They cultivated at the old village to some extent and at the new one since 1778, when it was commenced by Maillet It will be seen by the report of the United-States officers, sustained by positive proof, that one Antoine St. François had a family in Peoria in 1765 and cultivated a field of corn adjacent to the village. Other inhabitants also resided there at the same time and long before It is true, most of the citizens were Indian traders and those living on the trade, but this trade required support by men and provisions, which were both furnished to some extent by the settlers at Peoria.

Ke-kauk-kem-ke was the Indian name of Peoria. The Pottawatomie Indians, who occupied the country after the Peorias were driven off, and all the surrounding Indians have recognized the above name. The meaning of the name in English is strait, frith, or narrow. The old Indian name of Detroit in Michigan is the same. The French recognize the meaning in the name of Detroit, but not the Indian word of *Ke-kauk-kem-ke* Detroit in English is a strait, frith, or a narrow defile, which is the meaning of the above Indian word.

The French gave the name of Peoria to that place on account of the Peoria tribe of Indians, who resided at the strait or outlet of the lake when they first explored the country.

Thomas Forsyth settled in Peoria in 1809. He was of Irish extraction and born at Detroit, December 5, 1771. His father, Robert Forsyth, emigrated from Ireland to Philadelphia in 1757; went to Canada and was wounded in the battle at Quebec, where both Wolfe and Montcalm fell. He married in Canada and emigrated to Detroit, then a British province.

John Edgar, the same that lived and died at Kaskaskia, Jas Abbot, and Robert Forsyth were three prominent Irishmen at Detroit, whose friendship for the American Revolution caused at least two of them, Edgar and Forsyth, much hardship and suffering.

The British governor of Detroit, hearing these Irishmen condemning the war against the Americans and particularly that brutal conduct of exciting the Indians to murder the American women and children on the frontiers, seized Edgar and Forsyth and cast them into a dark and loathsome dungeon at Detroit.

The British, not repenting of their barbarous conduct toward these noble Irishmen, became more enraged and put them in irons for merely expressing their opinions in favor of the American Revolution and condemning the murder of the women and children. The British governor of Detroit sent Edgar in irons to Quebec; but on his passage he escaped near Montreal and went to Boston. He continued his march until he reached Kaskaskia, as heretofore stated. The enraged British retained Forsyth for a long time in prison, and at last, finding nothing against him, turned him out. James Abbot was a little more cautious and was not imprisoned, but the frowns of the government were heavy and strong against him.

Thomas Forsyth, the subject of this sketch, was raised and educated at Detroit until he was seventeen years old. He received a plain, common education, which qualified him in after-life for both the public and private business in which he was engaged. In 1793, he left Detroit with his half-brother, John Kinzie,* the founder of Chicago and the father of John H.

* John Kinzie—son of a Scotchman named John Mackenzie, who lived in Quebec, and later moved to Detroit, where he died—was born in Quebec in 1763; his mother had previously been married to a gentleman of the name of Haliburton, whose only daughter by this marriage was the mother of Gen. Fleming and Nicholas Low of New York. John Kinzie was the only child by this second marriage; his father died during his infancy, and his mother married, 3d, Robert Forsyth, a Scotch-Irishman, from Blackwater, Ireland, arriving in New York about 1750; was a soldier under Wolfe at Quebec, and was twice wounded, was later stationed at Detroit and where, after his discharge, married and settled; kept a tavern some years; engaged in the fur-trade; and died about 1790

John Kinzie, when about eleven years old, ran away from a school at Williamsburg, L. I., where he and two younger half-brothers were, to Quebec, where he acquired, during the three years he remained there, a knowledge of silversmithing, that he turned to account in connection with the Indian-trade at which he commenced early in life, having establishments at Detroit, 1795-7, Sandusky, Maumee, and later, 1800, at St Josephs. As early as May 12, 1804, he was sutler for Fort Dearborn, later, trading-posts were established by him at Milwaukee, Rock River, on the Illinois and Kankakee rivers, and at LeLarge in Sangamon County, Ill. About 1810, his partner was John Whistler, Jr., and the same year his half-brother Thomas Forsyth, they continued together as late as 1815.

After the massacre, August 15, 1812, he returned to Detroit, and again to Chicago in 1816. In 1800, he married (2d) Mrs Eleanor (Lytle) McKillup, the widow of a British officer, having previously married Margaret Mackenzie, by whom he had William, James, and Elizabeth. The children by the second marriage were John Harris; Ellen Marion, born at Chicago, Dec, 1804, married (1), July 20, 1823, Dr Alex. Wolcott, Indian agent, (2) Geo C Bates, May 26, 1836, and died at Detroit, Aug 1, 1860, Maria, born 1807, married Lieut, now Maj-Gen. David Hunter, U.S.A., of Washington, D.C.; Robert Allen, born Feb. 8, 1810, married a daughter of

Kinzie* and other children. He remained with Kinzie fifteen months and continued the Indian trade with a Scotch merchant, Mr. Sharp. After Sharp's death, in 1799, Forsyth commenced business himself and steered west thro the Indian country by St. Joseph, Chicago, Illinois River, to the Mississippi. He wintered one year at the Two Rivers, on the Mississippi, and traded with the Western Indians for several years

He married a lady in Upper Canada, near Fort Malden, and soon after removed to Peoria His wife was born in Hagerstown, Maryland, and her family name was Le Motte. Her father and family were captured on the Ohio River by the Indians as they were emigrating West, and this lady and others of the family were sent to Canada, where she married Mr. Forsyth

In the war with Great Britain in 1812, Mr Forsyth acted an important and efficient part in that contest, and at the same time a very dangerous and confidential part. In the beginning of the Indian troubles in 1811, he resided at Peoria and had a

Col. Wm Whistler, U S A , and died at Chicago, Dec 12, 1873. Shaw-nee-aw-ke—silver man—Mr Kinzie's Indian sobriquet, was U.-S. Indian interpreter, sub-agent, etc , and died at Chicago, Monday, Jan 6, 1828 —G. H. F.

* John Harris Kinzie, born July 7, 1803, at Sandwich, Canada, arrived with his father at Chicago, Oct , 1803, where he remained till 1812—when Fort Dearborn was abandoned—when the family returned to Detroit, and in 1816 returned to Chicago, where he remained till 1818, when his father apprenticed him at the Mackinac agency of the American Fur Co.; in 1824, he was transferred to Prairie du Chien; in 1829, he was stationed at Fort Winnebago, as sub-agent of Indian affairs, and was a subscribing witness at many of the treaties made with the Indians Aug. 9, 1830, at Middletown, Conn , he married Miss Juliette A., daughter of Arthur Magill of that place, later of Chicago, Ill In 1833, Chicago again became his home, and was engaged in the forwarding business; later, his brother-in-law, now Maj.-Gen. David Hunter, was his partner In 1841, he was appointed registrar of public lands by Pres't Harrison, and removed by Tyler In 1848, when the Illinois-and-Michigan Canal was completed, he was appo nted canal collector In 1849, President Taylor appointed him receiver of public moneys The office of canal collector he held until commissioned by President Lincoln paymaster in the army, in 1861; and this latter appointment he held at the time of his death, which occurred on the cars approaching Pittsburg, Pa , June 21, 1865. His widow, born Sept. 11, 1806, died Sept 15, 1870; their children Eleanor L . wife of W W. Gordon, and lives at Savannah, Ga ; John Harris, Jr , killed at Fort St Charles, Ark., June 18, 1862, aged 23; Arthur M., married Caroline Gilbert, third daughter of John Lush and Maria E. (Whipple) Wilson, now living at Riverside, Cook County, Ill.; and George H , 1st lieutenant, 15th Infantry, U.S.A.—G. H. F.

great influence over all the Indians, but more particularly with the Pottawatomies. He had been raised with this nation, spoke their language well, and was well acquainted with their character. His position, Peoria, was in their midst, so that he had a knowledge of all their movements and even their councils relative to war

He was on business at St Louis in the early part of 1811, and became acquainted with Gen William Clark, the superintendent of Indian affairs. He related to Clark, on being requested, the state of the Indian disposition and their intended hostile movements His character and merit were immediately appreciated and he was appointed an Indian agent at Peoria, but this appointment was not made known, for wise and prudential considerations If the Indians were to know it, he would lose all his influence with them, but by retaining his standing and influence with them, he could ameliorate much of the horrid barbarities that are commonly practised on both sides in an Indian war Forsyth had not the power to avert the Indian war, but he aided much in its amelioration.

In the fall of 1811, he understood that the Sac and Fox Indians were about to make an attack on the frontiers of Missouri, and he sent down to the officer in command at St Louis, a confidential Frenchman, Antoine Le Pense, who gave the information to the officer and much of the calamity was avoided.

Early in the spring of 1812, when a kind of *quasi* war existed between the Indians and whites, he descended the Illinois River to St Louis to consult with Gov. Howard, and also proceeded to Kaskaskia to see Gov Edwards He laid the whole Indian affairs in relation to the approaching war open to these two executive officers of Illinois and Missouri, which gave them the true state of matters, so they might make arrangements according to the exigencies

On August 15, 1812, the Indians massacred most of Capt. Nathan Heald's company at Chicago, Illinois, and Lieut Lina T. Helm was wounded and taken prisoner Helm was the first lieutenant in the company of Capt. Heald The Indians took him to the AuSable on the Illinois River

Mr. Forsyth, hearing of the massacre of the troops at Chicago, at the risk of his life, went directly to the Indian towns on the Illinois River to see and ameliorate the condition of the prisoners He found Lieut. Helm at the AuSable with the Indians and had the influence with his captors to ransom him He advanced the amount of the ransom out of his own funds, and perhaps all of it was never returned to him. He ransomed the lieutenant and had him sent in safety to St Louis.

Mr. Forsyth risked his life every moment he was engaged in this important and truly dangerous service If the Indians, the Pottawatomies, were to receive a bare hint of his Indian agency, he would have been burnt at the stake He risked his life for his country and was in extreme and imminent danger for a great portion of the war. It required the utmost sagacity and great propriety of judgment to manage the matter so as to retain the confidence of the Indians Much of their friendship was for him personally. His personal influence was the great cause of his success. He had been uniformly kind and benevolent to them

To show his confidence and friendship to them, he took with him a few of the old friends of the Indians, who had married squaws and had before the war resided at Peoria He also took with him some of the half-breed children to see their Indian cousins. They had no weapons, guns, or powder with them. They carried in the boat such articles as the Indians needed and such as Forsyth had heretofore sold to them, except ammunition They asked Forsyth the reason why he did not have powder and lead with him in his boat, as he used to have He told them that in a war all the powder and lead belonged to the great father, the president, and he would not let any of his children have it until the war was over. He said Craig had seized him and all their old friends in Peoria by force and dragged them down to St. Louis, for fear their friends would do the Indians some good

What made it the most dangerous was the influence Dickson had with the Indians, and he all the time tempting the Illinois-River Indians either to kill him or take him prisoner

While Forsyth was on one of these missions of benevolence from St. Louis to his old friend, a Pottawatomie chief whose name in English was Sugar, he very narrowly escaped losing his life He went to his friend, the chief, at AuSable village, above Peoria, and staid with him all night In the night he discovered his friend, the chief, very uneasy He could not sleep and was frequently up, looking round his camp Forsyth asked what was the matter The Indian said: "I am afraid for you Dickson tried to get me to take you prisoner I told him you were my friend and I would not hurt you; but," he said, "there are some Winnebagoes not far off, they are drinking and I am afraid they may come to take you They shall not take you; but in the conflict they might kill you"

No Indians came that night; but the next night Dickson had a host of Winnebagoes at the camp of the chief, but Forsyth had left the same day If he had remained he would have been killed or taken prisoner.

Late in the fall of 1812, Craig was in the Peoria Lake with a boat and some Indians came down the lake in a boat and fired on his boat. The conduct of these Indians enraged Craig against the citizens of Peoria. He said they were friendly to the Indians He forced all the inhabitants of Peoria—Forsyth, the Indian agent, as well as the rest—on board of his boat and landed them at Savage's Ferry, opposite the mouth of the Missouri.

These poor people were harmless, unoffending inhabitants of Peoria and were forced from their homes and living to almost starvation Many of them soon returned to Peoria and some the same winter They had left their cattle and all their support at the village. Craig, in his rage, also burnt most of the houses in the village of Peoria While Craig was kidnapping Forsyth, he did not inform Craig of the fact that he was Indian agent, residing at Peoria for the public service and at the request of the general government.

Mr Forsyth continued to act as Indian agent for the Illinois Indians during the war; but when peace was restored, he was entrusted with a very important agency—that of agent for the Sac and Fox nations of Indians. He attended faithfully to his public duties in this office He was entrusted with large sums of money and great amounts of merchandise for these Indians, and his accounts and duties were always approved by the government He was an excellent and faithful officer He made treaties with the Sac and Fox nations, which were

always ratified by the government. But his services in the war
and his benevolent and humane conduct to the wounded and
distressed prisoners on the Illinois River, deserve the lasting
gratitude and esteem of the government, as well as those whose
sufferings he so kindly relieved.

He retained the office of the Indian agency of the Sac and
Fox Indians for many years, and if he had been continued in
the office it is not very probable that Black Hawk would have
attempted a war against the government. Forsyth had such
influence over the Indians that it is quite certain he could have
quieted their feelings and no blood would have been shed.

After the war, in 1815, Dickson and Forsyth met in St Louis
and talked over their doings in the war. Dickson confessed he
was near making Forsyth a prisoner, while Forsyth said Providence and justice prevented it.

In the decline of life, Mr Forsyth purchased a fine farm west
of St Louis and improved it. He died on it in 1852. His
death was a loss to the community and as such and for the respect and esteem entertained for him by the people, his friends,
family, and the public generally, lamented his death with heart-
felt grief and sorrow. Nature bestowed on him a sound, well-
balanced mind, and benevolence and kindness of heart were his
predominant traits of character. His person was large and
portly. He occupied a prominent standing in community and
well did he deserve it by his uncommon services to the public.
His private life was amiable and kind. His duties as husband
and father he performed in that amiable and benevolent manner
that showed a heart overflowing with "the milk of human kindness" He possessed many virtues and traits of character to
be admired and approved, while he had very few to be condemned

In 1795, the territorial legislature erected a new county out
of the southern part of St Clair and called it Randolph, in
honor of the governor of that name of Virginia. The line
dividing Randolph and St Clair counties runs nearly east and
west to the head of Ryan's Creek, pursued that creek to the
Bottom, and thence to the Mississippi. Kaskaskia was made
the county-seat of Randolph County and Cahokia that of
St Clair.

CHAPTER VII.

The Religion and Morals of Illinois prior to 1818.

FOR the following sketch of the early American pioneers, their religious and moral character, and the pioneer efforts to form religious institutions in this territory, cultivate the minds and morals of the people, I am indebted to my friend, Rev. John Mason Peck* of this [St. Clair] County. The brief reply to the request made him precedes the sketch:

* John Mason Peck, the only child of Asa and Hannah (Farnum) Peck, was born Oct. 31, 1789, at South-Farms Parish, Litchfield Co , Conn He came of Puritan stock, his ancestors Dea. Paul and Martha Peck emigrated from Essex Co., Eng., 1634, and settled at Hartford, Conn., of which place he was one of the proprietors and where he died Dec 23, 1695 John M. lived on his father's little farm and after his fourteenth year a large share of its cultivation was performed by him. During the winter months a part of his time was spent at a common-school that must have been inferior to the average institutions of that kind then in New England, as he complained that after he was eighteen, and had began to teach school, his own spelling and writing were sadly deficient and he did not pretend to understand grammar. At this age he was brought under a strong religious influence, and soon it became a serious alternative choice with him whether it was his duty to prepare himself for the ministry or remain upon the farm as the chief reliance of his poor and infirm parents. It was perhaps to reconcile his conscience to the latter choice that he took to himself a wife, and married, May 8, 1809, Sarah Paine, born in Green Co , N.Y., Jan. 31, 1789, who, after her father's second marriage, went to her mother's relatives in Litchfield, Conn ; and died at Rock Spring, St. Clair Co., Ill., Oct. 24, 1856. Their children were: Eli Paine, born July 28, 1810, at Litchfield, Conn., died near St. Charles, Mo , Oct. 5, 1820; Hannah F., born July 10, 1812, married Ashford Smith of Rockville, Iowa; Harvey Y., born Sept. 28, 1814, died Dec 17, 1855, leaving a widow and six children; Wm C , born Feb. 11, 1818, died Sept 14, 1821; Mary Ann, born Sept 18, 1820, wife of Sam G Smith, resides on the old homestead in St Clair Co , Ill.; Wm. S , born Nov. 13, 1823, lives in Iowa; John Q A , born Aug. 27, 1825, lives at Rock Spring; an infant, born Dec. 10, 1827, died *sin nomine,* Henry M , born May 7, 1829, resides at Rock Spring; James A., born Sept 21, 1831. Two years later, 1811, he moved with wife and one child to Windham, Green Co., N.Y., then known as Big Hollow; the six following years were devoted to preaching, school-teaching, and organizing churches and Sunday-schools in that sparsely-settled vicinity; in 1817, with wife and three children, he journeyed by land in a small wagon drawn by one horse to Shawneetown, Ill , arriving late in the fall, thence in a keel-boat, commanded by Capt. Nixon, late of Calhoun Co , Ill , his brother-in-law, to St. Louis, Mo., where, or near St. Charles, his family resided for the next five years, while he traveled through Missouri Ter'y, preaching, organizing churches and Sunday-schools, distributing bibles and other religious matter, except

253

"GOV REYNOLDS:—Your letter of March 1st, requesting from my pen sketches of the religious and moral history of

for a short time when he taught school at St Louis and St Charles, in the spring of 1822, he purchased from the U. S. sec 27, T 2, N R 7, W., about 3 miles west of Lebanon, St Clair Co., Ill., Rock Spring, so named by him from a spring gushing from the cloven rock, near which the same year he built his first double log-house. In Feb., 1825, he went East and secured funds and arranged for the establishment of a Baptist seminary; with the aid thus secured, together with his personal contributions of money and labor, a two-story frame building with two one-story wings was completed in 1827, near his residence, and with 25 students, soon increased to 100, was opened the "Rock-Spring Theological Seminary and High-School," the first institution in the State of a higher dignity than a common county-school Dr. Peck was professor of theology; Rev Joshua Bradley, president, and Rev. John Messinger, professor of mathematics, in 1831 it was closed, and was reopened at Upper Alton in 1832 as the Alton Seminary, a charter was granted in 1833, and declined by the projectors on account of its restrictions, intermediate legislation in 1835-6 and the session of 1841 repealed the objectionable provisos; Dr Peck had in the meantime induced Benj. Shurtleff, M D., of Boston, Mass., to contribute $10,000, in consideration the name was changed and is still known as Shurtleff College. About 1822, Dr. Peck became the general western agent of the American Bible Society for western half of Indiana, Illinois, and Missouri, he had strong anti-slavery sentiments and took an active, prominent, and leading part in the struggle of 1823-4 that prevented the introduction of slavery into the State, in 1826, was a year at college in Philadelphia, where he acquired a knowledge of Greek and Latin, the sciences, and something of medicine. April 25, 1829, at Rock Spring, was issued the first number of *The Pioneer*, Rev. Thos. P. Green, publisher, and Dr Peck, editor; it was a five-column, single-sheet newspaper, the second established in St. Clair Co ; in the fall of the same year, Dr. Peck, by purchase of Green's interest, became sole proprietor, in 1836, *The Pioneer* followed Rock-Spring Seminary to Alton, where it reappeared as *Western Pioneer and Baptist Standard-Bearer*, Dr Peck continuing as editor and Ashford Smith, his son-in-law, having charge of the printing; in 1839, it was merged in the *Baptist Banner* of Louisville, Ky., to which the goodwill and subscription lists were turned over In addition to his many and varied duties, besides being a prolific lecturer on agriculture and aboriginal and early Western history he found time to contribute to newspapers and many lengthy and studious articles to magazines, as well as to write the following: "Guide for Emigrants, containing sketches of Illinois and Adjacent Parts Boston; Lincoln & Edmunds, 1831" "Gazetteer of Illinois, in Three Parts, containing a General View of the State; a General View of each Town, Settlement, Stream, Prairie, Bottom, Bluff, etc., Alphabetically Arranged. Robert Goudy, Jacksonville, 1834" Another, "Second edition, entirely revised, corrected, and enlarged, Grigg & Elliot, Phila., 1837" "New Map of Illinois J. H. Colton, N. Y., 1837." "Life of Daniel Boon," 1846, and edited the "Annals of the West Second edition St Louis, 1850"

While in charge of a Baptist college at Covington, Ky., in 1854, he was afflicted with a fever from the effects of which he never fully recovered, and died four years later at Rock Spring, March 15, 1858, as he said "literally worn out"; his remains rest beneath a beautiful monument erected to his memory in Bellefontaine Cemetery, St Louis, Mo.—H W BECKWITH, Danville, Ill., July 17, 1884

the early American immigrants to Illinois, especially those about New Design and its vicinity, has received due attention In compliance therewith, I have prepared the following sketches previous to 1818, the period when your history terminates; which you are at liberty to use as you may deem expedient for your forth-coming work

"Respectfully yours, J. M. PECK.
"ROCK SPRING, ILL, March 20, 1852."

The conquest of Illinois by Gen G. R. Clark, in 1778, and the organization of a civil government by Virginia, prepared the way for American immigration to this country, and by 1786, a number of families had settled in the American Bottom and in the uplands of what is Monroe County The settlement on the hill country at an early period obtained the name of New Design, the centre of which was some three or four miles south of Waterloo Contiguous to the present county-seat and near the residence of the late John Milton Moore was another early settlement, called Bellefontaine from a celebrated spring, which still throws out a residuum of its salubrious water. A third settlement, which originated a few years later, was Whiteside's Station, a few miles north of Waterloo Three other neighborhoods or settlements, as a few contiguous families were called, were in the American Bottom—all within the present boundaries of Monroe County.

The immigrants that require notice came principally from Western Virginia and Kentucky A number of these pioneers had visited the Illinois country as volunteers under Col Clark, seen its rich and fertile soil, gazed with wonder on its prairies, and after their discharge, returned with their families and in the company of neighbors and relatives

The first class of these immigrants came out in 1781, of whom we can give the names of J. Moore, Shadrach Bond, Sr., Robert Kidd, James Garrison, Larkin Rutherford, and J. Piggott. Nothing deserving note occurred among this little band of pioneers until 1785, when they were joined by Capt Joseph Ogle, Joseph Worley, and Jas Andrews, all with large families from Western Virginia and but a few miles from Wheeling

In 1786, they were reinforced by the arrival of James

Lemen, Sr., James McRoberts, George Atchison, and David Waddle, and their families There were probably others whose names are not mentioned; but I am not able to give definitely the dates of their arrival in the country or of their religious and moral influence

None of these persons were members or communicants in Christian churches at the period of their arrival in this wild country; but many of them had been trained up by moral and religious parents or guardians, taught to regard the Sabbath as a day of worship and the propriety of doing justly and being merciful to their fellow-men and keeping the commandments of the Lord Tradition says there was a female, Mrs. Bond, who had been a member of the Presbyterian church

Their Sabbath meetings were held alternately at each others cabins and were conducted by Shadrach Bond, Sr., (called Judge Bond), James Piggott, and James Lemen, Sr., who read the Scriptures, especially the psalms, and sermons from books and sung hymns. No prayers were offered. In this way, order and good morals were preserved in the settlements.

There was a class of Americans who paid no regard to the Sabbath, but engaged in sport and pastime, drank intoxicating liquors, used profane language, and were careless of moral duties and the fear of the Lord; but at this distant period they and their posterity are unknown

In the summer of 1787, James Smith, a Baptist preacher from Lincoln County, Kentucky, visited New Design and preached to the people repeatedly. His labors were successful and several of the leading pioneers professed to be converted, among whom were Joseph Ogle and James Lemen, Sr, their wives and other connections Elder Smith returned again in the spring of 1790, and preached several times and many more became deeply interested about the gospel of Jesus Christ

On May 19, as Mr. Smith was proceeding from the blockhouse, as it was called, to Little Village, in company with a Frenchman and a Mrs. Huff, they were fired on by a party of Indians who were concealed in a thicket near Bellefontaine His horse and the one rode by the Frenchman were shot and the woman wounded Smith had the presence of mind to throw his saddle-bags, which contained papers of value, into a thicket and retreated to the foot of the hill, fell on his knees, and prayed for Mrs. Huff, whom the Indians were butchering and who had been seriously exercised about her own salvation under the preaching for several days. The Frenchman made his escape and Smith's saddle-bags were found next day by his friends. The Indians made the preacher a prisoner, loaded him with a pack of plunder they had taken from the settlements, and began their march thro the prairies. Smith was a large, heavy man and under his heavy load and a hot sun, soon became fatigued.

Consultations were held by the Indians how they should dispose of their prisoner. Some proposed to kill him, fearing the white people would follow them, and pointed their guns at his breast. Knowing well the Indian character, he bared his breast, as though he dared them to shoot him, and then pointed upward, to signify the Great Spirit was his protector. Having caught him while in the attitude of prayer and hearing him sing hymns on his march, which he did to relieve his mind from despondency, they concluded he was a "great medicine" and held intercourse with the Great Spirit, and must not be killed.

They took him to their town on the Wabash, from whence, thro the agency of the French traders from Vincennes, he obtained his freedom—the people of New Design paying one hundred and seventy dollars for his ransom. He visited Illinois the third time, obtained his saddle-bags and papers, which contained some evidence of land-titles for his friends, and returned to Kentucky, where he lived and died

The next preacher who visited the Illinois country was Rev. Joseph Lillard, a Methodist Mr Lillard had been in the "traveling connection" of the Methodist Episcopal for several years. In 1790, he was placed on Lime-Stone circuit, Kentucky, a new one, and in 1791, on Salt-River circuit. In 1793, he visited the Illinois country, preached to the people, and spent some time there. Either then or at a future time he withdrew from the traveling connection, not being in favor of the government of that church He organized the first Methodist class ever formed in this territory and appointed Capt.

Joseph Ogle class-leader. The captain not being a ready writer, his sister, Mrs. Tolin, kept the records for him

Mr. Lillard was esteemed by all as a pious and exemplary man; but while in Illinois, he became afflicted with aberation of mind, made his escape from the house, and tho pursued, he outran his friends and followed the trail toward Kaskaskia On the route, he came across the body of a man by the name of Sipp, whom the Indians had killed and scalped While looking on this horrid picture, he became calm, his consciousness was restored, and he returned to his friends at New Design and made report of the discovery The people made up a party, visited the spot, and buried the unfortunate man. Mr. Lillard continued to preach the gospel as a kind of independent Methodist in Kentucky. About twenty years or more since, he made another visit to Illinois and preached in this county.

After the visits of Elder James Smith, meetings were held more regularly, unless in times of Indian alarm, and were conducted with singing, prayer, and reading discourses. The late Shadrach Bond, Sr., called Judge Bond, frequently led in these meetings and read the discourses

It was probably in December, 1793, or January, 1794, while Judge Bond was officiating in this informal manner on Sabbath, that a stranger came into the meeting. He was a large, portly man, with dark hair, a florid complexion, and regular features. His dress was in advance of the deer-skin hunting-shirts and Indian moccasons of the settlers, his countenance grave and his aspect so serious that the mind of the reader was impressed with the thought that he was a man, perhaps a preacher, and an invitation was given for him to close the exercises, if he was a "praying man" The stranger kneeled and made an impressive, fluent, and solemn prayer. There was a man in the company of small talents and rather narrow views, who from his national origin bore the *sobriquet* of Dutch Pete among the people; or Peter Smith, as his name appears in the land documents Pete was a zealous Methodist and when his own brethren or preachers prayed, he felt moved by the spirit to utter amen at the close of every sentence While the people were on their knees or with their heads bowed low on their seats, Pete manifested uneasiness during the prayer of the stranger. He fidgeted one way and then another; uttered a low but audible groan and to those near him seemed in trouble. The very impressive and earnest prayer of the gentleman excited his feelings beyond suppression He might not be a Methodist; but Pete could not hold in no longer and bawled out at the top of his voice. "Amen, at a venture!"

The stranger proved to be Rev. Josiah Dodge from Nelson County, Kentucky, who was on a visit to his brother, Dr. Israel Dodge of Ste. Genevieve and the father of Henry S. Dodge, late governor and now United-States senator of Wisconsin. Hearing of these religious people being entirely destitute of ministerial instruction, he had arrived opportunely to preach to them. Mr. Dodge spent some time in the settlement, preached frequently, and in February the ice was cut in Fountain Creek and he baptized James Lemen, Sr., and Catherine, his wife, John Gibbons and Isaac Enochs, who were the first persons ever baptized in this Territory.

During the next two years the people remained without preachers; but both Baptists and Methodists, without organized societies, united in holding prayer-meetings, in which, as formerly, the Scriptures and sermon-books were read, prayers offered, and hymns sung in praise to God.

In the spring of 1796, Elder David Badgley from Hardy County, Virginia, made a visit to this country He arrived in the New-Design settlement on May 4, and preached day and night until the 30th, during which time he baptized fifteen persons on a profession of faith in Christ. Baptist immigrants had come from Kentucky since the visit of Mr. Dodge, among whom was Joseph Chance, who had been set apart as a lay-elder in Kentucky. He and Mr Badgley organized the first Baptist church in the country, of twenty-eight members, which was called New Design. This church, with various fluctuations, continued until 1821, when, having been reduced by removals, deaths, and the formation of other churches, it became extinct and the remaining members joined Fountain-Creek church in the same vicinity

Rev. David Badgley returned to Virginia and in the spring of 1797, removed his family to Illinois and took the pastoral charge of this church A revival of religion followed and in April, 1798, Badgley and Chance formed another church of fifteen members in the American Bottom, a few miles above Harrisonville

In 1796, the late Rev Hosea Riggs, then an exhorter in the Methodist-Episcopal church, came to Illinois and settled in the American Bottom near Chaffin's old place. The class formed by Rev. Joseph Lillard had been dissolved or ceased to hold regular meetings, and Mr. Riggs gathered together the old members, the Ogles, Casterline, William Murray, and others, and formed the class regularly at Mr Ogle's in the bottom, Monroe County. Subsequently, he formed another class in Goshen Settlement. Both of these subsequently ceased as social organizations and the members who maintained a Christian character were merged in other classes.

Mr Riggs was born in Western Virginia, April 4, 1760 He was a soldier in the Revolutionary war, and when twenty-two years of age, enlisted in the army of Christ and joined the Methodist church He soon became an exhorter and proved a diligent and faithful soldier. In 1803, he went to Kentucky to attend the Western Conference and to solicit a preacher for Illinois, and the conference appointed Rev. Benjamin Young to form a circuit Mr. Riggs was subsequently ordained and for a long series of years maintained a respectable character and standing as a local preacher He removed to St Clair County at an early period, settled two miles east of Belleville, and died October 29, 1841, aged eighty-one years, at that time the oldest man in the county.

In 1804, Benjamin Young came to Illinois as a missionary preacher and was the first Methodist preacher who rode circuit here under direction of the conference.

The Western Conference, as it was called, was the only annual conference in the Methodist organization in the Mississippi Valley, and in 1805, contained four districts, Holton, Cumberland, Kentucky, and Ohio, and 11,877 members in society. At that period there were a number of respectable men, possessing more than ordinary intelligence, in the Illinois country who openly professed to disbelieve the sacred truths of revealed religion. At one period an effort was made to organize an association and adopt a code of morality in which nothing was to be introduced from that antiquated and superstitious book called the Bible. Tradition says the organization was defeated by the unlucky mistake of the committee unwittingly introducing the moral principles of the Scriptures, which a waggish member exposed. It is a lamentable fact that some of the fraternity bewildered the mind of the unfortunate preacher by their wild speculations and he was caught in the snare of scepticism. This was regarded, of course, as a splendid triumph and produced a disastrous effect on some others, especially untrained minds.

Young was expelled from the conference and for a number of years was in darkness and doubt and sustained sore trials. After years of wandering and unbelief, afflicted in body and more wretched in mind, he became a penitent, sought an interest in the prayers of the preachers, cast himself on the mercy of God in Christ and died in peace.

Dr. Joseph Oglesby was the preacher on this circuit in 1805. He was a man of vigorous mind, good preaching talents, and a successful laborer. He is still living in Indiana.

Rev. Charles R. Matheny* followed him in 1806, who married a daughter of Capt. Joseph Oglesby and settled in the county of St. Clair. He turned his attention to law and politics, but retained his ministerial and Christian profession; was appointed clerk of the county of Sangamon, settled in Springfield, where he sustained an honorable and upright character as

---

* Rev. Charles R. Matheny was a member of Capt. James B. Moore's company of "rangers" during the months of July and August, 1812. He was afterward a member of the territorial legislature, representing St. Clair County in the lower house of the third and last assemblies, in 1816-8, and was also a member from the same county in the second general assembly in 1820-2. "In 1817, the territory of Illinois was divided into three circuits, and in the first circuit, including the counties of St. Clair and Randolph, presided over by Jesse B. Thomas as judge, Charles R. Matheny was prosecuting-attorney. In this capacity he attended the first circuit-court held in Monroe County, at Harrisonville, July 21, 1817. He was succeeded by Daniel Pope Cook, beginning at the fall term, 1819; the latter being the first prosecuting-attorney under the new State organization."

Removing to Sangamon County on its organization, in 1821, he became its first county clerk, a position he held uninterruptedly until his death, Oct. 10, 1839. He was also circuit clerk until 1835. His wife survived him many years, dying at a ripe old age in 1858. Mr. Matheny was succeeded in the county clerk's office by his

a citizen and a faithful and devout Christian, and died a few years since, beloved and revered by all his acquaintance.

Among the useful men and successful pioneer preachers of Illinois we must not overlook Rev. John Clark. He was by birth a Scotchman, was well educated, followed the seas in early life, and was pressed on board a British man-of-war, which lay off Charleston harbor in 1781. Being a high-toned liberty man, he was so opposed to being compelled to fight the Americans that, at the risk of his life, he swam ashore and escaped with one of his comrades and made his way into the country, where he taught a school. For about one year he was under much distress on account of his sins and guilt, without anyone to give him instruction. At last he was delivered from this state of mind and obtained peace in believing.

An old Scotch divine, on being asked for the "best evidence of a gracious state," promptly replied, "forty years close walk with God." Our venerable friend bore this testimony, unquestioned by every class of persons who knew him, for fifty years. At that period he was on Broad River and joined a Methodist class under the preaching of John Major and Thos. Humphries, who first introduced Methodism into that part of South Carolina. After this he made a voyage to his native country, saw a beloved sister who was living, and received a little legacy left by his pious mother with her dying benediction. It was his wages while on the seas, which he had given orders to be sent

second son, Noah W., who held the position continuously for thirty-four years, retiring in 1873 to accept the presidency of the First National Bank of Springfield, Ill., a position he held until his death, April 30, 1877. His eldest son, Dr. L. D Matheny, a physician of bright promise, died before his father, in 1837. The third son, Hon. James H. Matheny, is at the present time county judge of Sangamon County, having been elected for three successive terms, by an almost unanimous vote. Judge Matheny was a member of the constitutional convention of 1847, and a colleague of Ninian W. Edwards and Stephen T. Logan; he was also lieut.-colonel of the 130th Illinois Infantry during the war of the Rebellion. The fourth son, Charles W. Matheny, was engaged in mercantile business for many years in Springfield, and was also president of the First National Bank of that city at the time of his death, April 16, 1879. The youngest son, E. Cook Matheny, is connected with the U S. revenue department as a gauger, a position he has acceptably filled for many years. The family, in its numerous descendants from Mr Matheny's five sons and three married daughters, is one which has maintained the reputation of their lamented progenitor, socially and morally as well as politically —J H G.

her. He visited London, heard Rev John Wesley preach, became more confirmed in his peculiar doctrines, returned to South Carolina and entered the ministry of the Methodist-Episcopal church, was received on trial in 1791, and commenced traveling the circuit. In two years he was admitted in full connection and ordained to that order of their ministry called deacon.

Being conscientiously opposed to slavery and not satisfied with the government of the Methodist-Episcopal church, he withdrew from the traveling connection in an orderly manner in 1796, traveled on foot to Kentucky, and there for several months made it his home with Elder Jolliff,* a Baptist preacher

---

* Elder Abner Jolliff, who lived and died in Barren Co., Ky., was born in Greenbrier Co., Va., and came of an old English family of Norman descent, who settled in Virginia in the seventeenth century, his four sons, Abner, Richard, James, and Elijah, and three daughters, Rachel, Elizabeth, and Jehoida, emigrated to Illinois in early days and settled in Jefferson, Clinton, Marion, and Washington counties, where they now have a large number of descendants.

Abner, the oldest son, in 1824, settled about three miles north of the present town of Richview, Washington Co; raised a large family, nearly all now dead; his son, Richard, was somewhat noted as a Baptist preacher of promise, and died young.

Richard, the second son, settled the same year near by his brother, both being on the old Vincennes trace; raised a large family, and his son Jacob, born on the claim the first year of the sojourn of the family in this State, yet owns and occupies the old homestead, one of the finest farms in Southern Illinois. Elizabeth, his oldest daughter, married an Englishman named Edward Russell; their sons, Thomas and J. K. Russell, are well-known citizens of Washington County. Martha, his second daughter, married Reece Williams, and raised a large family, and surviving her husband, now lives in Texas with her children. James E., the oldest son, lives near Fort Scott, and was a soldier in the Mexican war in Capt. Coffee's company of Col. Bissell's regiment (2d) Ill. Vols. Aaron, the second son, lived and died near the old home farm in Washington Co., was a soldier in Co. E, 14th Reg't U.-S Inf'y, during the Mexican war. His daughter, Mrs. T. B. Afflock, resides in Richview. Abner, the third son, was drowned when a young man, in crossing Grand-Point Creek when the stream was in a swollen condition. Richard, the fourth son, married Elizabeth Taylor, daughter of Press Taylor, a well-known pioneer of Washington Co., was a soldier in the war of the Rebellion in Co. B, 62d Ill. Infantry, and died at Pine Bluff, Ark, August 2, 1864. Jacob, the fifth son, the youngest and only surviving member of his father's large family, was born Feb. 5, 1825, on the farm he now lives on and owns, one mile south of Irvington, Washington Co., at the crossing of the Illinois-Central Railroad over the old Vincennes and Kaskaskia "trace", married Elizabeth Willard, and has a family of four sons and one daughter, who have all survived their mother.

Col James, the third son, settled about 1828 on Crooked Creek, Clinton Co, a few miles s.-w. of the present city of Centralia, and built a water-mill, about 1830,

and father to Col. James Jolliff of Marion County, Illinois. His peregrinations were made on foot—the mode in which he traveled his circuits in South Carolina—and in this way he arrived in Illinois in 1797. Here he preached with great acceptance on that stream near the site of Sherwood's horse-mill, erected in 1817, was a Virginia soldier in the war of 1812, and with his brother-in-law, James Rhea, served with Perry on Lake Erie, being among the contingent of one hundred and fifty men furnished by Gen. Harrison to Com. Perry to complete the crews in his fleet, and were both afterward engaged in the battle of the Thames, Sept 17, 1813, where the celebrated Indian chief, Tecumseh, was killed. They were both celebrated Indian fighters in the early days of the Northwest. Col. Jolliff was twice married and left numerous descendants. His oldest son was Jackson Jolliff. Reuben W. Jolliff, his second son, was captain of Co. G, 111th Ill. Inf'y, in the war of the Rebellion, his younger brother, Samuel A., being second lieutenant of the same company, who, with his brother Abner, are now living in Patoka, Marion Co. Col. Jolliff's daughter, Elizabeth, married E. Orvis, and lives near the old Jolliff mill in Clinton Co., where they have raised a numerous family. Another son, Elijah, served in Co. B, 62d Ill. Vol. Inf'y, in the Rebellion, and died at Pine Bluff, Ark., July 28, 1864.

Elijah, fourth son, settled in Jefferson Co. in the spring of 1825, had previously married in Kentucky and had several children, was accidentally killed, Christmas, 1832, at the home of in Jefferson Co. and by his nephew, Capt. James Rhea—a tow wad from a Christmas gun severing the femoral artery. Of his sons, Randall and William, and his daughter Elizabeth, married to James Willard, live in Oregon Co., Mo. Elijah Jolliff, his third son, lives near Irvington, Washington Co.

Rachel, the oldest daughter, born in Greenbrier Co., Va., Oct. 16, 1783, married Nov 20, 1801, James Rhea, born in the same county, June 3, 1780, moved to Barren Co., Ky., had ten children, then moved to Jefferson Co., Ill., to the old Rhea place, four miles northeast of Richview, in 1824, where their youngest child, Thos F., was born, July 27, in 1827, Jas. Rhea and most of his family moved to Island-Grove township in Sangamon Co., where he died in 1843, his widow in 1851. Of their children the oldest was Elizabeth, born in 1802, in Barren Co., Ky., and married there to George May, emigrated from thence with their parents first to Jefferson Co., then to Sangamon, moved afterward to Mason Co., where she died, her husband and children then moved to Gentry Co., Mo. The oldest son was James, who was born Aug. 27, 1804, married in Jefferson Co., Ill., in 1826, Susan Mattox, was a soldier in Capt. Bowman's company in the Black-Hawk war; a captain of militia in 1832-3, after killing his uncle accidentally in 1832, moved near Little Rock, Ark., in the fall of 1834, and died there in 1840, leaving a widow and three children. William, the second son, born March 10, 1807, married Dec. 11, 1828, Susan Foutch, in Sangamon Co., had twelve children, nine of whom lived to maturity, and died Feb. 8, 1860, his widow lives near New Berlin, Ill. Richard, the third son, born Jan. 14, 1809, married to Eliza Rhea and had three children, when he died, his widow married William Etheridge, and moved to Iowa. Jehoida, born Oct 11, 1813, married in Sangamon Co., John Foutch, in 1827, and had four children, and died about fifty years ago. Rachel died at the age of ten. John, born July 14, 1817, married Nov. 14, 1839, Julia A. Stark, born June 21, 1823, in Rutland, Vt., they had seven children, and with their children and descendants, live among various classes of the people in the settlements about New Design and the American Bottom; formed one or more classes and taught the children and young men in science and literature. Of his first pupils, several are yet living and hold

near New Berlin, Sangamon Co. Mahala, born April 25, 1820; married in Sangamon Co., Joseph Pulsifer; had twin sons, Nevo and Nevi, who are married and live in Gentry Co., Mo.; their mother died soon after their birth, and their father disappeared, it is thought was murdered for money while on a business trip to St. Louis. Mary A., born Oct. 27, 1822, died April 28, 1851; married E. R. Alsbury; had one child, Lucinda, who married James Shuff. Thomas F. Rhea, the youngest son, born in Jefferson Co.; married Oct. 3, 1844, Lucinda Wilcox; has five children living, all daughters, is a stock-raiser and dealer at New Berlin, Sangamon Co.

Elizabeth, second daughter, is a most noted pioneer matron of Southern Illinois; was born in Greenbrier Co., Va., about 1803, and is now over eighty years of age; was married in Virginia to John Faulkner, a member of the celebrated family of that ilk which has furnished to Virginia many able men, one of whom was governor of that State; shortly after their marriage, they removed to Kentucky and afterward to Illinois, settling near her brothers, Abner and Richard, in 1830, when Mr. Faulkner soon afterward erected a horse-mill, which furnished the settlers in that region their bread for many a year. This couple raised a numerous and historic family, and the husband and father died in 1853. Mrs. Faulkner still lives with her son Abner on her old homestead, where her family of thirteen were, some of them, born and all raised to maturity. John, the oldest son, was a Baptist preacher, and died young. Katharine, the oldest daughter, married Matthew Pate, and died many years ago, her son, John Pate of Jefferson Co., is a well-known lawyer, who formerly resided at Richview. Richard, the second son, died some years before the war, leaving a family. Aaron also reared a family on Grand Point, and died some years ago. Elizabeth married L. B. Baldwin, who live at Irvington and have raised a large and interesting family, among whom is R. D. Baldwin, a successful farmer of Irvington township. Gilbert, the fourth son, was a soldier in Capt. Coffee's Co. A, Col. Bissell's regiment (2d Ill.), in the Mexican war, and now lives near the old homestead in Washington Co. Margaret married Meg. Taylor and lives in Kansas. James, the fifth son, died before the late war, although married, he left no descendants, was of large stature, as were all of the Faulkner and Jolliff families. Abner, the sixth son, was a soldier in Co. B, 62d Ill. Vol. Inf'y, and lives with his family at the old homestead, a mile south of Irvington, on the Illinois-Central Railroad, and cares for his aged mother. Alexander, the seventh son, who was first-sergeant in Co. B, 62d Ill. Vol. Inf'y, in the war of the Rebellion, lives near and has a wife and several children. Charles J., the youngest son, was also a soldier in the war of the Rebellion, in Co. F of the 44th Ill. Inf'y, and died since the war. Angeline married Clark W. Mitchell, a soldier in Co. B, 62d Ill. Inf'y, and with her husband lives near Irvington. Caroline, the youngest daughter, married Jackson Trout, and died a few years since in Irvington, where her husband still resides.

Jehoida, the youngest daughter, married Enoch Holsclaw in Kentucky, and afterward removed to Illinois, settling near Mt. Vernon in Jefferson Co., from whence they again removed to Clinton Co., near the town of Central City, where both died many years ago, leaving numerous descendants.—J. H. G.

the memory of Father Clark, as he was familiarly called, as precious. Among those who are indebted to him for their education are those venerable men of this county: Robert Lemen, Esq., once marshal under the territorial government, and Rev Joseph and James Lemen.

At that period, Missouri, called Upper Louisiana, was under the dominion of Spain and of course the Roman-Catholic religion only was sustained and tolerated by law But the commandants and other officers, being disposed to encourage emigration from the United States to that country, permitted Protestants, after a vague and general examination, as a mere matter of form, to settle in that country, and large numbers had expatriated themselves to obtain grants of land. It is but just to the memories of these people to state that a presentiment existed in their minds that the country would come under the American government and they, or at least their children, would enjoy equal rights.

Father Clark was the first preacher of the gospel to cross the Mississippi and to preach to the American people there. This was in 1798 His excursions were regular and frequent, during which he would spend from two to three weeks. There were three settlements which he visited: one near the Spanish Pond, north of St Louis, one near Owen's Station, now Bridgeton, and the other on Feef's Creek He was a man of singular simplicity of manners, unaffected piety, and wholly disinterested, and took no pains to conceal his visits or his object in the Spanish country. The late Zenoe Trudeau, commandant at St. Louis, knew his character, his habits, and his purpose in crossing the river. He was friendly to the American residents and not disposed to molest them; but he must make a show of enforcing the laws and about the time Clark's appointments were finished, he would send a threatening message into the country that Mr. Clark must leave the Spanish territory or he would put him in the *calabozo*—the prison No personal molestation was ever offered

At a subsequent period, when the laws of the United States were extended there and settlements greatly enlarged, he made his home on that side of the river, but continued his visits to Illinois during his life, which terminated in 1833, at the age of seventy-five years. Early in the present century, he became a Baptist and subsequently was connected with that class who were termed, from their opposition to slavery, "Friends to Humanity"

Among the early pioneers of Methodism in this territory, the late Rev Jesse Walker deserves a conspicuous place. His birthplace was the vicinity of Petersburg, Va., but his youth was spent in North Carolina, where he was accustomed to labor on a farm. This was in a settlement of wealth, aristocratic and irreligious people, where the Sabbath was spent in amusement and excursions to other settlements. It was while on such an excursion he heard a Methodist preacher, whose pungent exhortations arrested his conscience and went to his heart After some two or three, weeks of agonizing distress, he obtained relief and rejoiced in the forgiveness of his sins He immediately joined a Methodist class, became an efficient member, then a leader and exhorter, and soon after a laborious and successful local preacher He was received on trial by the Western Conference, held at Cumberland, Tennessee, in October, 1802, ordained deacon and performed circuit duties on the borders of that State and Kentucky four years.

He was emphatically a *pioneer*, continually advancing into new settlements that were unprovided with gospel administrations; for in 1806, by his own request, he was sent to Illinois, and the same year Rev. John Travis was sent to Upper Louisiana, as Missouri was then called, being the first circuit preacher sent into that field by the Conference The next year Mr Walker returned two hundred and twenty members from Illinois, including a society of twenty on Coldwater in St Louis County This was a gain of eighty in Illinois in one year under his labors.

It was in the summer of 1807 that the late Bishop McKendree, whose name has been perpetuated in the Methodist college at Lebanon, made his first visit to this territory, and as presiding-elder, with Mr. Walker for an assistant in preaching, held two camp-meetings: one in Goshen Settlement, near Edwardsville, and the other at Shiloh, six miles northeast from Belleville, where a log-house was erected for a chapel. This was the first meeting-house and these were the first camp-meetings in Illinois

From 1813, Rev. Jesse Walker was presiding-elder in the Illinois district and continued in that department in this territory until near the period of the close of this history. His residence was in Alexander's Settlement, as then called, seven miles northeast from Belleville.

Of the Methodist pioneer preachers in the traveling connection, before the organization of the State government, who followed successively on the circuit, or who were local preachers, our information is too imperfect to follow the line accurately. Rev. John Scripps, now living in Illinois, then a young preacher, accompanied Mr. Walker on his round as presiding-elder in 1814.

Rev Jacob Whiteside of this county commenced the ministry about that time, and Rev. Josiah Patterson was also a faithful laborer in the settlements near the Ohio River. Rev. J. Nowlen is another who began to preach about that time.

In 1815, there were four circuits in Illinois, called Illinois, Okaw, Massac, and Wabash. Indiana, west of a meridian line at Madison, and Illinois made one district, over which Rev. Jesse Walker traveled as presiding-elder

Rev Abraham Amos came to Illinois Territory at an early period, either in the character of a circuit or a local preacher. He was a circuit preacher on the Mad-River circuit, Ohio, then a new one, in 1805. He was appointed a member of the legislative council of Illinois Territory, and while sustaining that office, died, April 11, 1818, much respected and universally regretted as a preacher, a Christian, and a citizen

In 1816, Rev. John Dew arrived in Illinois as the traveling companion of Bishop McKendree and soon proved himself to be an intelligent and successful preacher. The General Conference of the Methodist-Episcopal church had divided the Western Conference into two Tennessee and Ohio. Tennessee Conference included Arkansas, Missouri, Illinois, and Indiana to the meridian of Madison.

This year, 1816, the General Conference had set off all this field into another conference, called Missouri, and its first session was held at Shiloh, commencing September 23 At this meeting Rev. Samuel H. Thompson appeared for the first time. He had traveled a circuit in Missouri for the preceding year.

Mr. Thompson was born in Westmoreland County, Pa.; professed religion and joined the Methodists in Kentucky in 1807; became a preacher and entered the traveling connection in 1809. He was married in February, 1816, and the next autumn, settled at Union Grove, south of Lebanon. Mr. Thompson became a prominent and useful man in the ministry.

Among the local preachers, Rev Josiah Randle of Edwardsville was among the prominent men in the Methodist ranks in early times, and for many years clerk of Madison County. As the first Baptist preacher who settled in the country we have already mentioned David Badgley, who, with Joseph Chance, constituted the first church in the territory. Mr Badgley was born in New Jersey in 1749; removed with his parents to Virginia in 1768; made a profession of religion, and was baptized by Elder William Marshall in 1795, and a few years after, became a preacher He was ordained in 1795. Mr. Badgley aided in forming a number of churches and died December 16, 1824, at the advanced age of seventy-six. His descendants and connections are numerous in this county, and his youngest son is now one of the justices of the county-court.

Elder' John K. Simpson was one of the pioneer Baptist preachers in Illinois. He was a native of England and born near London, October 2, 1759. He was brought up an Episcopalian; married Ann Rider; removed to America and reached Vincennes in 1788; came to Kaskaskia in 1789, and next year settled near Bellefontaine. He was a religious man and joined the Methodist class under Mr. Lillard; but under the preaching of Elder David Badgley, he became a Baptist and was one of the fifteen baptized previous to the constitution of the church. He took an active part in church-meetings and social worship; commenced preaching and was ordained, probably, about 1803. Some may have deemed him too rigid and not sufficiently forbearing and tender of the imperfections of his brethren, for his name occurs frequently on the old book of records in connection with cases of discipline.

His decease, January 11, 1806, was singular For some time previous, he told his brethren and friends he should die soon and even named the day. A little time before his death, he visited and preached to Richland church and bid his brethren farewell, assuring them they would see him no more on earth. He complained of no illness, but was serious and devotional. A short time after, on Sabbath morning, he rode ten miles from his residence to the house of Judge Bond in the American Bottom, preached with much power and effect from Rom viii, 14, and died the same evening while sitting in his chair. The last words he uttered were: "Lord Jesus, thou hast promised to save me; come and receive my spirit." He was the father of Elder Gideon Simpson of this [St Clair] county.

Elder Joseph Chance, already mentioned, was born in the State of Delaware in 1765 His father died when he was a small boy, his mother married John Gibbons and moved to North Carolina, where young Chance was raised without much opportunity for education He married for his first wife Jemima Morris and moved to Kentucky, where he professed religion, was baptized, and commenced exhorting. In 1794, he removed his family to Illinois and became connected with the New-Design church. He afterward settled in Horse Prairie, where he preached to a little society; removed and settled east of Silver Creek, where a small church was organized in 1807

He made an excursion to Indiana and while there, was ordained Mr. Chance was not a man of great talents, but he was faithful in the improvement of the gifts bestowed upon him; devoted much time in preaching and visiting destitute settlements; raised a large family; and while on a preaching tour, died, in Washington County, Illinois, April 20, 1840, aged seventy-five years.

Among the good men and ministers in the Baptist ranks, we must not omit Elder William Jones, who came to the territory and settled near Rattan's Prairie, east of Alton, in 1806. He was born in North Carolina, but professed religion and entered the ministry in East Tennessee, and in company with John Finlay, another pioneer, came to this region to do good. Before the war, he removed to Shoal Creek, but the Indians becoming troublesome, he returned to Madison County. He was a preacher of moderate abilities and was moral, grave, peaceable, and pious in his habits. He represented Madison County in the legislature one term and died at his residence, in the hope of eternal life, January 2, 1845, aged seventy-three years.

The name of James Lemen, Sr., has been mentioned among the early pioneers of Illinois. He was born in Berkeley County, Virginia, in the autumn of 1760. His grandfather was an emigrant from the north of Ireland His father belonged to the Church of England, a branch of which existed by law in Virginia before the Revolutionary war, and died when James was a year old. His mother married again and he was raised by a strict Presbyterian In 1777, he entered the army under Washington; went north; was in the action of White Plains, and continued in service two years, when he was discharged and returned to Virginia He then went to the vicinity of Wheeling, where he resided for a time and married Catharine Ogle, daughter of Capt Joseph Ogle, already noticed

There are some amusing traditions among their descendants, relative to their early acquaintance. Both were young, moral persons, religiously educated, and early and simultaneously became impressed they were destined for each other. It seems this mutual attachment was strong, steady, and lasted thro life. Not a jar in feelings or an unpleasant word ever occurred between them

James Lemen was a rigidly honest, humane, kind-hearted, and benevolent man, independent in judgment, very firm and conscientious in what he believed right, and exhibited much decision of character He was opposed to war as an aggressive measure, not combative or cruel, but would fight like a hero when impelled by a sense of duty in defending the frontiers from Indian depredations. He followed his father-in-law to the Illinois country in the spring of 1785, by descending the Ohio River in a flat-boat. The second night the river fell while they were tied to the shore, and his boat lodged on a stump, careened and sunk, by which accident he lost his provisions, chattels, etc. His oldest son, Robert, a boy of three years old, floated on the bed on which he lay, which his father caught by the corner and saved his life Tho left destitute of provisions and other necessaries, James Lemen was not the man to be discouraged. He had energy and perseverance, and he got to the mouth of the Ohio and from thence up the Mississippi to Kaskaskia, where he arrived July 10, 1786.

The Indians caused frequent alarms, provisions and all other necessaries of living were scarce. He subsequently settled at New Design, on the old hill-trace from St. Louis to Kaskaskia, and his house became the half-way stopping-place for many years, and none were turned away. He had been subject to religious impressions from his childhood, but was not clear in his mind to make a profession of religion until James Smith arrived and preached to the people. He was generous and hospitable, would divide corn with the destitute, observed the Sabbath strictly, kept perfect order in his family, and yet was never harsh or severe with his children.

He was an acting justice-of-the-peace for many years under the territorial government and for a time one of the judges of the county-court. He took an active part in the lead of religious meetings many years before he was licensed to preach He was an opponent to slavery both from principle and policy and came to this territory to live in a free country. From some strong expressions he made on this subject while preaching at Richland Church in 1809, which ought to have been passed without notice, Larkin Rutherford, one of the members, took offence and brought a complaint into the church and the consequence was an illustration of the Scriptures: "Behold how great a matter a little fire kindleth." The little church became divided; the association of churches also divided, and the issue was three parties of Baptists, who existed for ten years and two parties much longer. The association was formed in 1807, of the five following churches, to wit: New Design, Mississippi Bottom, Richland, Wood River, and Silver Creek. There were three ordained preachers and sixty-two members in these churches. At the division of 1809, there were ten churches, of which three were in Missouri, eight ordained preachers, two in Missouri, four licentiates, and four hundred communicants of the three parties of Baptists, including six churches on the eastern and southeastern parts of the territory.

Presbyterians.—At the date of the constitution in 1818, there was no Presbyterian minister residing in the State, nor had there been a church organized in this part of the State. One or two small churches had been constituted in the southeastern part of the State under the jurisdiction of the Presbytery of West, now Middle, Tennessee. Two Presbyterian missionaries from the general assembly of the Presbyterian church had visited the territory and preached at Kaskaskia, Shawneetown, and other settlements.

In 1814, Rev Messrs Samuel J Miles and Daniel Smith, Congregationalists from New England, performed an exploring mission thro the Southwestern States and territories, with a twofold object: providing for the distribution of the Scriptures to the destitute and future missionary labors. They were at St Louis November 7, at Kaskaskia on the 12th, and Shawneetown after New-Year, on their way down the Ohio and Mississippi to New Orleans.

A subscription was started to form a Bible society at New Design and Kaskaskia, to which the names of James Lemen, Sr, James Lemen, Jr., Gov. Edwards, Nathaniel Pope, and many other gentlemen then living in Illinois were appended, with subscriptions of five dollars and under for the object. Nearly one hundred dollars were subscribed; but it appears they never organized or paid their subscriptions. At that period, Bibles and school-books were very scarce and not to be obtained without sending to the Atlantic cities. Another similar but abortive effort to form a Bible society was made at Shawneetown in 1816, a constitution adopted and directors chosen, which failed from lack of a little further effort

The late John Messinger, who was a philanthropist as well as mathematician, tho never a member of any church, obtained subscribers for the quarto family Bibles, published by Matthew Carey of Philadelphia in 1814, and circulated copies in many families in St. Clair County. Mr Messinger taught many young men the theory and practice of surveying and he frequently taught an evening-school for young and old, and it is no disparagement to some gentlemen, who have since been distinguished in the State, at the bar, and in the pulpit, to have it known that they received the ground-work of their education, after they had families, from Mr. Messinger.

There was a small colony of Tunkers and Dunkers, who settled in Union County and had a preacher of their own in early times

I will close this protracted sketch by a biief description of the manners and customs of the American pioneers I have noticed. They were rough in personal appearance and unrefined, yet kind, social, and generous. They were hunters and stock-growers, and confined their agricultural operations chiefly to corn and a small amount of wheat. They were brave, prompt, and decided in war, yet liberal and magnanimous to a subdued foe They showed great energy and a just spirit of enterprise in removing from five to fifteen hundred miles into a wilderness country and pioneering out the way for the future prosperity of their descendants They were hospitable, generous, and ready to share with their neighbors or newly-arrived strangers their last loaf They were guided by Providence, preserved amidst dangers, sickness, and savage assaults, and thus became the pioneers of civilization, the founders of a free government, and the extension of pure Christianity. They turned the wilderness into a fruitful field and prepared the country to sustain a more dense population and to increase in wealth and prosperity.

Their habits and manners were plain, simple, and unostentatious Their dwellings were log-cabins of the rudest and most simple structure Their furniture and utensils and dress were the most simple and economical possible; for such only could be obtained. For clothing, dressed deer-skins were extensively used for hunting-shirts, pants, leggins, and moccasons, and the red skin of the prairie-wolf or fox was a substitute for the hat or cap Strips of buffalo-hide were used for ropes and traces and the dressed skins of the buffalo, bear, and elk furnished the principal covering of their beds at night. Wooden vessels, either dug out or coopered, and called noggins, were in common use for bowls, out of which each member of the family ate mush and milk for supper A gourd formed the drinking-cup. Every hunter (and all the men were hunters) carried his knife in his girdle, while not unfrequently the rest of the family had but one or two between them If a family chanced to have a few pewter dishes and spoons, knives and forks, tin-cups and platters, it was in advance of the neighbors Corn was beaten for bread in the mortar, ground on a grater, or in a hand-mill.

From the cession of the country by Virginia to the continental congress in 1784, to the organization of the county of St. Clair by the government of the Northwest Territory in 1790, there was in fact no civil government in existence in the Illinois country, yet the people were a law unto themselves. Their morals were pure and simple, the grosser vices were rare, and there was very little use for the administration of either civil or criminal law. Ardent spirits, that outrage upon morals, social order, and religion, had been introduced into the country but in small quantities before the commencement of the present century. Theft and other crimes against the peace of society were rare and fraud and dishonest dealings seldom practised.

In the French villages, as in most Catholic countries, the Sabbath was a day of hilarity and pleasure. The Catholic population, being principally French, attended mass in the morning and practised their devotions in the church, and in the afternoon, assembled in parties at private houses for social and merry intercourse. Cards, dances, and various sports made up the pastime. The French people in Illinois in those times were not intemperate in eating or drinking on such occasions. The wealthier classes used, moderately, light-red wines, especially claret, while the poorer classes, in convivial parties, drank tafia and a liquor called *noyau*. I have often heard the old French settlers deplore the habits of intoxication and other vices, which, as they fancied, were introduced by the immigration that came after 1800. But old men always imagine the morals of the people grow worse and fraud and dishonesty increase as they advance in life.

CHAPTER VIII.

Illinois under the Government of Indiana Territory.

THE Northwest Territory being so large—extending from the shores of the Mississippi to the western line of Pennsylvania, and from the Ohio to the lakes and the northern limits of the United States—the people became uneasy and restless in their situation., One other consideration was that Gen. St. Clair, the governor of the territory, was very unpopular. The whole community, for various and for different reasons, was anxious for a change in the government.

The Northwest Territory was divided May 7, 1800, by act of congress and the western section was called Indiana Territory The eastern boundary of Indiana was a line beginning on the Ohio, opposite the mouth of Kentucky River; thence to Fort Recovery, and thence to the northern limits of the United States Indiana Territory included the Illinois country.

William Henry Harrison was appointed by the general government the governor of the territory He was born twenty-five miles from Richmond, Va, February 9, 1773. His father, Benjamin Harrison, was the governor of Virginia and acted a great and noble part in the Revolution.

Young Harrison was educated at Hampden Sydney College and left it at the age of seventeen. He was placed, by his kind father, the governor of Virginia, at the medical college in Philadelphia in 1790; but remained there not a long time. The defeat of Gen. Harmar in the West and the excitement to sustain the honor of the stars and stripes had reached the young and patriotic heart of Harrison in Philadelphia. The eloquent entreaties of his guardian and friend, the celebrated Robert Morris of that city, had no effect to retain him to the study of medicine The mortar and pestle were exchanged for the sweet music of the drum and fife and he became a soldier in the war against the Northwestern Indians. He urged his pretentions on President Washington so strong that he was appointed an ensign in the army in 1791, when he was only eighteen years old He repaired to the West, but too late to participate in the disastrous defeat of St Clair, November 4, 1791. He continued in the army and was aid-de-camp to Gen. Wayne. He was in all the active military operations for several years previous to the celebrated battle of Gen. Wayne against the Indians, in August, 1794 In this engagement, young Harrison was found fighting always in the hottest conflicts.

After the treaty at Greenville in 1795, Capt. Harrison—as he had been promoted to that office—was left in command at Fort Washington, the site of the present City of Cincinnati, where he married that year the daughter of Judge Symmes He then left the army and turned his attention to civil employment. At twenty-four, he was appointed secretary of the territory under Gov. St Clair. He executed the duties of this office with punctuality and honesty. In 1799, he was elected by the general assembly of the territory to the office of delegate to congress. This office was one of great responsibility and the duties onerous and interesting to all the country northwest of the Ohio River. His first attention was imperiously called to the subject of the public lands.

A heavy emigration commenced to the territory and the public domain at that day could not be sold in less tracts than four thousand acres, except fractions on the rivers. To poor settlers the land-system was a curse rather than a blessing, as it is at this day. Harrison was appointed chairman of the committee on the public lands in the house of representatives and he reported a bill, which passed into a law, authorizing the sale of the public lands in tracts of three hundred and twenty acres This was the smallest tract that could be sold in 1800. The new law required one-fourth paid down and a credit given for the balance of one, two, three, and four years. This was considered at that day a public service which Harrison performed in congress, of the greatest importance to the country.

To contrast the present system of the public lands with that of 1800 and before, is comparing night to day. Now tracts of forty acres may be sold, and before 1800, not less than four thousand could be entered by any settler. The passage of this law rendered Harrison extremely popular. He also obtained the division of the territory and was appointed governor of Indiana, which is narrated above.

Extraordinary duties were imposed on Gov. Harrison. Besides the ordinary duties of a governor of a territory, the additional and important trusts of the general agency of all the Indians and the duty of investigating the ancient land-claims in the territory were also confided to him. More treaties with the Indians were made and more land purchased by him from them than by any other man in America. His various duties, civil and military, required much energy and business habits in the office to enable him to perform them. These extraordinary trusts were executed with much ability and much to the satisfaction of the people and the government. It is truly astonishing, the many, the various, and the important offices which Gen. Harrison held and the duties of them he performed. His military career of itself would fill volumes, and his civil employments were numerous and highly important to the country.

In 1791, when he was eighteen years old, he was first, ensign in the army, then secretary of the Northwest Territory; delegate to congress, governor of Indiana and superintendent of Indian affairs; commissioner to adjust land-titles; major-general in the army; a farmer in the North Bend; in 1824, a senator in congress; minister to Columbia, South America; then the prothonotary of the court of Hamilton County, at Cincinnati, the county-seat; and next, the president of the United States.

No man in America ever filled as many high and responsible offices as Harrison did. He experienced thro life a continual scene of hurried and important events, and nothing in it of monotony. It is the events in a life that makes it important and conspicuous. A monotonous life has but two events in it and those scarcely worthy of notice—the birth and death of the individual. A life of monotony is a species of vegetation.

Harrison was in office for almost half-a-century and at last died in the presidency—the highest station known to man on the globe. The duties of these offices were performed in a new and rising community in the West, where parts of almost all nations, kindreds, and tongues were assembled together, and the duties as varient as the population. Under all these events and circumstances, he acted well his part. These facts demonstrate Harrison to be no ordinary man; but at the same time, he did not possess the highest order of intellect. He was a safe, prudent, and cautious man and one quality he enjoyed in an eminent degree and that was exhibited in all his transactions, public and private—a rigid and positive regard to honesty and integrity. This part of his character was tried in the fiery furnace of party politics and came out, like Daniel did out of the den of lions, unhurt.

In the presidential canvass of 1840, between him and Van Buren, he did not encourage those disgraceful proceedings of hard cider, coons, canoes, etc. He had been in the presidency but a very short time, and died at Washington, D. C., April 4, 1841. His death was truly a great public calamity and as such the community regretted and mourned his decease.

It has always been my opinion that his death was occasioned by the ardent duties of the office and the host of office-seekers hovering around him night and day until death relieved him from the importunities of these vultures for office. The love of God and his country were in his heart the last and his lips gave utterance to these sentiments in the transit from earth to eternity. Almost his whole life was spent in the service of his country and the last efforts he made when death was upon him was in praise of that country.

Harrison possessed an extraordinary energy and activity in business. He was very moral and correct in his habits and all his energies of mind and body were preserved for the service of the country. He possessed in an eminent degree both physical and moral courage; but he did not possess that high order of military talents to command that under almost all circumstances ensures success and victory to the army. He was plain and unostentatious in his manners and never paid much attention to his private financial affairs. He lived and died in moderate circumstances.

Emigration from the States commenced in earnest to flow into Illinois after the division of the territory in 1800. The American and even the French settlements began to extend throughout the western section of Illinois. Peace and plenty prevailed in every section of the country, which, together with its natural advantages, encouraged immigration.

In this year, 1800, the first man, Ephraim Conner, located himself in Goshen, twenty odd miles in advance of the settlements. His settlement was made in the American Bottom, near the bluff some five or six miles southwest from the present town of Edwardsville. Col. Judy purchased Connor out in 1801, lived there more than the third of a century, and died on the same place.

Rev. David Badgley and some others, in 1799, explored the country at present embraced in the county of Madison and called it Goshen. They gave it this name on account of the fertility of the soil and consequent luxuriant growth of the grass and vegetation. It was, in truth, a land of promise, and some years after it was the largest and best settlement in Illinois. Goshen Settlement, so called in ancient times, embraced about all the territory of Madison County and was in its early life, as it always has been, a compact, prosperous, and happy community.

A small impediment to the growth of the settlement was the killing of Dennis and Van Meter by the Indians in 1802. Turkey Foot, an evil-disposed and cruel chief of a band of the Pottawatomie Indians, and his party, returning home from Cahokia to their towns toward Chicago, met Dennis and Van Meter at the foot of the Mississippi Bluff, about five miles southwest of the present town of Edwardsville. The country contained at that day very few inhabitants above Cahokia, and Turkey Foot, seeing the Americans extending their settlements toward his country, caught fire at the spectacle and killed these two men. These Indians may have been intoxicated, as they were frequently drunk when they were trading in Cahokia. This was not considered war, but a kind of Indian depredation.

The first two white men that settled in the Six-Mile Prairie, in the present county of Madison, were Patrick Hanniberry and Wiggins. The latter had a family, but Hanniberry was a single man. They resided together in 1801, near the present residence of William Atkins. This settlement was called the Six-Mile Prairie, because it was six miles above St. Louis, in Upper Louisiana. The immigrants to the country were mostly from the Western and Southern States Very few Eastern people or Yankees settled in Illinois at that day The Ohio River was the main channel on which the hardy pioneers reached the country The old Fort Massac was a depot for immigrants Almost time immemorial, a few families and settlers resided in and adjacent to the fort.

In very ancient times, a military road was opened and marked, each mile on a tree, from Massac to Kaskaskia. The numbers of the miles were cut in ciphers with an iron and painted red. Such I saw them in 1800 This road made a great curve to the north to avoid the swamps and rough country on the sources of Cash River, and also to obtain the prairie country as soon as possible This road was first made by the French when they had the dominion of the country and was called the old Massac road by the Americans. A road also extended from Fort Massac to Cape Girardeau, in the then Spanish country

In olden times, two great crossing-places on the Ohio for the immigrants were at Lusk's and Miles' ferries These pioneers were both most excellent, worthy men; yet they had, as is quite common, a rivalship with their ferries. The ferry of Lusk was opposite the present town of Golconda, Illinois, and that of Miles only six or seven miles above.

It will be recollected that Nathaniel Hull descended the Ohio River in 1780, and landed at a place on the Ohio afterward known as Hull's Landing Miles established his ferry near it. Hull had opened a road from his landing to Kaskaskia This road did not intersect the Massac road, traveling west for eighty miles, altho the two roads were only a few miles apart at any one place from one end to the other. Miles adopted Hull's old trace and improved it. Many wagons and much travel crossed at these rival ferries and proceeeded on the respective roads to Illinois and to the Spanish country.

It must be recollected that the west side of the Mississippi was known as the Spanish country in early times, while the name of Louisiana might be recognized in the books, but not used by the people in common parlance In these times, no four-wheeled vehicles traveled the road from Vincennes to Illinois. This road was used by single horses, pack-horses, and footmen alone. It was a straight, narrow road, mostly traveled by the Indians and their fair sex on horseback, without the civilized invention of side-saddles.

The Indians are somewhat like the Arabs in their migrations They travel together with several families, more or less, according to circumstances They have their summer and winter residences similar to the gentry of large cities, but for different considerations. These natives travel with all their wealth, except at times they *cache* some articles in the earth, as the French call it that is, they hide the article in the ground until they return A family or a caravan of traveling Indians would make a good subject for a painter These moving parties are generally going or returning from their winter hunting-grounds and have with them their wives, children, dogs, horses, and all their assets of every description Each family has its own organization and government. In the evening when they camp, the females do all the work in making the camp, fire, etc., while their lords take their ease in smoking. The whole Indian race of the males is grave, sedate, and lazy Some may go out to hunt while the squaws are working. They generally stop early in the evening to prepare for the night

This traveling with the Indians is a living as much as if they were stationary in their towns. They have nothing changed in their peregrinations, only a very short distance of latitude or longitude, or a little of both, on the surface of the earth. Therefore their migrations may be termed traveling residences. Under this system, they make as much improvement at each camp as they do at their winter hunting-grounds or in their towns. The small children are often tied on the horses' backs to pack-saddles, so they can not fall off; the still younger ones are tied on boards, and while traveling, the boards are suspended by the side of the horse. These boards answer a valuable purpose to the Indians in traveling as well as at home. They are light and nicely made; are longer than the child and some wider. A hoop of strong hickory wood is bent over the face of the papoose and the ends made fast in the plank Holes are pierced in the edges of the board, thro which straps are passed to secure the bed and the child fast to the plank. Blankets and other clothes are placed between the infant and the wood and likewise around the small one; so that it and its bed are safely and securely made fast to the board. The hoop is often covered with a cloth or small piece of a blanket, so that the child is perfectly at its ease and safe from external violence At the end of the board a strap is passed thro a hole and the ends tied together When the squaws are busy, they hang the boards and children up out of the way from a limb of a tree; so the infants are safe while the mothers do the work. Sometimes they lean the board and child against a tree or post for safe-keeping This is better for the child than sleeping in a cradle Children placed on these boards grow straight, which is the reason the Indians are generally more erect than white men

The Indians, in their diet, are not fastidious or tasty. They display no unfriendly feelings to dirt or filth. When they kill a deer or buffalo, the choice parts are the entrails and they labor not much to discharge from this delicacy the inner substance. They throw these entrails on the coals and eat them when they are barely warm They often pack their meat, in their journeys, by running a tug-rope thro each piece, which is cut six or seven inches square, and tying the tug to the saddle, the meat is suspended on the side of the horse, exposed to flies, dirt, etc. In their journeys, the males mostly ride and make the females walk. The manner in which the females are treated in any country is an exact index to the barbarity or civilization of the community

There are no Indian nations so barbarous and ignorant that they have not some notion of a Supreme Being. They all believe in a Great Spirit, "the master of life," as they term it. They, for the most part, believe also in a bad spirit as well as a good one. They perform their devotions to both powers, to court their friendship or to appease their anger. They believe in a future state of existence and, of course, in the immortality of the soul They also believe in rewards for virtue and punishment for crimes committed on earth. Guns and other articles and even at times their horses are buried with the dead to enable them to go to and hunt in the spirit land Their notions are that a wicked man will be placed in a cold, dreary land, where the briars and flint-rocks will tear the flesh from his bones and the game will be within his reach and altho he is starving with hunger, he can not kill anything. A good man will have a fine, warm climate, good hunting, and many wives.

The Indian belief of a future state in a dreary region is somewhat similar to the "*Avernum*" of Virgil, described in his "Sixth Book of the Æneid." Roman intelligence can not reach further on this subject than Indian ignorance. It is prohibited to man, learned or unlearned, to look into futurity.

Religion seems to be a constituent part of every rational being The fundamental principles are recognized by all mankind that there is a great First Cause and that religion and adoration are due that Being from all His creation. Thus far all human beings agree; but when this adoration or religion is reduced to practise, nearly all the world disagree in the details. The variety of religious opinions among mankind arises from our ignorance of the Supreme Being; yet all nations know enough to make themselves happy or miserable, as they may act. There is no mathematical problem more conclusive than that virtue produces happiness while crime causes misery.

A difference of opinion will always exist on this subject among men, and it is the duty of man not to condemn his brother for opinions different from his own. Therefore, I consider, a liberal and charitable toleration of all sects and denominations of religions is the enlightened platform of modern churches, and a departure from it, demonstrates the want of religion and also the want of every virtue that adorns and elevates the human family. It is impiety and blasphemy for a frail man to condemn his brother to perdition because he does not worship the Supreme Being in the same manner as he does.

Toleration, forbearance, and charity are taught in almost every page of the New Testament "Father, forgive them; they know not what they do," should teach the human family a lesson on these virtues that exalt and elevate mankind A religion that is based on proper and liberal principles should be taught, advanced, and urged on frail mortals; not by the sword, but by benevolence and charity and love. The more mankind are advanced in a pure and proper religion, the more elevated and dignified stand will the human family occupy. The more we love, revere, and worship God, the fountain of happiness, the nearer we approach Him and thereby the more happiness we must enjoy. Enlightened religion and virtue are correlatives with happiness. One can not exist without the other An austere, ignorant sectarian can not enjoy the same happiness that a liberal and enlightened believer is blessed with.

Many nations in ancient and some in modern times sacrificed animals to court the favor of the Great Spirit. Blackhawk and his band, in 1832, when they marched up Rock River, immolated a dog every night to appease the wrath of the Great Spirit. The dog was tied to a tree a short distance from the ground, with his nose uniformly pointed in the direction the Indians were marching He was cut open and a small fire was made under him; so his nether end was, in a small degree, burnt. The sight of this sacrifice excited sympathy for both the dog and the Indians. The Indians resort to this when they are overwhelmed with a great national calamity.

The Indians pay considerable attention to the burial of the dead. When a member of the family dies while they are out from the towns, where the common graveyard is, they often cut a trough out of a log; make it light and neat and tie it in the top of a tree, so the corpse in it may remain safe from wolves, etc., until they return. They then carry it to the common burial-ground and inter it with its forefathers. It was a matter of curiosity to see these coffins fastened in the trees when we were ranging on the frontiers in the war of 1812. These poor Indians and most of their customs have passed away and are almost forgotten.

In 1799, four Indians, Shawnees, were loitering about Lusk's ferry on the Ohio, and were in search of a man in that region, to kill. It is supposed that some one at Fort Massac wanted to destroy a man named Duff, who resided on the bank of the river, and hired these Indians to commit the murder. They came to the house of Mr. Lusk and examined him minutely, but did not molest him. He was not their victim. At length, they killed Duff, who resided at the mouth of Trade Water, on the Ohio. They escaped and there the matter ended. It was rather common in these times to employ Indians to commit those crimes.

In 1800, Lusk built a decent house on this shore of the Ohio, where Golconda now stands, to accommodate the travelers. A few years after, Gen. Lacy established on the Ohio another ferry, a short distance from Miles', and some time after, Ford occupied Miles' old ferry. In Ford's day, this ferry and the country adjacent to it, on the west of the Ohio, became notorious for the violation of the peace and order of society.

In 1806, at the place, ten miles from the Ohio, where Potts resided afterward, on the road west of the river, a bloody tragedy was acted. A man by the name of Steagall—the same who assisted to kill one of the Harps in Kentucky—eloped with a young girl and made the above place his residence. Our country at that day was new and almost without inhabitants; so that Steagall supposed that neither law or gospel could reach his crimes, but far otherwise. Two or three of the brothers of the seduced girl and her father followed them from Trade Water, in Kentucky, the residence of the father, and after dark, shot Steagall to death and brought back the deluded girl to her home and family. They found Steagall and the others sitting up under a gallery outside of the cabin, with a lamp burning. The assailing party advanced in silence and secrecy near Steagall and shot him without doing any of the others any injury whatever.

In 1756, Jean Baptiste Saucier, a French officer at Ft. Chartres, and married in that vicinity. After the country was ceded to Great Britain in 1763, he located himself and family in Cahokia, where he died. He had three sons. Jean B., Matthieu, and Francis Saucier, who were popular and conspicuous characters in early times in Illinois. These brothers, while they resided in Cahokia, were employed in various civil and military offices and bore a conspicuous part in the transactions of the country at their day. Jean B. Saucier died in Cahokia, while the other two founded the village of Portage des Sioux in Upper Louisiana. This village is situated on the Mississippi, at a narrow place between that river and the Missouri, where the Indians made a portage between the two rivers, which gave it the name of the Sioux Carrying Place. Both Matthieu and Francis Saucier raised large families at this place. Francis had five educated and accomplished daughters, whose marriages united him to that number of conspicuous families. Cols. Menard, Chouteau, Sr, James and Jesse Morrison, and George Atchison were the sons-in-law of Saucier. The two aged patriarchs (the Sauciers) died in this village.

In 1792, Jean Francis Perry emigrated from France and settled in Illinois. He was a native of the city of Lyons in France and was the descendant of a very respectable and wealthy family of that famous city. His mother was a branch of the French nobility and his father a judge of dignity and high standing in Lyons. Young Perry received a liberal and classic education. He also studied and practised law in France. He was gifted by nature with a strong mind and improved it by the best education the old country could bestow on him, which made him a very superior man. He was forced away from the bright prospects before him, of wealth, honor, and high standing with his countrymen, and left his native land, his father's house and family, for an asylum in America. The French Revolution breaking out, caused him to migrate to the United States. His father decided that his son must retire from the scenes of bloodshed for safety in the new world. He was fitted out with money and came to the United States. He associated with him M. Claudius, a Frenchman, in merchandising and they started from Philadelphia to the West. They passed the new settlement of Gallipolis on the Ohio, but the good-sense of Perry advised him that that settlement was too new and too poor for him. He and partner reached Cahokia with their small store of goods; but soon after settled in Prairie du Pont.

In a few years after they had opened their store, Claudius went to Philadelphia to purchase goods and was killed by being thrown from his horse in the streets of that city. His foot caught in the stirrup and he was dragged and torn to death on the pavements.

Perry purchased the ancient mill-site on Prairie-du-Pont Creek, where the Mission of St Sulspice first erected a mill, long before the cession of the country to Great Britain in 1763. He built on this site a new and profitable mill and occupied the dwelling near it with himself and family. About this time,

1794, he married a young and beautiful creole, a daughter* of Jean B. Saucier, above mentioned This union was prosperous and happy. Altho Perry was a sound and well-read lawyer, yet he never practised in our courts He availed himself of the intelligence of the law and his great energy and activity in business; so he amassed a great fortune in a very few years. He started into operation his mill and kept his store also in profitable order, so that both these means advanced his fortune; but the greatest part of his wealth was acquired by his profitable commerce in lands His strong mind, together with his knowledge of the law, enabled him to enter the arena of land speculation with the power to contend with a giant in that traffic

* Adelaide Saucier, was born in the village of St Philip, that adjoined Fort Chartres, in 1758, and died at Belleville, Ill., in 1833; of her two daughters by this marriage, the eldest, Adelaide Perry, born at Prairie du Pont, St. Clair County, January 24, 1803, died at her home in Belleville, May 13, 1881, and married, Oct 18, 1820, Adam W Snyder, son of Adam Snyder, a German house-carpenter, who emigrated to America from Strasburg, in the then French province of Alsace, and located in Reading, Pa , later he removed to Connellsville, where he resided until his death, in 1836

Adam Wilson Snyder was born in Connellsville, Fayette Co , Pa , Oct 6, 1799, in boyhood he was physically incapable of hard labor, tho necessity compelled his exertion, and he supported himself by wool-carding during the long summer vacations between the winter terms of school, where he acquired the elementary English branches with a slight knowledge of Latin In 1815, when scarcely 16, prompted by a desire to try life in the West with wider opportunities, he visited a half-brother near Columbus, Ohio, where he soon became a clerk in the country store of McFarland, who afterward settled in Ridge Prairie, St. Clair Co., Ill ; shortly after, while visiting his former home, Jesse B Thomas, at that time one of the judges of Illinois Territory, residing at Cahokia, the county-seat of St Clair County, and later at Kaskaskia, the most important town in the Territory, called upon him and offered him a situation in a wool-carding and fulling-mill that, to supply a long-felt want, he had decided to erect at Cahokia Accordingly in the spring of 1817, with all his earthly possessions in a moderately-sized bundle, he accompanied Judge Thomas, to whom he had been highly recommended, to Cahokia, and on his arrival immediately commenced mixing mortar and carrying stone for the first wool-carding mill in Illinois, with the advice and encouragement of his employer, he commenced and diligently prosecuted the study of law during the hours of labor, until he was admitted to the bar in 1820, with the assistance and influence of Judge Thomas, then U -S. senator, he readily gained a professional, political, social, and, and financial position, and in 1830 was elected State senator from St Clair County, serving in the seventh, eighth, and ninth general assemblies; was in the Black-Hawk war as a private in Capt John Winstanley's Co , enlisting April 18, 1832; on the 29th was appointed adjutant of his (1st) regiment, and upon the second call raised a company of which he was elected captain, enrolled May 27, mustered out June 21, 1832. Among the

He owned at his death choice selected lands all over the country, and what is the best evidence of his sound judgment, he owed not a cent at his decease.

Perry was, with all his wealth, a plain, unostentatious man, and lived and dressed in true republican style He paid due regard to all the various rules of economy and was amiable and benevolent in an eminent degree. His house was always open to the poor coming from a distance to his mill, and he entertained and made them comfortable and happy with everything his means afforded. He was very popular and much esteemed by all classes of people. His friends forced him into public employments. he acted for a long series of years as a judge of

high privates of his company were Hons Joseph Gillespie; James Semple of Madison County, afterward U.-S. senator, Pierre Ménard of Randolph County, and Col. John Thomas of St Clair County. The county-seat of St. Clair Co having been removed from Cahokia to Belleville he purchased and occupied the former residence of Gov. Edwards in 1833, in 1834, was defeated for congress by Gov Reynolds—both were democrats; in 1836, he defeated Reynolds for congress; in 1838, was again defeated for congress by Reynolds; in 1840, was elected State senator; and in Dec , 1841, received the democratic nomination for governor; the election was held in August, 1842, but on May 14 previous he died at his home in Belleville; and Judge Thomas Ford was selected to fill his place on the successful ticket. Of his family who survived him, the widow and three sons:

Hon William H , his eldest son, born July 12, 1825, has resided all his life in St. Clair Co , and in Belleville since 1833; was graduated from McKendree College in 1845, and immediately commenced the study of law in the office of Gov. Koerner, and was admitted to the bar in 1846; was postmaster of Belleville by appointment of President Polk, during the Mexican war he was enrolled at Alton, May 26, 1847, as 1st-lieutenant of G. W. Hook's Company E, and June 8, was adjutant of his regiment—Col Newby's; was twice prosecuting-attorney of the Belleville circuit, represented St Clair Co. in eighteenth and nineteenth general assemblies; was appointed and declined a lieutenancy of dragoons in 1856; member of the constitutional convention of 1870, and is now serving his third term as judge of the circuit (3d) court

Frederick Adam, second son, born Dec 8, 1827; graduated at McKendree College at age of 17; was admitted to the bar two years later; in 1847, received appointment of 2d-lieutenant, Co. G, 16th U.-S. Inf'y, in Mexican war, disbanded August, 1848; practising his profession till 1849, he crossed the plains to California, and after a brief mining experience, located in San Francisco; in 1853 was a member of the legislature and one of three of its members appointed to revise the statutes of California, died *en route* to Lake Bigler in July, 1854, in his 27th year.

Dr. John Francis, youngest son, born March 22, 1830, at an early age commenced the study of medicine, and has so far devoted his life to its practice; resides at Virginia, Cass Co , Ill.; was elected a member of the legislature in 1878 from the 36th district; is known in the scientific world by his contributions to American ethnology and archæology.

the court of common-pleas. He also acted as a justice-of-the-peace in and for the old St. Clair County almost all his life after he reached Illinois Perry learned well the English language; so he was at home in that as well as the French. He was prevailed on to serve one or more sessions in the legislature of Indiana Territory. He was there in one session at Vincennes with Judge Bond and Major Murdoch, members of St. Clair County. He acquitted himself in all these various offices with honor to himself and advantage to the public.

Some years before his death, by some excessive exertion, he injured his constitution, which caused his death. His system was so deranged that the blood-vessels refused to perform their ordinary functions. He wrote to Dr. Rush of Philadelphia on the subject and had directions from that celebrated physician who to manage the case. He lingered in this situation for several years and became, by the disease or by some other means, very corpulent. Blood was taken from him every month or oftener, to save his life. He died* in 1812, in Prairie du Pont, where he had resided for nearly twenty years. His decease was a sore calamity to his family and the public of that section of the country. His family† lost a kind, amiable, tender parent and husband, and his neighborhood was deprived of their best friend

His mind, as it has already been stated, was of the first order for strength and solidity. It was improved and trained by education and by profound meditation. He had nothing of the gaudy or tinsel character in his composition; but his talents and energy, in this new and poor country, had not the appropriate theatre in which to act. He was forced off from his country and settled in an obscure corner. His talents at Prairie du Pont were like "the rose that wastes its fragrance on the desert air." He possessed great energy and activity in business, and with these qualifications, he reached the *ne plus ultra* of his situation. He was placed in the highest offices in the country and became

---

* His widow married, in 1815, Augustine Pensoneau, who died in the fall of 1819; his widow and two children—Felicite and Augustine—surviving.

† Henriet, his younger daughter (who died in St. Clair Co., April 22, 1882), married, in the fall of 1822, Louis (died February 22, 1826, at Point a la Pierre), son of Louison Pensoneau; their only child, Louis Perry Pensoneau, now lives with his married daughter—*his* only child at East St. Louis, Ill.

very wealthy, so he acted well his part in the limited sphere in which he was situated. He was upright and correct in his morals, but never identified himself with any church His church was nature's creation before him and God the teacher

Toward the close of the last century, three brothers, Pierre, Hypolite, and Francis Ménard, emigrated from Canada and settled in Kaskaskia These French pioneers were conspicuous and very influential characters They were natives of Quebec in Canada, and were of respectable family Their father had been an officer in the French service and was in the military operations near Fort Duquesne about the time of Braddock's defeat

Pierre Ménard, the oldest brother, was born in 1767, and received a common, plain education in Canada He was, like many of the young Canadians, filled with adventure to come to the West He reached Vincennes in 1786, and entered the employment of Col Vigo He was an agent for Vigo in the Indian trade. He was employed that year and several others subsequent, to procure from the Indians supplies for the army under Gens. Clark and Scott He headed many parties out from Vincennes to the Indian hunting-grounds and packed meat back for the troops. Col Vigo and Ménard crossed the mountains to Carlisle, Pennsylvania, to see President Washington on public business in regard to the defence of the country. This was in 1789, and they met the president at Carlisle In 1790, he and Du Bois of Vincennes became partners in merchandising and established a store of Indian and other goods in Kaskaskia. This year he located himself, a young, single man, in old Kaskaskia At this time, his mind and body had reached man's estate He had been mixing with the world for several years and had some experience in the affairs of men.

Nature and education had conspired to make Ménard a conspicuous and very popular character He was endowed with a strong, vigorous intellect and was also blessed with an energy that never tired or ceased exertion, only to enjoy rest, so as to be able again for redoubled activity But nature and education had also given to him the most candid, frank, and honest deportment, of which very few men are blessed in such an eminent degree His words, actions, and all his movements indicated a pure and upright heart, where neither guile, deceit, nor cunning had any resting-place

With these traits of character, he was one of the most conspicuous and influential personages in the country. Few men in Illinois ever enjoyed the honest and sincere affections of the people in such degree as Col. Ménard did. Not only did the the white population admire and respect his character, but the Indians almost worshiped him as they did the Great Spirit At any time, an Indian would prefer giving Ménard his peltry for nothing than to receive double value for it from a long-knife American He was the United-States agent for the Indians for many years and acted in such an honorable and upright manner that both parties were highly pleased with his conduct No man in the West had more influence with many of the Indian tribes than he had He was appointed by the government in many cases to treat with the red-skins.

He and Lewis Cass were at the Lower Rapids on the Mississippi in 1826, on July 4, preparing for a treaty with the Indians, and during the festivities of the day, he named the town at the foot of the Rapids, Keokuk, which it has retained to this day This place was then just started and was christened Keokuk by Ménard, one of the most popular and influential pioneers that ever was in Illinois. It will be recollected that Keokuk, for whom this town was named, was a great and talented chief of the Sac and Fox Indians He was by nature not far behind any of the great Indian chiefs He had the good-sense to know the red-skins could not contend with the whites and always on this consideration inculcated peace in his braves

Keokuk was made a war-chief by his merit and not by birth In the late war with Great Britain, the Sac and Fox Indians were about to be destroyed, as they supposed, by the army under Gen Howard in 1813 The whole nation at Rock Island, except a very few, commenced lamentations and shedding tears of distress, thinking the Long Knives were about to kill them all. Keokuk was then a mere youth, but his great native mind and his true patriotism made him stand out the champion of the nation to defend them and country against Howard and his army A few other choice spirits of the young warriors joined him and marched out to meet the American army, preferring death to the surrender of their country.

It so happened that the Americans were not near them and the panic arose without foundation. I was with the army under Gen. Howard and we were almost as much alarmed at the Indians as the Indians were at us. They had three or fourfold over our number. This movement made Keokuk a war-chief of the nation and Gen. Scott and myself, as commissioners at the treaty of Rock Island in 1832, with the Sac and Fox Indians, confirmed him in this office. Keokuk had sound, good sense. He took the newspapers and got them explained to him.

Col. Ménard was almost all his life, after he left Canada, engaged in the Indian trade. He was never idle. He consented on many occasions to serve the people in the general assembly and was elected to represent Randolph County, with two others, Robert Morrison and Robert Reynolds, my father, in the legislature of the Indiana Territory in 1803. He was then quite a young man, energetic and well acquainted with the country between Kaskaskia and Vincennes. This assembly convened at Vincennes in the winter and the traveling across the wilderness, a hundred and fifty miles, between the Mississippi and Wabash rivers, was excessively bad. The creeks were swimming and the weather extremely cold. At that day, not a house stood between the small settlement near Kaskaskia and the Wabash River.

Ménard was first in almost every enterprise in pioneer times in Illinois. He was in the first legislatures of both the territories of Indiana and Illinois and was the first lieutenant-governor of the State in 1818. He was elected to the legislative council, so called at that day, of the first Illinois legislature from Randolph County, in 1812, and was elected speaker of that body. He presided in that assembly, as he did in many subsequent cases, with good, common-sense, but without pomp or parade. He was continued in the legislative council of the Illinois Territory from the first assembly in 1812, to the close of the territorial government in 1818, and always elected the presiding-officer. He had a sound, solid judgment and true patriotism to govern his actions in these legislative assemblies. He never made speeches of any length, but, like Franklin, told anecdotes that were extremely applicable and made remarks that showed both his good sense and patriotism. Many of the wise and equitable laws which have made Illinois so prosperous, came out from under his fostering care.

After the close of the term of his office as lieutenant-governor, he almost always declined any further public employment. He accepted the office of commissioner to treat with the Indians, but longed for retirement, so as to attend to his private business and family. He gradually declined any public office and turned his attention to acts of benevolence and kindness, which were so congenial to his heart.

It was not in public life where he excelled; but it was in his private and domestic conduct where his true and genuine benevolence displayed itself and all the virtues that adorn and ennoble the human family had a proper theatre in his heart for their action. The poor and distressed always received charity at his hand. The "milk of human kindness" never reigned more triumphant in any heart than it did in his. In his younger days, he had, as most others did, purchased lands of the citizens. These lands, together with his Indian trade and other means, made him a princely fortune; but his amiable and kind disposition diminished it to some extent. He could not refrain from being security for many individuals whose debts he was compelled to pay, but at last he died, seized of much wealth. The legislature of Illinois, in 1839, as a marked honor to him, called a county Ménard, which is at this time a flourishing county, situated northwest of Springfield. He was extremely active and energetic during a long and eventful life. He was a partner, in 1808, in the mammoth company of Emanuel Liza and others and remained in the Rocky Mountains a year, doing business for the company.

Ménard died at Kaskaskia in 1844, aged seventy-seven years. In his death, the country lost a great and good man and his family a kind and affectionate parent. He had no enemies to rejoice at his death, but a host of friends to mourn their loss. The blessings of the people rest in the grave with him. He was a liberal and enlightened member of the Catholic church, and died happy, confiding in the doctrines of that church.

In 1795, Francis and Hypolite Ménard left Canada when they were young men and settled in Kaskaskia. Hypolite was quite a youth when he came to Illinois. Francis soon became a great and conspicuous navigator of the turbulent and headstrong Mississippi. He had the strong and energetic talents equal to the emergency to master the river and to conduct his gallant vessel, with fifty or eighty men on board, with safety from port to port. A commander acts under an immense responsibility in this service. Property to a great value and the lives of his crew were confided to his judgment and discretion. A wilderness of five or six hundred miles extended along the river between the upper and lower settlements. Under all these circumstances, it required great and energetic talents to succeed over all these difficulties of the Mississippi.

Ménard had the capacity to perform these hazardous and perilous voyages and thereby he obtained a reputation not equaled in the West for his judgment and courage in navigating this dangerous river. He had such extraordinary judgment and corresponding energy that he took advantage of circumstances that a man of less intellect and firmness would not dare undertake. On many occasions, when there were storms on the river, little less than tornadoes, blowing up or down, let it be night or day, Ménard would unfurl the sails of his well-organized craft and run before the wind, perhaps eighty or a hundred miles, before he would land his vessel. In these great emergencies, he assumed without effort a calm and composed dignity. The high order of talent and firmness which he so eminently possessed occupied the commander to the exclusion of the common traits of human nature. He dressed himself in his favorite capote and red cap; invoked the favor of the Savior and promised masses. In such crisis, he showed himself the greatest of the great in his profession. His features indicated intelligence and extreme firmness on these occasions, bordering on recklessness.

In these perilous storms, he took the helm in person and seemed almost as solid and firm as the rocky bluffs of the Mississippi which he passed in his barge. He often sailed his vessel against the strong current of the river to a great distance before he touched land. By this he gained eight or ten days' hard labor. In one of his voyages to New Orleans, when his character was well known in that city, as in Kaskaskia and also on the river, one of his young men from Prairie du Rocher got a little tight just on the eve of their departure from New Orleans to Illinois, and saw a cage of birds a Spaniard had to sell. The creole from Prairie du Rocher took it into his head that the birds would do better to be free and turned them out of the cage. The officers seized Ménard's man and were about to commit him to the calaboose. Ménard was ready to start home and disliked to lose his man or to wait for his trial.

Boatmen in olden times were rude and the police had much trouble with them in New Orleans. For this reason, a guard of soldiers was put over the bird liberator Ménard was never one day in place but all his acquaintances were his devoted friends. This was the case at New Orleans. There was something unaccountable and indescribable in the frankness and candor of Ménard to gain him friends wherever he was known His honesty and disinterestedness seemed to aid in his popularity, but such was the fact. The boatmen of that day always carried their arms. He ordered his men to parade under arms One or two were left with the boat to guard it and a swivel or two were charged to fire on the police, if necessary. He marched at the head of his corps to the place where the guard and police-officers had his man in custody. It will be recollected that nine-tenths of the citizens of New Orleans were French. Ménard informed the guard, he came for his man; he would pay for the birds and would have his comrade. The die was cast—he must succeed. In his loud, commanding voice, he told the assembly in French, who had crowded around the prisoner, to withdraw. He ordered his boatmen to cock their guns, and then in a decisive manner, he ordered his creole to leave the police and the first man of the guard that tried to prevent it, should be shot. The prisoner left; the guard was intimidated and Ménard marched his man to the boat amid the loud cheers of the people. The Spanish government, just before the cession in 1803, was becoming very unpopular.

Ménard was attentive to his religious duties. He and crew performed their church devotions in both Kaskaskia and New Orleans, before and after a voyage, with sincerity. He always had masses said in both churches, returning thanks to God for his success. It was a sublime spectacle to see these rough, hardy boatmen, who bid defiance to all creation but God, kneeling at the altar in sincere devotion to Him on high.

Ménard had mostly on the boats he navigated, some part of the freight, by which he managed so as to make money. He purchased fine farms near Kaskaskia and became quite wealthy altho he was extremely liberal He lived to an old age and died at Kaskaskia. No death was more lamented than his. Everyone considered they had lost their best friend. He possessed a strong, uncultivated mind, with a heart, under an exterior of no great polish, that did honor to human nature These two Ménards were descendants of the ancient and noble Barons of Normandy, and if they had lived in olden times, they would have been knighted on the field of battle or buried there with the honors of war.

Hypolite Ménard was an excellent citizen; raised a large family and was a good farmer in the Point, so called, between the Kaskaskia and Mississippi rivers. He was quite respectable and at times, represented Randolph County in the general assembly. He was an honest, correct man in all his actions, public and private, and possessed more French vivacity than his brothers. He also lived to an advanced age and his remains rest in peace in the old cemetery at Kaskaskia.

In olden times, the whole country between Lower Louisiana and Canada was called Illinois, and the French citizens, down to 1810, or thereabouts, called the United States, America, and did not consider themselves *dans l'Amerique*, as they termed it. It seemed strange to my ear to hear the French, in 1800, speak of America as a different country than theirs on the Mississippi. In fact, the people, their dress, language, houses, manner of living and doing business were so different from the Americans in the States that it almost made us believe we had traveled out of America Add to this, a great number of Indians—perhaps two to one white man—were, for the most part of the year, in and camped around Kaskaskia The other Indians forced all the Illinois tribes to remain near the whites for protection.

It will be recollected that the Spanish government, in 1795 and after, when the difficulty about the navigation of the Mississippi River was settled between us and Spain, encouraged the Americans from the States to settle in Upper Louisiana. This policy was to build up a barrier of Americans against British encroachments from Canada. They knew the Americans disliked Great Britain and would not permit that nation to trample on them. Thus it was that liberal donations of lands were given to the settlers. In East Tennessee, about 1800, it became quite popular to move to the Spanish country in Illinois, as it was then called. The Birds and Murphys, two respectable and numerous connections of people, emigrated from East Tennessee to the west side of the Mississippi.

The neighbors of my father had been out to see the country and put the people on fire to move. My father, Robert Reynolds, caught the mania. He emigrated from Ireland—was brim full of energy and disregarded moving. The travel at that day from East Tennessee to the Mississippi was considered more troublesome and dangerous than the journey is at this time to California. The intelligence of the people and the facilities for traveling have been much improved within fifty years past. Our traveling caravan consisted of my two parents, six children (I the oldest), one negro woman, three hired men, eight horses, two wagons, and the appropriate number of dogs for a new country. We started from the northern section of Knox County, Tenn., for what was then literally true, the Far-West.

To show the unparalleled improvement and growth of the West since 1800, I state that we crossed Clinch River at the southwest point, into a wilderness country belonging to the Indians. We saw a great abundance of cane near the Cany Fork of Cumberland River, where we crossed it at Walton's ferry. At that day there was no Carthage there. We passed Dixon's Spring, Bledsoe's Lick, and Betts' tanyard at the Red-River Ridge, so called at that day. We traveled thro the Red-River country to the place where Hopkinsville now stands. At that day there was not a house there, except a jail. We passed the residence of Judge Prince and Richie's horse-mill. Here my father purchased considerable provisions and the next point was Lusk's ferry on the Ohio, where my father's three hired men left us.

The first Illinois soil I ever touched was on the bank of the Ohio, where Golconda now stands, in March, 1800. When we were about to start from the Ohio, I asked Mr. Lusk "how far it was to the next house on the road," and when he told us that the first was Kaskaskia, one hundred and ten miles, I was surprised at the wilderness before us. My father hired a man to assist us in traveling thro the wilderness. We were four weeks in performing this dreary and desolate journey. The first difficulty we encountered was a terrible hurricane that prostrated the timber and filled the road for miles with the trunks and branches of the trees. This detained us considerably, to cut a new road round and over this fallen timber. The next great obstacle was Big-Muddy River. That detained us several weeks. We first waited for it to fall; but at last we were forced to raft it and swim the horses The horses became poor for the want of gra n or grass, as it was then in the month of March and scarcely any grass was up to support them. A small matter in a crisis is much regarded. We had two axes, but lost one in Big Muddy. The axe fell into water twenty feet deep, so we could not regain it If we had lost the other, surrounded with high water as we were, we might have been numbered, if not with the dead, at least with the distressed

The next creek was Little Muddy We had learned the arts and mysteries of rafting and so we did better The next creek was that small stream a few miles east of Beaucoup We rafted that and Beaucoup, making four in all which we thus crossed. After that we reached Kaskaskia without much difficulty. We saw plenty of buffalo sign between Big and Little Muddys; but were no hunters and killed nothing. The citizens of Kaskaskia, Messrs. Edgar, John R. Jones, Robert Morrison, Ménard, and others were anxious that my father should settle on this side of the river, but he went to St. Genevieve to obtain some permit or license from the commandant to settle in the country. The regulations of the government requiring him to raise his children Catholics determined him not to live under such government. My father and mother were born and raised in Ireland in the Protestant faith and would not consent to live in a Catholic country. We were destined for the Murphy's Settlement, on the St. Francis River, but the above caused us to settle in Illinois We made a plantation a few miles east of Kaskaskia, in the settlement already described, and resided there until 1807, when we moved and settled in Goshen Settlement in the American Bottom, four miles southeast of the present town of Edwardsville.

My father was born and raised in the county of Monohon, Ireland, and my mother in the City of Dundalk. They landed at Philadelphia not long after the Revolution and I was born in Montgomery County, Penn., in 1788. The same year I was born, my parents moved to Knox County, Tenn., where they left for the Spanish country, as before stated. My father was a man of strong mind and possessed a good English education. He was ardent in politics and restless when young. In his matured age, he read much and wrote essays for the papers. He was a great admirer of Jefferson and hated the government of Great Britain with a ten-horse power. I never knew any man who loved the government of the United States more than he did. In his younger days, he was elected representative from Randolph County to the Indiana legislature and held the offices of judge of the court of common-pleas of the county and justice-of-the-peace.

Judge James McRoberts* of Monroe County was a very early and respectable pioneer of Illinois. It was by him and similar citizens of moral and correct deportment that Illinois has taken a stand in her infancy which bids so fair to prosperity in maturer days. James McRoberts was born in Glasgow, Scotland, May 22, 1760. He emigrated to America and settled in Philadelphia at the age of twelve years. At the tender age of seventeen, he entered the tented field in the Revolutionary war and became a soldier in that most glorious struggle that not only broke to atoms the chains of bondage from our limbs, but it

* Judge McRoberts' family came to America in 1772, residing at Philadelphia a short time, thence to Washington, Pa., where a permanent home was established; at 17 years he joined the army at Brandywine, was in the battle of that name, at the siege of Yorktown, and witnessed the surrender of Cornwallis, Oct. 19, 1781, remained in the service fighting Indians on the Ohio until discharged in 1783. Of his nine children, five of whom were daughters, six survived him; of the four sons· James, Jr., Samuel, Thomas, and Josiah, the three younger reached maturity and filled various State and national positions. At this time but two of the nine are alive— Mrs. Mary Trail of Waterloo, Monroe Co., Ill., born February, 1818, married 1841, Maj. Xerxes F. Trail, major, July 1, 1846, of Col. Bissell's regiment 12-mo vols., in the Mexican war, and fought in every battle from Buena Vista, where he distinguished himself while in command of three companies in the conflict at the mountain on the left, to the final surrender of the city of Mexico, their two children: Mary Francis, wife of Col. Milton Moore, and Samuel, now living in Austin, Texas, and Circuit-Judge Josiah McRoberts of Joliet, Ill.

will, in the end, liberate and free all mankind from oppression. It is a proud honor to have an opportunity to serve in such a glorious war and the children of the Revolutionary fathers will hold sacred that honor transmitted to them under all vicissitudes of life Judge McRoberts remained in the Revolution until the eagle mounted high over the fallen lion and was honorably discharged in 1783.

In 1794, he married a lady of excellent, strong mind and high sense of propriety and proper deportment He settled in 1788 on the Ohio River in Kentucky and the next year, 1789, he visited Kaskaskia in search of a new country. McRoberts and comrades explored thoroly the Northwest and the Spanish country west of the Mississippi, and returned to Kentucky and remained there until 1797 He had seen the advantages of Illinois and was determined to reside in it This same year he came to Kaskaskia and the next year, he located himself on the plantation whereon he lived almost half-a-century and died. It is remarkable that in this new country where everything is so changeable that the same dwelling-house he built in 1798 is in existence and tenantable repair In this same house, all his numerous family of children were born and raised This is the birthplace of Hon Samuel McRoberts,* who died while in the

* Samuel McRoberts, born in Monroe Co , Ill , Feb 20, 1799; after receiving such instruction as the country afforded, at an early age entered Transylvania University, Lexington, Ky , while Horatio Holly was its president, and taking high rank in all his classes, was graduated in 1819 in classical and law departments, returning to Illinois, he was in 1821 elected the first circuit-court clerk of Monroe Co ; in 1825, he was appointed circuit-court judge, and held the office three years; presiding at the trial of the People vs. Solomon H Winchester for the murder of Dan'l D Smith, held at Edwardsville, March, 1825, in which Felix Grundy of Tennessee successfully defended, in 1828, was elected State senator, representing the district composed of Monroe, Clinton, and Washington counties, was later appointed by Prest Jackson U -S dist -att'y of Illinois, this office he resigned; was appointed by Prest VanBuren receiver of public moneys at Danville, and on making his final settlement with the treasury it owed him $1 65, for this amount Secretary-of-the Treasury Robt J Walker drew a treasury-warrant and remitted to him in 1839, VanBuren appointed him in 1839 solicitor of the general land-office at Washington, he resigned in the fall of 1841, and at the ensuing session of the legislature was elected U -S senator, serving through the 27th congress; died at Cincinnati, O , March 27, 1843 from the effect of a cold contracted while crossing the Alleghany Mountains On Dec 13, 1843, Sen Breese, his colleague, introduced resolutions and eulogized his memory in the senate, and later Hon. John Wentworth introduced them to the house, and paid a glowing tribute to his memory His only son died in 1874 in Washington, D. C

senate of the United States. It is also the birthplace of the talented and interesting member of the bar, Josiah McRoberts* of Joliet, Illinois—both the sons of Judge McRoberts.

Judge McRoberts was a practical farmer and supported himself and family by his agricultural industry. Of all the professions pursued by man, farming is the most honorable and independent. In the case of mechanics, professional men, sailors, soldiers, etc., they must of necessity depend on others for support; but the farmer does not depend on man for his bread. He depends on the earth and Providence and if he does his duty they will not desert him.

Judge McRoberts was a conspicuous settler in his section of country, which induced others to locate around him, and thro all vicissitudes of the country, he remained on his plantation almost as firm and as regular as the days and nights succeed each other. His wisdom and good sense were appreciated by the people and he was called on in many cases to serve the public. To accommodate the neighborhood, he acted as justice-of-the-peace for many years. He was also elected to the office of county-judge under the State government. In all these offices, he acted with sound, good sense and acquitted himself much to his honor and to the benefit of the country. When he was on the bench of the county-court, the finances and the policy of the county were managed with good sense and with great advantage to the public. The duties of this court are

* Josiah McRoberts, born in Monroe Co., Ill., June 12, 1820, was placed under James Charters, a Scotch schoolmaster, a profound scholar and superior linguist, who laid the foundation for his classical education, in 1836, he entered St. Mary's College, Mo., Rev. John D. Timon, president; after being graduated in 1839, he began his legal studies at Danville, Ill., under his brother Samuel, in 1842, he entered the law-school at Transylvania University, Lexington, Ky., and after receiving his diploma, returned to Danville in 1844 to practise; was elected State senator from the Champaign-and-Vermilion district in 1846, and at the expiration of his term moved to Joliet, Ill., where he now resides, was appointed by Gov. Matteson State trustee of the Illinois-and-Michigan Canal in 1852, holding this four years; in 1866, was appointed by Gov. Oglesby circuit-court judge to succeed Sidney W. Harris, resigned, this office he now fills, having been elected three successive times. Judge McRoberts married at Joliet, Aug. 9, 1849, Gertrude Helmer, dau. of Robert and Catherine (Myers) Shoemaker, born at Herkimer, N.Y., March 6, 1828, came to Illinois in 1836, and died at Joliet, July 11, 1883. Of their eight children but three are now living: Louise M., wife of Edward C. Aikin, Frank H.; and Josiah, Jr., Elizabeth, the second daughter, having died Nov. 2, 1880, aged 25 years.

important to the community and they require the most experienced and wise men in the county to perform them in a proper manner. Judge McRoberts possessed the sound mind, with long experience, and practical good sense to fill such office and he did so to the improvement of both the county and the morals of the people.

This venerable patriarch, after living a long and useful life and seeing his family raised and doing well, died on his farm, in September, 1846, aged eighty-six years. He was moral, punctual, and correct in all his acts, public and private. He lived a long and interesting life. His life may in truth be said to be eventful, altho he resided in one and the same locality for nearly fifty years. His emigration to America was an important event; the next was his services in the great and glorious Revolution; the next was exploring and settling in Illinois at such an early day; and the last and greatest was his continued and uninterrupted residence on the same place for forty-nine years. This pioneer seemed to me to have performed all the ordinary duties assigned to man.

The aged and respectable matron, the widow* of Judge McRoberts, is still alive, a monument of female worth and usefulness. This lady possesses a strong mind and a just sense of the independence of character. She gave her tender offspring the proper impressions when they were prattling around her knee and they never departed from those wise and proper instructions. Her descendants for the most part are respectable and interesting. The conduct of this matron in her family proves the propriety of paying particular attention to the moral and correct education of the females; as it is the mothers who give their children the first impressions. If these impressions are good and wise, the children will become worthy and respectable citizens.

Altho emigration into Illinois had commenced in good earnest in and about 1800, yet the country was new and much infested with reckless savages. In 1802, a single young man was returning from Kaskaskia to the States and about fifteen miles east from Kaskaskia, on the Massac road, an Indian shot him

* Mary Fletcher, born in Nashville, Tenn., in 1776, married in 1794, and died in the spring of 1862, aged 86, surviving her husband 16 years.

This murder was committed on the waters of the river Mary No inhabitants were living near the place and the whole country was a wilderness and crowded with Indians The murderer was a straggling Delaware from the west side of the Mississippi. When he committed the murder, he took the man's saddle and some other articles and escaped toward the mouth of the Big Muddy, in the Mississippi Bottom The whites discovered the outrage and employed the Kaskaskia Indians to assist in the search for the murderer. The Indians found the Delaware in the Mississippi Bottom and brought him to Kaskaskia The friends of the murdered man proved certain articles the Indian had with him, which, with other circumstances, convicted the Indian It was rather a sham to try an Indian, as the juries would always convict them if there was the semblance of evidence against their old enemies. Late in the fall, this Delaware was hung by George Fisher, the sheriff of Randolph County, on a honey-locust tree on the bank of the Kaskaskia River, a mile or so above the village of Kaskaskia This was the first man I saw hung and the revolting spectacle made a lasting impression on my mind against capital punishment I recollect, the poor savage in his death-struggle reached his hand to the rope around his neck and it was with great difficulty the sheriff could extricate the Indian's grasp, so he could be hung until he was dead How revolting it is to Christian principles, properly understood, to execute a human being!

Another barbarous execution was committed in Kaskaskia in 1804 Emsley Jones killed a man of the name of Reed in the Mississippi Bottom, some twelve or fifteen miles below Kaskaskia. Jones was executed in the commons, south of Kaskaskia, in the presence of a great concourse of people I never would witness another execution after those of Jones and the Indian.

In the early settlement of the country, when the people were too poor to erect suitable prisons to confine these malefactors, they were compelled, in self-defence, to resort to capital punishment; but at this day, there is no excuse for this barbarous and anti-Christian practice I think it is horrid to force the murderer before his God with his brother's blood red on his hands. The convict should enjoy his natural life for reflection and repentance Let him be put in a dungeon, so that he has an opportunity to prepare himself by penitence, contrition of heart, and such other changes as will fit him for the presence of God. Vengeance belongs to God and not to man. Moreover, I think, life belongs to the Creator and we have no right to destroy it. We are tenants at sufferance, we may use the premises, but not commit waste on them.

I can say, at least, in early times, Illinois was honored and blessed by the policy and services of great and wise men. LaSalle, Tonty, and many of the missionaries were great and good men. So were Renault, Vincennes, Artaguiette, and others. These were conspicuous characters in the discovery and early settlement of the country. For his Revolutionary services west of the mountains, Gen. Clark might with propriety be termed "the Washington of the West." Vigo and others acted well their part in the conquest of Illinois, and Charles Gratiot performed such great and important services for his country in the Revolution that he is entitled to the rank and standing of almost any of the above-named Illinois patriots. He is raised, by his meritorious services, to the dignified and elevated standing of a Revolutionary patriot—the highest elevation that adorns the human character.

He was born in the celebrated city of Lausanne, Switzerland, in 1747. His family and connections were of the first respectability and wealth of that city. They were strong Huguenots and supposed it to be their duty to educate their son, Charles Gratiot, in that faith in London. At the age of ten years, he was placed in the care of a friend in the metropolis of the British Empire to receive his education. His talents were soon developed, so that he was discovered to possess an extraordinary strong mind. He was in the hands of influential and wealthy merchants, who believed the *summum bonum* of human happiness to consist in two things: neatly-kept books and great wealth. Under these influences, young Gratiot was mostly prepared for commerce; but his genius disdained the sordid shackles of traffic when the freedom of man came in contact. After receiving his education, at the age of eighteen, he sailed from London for Canada and joined, at Montreal, a wealthy uncle. He immediately formed a partnership for the Northwest Indian trade with Messrs. Kay & McRae.

It must be recollected that in early times, and particularly with the British in Canada, the Northwest trade with the Indians was the main channel to wealth and fame, and in fact almost all the enterprising and active young men of that day, whose energies and talents entitled them to fame and honor, turned their attention to the Northwest trade

Charles Gratiot,* in 1767, when he was only twenty years of age, embarked in this trade and bade Canada a long farewell. His partners were stationed, one at Mackinac and the other in Montreal, while he himself was the active, intelligent, and business partner that extended the commerce of the company from the lakes and the waters of the Maumee, across the Wabash country to the Mississippi and from the Falls of St Anthony to the mouth of the Ohio. As his business increased, his mind and energies in the same proportion improved and developed themselves. He was the master-spirit in commerce throughout this vast region of country and the company of which he was partner employed seventy or eighty thousand dollars in their Indian trade. Charles Gratiot had the entire control of this great sum of money and all the commercial transactions within this extended territory. He remained in the region of country near Lake Superior for some years, trading with the Indians, receiving his supplies of goods from Mackinac and returning the proceeds of sales also to that place. In 1774, he turned his attention to the Illinois country and established stores at both Cahokia and Kaskaskia. He also extended his Indian trade across the Wabash Valley to the waters of the Maumee, so that his vast operations embraced four or five States of the present Union in the Northwest. His grand depot of the Indian trade was at Cahokia for many years and from this point he extended the ramifications of his commerce in various quarters over this vast region.

I have been favored with an examination of his commercial letters, dated at Cahokia, St Louis, and the Riviere des Peres, in 1775 and down to 1785, which exhibit his commercial trans-

* When the transfer of sovereignty took place at St Louis, March 10, 1804, under the treaty which annexed Louisiana Territory, and the French flag was lowered, he unfurled the first American flag in Upper Louisiana, from the balcony of his residence.

actions throughout a great portion of the Mississippi Valley. The old village of Cahokia he termed Cahos at that day in his letters While Mr Gratiot was engaged in successful commerce in Illinois and having great influence with the white and Indian population of the country, in 1778, Gen. Clark invaded the country with a small army, bearing on its banners liberty and independence Altho Gratiot had been educated in England, yet the spirit of his dear native Switzerland burned strong in his heart for liberty and without hesitation, his sound judgment and his generous impulses for freedom declared for Clark and the American Revolution This was not an empty declaration, but he embarked his whole energies and fortune in the cause of the Revolution.

It is known to all that Clark had received scarcely any means from Virginia to conquer and retain the Illinois country. The army commanded by Clark was in a starving and destitute condition, except they were supported by the resources of the country They remained in the Illinois and Wabash countries for several years and were sustained by the inhabitants of the country during that time The French inhabitants were too poor to give away their substance and the support of the army fell on Gratiot, Vigo, and other such choice spirits, for the most of the above crisis If these supplies were not given by Gratiot and others, the great and glorious campaign of Clark must have failed for the time being, but the generous heart of Gratiot hesitated not a moment and he came to the rescue. Gratiot paid to the citizens and became accountable to them to the full amount of his vast estate for supplies for the American army. His heart and soul were enlisted in the cause of human freedom. The blood of the country of Tell burned in his veins and all his means were exhausted in the glorious conquest of Illinois. He paid at several times for army supplies as much or more than he was worth at the time of the conquest of the country; but his talents and energies soon enabled him to become wealthy again.

At the time, both Virginia and the colonies, and for a long time after, were unable to refund to him the amount of money he so generously expended in the conquest of Illinois, and in fact not much if any has ever been paid back to him or his family by the government to this day. Virginia, always noble and generous in her councils, agreed to give Gratiot thirty thousand acres of land on the southeast bank of the Ohio, including the present City of Louisville, but before the grant was completed, Kentucky was organized as a State over the country and the promise to Gratiot was never completed—more for the want of application than otherwise. The general assembly of Virginia placed the claims of Gratiot on the list to be paid prior to many other debts; but his claims remain unpaid, with many others of a similar character, to the present time.

Not only the operations of the army under Gen. Clark would have been crippled for the want of supplies if Gratiot and others had not given them, but the various treaties made by that great and talented general, Clark, would not have been so many or so favorable if it were not for the aid these great and eminent patriots afforded him. When Gratiot saw his country free from British despotism and his exertions for the independence of America crowned with success, he retired from the public service and confined himself more to domestic enjoyments. Altho he employed his exertions and expended his fortune for the emancipation of his country, without pecuniary compensation, yet his heart exulted with great joy to see the colonies free, which was superior to any other payment that earth could bestow on him.

He married, in 1781, a Miss Chouteau, a sister of Auguste and Pierre Chouteau of St. Louis, Upper Louisiana. This family were the founders of St. Louis in 1764, and were of the first standing and respectability in the West. Gratiot, after his marriage, made St Louis his residence for life and became one of the most conspicuous characters in Upper Louisiana. In the decline of life, he abandoned the Indian trade and turned his energies to more domestic employments. He was engaged in manufacturing salt on the Merrimac, west of St Louis, and turned his attention to the lead-mines of the Upper Mississippi. He also acquired a large quantity of land west of St. Louis and made a plantation on it near the Riviere des Peres. He purchased slaves in Virginia and cultivated this farm. He resided on it at intervals and improved on it a very large plantation for that day.

Your Obt Servt
Henry Gratiot
Sub. Ind. Agent.

After enjoying life for sixty-five years and the most part very active and important transactions he performed, he died in St. Louis in 1817, amidst the tears and lamentations of his family and friends for the affection and respect they owed him and for the loss they sustained in his decease He was frank, open, and candid in all his transactions, public and private, and his honesty and integrity were always above suspicion. He was moral and exemplary in his deportment, and altho he was never a member of any church, yet his conduct was approved by the wise and good of all denominations

He raised a large and interesting family.* One of his sons, Henry Gratiot,† was an Indian agent for the Winnebagoes for many years and died in that office. Charles Gratiot,‡ another son, was placed in the military academy at West Point and graduated in that institution with much honor and high reputation for his talents and the progress he made in the sciences taught at that academy, and was, after long and arduous services, promoted to the head of the engineer corps of the United

* His family, who survived him, consisted of four sons and five daughters

† Henry Gratiot, second son, born St. Louis, Apr. 25, 1789; moved to Fevre-River Lead-Mines, now Galena, Ill , Oct., 1825, on account of his aversion to slavery and a desire to bring up his family in a free-state; married, June 21, 1813, Susan, dau of Stephen Hempstead—a Revolutionary soldier, and one of the earliest (1811) emigrants from Conn. to St. Louis, Upper Louisiana ter'y—father of Hon. Edward Hempstead, first delegate in congress from Missouri Terr'y, and of Chas. S. Hempstead, one of Galena's early lawyers, as well as of Wm. Hempstead, a prominent and influential merchant of early Galena. Henry with a younger brother, Jean Pierre Bugnion Gratiot, were among the first to develop the Fevre-River Lead-Mines, and for a long time maintained a large mining-and-smelting business at Gratiot's Grove, now in Lafayette Co , Wis , enjoying the Indians' confidence, he was enabled to exert great influence over them during the Blackhawk war, rendering inestimable services to the entire white population; d. Barnum's Hotel, Baltimore, Md., Apr. 27, 1836; four sons survived him: Chas H Gratiot, b. St Louis, Jan 9, 1814, d. Gratiot, Wis , Mch 15, 1883; Lt.-Col. Edw. Hempstead Gratiot, b. St Louis, June 19, 1817, late ass't-pay. U.-S. A., d. Platteville, Wis., Dec. 17, 1882; Henry Gratiot, b St Louis, Oct. 25, 1824, resides at Smartsville, Cal.; and Stephen Hempstead Gratiot. b. St Louis, Nov 21, 1831, d. Wash., D. C., Dec. 17, 1864; his only surviving daughter, Adèle, is the wife of Hon. E B Washburne, late U -S. minister to France, and now living in Chicago.

‡ Gen Chas Gratiot, eldest son, born St Louis, Aug. 29, 1786; admitted to West Point from Missouri Terr'y, July 17, 1804; 2d lieut eng'rs, Oct. 30, 1806; capt , Feb. 23, 1808; chief-eng Maj -Gen Harrison's army in 1812-3; bvt.-col Mich militia, Oct. 5, 1814; eng. in defence of Ft. Meigs, April and May, 1813; married Ann Belin, Phila , Apr 22, 1819; attack on Ft. Mackinac, Aug. 4, 1814; maj., Feb. 9, 1815; lieut.-col , Mch. 31, 1819; col and prin. eng., May 24, 1828; brevet brig.-gen , "for meritorious service and general good conduct," May 24, 1828 (Sept. 29); inspector to military academy, May, 1828, to Dec., 1838; died at St. Louis, Mo., May 18, 1855.

States and honored with the office of general of that scientific department. He remained in this high and dignified station for many years, performing the most scientific and difficult duties the government had to transact in this department. He was the officer that directed and governed the construction of Fortress Monroe, at old Point Comfort on the Chesapeake Bay, which will remain for ages, a splendid monument of the talents and science of Gen. Charles Gratiot. For durability and for scientific proportions and work, there is no fortification, perhaps, in America which surpasses that of Fortress Monroe. The war department ordered Gen. Gratiot to take into custody the amount of money necessary to construct the fortress and disburse the same. Under the order of the department, the general took charge of the funds and paid out, in the construction of the fortification, perhaps two or three millions of dollars. It had been the uniform practise of the disbursing officer, for his responsibility and care in keeping and paying out the money in such cases, to retain a certain percentage on the money disbursed. Gen. Gratiot retained the customary percentage and without trial or explanation was dismissed from the service for the above-supposed offence.

Others of his children were also conspicuous and respectable citizens. Judge Gratiot of St. Louis County, Missouri, held the office for many years of county judge and acquitted himself well in that office. One of his daughters married J. P. Cabbanne, who was a talented, efficient business man. Another married Pierre Chouteau, Jr., who is one of the most talented and enterprising merchants in the country. He was for many years the head of a large company that traded to the Rocky Mountains, and by his commerce and other industry, he has acquired an immense fortune. The descendants of this Revolutionary patriot and meritorious pioneer are numerous and respectable, located in St. Louis and in many other sections of the Union. They may all look back with honest pride and exultation to their illustrious ancestor and say of him with the great poet.

"An honest man is the noblest work of God."

John Beaird and family emigrated from Wayne County, Ky., to Randolph County, Ill., in 1801, and settled on the east side of the Kaskaskia River, four miles northeast of Kaskaskia village. Beaird was born in Virginia and raised in the mountains of New River of that State. He came to Tennessee in 1787, and married a connection of my father. He was located on the frontiers of Knox County, Tenn., while the Cherokee Indians were hostile and did much damage to the settlements in the northern section of Knox County. Beaird was uniformly elected a captain to pursue the Indians when any depredations were committed. He was brave, energetic, and decisive in his character and possessed a strong, uncultivated mind, but had not attended to an early education. His person was stout and comely and his courage was never doubted; but on the contrary, this trait of his character was often tested in both private and public acts.

In 1793, the Creek Indians intended an invasion of West Tennessee, called at that day, Cumberland, and William Blount, the governor of the Southwest Territory, gave Major Beaird the following order, dated at Knoxville, April 18, 1793.

"SIR:—The object of your command is to relieve the Cumberland inhabitants, Meroe district, from a powerful invasion of the Creeks."

Major Beaird had under him one hundred and twenty-five men. He marched from Knoxville to Nashville, two hundred miles, met some Creek Indians; killed a few, and returned home in good order with his command. On May 28, 1793, Gov. Blount ordered Beaird to pursue certain Indians with fifty mounted men and scour the Cumberland Mountains. The Indians had killed two citizens near Clinch River, of the name of Gillum. The country at that day was in a singular situation. On one side of the Tennessee River, the Indians pretended peace and the government prevented the troops from crossing the river in search of those Indians committing murders on the frontiers. When an Indian committed any aggression on the whites, he would flee to the peace side of the Tennessee and be secure from the whites. The Cherokees, who resided on their side of the river, concealed the murderers and put the crime on the Creeks. The policy of the government and the practise of the Indians inflamed the minds of the people to the utmost excitement.

When Capt. Beaird organized his company of fifty mounted men, to pursue the murderers of the Gillums, he, in defiance of his orders, crossed the Tennessee and chastised the Indians at Hanging-Maw's Town, so called. He killed several Indians there. Beaird was daring and decisive and took the responsibility. Nine-tenths of the people approved of his course. The government ordered a court-martial to try him, but he laughed at a trial. He and company found in the nation a quantity of Indian goods which the government had there to present to the Indians if a treaty were made with them. Beaird and men took the goods from the guard and burned them. All these proceedings were sustained by the people, but highly condemned by the government.

In all the Indian wars on the frontiers of Knox County, Tennessee, Beaird was the most efficient, bold, and daring officer in the service. He did more service with the least means than any other officer on the frontiers. When the State government was formed, he was elected from Knox County to the general assembly of the State and his public services were always held in high estimation by the people of Knox County. He moved from Tennessee to Kentucky and thence to Illinois, as above stated. He made an excellent citizen in this new, wild country, improved a large plantation and assisted to change the habits and customs of the people from hunting and idleness to work and industry, which the country at that day much needed. He died in 1809, leaving a large family of children.

One of his sons, Joseph A. Beaird, in after-days, became a conspicuous and respectable citizen. He represented Monroe County in the general assembly for many sessions and made an efficient and conspicuous member. He possessed a sound mind, with much polish of manners. Gentility and urbanity of manners seemed to be natural with him. He was honorable and rather chivalric in his character; his probity, punctuality, and honesty always ranged high and above suspicion. His neighborhood made him their executor-general, while he would consent to do the business appertaining to that troublesome situation. He died in 1829, aged forty years, leaving a considerable property and several children.

Another son, William A. Beaird, the old sheriff of St. Clair

County, almost every one in the county knew. He was blessed with a sound, solid judgment, altho he did not use it as it seemed to his friends he might have done. He obstinately refused to become educated or to receive any information thro the medium of books or from print in any manner whatever. He possessed much practical knowledge, which he acquired by observation and his intercourse with the people. He never married. He was kind and benevolent, particularly to the poor and distressed. Any one in distress, no matter what color, nation, or kindred, were sure of Beaird's assistance if he knew of the case. He was appointed deputy-sheriff in 1815, and continued in that situation until the State government was organized, in 1818; then he was elected by the people and continued in that office by biennial elections for twelve years. In all, he performed the duties of that office for about fifteen years. He was at one time very popular; his kindness to the people made a lasting impression on them. Many in the county owe their taxes to him at this day. He died in Belleville in 1843.

In 1801, that dreadful scourge, the small-pox, made its appearance in St Louis. Many of the citizens of Cahokia were inoculated by Dr. Sougrin of St. Louis and were lodged in his hospital in that city. It never came into Cahokia so as to sweep entirely over the village. It reached the vicinity of Kaskaskia some few years after and was principally confined to a house of refuge, erected by Dr. Fisher at his plantation, six miles out of town, at the foot of the bluff, on the road from Cahokia to Kaskaskia. Here the doctor provided a hospital, with all things necessary, and almost the whole French population passed thro this dreadful malady at this place under the the treatment of Dr. Fisher. I think very few died in this hospital. The citizens of Kaskaskia kept up a guard all summer at the outskirts of the village to prevent the contagion reaching the town. This disease did not reach the American settlements at all. The small-pox never raged thro the country and at last were rendered harmless by proper vaccination.

In 1797, Abraham Eyeman, John Teter, William Miller, Mr. Randleman, and a short time after, Daniel Stookey, located themselves and families in a settlement a few miles southwest of the present City of Belleville. This colony was composed of industrious, moral, and upright citizens and it grew and prospered in the same proportion In 1802, the whole country extended its borders. Many citizens—the Ogles, Enochs, and Whitesides—left the older settlements and located themselves in the fine, healthy country northeast of the present City of Belleville This colony settled on that beautiful tract of country known as Ridge Prairie, extending from two to eight or ten miles from Belleville In this same year, 1802, the Goshen Settlement was enlarged and improved The Gilham and Whiteside families settled there. These two large connections embraced nearly all the inhabitants of the settlement The Casterlands, Seybolds, Groots, and some others located at the foot of the bluff, above the Quentine Creek. In 1803, Samuel and Joel Whiteside made the first improvements on the Ridge Prairie, six or eight miles south of the present town of Edwardsville.

These settlements were made mostly by the pioneers who had been already in the country for many years and who had been accustomed to a frontier life. This frontier was exposed to Indians not entirely friendly to the whites and it required the most hardy and brave old settlers to brook the fierce and savage bands of Indians that infested the settlements at that day. Dennis and Vanmeter had been recently killed and the whites were distrustful of the Indians for many years in the early settlement of the country.

It must be recollected that fifty years ago the whole country was crowded with aborigines and there was a very small amount of white population in proportion. On the frontiers in Randolph, the inhabitants were not so much exposed to the fierce and hostile bands of Indians as those in the north. What also prevented the growth of the country was the want of mills, schools, and houses of worship All these difficulties taken together were adverse to the speedy growth of the country These colonies in Illinois lingered in this condition for many years When a brave, hardy, independent family came and settled among these original pioneers, it was hailed as a jubilee and all treated the new-comers as brothers.

The most trouble and labor was in either obtaining corn-meal or doing without it Flour at that time was not much in use All the frontiers of Goshen Settlement and in fact all the upper colonies were compelled to go to Cahokia or to Judy's mill, near Whiteside's Station, for their grinding. The extreme settlements were forced to travel fifty miles or more for their meal for many years. This is the necessary result of a pioneer's life To relieve absolute want, the band-mill, propelled by horsepower, was the pioneer that made its appearance and was hailed as a kind of Godsend. Several of these mills were erected in Goshen Settlement. The Pruits built one at the edge of the prairie a few miles east of the present town of Collinsville. Talbot had first a horse-mill and afterward a small water-mill on the Quentine Creek, south of Collinsville Cornelius built a water-mill on the same creek, below Elliot had a horse-mill south of the present Edwardsville about three miles. Carpenter kept one in the Six-Mile Prairie and Thomas Kirkpatrick built a water-mill many times on Cahokia Creek, adjoining the present Edwardsville. These were the pioneer mills of the frontiers for many years and were built before 1807 I have myself rode on bags to the most of them when I was a lad residing with my father in Goshen.

In early times, McCann owned a horse-mill of much celebrity and standing This mill was situated a few miles east of Turkey Hill and was attended by its customers far and near The mill of Hosea Rigg was a few miles west of that of McCann. About this time, Chapman built a small water-mill on the creek west of Belleville and old Mr. Schook erected a still smaller one on the small branch west of the mill of Chapman. These water-mills were like faith without works, not worth much In the southern settlements, the people procured their grinding at the New Design, Levens', or at Kaskaskia Under these circumstances, what great rejoicing it was with the people when green corn and potatoes made their appearance and were fit for use To procure grinding was the greatest trouble and inconvenience of the new settlements. This want of mills retarded the improvement of the country in early times more than all other considerations Schools and preaching could be dispensed with better than corn-meal

The country at that day was more sickly than it is at present, but the only disease then was the bilious fevers with the pleur.sy at rare intervals. The bilious attacks showed themselves mostly in the form of fever and ague. The fever without the ague or some chill with it was not frequent. These diseases attacked the people in the latter part of the summer and in the fall and were very common, but not often fatal. The sickness at this time is not so common, but more malignant and dangerous. Many in olden times were sick in the fall, but few died. By improvement or by some other means, the diseases of the country have changed within the last fifty years to be much fewer cases, but more fatal. The remedies to cure the bilious fever and ague in the first settlement of the country were tartar-emetic, calomel, and jalap and peruvian barks These were the uniform and universal medicines and they generally succeeded. When the patient was weak after the fever, the doctors prescribed *stimulus* of wine, etc But in the fall, after the sickness disappeared and all things were plenty, the citizens soon forgot the disease and turned their attention to fun, frolic, and hunting.

In pure pioneer times, the crops of corn were never husked on the stalk, as is done at this day; but was hauled home in the husk and thrown in a heap, generally by the side of the crib, so that the ears when husked could be thrown direct into the crib. The whole neighborhood, male and female, were invited to the shucking, as it was called The girls and many of the married ladies generally engaged in this amusing work In the first place, two leading, expert huskers were chosen as captains and the heap of corn divided as near equal as possible Rails were laid across the pile, so as to designate the division, and then each captain chose alternately his corps of huskers, male and female. The whole number of working hands present were selected on one side or the other and then each party commenced a contest to beat the other, which was in many cases truly exciting One other rule was that whenever a male husked a red ear of corn, he was entitled to a kiss from the girls. This frequently excited much fuss and scuffling, which was intended by both parties to end in a kiss

It was a universal practise that tafia or Monongahela whisky was used at these husking frolics, which they drank out of a bottle—each one, male and female, taking the bottle and drinking out of it and then handing it to his next neighbor, without using any glass or cup whatever. This custom was common and not considered rude. The bread used at these frolics was baked generally on johnny or journey-cake boards and is the best corn-bread ever made. A board is made smooth, about two feet long and eight inches wide, the ends are generally rounded. The dough is spread out on this board and placed leaning before the fire. One side is baked and then the dough is changed on the board, so the other side is presented in its turn to the fire. This is johnny-cake and is good if the proper materials are put in the dough and it is properly baked. Almost always these corn-shuckings ended in a dance. To prepare for this amusement, fiddles and fiddlers were in great demand and it often required much fast riding to obtain them. One violin and a performer were all that was contemplated at these innocent, rural dances.

Toward dark and the supper half over, then it was that a bustle and confusion commenced. The confusion of tongues at Babel would have been ashamed of those at the corn-shuckings. The young ones hurrying off the table and the old ones contending for time and order. It was the case nine times out of ten that but one dwelling-house was on the premises and that used for eating as well as dancing. But when the fiddler commenced tuning his instrument, the music always gained the victory for the young side. Then the dishes, victuals, table, and all disappeared in a few minutes and the room was cleared, the dogs drove out, and the floor swept off, ready for action. The floors of these houses were sometimes the natural earth, beat solid, sometimes the earth with puncheons in the middle over the potato hole, and at times the whole floor was made of puncheons. Sawed planks or boards were not at all common in early times.

The music at these country dances made the young folks almost frantic and sometimes much excitement was displayed to get first on the floor to dance. Generally the fiddler on these occasions assumed an important bearing and ordered in true professional style so and so to be done, as that was the way in North Carolina, where he was raised. This decision ended the contest for the floor. In those days they danced jigs and four-handed reels, as they were called. Sometimes three-handed reels were also danced. In these dances there was no standing still. All were moving at the same time, at a rapid pace, from the beginning to the end. In the jigs, the by-standers cut one another out, as it was called, so that this dance would last for hours at times. Sometimes the parties in a jig tried to tire one another down in the dance and then it would also last a long time before one or the other gave up. The cotillons or stand-still dances were not then known. Waltzes were introduced into the country at a late day by the Europeans.

The dress of these hardy pioneers was generally in plain homespun. The hunting-shirt was much worn at that time, which is a convenient working or dancing-dress. Sometimes dressed deer-skin pantaloons were used on these occasions and moccasons, rarely shoes, and at times, bare feet were indulged in. The bottle went round at these parties like it did at the shuckings and male and female took a dram out of it as it passed around. No sitting was indulged in and the folks either stood up or danced all night, as generally daylight ended the frolic. A great deal of good feeling was enjoyed in these innocent parties and very little of the green-eyed monster was displayed on these occasions. Mothers could then praise with sincerity the beauty and the grace in the dance of their neighbors' daughters, while at this refined and civilized day, such praises come only from the lips and scarcely that deep. Excessive refinement and accomplishments may polish the outside; but it is doubtful if the inside is made better by the operation.

Many a sweet love-story was told over, in a laughing manner, by the young hunters or farmers to their sweethearts during these nights of innocent amusement. The young man of eighteen would cough, choke, and spit, look pale, and sweat when he was about to tell his girl the secret movements of his heart in her favor, while his heart thumped with almost as loud a noise as a pheasant beating on a log. The girl received these outpourings of her lover's heart with such sparkling eyes and countenance that it spoke volumes of love to her beau. These love contracts that ended in marriage were frequently made at the dances.

What ineffable pleasure it was to these young folks to dance together, who had in sincerity unfolded their hearts to each other. These honest, unsophisticated children of nature love with more sincerity and honesty than the excessively refined and educated do. In the morning, all go home on horseback or on foot No carriages, wagons, or other wheeled vehicles were used on these occasions for the best of reasons : because they had none.

The pioneers dropped slowly into the Illinois country. Jacob Judy was a very ancient and respectable pioneer in Illinois. He came and settled in Kaskaskia in 1788 He was born in Germany and emigrated to the United States when he was six years old. He married in Frederick County, Maryland, moved to Pittsburg, where he worked for the public at the gunsmith business for many years and received nothing for it He had three children. In 1786, he and family descended the Ohio River to Kentucky. On the river, at the mouth of the Scioto, he heard the Indians making noises to decoy him to land; but he kept straight on. He had but one man with him besides his family. His daughter, Nancy Judy, then eighteen years old—who is still alive and eighty years of age—steered the boat, while her father, her brother, Samuel Judy, his son, and the hired man rowed the craft with all possible speed by this dangerous section of the river. He remained two years near Louisville in Kentucky and descended the Ohio in a flat-boat He was forced up Cache River, in the present county of Alexander, for protection from the Indians and remained there for seven weeks until a boat could come from Kaskaskia to his relief. He resided at Kaskaskia four years and then moved, in 1792, to the New Design. In 1794, he settled at his mill and died there in 1807

Judy worked at his trade in Illinois and accumulated considerable property. He possessed a strong mind, with much enterprise and energy Samuel Judy, his only son, came with his father to Illinois in 1788, and became a conspicuous and enterprising citizen. He married into the Whiteside family and settled in Goshen, as before stated, in 1801. In his youth, he was active and vigorous and was always ready and willing to enter into any campaign against the Indians or to do battle with them

In 1794, Joel Whiteside was driving a yoke of oxen about

one hundred and fifty yards southwest of the public square in the present town of Waterloo and an Indian shot him. The ball passed thro his body, but did not kill him. Judy, Todd, Andy Kinney, and some others pursued the Indian with dogs and guns; overtook the murderer and killed him under a large tree which stood near the main road, about half a mile south of Whiteside's Station. The tree is now cut down and a field made round it. Young Samuel Judy was very active and energetic in the pursuit of this Indian and displayed the warrior in this, his first Indian skirmish In two desperate conflicts with the Indians—one on Shoal Creek with old Pecon and the other near the bluff and below the place where the macadamized road descends it—Judy showed himself to be the bravest of the brave

In the late war with Great Britain in 1812, he was always actively employed in the service. He commanded a company of spies in the campaign under Gov. Edwards in 1812, against the Indians at the head of Peoria Lake, and acquitted himself, as he always did, to the satisfaction of the public This service in the campaign of 1812 was arduous and at times dangerous The spies were in advance of the little army, a mile or more, and were ordered to fight the enemy, let him be great or small, until the main army were placed in the order of battle behind them. He shot an Indian near the Black Partridge's Town, at the upper end of Peoria Lake, and killed him.

In the next campaign, in the fall of 1813, he also commanded a company in the army of Gen Howard. Like all his military services, he did his duty to the entire satisfaction of the public. In many of the skirmishes on the frontiers, Judy was active and efficient, and at the same time, prudent and cautious He was always, in these military preferments, very modest and unassuming. He never solicited an office in his life and would always have preferred acting as a private in these operations against the Indians, but his neighbors and friends almost compelled him to take command, as above stated. He was elected to the legislative council of the Illinois Territory, in the fall of 1812, from the county of Madison This was the first legislature that convened under the territorial government and was a very important general assembly. This body convened at Kaskaskia and transacted very important business in organizing and starting the machinery of the new government into operation. The finances were to be regulated, taxes imposed, and the militia organized These subjects were of the greatest importance and interest to the people Judy performed his duties in this office much to his credit and also to the advantage of his constituents.

Nature had been bountiful to Judy and had bestowed on him a clear, sound, and solid judgment He had very little opportunities of education and could barely make out to read and write and knew but little of the arithmetic; but his condition in life and his strong mind, with his retentive memory, made him a very able and efficient member of the legislative council of the territory These qualifications, together with his merited character for honesty and probity, gave him a standing in the legislature which was not surpassed by any member in that body and which was always wielded for the benefit of the public. He remained in this office for four years and made an excellent member. The people of Madison County elected him to the important office of county commissioner for many years. His solid judgment, together with his positive honesty and practical economy, made him a most able and efficient member of the county-court. This was an office in which he displayed his talents. The county levies were to be made and the money expended on proper objects This required just the judgment, honesty, and economy which he possessed in such an eminent degree, to enable him to execute the duties of the office. The finances of Madison County were safe in the hands of Col Judy.

With these talents, he managed his own private business with great success. He became wealthy by the common operations of agriculture, without speculation or chicanery. He improved a large plantation and built a fine brick-house—the first erected within the limits of Madison County. This house he built in 1808, and much enlarged and improved his farm the same year. In this new country, he availed himself of its advantages and raised large stocks of horses, cattle, hogs, and sheep The cattle lived winter and summer in the range and the horses did the same, with a small amount of food in the bad weather of the winter.

In the matured age of Col. Judy, I, as the executive of the

State, appointed him, with three others, warden of the penitentiary at Alton. The duty of this board was to adopt a penitentiary system, erect a suitable building, and put the whole machinery into complete operation I was one of the board and found that Judy was a wise, prudent, and efficient member. The plan and system of the prison at Alton were based on that of Auburn, New York. This at Alton has succeeded admirably well He died at his residence in Madison County in 1833, aged seventy-five years The death of Col Judy was sincerely regretted by the public His large family and connections knew well his worth and mourned his death with heart-felt grief But mortality is born with all human beings It is the just law of God and we must and ought to submit to it with pious resignation

Few men had a mind more equally balanced than his was. It was moulded far above mediocrity No trait had the ascendancy to destroy the legitimate operations of the others His powers of judgment were strong; so was his perception clear and discriminating. His imagination was kept in proper bounds by his solid judgment and his kindness and benevolence were strongly marked in his actions thro life. His courage was of the unterrified order, which had been tested on many occasions in the service of his country He was moral and correct in his habits during a long life; never joined a church, but sustained all with his good-will and friendship He never indulged in any of the excesses so prevalent in his day—of gaming, drinking, or light and frivolous amusements Judy was a pioneer that gave standing and character to the country and it is the seeds sown by him and such characters that have produced such fruits in Illinois of her future power and greatness He left a large family of children and also a large estate

The stock of Col Judy was injured by that mysterious disease known as the milk-sickness It made its appearance in early times in his stock and remains to this day rather a mystery as to the cause of the disease That such malady does exist, there is no doubt The human family as well as animals are destroyed by it I had a sister whose death, it was supposed, was caused by it It is known that the disease is a poison. Dogs and other animals die with the poison when they eat in the dead

bodies—the victims of this disease. The human beings who die by the disease derive it from the milk, butter, or meat of the animal infected with the poison. The name of the disease arises from the milk the victims eat. This much is ascertained; but what *is* the poison, is not so well known. It is the general approved opinion that the poison is emitted from some poisonous mineral substance in the earth. It rises in a gaseous state; falls back on the vegetation; is infused in the water, and in the morning before the dew is evaporated, the animals eat the poison with the vegetation and thereby die. The disease only appears in the fall of the year and in shady, damp localities. A vegetable can not cause the disease because it would have been discovered, and in some cases, animals that are kept up and eat no green food, die by the use of the water impregnated with the poison. It makes its ravages on stock in many parts of the West. Sometimes for many years it almost disappears and afterward returns and assumes its former virulence.

The first governor of Illinois under the State government—Shadrach Bond—was a great, noble, and talented pioneer. He stood in the front ranks of that hardy and noble race of men, the ancient pioneers of Illinois. The few remaining of that class may look back at Gov. Bond with the proud recollection that he was one of them and was a sample of good sense, honesty, and most of the virtues that elevate and dignify the human character. Shadrach Bond was born in Frederick Co., Maryland, in 1773, and was raised by a pious father, Nicholas Bond, on a plantation. He was educated a practical farmer and such was his occupation during life, except the services in public stations he performed, which detained him from his farm for some portion of his time. In 1794, when he reached his majority, he emigrated to Illinois and resided in the American Bottom with his uncle, Shadrach Bond, Sr. He received in Maryland a plain English education, such as farmers generally bestow on their children. But Illinois, when he reached it, was a wild country, not much disposed to the improvement of the mind in science and literature. Yet man and his various actions were before him and he acquired the practical knowledge of mankind and the various springs of human action. He learned in his early life much useful knowledge of all the various moving principles of the human heart and availed himself of this information in after-life. Gov Bond was in his matured age an intelligent, practical man. He was not a lady-parlor scholar, who read the novels of lovesick swains and fainting girls; nor did he ever wash his face with cologne-water; but he was nature's nobleman, educated in the wide world of the human family, and his conscience and sound judgment were his unerring preceptors. Some think a man is not intelligent or learned if he were not cudgelled thro a college or read "Robinson Crusoe" or the novel of "Goody Two Shoes." The whole creation should be a man's school-house and nature his teacher. Bond studied in this college and Providence gave him a diploma

He for some years resided with his uncle after he first came to Illinois and indulged in much of the gayety and amusements of the country at that day, but when age and experience reached him, he changed his course and purchased a fine farm on the bank of a beautiful lake in the American Bottom and improved it in good style. He resided here for many years, a single farmer About 1800, the whole society changed its character to some extent to a more civilized and moral state; and the agricultural and other interests of the country changed in the same proportion. Bond was, by his example and precept, greatly instrumental in bringing about this desirable change He labored with his own hands on his farm, with such assistance as he could procure at that early day He felt an honest pride in being dependent on no one for his support except on his mother-earth and God, that giveth the increase He spent the happiest part of his life on his farm He possessed a jovial and convivial spirit, and with his friends he enjoyed much happiness These convivial parties were not based on gluttonness or intemperance; but they were sustained by the noble and generous hearts of the higher order of warm and congenial spirits. Bond possessed warm and ardent feelings and when excited in the society of his friends around the festive board, he not only was happy himself, but made all around him happy also. In these parties, he was the fountain of hilarity and good feelings and imparted it to all others around him He possessed a heart filled with true benevolence and good kind feelings to all the human race, and on these occasions the feelings that adorn the human character flowed deep and strong

He generally kept a large pack of hounds and with his friends, the fox-hunt was with him capital sport. The hounds, horn, and the voice of Gov. Bond made sweet music in the mornings on the commons near the village of Kaskaskia in olden times. He took great delight in this rural sport and in fact all his impulses and his disposition were inclined to the cheerful and bright side of human nature, so he generally enjoyed himself and made all around him happy, likewise. When he reached man's estate, in the American Bottom, on his farm, his person was large and portly. He weighed two hundred pounds and was six feet high. His person was erect, compact, and formed with perfect symmetry. His bearing was noble, dignified, and commanding and his features were regular, but marked, strong, and masculine. His complexion was dark and his hair a glossy jet-black. His eyes were large, brilliant, and of a hazel color. His forehead was large and capacious and his countenance denoted him to possess superior intellect, with many other marked traits of character that adorn human nature. Such was the person of farmer Bond.

With such character as Bond possessed and with his fine person, he was a great favorite with the ladies; yet his gallantries, altho many, were always circumscribed with propriety. He possessed the capital in this branch of business, but never traded in it to any great extent. In his early life, he was elected a member to the general assembly of Indiana Territory, which met at Vincennes. He made, as he always afterward did, a sound, solid member. He attended faithfully to the business of the people and mingled again with his constituents. In 1812, he was elected the first delegate from the Territory of Illinois to congress, and in this office he performed great and important services for his constituents By his exertions in that body, the first act of congress was passed in 1813, to grant the citizens the right of preëmption to secure their improvements. This was the first great lever that moved Illinois onward toward that glorious eminence she occupies at this time. The people, before this act of congress passed, had, nine-tenths of them, settled on the public lands and had no right or title to their plantations whatever. No one was certain of securing his improvement or labor and therefore small improvements were made.

This provision was hailed as the greatest and the best. It gave the country peace and quiet for the citizens in it and broke down the barriers against immigration to the territory. Ever after this act was passed—which not only secured the right of preemption to settlers, but brought the public lands into market —the flood of immigration was deep, strong, and constant. This act of congress was the great key-stone to the arch of the prosperity and growth of Illinois. This one act entitles Bond to the lasting gratitude of his country. "Men's evil manners live in brass, their virtues we write in water." How often do we hear, at this day, the young politicians casting slurs and disrespect on such respectable statesmen as Gov. Bond. Many of these modern politicians are manufactured in the colleges by the wealth of their fathers, in the same manner as a mechanic makes an axe-handle and with almost as little intellect as the handle. Yet, because the pioneer statesman did not graduate with a parchment diploma, he must receive the ridicule of these modern butterfly critics and calico politicians. Nature gave her richest diplomas to Cromwell, Hannibal, and Washington, without their being kicked thro a college like an unwilling jack is whipped to his labor. The gigantic talents of Jackson and Clay, two of the greatest men the nation has produced since the Revolution, were never cramped and degraded by the monotonous *routine* of a collegiate education. I am in favor of a proper education and opposed to the abuse of one. All I dislike is these tinsel scholars condemning men "whose shoes' latchet they are not worthy to loose."

Bond remained in congress only one term and was appointed receiver of public moneys at Kaskaskia. This was a laborious and responsible office. The commissioners to adjust the ancient claims to land in Illinois had not completed their work and Bond, together with Michael Jones, examined a great many of the claims; reported them to congress, and they were approved. This was a delicate trust to perform, as the inhabitants and commissioners in former days were unfriendly on the subject; but Bond, with his usual good sense and honesty, gave general satisfaction. About this time, 1814, he moved from his old plantation in the American Bottom to Kaskaskia and made a large farm near that village. The intercourse of the people with Bond made them know and appreciate his merits, and at the election for State officers, he was chosen governor of the State without opposition. The honest and sincere friendship of the people for him made him the first governor of Illinois without opposition. The duties of this office were important, onerous, and difficult to perform. The change of the laws, policy, and all, from a territorial to a state government, required prudence, circumspection, and much wisdom He possessed these qualifications and performed his duties to the general satisfaction of the people.

Gov Bond strongly urged on the people and the first legislatures of Illinois, during his term in office, the propriety and utility of constructing a canal connecting the waters of Lake Michigan with those of the Mississippi Some short time after his term of office as governor expired, he was appointed register of the land-office at Kaskaskia, wherein he remained in his old age, doing business to the satisfaction of the public On April 11, 1830, he expired in happiness and in peace with man His last breath was breathed in good will to the human family and praise to God He left a very blameless and unspotted character and as such, his friends and the public mourned his death To his respectable family, their loss was irreparable. He was a kind parent and an affectionate husband His earthly career is ended, but his worthy character stands strong in the hearts of the pioneers and others of Illinois *

Gov. Bond had two brothers, Nicodemus and Joshua Bond, who also settled in the American Bottom Joshua Bond remained in Illinois but a few years, went to St. Louis, in Upper Louisiana, and thence to Vincennes on the Wabash He raised a large and respectable family, who have for the most part settled in Illinois The descendants of Joshua Bond possess a

* Gov. Bond had six children Thomas S , Emily, Julia R , Mary A., Isabella F , and Benjamin N All are now dead except Dr Benjamin N Bond, who resides in Stanberry, Mo Julia R Bond married Col Frank Swanwick of Randolph Co ; Mary A. married Joseph B Holmes, a merchant of Chester, in the same county, Isabella F married James P Craig of the same place The descendants of Gov. Bond number many of the most respected and wealthy citizens of Randolph Co

In April, 1881, the remains of Gov Bond and his wife were removed from Kaskaskia to Chester and consigned to the same vault, over which a monument was erected by authority of the legislature of Illinois, act approved May 28, 1881.—J H G.

good standing in community. Several of the sons sustain a very respectable reputation at the bar as talented lawyers, and one of them, Benjamin, is at this time a sound lawyer and the marshal of the State of Illinois. One other, Thomas, was captain of a company in the Mexican war and acted well his part in that service. All the Bond family may look back with gratitude and honest pride to their illustrious and venerable relative, Shadrach Bond, Sr , who was the brave and daring pioneer that enrolled himself in the Revolutionary war under the banner of Col. Clark, and he may say, with Clark and his troops, as Cæsar said in ancient times. "We came, we saw, we conquered"—Illinois. He was the illustrious Columbus of his family that discovered the new world for them, and as such, this ancient patriarch receives their gratulations and sincere homage.

The country gradually increased in its population. In 1803, John Primm emigrated from Virginia and settled first in the New Design, made a crop there, and settled at the foot of the Mississippi Bluff, southeast of Cahokia; remained here several years and moved to his plantation, a few miles southwest of Belleville. He died there in 1836, aged almost eighty-seven years. Mr Primm was born in Stafford County, Va.; served in the Revolutionary war immediately under Gen. Washington, and assisted at the glorious capture of Lord Cornwallis at Yorktown in 1781. This was the crowning battle for the freedom of the human race and Primm enjoyed the honor of aiding in this great and glorious victory. He had a large family—seventeen children—four girls and thirteen sons. He lived the even, temperate life of an agriculturist and performed all his duties to the Creator and to man in a moral and correct manner. One of his sons was carrying the United-States mail in August, 1814, on horseback from Cahokia to Clinton-Hill post-office, two or three miles northeast of Belleville, and in the Derush Hollow, so called at the time, near the Bottom, he and his horse were killed by the lightning. His body was burnt black by the electricity.

In 1799, sailed down the Ohio River, Matthew Lyon and family, with John Messinger and Dr George Cadwell and their respective families. These last two named were the sons-in-law of Lyon and all settled at Eddyville in Kentucky. Matthew Lyon had obtained a considerable celebrity as a member in congress from the State of Vermont. He was a native of Ireland; had been in the Revolution, and was a warm advocate of Thomas Jefferson and republicanism against John Adams and federalism He possessed some talents and much ardor and enthusiasm. While he was in congress, he had a difficulty with a member of the federal party and spit in his face. He was up before congress for contempt; but speeches were the only result. He was extremely bitter against the administration of Adams and he was fined and imprisoned under the alien and sedition laws While he was in prison in the State of Vermont, his friends elected him to congress and took him out of confinement to serve them in the congress of the United States He represented his district in congress from Kentucky for several terms and was always, during a long and important life, an excessively warm and enthusiastic partisan in politics. He was at last appointed an Indian agent for the Southern Indians and died there at an advanced age. Long after his death, congress paid back to his heirs the fine he paid, with interest. It was considered by congress that the fine was paid under a void law and that it was due to principle, as well as to his descendants, to refund the amount paid and interest. I voted in congress to refund the fine and interest to his heirs

Matthew Lyon was a droll composition. His leading trait of character was his zeal and enthusiasm, almost to madness itself, in any cause he espoused. He never seemed to act cool and deliberate, but always in a tumult and bustle, as if he were in a house on fire and was hurrying to get out. His Irish impulses were honest and always on the side of human freedom This covers his excessive zeal.

Messinger and Dr. Cadwell left Eddyville in 1802, and landed from a boat in the American Bottom, not far above old Fort Chartres They remained in the Bottom for some time and Dr. Cadwell moved and settled on the Illinois bank of the Mississippi, opposite the Gaborit Island and above St Louis He was quite a respectable citizen, practised his profession and served the people in various public offices. He was justice-of-the-peace and county-court judge for many years, in both St. Clair County and in Madison also, after its formation. Since the establishment of the State government, he served in the general assembly from both Madison and Green counties, at different times, and always acquitted himself to the satisfaction of the public After a long life, spent in usefulness, he died in Morgan County, quite an old man He was moral and correct in his public and private life and left a character much more to be admired than condemned; was a respectable physician and always sustained an unblemished character

John Messinger was born in West Stockbridge, Mass., in 1771, and was raised a farmer. He was in his youth educated both to work and the ordinary learning derived from books at a school This system of farmers learning their children the science and practise of agriculture, as well as science from books, deserves particular consideration, and this mixture of education seems to me to be the best that a young American can receive

Messinger, when he advanced some years in age, in his agricultural pursuits, he commenced the study of mathematics with William Coit, who resided in the neighborhood of his father In 1783, he left Massachusetts and settled in Vermont and learned not only the art of farming, but also in his early life became acquainted with the business of a carpenter or housebuilder and the trade also of a millwright He possessed a strong and vigorous intellect and his mind, by either nature or education or by both, became quite solid and mathematical. He possessed also a great share of energy and activity; so that it was not a difficult task for him to acquire these different mechanical trades as well as to become deeply versed in mathematical science.

In maturer age, his whole delight and pleasure was found in the science of mathematics and the various practical branches arising out of that science. His whole life seemed to be tinctured with mathematics and I believe for many years he was the most profound mathematician and best land-surveyor in Illinois He moved to the New Design from the American Bottom and in 1804, purchased a mill and premises on Rock-House Creek, east of the New Design. He repaired the mill and resided there for some years and then moved to Clinton Hill, his late residence, a few miles northeast of Belleville.

John Messinger, by the force of his genius and energies, became an excellent English scholar and was always pleased to have an opportunity to instruct any of his neighbors or friends that would call on him for that object. He taught the science of surveying to a great many young men and has also taught many grown people, males and females, the common rudiments of education even after they were married. He reached Illinois in 1802, when there was scarcely a school in the country and it was honorable to both him and his students for one to give and the other to receive an education if it were after the parties were married.

Messinger was not large in his person, but compactly built, hardy and very energetic. With the talents he possessed and his activity, he was extremely useful, not only in teaching the art of surveying to others, but in the practical operations of surveying himself. He was the first person or among the first surveyors that, in 1806, surveyed the United-States lands in townships in this section of the State. In town six, south range seven, west, and in that region of country, the public domain was surveyed by Messinger in the above year. I think he was a subcontractor under William Rector. He surveyed much of the public domain in St. Clair and Randolph counties.

He not only was an excellent mathematician, but he wrote and published a book entitled, "A Manual or Hand-Book, intended for Convenience in Practical Surveying." This work was printed by William Orr in St Louis in 1821, and contains the whole science of practical surveying, together with the necessary tables to enable the practitioner to calculate the area of land without any difficulty whatever. This book shows deep research by the author and establishes the fact that he was a profound mathematician. He was professor of mathematics in the seminary at Rock Spring, St Clair County, for some time and performed the duties of this responsible station to the entire satisfaction of the public. In 1815, he was appointed deputy-surveyor under the surveyor-general, Edward Tiffin of the State of Ohio, and was authorized to survey the Military Tract in the forks of the Mississippi and Illinois rivers. He surveyed much of this tract, which was approved by the surveyor-general. He was appointed, with a gentleman of Hillsborough, Illinois, to survey, on the part of the State of Illinois, the northern limits of the State, in latitude forty-two, one-half degrees north. Hon Lucius Lyon of Michigan was the commissioner on the part of the United States to assist in the survey.

Messinger was an efficient and scientific astronomer and mathematician in calculating the latitude and surveying this line dividing the State of Illinois from Wisconsin He and Philip Creamer, a celebrated artisan, made surveyors' compasses that were as well calculated and as well finished in workmanship as any made in the United States Messinger was never ambitious of public office, yet the public called on him and he served them both in the general assemblies of the Indiana Territory and the State of Illinois He was elected, in 1808, from the county of St Clair to the legislature of Indiana Territory and did much toward obtaining a division of the territory, which took place the next year. He was elected from St Clair Co. a member of the convention that met at Kaskaskia and formed the State constitution in 1818 He made a cautious and prudent member, always wise without rashness In the first general assembly of the State of Illinois, at its organization in 1818, he was elected speaker of the house of representatives. He was a member elect from St Clair County and made an upright and impartial speaker. This was an important legislature and much business was done during the session.

He gave his children a common, good education and learned almost all of them the art of surveying. He never acquired any great amount of wealth, altho he had great opportunities to acquire property. He had no talent for speculation, was rigidly and scrupulously honest and possessed an ambition to appear plain and unassuming He seemed to be proud of his want of pride His morals and orderly bearing were above reproach and such as even a clergyman might be proud of. His mind was strong and mathematical and all its various movements seemed to be in search of some abstruse problem in that science that delighted him so much He died on his plantation in 1846, aged seventy-five years At his death, he had no enemies, but truly all friends that mourned his decease He had not time or disposition to attend to his farm He seemed resigned to leave this vale of tears with the hopes of being with his God to enjoy a happy immortality.

William Kinney was a great and talented pioneer of olden times and enjoyed a high and conspicuous standing in Illinois. He was blessed with a vigorous and strong intellect and also with great energy. Kinney was born in Kentucky in 1781, and emigrated, in 1793, with his father to the New Design, Illinois When he came to the country, he was thirteen years old and at nineteen he married. His youthful days he had spent with the young people of the country in gay and amusing society. The young folks at that day did not work much and received no book-education whatever. The occupation of the youths and sometimes of the aged of that day was pleasure and amusements of various descriptions. Young Kinney was never behind any one in these merriments and recreations He was the leader in these festivities and amusements and altho many of the young men were injured by them, yet Kinney learned by this course of life much of the human heart and the various movements of human nature. He inherited from nature great parts and he improved them in every situation he was placed in during a long and important life. His mind was strong and solid whenever he took time to reflect His judgment of men and things was good to a proverb. His memory was retentive, as he never forgot what he learned in either a frolic or under the droppings of the sanctuary. His energy and activity were boundless. These great and strong traits of character were all developed before he ever opened a book and in truth, he never went to school regularly as a scholar more than three months in his life. Both his natural disposition and his early education inclined him thro life to gayety and amusements of every character. He possessed a fund of pure attic wit and his satire, when called out on proper occasions, was severe and scathing, and his anecdotes were extremely pertinent on many illustrations and were boundless; but his sound judgment restrained these traits of character in their appropriate limits.

After he was married, he was taught by John Messinger to read and write. The arithmetic he mastered himself in his own way. This is the foundation of all his scholastic education and on it and his observation and reflection, he became intelligent and made one of the most prominent, popular, and influential characters of his day. It would be almost useless to remark that at his marriage and always before and for some time after, he was entirely destitute of worldly means, except a mere support. In his youth, his wild-oats were strong and rank, so that he had neither time or disposition to accumulate property; but being the head of a family and assuming a rank in society, he was forced to reflect and he changed his conduct. In 1803, he located himself on a beautiful and commanding eminence a few miles northeast of the present City of Belleville and commenced with his own hands to make a farm on these premises. His wife was a most excellent lady, of sound mind and amiable disposition. They were both, at that time, young, talented, and poor, so they possessed the elements of success and they used them much to their honor and advancement. His amiable and excellent wife, with her first-born, was often out in the clearings and in the field, assisting her husband to gain their daily bread. They placed the child on a blanket and the parents worked in its neighborhood to improve their farm. Mr. Kinney in those days went to market himself in St. Louis and Cahokia and sold his surplus articles raised by his own hands on his farm. He resided first in a small house south of his late residence a half-mile or more and it was there he and wife made the first improvement.

In 1809, Mr. Vonphul persuaded Kinney to take some few articles of merchandise and sell them; if he could not sell them, he might return them to Vonphul again. After some hesitation, he took the goods. They consisted of a few bolts of domestic manufactured cotton cloth and Kinney packed them before him on his horse from St. Louis to his farm. At that time, he could barely write and knew nothing of book-keeping, but his natural strong talents enabled him to invent a system of book-keeping for himself, without any previous knowledge of the science. This is the very humble and the very honorable commencement of the pecuniary career of Gov. Kinney. He began at this low foundation without any resources but his great mind and energies and he made a princely fortune in the same place and country where he commenced thus humble. He traded in merchandise, lands, horses, and almost everything that had any value attached to it and always made on the business he embarked in. He erected a comfortable house on the eminence where it now stands and in it, he displayed a kindness and hospitality rarely equaled in any country or in any age. His house was almost always crowded with his friends and they were always entertained with an unsparing hospitality

In matured life, he entered the political arena and was a warm and efficient politician. He was a Democrat, "dyed in the wool," and maintained the doctrines of the party without fear or affectation on all occasions He was often elected from St Clair County to the general assembly of the State of Illinois and made an efficient business member. In the first general assembly after the organization of the State government, he was a member and assisted to put the political machinery in operation In 1826, he was elected lieutenant-governor of the State and presided in that office in a manner to give character and standing to the State Altho he served the people in these public offices, he attended strictly in his early life to his private business and accumulated wealth all the time In the decline of life, he was appointed commissioner of internal improvements, which gave him much trouble and was a great injury to his fortune He died in 1843, aged sixty-two years, on his farm where he lived forty years His death was regretted by his friends and family In his early life, he became interested in religion and was baptized in 1809 He not only became a worthy and devout member of the Baptist church, but was authorized by the church to preach the gospel and became a distinguished and influential preacher His sound judgment displayed itself in this profession as well as in all his other transactions in life

The travel on the road from the Ohio to Kaskaskia increased and it became necessary and also profitable to make tavern stands on the road Comfort Joy, an Eastern man, in 1804, made the first establishment on Big-Muddy River where the old Massac Trace crossed it. He resided some years here He was on his way to the Ohio Salt-Works with his cart and and oxen and by some means, the oxen kicked him, causing his death The family broke up and left the stand

In 1803, Hays and some others formed the first settlements on Big-Bay Creek, some miles northwest of the present town of Golconda, Pope County. This settlement continued to increase. William Jones and John Finley stopped in it in 1804, and remained there two years before they moved to Madison County. In early times, in this settlement a murder was committed. The accused was brought to Kaskaskia for trial, as all that section of country was embraced in the county of Randolph at that day and Kaskaskia the county-seat. The man accused of the murder escaped. In 1805, Phelps, Daniels, and some others made a settlement on the Massac road, ten miles east of Big Muddy. Two settlements were made on Silver Creek in 1804, which were the first on the creek. One was made a few miles from the mouth, in this year, by Abraham Teter, Peter Mitchel, and a widow Shook—the sister of Teter They were the first families that located in the neighborhood of the present Solomon Teter, who is the son of Abraham Teter The other was made by the Bradsby family,* about three miles north of the present town of Lebanon, at the edge of the Looking-Glass Prairie.

William H. Bradsby, the oldest son, with two other young men, came out in the spring of 1804 from Kentucky, made an improvement and raised corn on the place above mentioned. The family moved in the fall. The settlement of the Bradsbys

* John Bradsby and William, his brother, soldiers of the Revolution, came to this country from Ireland about the middle of the 18th century, William was never heard of after entering the army, and it is supposed died in the service, John married Mary Higgins, a native of Virginia, in Bedford Co., Va., in 1785, and shortly after the birth of their eldest child, 1787, moved to Barren Co., Ky., where he taught school and preached for several years; and their children were:

Dr. Wm. H. Bradsby was born in Bedford Co., Va., July 12, 1787, married, Nov. 6, 1818, Catharine M. Higgins (born in Barren Co., Ky., 1801); of their ten children 3, Eloise, wid of Wm. Adams, living near Lebanon, 8, Henry Clay of Effingham, Ill., born Feb. 29, 1832, Covington, Washington Co., Ill; was educated at McKendree College, Ill., and Jefferson College, Pa., a lawyer, was married July 28, 1858, to Melinda, youngest child of Hon. Elijah C Berry, first State auditor, and have two children—the eldest married F. W. Burnett, attorney, Springfield, Ill., 9, Indiana, wid of J. H. Williams, residing in Lebanon, Ill; 10, Catharine, wife of Addison Pyle, residing near Lebanon, Ill., the others died young without issue. The Dr was the first postmaster in Washington Co (at Covington), the first school teacher, also the first circuit and county clerk and recorder, was probate and county judge when he died, and during many years was deputy U S surveyor, and surveyed much of this portion of the State, his labor extending as far east as Wayne and Clay counties, besides being clerk of all the courts he was virtually county treasurer, having the custody of the county money. All of the early records show his neat and elegant hand. He died in Nashville, Ill., August 21, 1839.

was in advance of the other inhabitants seven or eight miles. The Bradsby family were brave and energetic pioneers. They possessed good talents and were fearless and intrepid. They were firm and decisive when they took a stand and were also moral and correct and made excellent citizens. The old sire taught school in various neighborhoods. He had a school, in 1806, in the American Bottom, almost west of the present Collinsville, and the year after, he taught another in the Turkey-Hill Settlement. The other small colony on Silver Creek was also some distance from any other inhabitants. They likewise were good citizens

Peter Mitchell, in matured age, acted as a justice-of-the-peace and county commissioner. He was a moral, correct man and was one of the ancient emigrants from Hardy County, Virginia, who settled at the New Design in 1797. It would seem that there was a kind of fatality in colonizing a new country. Single families will frequently locate in advance of the other inhabitants, many miles in a wilderness, without obtaining any greater advantages than those enjoy in a more dense settlement.

The two oldest sons of Mr. Bradsby—William and James— were in the ranging service and made good soldiers. William H Bradsby, after he was here a few years, returned to the old

James, the second son, who served as a ranger in Whiteside's company, died at a ripe old age at the old home, near Lebanon, in 1868, left two sons, Addison and William, and three daughters, Mary, Priscilla, and Pauline, all dead except Addison, who lives on the old homestead

The third son, Richard, was 7 years of age when his father moved to Illinois; was married in 1831 to Lucinda Adams, and settled in Looking-Glass Prairie, was in the Black-Hawk War, first enlisting in Capt Wm Moore's company of Buckmaster's Odd Battalion in 1831, joining a spy company on the 19th of June, no record of his later service has been preserved; in 1848, he was elected one of the county board of St Clair Co , a position he held for many terms, and died Sept 5, 1875, leaving one child, Virginia, the wife of Dr James L Peryman of Belleville

Mary married Richard Higgins, both died several years ago, leaving three daughters who, with their descendants, live near Lebanon.

Priscilla married Thomas Chilton, and removed to Sangamon Co in 1819, and from thence to Wisconsin, where both died, leaving several children

Jane married Jesse Bayles, and was massacred with Lucinda Higgins, a sister of Mrs. W. H. Bradsby, by the Indians on Sugar Creek, in the fall of 1814

John married Naomi Faris, died in 1845, on his farm near Lebanon, leaving two sons, Francis and William, and a daughter Francis died in 1880, and William now resides in Greenville, in Bond County.—J H G

settlements; qualified himself and studied medicine. He was a good physician and practised some time, but disliked the profession and became rather a public character. He was elected to the State legislature from St Clair County in 1814, and made a good member He was appointed to most all or quite all the small offices in Washington County when that county was organized. He made his residence at Covington for many years and when the county-seat was moved to Nashville, he still held the offices and died about that time.

Dr Bradsby sustained well the reputation of a pioneer. He possessed a strong mind with a courage that quailed at no danger or disaster. We were United-States rangers* together in the same company, commanded by Capt. William B Whiteside in the war of 1812, with Great Britain. We were both sergeants and ranged together around the frontiers of the infant settlements of Illinois to defend them from Indian depredations By this occurrence, I became intimately acquainted with the merit and worth of Dr Bradsby and no man ever possessed a purer, better heart than he did His attachments and friendships were ardent and firm. He was generous and benevolent and always ready to relieve distress. His love of country and its free institutions was ardent and strong. When he was quite a lad, in 1804, when the stars and stripes were first raised in St. Louis, after the cession of Louisiana to the United States, on July 4 of that year, he quit his plow on Silver Creek and joined heart and soul in the celebration He rejoiced to see the free institutions of the United States extended over the country where Spanish tyranny had heretofore been sustained by that despotic government

David Philips, the head of a numerous and respectable family, emigrated from North Carolina, stopped in Tennessee and finally settled in Illinois He located himself and family on Richland Creek, a few miles south of the present City of Belle-

* Congress, in 1811, passed an act authorizing the organization of ten companies of rangers which afterward formed a regiment, known as the 17th U S Infantry, placed under the command of Col Wm Russell of Kentucky, a renowned Indian-fighter. Of these companies four were raised in Illinois Territory, those commanded respectively by Captains Samuel Whiteside, Wm. B Whiteside, James B Moore, and Jacob Short —J H. G

ville, in 1803. Mr Philips was born in Orange County, North Carolina, in 1755, and was a soldier in the glorious war of the Revolution He spent much of his youthful vigor in the tented field and reposed in proud defiance of British tyranny under the stars and stripes He trusted his all to God and liberty and he was victorious He heard of Illinois and when he saw it in 1803 he realized all his fond hopes of the promised land He emigrated to settle his large family in a new country. There are seven of his sons alive at this time and the youngest is upward upward of fifty years old He has also one daughter alive His descendants are numerous and respectable He and all his sons were raised farmers and they generally support themselves by that ancient and honorable profession to this day The aged father died at his residence, south of Belleville, in 1826, full of years and respected by his family and neighbors He led his large family thro the wilderness; settled them in a fine country and died happy

After the conquest of Illinois, the State of Virginia instructed Gen Clark to establish a fort at the Iron Banks on the Ohio River He executed this command as he did all others, with great wisdom and celerity He promised lands to all who would emigrate to the Iron Banks and settle there with or without their families This was a kind of armed occupation of the country. These promises of Clark and his extraordinary influence caused many families as well as many single men to locate at Fort Jefferson, which was the name of the fort at the Iron Banks. Toward the close of the Revolution, Virginia was not very able to sustain this garrison and the troops and families were compelled to leave it for the want of support The officers of the fort first quartered the soldiers on the citizens of the French villages and at other places for support, but not calling for them, they were compelled to shift for themselves Thus it was that many of Clark's men, as they were termed, as well as families, after 1780, were residents of the metropolis of the country, Old Kaskaskia

Pickett, Seybold, Groots, Hiltebrand, Dodge, Camp, Teel, Curry, Lunceford, Anderson, Pagon, Doyle, Hughes, Montgomery, and others were soldiers who had been in the service of Virginia under Clark, either at Fort Jefferson or in the conquest of Illinois It was part of these men who established the small colony on the east side of the Kaskaskia River, not far from the old town of Kaskaskia, after 1780

It was in this settlement, in the early part of the spring of 1788, that a most singular battle and siege occurred. David Pagon, one of Clark's men, had made a house two miles from Kaskaskia, on the east side of the river, and had finished it in a strong and substantial manner, so as to withstand an Indian attack Levi Teel and James Curry, also two of Clark's soldiers, had been out hunting on the east side of the river and had encamped in this house for the night The door of the house had three bars across it, to secure it against Indian assault, and in the door was a hole cut for the cat to go in and out Toward day, Curry informed Teel that there were Indians about the house and that they must fix up their guns for defence Teel was rather inclined to open the door and give up as prisoners, while Curry would not listen to it at all Teel went to the door to either open it or to make discoveries and stood with his foot near the cat hole The Indians outside stuck a spear thro his foot and fastened him to the floor. The Indians, in their war expeditions, always carry spears with them By a kind of instinct, Teel put his hand to the spear to draw it out of his foot and other spears were stuck in his hand They cut and mangled his hand in a shocking manner, so that he was not only nailed to the floor of the house, but his hands were rendered useless

It was ascertained afterward that it was the Piankeshaw Indians and there were sixteen in the band Curry was an extraordinary man; brave to desperation and inured to broil and feats of battle until he was always cool and prepared He jumped up in the loft of the house to drive the enemy off before Teel would open the door and by a small crevice in the roof, he put his gun out and shot into the crowd of Indians He shot three times with great rapidity, for fear Teel would open the door It was discovered afterward from the Indians that Curry had killed three warriors He then got down to see what Teel was about and found him transfixed to the floor, as above stated He then got up again in the loft and tumbled the whole roof, weight-poles and all, down on the Indians standing at the door with spears in their hands It will be recollected that in olden times the roofs of cabins were made with weight-poles on the boards, to keep them down. The pioneers used no nails as they do at this day. The roof falling on the enemy killed the chief and the others ran off. Day was breaking, which assisted also to disperse the Indians Curry took both guns and made Teel walk altho he was almost exhausted on account of the loss of blood. They had a hill to walk up at the start, which fatigued Teel and he gave out before they reached Kaskaskia altho they had only two miles to travel. Curry left Teel and went to Kaskaskia for help and at last saved himself and comrade from death.

To my own knowledge, the houses in times of Indian wars were fixed so the roofs could be thrown down on the enemy and sometimes large round timbers were laid on the tops of the houses on purpose to roll off on the Indians below.

James Curry came with Clark in 1778, and was an active and daring soldier in the capture of Forts Gage and Sackville. He was large, strong, and active and was always foremost on the list of those who contended for the prizes in foot-races, leaping, wrestling, etc. He was a similar character to the celebrated Thomas Higgins of modern pioneer memory. In all desperate and hazardous services, Clark chose him first to act in these perils and dangers.

The citizens of Illinois of olden times were compelled to hunt for a support. Curry and Joseph Anderson, who afterward lived and died on Nine-Mile Creek, Randolph County, were out hunting and the Indians killed Curry, as it was supposed; as he went out to hunt from their camp and never returned. Thus was the closing scene of one of the brave and patriotic heroes, the noble-hearted James Curry, whose services were so conspicuous in the conquest of Illinois Not only a burial was denied to this gallant soldier, but his remains are mingled with the mother-earth; so that even the place of his death is not known His blood was spilt in Illinois and it may produce, when the occasion demands it, a race of heroes whose services for their country may equal those of the lamented Curry

Another of the gallant soldiers of Gen Clark, William Biggs, lived a long and eventful life in Illinois. He was born in Maryland in 1755, and at the age of twenty-three years, he enrolled himself in the Revolutionary war under Gen. Clark. He acted as a subaltern officer in the conquest of Illinois in 1778 and 1779 He was hardy, energetic, and brave and used these qualities for the redemption of not only the United Colonies from bondage, but of the whole human race He withstood the perils and "hair-breadth 'scapes" incident to the campaign under Clark with the heroism of a veteran warrior. He received no bounty in land in the grant made to Clark and his soldiers, but the congress of the United States, recognizing the honorable services rendered to the colonies in the Revolution by Lieut Biggs, granted him, in 1826, three sections of land The congress of the United States gave Judge Biggs this public and honorable testimony of his important services bestowed on his country for its liberation from British despotism. Soon after the close of the Revolution, he returned and married in West Virginia. Not long after his marriage, he, with two brothers, emigrated to Illinois and settled at Bellefontaine.

In the spring of 1788, he had been out hunting and had got some beaver fur, which he was desirous to sell in Cahokia He then resided at the Bellefontaine and started with his beaver fur, in company with John Vallis, to Cahokia. John Vallis was from Maryland near Baltimore Early in the morning of March 28 of the above year, Biggs and Vallis were riding on the main road from the fountain to Cahokia—the same road that is at present traveled—about six miles from Piggot's Fort in the Bottom, and they heard the report of two guns. Biggs supposed them to be hunters, but soon after, he saw sixteen Indians with their guns presented. He and Vallis whipped their horses, but in vain; all the Indians fired their pieces at him and comrade The bullets riddled the horse of Biggs, killed him and shot four holes thro Biggs' overcoat, but did not hit him. A ball entered the thigh of Vallis and of which wound he died six weeks after The horse of Vallis carried him to the fort Biggs, his furs, saddle, and all fell off his horse and after running some distance the Indians caught him and made him a prisoner.

When Vallis reached the fort, they fired a swivel to alarm the neighborhood At the report, the Indians run with Biggs for six miles. They were Kickapoos and started direct to the

Weastowns or Ouitenon on the Wabash River, two hundred miles above Vincennes One of the Indians that captured Biggs attempted to kill him, but to get rid of this Indian, his comrades killed him. These savages have no regard for life except it be their own The first day, they traveled with Biggs forty miles. They had no horses and must have traveled fast on foot. Sixty-four years ago, Biggs, as a prisoner, must have passed not far south of Belleville and Lebanon and traveled almost three hundred miles to the Wabash, opposite the Weastowns, in ten days The Indians were very severe on him in tying him at night, for fear of his escape; so he was almost unable to walk After he reached the Indian towns, he was ransomed by agreeing to pay a Spaniard, Bazedone, two hundred and sixty dollars ransom and thirty-seven more for other necessaries on which to enable him to reach home He descended the Wabash and the Ohio to the Mississippi, up that river to Kaskaskia and on home to the Bellefontaine.

It was a miracle that so many Indians fired at Biggs and Vallis, and within forty yards, did not kill them both. Biggs suffered much, but he saved his life. He was a fine, handsome man and his beauty had its effect even on the untutored females of nature, as many of the Indian belles offered their hearts to him in wedlock, but he acted the second Joseph with them on the Wabash River as his illustrious predecessor did in Egypt Mr Biggs wrote a narrative in 1826 of his captivity and had it published.

Gov St Clair in 1790 appointed him the sheriff of St Clair County, which office he held and did the business of it for many years, as the ancient records testify He had received a plain, common education and had mixed so much with men, danger, and war that he was well qualified to execute the duties of this office. He was kind and obliging, so that the office of sheriff sixty years ago, as it does to this day, enabled the incumbent to become popular, if he be an honest, agreeable man, with common business talents He was popular and the citizens of St. Clair elected him to serve in the legislature of the Northwest Territory for two different terms He attended twice and rode on horseback to Vincennes, thence to Louisville, thence thro Kentucky and the territory to the seat of government of all the country northwest of the Ohio River

At a time when Bond and Biggs were doing military service in Illinois, in 1778, under Gen Clark, they concluded to return to Illinois after the war was closed. They said in a joke that they would like to represent this country in the legislature; and behold, they both did realize their waking dreams expressed in the war. They were in the first general assembly of the territory, convened west of the Ohio, after the Revolution.

Biggs acted as justice-of-the-peace and judge of the court of common-pleas of St Clair County for almost time out of the memory of man and made an honest, safe officer. He was elected from St Clair County to the general assembly of the Indiana Territory in 1808, and acted well his part in obtaining a division of the territory Illinois Territory was established soon after and the legislature of which Biggs was a member gave motion to the ball Judge Biggs was elected, in 1812, from St Clair County to the legislative council of the general assembly of the Territory of Illinois, remained in this office four years and made a solid and useful member He was acting in the first organization of the first territorial government. We are now enjoying the fruit of his and others' labors Toward the close of his life, he manufactured salt in Madison County, on Silver Creek, and died at Col Judy's in 1827, an aged and respectable pioneer of Illinois. Few men have had the good fortune to live in the age and had so many opportunities to perform services for the human family as Judge Biggs had; but in all these public transactions, he did not attend to his private interests He never was wealthy—only possessed a reasonable competency. His remains now repose in peace in a country wherein he acted in such important scenes.

After the Indian war had closed in 1795, the citizens of Illinois turned their attention to the improvement of their stock The breed of horses were advanced and many good ones raised in the country. Illinois at that day, as it has been ever since, was a good climate for horses Col. William Whiteside, in 1796, introduced into the country a fine blooded-horse of the Janus stock It is supposed by the best judges of horses that a better horse has never since stood in Illinois. Many of his colts made turf nags that won races not only in Illinois, but in many parts of the Union. The owners of two of these horses, both sired by Whiteside's horse, made a large bet on a race between them, of three miles and repeat. The race took place in the Horse Prairie in the spring of 1803. The people of Illinois at that day were all comprised within St Clair and Randolph counties and were not numerous The whole country, with a few exceptions, were great amateurs of the sport and the race, and the horses were as much discussed, to the number of people, as the late Mexican war was. I would not be surprised if one-third of all the males of Illinois attended the race and part of the females. The celebrated race-horse, Sleepy Davie, whose famous character all the ancient pioneers recollect, won the race, beating a fine gray horse much larger than himself.

These races were in their character something similar to the Olympic games in Greece and the railroad conventions and mass-meetings of modern times. It is essential for the people to assemble together to form friendly acquaintances and wear off unfounded prejudices. This is a great and important element in the congress of the United States. It gets the extremes of the nation together, and by a friendly intercourse among the members, the Union is made more permanent By the Olympic games, the Grecian States were preserved and the people improved Our Illinois races were nothing more in a small way than part of the Olympic games. The people came together from all parts of the inhabited Illinois and had a friendly interchange of sentiment; became acquainted with each other, and returned home as friendly as brothers. At that day, 1803, less than sixty miles north and south and fifteen or twenty from the Mississippi, east and west, embraced the whole settlements, French and Americans, in Illinois

At these races almost every description of business was transacted. Horses were swopped and contracts made. Debts paid and new ones contracted. Amusements of various species were indulged in. Foot-racing, wrestling, and jumping were not neglected. Sometimes shooting-matches were executed; so that in old pioneer times these horse-races were names for meetings where much other business or pleasure was transacted and experienced. Small kegs of whisky were often brought to the races; a keg in one end of a bag and a stone in the other Sometimes a keg in each end was the manner of getting the liquor to the races Old females at times had cakes and metheglin for sale. This race in the Horse Prairie was the most celebrated match-race that occurred in Illinois in early times and drew to it the greatest concourse of people I think, in a moral point of view, the community was improved by it; not on account of the race, but by the friendly intercourse among so vast an assemblage of people at that day

I presume, in 1803, there were scarcely three thousand souls, French and Americans, in all Illinois. No census at that day was taken and it is difficult to be certain in the number; but judging from the best *data* in my power and my personal observation, I think the above is correct. This estimate is allowing an increase of one thousand souls in fifteen years—since 1788 to 1803 The French during this period were diminishing and the Americans made up the increase to scarcely three thousand inhabitants,

About this time, 1800, and onward, the inhabitants changed to some extent their mode of business and living They assumed more the agricultural pursuits and abandoned hunting. A commerce had commenced to New Orleans in flour, tobacco, and live-stock, which induced the people to change their employments The game was more exhausted, so that hunting was not so profitable as heretofore. This change gradually took place after 1800 to the war of 1812, which checked its progress to some extent. The immigrants were mostly from the Southern and Western States and had been in the habit of cultivating cotton and they continued its cultivation in Illinois It was supposed fifty years since that Illinois was a good medium cotton country. Tobacco was also cultivated. Flax was raised and manufactured into clothing Wheat was more cultivated than in former days The range was good; so that cattle, hogs, and horses were raised in abundance The only misfortune of which farmers complained was the want of a market for their surplus produce.

This change in the industry of the people justified the erection of more mills Tate and Singleton, in 1802, built a good water-mill for that day on the Fountaine Creek, a few miles northwest of the present town of Waterloo The mill-house was made of stone and the capacity of the mill was made in proportion to the demand of the country at the time. Edgar's mill continued to do the most of the merchant business of the country then and for a long time after.

Madame Beaulieu, a pioneer lady, was born in the village of St Phillippe in 1742, and was educated in Quebec, Canada. Her father, a subaltern officer, came with the French troops to Fort Chartres and located in the above village, sometimes called the Little Village. His name was Chouvin. He settled afterward in Cahokia, where his daughter married M. Beaulieu. This lady was educated and intelligent. She was the director-general in moral and medical matters She possessed a strong, active mind and was a pattern of morality and virtue. She was the doctress in most cases and the sage *femme* general for many years. She was extremely devout and an exemplary member of the Catholic church This, together with her merit generally, enabled her to fix up many of the male and female delinquencies of the village. She was sincerely entitled to the praise due a peace-maker. Many of the young and accomplished ladies courted the society of this old lady for improvement. She lived a long and useful life and died in Cahokia in 1826, eighty-four years of age, much lamented by all classes

On June 5, 1805, a terrific hurricane swept over a part of Illinois. It was one of those tempests of the whirlwind order. The tornado moved from the southwest to the northeast and crossed the Mississippi about a mile below the mouth of the Merrimac. It was about three-quarters of a mile wide, and to that extent, for several miles in Illinois, it prostrated trees and even swept the water out of the river and the lakes in the American Bottom to that width. William Blair had a boat moored on the river near the place where the storm crossed it and was certain that most of the water to the above extent was raised out of the river by the violence of the tempest. It also took the water out of the lakes Fish from the river and lakes were scattered all over the prairie in the course of this storm. It occurred about one o'clock of the day and the atmosphere before was clear and the sun shining.

Col. James A. James resided with his father nearly in its course and was an eye-witness to this terrific storm Dr. Cairnes and family were directly in its course, and when they saw it approaching, they made an effort to escape it and succeeded in saving their lives. James and family retired out of its violence. It reached the doctor and family, but it seemed they were saved by a kind of miracle His wife was behind in their flight and she lay flat on the earth, holding on to a bush, but the rails, tree tops, and almost every moveable thing were dashed around her with great force. She was wounded in the head, but not mortal. The doctor and the rest of the family escaped unhurt James and family were farther out of its violence and were saved. The cattle of the doctor came home before the hurricane reached the premises, bellowing and much terrified. They all perished by the violence of the tornado The doctor had a horse in a lot near his house, which was killed by a fence-rail running thro him The lowest log in the house and last rock in the foundation of the chimney were swept off by the force of the wind. The vegetation and all and everything moveable in the course of this storm were destroyed and torn to pieces. A large bull was raised up high in the air; carried a considerable distance, and every bone in his body was broken The force of the storm was measurably spent by the time it reached the Mississippi Bluff. It must have struck the bluff not far from the place where the township line descends into the bottom; but no injury was done on the hills. The clothes and all the household furniture of the doctor were destroyed and scattered far and near One of his waistcoats was found at the Little Prairie, where his father resided, six or eight miles from his demolished residence. The storm carried in it pine tops from Missouri, which do not grow nearer than fifty or sixty miles from the American Bottom. This was the most violent tempest that ever visited Illinois. Others have occurred, but none so violent. In the midst of the storm it was very dark. In 1814, Kaskaskia was assailed with one; but not so severe as that of 1805 It did not much injury to the old town, as it did not pass directly over it. We hope for good weather and no storms

In 1805, Philip Creamer emigrated from Harper's Ferry, Maryland, and settled in the American Bottom a short distance east of Prairie du Pont. He was born in Taneytown in the above State and learned the trade of gunsmith at Harper's Ferry.

Nature and education together made this pioneer one of the greatest mechanics in America. The work of this eminent artisan will compare favorably with the work of any mechanic in the Union. He possessed a natural and great genius to work in metal. Anything done in metal, he could accomplish by a short apprenticeship. But he was the best in making a gun, as he practised that part of the profession the most, and he made all parts of a gun and put it together as if it had grown fast there by nature. His gunlocks scarcely ever missed fire. It was a proverb in olden times, "he is as sure as a Creamer lock." In the war of 1812, he was very useful in repairing and making guns for the troops defending the frontiers. Government appointed him to work at his trade for the Indians. Some of his friends induced him to make a pistol for Hon. John C. Calhoun when he was secretary of war. The workmanship so surprised Calhoun that he wrote Creamer a letter requesting to know where he learned his trade and a sketch of his life. Creamer was a singular man and would not answer it, as he said "he was no showman or stud-horse to be advertised." He lived to an old age and died a few years ago, much respected.

In a new country I think there are more original and eccentric talents than in an old settlement. It seems that all the latent sparks of genius are called forth by the circumstances of the country. These singular talents were often exhibited by the pioneers in their games and sports.

In 1806, Robert Pulliam of Illinois and a Mr. Musick of Missouri made a bet of two hundred dollars on a horse-race of one-quarter of a mile. This race was agreed to be run on the ice in the Mississippi a short distance above St. Louis. It was a singular place—on the ice—to run a horse-race; but the parties run it and were not injured. Another strange wager was made in Kaskaskia by two very respectable citizens. This bet was made in perfect good humor and for sport. A dozen bottles of Champagne were wagered on the following game. The snow was four inches deep and the bet was that the gamesters were to go out in the commons of Kaskaskia, strip off their boots and socks to the bare feet, and whoever killed the first rabbit on the snow in their bare feet, won the wine. It would puzzle Hoyle to define the principles on which this last game was based.

In 1800, an enterprising and talented pioneer, Michael La Croix, settled in Peoria and extended his trade mostly with the Indians throughout the Upper Illinois country. He frequently visited Cahokia, but his main residence was at Peoria He was a Canadian-Frenchman and had received a liberal education The person of La Croix was stout, dignified, and prepossessing, and his appearance indicated what he really was: a man of sound mind and great energy. He was a successful Indian trader for many years and was in Canada to purchase goods when war was declared in 1812 against Great Britain, and he was detained in Canada, a British province, to defend it. He was also forced out into the service against the United States This he disliked; yet, if he had deserted to the Union, his goods and estate, which were considerable, would be forfeited to the king. He remained on the side he disliked and the government pressed him into the military service. While he was forced into the army, he accepted a lieutenancy, merely to raise him from the ranks. When peace was restored, he returned to the United States, and in 1815, he was naturalized.

Before he went to Canada in 1812, he built a fine house in Peoria and when Capt. Thomas E. Craig was at that place in the fall of 1812, he became excited against the citizens of Peoria and burnt the house of La Croix and many others. This burning by Craig was considered by all reasonable men as a wanton act of cruelty. After the war, the Indian trade was not so good as heretofore The whole country on the Illinois River was being settled with a white population, which took the place of the red-skins. M La Croix died in 1821, in the village of Cahokia, much regretted by his family and acquaintances

It will be recollected that Virginia, in her cession of the Illinois country and the Northwest Territory to the United States in 1784, a compact was made that "the French and Canadian inhabitants and all other settlements of the Kaskaskias, St.Vincents, and the neighboring villages, who have professed themselves citizens of Virginia, shall have their possessions and titles confirmed to them and be protected in the enjoyments of their rights and liberties In June, 1788, a resolution of the old congress passed, granting a donation of four hundred acres of land to each head of a family in Illinois and also confirming them in their possessions, as required by Virginia An act of congress passed in 1791, granting a donation of one hundred acres to each militia-man who was enrolled in the militia service of that year. The governors of the territories of the Northwest and Indiana were authorized to adjust the claims arising out of these various acts of congress. They had granted some of the claims, but many were still unadjusted To remedy this evil, an act of congress was passed in 1804, establishing land-offices at Kaskaskia, Vincennes, and Detroit, to adjust these old claims and to sell the public lands after the private titles were set apart to the proprietors.

The great *desideratum*, something devoutly to be wished for, was the settlement and improvement of the country. This was the universal prayer of all classes of people in Illinois, to my own knowledge, for almost half-a-century It was quite natural. The country was so thinly populated that the inhabitants did not enjoy the same blessings of the government, schools, and even the common comforts of life that were enjoyed by the people of the old states. The adjustment of these old land-titles must be made and the public lands surveyed before the citizens could procure good titles to their lands, and before that, not much settlement of the country could be expected. Therefore the citizens were extremely anxious to have these matters all arranged; so that the country could fill up with families living on their own lands, with good titles to them

Under the act of congress of 1804, Michael Jones and E. Backus were appointed register and receiver of the land-office at Kaskaskia These commissioners entered into the duties of their office, but made no report of confirmations of titles before 1809. This delay excited the people and a very bitter and rancorous feeling was engendered between the commissioners and many of the inhabitants About that time, an excessive and virulent party-spirit, without any great principle to found it on, also existed Jones, one of the commissioners, entered warmly into these party politics. Michael Jones was born in Pennsylvania and came to Kaskaskia, the register of the land-office in 1804 He was a sprightly man, of plausable and pleasing address. He possessed a good English education and was, in his younger days, well qualified for business if he had been clear of excitement. His temperament was very excitable and rather irritable. His mind was above the ordinary range; but his passion at times swept over it like a tornado His colleague, E Backus, was an excellent man, kind and benevolent, and entered not much into the feelings of either side He permitted Jones to take his own way in the reports made in the land-office to the secretary of the treasury

An act of congress passed in 1812 which pretended to authorize the commissioners to revise the former decisions of the governors and the commissioners themselves With these excited feelings against his political enemies, Jones not only reported against many of the claims, but branded the parties with perjury and forgery to an alarming extent. With these party-excited feelings, many of the best citizens in the country were stigmatized with the above crimes, without cause and when they had no means or manner of defending themselves For nine years the delay to adjust the land-titles and to get the public lands into market was kept up throughout the country and the immigration considerably delayed on that account. It was not until the act of congress passed in 1813, granting the right of preemption, that the country in true earnest commenced to populate and improve. The public lands then were brought into market and the improvements of the people secured

In 1802, and for a few years after, the settlements on the east side of the Kaskaskia River increased considerably Fulton with his large family located there; so did the Huggins, Bilderbacks, Hill, and Livelys, and in 1805, about fifteen families from Abbeyville District, South Carolina, located in the same settlement, from five to fifteen miles from Kaskaskia. The Andersons, Thompsons, Erwin, McDonald, McBride, Cox, Miller, Couch, and others composed this settlement, and during the next few years, this colony from South Carolina increased to forty families or more These South-Carolina emigrants were hardy, energetic people, well qualified to sustain themselves in a new and frontier country. They were honest and patriotic, of Irish descent, and were warm and impulsive The old ones were generally of the Presbyterian church; but the younger class was moral, yet joined no church.

In 1806, when the United-States lands were to be surveyed, the Rector family reached Kaskaskia and remained there for several years This family in Illinois was numerous and conspicuous in pioneer times There were nine brothers and four daughters of the family. They were all born in Fauquier County, Virginia, and many of them raised there. Some of them had emigrated to Ohio and others direct to Illinois. The family were singular and peculiar in their traits of character. They were ardent, excitable, and enthusiastic in their dispositions. They possessed integrity and honesty of purpose in the highest degree. Nature had endowed them with strong and active minds, but their passions at times swept over their judgments like a tempest They were the most fearless and undaunted people I ever knew. Dangers, perils, and even death were amusements for them when they were excited. They were impulsive and ungovernable when their passions were enlisted. They were the most devoted and true-hearted friends and the most energetic and impulsive enemies to any one they thought deserved their hatred. The family in their persons were generally large and formed with perfect manly symmetry. They were noble, commanding, and elegant in their bearing and their personal appearance was, for manly beauty, not surpassed in the territory They possessed an exquisite and high sense of honor and chivalry An insult was never offered to any one of them that went unpunished.

William Rector was the oldest brother and a monitor for the balance. He was a deputy-surveyor and all were respectable gentlemen Stephen Rector was a lieutenant in Capt. Moore's company of United-States rangers in the war of 1812, and performed well his duty to his country.

Nelson Rector was captain of an armed boat in 1814, and had an engagement with the British and Indians at Rock sland He possessed the noble bearing of the ancient knights. It became necessary at the battle-ground to leave the boat and rout some Indians from an island in the Mississippi. Capt Rector was dressed richly, with a splendid military uniform, epaulettes, and a large red feather in his hat. Thus equipped, he drew his sword and walked deliberately on an open sand beach, in a short distance of the enemy, and ordered his company to follow him. Many Indian guns were fired at him, which he disregarded as if they were pop-guns. He escaped, but it was miraculous, as he was alone, in advance of his company, and such a distinguished object, an officer so gayly dressed, without a gun to return the fire. But all the Rectors were strangers to fear.

Thomas Rector, one of the younger brothers, had a duel with Joshua Barton on Bloody Island, opposite St. Louis, and was as cool in that combat as if he were shooting at a deer in the prairie. These young men espoused the quarrel of their older brothers and Barton fell in the conflict. William Rector commanded a regiment as colonel in the campaign of 1812, against the Indians at the head of Peoria Lake, and in the same campaign, Nelson Rector acted as an aid-de-camp to Gov. Edwards.

The whole Rector family were patriotic and were always willing and ready, on all proper occasions, to shed their blood in the defence of their country. Nelson Rector had a company of surveyors out on the waters of the Saline Creek in Gallatin County, Illinois, and on March 1, 1814, he was fired on by the Indians and severely wounded. His left arm was broken; a ball entered his left side and another touched his face His horse carried him off and he recovered from his wounds In 1816, Col. William Rector was appointed surveyor-general of Illinois, Missouri, and Arkansas. He made St. Louis his residence, where the whole family assembled and resided also.

The Goshen Settlements were extended north in 1804. In that year, James Stockton and Abraham Pruitt settled at the foot of the bluff, not far below Wood River. These two families were the first that located in the Wood-River Settlement, so called afterward. These emigrants came from Knox Co, Tennessee, and were the pioneers of a large connection that followed in a few years after. They were honest, correct farmers About this time, the Six-Mile Prairie Settlement increased also.

In this year, 1804, Delorm, a Frenchman from Cahokia, settled at the edge of the timber east of the Big Mound in the American Bottom, near the Quentine Creek. The French had resided on the Big Island in the Mississippi, below the mouth of the Missouri, at intervals, for fifty or sixty years before. Squire La Croix, who died in Cahokia an old man a few years since, was born on that island.

The Quentine Village commenced its existence soon after Delorm settled east of the Big Mound in 1804. It extended from the mound west, along the margin of Cahokia Creek for some miles, and was at one time a handsome little village. They mostly emigrated from Prairie du Pont. About the same time, 1805, Nicholas Turgion, August Trotier, Dennis Vallentine, and others commenced the French Village, which is situated in the American Bottom on the banks of a lake It extends west from the bluff and the macadamized road now passes thro it. Vallentine built a horse-mill in this village. This little French colony, like that of the Quentine, flourished for several years and both were neat little French settlements. The Quentine has been declining for some time and has almost disappeared as a village The country around it is assuming an agricultural existence and that of a French village is merged in farms

It was in the neighborhood of this village that the monks of La Trappe established themselves in 1810, at the Big Mound in the American Bottom. It seems that this order of religionists carries on a crusade against human nature in their own persons. We read of the bravest of the brave, but they were the most rigid of the rigid. They carried out the *ne plus ultra* of fanaticism Two of their vows were celibacy and perpetual silence. It is strange they did not declare against eating. Females were not permitted to enter on their premises. It is said they swept off their tracks if any came within their walks by mistake This order is a branch of the Cistercian monks and was first founded by Rotrou I., count of Perche, in 1040. It relaxed in its severe discipline until Abbe Rancé reinstated it in its vigor in 1664. It was situated first in the most gloomy and wild province of France—that of Perche. Its last founder, Rancé, got soured at the world and particularly against his mistress, who discharged him for another lover, and he commenced a war against himself. He lay on a rock, lived on bread and water alone, and removed a handful of earth from his grave each day of his life, and what is strange, he had followers. I have myself addressed many of the monks at the mound and they were as silent to me as the grave. The New Testament teaches no such doctrine as that. The Revolution in France removed them from that nation and public opinion, which is more powerful than a revolution, discharged them from the American Bottom. They located themselves first in the United States in 1804, at Conewago, Pennsylvania, then in Kentucky, then at Florisant, St Louis County, Missouri, and lastly, as above stated. They were sickly at the mound, sold out and disappeared in 1813.

Soon after the purchase of Louisiana, President Jefferson projected a peaceable campaign across the continent to the Pacific Ocean. The object of this exploration was to acquire information of the country between the two oceans and secure the friendship and trade of the Indians. Merryweather Lewis and William Clark, brother of Gen G R. Clark, were appointed the leaders of the expedition. The exploring party, consisting of thirty-four men, camped the winter of 1803 and 1804 in the American Bottom, not far from the Mississippi, below the mouth of Wood River. This camp was the *ultama thule* of the white settlements in Illinois at that day. Lewis was a captain and Clark a lieutenant in the United-States army. They visited Cahokia, St Louis, and the settlements around in Illinois during this winter. They embarked on the Missouri River on May 14, 1804, and returned to St Louis in December, 1806. Many of the party, John B. Thompson, Collins, Willard, Newman, Windsor, Frazier, Gibson, and perhaps some others settled in Illinois and most of them remained there.

In the years progressing from 1804, the settlements of both Randolph and St Clair counties enlarged considerably. Lacy, Tindale, Gaston, Franklin, Herd, Cochran, and others located in the settlement east of the Kaskaskia River, in Randolph

County. Smith and Taylor located in the American Bottom, between Prairie du Rocher and Kaskaskia, in 1801, and both raised large families there. Henry Noble and Jesse Greggs were the two first families in 1804 that settled on Big-Muddy River. They were the pioneers of Big Muddy. Going, Pulliam, Griffin, Chance, Ratcliff, Gibbons, and some others were added to the outside settlements of Kaskaskia River and Silver Creek in these times. Chiltons, Brazell, Lorton, Moore, Downing, Lemen, Copeland, Lacy, Gregg, Vanhoozer, Rattan, Hewitt, Hill, Stubblefield, Jones, and many others were attached to the eastern and northern parts of what was then known as the Goshen Settlement.

In these days, 1805, John T. Lusk emigrated from Kentucky and settled in Goshen, Illinois. He was born in South Carolina and had lived with his father at Lusk's Ferry on the Ohio, opposite the present town of Golconda. He has been engaged the greater part of his life in the administration of the laws. He served in the military in the war and has performed his duties well in both civil and military offices.

The Six-Mile Prairie Settlement was enlarged by Waddles, Griffin, Squires, Cummins, Carpenter, Gilham, and others. About this time, some efforts were made to ship the produce to market by the farmers themselves. The same energies that defended the country in times of war were now turned to commerce. Several flat-boats were constructed; laden with corn, hogs, cattle, etc., and started to New Orleans from the head of the Big Island, in the present county of Madison. Some reached the destined port, but others were wrecked on the voyage for the want of skill in the navigation of the river. Boats were also started down the river from the Big Prairie, in the present county of Monroe. The lead-mines in Missouri were a market for live-stock, hogs, and beef-cattle.

School-houses were "few and far between" at that day. The immigrants were from the Southern and Western States, as it has already been remarked, and were not as efficient to advance education as their duties to themselves and country demanded at their hands. A school-house, a log-cabin, in ancient times stood at the foot of the bluff, half-way between Judy's and William B. Whiteside's; but more than half the time it was not occupied. About half the time, a log schoolhouse was tenanted by a school, which stood east of the spring of John Fulton of Ash Hill, Randolph County. Doyle, the brave old soldier of Gen. Clark, kept a school in Kaskaskia for many years after 1790. In 1805, Edward Humphrey taught a school in the American Bottom, near the Chaffins. In the French Villages, common education was very much neglected. The priests and the old ladies at times taught the children, but not often. At the New Design and in the American Bottom, schools were to some extent sustained. About this time, 1805, and onward, the country commenced to have frontiers. Before that, inside and outside of the American settlements were all frontiers.

In pioneer times, professional characters were not numerous. The country was poor and sparsely settled; so that many of them could not make a living by their practice.

George Fisher was a physician who was considered the best of his day. He emigrated from Hardy County, Virginia, and settled in Kaskaskia in very early times. He was also a merchant; but he did not long continue in that profession. Dr Fisher was a gentleman of common education, and had been a well-read physician, but depended more on his natural abilities than books. He possessed a good, sprightly mind, and a great share of activity. He was an agreeable and benevolent man. Soon after the territory of Indiana was established, Gov Harrison appointed Dr. Fisher the sheriff of Randolph County. He executed the duties of this office to the satisfaction of the public for many years. He was elected to the first general assembly of the Illinois Territory. He was a great favorite with the people—kind to the poor and indulgent to all. He was elected the speaker of the house of representatives. This is an office of standing and dignity, no matter where the assembly may be. Dr Fisher was elected to the convention in 1818, from Randolph County. He acted in that celebrated convention that formed a Constitution, which secured the prosperity and happiness of the State for many years. He died on his farm, at the foot of the bluff, in 1820, much lamented by the people.

Dr. Wm. L. Reynolds emigrated from Kentucky, Bracken

County, in the year 1809, and settled in Kaskaskia. He possessed talents of a high order, and a probity and integrity that dignify human nature in any condition in life. He had received a collegiate education, and was well versed in the science of medicine. He had studied with great assiduity, and his labors were crowned with success. For many years he reigned triumphant in his profession in Kaskaskia and vicinity. Dr. Fisher had retired to his farm, and did not practise much. Dr. Reynolds moved to Cahokia, and practised there with a high reputation, as he had done in Kaskaskia. He returned to Kaskaskia, and practised his profession there for many years. He was elected to the territorial legislature in 1815, and was instrumental in establishing Jackson County, and giving it the name of Jackson, and the county-seat, Brownsville, in honor of those two great generals in the United-States army. He became sickly, and died in 1823 with the consumption, without seeing many years. His death was much regretted, not only for his sake, but for a more sordid consideration, the loss of him as a physician.

A more ancient pioneer doctor was Trueman Tuttle. Dr. Tuttle was an Eastern man, with classic education, who came as a surgeon of the United-States army with the troops that came to Kaskaskia in 1802. He was considered a good physician, and accordingly got a good practice with the citizens while he remained in the army. When the army left, he resigned [1808] his office as surgeon, and remained to practise at Kaskaskia. After some years he established himself in Cahokia, and there also maintained an excellent character. He was appointed judge of the court of common-pleas of St. Clair County, and justice-of-the-peace. He was honest and correct in these offices, as he had been in all his acts, public and private.

There was a Dr. Wallace, who attended to the dreadful sickness of the New Design in 1797; but his character was little known then or at present. Dr. Lyle resided in Cahokia in very early times, and was considered a good physician, but excessively ill-natured and cross.

Dr. James Rose emigrated from Kentucky, and settled in Kaskaskia in 1805. He possessed some talent and made a good physician in his early life. He was a little lame, but before he forgot himself for his friendship for alcohol, his mind was not lame. He enjoyed a good practice at Kaskaskia and vicinity. He did reside in Belleville; but toward the close of his career he neglected his profession, and it in turn neglected him.

Dr. Caldwell Cairnes was a sound, good physician in olden times in Illinois. He emigrated from Pennsylvania about half a century ago, and located in Illinois. In 1805, he was in the tornado already mentioned. He possessed himself of a splendid farm, which he styled Walnut Grove. He farmed on a large scale, and attended likewise to his profession. He was a judge of the court of St.Clair County, and justice-of-the-peace. When Monroe County was organized, he was elected from it one of the members that formed the State constitution. He made a solid business member in that body. He died on his plantation, much regretted by the public. Dr. Cairnes was a sound, clear-headed man, and was honest and correct. He left behind him a good reputation and a large estate.

Benjamin H. Doyle, an attorney-at-law, emigrated from Knox County, Tenn., and settled in Kaskaskia in 1805. He practised in the courts of Randolph and St.Clair counties. He possessed a good address, and would have made a good lawyer if he had attended to his studies. He was appointed attorney-general, but resigned his office in 1809, and left the country.

James Haggin was born in Kentucky, and emigrated to Kaskaskia in 1804. He practised law some years in the courts of both Randolph and St Clair, and was a promising young man. He built a house, not in the settlement, but, at that day in the wilderness, four or five miles east of Kaskaskia, at the head of Gravelly Creek. He remained in Illinois but a few years, and went back to Kentucky, where he became a very eminent man.

John Rector, a lawyer—one of the Rector family before mentioned—located in Kaskaskia in 1806; opened a law-office, and attended the courts at Kaskaskia and Cahokia. He practised his profession for a few years in Illinois, and left the country.

The first attorney who made Cahokia his permanent residence, after Darnielle, was William Mears. He came to this village in 1808, and there commenced the practice of the law. He was born in Ireland in 1768, and emigrated to the United States. He landed at Philadelphia, and taught school some time in Pennsylvania. He came to Cahokia, about forty years of age, as if he had dropped down from the clouds—without horse, clothes, books, letters, or anything except himself—a rather singular and uncouth-looking Irishman. He had read law while he taught school in Pennsylvania. He possessed a strong mind and retentive memory. In his early days he was not a scholar, but by application and severe study he not only acquired a profound knowledge of the law, but also became a learned and intelligent man. He was appointed attorney-general for the territory of Illinois in 1814, and, to my own knowledge, he made an able and efficient prosecuting-attorney. He moved to Belleville when the county-seat was taken there, in 1814, from Cahokia, and remained in this place during his life. He was elected clerk of the house of representatives of the general assembly. He married a respectable lady in Missouri—built a house in Belleville, and died there in 1824. Mears had no talent for speculation or acquiring wealth; but lived decently on his practice, and died about even with the world.

In 1809, Samuel D. Davidson, a lawyer from Kentucky, came and settled in Cahokia. He was a decent young man—moral and correct—but made no impression on anything where he lived, moved, or had his being. He wrote a beautiful hand, which was about the beginning and ending of his talents. I think he taught a school in Cahokia, and he entered the military service in 1812. In the campaign of 1813 he was appointed to some office in the quartermaster's department. Some time after the war, he left Cahokia to parts unknown.

Russel E. Heacock practised law in St. Clair County in 1808, and moved to Jonesboro', south of Kaskaskia. He married in that vicinity, and practised law for several years in that section of Illinois. He moved to Buffalo, New York, and then to Chicago, and acquired considerable property in and near Chicago, [where died of cholera in 1849.]

Joseph Conway emigrated from Kentucky, and settled in

Kaskaskia, as a lawyer, in 1812 He acted in the contractors' department for some time on the frontiers during the war. He practised law in the courts in and south of Kaskaskia for some time after he settled there Judge Thomas, one of the United-States judges for the territory of Illinois, appointed him clerk of the circuit-court of Madison County in 1816 He remained in this office until 1825. Politics then was warmly agitated by the people, and Emanuel J. West was put in the office of clerk of the Madison circuit-court. Conway was popular, and the people elected him to the State senate for four years Then he was appointed clerk in Rock-Island County He remained in this office for several years—went down the river and died.

Three brothers,* Louison, Etienne, and Louis Pensoneau,

---

* Diligent inquiry has so far failed to discover the descendants of Etienne and Louis Pensoneau, and it is not known if they left any. After Etienne purchased from Blair the land upon which the city of Belleville stands, he built a water-mill on Richland Creek about two hundred yards south of the present site of the great Harrison steam-mill and continued to operate it until he sold out to Gov Edwards He then returned to Cahokia, and from there removed to St Louis, where he engaged in business and remained until his death

About 1794, Louison Pensoneau married Miss Lizette Le Compt in the village of Cahokia, and after residing some years in Peoria, settled on a farm at Point a la Pierre, near the Grand Marais, four miles east of the Mississippi, on the Belleville road. At that place he died in 1832, and his widow continued to reside there until her death in 1841 Of this union there survived ten children, three daughters and seven sons The daughters were Bridget, Marie, and Louisa, the sons were Louis, Paschal, Laurent, Edward, Narcisse, Charles, and François, the two last being twins.

Bridget was married to Amable Tramble in 1818, and died in 1831, and her husband, a Canadian-Frenchman, survived her but three or four years. They left two sons, Louis and François Tramble, who both died without issue Louis, a journeyman printer, dying in San Francisco, Cal , in the spring of 1850, and François was drowned in the Missouri River, near Fort Leavenworth, in the same year, on his return from the Yellowstone as an employé of John P. Sarpy & Co , fur traders of St Louis

Marie married John Valentine, and both died in a few years after their marriage, leaving one daughter, named Louisa, who subsequently married Octav Born, a Canadian, and with him emigrated to New Orleans.

Louisa married Joseph Trotier in 1820, and lived and died in Cahokia She had two children, Mary and Joseph Mary Trotier was married to Col Vital Jariot in 1845, and died in 1852. Her brother, Joseph, wandered to the Far-West, and is perhaps still living

Of the sons of Louison Pensoneau and Lizette Le Compt—now all dead—Louis, born in 1800, married Henriet, youngest daughter of Jean François Perry, in the fall of 1822, and died where he had always lived, at Point a la Pierre, Feb 22, 1826 His only child, Louis Perry Pensoneau, born May 1, 1824, is now residing at East

emigrated from Canada, and settled in Cahokia in 1798. They were born at the old Prairie Fort, so-called, in the Three-River Settlement, Canada, between the years 1772 and 1776. These brothers married in Cahokia and made excellent citizens. Louis occupied the ferry between Cahokia and St. Louis for many years. In olden times the ferry between these two villages was kept below the mouth of the old Cahokia Creek. This was west of Cahokia and Louis Pensoneau was the ferryman for a long time. Etienne was a very active and business man. He possessed extraordinary energies, and improved the country considerably. He made the first house, "the brick-house," so-called, in olden times in Illinoistown. He then purchased the site of Belleville from George Blair, and sold it to Gov. Edwards. He went to St Louis, purchased property, and died in 1821

St. Louis with a married daughter, *his* only child. The widow of Louis Pensoneau, with her son and widowed mother (*nee* Perry), removed to Belleville in 1833, and she died at Mascoutah, St. Clair County, April 22, 1882

Paschal Pensoneau, the next son, in early manhood became identified with the Kickapoo Indians, married one or more of them, and died a few years since on the reservation of the remnant of that tribe, in the Indian Nation, leaving several half-breed children.

Laurent, the next son, born in 1805, married Elizabeth Hays, daughter of John Hays, Esq., and died at Point a la Pierre, without issue, July 18, 1848. His widow afterward married Bradford Broulette, and removed to Vincennes, Ind , where she still resides, her second husband having died several years ago.

Edward Pensoneau was born in 1810, and married Miss Isabella Boismenue in 1843, who died in 1846, leaving one son, Edward, now residing near East St. Louis. Edward, Sr., was again married in 1853 to Margaret Saucier, daughter of Matthieu Saucier, who, with three children, survived him, and still resides in or near Cahokia Edward Pensoneau, Sr., died in 1860.

Narcisse Pensoneau was born in 1812, and married Felicite Pensoneau in Belleville in 1835, and died at Mascoutah, Ill , Oct 8, 1878. His wife died at the same place, November 28, 1876. Of several children they had, but two survived them: Felicite, born in Belleville, July 22, 1836, who is living and unmarried, and William Bissel Pensoneau, married and residing in Jackson County, Ill.

The twin sons, Charles and François, were never married Charles died in Belleville in 1860, and François about the same time, in Louisiana

About the time the three brothers, Etienne, Louis, and Louison Pensoneau, arrived in Cahokia, two other Pensoneaus—second or third cousins of theirs—who are not mentioned in the "Pioneer History," came to that village from Canada They were brothers and named François and Augustine They were citizens of Cahokia for many years, and both died and were buried there. Augustine Pensoneau married the widow of Jean François Perry in 1815, and died in the fall of 1819, leaving his widow and two children: Felicite, born in 1817, who married Narcisse Pensoneau, and Augustine, born in 1819, who was raised in the family of Hon. Adam W Snyder, and is now residing in Belleville

Louison Pensoneau, when he arrived in Illinois, embarked in the Indian trade, and remained in it almost during life He made the Illinois River the scene of his operations, and the Kickapoo Indians were his customers. Peoria was his main depot, and the prairies round about were his counters where he sold his goods He was the first person that moved in the adjustment of the old Peoria claims. He got up a petition from the Peoria inhabitants and sent it to Hon Daniel P Cook, representative in Congress, and the consequence was the act of congress of 1820, authorizing the register of the land-office at Edwardsville to hear evidence and report on the claims His report was confirmed by another act of congress, passed in 1823. These Peoria claimants stand in the same situation as any of the ancient inhabitants of Illinois who have had lands granted to them by the government. Louison Pensoneau died in 1832, much regretted

The settlements in the two counties, St Clair and Randolph, enlarged considerably for some years before the territory of Illinois (in 1809) was created The inhabitants had located themselves on the frontiers, so that the Wood-River Colony was made stronger and enlarged The same of the settlements on Silver Creek and the Kaskaskia River, from Going's Settlement down Some few had located on the River Mary, in Randolph, and in the Mississippi Bottom below the creek called Gagnie. Hickman, Manscoe, and some others settled in this bottom as early as 1806 About this time Bowerman and Steel settled on the Massac Road, some fourteen miles east of Kaskaskia. Two or three of the Bird family located at the mouth of the Ohio—the present Cairo The Birds were engaged in the commerce on the rivers, and made this establishment to accommodate themselves and others navigating the western waters in 1805

Near the Ohio Saline, as it was called, a settlement was formed in very early times, which increased for several years before the year 1809 A few families were residing on the west side of the Wabash, near Vincennes, some time before the war of 1812; but they left during the war In 1809, Macauley emigrated from Kentucky, and located on the Little Wabash where the Vincennes road crossed He abandoned this place in the war, but returned afterward

CHAPTER IX.

Illinois under the Government of the Illinois Territory.

THE settlements were so remote from Vincennes, the seat of government of Indiana Territory—and they being a small strip scattered on the margins of the Ohio and Mississippi rivers—that the people in Illinois clamored much for a new territory. Nine-tenths of the country composing the Illinois Territory at that day was uninhabited and a wilderness

In the general assembly of the Indiana Territory, in 1808, Jesse B. Thomas, a member of the legislature, was elected a delegate to congress, and instructed to obtain a division of the territory On February 23, 1809, the territory of Illinois was established The boundaries of the Territory were the same as those of the State at present, except the Territory extended north to the northern limits of the United States The Federal government organized the territorial government and appointed the officers to administer the laws in it Ninian Edwards was appointed governor, Nathaniel Pope, secretary; and Jesse B. Thomas, William Sprigg, and Alexander Stuart, the judges. Stuart soon resigned, and Stanley Griswold was appointed These officers, for the most part, were great, talented men, and gave character and standing to the country.

Nathaniel Pope being present, entered into the administration of the government in the absence of Gov. Edwards Secretary Pope, acting as governor, appointed the proper number of justices-of-the-peace and other officers in the two counties John Hays was appointed sheriff, and John Hay clerk of the court, and John Moore, coroner. Gov. Edwards arrived at Kaskaskia, and he, with two of the judges of the Territory, by the authority of the Ordinance of 1787, constituted a legislative body in the first grade of territorial government They reenacted the laws of the Indiana Territory, which were applicable to the territory of Illinois

The establishment of a separate government in Illinois, in 1809, had great influence on immigration. The country was then better known and its merits appreciated. A great many adventurers followed the government, and Gov. Edwards was greatly instrumental in procuring immigration.

Matthew Duncan, an editor and proprietor from Kentucky, established the first newspaper in the Territory. The paper was published at Kaskaskia in the fall of 1809, which was a great lever to make known the advantages of Illinois. In 1815, Robert Blackwell and Daniel P. Cook purchased this paper,* and published it for several years at Kaskaskia.

Col. Benjamin Stephenson and many other immigrants came to the country under the patronage of Gov. Edwards.† The Rector family being already there, with many others, and together with the colony arriving with the new government, made old Kaskaskia a gay and fashionable place again. Never did Kaskaskia witness as much gayety, carousal, and amusement since the winter of 1809 and 1810. It is stated that the number of inhabitants in 1810 was 12,520. I think this number is swelled a little for effect, but the country was populating

---

* In McDonough's "History of Randolph, Monroe, and Perry counties," published in 1883, we find the following:

"Writers disagree as to the date of the first appearance of a newspaper in Illinois. Reynolds says that it was as early as 1809, while others equally reliable fix the date in 1814. All, however, agree that the *Illinois Herald* was the first paper published in the Territory, and that, Matthew Duncan was the publisher and editor. These points being settled, we are prepared to fix positively the date of its first appearance. We are in possession of No. 32 of Vol. II. of the *Illinois Herald*, published at Kaskaskia (Illinois Territory), Thursday morning, April 18, 1816. Presuming that its publication continued without interruption up to the date above named, the first issue was made September 6, 1814, page 194. On the same page, we are informed that the date of the transfer of the *Herald* to [Daniel P.] Cook & [Robert] Blackwell was August 25, 1817. They changed the name of the paper to the *Illinois Intelligencer*."

A careful examination of the files of the *Missouri Gazette and Illinois Advertiser*, now in possession of the *Missouri Republican*, at St Louis, fails to show any mention of the *Illinois Herald* prior to 1814.—J. H. G.

† "NOTICE.—I have for sale 22 slaves. Among them are several of both sexes, between the years of 10 and 17 years. If not shortly sold, I shall wish to hire them in Missouri Territory. I have also for sale a full-blooded stud-horse, a very large English bull, and several young ones.   NINIAN EDWARDS.

"October 1, 1815."—*Illinois Herald*, Kaskaskia, Oct. 1, 1815

fast at that time to what it was in former days. All the influence of these officers of the Territory that they could exercise were exerted for the welfare and growth of the country

In 1809, Gov. Edwards appointed John J. Crittenden attorney-general of the Territory, and, on his resignation, his brother, Thomas T. Crittenden, was appointed to the same office. These gentlemen did not remain long in the country, but returned to Kentucky. Gov. Edwards was born in Montgomery County, Md., in March, 1775. His parents were wealthy and respectable, and his education was commenced under favorable auspices. He was a companion at school of the celebrated William Wirt, and prepared for college under the tuition of a respectable clergyman—Mr. Hunt. He then was sent to the college at Carlisle, Pennsylvania. He did not graduate, but left the college and his home at the age of nineteen years for Kentucky.

Nature bestowed on Edwards many of her rarest gifts. He possessed a mind of extraordinary compass and an industry that brought forth every spark of talent with which nature had gifted him. His intellect was naturally strong and vigorous, and these qualities, together with his assiduity in his studies, made him a very superior man. He rose in Kentucky to the high and important office of chief-justice of the State. He was appointed governor of the territory of Illinois by President Madison, and by appointments continued in that office to the organization of the State government, in 1818.

Gov. Edwards, by proclamation, established in 1812 the counties of Madison, Johnson, Pope, and Gallatin; and having had a vote of the Territory in favor of a second grade of territorial government, he ordered, on September 16 of the same year, an election for members of the legislature. By his proclamation this assembly was convened at Kaskaskia, November 25, 1812. This was the first legislative body elected by the people that ever assembled in Illinois. The whole Territory contained six counties, and the general assembly twelve members—five in the council and seven in the house of representatives; as it seems Pope County had no member in the council that session.

John Thomas of St. Clair County was elected clerk of the council, and William C. Greenup of Randolph, clerk to the house. One door-keeper attended on both houses, and each branch occupied a room in the same building It is said that the whole assembly boarded at one house and slept in the same room in Kaskaskia. The members of the council were Samuel Judy of Madison, William Biggs of St Clair, Pierre Ménard of Randolph, Thomas Ferguson of Johnson, and Benjamin Talbot of Gallatin. The members of the house were William Jones of Madison, Joshua Oglesby and Jacob Short of St. Clair, George Fisher of Randolph, Philip Trammel, and Alexander Wilson* of Gallatin, and John Grammar of Johnson. This legislature did much business, and made a short session

Soon after Gov Edwards and other territorial officers arrived at Kaskaskia, they organized a colony of themselves and located in the prairie below Prairie du Rocher. All made habitations

* Alexander Wilson, native of Virginia, came to the State in 1809 or 1810, from Kentucky, and settled at Shawneetown. Was appointed a justice-of-the-peace of Randolph County by Gov. Edwards, July 20, 1810 Was a member of the first territorial legislature assembled by Gov Edwards at Kaskaskia, and with Phillip Trammell represented the then new county of Gallatin He took his seat November 25, 1812, and died while a member of the legislature His son, Harrison Wilson, altho but a youth, was a volunteer in the war of 1812, and served as ensign of Capt Thomas E Craig's company of territorial militia in the expedition against Peoria After his father's death he was active in his section on all matters relating to the protection and development of the new territory, was appointed treasurer of Gallatin County, Dec 28, 1813, and justice-of-the-peace in 1817. As the friend of Gov Bond, he seems to have been well esteemed by the latter. His inclinations were for the military service, and after the close of the war of 1812, altho colonel of a militia organization, he had no opportunity for further duties until the Black-Hawk War of 1832, in which, as captain of one of the companies of Posey's Brigade, he served with credit to the end After the end of the Indian troubles, he settled down upon his farm in Gallatin County and lived a quiet and uneventful life until his death, at Shawneetown, in Feb., 1852, at the age of 63.

Alexander Wilson was succeeded in the legislature by Thomas C Browne, and at his instance, in recognition of the services of his predecessor, as one of the pioneers and founders of the territory, the legislature by a unanimous vote, with the full approval of the council and Gov Edwards, Nov 29, 1814, granted the heirs of Alexander Wilson a right of ferry-franchise across the Ohio River at Shawneetown This franchise has ever since remained in the family and is now owned and operated by the heirs of Harrison Wilson, whose sons, John Andrew Wilson of Hamilton County, Maj-Gen James Harrison Wilson of the regular army, and Maj Henry S Wilson, 18th Ill Cavalry, and Maj Bluford Wilson, late solicitor of the treasury, have all served the State or national government with credit, and Gen Wilson with distinction in the war of the Rebellion Gen Wilson and Bluford Wilson alone survive, and since the war have been the promoters and builders of the St Louis-and-Northwestern, Cairo-and-Vincennes, and Louisville,-Evansville-and-St. Louis railroads, in their native section of the State —J. H. G.

in this neighborhood, and many of them resided there Gov. Edwards, Judge Thomas, Judge Stuart, some of the Rectors, Stephenson, and perhaps some others, resided in this colony. It at last broke up, and all the first pioneers left it.

Gov. Edwards was very energetic and active in his youthful days; and the war of 1812 gave him an ample theatre in which to exercise his talents and energies. The country was weak and the enemy—the numerous bands of Indians—were strong, and were abundantly supplied by their allies, the British, with the means of annoying the settlements. The inhabitants were so extended over such a large country, which made it more difficult to defend them than a small territory would be, and the general government had not the power to relieve the Territory to any great extent. Edwards was equal to the emergency, and performed his duty nobly to his country. He attended to the defence of the country in person, and was present in all the important transactions, guiding and directing the whole. He remained at home with his family a very small portion of his time during the whole war.

He was elected to the senate of the United States in 1818, and was shortly after reelected, as his term soon expired. The duties of this high and important office he performed with an ability and force of character that gave him and the State much standing and reputation. In 1826, he was elected governor of the State, and gave to this high and confidential trust all his experience, talents, and energies. He was the fast friend of the canal, not only in the senate of the United States, when the law passed granting so much land to the State for that noble improvement, but also while he was the chief executive of the State he urged that measure with all his great abilities. At the close of the war of 1812, he was appointed, with August Chouteau and William Clark of St Louis, a commissioner to treat with the Indians; and in 1815, many humane and equitable treaties were made with them.

While the cholera was raging in Belleville, in 1833, he was out, attending night and day to the afflicted with that scourge. With his knowledge of medicine and his true benevolence, he was a kind and efficient friend to the sick. It was his great anxiety and exertions in time of the cholera to save the distressed that caused him to take that disease. He was aged and his constitution some shattered, so that he fell a victim to the disease in a few hours after it seized on him. He died in Belleville, July 20, 1833. In the death of Gov Edwards* the country lost one of its ablest and best friends, and his family a kind parent and husband

Judges Thomas, Stuart, and Sprigg were, under the new Territorial organization, authorized and required to hold courts in all parts of the Territory under the judiciary system prescribed by the Territorial legislature. Judge Stuart remained on the

* Gov Edwards left two sons whose connection with the history of the State was of scarcely less importance than his own. His oldest son, Ninian Wirt Edwards, was born April 15, 1809, near Frankfort, Kentucky, and removed with his father to this State. Was married to Elizabeth P Todd, at Lexington, Ky , February 16, 1832 He graduated at Transylvania University in the law department in 1833 Was afterward appointed attorney-general by Gov John Reynolds in 1834 Confirmed by the legislature in 1835 Disliking Vandalia as a residence, he resigned shortly afterward and removed to Springfield, in the latter part of the year 1835. He was the next year, 1836, elected to represent Sangamon in the 10th general assembly as a colleague of Abraham Lincoln, Gen E D Baker, and six others—known in the State's history as the celebrated "long nine", who encompassed the removal of the capital to Springfield Mr Edwards was reelected in 1838, in the first legislature which met in the new capital, was senator from Sangamon County in 1844-8, and again to the house in 1848-50, and reelected to the latter position in 1850-52 During Mr Edwards' term of office, as state senator, he was elected one of the delegates to the constitutional convention of 1847. Before the expiration of his last legislative term he was appointed, March 24, 1854, by Gov. Matteson to be the first State superintendent of public instruction, under the new free-school law, a position he filled ably and worthily, giving the benefit of his ripe experience and extensive acquaintance, as well as his thoro scholarship to the proper organization of what has since proven to be one of the best systems of public education the land can boast Mr Edwards is still living in Springfield, where he occasionally appears as an attorney in the courts where he has practised for nearly fifty years. His rank as a lawyer was deservedly high, he was one of the attorneys representing the State before the board to investigate the claims of the canal contractors in 1852-3-4 He was the author of the first free-school law, approved Feb 15, 1855 He also edited his father's letters and published many of them, with a sketch of his life, in the year 1870 Mr Edwards had two sons and two daughters, who are all married, and most of their descendants are living near him in Springfield, Illinois

The younger son of Gov. Edwards, Hon Benjamin Stephenson Edwards, is also a prominent member of the Springfield bar, and at the present writing a member of the firm of Stuart, Edwards & Brown Judge Edwards was elected judge of the thirtieth circuit in 1869, a position he filled acceptably until his resignation the year following He has filled many minor positions acceptably, and is today one of the acknowledged leaders of the bar of the capital city J H G

bench in Illinois but a short time, and was appointed judge in the territory of Missouri. Stanley Griswold was appointed in his place in Illinois, as before stated. Judge Thomas presided in three upper counties in the Territory, Sprigg in the centre, and Stuart or Griswold on the Ohio and Lower Wabash. This system greatly improved the judiciary of Illinois, which was very much needed

Nature has been as bountiful to her native-born sons in Illinois as she has been generous in providing the fairest and finest country for their support. Samuel McRoberts, one of nature's loftiest sons, was born on his father's plantation in Monroe County, February 12, 1799. The natural gifts of Samuel McRoberts were great, and he added to them by an assiduity and intense application to study that would almost overcome any obstacle. Three great leading elements composed his character: a strong and vigorous intellect, an untiring energy and industry, and an unbounded ambition. These traits, while yet a young man not much over forty years, raised him from an obscure and humble situation in life to the senate of the United States, which is one of the most elevated and most important stations that is known to man.

In his tender years a tutor in his father's house instructed him in the rudiments of education. When he was of the proper age, he assisted his father to cultivate the farm for their support. At maturer age he was placed under the care of a very competent teacher, the late Mr. Edward Humphry. Mr. Humphry was an excellent citizen and a fine scholar. He commenced a school in the American Bottom, near the residence of Mr Chaffin, in 1805, and continued to teach for many years. His merit raised him to the kind consideration of the people, and he held many important offices—member to the general assembly, register of the land-office, etc

Young McRoberts received at this school an excellent English education, and also studied the Latin language. He delighted in mathematics, in which science he became well versed at this institution. He continued to prosecute his studies with his means and under the circumstances of the country until he was twenty years of age, then he accepted the clerkship of the circuit court of Monroe County. While in this situation, he acquired the means and opportunity to improve his mind, and he let no opportunity escape; but read day and night, while other young men of his age and condition were enjoying themselves in society and amusements At the age of twenty-two years he entered the law department of the Transylvania University, at Lexington, Ky. The faculty at this time were William T. Barry and Jesse Bledsoe, whose fame and characters are known all over the nation. He attended three full courses of lectures, and had the degree of bachelor of laws conferred on him by the president and faculty For classmates he had ex-Senator Morehead of Kentucky; H. C. White, Jr., of Tennessee; Senator Sevier, Arkansas; Mr. Harrison, late member of congress from Missouri; Mr. Speaker White of Kentucky; Gov Boggs of Missouri; Hon. Mr. Howard of Indiana, and many others, who became distinguished characters on the American theatre of great men.

After his return to Illinois, he commenced the practice of the law at a strong bar—Kane, Cook, Star, Blackwell, Mears, Thos Reynolds, Mills, Baker, and others composed the bar of this section of the State where McRoberts commenced the practice of the law, but he succeeded to the admiration of the public. In 1825, he was elected by the legislature circuit-judge of the second circuit in the State. In 1827, the judiciary was changed and he was placed again at the bar. In 1829, he was elected by the counties of Monroe, Washington, and Clinton to the State senate In 1830, he was appointed, by President Jackson, district-attorney for the district of Illinois; and in 1832, he was appointed receiver of public moneys at the Danville land-office.* In 1839, he was appointed solicitor of the general land-

* Prior to 1832, the land-office for Eastern Illinois, north to the Wisconsin line, was at Palestine, Crawford Co ; all north to the dividing line between townships 16 and 17, and west to the 3d principal meridian, was cut off of the Palestine district in 1831, and formed into the Danville land-district, with Mr McRoberts as its first receiver, and on June 26, 1834, the Danville land-district was subdivided by an east-and-west line between T. 30 and 31 (now the northern boundary of Iroquois and Livingston co's), the territory north of which composed the Northeastern land-district, and opened for business at Chicago, May 28, 1835. This explains why early settlers within the limits of the last-named district had to go, successively, to Palestine, Danville, and Chicago to enter government lands Judge McRoberts remained receiver of the Danville land-office until his appointment as solicitor of the general land-office at Washington in 1839, the house he lived in from 1832-9, a two-story frame, still stands on S. Vermilion St., Danville —H. W. B.

office at Washington City, and in 1841, he was elected to the senate of the United States.

While a member of the senate, March 22, 1843, he died at Cincinnati, on his return from Washington to Illinois The whole 'State, and the public generally, mourned and regretted his death: that so young a man and one so promising for future greatness should be cut off in the zenith of his usefulness and promise His family and relatives were overwhelmed with sorrow and grief; but such is the mysterious ways of Providence. Excessive energy and intense application to study and business impaired his health, and at last shortened his days Few men in any country or in any age run the brilliant career he did in so short a time. He was very kind and attentive to his brothers and sisters, and aided to give them an education.

George Forquer and Thomas Ford—half-brothers—were ancient and respectable pioneers of Illinois Forquer was born near Red-Stone Old Fort, now Brownsville, Pennsylvania, in 1794, and Thomas Ford in or near Uniontown, in the same State, in 1800. The father of George Forquer was an officer in the Revolution, and served in that disastrous campaign to' Canada under Gen. Arnold. After his return from Canada, he was appointed collector of the revenue of Bucks County, Pennsylvania, and was robbed by the tories; so that he lost all his private fortune, which compelled him to seek an asylum in the West He located near the Red-Stone Old Fort, and there he was killed by a coal bank falling on him. Mrs. Forquer, two or three years after, married Robert Ford, and in 1802, her husband was killed, as it was supposed, by robbers in the mountains. The old lady had a large family and scarcely any means for their support.

It was the custom of the Spanish government to give lands to actual settlers; and with the object to obtain land, Mrs Ford set sail in a keel-boat from Red-Stone Old Fort, in 1804, for St. Louis, in the Spanish country When she reached St. Louis the country was ceded to the United States, and she received no land. She remained in St. Louis some time, and then she and most of the family were taken sick. After their partial recovery, they moved to the New Design, in the fall of the same year they reached St Louis. They located themselves about three miles south of Waterloo. The next year they moved near the bluff, where for the first time Forquer and Ford walked upwards of three miles to school. They were under the same teacher (Mr. Humphry), who had the charge, likewise, of young Samuel McRoberts, and at the same time.

Mrs. Ford had a large family, mostly females, and not much means to support or educate them; but used her utmost exertions to accomplish that most desirable object—the education of her children. This lady possessed much talent, energy, and firmness of character. She observed system and economy in her family. It is supposed by many that much of the celebrity and standing of her two sons were caused by the sound moral principles with which she impressed them when they were under her maternal care.

Forquer being much older than Ford, was compelled to leave school to assist to support the family. He was forced to work out when he was only nine years old, and his schooling altogether was very little more than one year. He learned the trade of a house-joiner or carpenter in St. Louis, and worked at his trade for several years in that city. He returned to Illinois and purchased the tract of land on which Waterloo was located, in 1818. Daniel P. Cook and Forquer laid out this town, and Forquer purchased a stock of goods. He afterward projected the town of Bridgewater, on the Mississippi, one mile above Harrisonville. He was injured by these goods, which was the reason he studied law. He commenced the study of the law with a defective education; but he possessed a vigorous and active intellect, which supplied all deficiencies. He attended the Polemic Societies in Monroe County, and he learned the arts and mysteries of a fluent and elegant speaker. He had a good voice, and was a pleasant orator. This was a great lever in his extraordinary success. He possessed, as most of the pioneers of olden times did, an unbounded ambition. It was with him as Lord Nelson said, before the battle of Trafalgar. "Victory, or a grave in Westminster Abbey." Success or death, was imprinted on Forquer's banner.

In the year 1826, he was elected to the legislature from Monroe County, and was at the end of the session appointed secretary of the State. Some years after he was elected attorney-general of the State of Illinois. Afterward he moved to Sangamon County, and was elected to the State senate from that county After that he was appointed register of the land-office at Springfield He died of a pulmonary disease at Cincinnati, in 1837, aged forty-seven years

Altho he commenced in the world poor, and embarrassed with his merchandizing debts, yet he accumulated a considerable estate and died wealthy. He was blessed with the amiable and benevolent virtues in an eminent degree He was generous and hospitable, which flowed from the pure fountains of his noble heart. He made a good and successful practitioner at the bar, and had acquired a reputation and character by his merit that extended all over the country. The community sincerely mourned his death, as they had lost a great and good man, but it was his family that shed sincere tears of affliction and sorrow for their loss

Ford being younger, had a better opportunity than his brother Forquer to obtain an education, altho it was quite limited He might be considered as having received a good common education for the wilderness state of the country, forty years since, in Illinois In his youth his mind was developing itself, so that he gave great promise of his future success At school he was ardently attached to the science of mathematics. Daniel P Cook became acquainted with Ford, and saw at once that he possessed a vigorous and strong mind, and was his sincere and efficient patron ever after.

Cook provided and made the arrangements for Ford to study law. Forquer considered Ford's education defective, and sent him to Lexington, Ky, to improve it. But he remained there not a year. His brother Forquer being broken up, he returned home and commenced the practice of the law, in 1823 He was compelled on many occasions, when he was reading law, to stop and teach school for a support In 1829, he was appointed prosecuting-attorney for a judicial district. In 1831, I appointed him again prosecuting-attorney—Gov Edwards having first appointed him In 1835, he was elected by the legislature a circuit-judge, and in 1840 an associate-judge of the supreme court. In 1842, he was elected governor of the State of Illinois.

Gov Ford possessed many of the high and noble traits of character that constitute an eminent man. He was gifted with a strong and investigating intellect, and also possessed a firm, open, candidness of character that was admired by all. His mind was original and self-sustaining. Being in his infancy thrown on his own resources strengthened this trait of character. His firmness, moral and physical courage were never doubted by those who knew him. His ambition was prudent and well regulated by his sound judgment. His imagination was barely sufficient for a great man. The great governing element that gave him the high standing and celebrity which he so justly deserved was his strong mind. This kept his whole mental machinery in operation, and produced the results which are so much admired by mankind. But at last one trait was defective —he *could not resist the temptation* of refined and intellectual society. God in his wisdom has made this the weakest point in the human character, and more are shipwrecked on this rock than all others in the voyage of life.

Gov Ford possessed a nice sense of honor, bordering on the chivalric notions of olden times. His notions of probity and integrity were refined and well defined. With these notions, speculation, talented financiering was foreign from him; and he never cared for wealth more than a support, and scarcely that much. It is a difficult medium to reach, between ethereal philosophy on one hand and sordid money-making on the other. Two of the greatest men—except Washington—the nation ever produced were entirely dissimilar on this subject—Franklin acquired an estate and Jefferson lost one.

The mind and character of Gov. Ford qualified him for a judge better than for any other station. He was frank, open, and firm on the bench, and at the same time learned and competent in the exposition of the law. He was a good and sound lawyer, but not the advocate some others were at the bar. His honesty and warm friendly attachments to friends when he was governor enabled the cunning and shrewd hangers-on at the seat of government to mislead him at times. The Mormon war was a trouble to him, and it would have been to almost any governor placed in similar circumstances. That he acted with honesty and moral and physical courage in this nondescript war, I have no doubt. Ford not only possessed a strong mind generally, but his intellect was clear and discriminating. With these talents he made a good writer, and has written the history of Illinois, which is not yet published * Those having the manuscript say this history will be valuable for its information, and add credit to its author. After the close of the gubernatorial office, he resided in Peoria and practised his profession. He died there in 1849, sincerely regretted by the public.

It has been stated that George and William Blair emigrated to Illinois in 1796. George occupied a place on the main road from Whiteside's Station to the Fountain, where the late Mr. Eberman resided, and erected a distillery on the spring branch, west of the road. He was appointed sheriff of St. Clair County, and held that office for many years In 1802, he moved with his family to the present site of the city of Belleville, and erected a log-cabin about the place where the house of the late John Hay stands at present, in this city. He owned two hundred acres of land on which the town of Belleville, in the year 1814, was located.

The county-seat of St. Clair County had been at Cahokia for many years previous, but the country being settled by the Americans out of the French villages, gave the preponderance of population to the East, and on Dec. 10, 1813, an act of the legislature of the territory passed, authorizing James Lemen, Caldwell Cairnes, John Hays, Isaac Enochs, William Scott, Nathan Chambers, and Jacob Short to select a suitable site for the county-seat of St. Clair County. On March 10, 1814, the commissioners selected the plantation of George Blair for the county-seat. The public-square was staked off, one acre of land in Blair's field, which the report of the commissioners says "is twenty or thirty rods northeast of the house of George Blair." Blair agreed to give the county not only the public-square but also every fifth lot taken out of twenty-five acres of land around the public-square. It was agreed that the public-square "is given for the purpose of erecting public buildings thereon."

* "A History of Illinois, from its commencement as a State in 1818 to 1847. Containing a full account of the Black-Hawk War, the rise, progress, and fall of Mormonism, the Alton and Lovejoy riots, and other important and interesting events. By the late Gov Thomas Ford. Chicago: Published by S. C. Griggs & Co. 1854."

Blan agreed further that arrangements would be made so that the court in June of the above year may be held in Belleville George Blair had the honor to give the name of Belleville to the town and county-seat of St Clair County. The court of St Clair County, on August 8, 1814, recognized the name of Belleville and dated their sessions ever after at it. Belleville is a French word, which in English means a fine city, and it has realized the name Edwardsville was located about the same time and was made the county-seat of Madison County. It has remained the seat of justice of that county to the present time I recollect of attending the court there in an old fort made by Thomas Kirkpatrick near the Cahokia Creek, late in the fall of 1814. The house which is the most conspicuous for its age and public services in Belleville is the hotel built by James Tannahill in 1816 It was in pioneer times the *hotel de ville* of Belleville. It stands on the west side of the public-square—grows with the country and is now more popular than ever

Thomas Higgins was born in Barren County, Ky., in 1790 He came to Illinois with his relatives in 1807, and located on Silver Creek, St. Clair County, near his folks, the Bradsbys. He received a very limited education, as his parents were in humble circumstances and he himself had not much love for a school-house. He possessed a good mind, but he would in defiance of danger or anything else, employ himself in harmless mischief and merriment He had nothing savage or cruel in his disposition, yet he was as brave a man as ever existed. He was in his manhood very strong, muscular, and active He was not so very tall, but compactly formed for great strength and activity During the whole war of 1812, he was actively engaged on the frontiers in defending the settlements. I personally knew him to be a member of the company commanded by Capt William B. Whiteside in most of the war In 1814, he joined another company,* and was one of the party under the command of Lieut. John Journey at Hills Fort, situated six or eight miles southwest of the present town of Greenville, Bond County. Journey had eleven men in his corps, and on August 20, 1814, Indian sign was discovered near the fort, and the next morning

---

* Capt. Jacob Short's company.—Edwards' "History of Illinois," pp 347-8

at daybreak, Journey and party were mounted and out to reconnoitre the country They had not marched far before they entered an ambuscade of a large party of Indians The warriors fired on them and Journey and three of his men were instantly killed. William Burges and John Boucher[*] were wounded—Boucher slightly The horse of Higgins was shot in the neck and fell to the ground, but soon rose again Higgins remained a moment "to get a pull at them," as he said He took deliberate aim at an Indian and shot him dead. He then mounted his horse and was about to return to the fort, when a familiar voice hailed him from the grass and said, "Tom, you wont leave me?" Higgins hollowed out to him to "come on." "I can't come, my leg is smashed to pieces," answered Burges Higgins dismounted instantly and was getting the wounded man on his horse, but the horse scared and ran off. Higgins told Burges "to limp off on three legs, and he would protect him." Burges crawled off thro the grass and saved himself, while Higgins was left behind to fight the most bloody and terrible battle that ever the same number of men—three Indians and one white man—were engaged in Higgins had loaded his gun as soon as he had killed the Indian and was ready for the enemy again, but all at once three Indians made their appearance near him. He saw a small ravine close to him and ran for it; so he could defend himself against so many Indians While he was run-

---

[*] John Boucher, son of a Frenchman, was born in Kentucky in 1782, came to Illinois Territory in 1801; was married, Sept , 1817, to Margaret, a native of Hardy Co , Va , and with her parents came to New Design in 1796, daughter of Solomon Shook; was a man of great physical strength and activity, and after moving about the then settled parts of Southern Illinois, he finally settled down, in 1836, in Washington Co , a few miles west of Nashville, where he resided until 1851, when he removed to Jones Co , Iowa, where he died three years later, aged 72, his wife died at Monticello, Iowa, Oct 4, 1866, aged 75 Of their six children, four sons and two daughters, three survived their parents 1, Thomas, still resides on the old homestead in Iowa, 2, John Vincent, born Sept 27, 1818, married, March 5, 1844, Mary B , daughter of Allen Rountree, enlisted in the late war as orderly sergeant of Co E , 10th Missouri Inf'y, and contracting a dangerous illness, started home on a sick furlough, and died at Richview, Aug. 30, 1863, his oldest son, Geo O , aged 17, enlisted in Co I, 80th Ill , and served for three years, and is at present engaged in mercantile pursuits at Joplin, Mo Two other sons, Hiram and John, were engaged many years in merchandising in Nashville, where they still reside P H and Lyman T. are practising law at Boulder, Colorado The only daughter married Dr Salem Goodner and lives at New Minden, Washington Co —J H G

ning, he discovered for the first time his leg failed him—he was wounded at the first fire, but did not know it at the time.

One of the Indians was a very large, stout man, as large as Higgins. The others were small and not so courageous as the large one. Higgins was satisfied he must receive the fire of the large Indian and attempted to dodge it, but the bullet lodged in his thigh and he fell; but rose instantly. By this time, the other two had also fired at him and both balls hit him; he fell, badly wounded, but soon again was on his feet, with his loaded gun in his hand. The Indians threw down their guns, as they had not time to load them again, and rushed, whooping and yelling, on Higgins, with their spears, tomahawks, and knives. When they advanced near him, he presented his gun at them, and that would keep them off awhile. Higgins often told me that the large Indian was as brave as a lion—he could not daunt him or intimidate him in the least; but when the small ones came near him, they quailed under his furious looks. They could not look him in the face, "but the large Indian could look the devil in the face," as Higgins expressed it. The bold Indian was rushing on him and he shot him dead. It is supposed the large Indian did not believe Higgins' gun was loaded, or he would not have rushed on certain death. The Indian had a great soldier—Higgins—to contend with. When the other Indians saw their main man killed, it made them more fierce. They raised the warwhoop the louder and rushed with greater vigor on poor wounded Higgins, who had in his body four Indian balls and had lost much blood; was weak and almost exhausted; had an empty gun and no other weapon; was near many Indian warriors besides the two pressing on him, who were armed with spears, tomahawks, and knives, and were strong, having lost no blood, nor were they wounded, as Higgins was. They gave Higgins many flesh-wounds, as his shirt and body were literally cut to pieces. One of the Indians threw a tomahawk at him; cut his ear nearly off and laid the bone of his head and side of his neck entirely bare. This blow knocked him down, and when they rushed on him with their spears, he kicked them off. When one of the Indians presented his spear at the breast of Higgins while he was stretched on the ground, he caught the spear, and the Indian pulling it, raised Higgins up by it. Then it was that he took his gun and literally knocked the brains out of one of the Indians This blow broke the skull of the Indian and likewise Higgins' gun. It was shattered all to pieces and the barrel was bent. Then he had but one Indian to fight, but he was nearly exhausted During most of this fight, it was in sight of the fort, and a woman—a Mrs. Pursley—became excited and said "she could not stand and see so brave a man as Higgins murdered by the Indians." She mounted her husband's horse and started to his rescue. The men in the fort could not see a woman go alone and followed her As soon as the Indian fighting Higgins* saw the rangers coming, he fled, and they found Higgins prostrated on the ground, nearly dead—cut and mangled and almost torn to pieces. It is supposed, when the Indian fled, the excitement of Higgins subsided and he fainted In fact, he was nearly dead when his friends relieved him He barely escaped death from his wounds and never entirely recovered from them altho he lived many years after. He received a pension to the full amount of the law.† He was appointed door-keeper to one of the houses of the general assembly of Illinois, and resided in Fayette County; was a farmer and raised a large family He died at his residence, above Vandalia, in 1829 Higgins was a generous, open-hearted pioneer.

In the war of 1812, the exposed situation of the country, the weakness of the population, and the strength of the Indian

* Gov. Reynolds in his later work, gives an amusing account of a duel fought with rocks, between Higgins and another man, at the lead-mines, in which the celebrated Indian-fighter was victorious —"My Own Times", (2d ed) page 169 —J H G.

† I was well acquainted with Hiram Arthur, a remarkably honest and truthful man, who was in the fort near the scene when it took place, and observed it all He gave me a written account of it, which is now among my papers, from which it appears that about nine-tenths of the amount of the melée is all bosh "Higgins," he says, "was a brave fellow, but the trouble with the story we read of is that but a small percentage of the facts stated ever occurred. The account originated with Higgins himself. After the war, he lived in Fayette County, Ill., and there he met with a Mr Hall, who wrote or contributed to the 'Annals of the West,' and gave him his version of the affair, and it took wings and has flown ever since All that can be said is that the account is altogether overdrawn " I knew Tom Higgins well, and he was in the habit of telling tremendous yarns, and was a capital hand at making himself the hero of all his adventures, particularly when he was in his cups.—J. GILLESPIE, Jan 25, 1883.

enemy brought into actual operation the whole capacities of the country, physical and mental, for its defence, and among the pioneers that came to the rescue was Thomas Carlin, who emigrated to Illinois in 1811 and became a conspicuous and popular character. Carlin was born in Fayette County, Ky., in 1789, and moved with his father to Shelby County, in the same State, in 1793. The family moved in 1803 to the Spanish country, Platin Creek, St Louis County. The father of Carlin died the same year he settled in St. Louis County, leaving his widow and seven children—Thomas the oldest. The parents of Carlin on both sides were of the Irish extraction. The circumstances of the father were very limited, so the son had no opportunity of an education. In fact, the county where they resided, in Upper Louisiana, was destitute of schools at that day. Carlin attended school at rare intervals; but such long periods passing between that he forgot almost as fast as he learned anything at school. At school his only guide was the Dilworth spelling-book and the Barlow knife to make pens, but Nature came to the rescue and recognized Carlin as her favorite son. She spread before him her ample creation and she herself became his teacher. He was highly favored with a strong and vigorous mind and an untiring energy. He possessed strong and excitable feelings; but his firm and decisive judgment compelled all these turbulent and violent passions to revolve around it like the planets do around the sun, the common centre. He possessed a marked and decided character and one of great force and influence. By mere accident, he got hold of an arithmetic, and without a teacher, he became well acquainted with that noble and grand science

On June 3, 1812, he entered the military service of the United States as a private in the company commanded by William B Whiteside. The war was about commencing and the prospect was gloomy; but this was no impediment to Carlin to deter him from the defence of his country. Among his other decided traits of character, he had courage and firmness, even to desperation. He made an excellent soldier; always prepared for any service, let it be perilous or not. In the fall of 1812, he was in the campaign to Lake Peoria, and the army under Gov. Edwards halted and camped within a few miles of the Black-

Partridge's Town, on the east side of the Illinois River, nearly opposite the upper end of Lake Peoria. It was necessary to select some choice spirits to reconnoitre the Indian town at night. This was considered a dangerous and perilous service. Carlin volunteered as one of four to reconnoitre and report, and he and three Whitesides—Robert, Davis, and Stephen—were entrusted with this delicate service. They proceeded to the Indian village and went thro every part of it without detection. If a dog were to bark or other alarm made, these brave men must have perished, being thus caught in the midst of a great number of hostile Indians. They reported the strength and situation of the enemy, so that the army could the next morning be conducted with certainty to the attack. The United-States Rangers were established for the defence of the frontiers and they accomplished that object to the fullest extent, but in performing this service, great battles or long campaigns were not contemplated or required; yet all such services as were required, Carlin and others performed to the satisfaction of the public. Carlin marched in the campaign under Gen Howard in 1813, thro the country between the Mississippi and Illinois rivers.

Toward the close of the war, he married a beautiful young lady of Madison County, of strong mind and of pleasing and agreeable manners. This lady being matured by age and experience, developed a sound judgment and an amiable and happy disposition, and was to her husband in truth a helpmate during his life. They raised a large and respectable family.

In 1815, Carlin emigrated north from Madison and located on the high land between Macoupin and Apple creeks, and was about the first family that settled north of the Macoupin Creek. When Green County was first organized, the county-seat was laid off on his land and the seat of justice called Carrolton. Carlin was elected the first sheriff of Green County and performed the duties of the office with punctuality and fidelity. This was the first office he ever held and he then gave proof of his efficiency, integrity, and activity to be useful to the people, and they always thereafter appreciated his merit. He was often elected to the general assembly of the State from Green Co., always his public services were approved and he became still more popular. He was a cautious business member. When the county of Macoupin was established, the county-seat, Carlinville, was named in honor of him. He was appointed receiver of public moneys at Quincy and remained in that office many years. This was a very responsible office, as great amounts of money were received in that office for the government, and the accounts were settled to the perfect satisfaction of all. In this office, as well as in all others, he exhibited a positive honesty and integrity, which is one of the brightest ornaments in the human character.

In 1838, he was elected the governor of Illinois. This was a high and important trust, and he performed the duties of that station with a sound judgment and practical common-sense. He was sworn into office at Vandalia in 1838, and on Dec 7 of that year, he delivered a chaste and statesman-like message. It is short and well adapted to the situation of the country in its embarrassed condition. He appealed with warmth and sincerity to the people and the legislature to promote education. He also urged the completion of the canal and the necessity to legislate with care and caution on the subject of State banks. His measures and policy will be at some day admired for his wisdom and good sense. It must be recollected that Gov. Carlin* was a warm and ardent politician, and in fact he was ardent and enthusiastic in all his actions; but in politics, was firm, consistent, and ardent. He was one of the deepest dye in the democratic party, and was a great friend to Gen. Jackson He was in his politics, as in all other transactions, honest and correct. His course in politics gave him great standing with his party

* In 1814, Gov. Carlin married Miss Rebecca Huitt, and resided on the Mississippi, opposite the mouth of the Missouri, and four years later removed to Greene County. After retiring from public life to his Carrolton farm, he was again called from his retirement to serve out the unexpired term of Hon John D. Fay, who had resigned his seat in Illinois legislature, 1848-50

His death occurred Feb. 14, 1852, aged 63, leaving a widow and seven children, six having died

Gov. Carlin was captain of a company in the Odd Battalion of Spies, commanded by Maj John D. Henry in Gen. Whiteside's brigade, in the Black-Hawk war, and which served from April 20 to May 27, 1832. James Carlin, a brother of the governor, was a private soldier in this company, and was at one time clerk of the circuit-court of Greene County, and died leaving considerable property in real estate in that

After Gov. Carlin was married, became the head of a family, and had arrived at full maturity of mind, he became seriously concerned in religious matters. He received his first impressions of religion from the preaching of Rev. John M. Peck of St. Clair County, and became a member of the Baptist church. He was kind and benevolent to all, but to his family he was affectionate and sincerely devoted. He gave his children an excellent education and they profited by it equal to the efforts made by the parent. He died at his residence in Carrollton in February, 1852, full of years and full of honor. His death was lamented and regretted by the public and his family experienced an irreparable loss, and as such they mourned his decease. Carlin was, in the true sense of the word, a self-made man. He commenced humble in life, and by his talents, energy, and integrity, he reached the highest office in the gift of the people in the State, and has reached still a higher station: that of a large place in the hearts of the people.

About the time (1809) the territory was organized, the country on the margins of the rivers down the Mississippi from Kaskaskia and up the Ohio and Wabash rivers almost to Vincennes, commenced to settle and improve. Samuel Omelvany* and

county, he was the father of Gen. William P. Carlin, whose record as colonel of the thirty-eighth Illinois infantry and afterward a brigadier-general in the army of the Cumberland, is part of the proud achievements of Illinois, in the late war. At the close of the war Gen. Carlin had attained by successive promotions the rank of major in the regular establishment, and brevet-major-general of volunteers. He is yet in the regular army, being colonel of the 4th Infantry. His younger brother, Hon Walter E. Carlin of Jerseyville, was also a lieutenant in the thirty-eighth during the Rebellion, and at the age of nineteen refused a commission as captain of his company, tendered him by Gov. Yates. He represented Scott, Greene, and Jersey counties as one of their Democratic members in the thirty-third general assembly. He is a banker by occupation, a member of the firm of Carlin and Bagley, and as a financier ranks high, having when chairman of the county board caused to be liquidated under his management a heavy county debt —J. H. G.

* John Omelvany, with his wife, two younger sons, Patrick and William, and a daughter Mary, who married a McConnell and settled in Tenn., came from Ireland about 1798-9, and, after a few years residence in Ky., settled in what later became Pope Co., near his oldest son Samuel, who landed in Charleston, S C , in 1797 or 8, where he married and soon after (Reynolds says in 1805, see next p., 386) came to Illinois Territory, settling in Pope Co., on the Ohio River. In addition to farming, trading, and flat-boating to New Orleans, he was for that day an extensive dealer in the products of the country—corn and hogs. Later he removed to Randolph Co. and was a member of the county-court in 1819. Still later he resided in and repre-

others formed a colony on the Ohio River, near the mouth of the Grand-Pierre Creek, as early as 1805. The margins of the rivers commenced settlement as early as 1804 or '5, and continued to increase rapidly. A family of Quakers from North Carolina of the name of Stokes settled some miles east of the present town of Jonesboro' in 1808. It was called for years after, Stokes' Settlement.

The Logan family emigrated from Missouri and settled on Big Muddy in pioneer times. Dr. Logan* is still alive and a

sented Union Co in the legislature in 1820-2, contesting successfully the seat occupied by Samuel Alexander, and died about 1828 His mother died the year of their arrival, and his father and younger brother Patrick the year following His children: George died at 30, and John still lives in Pope Co., a successful merchant and trader; Margaret, married Wood, and Mary are long since dead.

William, the youngest son of John, born 1775, married 1799, Susan McKee of Ireland, in So Carolina, moved to Ky in 1804-5, settling near Elkton, Todd Co, Ill He had six sons and five daughters (1) John, born in Ky 1800, lawyer, settled at Carlyle, Clinton Co, Ill, in 1830, where he practised law till he died in 1836; served in Capt Andrew Bankson's company in Black-Hawk War (2) William W., born in Monroe Co, 1829, brought up to the law, county-clerk, 1843-8; now living in Centralia (3) James M, bred to his father's trade, brick-making, in 1853 entered the mercantile business in Centralia, was postmaster for several years, and now lives at East St Louis, where one of his sons is city attorney. (4) Edward, lawyer, represented Monroe Co in the legislature of 1846-8, was presidential elector in 1852 on the Pierce ticket and died before the Rebellion (5) Harvey K. S, also a lawyer of Centralia, was judge of the second circuit from 1858-61, filling the vacancy occasioned by the resignation of Judge Breese, moved during the late war to California, where he is now practising law. (6) Constantine was killed in his 18th year at Waterloo by the accidental discharge of a gun Of the daughters, Nancy, born 1802, married, 1828, W. W Moore in Monroe Co, and died at Oakland, Cal., Feb, 1883, Martha and Mary, twins, born 1804, married, and have descendants in Marion and Jefferson counties; Susan, 4th, died at San Jose, Cal, 1864; Elizabeth, 5th (Concannon) is living in Oakland, Cal The mother of this numerous family died in Marion Co, Feb, 1875, aged 93

* Dr John Logan came to this country from Ireland early in this century, and married, in 1824, Miss Elizabeth Jenkins, a sister of Hon Alexander M Jenkins, afterward lieut -governor of the State, a lawyer of high rank, and a judge eminent for his probity and legal acquirements Dr Logan raised a family of eleven children, several of whom have shown marked ability, and the oldest son, distinguished as a soldier and a statesman, is Hon John A. Logan, at present a United States senator from Illinois. Dr. John Logan was a man of great force of character and served in many public positions with satisfaction to the people and credit to himself. He was a member of the house of representatives in the tenth general assembly, serving with Abraham Lincoln, John J. Hardin, James Shields, Stephen A. Douglas, Augustus C French, John A. McClernand, John Dement, Jesse K Dubois, and many other political celebrities He was reelected to the eleventh and twelfth and again in 1846

respectable and living monument of the pioneers of Southern Illinois. This gentleman has been in much public service and acted to the advantage of the public interest and much to his own honor

to the fifteenth general assembly, his last appearance in public life. He "was a corporal in Capt. A M. Jenkins' company in the Black-Hawk War, serving throughout June and July, and was mustered out August 10, 1832, at Fort Hamilton."

John Alexander Logan was born Feb. 9, 1826, at Murpheysboro', Jackson Co ; his early education was limited by the resources of the country, but he had passed through a course at Shiloh College when the breaking out of the Mexican war called him from his studies to the field. He enlisted at Alton, and was enrolled May 29, 1847, in Company H of Col. Edward W. B. Newby's (5th) Regiment of Illinois Volunteers; was elected 2d-lieutenant of his company and afterward served for a time as adjutant of his regiment After the close of the war, he studied law in the office of his uncle, Gov Jenkins, was elected county-clerk of Jackson County in 1849, serving one term, continued his law studies and graduated from the law department of the University of Kentucky at Louisville in 1851 He went into the law practice with Gov. Jenkins in 1852. In June of that year he was elected prosecuting-attorney of the first judicial circuit, and removed to Benton, Franklin County. He was the same fall elected to represent Franklin and Jackson counties in the eighteenth general assembly; was married, Nov 27, 1855, to Miss Mary Cunningham of Shawneetown, Ill. In 1856, was chosen a presidential elector for the ninth congressional district on the democratic ticket; in 1858, was elected to congress from that district and again reelected in 1860. He was an ardent supporter of Stephen A. Douglas, and followed the lead of that able statesman in his support of all necessary measures adopted by President Lincoln on the suppression of the Rebellion While yet a member of congress, he took a musket and went into the ranks, participating as a volunteer private in the memorable battle of Bull Run. Returning to Illinois, he raised the 31st Regiment of Volunteers and became its colonel, and made his next record on the field of Belmont. On March 5, 1862, he was made brigadier-general of volunteers, and declining a reelection to congress in 1862, was made a major-general in November of that year, and devoted himself arduously to the task of putting down the Rebellion. He participated in nine of the battles about Vicksburg, afterward at Resaca, at Kenesaw Mountain, at Atlanta, at Dallas, and in many of the hotly-contested fields of the campaigns of 1863 5 His promotions were rapid, from a division he rose to a corps commander, and finally, on May 23, 1865, he was advanced to the command of the Army of the Tennessee. In 1865, he was appointed minister to Mexico, but declined. In 1866, Gen. Logan was elected congressman-at-large from the State of Illinois, and reelected to the same position in 1868 and again in 1870. In 1871, he resigned his seat in congress to accept the succession to Gov. Richard Yates in the United-States senate. His term expiring in 1877, he was the candidate of the republican party for the succession, but was defeated by David Davis. Two years later he was again elected and succeeded Gen Richard J Oglesby to the seat he now fills Gen Logan was nominated by the Republican National Convention as their candidate for vice-president, at Chicago, June 6, 1884

Wm. H. Logan, a younger son of Dr. Logan, and a lawyer of much promise, died soon after the war. He represented Jackson and Williamson counties in the 24th general assembly, possessed oratorical powers of no mean order, and acted as a Union independent democrat.—J. H. G.

Alexander M. Jenkins,* who was partially raised in Southern Illinois, is a talented and conspicuous citizen. Jenkins, like most of the pioneers, had no opportunity of an early education; but in after-days, he improved himself, so that he is at this time not only a good scholar but an intelligent and well-read man. He was when a youth compelled to work on his own hook for the means to obtain an education, and succeeded well. He has been elected many terms to the general assembly of the State, and commanded a company from Jackson County in the Black-Hawk war. In 1834, he was elected lieutenant-governor of the State. He was appointed receiver of public money in the land-office at Edwardsville and resigned that office. For some years before, he had been merchandising and afterward he studied law and commenced the practice in the southern counties of Illinois. He was elected a member from Jackson County of the convention that formed the new constitution in 1847, and is at this time a practising lawyer.

John Dougherty was also raised in Southern Illinois and has, by his merit and exertions, become a good lawyer and respectable citizen. He labored under embarrassing circumstances in his youth; but by his natural resources and his exertions, he has surmounted all obstacles and is now enjoying the rich re-

* Mr. Jenkins was elected to the legislature to represent Jackson County in 1832-4, at the expiration of which term he was elected lieutenant-governor, holding that position until his resignation, which occurred in 1836, to accept the position of president of the first Illinois-Central Railroad Company, chartered January 16, 1836. When the State adopted its ill-fated system of public improvements, February 27, 1837, the surrender of this charter was demanded, and although the company had already expended considerable money and Mr. Jenkins given much time toward the preliminary arrangements, necessary before the building of the road should be begun, the charter was cheerfully surrendered. After the State had expended over one million dollars on this road it was abandoned, and on March 6, 1843, the State, as an act of justice, returned the franchise to the representatives of the old company. The Cairo City-and-Canal Company reincorporating them for this particular purpose as the Great-Western Railway Company. A failure to secure the passage of a preemption grant in congress, and the grant at a later day, of a large quantity of land to the State in aid of the building of this road, resulted in the incorporation of a new company (February 10, 1851), that finally completed the road.

Mr. Jenkins was elected judge of the third judicial circuit in 1859, to fill the vacancy caused by the resignation of W. K. Parrish, and was reelected at the close of his term in 1861. He "died in the harness", before the expiration of his official term, February 13, 1864.—J. H. G.

ward that is always given to an energetic and proper course of conduct. His father was limited in his means and his son was compelled to rely on himself for his education and the study of the law before he commenced practise. He worked, taught school, and used all honorable means in his power to obtain an education. He has been elected time and time again to the general assembly of the State from Union County and often from both the counties, Union and Alexander, when they voted together. Dougherty has a good voice, a pleasing, eloquent speaker. He possesses a good mind and a kindness and benevolence of heart.

George Hacker was appointed a justice-of-the-peace in Randolph County in 1810. He resided then on Cache River.

John S. Hacker was an early pioneer of Illinois and has, by his natural talents and exertions, become a conspicuous and popular man in Illinois. He was thrown on his own resources in his infancy and was compelled "to buffet the storms of life" without aid or assistance from any quarter, but his natural talents are good. He possesses a quick and discriminating mind, and he has had such incessant intercourse with the people that he is well acquainted with the human character. Mankind seemed to be the school-house in which he received his education. He married a lady of fine common-sense and of mild and amiable disposition. She has acted in the family the part of a wise and dignified matron, to whose proper conduct much of the success of the family is attributable. Hacker was about the first settler in the pleasant town of Jonesboro', the county-seat of Union County, and has remained there thirty years. He makes a good speech and is listened to with pleasure; is original in his ideas and so utters them in his stump-speeches

Samuel Omelvany was a popular pioneer in his settlement and in fact throughout the south of Illinois in his day. He was a native of Ireland; had resided in Kentucky, but ended his days in Southern Illinois. He was blessed with a very strong natural mind; possessed not much education or book intelligence; but the strength of his mind was visible in all his actions, public and private. His person was large and he had no parlor polish in his manners; his mind corresponded with his exterior, strong and natural. He was a member-elect from Pope County to the convention in 1818 that formed the first constitution of the State, and he has been elected often from the same county to the State legislature, and has served the people in various other stations with ability.

Hamlet Ferguson resided in pioneer times at or near Golconda, Pope County, and was a respectable citizen He filled various offices and was a member in the State convention that formed the constitution in 1818 "He acted well his part, there all the honor lies."

A great many worthy working emigrants from North Carolina, Pennsylvania, and some from Kentucky settled in the region of country below Big Muddy and not far from the Mississippi. They were of German descent and formed a moral, excellent settlement A very conspicuous and talented man among them was Rev George Wolf, who was a preacher of the gospel and was nature's great man He was raised on a farm and pursued that profession for a living for himself and family He is one of the Universalian Baptists and preached his sermons to contain the scriptures and reason together

In early times, large settlements were made in the present limits of Gallatin County, and the old Shawneetown, that the aborigines had occupied for ages past and Col Croghan visited in 1765, was again brought into modern existence It received the name of Shawneetown on account of a band of Indians of that name having lived there in olden times. This town was first settled by talented, great men John McLean, Thomas C Browne, Jeptha Hardin, Joseph M Street, Marshall, Jones, Hubbard, Rallings, Gatewood, Kirkpatrick, Posey, Vanlavingham, and others of talents and enterprise, located in Shawneetown at different times during its pioneer days. At the Licks, as the salt-works were then called, were settled Isaac White, the United-States agent, Guard, Philip Trammel, Leonard White, John Lane, and others About the close of the war in 1814, several fine water-mills were erected on the Little-Wabash River a few miles above the mouth The town of New Haven has been built in the neighborhood.

Isaac White was a resident of the West for many years before the battle of Tippecanoe, where he perished in the cause of his country. White was agent for the United States at the Ohio saline for some years. Gov. Edwards appointed him captain of a company in 1810 He was with Gov Harrison in the campaign up the Wabash in 1811, and was killed in the battle of Tippecanoe in November of that year. The death of this brave soldier was very much regretted generally. The legislature called a county White in honor of him and to perpetuate his name.

Probably of all the pioneers of Illinois, nature did the most for John McLean of Shawneetown. His gigantic mind, his form of noble and manly symmetry, and his lofty and dignified bearing, all demonstrated him to be the "noblest work of God." His person was large and formed on that model of natural excellence that would at once attract the attention and admiration of all spectators The vigor and compass of his mind were exceedingly great and other traits of character equally strong His eloquence flowed in torrents, deep, strong, and almost irresistible. Nature did so much for him that he depended too much on his natural abilities and did not as much for himself Yet without effort, he naturally took the highest stand in any situation in which he was placed

McLean was born in North Carolina in 1791 His father and family emigrated to Logan County, Ky., when his son John was only four years old He was raised there until he was twenty odd years old, and then he settled in Shawneetown in 1815 This pioneer, like most of the others, was raised in a country destitute of schools, and thereby had in his early days not the advantages of an education His mind was permitted to exercise its own originality, without restraint or discipline, but it was so great and powerful that it would, to speak in sailor phrase, "right itself when thrown on its beam's ends" He studied law in Kentucky and commenced the practice in Shawneetown as a lawyer should be: poor, talented, and ambitious. When he reached Illinois, he had nothing to depend on but God and himself, and on this foundation, he soon became one of the most conspicuous and popular men in Illinois Besides his great strength of mind, he was possessed with a lively imagination and much eloquence There was no man in Illinois, before or since his day, that surpassed him in pure natural eloquence Nature made him a great orator.

The first great trial of his strength was with Hon Daniel P Cook for a seat in congress. This was the first congressional election in the State. The country was much excited and two of the greatest men then in the State, or ever have been in it since, were started on this track of honor They were both open, noble-hearted Kentuckians, generous and chivalric, so that the canvass was conducted on honorable principles The fashion at that day and ever since has been to have political meetings and address speeches to the people, literally from a stump of a tree This custom was introduced here from the Southern and Western States From the stump, these two young orators, both favorites of nature, addressed the audience in such streams of eloquence that has never been surpassed in Illinois before or since These two young politicians were pioneers for whom any community would feel an honest pride. McLean was elected then; but Cook beat him the next election.

McLean was elected many times to the general assembly from Gallatin County, and was almost always made speaker of the house of representatives He was elected to the United-States senate twice. The first time for one session to fill a vacancy and the next was for a full term But in 1830, at Shawneetown, he died No man possessed a stronger hold on the people than he did, so that his death was considered, as it really was, a great public calamity, and mourned for with tears of sincere affection and sorrow A county in Illinois bears his name, to do him honor. He was not wealthy, left a wife and many friends

In the fall of 1808, a wagon-road was laid off from Goshen Settlement to the Ohio salt-works This road crossed the Kaskaskia River where Carlyle is situated at present, by the Walnut Hills, and so on to the salt-works. This was in olden times called the Goshen Road

Thomas C Browne, a living and conspicuous pioneer of Illinois, was born in Kentucky, emigrated to Illinois and settled in Shawneetown in 1812 He studied law in Kentucky and commenced the practice as soon as he reached the northwestern shores of the Ohio River The first courts in Gallatin County were held at the county-seat, Shawneetown, in flatboats, as they had at first no court-house. Boats were plenty, being floated down the river and moored to the bank at the county-seat The grand-jury occupied one, while the court, bar, suitors, witnesses, etc, sat in another.

Thomas C. Browne possesses many excellent traits of character; he is endowed by nature with a strong intellect and with a benevolence and goodness of heart that have marked his whole progress thro life. With these traits of character, he delighted to mingle with the people and he obtained much of his education and intelligence in this manner With the solid mind he possessed, he was in an academy of human knowledge every day and he profited well by the occasion In 1814, he was elected with Philip Trammel to the legislature of the Territory of Illinois from Gallatin County, and made a wise and discreet member altho he was very young In 1815, he was appointed prosecuting-attorney for the counties of Gallatin, Pope, Edwards, and others in the eastern part of the territory. All these duties he performed to the satisfaction of the public. In 1816, he was elected from the same county to the legislative council of the territory. This office continued to the organization of the State government in 1818. By being in the legislature so long, and being a sound, solid member, and becoming so well known and popular throughout the country, the first legislature under the State government elected him one of the justices of the supreme court of the State, without much opposition He remained in that office for nearly thirty years Honor, integrity, and fidelity are prominent traits in his character

Nathaniel Pope was a younger branch of a great and talented family in the West He emigrated from Kentucky to Upper Louisiana in 1804, and remained on the west side of the Mississippi for some years For some time, he made Ste Genevieve his home and attended the courts on this side of the river. In 1809, he was appointed secretary of the territory of Illinois, and then made Illinois his residence during life. He was born in Louisville, Ky, in 1784 At an early age, he was placed in the Transylvania University at Lexington, Ky, and received a classic education. He also learned well the French language and spoke it fluently At college, he attended assiduously to his studies, which gave presages of his future greatness, and he graduated with a high reputation for his learning and abilities. He studied law with his brother, John Pope of Kentucky, and soon became well versed in the laws of the country, for a young man.

Nature had bestowed on him rare and great talents; his judgment was strong and profound, and his great natural intellect was thoroly trained and disciplined by study. Nature gave him also an unbounded benevolence and kindness of heart. Nothing savage or cruel lurked in his breast, but the sunshine of kindness to all mankind illuminated his path thro life. He possessed a noble dignity of character that gave him a due degree of self-respect. With these admirable traits of character and his profound knowledge of the law, he stood at the head of his profession and enjoyed an extensive practice. He married a lady of accomplishments and beauty. She also possessed a strong mind and an amiable and benevolent disposition. These worthy parents were the progenitors of a respectable family of children. In 1816, he was elected a delegate to congress from the territory, and I think he did more important services for the people than any one man has done since in so short a time.

Among various other measures, he procured the northern boundary of the State to be extended north from the southern bend of Lake Michigan to latitude forty-two and a-half degrees north. On this globe, to the extent, there is not a better tract of country; and when there were barely forty thousand souls in the territory, he had passed an act of congress authorizing the people of Illinois to form a State government. When the State was admitted into the Union, he was appointed the United-States judge of the district of Illinois. In this offrce he remained upward of thirty years and made a judge that added dignity and respectability to the office and State. It was in the social, convivial parties where he was the greatest of the great. When the society was composed of learned, brilliant, and witty, he was among them, the centre of attraction. It was in his own family circle, with a few accomplished friends, men of science and talents, where he displayed his great social qualities. Pope County was called by that name to honor him and to perpetuate his memory. He died Novem-

ber, 1850, with great coolness and composure; conversed of death itself with respect, but with as much calmness and Christian resignation as upon any other subject. He was much esteemed by the public and his decease was in fact, as they considered it, a public calamity.

In early times, before the New-Orleans sugar was sold so cheap in this market, the inhabitants—French, Americans, and Indians—made maple-sugar Quantities were manufactured not only for domestic use but as an article of commerce Molasses was also made. In early times, horse-flies were extremely annoying to animals. In the summer, horses were often killed by them between Kaskaskia and Vincennes A green prairie-fly was the most numerous and annoying In the heat of the day they were the worst. Sometimes farmers could not plow in daytime and at times they covered the horse with a blanket. Millions of these flies were produced in the prairies. When the country became settled and improved, they disappeared.

It is almost forty years since Daniel Pope Cook, another great favorite of nature, commenced his brilliant career in Illinois. He rose high, shined bright, and died soon. He was at one time the darling and idol of the people; he was great, brilliant, and active in his mind, his qualifications of heart were noble, generous, and benevolent. The name of Daniel P Cook is yet sweet music in the ears of many an old pioneer of Illinois They almost involuntarily cry out: "When is the election?" His genius, vigor of intellect, and versatility of talent were rarely surpassed and not commonly equaled in any country. He was born in Scott County, Ky., in 1793 His parents were pious, respectable citizens and obtained their living by cultivating a farm. Cook was, from his infancy, a sickly, weakly child, which was one reason, together with the circumscribed means of his father, that his education in his youth was not much attended to. He started in the world with a very limited education

In 1811, when he reached his eighteenth year, he visited Ste. Genevieve, Mo, a poor, sickly youth, without friends, wealth, or any influence except his native talents, energy, and honesty He was employed as clerk in the store of William Shannon at

Ste. Genevieve for several years In this situation, his mind developed itself and he acquired friends by his agreeable address and amiable disposition He attended punctually to his business and displayed those great abilities that in after-days were the admiration of the country. In 1813, he commenced the study of the law with Judge Pope in Kaskaskia, and by extraordinary exertions, he obtained license to practise in 1815. By intense study, his health was injured; so that he was compelled to take a voyage to restore it. In 1817, he went to the city of Washington and was appointed the bearer of dispatches to our minister, John Quincy Adams, at the court of St James. Cook became acquainted there with John Q. Adams and returned with him to the United States. In 1818, he was appointed judge in the western circuit of the State, and became very popular in that office. The same year, he was a candidate for congress. In this canvass, he displayed the highest order of talents in his masterly appeals to the people, and demonstrated a statesmanship that was surprising in so young a man. He did not succeed, but was elected attorney-general of the State after the August election At the next election to congress, he was elected over McLean. He remained in congress many years and made an efficient and able member.

About this time, his health became enfeebled and he was sinking fast under a pulmonary complaint On his return from Washington the last time, he visited Cuba and New Orleans for his health, but to no effect. He returned to Kentucky and died at his father's residence [Oct. 16, 1827], aged thirty-six years. "Alas, poor Yorick" His bad health and death were regretted by all classes of citizens His opponents ceased their political warfare and joined in the sorrows and lamentations of the people for the death of so young a man and one of such high order of talents His delicate frame and constitution would not admit of intense application to business or study Confinement universally made him sick, which was a great impediment to his intellectual improvement. He possessed a genius of such capacity that he acquired information as if by intuition. His mind was rapid as well as deep in its researches He was ready and prepared on short notice for all ordinary subjects. He was eloquent and fascinating in his speeches. Nature blessed him with a benevolence and a good will to all mankind in a superior degree, and he was a most amiable and interesting companion in society His career was short but very brilliant As he could not, on account of his bad health, study books, he studied men and was a profound philosopher in the science of the human family. It was this information and his native eloquence that gave him such power at the bar over the jury and on the stump over the masses. The county of Cook is called in honor of him.

Jeptha Hardin was a branch of the large and respectable family of Hardins in the West; was a half-brother of the celebrated Benjamin Hardin of Kentucky, and also a relative of the late John J. Hardin* of Illinois, and he possessed traits of character in common with that talented family. In 1815, he came to Shawneetown a lawyer from Kentucky and remained there during life. He possessed a strong, original mind, and seemed to disdain scholastic education. He studied the law-books no more than answered his purpose at the bar and on the bench; but mostly applied his strong mind to men and measures as they passed before him He practised law to a considerable extent and became wealthy. He resided on a fine farm and enjoyed himself in scientific agriculture. He was appointed circuit-judge of the court and performed the duties of the office with ability and integrity. He sustained an irre-

* His grandfather, John Hardin, born in Fauquier Co., Va., Oct 1, 1753, died in 1792. He early became an excellent marksman; served with distinction in the Indian wars of Virginia, and as a lieutenant in Morgan's Rifle Corps in the Revolution, settled in Washington Co., Ky., in 1786. He commanded a detachment of Kentucky and Pennsylvania militia under Gen Harmar at his defeat, Oct. 19 and 22 1790; commanded Brig.-Gen. Chas. Scott's advance, and distinguished in his successful expedition against the Indians on the Wabash, in May, 1791. Murdered by the Indians while bearing a flag of truce, near Shawneetown, O., for his horse and equipments, which were very fine; was the father of Martin D. Hardin, lawyer, born on the Monongahela River, Pa., June 21, 1780; died Oct 8, 1823; educated at Transylvania Academy; studied law, several years a member of the Kentucky legislature; secretary of state in 1812; a major under Maj.-Gen Harrison in the Northwestern army in Lieut.-Col John Allen's Rifle Reg't of Aug., 1812; U.-S senator in 1816-7 He published reports of Laws in Kentucky Court of Appeals, 1805-8, Frankfort, 8vo, 1810 His son, John J. Hardin, born in Frankfort, Ky., Jan 6, 1810; educated at Transylvania University; practised law at Jacksonville, Ill.; was prosecuting-attorney; member of the Ill. legislature, 1836-42; representative in congress from Ill., 1843-5; col. first reg't 12-month volunteers in Mexican

proachable character, and in his old age, died wealthy at his residence near Shawneetown.

Thomas Harrison is a noble and existing monument of the worth and merit of the ancient pioneers of Illinois. He and many others may look back with great satisfaction to their lives spent in the performance of their duties to God and man, and say: "We are the pioneers that first improved the country; defended it in times of peril, and are now about to transmit it, the finest country on earth, to our posterity."

Thomas Harrison was born in York District, South Carolina, in 1779 His parents were respectable and obtained their living by cultivating the soil, which is the most ancient and honorable occupation on earth. His father moved to Rutherford County, North Carolina, and resided there some time, then settled in Georgia; afterward he resided in Buncomb County, North Carolina, and from that point, Thomas Harrison, the Galbreaths, and some others emigrated to Illinois in July, 1804. They camped on the bluff near Kaskaskia and from whence they explored the country. At last Mr. Harrison and some others of the immigrants settled the same year three or four miles southwest of the present city of Belleville He improved a plantation, and in 1813, built on it the first cotton-gin that ever was established in Illinois. It was propelled by horsepower; but when the price of cotton was reduced so low, the

war, June 30, 1846; killed, Feb. 23, 1847, in battle of Buena Vista, while leading his reg't in a charge at the latest conflict. His son, Gen. Martin D. Hardin, great-grandson of John Hardin, born at Jacksonville, Ill, June 26, 1837, graduate of West Point; brevet 2d lieut. 3d artillery, July 1, 1859; 2d lieut, Jan. 2, 1860; 1st lieut., May 14, 1861; lieut.-col. 12th Penn. Reserve Veteran Corps, July 8, 1862; brevet-capt , Aug 29, 1862, for gallant and meritorious service in the battle of Groveton, Va., brevet-maj ; Aug. 30, 1862, for gallant and meritorious service in the battle of Bull Run (2d), Va.; col 12th Veteran Reserve Corps, Sept. 1, 1862, brevet lieut.-col , Dec. 14, 1863, for gallant and meritorious service in an encounter with a band of guerrillas; brevet-col , May 23, 1864, for gallant and meritorious service in the battle of N. Anna River, Va., mustered out of volunteer service, June 11, 1864; brig.-gen. of volunteers, July 2, 1864, brevet brig.-gen , March 13, 1865, for gallant and meritorious service in the field during the war; mustered out of volunteer service, Jan. 15, 1866; maj. 43d Inf'y, July 28, 1866; transferred to 1st Inf'y, Mch 15, 1869; retired with rank of brig -gen., Dec. 15, 1870, loss of left arm and wounds in line of duty (under acts of congress, Aug. 3, 1861, and July 28, 1866).—GARDNER, DRAKE, HAMERSLY.

cotton business and his gin were abandoned. Soon after, he purchased an ox tread-mill in Belleville and carried it on for some time; then built a small steam-mill, and then a larger one at the west end of the town. This mill, with sixty odd thousand bushels of wheat, or more, were burnt. Then they erected the splendid mill that they own at present. This mill is one of the best in the State, with four run of burrs and a capacity to manufacture two hundred barrels of flour in twenty-four hours. He has raised a large and respectable family, natives of St. Clair Co., and the males are associated with their honored sire in the mill business.

Mr. Harrison and family possess strong and vigorous minds and great energy and industry. Their probity, honesty, and punctuality have gained them a high standing throughout the country. They have a large capital vested in their business. By their sound judgment and economy, they have amassed a fortune. Mr. Harrison embraced religion when a young man, joined the Methodist-Episcopal church, and has been an efficient and talented local preacher in that church for about half-a-century.

On Dec. 16, 1811, an earthquake visited Illinois. A convulsion of nature of this character was never before experienced in Illinois. The first occurred in the night and many of the inhabitants on the frontiers supposed it was the Indians throwing the houses down. On the Kaskaskia River below Athens, the water and white sand were thrown up thro a fissure of the earth. The violence of the earthquake was so great that it threw down chimneys and injured houses.

In the early spring of 1811, Jacob Short and Moses Quick*

---

* Moses Quick was one of three sons of Isaac Quick, who emigrated in the latter part of the last century from New Jersey, where his sons were born, to Pennsylvania, and from thence to Illinois, settling near the present town of Mascoutah, in St Clair County, in the year 1806. Isaac Quick brought with him his sons, Thomas and Moses. Isaac Quick was married to Lucretia Runyon in 1777. Aaron Quick, his eldest son, was born October 19, 1778, and was married December 9, 1800, to Lucy Preston, a native of Virginia. Aaron Quick came to Illinois in 1809, he settled near Belleville, where he entered a thousand acres of land in an early day. He was one of the first school-teachers of St. Clair County, and is described as a man of a high grade of intelligence, and altho a self-cultured man, one of a vast fund of general information. He left at his death a considerable estate, accumulated by judicious investments in lands of St Clair County. In McDonough's "History of

Randolph County", in a list of entries, Aaron Quick appears to have entered 160 acres of land near the present site of Palestine, on November 17, 1816. The second son, Thomas, was never married. He was a man of fine social qualities, and died in Belleville in the spring of 1837, lamented by a large circle of friends and relatives.

Moses Quick, the youngest son, was of an adventurous, speculative disposition, besides the enterprise to which Gov. Reynolds alludes. He also owned a mill near Belleville, on Richland Creek, and a farm adjoining, which he sold in the fall of 1816, to Major Washington West. On this mill was ground the first flour manufactured in St. Clair County. A shipment of 200 barrels was made by Quick to New Orleans in the year 1816. The following advertisement is from the *Missouri Gazette and Illinois Advertiser*, of Saturday, April 27, 1816·

"FOR SALE

A SAW MILL, now in full plight, and equal if not superior to any in the territory, and a GRIST MILL partly built, which can be put in operation at a small expense. Also, 167 acres of well-timbered land, situated one mile from Belleville, Illinois Territory.

April 26.
MOSES QUICK "

The consideration for which this property was sold is shown by the deed-records to have been three thousand dollars. Moses Quick removed shortly afterward to Mississippi, where he became largely interested in the steam navigation of the Mississippi River, owning at one time several boats which plied on that river and Lake Ponchartrain. He died in 1835 or '36, while making a trip on one of his boats to St. Louis, his descendants, who are numerous, all reside in the States of Louisiana and Mississippi.

Isaac Quick had also fourteen daughters, five of whom married and left descendants, eight of whom died young, and one of whom never married. His daughters married as follows · MARY, to Cornelius Rettinghous, and a second time, to George Harris, having several children by each, AMY, married to Charles Messenger, leaving many descendants, RHODA, married to George Harrison, by whom she had five sons and five daughters, SARAH, married Henry Allyn, and with her children and descendants live in Washington Territory; LUCRETIA, married George Allen, and with her descendants live in Rock-Island County, Illinois.

Hon Thomas Quick, now a prominent member of the St Louis bar, is a son of Aaron Quick, and one of twelve children, ten of whom lived to maturity; he was born Oct. 13, 1823, and is the youngest of the family. He was educated at McKendree College, and admitted to practise in 1846, and practised law in Waterloo from 1847-55. He represented Monroe County in the legislature in 1850-2. He returned to Belleville in 1855, and formed a law partnership with Jehu Baker. He was appointed bank examiner by Gov. Bissell, and reappointed by Govs. Yates and Oglesby, and did much to successfully wind up the business of the system of unstable banks with which Illinois was then afflicted. He purchased a farm in Washington County in 1858, and removed to it, giving up temporarily his large and lucrative law practice. He was, in 1861, one of the incorporators of the Irvington Agricultural College, and was afterward one of the first board of trustees for the Agricultural College at Champaign. He had six children—four of whom—three sons and one daughter—are yet living, his oldest son, Orlando T., died in the army in 1865, his oldest living son, Edwin, is a promising young lawyer, in Chicago. The descendants of the Quick family form today the strongest and perhaps the largest body of relations among the American residents in the St Clair County.—J. H. G.

made a flat-boat on the north side of the Kaskaskia River, about three-quarters of a mile below the present town of Athens, and loaded it with beef, cattle, and corn. In March, they set sail down the river to New Orleans They sold out and returned on horseback This was the first boat built on the river above Levens

It has been stated that the judiciary of the territory was much improved by the United-States judges holding the courts; yet the old system was retained to some extent These judges were required to hold courts twice in every year in each county and a court of *dernier resort* at the seat of government. These judges were gentlemen of high standing and character, which added much to the reputation of the country

Jesse B. Thomas* was a man of talents, but did not particularly employ his mind on the dry subtilties of the law. He was born a politician and never ceased the avocation until death closed the scene with him a few years since, in the State of Ohio. In 1818, he was elected a member from St. Clair Co. to the convention that formed the State constitution, was elected the president of that body, and gave general satisfaction in the performance of his duty. He was also elected to the United-States senate the same year; made a good business

* Jesse Burgess Thomas, a descendant of Lord Baltimore, was born in Hagerstown, Md., in 1777, moved west in 1779, studied law with his brother, Richard Symmes Thomas, in Bracken County, Ky., where he was married—his wife dying within a year after marriage On the organization of Dearborn Co, Indiana Territory, March 7, 1803, he located in Lawrenceburgh as a practising attorney, and was elected, Jan 3, 1805, to represent that county in the legislature which convened at Vincennes, Feb. 1, by proclamation of Gov Wm H Harrison, to choose members of the legislative council, from the ten names thus selected, congress appointed five, again, on proclamation of the governor, the legislature assembled at Vincennes, July 29, 1805, and at this, its first session, he was elected speaker, and Benj Chambers of the same county, president of the council; he presided as speaker of the first and second sessions of the general assembly at Vincennes, from Sept. 26, 1805, to Oct 24, 1808—three years and one month, when he was elected by the assembly as delegate to the 10th congress, to succeed Benj Parke, resigned, serving from Dec 1, 1808, to March 3, 1809, was appointed and commissioned, Aug 24, 1805, by Gov Harrison, a captain of militia of Dearborn County, during his legislative term, he married the widow of Maj. John Francis Hamtramck, and moved to Vincennes, residing there a short time, on the organization of Illinois Territory, Mch 7, 1809, President Madison appointed him one of its judges, he then moved to Kaskaskia, thence to Cahokia, and later to Edwardsville; in July 1818, he was a delegate from St

member; was a great friend of Crawford for the presidency, and did much in the compromise of the Missouri question He was a gentleman of fine appearance and address He had a saying on which he acted considerably: that "you could not talk a man down, but you could whisper him to death." On the bench or in the senate, he possessed a dignified and respectful bearing, which added much standing to his character

William Sprigg possessed a strong, discriminating mind, and made an excellent judge, was a fine classic scholar and a well-read and profound lawyer He was born in Maryland and was of excellent family His brother was the governor of Maryland and other relatives occupied important stations in that State He had an utter contempt for street politics A purer heart or one with more integrity never found its way to the bench. He was a spectator in the campaign of 1812 under Gov Edwards to Peoria Lake, as he had no gun or weapons that indicated belligerency His pacific and sickly appearance, together with his perfect philosophic indifference as to war or peace, life or death, made him the subject of much discussion among the troops. He was the only *savant* in the army, to my observation

Stanley Griswold was a correct, honest man, a good lawyer; paid his debts and sung David's psalms He was transferred to Michigan Territory and in his place Thomas Towles was appointed, who presided on the east of the territory

Clair Co to and president of the convention that formed the constitution of Illinois and suggested its name, was elected by the first general assembly of Illinois one of its first two United-States senators, serving from Dec 4, 1818, to March 3, 1828; in 1820, while in the senate, he introduced the Missouri Compromise, was chairman of the committee of conference on this measure, and as adopted was his work, this he regarded as the most important act of his life, in 1824, he was a member of the caucus that nominated his friend, William H. Crawford, for president, in 1840, he took an active part in effecting the nomination of his old friend, Gen. Harrison, for president, and attended the convention held that year at Columbus, Ohio, in 1829, he assisted in the organization of St Paul's Episcopal church of Mt Vernon, Ohio, of which he was a consistent member, where he had moved at the close of his last term in the senate, and owned a large property, he was also one of the town proprietors of Brookville, Franklin Co, Ind In stature, he was full six feet, with florid-brown complexion, dark-hazel eyes, dark-brown (nearly black) hair, with a well-developed muscular system, and weighed over two hundred pounds; was very particular in his personal appearance, and had the mode of a refined gentleman of the last century; was very considerate of the rights and feelings of others, and would not buy at a sheriff's sale He died, childless, at Mt. Vernon, O, leaving a large estate, May 4, 1853, aged 75 years.—SAMUEL MORRISON, Indianapolis, Ind., Sept. 4, 1884.

After the close of the war of 1812, Joseph Duncan emigrated to Illinois and settled at the high bluff in the Mississippi Bottom, near the Grand Tower in Jackson County. Duncan was young, unassuming, and of genteel deportment. He was born and raised in Paris, Ky., and was an ensign in the United-States army in the campaign to Canada in 1813, under Gen. Harrison. He was in the defence of Lower Sandusky, with Maj. Croghan, and behaved gallantly. He was governor of the State and in congress for many years. He died a few years since, much regretted by his family and friends.

President Madison, on June 1, 1812, recommended war against Great Britain, and on the 18th of the same month, war was declared. John C. Calhoun made an able and dignified report, appealing to the people to defend the honor and character of the nation and recommending war—the last resort to sustain our national honor.

The Indians had been growing sour and hostile to the inhabitants for years before the declaration of war. Tecumseh and the Prophet, his half-brother, were exciting their brethren against the Americans for years before. It is surprising how quick and correct the information is that the Indians receive of the relations between us and Great Britain.

A very great chief, Tecumseh, appeared among the Indians at this time. His father was a Shawnee and his mother an Ottawa woman. At rare intervals, extraordinary men will arise among the Indians. Any one that will study the character of this great chieftain will sincerely deplore his situation and that of the aborigines generally. This great man was almost or perhaps equal to any of the renowned warriors and statesmen among the North-American Indians. He possessed an extraordinary strength and vigor of mind. Tecumseh had a magnanimity of character of which few of the great men of the nation were gifted. There was something noble and grand about him; he disdained the friendship of the British, except he wanted to use them to save his country from destruction. This Indian Napoleon had his Talleyrand, the prophet. This last-named man was educated in Canada and was a cunning knave. He used, as well as counsel to the Indians, incantations, dreams, and juggling to rouse the red men against the whites.

Robert Dickson, a talented Briton and Indian-trader, whose residence was at Prairie du Chien, had great influence over all the hordes of the savages in the North. He had prepared three or four thousand warriors ready to attack the frontiers of Illinois and Missouri. But these warriors were more needed in Canada. They were sent there and thereby we were saved. The war in Canada was our defence. While Dickson was preparing his Northern warriors, Tecumseh was South, rousing up the natives there to war against the government

Some few murders were committed on our frontiers before war was declared. On June 2, 1811, a family of the name of Cox resided on Shoal Creek, near the forks, and the Indians discovered the family from home, except a young man and woman. They killed the young man and mangled his body cruelly. The girl they took prisoner and also took several horses. Col. Pruit acting as captain, Henry Cox, Ben Cox, and some others, to the number of eight or ten men, pursued the Indians and overtook them and the girl about seven miles from their town and fifty miles north of Springfield. A kind of bashful fight ensued. In the scramble, the girl broke from the Indians toward the whites, and as she ran, an Indian wounded her severely in the hip, by throwing a tomahawk at her. The whites got some of the stolen horses and the girl. They reached home in safety.

The next murder of the same year was Price, a relative of the Whitesides. Price was killed on June 20, near the spring in the lower end of the present city of Alton. Price and another man were plowing their corn and they saw the Indians approaching them at the spring, where there was a small cabin. The horse was unhitched and the whites had a gun. As the Indians came near the spring, the Americans asked them if they were for war or peace. One of the Indians, who was very large and tall, laid down his gun and gave his hand to Price, but held him fast and the other Indians murdered him. While the conflict was going on, his companion jumped on the horse and was wounded in the thigh in making his escape.

This was war, and the frontiers commenced building forts and preparing for the contest. During this summer, Tecumseh was in counsel with Gov. Harrison at Vincennes, and his conduct breathed war. The Prophet had assembled at his town on the Wabash at Tippecanoe all the hostile and straggling Indians in the Northwest, and had them in a rage against the United States. For the protection of the country, Gov. Harrison was compelled to disperse them or make them quit in some manner. He marched an army of seven or eight hundred strong against this town and encamped near it on November 6. The Indians made a furious attack on the army some time before day. If it had not been for the regulars, it would have been another St. Clair defeat. The regulars saved the army. The volunteers fought well, but they could not escape, as the enemy had almost surrounded them. This battle put the frontiers into a still greater panic. Indian war was considered to be declared by this battle.

In the early spring of 1812, several mounted companies were organized for defence of the country. Small block-houses, family forts were erected all around the frontiers from Wood River to the mouth of the Ohio and up the Ohio and Wabash rivers. Camp Russell was erected about a mile and a-half northwest of the present town of Edwardsville, and was called for William Russell, who was colonel of a regiment of ten ranging companies. This was the great military depot for men and other material. Campbell, a United-States officer, erected a small block-house on the bank of the Illinois River, on the west side, twenty odd miles from the mouth. Another military station was on the Mississippi, opposite the mouth of the Missouri. This stand was to guard the river, as well as to range on the frontiers. Another was established on Silver Creek, northeast of the present town of Troy. At the site of the present town of Carlyle, a block-house fort was built. The same class of forts were built, one a small distance above the present town of Aviston, in Clinton County. This was called Journey's fort. Two were erected on the east side of Shoal Creek, known as Hill and Jones' forts. One on the west side of the Looking-Glass Prairie, a few miles southeast of the present town of Lebanon, and known as Fort Chambers. On the Kaskaskia River, at Middleton's and Going's, were block-houses. Another block-house was erected on Doza Creek, a few miles from the mouth, at Nathaniel Hill's. All around the southern frontier some security was made against Indian depredation. These forts were all erected in the spring of 1812

In the Jourdan settlement, Thomas and Francis Jourdan, both, with the assistance of the militia from the salt-works, erected two forts in 1811 They were situated eight or nine miles on the road east of old Frankfort. The settlement had commenced in 1808 or '9

Andrew Moore and family went from Goshen Settlement in 1810, and settled on the road of that name, southeast, ten or fifteen miles, of the present town of Mount Vernon. He and his son were killed by the Indians in 1812. The father and son went to Jourdan's fort and returned toward home to the middle fork of Big Muddy, and camped all night. After much bloody fighting, both he and his son were killed by the Indians and his horses taken. A prairie where he resided is called Moore's Prairie. After dark at Tom Jourdan's fort, Barbara, Walker, and James Jourdan, three men, stepped out for some wood. The Indians lay concealed in the brush, and shot Barbara dead, wounded Jourdan in the leg, and missed Walker.

Several officers distinguished themselves in the war in Illinois and showed strong minds as well as great devotion to the country. Capts Samuel Whiteside, William B. Whiteside, James B Moore, Jacob Short, Nathaniel Journey, Willis Hargrave, and William McHenry were efficient and very active in the defence of the country. Samuel Whiteside is still alive, a venerated and respected pioneer. Samuel and William B. Whiteside are two of the sons of the two gallant soldiers of King's Mountain memory. Each of these brave men commanded companies in the defence of the country James B. Moore emigrated to Illinois with his father in 1781, and grew up a soldier amidst the wars and perils of the country. He also commanded a company in 1812. The father of Jacob Short emigrated to Illinois in 1796, while his son Jacob was a youth, and he too, like those already mentioned, was enured to the hardships and difficulties of a new country from his infancy. These four patriots were captains of four ranging companies, organized by act of congress for the defence of the country. Nathaniel Journey was a great and talented man and was a captain during most of the war He mostly protected the settlements near to the fort bearing his name. Hargrave and McHenry were officers in the service of the government and for the most part guarded the frontiers in the eastern section of the State.

During the summer of 1812, four mounted companies under the above-named captains, ranging throughout the country as far as the Wabash, gave the country ample protection. In the fall of 1812, the fort at Hill's station was attacked and one man was wounded. An Indian shot thro the back wall of a chimney to one of the block-houses and thus wounded the man. An Indian was also killed or wounded, as blood was left where they were.

In the fall of 1812, all the troops that could be mustered up for a campaign against the Indians were about three hundred and fifty men. Gov. Edwards was the commander and under him were Cols. Russell, Stephenson, and Rector. Samuel Judy was a captain over a company of twenty-one spies and of this corps I was a member. For these no baggage-wagons were provided, but each man packed his own provisions for twenty or thirty days, and the horses lived on the grass. The army marched from Camp Russell up the Cahokia Creek, by the head of Macoupin, and crossed the Sangamon River a few miles east of the present city of Springfield, and then on to the Black-Partridge Town. This Indian village was situated near the Illinois-River bluffs, opposite the upper end of the lake. In the morning before we reached the town, the spies met an Indian and his squaw before they perceived us. Judy killed the Indian, who, while dying, shot Right, who died of the wound soon after. The squaw was taken prisoner. Several Indians were killed and some whites were wounded. Three men, Peter St Jean, John Howard, and Charles Kitchen, crossed the river in pursuit of the Indians.

As Edwards did not meet Gen. Hopkins, as he anticipated, our army returned home with all convenient speed. Capt Craig went in a boat from Shawneetown to Peoria with provisions for the troops of Hopkins and Edwards, but none were needed. Gen. Hopkins marched from the lower part of Kentucky with a large army to sweep over the Illinois country, down that river, and meet Gov. Edwards toward the head of Peoria Lake.

On Feb. 9, 1813, two families were destroyed near the mouth of Cash River. The Americans followed the Indians south into the State of Kentucky, and a snow fell, so that the party could not follow the trail and the Indians escaped.

In the month of March, two travelers, Young and McLean, crossed the Kaskaskia River at Hill's ferry, where Carlyle is situated at this day. The Indians, soon after they had crossed the river, killed Young and had a severe combat with McLean. They shot seven times at him, but he swam the river and escaped. Boltenhouse was killed a few miles south of Albion, toward the Wabash.

Howard was appointed brigadier-general and took the command of the troops into his own hands. Another campaign was decided upon in the northern section of Illinois, and the Illinois troops, to the number of three or four hundred, left Camp Russell about August 1, 1813. I was sergeant in Capt. William B. Whiteside's company of United-States rangers, and marched in this campaign. At Fort Mason, the Missouri troops all swam over the river and joined us. The army was reorganized at this station, Gen. Howard in command, Cols. McNair of St. Louis and Stephenson of Randolph, Ill., were the two colonels, Comdts. Wm. B. Whiteside, Nathaniel Boone of Missouri, John Murdoch, and others were made majors. Col. Desha of the United-States army was in some command. Col. Clemson was the inspector. The whole force amounted to not more than eight hundred men. The army marched up the Mississippi Bottom to a point above Quincy, thence across the country and struck the Illinois River forty odd miles below Peoria. The army reached Peoria on a calm, pleasant evening and the beauty of the situation was admired by the whole army. The lake and the scenery around made a pleasing impression of its grandeur and beauty even on the stern, rugged soldiers of the army. A young man was shot here during the night by accident. The army marched to the upper end of the lake and returned next day. The troops camped on the south side of the lake for three or four weeks. It was here that the logs were cut for Fort Clark. With a proper truck-wagon and ropes with cross-pieces of wood tied at the proper intervals, eight men can draw as many logs as four horses. The logs were thrown into the water and the regulars under Capt. John Phillips rafted them over the lake and made Fort Clark with them. The army returned to Camp Russell in safety late in November. These campaigns did much good in checking the aggression of the Indians.

In 1814, Mrs. Reagan and six children were killed in the forks of Wood River, a few miles east of the present city of Alton. A party of whites followed them, commanded by Capt. Samuel Whiteside. One Indian was killed in a tree-top by Pruitt, and the rest escaped.

In August, Henry Cox and son were killed by the Indians on his farm near Hill's fort, Shoal Creek. This was the brave soldier that saved the life of the girl some years before.

In 1814 [July 19], Maj. John Campbell commanded a squadron of boats that ascended the Mississippi to Rock Island, and had a severe engagement with Sac and Fox Indians. Campbell was wounded and many of his men killed in his boats. He was relieved and the whole armament was drove down to St. Louis again. The men fought well, but the Indians were numerous and had almost captured the whole force.

Major Taylor, the late president of the United States, sailed on August 3, 1814, with three hundred and thirty-four men, in boats to Rock Island When they reached the island, the British, with a number of redcoats and more than a thousand Indians, met them The enemy had also a six and three-pounder cannon. After much hard fighting, the Americans retreated, with a loss of several killed and wounded In the same year, the British from Mackinac, with redcoats, cannon, and Indians, captured Prairie du Chien and the Americans burned Fort Madison and Johnston, and retreated to *Cape au Gris.*

In the fall of 1814, the wife of Jesse Bayles was killed by the Indians in Sugar-Creek Bottom, not far above the present town of Aveston. She and husband went out to look for the hogs and she was killed

In the winter of 1814 and '15, the Indians, as well as their ally, the British, ceased hostile operations in the Northwest, and in the summer of 1815, peace was established between all the Indians of the Northwest and the United States. This Indian war and peace were the key-stone to the prosperity and improvement of Illinois. The soldiers from the adjacent States, as well as those from Illinois itself, saw the country and never rested in peace until they located themselves and families in it. Moreover, many of the citizens that were in the military service saved some of their wages and with it bought themselves farms. Illinois, since the peace of 1815, grew as if by magic to the present time, and within a reasonable short time, not a State in the Union will have a population that can be numbered equal to the Prairie State.

At the termination of the war, with the influx of population, professional men also appeared in the country. Elias Kent Kane emigrated from the State of New York, touched at Tennessee, and finally, in 1814, settled in Kaskaskia. He was a native of New York and came to Illinois when quite young. He received a classic education and studied law in his native State. He possessed a strong mind and a benevolence and kindness of heart that are rarely surpassed. He was a profound lawyer and an agreeable and eloquent speaker. In 1818, he was appointed secretary-of-state and remained in this office for some time. He was elected to the general assembly of the State from Randolph County and then to the senate of the United States in 1824. In 1830, he was reelected, and [Dec 12], 1835, while in the senate at Washington, he died. The death of Mr. Kane was very much lamented in congress and also by the people of Illinois. His talents and amiable disposition endeared him to his friends and family, so that his death rendered them inconsolable. His career in Illinois was brief but elevated and conspicuous.

Alonzo C. Stuart, a lawyer, emigrated from Reading, Pa., and settled in Belleville in 1816. He was a fine classic scholar and a well-read lawyer. Mr. Stuart was born in Clermont, N.H., and was a regular graduate at Dartmouth College; he received a diploma from that institution of learning. He obtained license in Pennsylvania in 1812 to practise law, and in Illinois in 1817, but soon after he experienced an accidental death that put an end to his usefulness and promise. His decease was very much regretted by his family and friends.

Robert K. McLaughlin, a lawyer, emigrated from Kentucky

and settled in Illinois in 1815. McLaughlin possessed a sound judgment and much energy and industry. He married a lady of excellent sense and an amiable disposition. He resided for a time in Belleville, but finally located in Vandalia, where he has been the balance-wheel (to speak in boat phrase) of the town for many years. He is now enjoying, in ease and wealth, the respectable life of a pioneer. He has a wife, wealth, and no children.

Col Benjamin Stephenson moved with his family to Illinois from Kentucky in 1809. He was sheriff of Randolph County for many years. In the war of 1812, he acted as colonel in two campaigns. Stephenson was elected a delegate to congress from the territory of Illinois in 1814, and was appointed register of the land-office at Edwardsville. In public or private life, he was a polite and agreeable gentleman. Death closed his earthly career some years since [at Edwardsville].

Major William George Brown is a respectable and living pioneer of Illinois. In the Old Dominion and Prince Edwards County, he was born in 1777. The father of Maj Brown emigrated to Kentucky in early times and the major moved to Illinois in 1816. At the Long Point, so called, he settled and has resided there for more than one-third of a century. The county of St Clair has been represented by him in the State legislature for many years, and he has been active in the defence of the country in all the Indian wars of his day. With the public, his character stands high for his good sense and honesty.

James Lemen, Sr, was blessed with a large family of children.* Most of his sons are members of Christian churches

---

* The "U. S. Biog Dict," Chicago, 1876, gives the following additional facts concerning this celebrated family. James Lemen, Sr, was born near Harper's Ferry, Va, in 1758; was married in Virginia in 1782, and had born to him eleven children, of whom three died in infancy and eight lived to be over sixty. This remarkable family consisted of six sons and two daughters. James Lemen, Sr, lived to be 64, and died in 1822. His sons were as follows:

1 Robert Lemen, born near Harper's Ferry, Va, Sept 25, 1783, married Hester Tolan in 1805, settled in Ridge Prairie, St Clair Co, Ill, and there reared a family of fifteen children, most of whom arrived at years of maturity; was educated under the instruction of that eccentric and able pioneer Baptist preacher, "Father" John Clark, and was far above the ordinary men of his day in native and acquired ability, was appointed by President John Quincy Adams U S marshal of the State of Illinois in 1825, was a member of the Baptist church, and died Aug 24, 1860, aged 77

and many of them preachers of the gospel. Robert Lemen, one of his sons, was engaged for many years in teaching school at a time when the country was in great need of schools.

2. Rev. Joseph Lemen, born also in Virginia, Sept. 8, 1785, married Mary Kinney, daughter of Rev. William Kinney, Sr., afterward lieut.-governor of Illinois, and with her raised a family of fourteen children, was a prominent Baptist preacher for more than half a century, lived in Ridge Prairie, St. Clair Co., and died June 29, 1861, aged 76. In McDonough's "History of St. Clair County" is a chapter written by Joseph B. Lemen, a member of this family, in which is given the history of the Baptist churches of that county. He says, speaking of the Richland-Creek Baptist Church, first organized June 14, 1806.

"In 1809, these people built a meeting-house on Richland Creek, some three miles northeast of Belleville, and at that time had a membership of about forty. Among the members were Benjamin Ogle, James Lemen, Sr., Wm. Lot Whiteside, William Kinney, Isaac Enochs, Larken Rutherford, Rev. Joseph Lemen, Robert Lemen, Polly K. Lemen, Catharine Lemen, Ann Simpson, Hetty Lemen, Ann Whiteside, Sally Whiteside, Ann Lemen, Elizabeth Badgeley, Mary Kinney, and others."

On July 8, 1809, Rev. James Lemen, Sr., who had been licensed to preach one year previous, arose in church and denounced slavery and the practise of holding slaves as one he could not tolerate, to this some of the membership objected, and the senior Lemen and four others withdrew, and with two others organized a new church under the name of "the Baptist Church of Christ, friends of humanity," afterward known as the Bethel Baptist Church. Their building was located two and one-half miles southeast of Collinsville, and is yet a flourishing society. Joseph Lemen sustained pastoral relations with Bethel Church for many years—except when his brother Moses was in charge—during almost the first half-century of its existence. He was assisted also by his brother James during many years of the time, who is described as "a man of much power."

3. Rev. James Lemen, born in Monroe Co., Ill., Oct. 8, 1787, was also a Baptist preacher of considerable renown, preaching in Illinois, Missouri, and Kentucky; married Mary Pullham, Dec. 8, 1813; reared a large family, and died Feb. 8, 1870, aged 82. "He was the second child born of American parents in the colony. Enoch Moore being the first." He was a member of the second territorial legislature from St. Clair Co. in 1814-15; again representing the county in the second general assembly, 1820-22; and was state senator from 1824-28. His widow died in 1876, aged 81.

4. William Lemen was born in Monroe Co. in 1791, and also belonged to the Baptist church from an early age; married in the same county Maud Miller, who bore him seven children, only two of whom lived to adult age, was a soldier in the Black-Hawk war, and died in Monroe Co. in 1857, aged 66.

5. Rev. Josiah Lemen, born in Monroe Co., Ill., Aug. 15, 1794, was also a Baptist preacher; married Rebecca Huff, reared a large family; and died near DuQuoin, in Perry Co., July 11, 1867, aged 73.

6. Rev. Moses Lemen, born in Monroe Co., Ill., in 1797, became a Baptist minister in early life, married first, Sarah Hull, by whom he had three children, second, married Sarah Varnum, by whom he had seven children. He represented Monroe Co. in the house from 1828-30, and died in Montgomery Co., Ill., March 5, 1859, aged 62.—J. H. G.

James Lemen, Jr, was born at the New Design in 1787, and was raised in Illinois. He has been elected at various times to one or the other branch of the general assembly of the State for twelve or fifteen years. Likewise, he was elected a member from St Clair to the convention that formed the first constitution of the State In all these situations in which the people placed him, he has acted with ability and fidelity The public awards to him an unblemished reputation

The Casey family, a numerous and respectable connection, emigrated mostly from Tennessee to Illinois and settled in several of the counties in the interior of the State Hon Zadoc Casey* is a conspicuous and worthy pioneer of the

* Zadoc Casey's father came from County Tyrone, Ireland, settled in North Carolina before the Revolution, and was a soldier under Marion and Sumpter. Zadoc Casey was born in Georgia, March 7, 1796, was brought up in Sumner County, Tennessee, where the family removed while he was quite young, was married in Tennessee, Aug 31, 1815, to Rachel King They have had seven children While his oldest child was an infant, Gov. Casey removed with his family to Illinois, in 1817, and settled in Jefferson County, near the present town of Mount Vernon, of which he was the founder, where his family was reared, and here he lived, died, and was buried Gov. Casey was elected to the house of representatives of the third general assembly, to represent the counties of Jefferson and Hamilton, in 1822-4, the first representative either of said counties had in the general assembly Two years later, Marion County having in 1823 been organized and added to the district, in 1824-6 he represented the enlarged district In 1826-30, he was in the State senate representing the district comprising Jefferson, Hamilton, Marion, and Clay counties In August, 1830, he was elected lieutenant-governor at the same election with John Reynolds as governor He resigned this position in 1833, to accept a seat as one of three members which Illinois was allowed in the Federal congress after the census of 1830, and served five successive terms in congress, being reelected at every election until the district was changed in 1842 He was a prominent member of congress and was chairman of the committee on public lands, and the State of Illinois is indebted to him for the land-grant which enabled them to build the Illinois and-Michigan Canal He also made the first report to congress in favor of a grant to aid in the construction of the Illinois-Central Railroad Senator Douglas, in a correspondence with Judge Breese in 1851, gave to Gov Casey the credit of the first official recognition of the importance of the road in a report made in 1837, to the house of representatives of the national congress, while chairman of the committee on public lands.

Gov. Casey was elected to 16th general assembly in 1848, and was speaker of the house, he was reelected to the house again in 1850-2, as a colleague of Gen. Hayme, representing Jefferson and Marion counties. In 1860, he was elected as state senator from the 20th district, composed of the counties of Jefferson, Wayne, Edwards, Wabash, Marion, Clay, and Richland, and was holding this position at the time of his death, Sept 4, 1862

Gov Casey's oldest son, Samuel K Casey, was educated at McKendree College,

family and has held many high and honorable offices in the State. In 1830, he was elected lieutenant-governor and has been a member of congress for many years; was a member of the last convention to form the State constitution, and is at the present time a member of our State legislature. In early youth, he did not attend to his education, but in after-life, he improved himself very much and is an intelligent man. Nature blessed him with an interesting family, many of whom bid fair to be useful and distinguished citizens.

Hon John A. McClernand* is a conspicuous pioneer of

Lebanon, Illinois; licensed to practise law in 1845, was warden for many years of the Illinois State penitentiary at Joliet; returned to Jefferson County after the Rebellion, and was elected to the State senate in 1868, and died during his term of office, May 31, 1871, at his house in Mount Vernon of hemorrhage of the bowels. Mahala, the oldest daughter of Gov. Casey, married Rev Lewis Dwight, and died in 1844; her son, S L Dwight, a prominent lawyer of Centralia, Marion County, was a member of the house in the State legislature of 1870-2. Hiram R Casey, the second son, died in Louisana in 1856. Dr. Newton R. Casey, the third son, was educated at the university at Athens, Ohio, is a physician and surgeon, and lives at Mound City. He was a member of the house in 25th, 26th, and 28th general assemblies, from Pulaski County. The fourth son, Thomas J Casey, was educated at McKendree College, taking the Master's degree in 1850, he was licensed to practise law in 1853; in 1856, he was elected circuit attorney of the twelfth circuit, to which he was reelected in 1860, in the summer of 1862, he raised the 110th Illinois Infantry, of which regiment he was elected colonel. Served with his regiment thro the fall campaign with Buell in Kentucky in 1862, with Rosecrans in the battle of Stone River, making a splendid record for personal gallantry in that severe engagement; and in May, 1863, he was mustered out at his own request on a consolidation of his regiment, his business interests, and those of his father, who had died in the meantime, requiring his personal attention. Col Casey was married in 1861, to Miss M. S. Moran of Springfield. He was a member of the house of representatives in 1870-2, and succeeded his brother, Samuel, in 1872-6, in the State senate. He was elected one of the judges of the second circuit in 1879, and was selected as the judge of the appellate court from his circuit, a position he now fills. Gov Casey's youngest son, Dr. John R Casey, was educated at McKendree College, and afterward received a thoro medical education, and is now a practising physician in the city of Joliet.—J. H G

* Gen. McClernand was born in Breckinridge County, Kentucky, in 1812. When four years of age he lost his father, and his early years were years of trial, hardship, and difficulty, which he surmounted with an indomitable will, and at the age of twenty he had placed himself in an honorable position in the profession of the law. He moved to Shawneetown, Illinois, in 1830; volunteered as a private in Capt. Harrison Williams' company in the Black-Hawk war, in the summer of 1832, and was promoted to the position of assistant quartermaster on the staff of Brig.-Gen'l Alexander Posey, commanding the 1st brigade. He established a Democratic newspaper in Shawneetown in 1835; was elected to the legislature in 1836-8, and again in 1840;

Southern Illinois. He was raised in Gallatin County and worked his way thro many difficulties to eminence and a high standing Law was his avocation and he practised his profession for some time in Southern Illinois In constructing the Illinois-and-Michigan Canal, he acted an efficient part as a State officer and has represented Gallatin County time and time again in the State legislature, but most of his public services were in the congress of the United States In this honorable body he made a conspicuous and efficient member. Nature gifted him with an active and vigorous intellect and much energy

was reelected in 1842; and in 1843 was elected to congress, to which position he was reelected in 1844, again in 1846, and still again for the fourth consecutive term in 1848. He declined a fifth reelection, and removed to Jacksonville in 1851 In 1840 he was elected a presidental elector on the Democratic ticket and in 1852 he was elector on the Pierce ticket In 1856 he removed to Springfield, where he engaged in the practise of his profession before the Federal courts In 1859 he was again elected to congress from the Springfield district, to fill the vacancy caused by the death of Maj Thos L Harris He was married in 1843 to Sarah, daughter of Col. James Dunlop of Jacksonville, Ill.

In August, 1861, Gen McClernand was commissioned as a brigadier-general by President Lincoln He immediately resigned his seat in congress and returned to Illinois, where he recruited a considerable force of volunteers in a short time He resumed command at Cairo Sept 5, 1861 After leading in many important campaigns and expeditions and distinguishing himself at Fort Henry, Fort Donalson, and Shiloh, in each of which engagements he commanded a division, and being promoted to a major-general after the surrender of Fort Donelson, he was next assigned to the command of an army corps, by Gen Halleck's order, and in this position did much to further the Union cause in 1862 Gen McClernand is undoubtedly entitled to much of the credit for planing the campaign of 1863 Unfortunate disagreements occurred between him and Gens Grant and Halleck, and after his victory at Arkansas Post, he was ordered back He afterward took part in the battles of Fort Gibson, May 1, Champion Hill, May 3, and Big Block, May 17, 1863; also in the siege of Vicksburg which followed and on June 18 was relieved from the command of the 13th corps Gen McClernand tendered his resignation Jan 14, 1864, which the President refused to accept, and he was replaced in command of the 13th corps, and assigned to the department of Gen Banks, on Jan 23, 1864 He took part in the ill-fated Red River campaign of 1864 until prostrated by sickness, and on June 12 was brought home shattered in health and unable to return to the field Altho he sought active service afterward his health was not in a condition to justify it, and unwilling to hold a position that he did not fill he again tendered his resignation in November, 1865, and it was accepted

He was president of the Democratic National Convention in St Louis in 1876; has always been an ardent politician of the old Jefferson school. He is still engaged in the active practise of his profession in Springfield, a member of the firm of McClernard & Keyes —J H G

Rev. John Mason Peck emigrated to the West in 1817, and has been extremely efficient and energetic in advancing the morality and religion of the country. This reverend pioneer was born in the State of Connecticut in 1787, and reached Shawneetown in 1817. For many years he resided in Missouri and he and family were much afflicted there with sickness. In 1821, he located in Illinois and has resided at his celebrated site, the Rock Spring, ever since.

Nature has endowed Mr. Peck with her choicest gifts and he himself has been indefatigable and energetic in his scientific and literary labors. A strong, vigorous, and discriminating intellect he possesses in an eminent degree. In addition to this great gift of nature, he is also blessed with an activity and energy that shrink from no labor and research that is within the compass of his power. With his efficiency and energy of character, he has accomplished much in the West. Education has been a favorite pursuit with him during his whole life in the Western country. The Sunday-schools may greet Mr. Peck as their most efficient supporter. The temperance cause may also hail him as its best friend and champion. Morality and religion itself were greatly advanced in this new country by his untiring exertion. The eminent talents of this divine are devoted mostly to preaching the gospel and writing books. Sermons of this gentleman are clear and strong and contain in them not only the theory of religion, but also the practical application to the actions of men. The writings of Mr. Peck exhibit much talent and research and do him and the country much honor. The literary character of this author stands eminent throughout the West and he promises much to advance his literary fame. The Baptist denomination of Christians he has joined and is one of their most efficient members.

William B. Whiteside, the captain of the company of United-States rangers in the war of 1812, was born in North Carolina, and when a lad, came with his father, Col. William Whiteside, to the country in 1793. He was raised on the frontiers and without much education, but possessed a strong and sprightly intellect and a benevolence of heart that was rarely equaled. All his talents and energies were exerted in the defence of his country. He was sheriff of Madison County for many years.

At his residence in Madison County, he died some years since

Chicago was known and visited by the explorers of the country from the earliest times to the present, but no regular village or colony was ever established there until modern date Indian-traders and the engage were often located there, but no continuous settlement was made The name is of Indian extraction and means in English the Land of Onions or Wild-Onion Field. The Indians, in 1812, [Aug 15], massacred almost a whole company of regulars there and kept the place until peace was declared.

Jean B Pont-au-Sable had a store of Indian goods there in 1795, and John Kinzie settled there about 1804 The Illinois-and-Michigan Canal gave Chicago the first start in modern times and now it bids fair to be the largest city in the valley of the Mississippi.

John D. Whiteside, another son of the aged Col Whiteside, was born at Whiteside's Station in 1794, and was raised, lived, and died there in 1850 This pioneer possessed a strong, solid mind Many important public stations he occupied with credit to himself. At various times, he has represented his native county in the State legislature and occupied for many years the office of treasurer of State; also the office of fund-commissioner. The business of this last office required his services in Europe, where he transacted important business for the State It is singular that he was born, lived, died, and was buried on the same locality, the Old Station, in the present county of Monroe

The Moore family emigrated from Georgia and settled in St Clair and were respectable citizens. The aged patriarch, Risdon Moore, was a popular and conspicuous man of his day. The county of St Clair was represented in part by him for many years and he was elected the speaker of the house of representatives of the general assembly He died many years since and left an unblemished character

A large connection of the Mitchells and Wests[*] emigrated

---

[*] The West family are of English ancestry, and the first of the name came with Calvert, Lord Baltimore, to Maryland in 1632 John West, a progenitor of the present family, lived and died in Maryland; his son, Benjamin, removed to Virginia before the Revolution, and served during that struggle on the military staff of Gen.

from Bortetot County, Va, and settled in St Clair County, east of Belleville in early times. This colony was composed of intelligent and worthy citizens and the descendants have spread over the country far and near

George E. Walker, a respectable and worthy pioneer, was born in Tennessee, and his father and family, in 1811, settled on the east of the Kaskaskia River, near the northern limits of Randolph County Young Walker in his early days started out into the wide world to make a living, and most nobly has he sustained himself He traded with the Pottawatomie Indians and the white population on the Illinois River to much advantage. Walker was an efficient member of the company that built a railroad from the Mississippi Bluff to the river. This road was constructed seven miles long in 1837, for the purpose of conveying coal to the St Louis market, and was the first railroad built in the State. In 1839, he commenced merchandising in Ottawa, Ill At this time, he is one of the most wealthy and efficient merchants in this State. He possesses a strong natural mind and energy and activity unequaled.

Washington; his son, Washington West, was born in Maryland, but was moved in infancy to Virginia, where he married Frances Mitchell of Virginia Their children were two sons and one daughter Benjamin Hillary West, the younger of these sons, was one year old when the family came to Illinois in 1818, he was married to Mara Catherine Hiel, also a native of Virginia, and from this union sprang a family of eleven children; all reside in St Clair County, among these is the third son, Dr Washington West of Belleville The elder son, Tilghman Hillary West, born in Montgomery Co., Md , Sept 20, 1773, married in 1803, Mary Mitchell, and moved to Illinois Territory with his brother, Benjamin H , and their families and sons in 1818 His son, Benjamin J. West, Sr , was married to Louisa A Mitchell, June 7, 1836, and settled in Belleville. From this union sprang Benjamin J West, Jr., born in July, 1846, he was educated at McKendree College and St Louis University, and did efficient service in the 142d Regiment Illinois volunteers —during the late war, was married June 12, 1869, to Miss L K. Gere of Alton, Ill ; and was mayor of Belleville, Ill , in 1881 Hon Edward M. West of Edwardsville, Madison County, Ill , an older son of Tilghman H West, born in Botetourt County, Virginia, May 2, 1814, is the head of the banking-house of West & Prickett In 1838, he was elected treasurer of Madison County, and reelected to a second term. In 1844, he was elected school superintendent of the same county, and was one of the delegates from his county to the constitutional convention of 1847, and was largely instrumental, as a member of the finance committee, in securing the adoption of those wise measures which protected the State from repudiation and placed its credit on a sound basis He has been a prominent member of the Methodist church since 1842, and held the position of chaplain, with the rank of captain, in the Illinois National Guard.—J H. G.

APPENDIX.

MEMOIR OF CHARLES GRATIOT, SR.

[Revised by the author, Jan 7, 1885 From the *St. Louis Republican*, Aug 24, 1878.]
COMPILED FROM AUTHENTIC DATA IN POSSESSION OF THE WRITER.

I have long had it in contemplation, from my connection with the family of the deceased, Charles Gratiot, Sr., to prepare an article relating to the above individual, who, from the date of his first establishment in the then little village of Cahokia in 1777 (but thirteen years after the commencement of the embryo village of St Louis by Laclede) to his death in 1817, a period of forty years, was, from his education, acquirements, and business capacity, one of the most influential residents of our early St. Louis.

I am more directly induced to commence this procrastinated intention from the perusal of an obituary in the Sunday *Republican* of July 21, of the recently-deceased (July 13, 1878, aged 81 yrs. 8 mo. 10 dys) Isabelle, relict of the late Julius DeMun, and the last-surviving child of Charles Gratiot, which obituary contains so many material errors of fact, particularly as regards Mr Gratiot, that I deem it but proper for the truth of history that these errors should be corrected while fresh before us

But little is known at the present day of the ancestry of Charles Gratiot but what was derived from himself in his lifetime. He was of French origin, his ancestors being of those Huguenots who were compelled to leave their native France after the revocation of the edict of Nantes by Louis XIV, at the latter part of his reign, toward the close of the seventeenth century, owing to the persecutions they experienced for their religious views and opinions. A large portion of these persecuted people crossed the eastern boundaries of France into Switzerland, where all religious opinions were tolerated, and many settled in that country; among these were the immediate ancestors of Charles Gratiot, who in his lifetime always claimed to be a Swiss, and not a Frenchman.

Charles Gratiot, the only son of David* and Marie (Bernard) Gratiot was born at Lausanne, Canton of Vaud, anciently Leman, situated on the north shore of the ancient Lac Leman, modern Lake of Geneva, Switzerland, in 1752. After his school-boy days he was sent to an uncle Bernard in London, a brother of his mother, in whose mercantile house he spent some years, and then came to Montreal, Canada, arriving May 30, 1769, to another uncle Bernard, a merchant of Montreal, with whom he served as clerk for some five years   In 1774, this uncle sent him in the Indian trade to Michilimakinac, and in 1775 to the Illinois country, with a venture of goods for this uncle's account, where he remained about a year, and took such a fancy to the country that he determined to return and settle in it. So in 1777, having left this uncle's service and formed a copartnership with David McCrae and John Kay, two young Scotchmen of Montreal, fur-traders like himself, under the style of David McCrae & Co , he came to Cahokia late in November   The

---

* Charles Gratiot in his marriage contract in the Spanish archives is called the son of *Henry* Gratiot and Marie Bernard, but in all his letters to his parents he addresses them to his father *David* Gratiot, which doubtless was his correct name

writer of this is the possessor of his first little ledger, in his own handwriting; the first entry therein bears date Michilimackinac, Sept. 24, 1777, on his route here, then follows entries at Green Bay, Portage of the Ouisconsin, Prairie du Chien, and the first at Cahokia, Dec. 2, 1777, where he must have arrived about the close of November, and remained over three years, removing to St. Louis early in 1781, previous to his being united in marriage to Victoire Chouteau, born in New Orleans, third and youngest daughter of Marie Therese Chouteau, *nee* Bourgeois, on June 21, 1781; Mrs. Chouteau, the mother, born in New Orleans, 1733, then residing at the southwest corner of our present Main and Chesnut streets, in the stone house that had been built for her residence, and which she occupied from its completion in 1766-7 to her death, Aug 14, 1814, aged 81 Here Mr G lived for a few years, and in this house then first child, Julie, afterward Mrs. John P Cabanné, was born, July 24, 1782

In 1783, about the close of the Revolutionary War, Mr G. made a journey to Virginia to urge his claims for indemnification partly for large losses he had sustained in some manner by the seizure and confiscation of his goods in some of his Indian trading expeditions, in which he was then extensively engaged, but mainly for supplies and assistance furnished by him to Gen Clark and the Americans. Here he met with Patrick Henry and other noted men of the day, and succeeded in obtaining grants for large bodies of land in Kentucky, then included in the territory claimed by Virginia From this journey he returned to St. Louis in the summer of 1784.

Mr. Gratiot purchased, Nov. 28, 1785, from the widow of Eugene Poure, dit Beausoliel, for $500, the north half of our present block 3, 120 feet on Main by 150 feet deep to the river, with a house of posts, 40 by 20 feet and another of 20 by 15. And subsequently, in 1787-8, the south half of the same block, upon which was also a small house of posts On this property he resided for some years, and here several of his first children were born

Between the years 1792-3, Mr. Gratiot was associated with one Solomon Abraham, a merchant of Montreal, in trading with some of the Indian tribes of the upper country, the goods for these outfits being procured by Abraham from London. In the prosecution of this business they met with heavy pecuniary losses, as did all others engaged in this trade at this particular time. This was caused by the revolution in France, involving that country in an immediate war with Great Britain, and subsequently with nearly all Europe, materially depreciating the price of furs in that country and enhancing the cost of the goods for the trade

At this period, 1793, Mr G. made a voyage to Europe, being absent about twenty months The facts connected with this voyage I derive from his letters from Canada and London (in my possession) to his brothers-in-law, the two Chouteaus, at whose instance principally the voyage was undertaken, they then having a large fur-trading establishment in Mackinac, from which it appears that Mr. Gratiot, having experienced heavy losses in business some time previously, and finding himself very much embarrassed pecuniarily, had conceived the project of this voyage, then no small undertaking from this remote point, induced thereto partly by the very liberal remuneration to be allowed him by these gentlemen and others, whose furs, etc , he was to dispose of in London, then the great fur-mart of the world, and there purchase for them the goods they needed in the prosecution of their Indian trade, instead of, as heretofore, at Montreal, but mainly by the confident hope that, from his business capacity and his knowledge of the English language, "something might turn up" that would enable him to retrieve his affairs, and again place him in a prosperous position. In this hope he was not disappointed, as will subsequently appear.

He left St Louis at the end of May, 1793 The route then was by canoe or periogue up the Mississippi and Ouisconsin rivers, through Green Bay to Mackina', thence down through the lakes to Montreal. He was in Mackina' in July and in Montreal about August 20, and embarked for Europe about the close of October. At this time, Mr G was in the prime of life—just forty years—and had been married about twelve years, leaving at home five children, his wife giving birth to their sixth on Oct 25, just as he was on the eve of his departure from Montreal.

Arriving in London at the close of the year 1793, he spent the winter in unceasing application to the interests of those parties for whom he had undertaken the voyage, as is shown by his letters from that city In attending closely to this business, he became intimately acquainted with a Mr. Schneider, a merchant of very large means, at the head of a commercial house having extensive business relations with some of the principal cities of Europe This gentleman conceived a warm friendship for Mr Gratiot He made him propositions to establish a house in St. Petersburg, Russia, where large quantities of furs were disposed of. He proposed to furnish the capital necessary therefor, would procure for him consignments from other European cities, and eventually give him an interest in his London house. This generous proposition Mr G gratefully accepted, as he states in a long business letter of March 30, 1794, from London, to his brothers-in-law, the two Chouteaus, covering some twelve or fourteen pages of large foolscap.

Nothing could better exemplify the honorable character, the innate sense of those qualities which constitute the gentleman, and the liberality and self-sacrificing disposition of the man, than a perusal of this letter—but as that would require too much space in this article, I will merely condense the substance. The largest portion of the letter is devoted to the business interests of those for whom he made the voyage. Then, as to his personal matters: Explains the considerations that induced him to accept the offer to establish himself in Europe; regrets the severance of the ties, perhaps forever, that bind him to his friends in America, gives specific instructions for closing and settling his affairs in St Louis, enumerating all those to whom he is indebted, with directions to pay all his debts and to dispose of all his property, etc.; desires his wife to prepare herself and the children for the voyage to join him in Europe "when she will have received his instructions to that effect, and concludes with the hope that his friends there will cherish his remembrance and his sincere affection for all." In view of his contemplated absence from St Louis, for possibly a long period of time, Mr Gratiot had executed to his brother-in-law, Aug Chouteau, before his departure, under date of May 24, 1793, a general power of attorney, clothing him with full authority to act for him in his absence in all matters, as if done by himself in person.—Archives, vol, iv 505, p 770.

At this period, his brother-in-law, Pierre Chouteau, had just lost his first wife, Pelagie Kiersereau, to whom he had been married some ten years, leaving him a widower, yet comparatively a young man of thirty-three, with four children. He then began to entertain the idea of a trip to Europe, as mentioned by Gratiot in the foregoing letter of the 30th from London, but it appears that Chouteau had abandoned the idea of this voyage, as he had just previously to the date of this letter taken to himself a second wife, Brigitte Saucier, of which fact, of course, Gratiot was not apprised when he wrote, expecting Chouteau to come over and bring with him under his protection Gratiot's wife and children It appears then the voyage of

Mrs Gratiot was abandoned, if ever entertained by her. Mr. Gratiot remained abroad some twenty months, returning to St. Louis at the commencement of 1795. He must have met with pecuniary success in his enterprise, as we find him subsequently in easy circumstances.

At the close of 1796, Mr Gratiot purchased from his brother-in-law, Joseph M. Papin, for $3000, the south half of our present block 32, 120 feet front on Main by 300 deep to Second Street, just across the street (now Chesnut) from his mother-in-law, Mrs. Chouteau, with a large stone house of 55 by 36 feet. This house was built by Papin, who had purchased this lot from Martin Duralde in 1780, built the house for his residence, and lived in it some sixteen years until he sold to Mr. Gratiot as above. Mr G moved into this house early in 1797, and in this house his six youngest children were born. As an instance of the kindness of heart and munificent liberality of the man, I relate the following circumstance. In Feb, 1797, not long after his return from Europe, Mr. Gratiot purchased from Bernard Pratte, for $560—then its full value—the northeast quarter of the block (now 32) north and adjoining his then residence on the south half of this block, with a large stone-house thereon. A few years thereafter, Mr. G. made to his wife's sister, Marie Louise Chouteau, wife of Joseph M. Papin, and her children, a "voluntary gift" (so expressed in the deed) of the above property, "in consideration of their near relationship, and having a large family in distressed circumstances, in consequence of the losses her husband has experienced in business, and the great affection she has always manifested for his family." This deed, executed Sept 12, 1801, is on record in the archives, vol 1 p. 442. On this property Mr and Mrs. Papin resided until their respective deaths some years thereafter, and with the growth of the city it became very valuable in after years.

After his return from Europe, Mr. Gratiot again embarked in business, in which he was engaged up to the period of his death, in 1817. In his later years, and after the country had passed into the possession of the United States in 1804, Mr. G., possessing a knowledge of the English language, was a prominent man in the affairs of our little town, filling various offices of trust, etc. He was the first presiding judge of the court of common pleas after its organization in 1804, having for his two associates on the bench Auguste Chouteau and David Delaunay. Subsequently a justice-of-the-peace, and afterward, upon the organization of the town, chairman of the board of trustees for 1811-3.

Mr. and Mrs. Gratiot continued to reside in the house above mentioned until their respective deaths; he died April 21, 1817, aged sixty-four, and his widow June 15, 1825, aged sixty-five, surviving her husband eight years. They were the parents of thirteen children, four of whom died in infancy, and nine—four sons and five daughters—grew to maturity, and were all married in this house with the single exception of their eldest son Charles, then of the United States army, who married in Philadelphia in 1819, some years before the death of his mother.

Mr Gratiot named in his will his widow and his eldest son-in-law, the late John P Cabanné, as his executors. The widow continued to reside in the old family mansion until her death. Her youngest son, Paul M. Gratiot, then a clerk in the employment of the French Fur-Company on the waters of the Upper Missouri, which occasioned his absence from St. Louis about nine months of the year, being then under an engagement of marriage with a sister of the writer, to take place at the expiration of the term of his engagement to the company, which had yet three years to run, being then in St. Louis on his annual return for two or three months,

COL FRANCIS VIGO

From a Lithograph by Mme. Mezzara   Drawn by Chas Alex Lesueur

and old Mrs. Gratiot, then very infirm, finding her end rapidly approaching and desirous of witnessing the nuptials of her last and youngest child, as she had those of all her elder children, desired that they might be united in her presence before she left this world. Accordingly the marriage ceremony took place on June 6, 1825, in the chamber of the old lady, where she then lay on her death-bed, the few persons present being the relatives and a few intimate friends of the two families—the writer of this being one, as elder brother and guardian of the bride. Mrs Gratiot survived this event but nine days, breathing her last on June 15, 1825, aged sixty-five.

FRED. L. BILLON.

FRANCIS VIGO.

Francis Vigo was born in 1747, at Mondovi, Sardinia. As a Spanish soldier, he was with his regiment, first at Havana, and afterward at New Orleans, when that city was a Spanish post. He left the army and came to St Louis, then the military headquarters of the Spanish for Upper Louisiana Here he became the partner of the commandant, Don Francisco de Leyba, and was soon extensively engaged in the fur-trade, acquiring great influence among the several Indian tribes between the waters of the Ohio and the Missouri. His sympathies, already enlisted in favor of the Colonies, took active form on the appearance of Clark at Kaskaskia His time, influence, and whole fortune were staked with an open hand upon the issue. He turned out his merchandise to supply Clark's destitute soldiers, and sustained the credit of the Virginia continental money, by taking it at par or guaranteeing its redemption, at its face, to those who exchanged their provisions or supplies for it. His advances or liabilities incurred in this way amounted to more than twenty thousand dollars, which, with Hamilton's, the British commander's confiscations at Vincennes, and losses through reprisals of Indians hostile to his side of the war, reduced him to poverty Living to a ripe, old age, he also gave much of his time, subsequently to the Revolutionary war, to the military and civic affairs of the old Northwest and Indiana territories, when the latter embraced all the former, except the present State of Ohio He was never recompensed for his pecuniary sacrifices, though the United States made a tardy and partial restitution to his heirs. Toward the close of his life, he lived upon his little homestead farm, near Vincennes, in great poverty and cheerful to the last. Recurring to his old age, he often said in a resigned, jocular way, "I guess the Lord has forgotten me " His wants were relieved often times by the kindly attentions of his neighbors, among all whom, particularly little children, he was a universal favorite The nearly effaced inscription upon an unpretending stone that marks the neglected spot where rest his remains, in the old cemetery at Vincennes, advises us that he died March 22, 1835.

The sketch of Vigo is a photograph copy, presented to the writer by Prof John Collett, Indiana-State geologist, and taken from the original, drawn by C. A. Leseure—the great artist and ichthyologist of the expedition of La Peruse, fitted out by Napoleon I to explore Australia—while he was associated with Rob't Owen at New Harmony, Ind The sketch was recognized by Vigo's friends as a very good and striking one This note is summarized from papers on Vigo, published by late Judges Law of Vincennes and Gookins of Terre Haute, Ind —both personal acquaintances, and the latter, Vigo's executor—Clark and Jefferson's correspondence, Prof. Collett, and reminiscences gathered by the writer while on a visit to Vincennes for that purpose. (September, 1884.)   H W. BECKWITH, Danville, Ill.

NAMES OF EARLY ILLINOIS SETTLERS.

In the "American State Papers, Public Lands," Vol 2 [Duff Green edition], pp. 132-4, is a statement, dated Kaskaskia, Dec. 31, 1809, of claims founded on "Improvements" in the district of Kaskaskia, which were affirmed by the board of commissioners appointed under act of congress to take evidence of all land-claims in the Kaskaskia district, under French, Spanish, or United-States grants. The commissioners were Michael Jones and E. Backus, and the following appear to be the names of English or American settlers who claim under "Ancient Grants":

William Arundel,	John Dodge,	Nathaniel Hull,	Henry O'Hara,
John Barton,	John Doyle,	John Jones,	John Peters,
James Biswell,	Clement Drury,	James Kinkead,	William Robins,
Thomas Brady,	Abram Flanary,	George Lunsford,	Elijah Smith,
Drury Bush,	Joshua Flanary,	Richard McCarty,	Henry Smith,
Robert Caldwell,	Thos. Flanary, Jr.,	John McElmuny,	Peter Smith,
George Camp,	Joseph Hanson,	Jno McElmuny, Jr,	Joseph Standlee,
Ichadod Camp,	Leonard Harness,	Thomas Marrs,	Robert Sybold,
Isaac Chaffin,	John Hiltebrand,	John Marshall,	David Wallis,
John Chambers,	David Hix,	John Montgomery,	Haydon Wells,
James Curry,	Michael Huff,	William Murry,	Isaac West.
Alexander Denis,	Thomas Hughs,		

In the same volume, pp 135-8, is a list of claims "founded on acts of congress granting donations of four hundred acres each to heads of families in the district of Kaskaskia," and which were confirmed by the board Of these acts of congress, one approved March 3, 1791, gave to each "head of a family" who had cultivated or improved land in Illinois prior to and including the year 1788, the right to four hundred acres of land. Of those claiming under these acts, the following were Americans or English, Irish or Scotch, naturalized Americans:

J. B Allary,	Alexander Douglas,	Nathaniel Hull,	Charles Robins,
William Arundle,	John Doyle,	Jacob Judy,	Mrs R Rogers,
George Atchison,	Clement Drury,	Patrick Kennedy,	Larkin Rutherford,
Thomas Bently,	Andrew Faggot,	James Kincade,	Catharine Ryan,
William Biggs,	Samuel Finley,	James Lemen,	Josiah Ryan,
James Biswell,	Elijah Flannery,	John Lyle,	John K. Simpson,
Shadrach Bond,	Thos. Flannery, Jr,	John McCormick,	Henry Smith,
John Boyd,	James Garrison,	Thomas Marrs,	Nicholas Smith,
Benjamin Byram,	Charles Gill,	James Mayfield,	John Sullivan,
Joseph Byram,	Samuel Hanley,	John Montgomery,	Levi Theed,
George Camp,	Joseph Hanson,	Mary Moony,	David Wallace,
Ichabod Camp,	Leonard Harness,	James Moore,	George Ware,
John Clark,	John Harris,	Joseph Morris,	James Watts,
Thomas Comstock,	James Head,	Joseph Ogle, Sr,	Isaac West,
John Cook,	George Hendricks,	Henry O'Hara,	James Wiley,
James Curry,	David Hicks,	David Pagon,	John Williams,
Alexander Dennis,	John Hiltebrand,	John Peters,	Joseph Worley,
Israel Dodge,	William Howe,	James Pigot,	William Wycoff,
John Dodge,	Thomas Hughes,	(Kaskaskia, Dec. 31, 1809)	

Congress also donated "one hundred acres* of land to each militia-man enrolled and doing duty in Illinois on Aug 1, 1790, within the district of Kaskaskia." The claims under this act were made mostly by French settlers, as they constituted the greater part of the militia force at that date The following are the names of the claimants other than those of French birth or origin affirmed by the commissioners, Kaskaskia, Dec 31, 1809 (same book, page 139-47):

William Arundel,	Edward Hebert,	William Murry,	Levi Theed,
Timothy Bellow,	John Jones,	Joseph Ogle,	Edward Todd,
George Biggs,	John Rice Jones,	Levi Piggott,	William Todd,
John Brady,	William Jones,	William Piggott,	Alexander Waddle,
Isaac Brasten,	Jacob Judy,	Daniel Raper,	David Waddle,
William Butts,	Samuel Judy,	William Robins,	Jesse Waddle,
Thomas Callahan,	Robert Kidd,	Benjamin Rogers,	Hardy Wear,
Isaac Chaffin,	Alexander McNabb,	John Sack,	Frederick Weiser,
William Chaffin,	Edward McNabb,	Ebenezer Sevans,	John Whiteside,
Alexander Dennis,	James Moore, Jr,	Daniel Shultz,	Wm F. Whiteside,
John Edgar,	John Moore,	John K Simpson,	William Young
Isaac Enochs,	William Moore,	Daniel Sink,	Whiteside,
Philip Gallaher,	John Moredock,	Christopher Smith,	James Wilson,
John Hays,	William Morrison,	Robert Sybold,	Thomas Winn

The commissioners (Michael Jones, John Caldwell, Thomas Sloo) afterward (Kaskaskia, Jan 4, 1813) reported another list of those who were, in their opinion, entitled to four hundred acres each under the act of March 3, 1791, as settlers prior to 1788 (page 189 of same volume) Of these the following appear to be Americans:

Joseph Anderson,	John Dimpsey,	Archibald McNabb,	James Scott,
George Atchison,	William Dove,	James McRoberts,	Ebenezer Severns,
Frances Bellew,	Raphael Drury,	Charles Martin,	Nicholas Smith,
George Biggs,	William Drury,	James Moore,	Abraham Stanley,
Thomas Biggs,	John Edgar,	John Moore,	James Stillman,
William Biggs,	Isaac Enochs,	Elisha Nelson,	John Sullivan,
Shadrach Bond, Sr.,	Daniel Flannery,	Benjamin Ogle,	Levi Theel,
Tobias Brashiers,	Elijah Flannery,	Joseph Ogle,	Thomas Todd,
Charles Burk,	James Garretson,	William Oglesby,	David Waddle,
Benjamin Byram,	Charles Gill,	David Pagon,	Robert Watts,
Peter Casterline,	James Gray,	Jonas Piggot,	George Wear,
William Chaffin,	Samuel Hanley,	William Piggot,	Layton White,
L. G Chamberlain,	George Hendricks,	George Powers,	James Wiley,
William Cheney,	Thomas Hughes,	Abraham Rain,	Thomas Winn,
Frances Clark,	James Lemen,	Larkin Rutherford,	Charles Wood,
John Clark,	Henry Levins,	Catharine Ryan,	Joseph Worley
Robert Creighton,	William Lewis,	Josiah Ryan,	

* The commissioners in confirming the four-hundred-acre grants deducted this hundred acres from all who received it The militia man of 1790 therefore received but three hundred acres of the congressional grant —J H G

The following advertisement appeared on Saturday, March 11, 1815, in the *Missouri Gazette and Illinois Advertiser*, published at St Louis, Mo.:

"JACKSONVILLE,

A Town, which the Subscriber has just laid out on a liberal plan, and offers at private sale, BUILDING LOTS to Mechanicks, Merchants, and others, who may incline to settle therein. JACKSONVILLE is situated on the easterly bank of L'Abbe, or Cahokia Creek, not more than four hundred yards from the Mississippi River, immediately opposite the flourishing town of St Louis

It is deemed unnecessary to go into detail of the many advantages that this situation possesses. Suffice it to say, that it is a good and beautiful site for a large town, and admirably well situated for commerce. That it is backed by an extensive tract of as fertile lands as any in the Western Country; where there are at present, many industrious and respectable farmers, and the country is rapidly populating by emigrants from the different parts of the United States

Jacksonville, St Clair Co , Ill. Ter , March 4, 1815.   ETIENNE PINÇENNEAU."

In the *Missouri Intelligencer and Illinois Advertiser* of Sept. 27, 1817, appears the law card of John Taylor and James H. Peck, in which they propose to practise their profession in the counties of Washington and St Louis in the State of Missouri. The advertisement states that "Mr. Peck will also practise in St. Charles and Howard counties in Missouri, and Mr Taylor will attend to business in the counties of Bond, Madison, St. Clair, and Harrison in Illinois Territory."

We are not certain whether this was the same John Taylor whose eccentricities as a traveling preacher and lawyer served as a basis for many tales of wondrous pulpit and bar oratory in the Southwest during the early part of the present century. We think it likely that he is the same, and that he afterward remained in Arkansas and Texas. The best known of his exploits which served as the basis of a newspaper story, very extensively copied by the western press at intervals during the last half century, represents him as having volunteered in behalf of a widow against a wealthy suitor who had bribed court, jury, and witnesses, and even the poor woman's attorneys, when Taylor appeared in the nick of time, and overthrowing all opposition by the scathing power of his burning oratory won her cause, and at the close of the trial announced in the court-room "God willing, John Taylor will preach in this courthouse at early candle-light."—J. H. G.

EARLIEST NATURALIZATION RECORD IN ILLINOIS.

[From Col John Todd's Record-Book, presented to the Chicago Historical Society by Edward G. Mason, and is the subject of one of his lectures before the Society.*]

"I do swear on the Holy evangelists of Almighty god that I Renounce all Fidelity to george the third, King of Great Brittan, his heirs and Successors, and that I will Lear true allegiance to the united States of America as free and Independent, as declared by Congress, and that I will not do, nor cause to be done any matter or thing that may be injurious or Prejudicial to the independence of said States, and that I will make Known to some one Justice of the Peace for the united States all Treasons, all Treatorous, Conspiracies, which may come to my Knowledge to be formed against said united States, or any one of them. So help me God

"Sworn at Kaskaskia, 10 July, 1782.   JAMES MOORE."

* "Illinois in the 18th Century," three lectures by E. G. Mason, of the Chicago Bar. No. 12 of FERGUS HISTORICAL SERIES

PIONEER HISTORY OF ILLINOIS.

INDEX.

A.

Abbeville, S C, mention, 352
Abbot, James, mention, 246, 247
Aboite River, mention, 124
Abraham, Solomon, mention, 420
Adams, John, mention, 120, 329
Adams, John Quincy, mention, 396, 411 n
Adams, Lucinda, marries Richard Brads by, 337 n
Adams, Samuel, mention, 120
Adet, P A, French minister to the U S, 220
Afflock, Mrs. T B., mention, 263 n
Agriculture under French, 67-9
Aiken, Edward, mention, 302 n
Aix-la-Chapelle, treaty of, 66
Albemarle County, Va, mention, 63
Alexander County, Ill, representatives, 389, mention, 131
Alexander County, Ky, mention, 319
Alexander, Samuel, mention, 386.
Alexander Settlement, mention, 268
Algonquin Indians, mention, 17
Allary, Jean Baptiste, entitled to land-grant, 424
Alleghany Mountains, name, 18; mention, 18, 50, 67, 75, 112, 157, 301
Alleghany River, mention, 63, 65.
Allen, George, mention, 400 n
Allewige Indian nation gave name to Alleghany Mountains, 18
Allouez, Claude Jean, missionary and first white settler in Kaskaskia, 41
Allyn, Henry, mention, 400 n
Alsbury, E R, mention, 265 n
Alsbury, Lucinda, marries James Shuff, 265 n
Alton, mention, 27, 190, 222, 244 n, 270, 387, 409, 418 n
Alton Penitentiary, mention, 322
American Bottom, why so called, 113; early settlers, 201; social life in the, 202-4, mention, 43, 46, 49, 66, 115, 131, 138, 146, 149, 167, 200, 201, 207, 214, 232, 255, 260, 265, 270, 299, 323, 324, 325, 326, 327, 329, 330, 337, 347, 348, 355, 357, 358, 371
American race, superiority of, 151-2

American settlers in Illinois, 112-8, 125, 127, 130, 137-44, depredations of Indians against, in 1786-95, 152-4, their social life, 273-5, principally from western and southern states, 346
Amherst, Gen Sir Jeffrey, 77
Amlin [Jean Baptiste], cruel death of, 122-3
Amos, Rev. Abraham, member of first Illinois Territorial legislature, 268
Anderson [David and James] family, mention, 352
Anderson, Joseph, one of Gen Clark's soldiers, 339, mention, 215, 341, entitled to land-grant, 425
Andrews, James, killed by Indians, 153, settler of 1785, 255, daughter (Drusilla) captured by Indians, 153
Andrews, Mrs James (Ogle), killed by Indians, 153
Antya, Pierre, resident of Prairie du Chien, 151
Apple Creek, mention, 383
Arcadians, British cruelty to, 66-7, finally settle along the Mississippi, 67
Arkansas, mention, 184, 426
Arkansas Indians, locality, 27
Arkansas Post established 1686, 40
Arnold's (Benedict) Canada expedit'n, 373
Arstugus, see Asturgus
Artaguiette, Pierre d', governor of Ill, 54, leads troops against Chickasaws, capture, death, 57-8, mention, 305
Arthur, Hiram, mention, 381 n.
Arundel, William, entitled to land-grant, 424, 425
Ash Hill, mention, 358
Assinnaboin Country, mention, 226.
Asturgus, Minard, mention, 215
Atchison, George, settler of 1786, 256, marries daughter of Francis Saucier, 287, entitled to land-grant, 424, 425.
Atchison, William ("Chape Wollie"), anecdote of, 162, mention, 201
Athens, Ill., mention, 401
Athens University, 414 n
Atkins, William, mention, 280
Anguel Anthony, surnamed the Picard du Gay, mention, 33.

427

Austin, Moses, partner of John Rice Jones, 171
Australia, mention, 423

B.

Bachus, Elijah, receiver of Kaskaskia land-office, 351, 424
Badgley, Elizabeth, mention, 412 n
Badgley, Rev. David, sketch, 259-60, notice, 269, mention, 236, 237, 269, 280
Bailey, Lieut [John], leads American forces against Fort Sackville, 104.
Baker, David Jewett, mem. of Ill bar, 372
Baker, Edw'd Dickinson, mention, 370 n.
Baker, Jehu, mention, 400 n
Balbec, ruins of, mention, 177.
Baldwin, L B., mention, 265 n.
Baltimore City, mention, 113, 165, 211.
Baltimore, Lord (Geo Calvert), 401 n.
Banks', Gen Nathaniel Prentiss, Red-River campaign, reference, 415 n.
Bankson's, Capt. Andrew, comp'y, Black Hawk War, 386 n
Baptist Banner, reference, 254 n.
Baptist churches and preachers, 115, 190, 256, 259, 263, ib n, 265 n, 269, 270, 272, 335, 385, 412 n, divided on slavery question, 272
Barbara, ——, killed by Indians, 406
Barbeau, Jean Baptiste, chief-justice of Ill under Northwest Territory, 180
Barbeau, Miss Marie C , marries Nicholas Jarrot, 214
Bark canoes, description of, 235.
Barlow knife, mention, 382
Barnum, should be Varnum, 156
Barre, Antoine Joseph Lefebere de la, 37.
Barren Co , Ky , mention, 263 n, 264 n, 336 n, 378.
Barry, William T , of Ky , mention, 372
Barton, John, entitled to land-grant, 424
Barton, Joshua, duel of, 354
Bates, George C , mention, 247 n
Battle of (references) Atlanta, 387 n, Belmont, 387 n, Big Block, 415 n, Brandy-Wine, 300 n , Buena Vista, 300 n, 397, Bull Run, 387 n, Champion Hills, 415 n, Cow Pens, 203, Dalas, 387, Ft Donelson, 415 n, Fort Henry, ib , Fort Gibson, ib , Groveton, 398 n, Guildford Court-House, 203, Kenesaw Mountain, 387 n, King's Mountain, 185, 203; N Anna River, 398 n, Pontotoc Creek, 57, Quebec, 246, Resaca, 387 n, Shiloh, 415 n; Stone River, 414 n, Thames, 264 n Tippecanoe, 163, 391, 404-5, Trenton, 156, Vicksburg, 387 n
Baton Rouge, mention, 80
Bay of Biloxi, fort established at, 43
Bayles, Mrs Jesse (Bradsby), killed by Indians, 409

Bayley, see Bailey.
Bayou Manchac, mention, 80
Bazadona, Laurence, a Spanish trader, ransoms Wm. Biggs, 343.
Bazedone, see Bazadona
Beard, John, settler 1801, sketch, 310-2.
Beard, Joseph A., notice, 312.
Beard, Wm A , notice, 312, 313.
Bear-Grass Creek, 191
Beaucoup Creek, mention, 299
Beaujeu, Count de, disagreement with LaSalle, 37, 38
Beauleau, Jean, mention, 347
Beaulieu, Mad.——(Chouvin), sketch, 347
Beauvais, Jean Bte [St Gemme], wealth of, 82
Beauvais, Miss Julia [St Gemme], marries, Nicholas Jarrot, 214
Beauvois, Jean B , mention, 215
Beck, Dr Lewis C , surveyed Ft. Chartres in 1820, op 46
Beckwith, Hiram Williams, sketch of Rev. John Mason Peck, 253-4, note on land-offices in Eastern Illinois, 372 n, sketch of François Vigo, 423
Bedford County, Va , 336 n
Bees in Illinois, 169-70
Bellew, Francis, entitled to land-grant, 425
Bellow, Timothy, entitled to land-grant, 425
Bellefontaine, location, 255, mention, 113, 131, 146, 182, 184, 185, 201, 205, 256, 269, 342
Bellefontaine Cemetery, St. Louis, 254 n.
Belleville, visited by cholera, 1833, 369-70, county-seat St Clair County, 377-8; name, 378, hotel of 1816, ib , mention, 115, 166, 188, 194, 195, 230, 260, 267, 268, 289 n, 290 n, 313, 314, 328, 330, 333, 339, 361, 362 n, 363, ib n, 377, 398, 399, ib n, 400 n, 411, 418, ib n.
Bently, Thos , entitled to land-grant, 424
Benton, Ill , mention, 387 n
Benton, Thomas Hart, U -S senator from Mo , 171
Berkeley County, Va , mention, 271
Bernard, ——, of London, mention, 419
Bernard, ——, of Montreal, mention, 419
Berry, Elijah C , first State auditor, 336 n.
Berry, Melinda, marries Henry Clay Bradsby, 336 n
Beshears, see Brashears
Bethel Baptist Church formed on anti-slavery principles, 1809, 412 n
Betts' (——) tanyard, mention, 298.
Bible Society, first, 273
Bienville, II , Jean Baptiste LeMoyne de, drives British out of the Mississippi Valley, 43; unsuccessful campaign against Chickasaws, 56-7, 59
Big-Bay Creek, mention, 335
Big Door, chief of Piankeshaws, 98.

INDEX 429

Big Island, location, 355
Big Mound, mention, 355
Big Muddy, settlers on, 357, 390, mention, 110, 299, 335, 336, 406.
Big Prairie thickly settled, 202
Big Spring, mention, 175
Biggs family of 1796, 201.
Biggs, George, entitled to land-grant, 425
Biggs, Thos, entitled to land-grant, 425
Biggs, William, sheriff, 1790, 180, sketch, 341-4, member of first territorial legislature, 368, entitled to land grant, 424, 425
Bilderback [John and Ephraim] family, mention, 352
Billon, Frederic Louis (historian of St Louis), Sketch of Chas Gratiot, 419-23
Bird, see Byrd
Bissell, Capt Daniel, commander of Fort Massac, 221
Bissell, Gov Wm H mention, 400 n, reference to regiment of, 265 n, 300 n
Biswell, James, entitled to land-grant, 424
Black Hawk, religious rites, 285; mention, 252
Black-Hawk County, reference, 368 n
Black-Hawk War excited by Sauk and Fox, 21; reference, 141, 264 n 289 n, 384 n, 386 n, 387 n, 388, 412 n, 414 n
Black-Partridge Town, location, 407, mention, 320, 383
Blackwater Island, mention, 247 n
Blackwell, Rob't, buys out *Illinois Herald*, 366, 1b n, member of Illinois bar, 372
Blair, George, sells site of Belleville, 377, mention, 202, 238, 377
Blair, Mrs George [Murdoch], mention, 202, 238
Blair, William, anecdote of, 347, mention, 377
Bland, Richard, mention, 120
Bledsoe, Jesse, of Ky, mention, 372
Bledsoe Licks of Tenn, mention, 298
Block-Houses, early, 114, 207, description, 131-4
Bloody Island, mention, 354
Blount, Wm, governor of S-W T'y, 311
Blue Licks, mention, 107, 143 n
Bluff Dale, Ill, mention, 27 n
Boggs, Gov Lilburn W, of Mo, 327
Boilvin, Nicholas, resident of Prairie du Chien, 1812, 151
Boisbriant, Pierre Duqué, commandant in Illinois, 46
Boismenue, [Nicholas?] sr, anecdote of, 90
Boismenue, Isabella, marries Edward Pensoneau, 363 n
Boltenhouse, Joseph, killed by Indians, 408
Bond, Di Benjamin, notice, 328
Bond, Benjamin N, mention, 327 n
Bond County, mention, 110, 337, 426
Bond, Emily, mention, 327 n
Bond, Isabella F, marries James P Craig, 327 n
Bond, Joshua, and descendants, 327-8 n
Bond, Julia R, marries Frank Swanwick, 327 n
Bond, Mary A, marries Joseph B Holmes, 327 n
Bond, Nicholas, father of Gov, mention, 323
Bond, Nicodemus, mention, 327
Bond. Shadrach, sr (Judge), early (1781) settler, 112, native of Md, 113, 255, member legislature of Ind and N.-W territories justice for many years, 114-5; with others erects block-house in Am Bot'om, 131, elected rep'sentative, 157, lay preacher, 256, 258, uncle of Gov., 323, with Gen Clark, 328, mention, 132, 149, 202, 270, 290, 344, entitled to land-grants, 425
Bond, Shadrach, jr (Gov), duel with Rice Jones, 173, Gov of Ill, portrait, sketch, 323-7; advocates Ill -and-Mich Canal, 327. descendants of, 327 n, mention, 368 n; entitled to land-grants, 425, 426
Bond, Mrs Shadrach, Jr, mention, 256
Bond, Thomas, notice, 328
Bond, Thomas S, mention, 327 n
Bon Succour, near Cahokia, 113
Boon, Daniel, mention, 84
Boon, Nathan, major in Gen Howard's expedition, 408
Boonsboro, mention, 87.
Boone's Lick, mention, 110, 140
Borer [Jacob], mention, 236
Born, Octav, mention, 362 n
Boscawen, Admiral Edward, mention, 155
Boston, mention, 247
Botetourt County, Va, mention, 184, 205
Boucher, Geo O, mention, 379 n
Boucher, Hiram, mention, 379 n
Boucher, John, wounded by Indians, 379, sketch and descendants, ib n
Boucher, John Vincent, mention, 379 n
Boucher, Lyman S, mention, 379 n.
Boucher, P H, mention, 379 n
Boucher, Thomas, mention, 379 n
Boulder, Colorado, mention, 379 n
Bouquet, Gen Henry, relieves Ft Pitt, 79
Bourgmont, Sieur de, erects fort on Missouri River, 52
Bowman, Capt James, his company in Black-Hawk War, 264 n
Bowman, Capt Joseph, at Cahokia, 98, visits Rock-River Indians, 98-9; mention, 92
Bowen, ——, settler 1780, sketch, 137
Bowerman, Jacob, mention, 364
Boyd, John, entitled to land-grant, 424
Bracken Co, Ky, mention, 358, 401 n
Braddock's [Gen Edward] Defeat, reference, 65, 76, 199

Bradley, Rev. Joshua, mention, 254 n.
Bradsby family, 336, 337, 378
Bradsby. Addison, mention, 337 n
Bradsby, Catharine, marries Addison Pyle, 336 n.
Bradsby, Eloise, marries William Adams, 336 n.
Bradsby, Francis, mention, 337 n
Bradsby, Henry Clay, mention, 336 n.
Bradsby, Indiana, marries J H Williams, 336 n
Bradsby, James, mention. 337, notice, ib n.
Bradsby, Jane, marries Jesse Bayles, is massacred by Indians, 337 n
Bradsby, John, and descendants, 336-7 n
Bradsby, Mary, marries Richard Higgins, 337 n.
Bradsby, Pauline, mention, 337 n
Bradsby, Priscilla, marries Thos Chilton, 337 n
Bradsby, Richard, notice, 337 n
Bradsby, Virginia, marries James L Perryman, 337 n
Bradsby, William (1st), mention, 336 n
Bradsby, William (2d), mention, 337 n
Bradsby, William (3d), mention, 337 n
Bradsby, Dr William II, and descendants, 336 n
Bradsby, Mrs Wm H, mention, 337 n
Brady, John, entitled to land-grant, 425
Brady, Thomas, captures St Joseph, 89, captured by Indians, 90, sheriff 1798, 128; marries LaCompt, 168, entitled to land-giant, 424, mention, 122, 126
Brady, Mrs Thos (LaFlamme) (St Ange) (LaCompt), sketch, 168-9
Branham, ——, of Ky, partner of Wm Scott, mention, 205
Brashears, Tobias, erects fort in American Bottom, 131, entitled to land-grant, 425
Brashiers, see Brashears.
Brasten, Isaac, entitled to land-grant, 425
Brazell, [Richard or Wm ?], mention, 357
Breckinridge Co, Ky, mention, 414 n
Breese, Sidney, U -S senator, 301 n, resignation as judge, 386n, mention, 413n
Bridgeton, Mo, mention. 266
Bridgewater, Ill, projected 374
Brisbois, Michael, resident of Prairie du Chien, 1812, 151
British, buy part of West from Iroquois, 61, colonization and conquest of Ohio Valley, 60-5, Empire, 305, government of Illinois, 73, 79-82
Brockville, Ind, mention 402 n
Broulette, Bradford, marries Mad Laurent Pensoneau, 363 n
Brown, Gen. Jacob, mention, 359
Brown, Maj Wm George, sketch, 411.
Browne, Thomas C, member of Territorial legislature. 368 n, settler at Shawneetown, 390; sketch, 392-3.

Brownsville, Pa, built 1786, 138, see Red-Stone Old Fort, 373
Brownsville, Ill, named for Gen. Jacob Brown, 359
Bryant, Guy, partner of Wm. Morrison, 161
Bryant (Guy) & Morrison (Wm), extensive business of, 161
Bryson, Wm., Indian scout, 175
Buchanan, James, mention, 139 n
Bucks County, Pa, mention, 160, 373
Buell, Gen. DonCarlos, mention, 414 n
Buffalo mention, 361
Buffalo Rock, tradition of, 35.
Buffaloes, 299
Buissoniére, Alphonse de la, governor of Illinois, 59-60
Buncomb County, N C, mention 398
Burges, Wm, wounded by Indians, 379.
Burk, Chas, entitled to land grant, 425
Burlington, Ia, mention, 139 n
Burnett, F W, marries daughter of H. C Bradsby, 336 n
Burr, Aaron, mention, 221
Bush, Drury, entitled to land-grant, 424
Butler, Gen Richard, 2d in command of Clair's expedition, 198, 199
Butts, Wm, entitled to land-grant, 425
Byram, Benjamin, entitled to land-grant, 424, 425
Byram, Joseph, entitled to land-grant, 424
Byrd family [Abraham and sons], mention, 298, 364

C.

Cabanné, Jean Pierre, manufacturer of salt, 110, mention, 310, 422
Cache River, Ky, mention, 319
Cadillac Antoine Laumet de la Mothe, mention, 44
Cadwell, Dr George, sketch, 329-30; mention, 328
Cæsar, Julius, mention, 79, 221, 328
Cahokia, established 1686, 40, missionaries and traders at, 41, growth, 1700, 43; flour and skins shipped from, 44, in 1721, 50-1, Pontiac killed in Cahokia, 75, 79, captured by Americans, 96, treaty with Indians at, 99, inundated, 113, 114; negro slaves hung for being witches in, 175, court held at, 180; county-seat of St. Clair Co, 252, 377; post-office at, postmaster at, 224; called Cahos, 307, mention, 18, 19, 23, 49, 67, 89, 90, 98, 122, 123, 127, 129, 131, 161, 167, 168, 170, 174, 185, 188, 189, 192, 201. 102, 211, 214, 215, 222, 223, 224, 225, 227, 245, 280, 287, 289 n, 306, 313, 315, 328, 333, 342 347, 350, 356, 359, 360, 361, 362, 363, ib n, 419, 420.
Cahokia Creek, 128, 214, 407, 426.

INDEX 431

Cahokia Indians, 18, 50
Cairnes, Caldwell, physician, anecdote of, 347, sketch, 360, mention, 377
Cairo, Ill., mention, 364, 415 n
Cairo City-and-Canal Co., mention, 388 n
Cairo-and-Vincennes Railroad, building of, 368 n
Caldwell, Robert, entitled to land-grant, 424
Calhoun County, mention, 253 n
Calhoun, John Caldwell, report 1812, 403, mention, 349
California, mention, 53, 289 n, 298
Callahan, Thomas, entitled to land-grant, 425
Calumet, mention, 90
Calvert, Geo. (Lord Baltimore), mention, 417 n
Camp s Creek, mention, 138
Camp, George, of Kaskaskia, 1783, 138; one of Gen Clark's soldiers, 339, entitled to land-grant, 424
Camp, Ichabod, of Kaskaskia, 1783. 138, one of Gen Clark's soldiers, 339, entitled to land-grant, 424
Camp Russell, location, 204, 405; name, 405, military depot for Illinois, 408, mention, 190, 407
Camp Spring, mention, 138
Campbell, Maj John, U.-S officer, erects block-houses on Illinois River, 405, commands expedition against Sac and Fox, 409
Campbell, ——, duel of, 234.
Camp-meeting, first in Illinois, 267
Canada settlers from, 21, 108, 127, 226, 246, 291, 347, 350, 362 n, 363; called New France, 65; mention, 17, 30, 37, 47, 83, 123, 155, 209, 223, 294, 297, 305.
Canoes, description of, 234-5
Cany-Forks, Tenn., mention, 298
Cape Girardeau, mention, 161, 281
Carey, Matthew, mention, 273
Carlin [W. E.] & Bagley, mention, 385 n
Carlin, James, notice, 384-5 n
Carlin, Gov Thos., sketch, 382-5; death, 384 n
Carlin, Walter E., notice, 385 n
Carlinville, name, 384.
Carlisle, Pa., mention, 291, 367
Carlyle, Ill., block-house near, 405, mention, 75, 79
Carolinas, mention, 75, 79
Carondelet, François Louis Hectore, Baron de, mention, 127
Carondelet Town, nicknamed *Vide Pouche*, "empty pocket," 82
Carpenter, Nathan, early miller, 315; mention, 357
Carr, Leonard, mention, 236, 237
Carrolton, Ill., county-seat of Green Co., 383; mention, 385 tion, 386 n, 392

Carthage, Tenn., mention, 298.
Casey family, mention, 413
Casey, Dr John R., mention, 414 n
Casey, Hiram R., notice, 414 n
Casey, Mahala, marries Rev. Lewes Dwight, 414 n
Casey, Dr Newton R., notice, 414 n
Casey, Samuel K., notice, 413-4 n
Casey, Thomas J., notice, 414 n
Casey, Gov Zadoc, notice, 413-4; sketch, 413 n
Cash River, mention, 281.
Cass County, Ill., mention, 289 n
Cass, Gov. Lewis, mention, 292.
Casterland, see Casterline
Casterline, Peter, entitled to land-grant, 425, mention, 260, 314
Cat Island, mention, 58
Catholic churches, priest, missions, 266, 275, 296, 299
Celeron, Louis, commander of French company, 59, deposited plates in Ohio Valley claiming country for France, 62
Central City, Ill, 265 n
Centralia, mention, 263 n, 386 n, 414 n
Cere, Gabriel, see Cerré
Cerré, Gabriel, merchant of St Louis, 114
Chaffin, see Chalfin
Chalfin, Isaac, entitled to land-grant, 143, 358, 371, 424
Chalfin, William, entitled to land-grant, 143, 358, 371, 425
Chamberlain, L G., entitled to land-grant, 425
Chambers, Benjamin, mention, 401 n
Chambers, John, entitled to land-grant, 424
Chambers, Nathan, mention, 377
Chance, Rev Joseph, settler of 1796, 259, sketch, 270 mention, 185, 269, 357
Chance, Mrs Joseph (Jemima Morris), 270
"Chape Wollie," see Wm Atchison.
Chapelle, Antoine la, of Kaskaskia, death, 163
Chapman, Elijah, early miller, 315
Charivari, description of, 178-9
Charleston, S C., mention, 220, 385 n
Charleville, Capt François, mention, 102
Charlevoix, Pierre François Xavier de, visits Marquette's burial place, 31; visits Kaskaskia, 50
Charters, James, mention, 302 n
Cheney, Wm., entitled to land-grant, 425.
Cherokee Indians, mention, 84, 311
Chester, Ill., mention, 327 n.
Chester, Pa., 225
Chesterfield, Lord Philip Dormer Stanhope, Earl of, mention, 223
Chicago, site inhabited by Pottawatomies, 17, Sainte Ange and wife, settlers of in 1765, 168; massacre, 249; land-office,

432   PIONEER HISTORY OF ILLINOIS.

372 n; early history, 417; name, ib n, see under John Kinzie, mention, 28, 90, 110, 247, ib n, 248, ib n, 361, 426 n
Chicago River, mention, 36
Chickasaw Indians, campaigns of French against, 56-9, 64
"Childe Harold," reference to, 147
Chillicothe, O, mention, 117, 181
Chills and fever, 315
Chilton family, mention, 357
Chilton, Thomas, mention, 337 n
China, mention, 30
Chippeway Indians, mention, 19
Cholera at Belleville, 1833, 369
Chouteau, Auguste, Indian commissioner, 369; judge of common pleas, St Louis, 422; mention, 308, 421
Chouteau, Marie Therese (Bourgeois), mother of Mrs Chas Gratiot, Sr, 420
Chouteau, Marie Louise, marries Joseph M Papin, 421; gift to, 422
Chouteau, Pierre, Sr, marries Pelagie Kierseran (see Kiercereau), and afterward Brigitte Saucier, 421, mention, 287, 308, 421
Chouteau, Pierre, Jr, mention, 310
Chouteau, Victoire, marries Charles Gratiot, Sr, 420, death, 423, mention, 308
Chouvin [Jean Baptiste Chauvin], mention, 347
Church, first in Illinois, 267
Church of England, 230, 271
Cincinnati, legislature meets at, 114, occuposition of Fort Washington, 197, mention, 50, 181, 198, 228, 278, 301, 373, 374
Clark County, mention, 244
Clark Francis, early teacher, 152, entitled to land-grant, 425
Clark, George Rogers, early life, portrait, 83, app't'd to organize Ky. militia, 87; appointed delegate to Virginia assembly, 88, conquest of Illinois, 90-8, thanked by Virginia legislature, 99, sketch, 129-30, recaptures Vincennes, 100-6, organizes government, 107, troops receive land-grant, 108, aided by Chas. Gratiot, 420, and François Vigo, 423, mention, 81, 85, 86, 87, 113, 115, 124, 128, 131, 137, 168, 216, 255, 291, 304, 307, 328, 342, 356
Clark, Rev John (Father Clark), early teacher and preacher, 152, 237, 262-6, 411 n, entitled to land-grant, 424
Clark, William, superintendent of Indian affairs, 249, Indian commissioner, 369
Claudius, Jean Antoine Alexis, trader, partner of J F Perry, killed at Philadelphia, 1792, 287
Clay County, representative, 413 n; mention, 336 n
Clay, Henry, reference, 326.

Clemson, Col Eli B, inspector Gen. Howard's expedition, 408
Clinch River, mention, 298, 311.
Clinton County, Ill, mention, 263 n, 265 n, 372
Clinton Hill, mention, 328, 330.
Cochran, Samuel, settler 1804, 356
Coffee's, Capt Elzey C., company, Mexican War, 265 n
Coit, William, mention, 330
Colbert, Jean Baptiste, French minister, mention, 30
Coldwater, Mo, mention, 267
Coles County, mention, 244
Collett, John, mention, 423
Collins, ——, settler 1806, 356
Collinsville, mention, 167, 315, 412 n
Colton, J H, mention, 254 n.
Columbia, Ill., mention, 131
Columbus, Ohio, mention, 289 n
Company of the Indies, see Company of the West, 48
Company of St Phillips organized, 47
Company of the West organized, 46; land-grants to, 48, united with Company of the Indies, ib ; returns charter, 54; mention, 44.
Comstock, Thomas, entitled to land-grant, 424
Congregationalists, 273
Connecticut, population 1774, 120, settlers from, 184, 253 n, 416; mention, 184, 309 n, 416
Conner, Ephraim, settler 1800, 280
Constitutional Convention of 1818, 358, 390, 401 n, 413, of 1847, 262 n, 370 n, 388, 418 n, of 1870, 289 n
Contonment Wilkinson, 221
Contrecoeur, Anthony Pecody, Sieur de, French commander, 63, 65
Conway, Joseph, early lawyer, 361-2
Cook County, name, 397
Cook, Daniel Pope, sketch, portrait, 395-6, mem congress from Ill, 364; proprietor of Waterloo, Ill, 374; canvass for congress, 392, mention, 261, 366, 372, 375
Cook, John, settler at Kaskaskia, 1783, 138, entitled to land-grant, 424
Copeland, ——, mention, 357
Cornelius, [Joseph ?], early miller, 315
Corn Island, locality, 92, mention, 98, 108
Cornmeal manufacture, 176-7
Cornwallis', Lord Charles, surrender, reference, 300 n, 328
Cotton-gin, first in Illinois, 398
Cotton in Illinois, 64
Couch, [James ?], mention, 352
County Tyrone, Ireland, mention, 413 n
Courts and suits, early, 74, 179-81
Covington, Ill, mention, 164, 167, 336 n
Covington, Ky., mention, 254 n

INDEX.   433

Cox [Absolam], mention, 352
Cox, Benjamin, bravery, 404
Cox family, mention, 404.
Cox, Henry, bravery, 404; killed by Indians, 409
Craig, James P., mention, 327 n
Craig, Capt Thomas E, mention, 250, 407, expedition against Peoria, 245, 350, his company in war of 1812, reference to, 368 n
Crawford, Col Wm, burning of, 86
Crawford, William Harris, nominee for president, 402, ib n
Crawford, ——, duel of, 234
Creamer, Philip, sketch, 348-9
Creek Indians, mention, 311
Creighton, Robert, entitled to land-grant, 425
Crittenden, John J, attorney-general of Illinois Territory, 367
Crittenden, Thomas T, attorney-general of Illinois Territory, 367
Crogan, Maj Geo, nephew of Geo R Clark, defends Lower Sandusky, 403
Croghan, Col George, agent of Sir Wm. Johnson, British commissioner, visits Shawneetown in 1765, 79, captured by Indians, 80.
Cromwell, Oliver, mention, 176, 326
Crooked Creek, mention, 263 n
Crozat, Antoine, of Paris, monopoly of Illinois commerce, 44; surrenders his charter, 46
"Crusoe, Robinson," mention, 324.
Cuba, Island of, mention, 396
Cumberland Mountains, mention, 311
Cumberland River, mention, 129, 298
Cumberland, Tenn, mention, 267
Cummins, Thomas, mention, 357
Cunningham, Mary, marries John Alex. Logan, 387 n
Cupid, mention, 222
Currency about 1783, 108.
Curry, James, one of Clark's soldiers, 339, anecdote of, 340-1, sketch, 341, entitled to land-grant, 424
Cushing, Thomas, member Continental Congress, mention, 120

D.

Dane, Charles, grant of land to, 50
Daniel, the prophet, mention, 279
Daniels, ——, 336
Danville land-office, 372, ib. n, mention, 254 n, 302 n
Darnielle, Isaac, second lawyer in Illinois, 181, sketch, 221-4
Dauphin Island, mention, 42, 43
Davidson, S D, early lawyer, notice, 361
Davis, David, U -S senator, 387 n [died, Bloomington, Ill, June 26, 1886, æ 71]

Deane, Silas, mention, 120
Dearborn Co, Ind, organization, 401 n
Decatur, Ill, mention, 244
Dehaut, Lancelot, assassinates LaSalle, 38, 39
Deists in Illinois, 260-1
Delaunay, David, judge, mention, 422
Delaware Indians, mention, 17, 18, 304
Delaware, letters from, 270
Delorme, [Hubert ?], settler of 1804, 355
Dement [Geo.], death, settler of 1792, 192
Dement, Henry Dodge, notice, 139 n
Dement, John, mention, 139 n, 386 n
Dement, Mrs John, notice, 139 n
Democratic National Convention, 1875, 415 n
DeMoulin, John, sketch, 180, 209-11.
Demountbrun, Timothy, comm'd't of Ill, 107, 144 [In John Todd's Record Book he signs his name, "Thimothe Demunbrum, Lt comd'g, par interem, etc."]
Dempsey, John, attacked by Indians, 154, 175, Indian fighter, 186, written Dimpsey, entitled to land-grant, 425
DeMun, Isabelle (Gratiot), decease, 419
Dennis, Alexander, murdered by Indians, 280, 314; entitled to land-grant, 424
Derush Hollow, mention, 328
Desha, Col Robert, in command in Gen. Howard's expedition, 408
DeSoto, Hernando, discovers the Mississippi, 25
Detroit beseiged by Indians, 73-9, size in 1765, 80, LaBalme's expedition against, 124, under control of British, 226; land-office, 351, mention, 54, 75, 88, 97, 102, 106, 107, 198, 216, 225, 245, 246, 247, ib n, 248 n
Dew, Rev John, mention, 268
Dickson, Robert, incites Indians against the Americans, 250, 251, 252, 404
Dillard, Capt Thomas, mention, 92
Dilworth's [Thomas] "Speller," reference, 382
Dimsey, John, see Dempsey
Dinwiddie, Robert, governor of Va., 63
Disunion measure, 1786, in Ill, 219, 221
Dixon, Ill, mention, 139 n
Dixon Ferry, mention, 141
Dixon Spring, Tenn, mention, 298
Dodge, Augustus C., sketch, 138-9 n, mention, 142
Dodge, Gen, Gov, and Senator Henry, manufacturer of salt, 109-10, sketch, 138-42, 138 n, mention, 259
Dodge, Dr Israel, settler of 1783, 138, 139, entitled to land-grant, 424, mention, 259
Dodge, John, settler of 1783, 138; entitled to land-grant, 424, one of Gen Clark's old soldiers, 339; mention, 215

28

434   PIONEER HISTORY OF ILLINOIS.

Dodge, Rev Josiah, preacher of 1794, 259
Dodge, Mary Louise, marries John Dement, 139 n
Donaldson, Col James L , mention, 165.
Dougherty, [George H. ?], miller of New Design, 146
Dougherty, John, lawyer, notice, 388-9
Douglas, Alexander, entitled to land-grant, 424
Douglas, Stephen Arnold, mention, 386 n, 387 n 413 n
Dove, Wm , entitled to land-grant, 425
Downing, [Jas or Wm ?], mention, 357
Doyle, Benj H , lawyer, mention, 360
Doyle, John, settler about 1780, sketch, 137, one of Gen Clark's soldiers, 339, early teacher, 358, entitled to land-grant, 424, mention, 215
Doza Creek, block-house on, 405
Drunkenness little known in early times, 111
Drury, Clement, ent'led to land-grant. 424
Drury, Raphael, entitled to land-grant, 425
Drury, Wm , entitled to land-grant, 425
Dubois, Jesse K , mention, 386 n
Dubois, Tousaint, partner of Pierre Ménard in 1790, [Indian trader and interpreter, major on Gen Harrison's staff, drowned in Kaskaskia River in 1821, a county in Indiana named for him, father of Hon Jesse K Dubois, who died at Springfield, Ill , Nov 24, 1876], 291
Dubreuill, ——, invents cotton gin and opens sugar plantation, 64
Dubuque, Ill , mention, 22, 127.
Dubuque, Julien, sketch, 21-2, 127; resident of Prairie du Chien, 151
D'Ucan, see Gay and Auguel
Ducharme, Dominique, brother of Jean Marie, 123
Ducharme, Jean Marie, expedition against St Louis, 123-4
Duché, Rev Jacob, chaplain to cong , 120
Ducoign, Jean Baptiste, chief of Kaskaskia Indians, 22-3
Ducoign, Jefferson, mention, 23
Ducoign, Louis, mention, 23
Duel between Crawford and Campbell, 234, Barton and Rector, 354, first duel in Illinois, 81-2
Duff, [John M. ?], killed by Indians, 1799 [?], 285
Duff, John, of Kaskaskia, 92
DuGay, see Gay, and Auguel
Duluth, Greyselon, Sieur de, comdt of trading party, 33
Duncan, Gov Joseph, portrait, sketch, 403
Duncan, Mathew, established first newspaper in Illinois, 366, ib. n
Dundalk, City of, mention, 300.

Dunkers, colony of, 273
Dunks, Andrew, mention, 215
Dunlap, Dr James, kills Rice Jones, 173-4.
Dunlop, Col James, mention, 415 n
Dunlop, Sarah, marries John A McClernand, 415 n
Dunmore's, Gov (John Murray, 4th earl of), expedition against the Indians, 83, 84, 86
DuQuoin, Ill mention, 412 n
Duralde, Martin, mention, 421
Dutisne, Claude Chas , explorations of, 43.
Dwight, Rev Lewis, mention, 414 n
Dwight, S L , mention, 414 n.

E,

Earthquake of 1811, 399
East St. Louis, mention, 386 n.
East Tennessee, mention, 298
Easton, Col Rufus, of St Louis, mention, 222
Eberman, Rev Wm , mention, 377.
Eddyville, Ky , mention, 328, 329
Edgar County, name, 117
Edgar, John, manufacturer of salt, 110; sketch, portrait, 116-8; chief-justice of Illinois under N W. Territory, 180, mill owner, 215, 347, imprisoned by British, 246-7; entitled to land-grant, 425, mention, 299
Edinburgh, mention, 155
Edwards, Benj Stephenson, notice, 370 n.
Edwards County, representative, 413 n; mention, 393, 413 n
Edwards, Gov Ninian, organizes legislature, 365; excites immigration, 366, advertises slave for sale, 366 n, sketch, portrait, 367-70, leads troops against Indians, 407, mention, 149, 249, 273, 289 n, 320, 354, 362 n, 368, 382, 391, 402
Edwards' "History of Illinois," reference, 378 n
Edwards, Ninian Wirt, sketch, 370 n
Edwards, Mrs. Ninian W , mention, 143 n
Edwardsville, land-office, mention, 364, 411, seat of Madison County, 378, mention, 190, 240, 267, 280, 299, 314, 315, 401 n, 405
Elk-Heart Grove, mention, 20, 244
Elliot, ——, early miller, 315
Emanuel, ——, a slave, shot, 175.
Embarras, The, mention, 101
England, settlers from, 128, 269.
English-Turn, mention, 43, 66
Enochs, Isaac, Indian fighter, 188, entitled to land-grant, 425; mention, 185, 259, 314, 377, 412 n
Episcopal Church, mention, 402 n.
Erwin, [Joseph ?], mention, 352
Essex County, England, mention, 253 n.
Etheridge, William, 264 n.

INDEX. 435

Everett, John, only inhabitant of St Philip in 1803, 125
Explorers of Illinois, early, 25-44
Exports of Illinois, early, 60
Eyeman, Abraham, settler of 1797, 313, mention, 236, 237

F.

Faggot, Andrew, entitled to land-grant, 424
Falling Spring, location, 128; mention, 210
Falls of the Ohio, mention, 219
Falls of St Anthony, mention, 211, 306
Faris, Naomi, marries John Bradsby, 337 n
Farmer, Maj Robert, succeeds Capt Stirling at Ft Chartres, Dec 4, 1765, mention, 74   See "Maj Frazier."
Fauquier Co , Va , mention, 353, 397 n
Faulkner, Aaron, mention, 265 n.
Faulkner, Abner, mention, 265 n
Faulkner, Alexander, mention, 265 n.
Faulkner, Angelina, marries Clark W Mitchell, 265 n.
Faulkner, Caroline, marries Jackson Trout, 265 n
Faulkner, Charles J , mention, 265 n
Faulkner, Elizabeth, marries L B. Baldwin, 265 n.
Faulkner, Gilbert, mention, 265 n.
Faulkner, John, and descendants, 265 n
Faulkner, John (2d), mention, 265 n
Faulkner, Katharine, marries Matthew Pate, 265 n
Faulkner, Margaret, marries Meg Taylor, 265 n
Faulkner, Richard, mention, 265 n
Fay, Hon John D , mention, 384 n
Fayette Co , Ky , mention, 143 n, 381, ib n, 382
Fayette, Ill , mention, 183, 184.
Feef's Creek, Mo , mention, 266
Fergus, Geo Harris, note on John Kinzie and descendants, 247-8 n; note on John Harris Kinzie and descendants, 248 n
"Fergus Historical Series," reference, 175 n, 462 n
Ferguson, Hamlet, notice, 390
Ferguson, Thomas, member of first Ill territorial legislature, 368
Ferrell, John, killed by Indians, 1789, 154
Ferry at Shawneetown, 368 n
Fevre-River lead-mines, mention, 309 n
Finlay, John, see John Finley
Finley, Rev John Evans, mention, 270, 336
Finley, Samuel, entitled to land-grant, 424
Fisher, George, sheriff of Randolph Co , 304; early physician, 358; member of first Illinois territorial legislature, 368
Fisher, Myers, mention, 170

Flanary, Abram, entitled to land-grant, 424
Flanary, Joshua, entitled to land-grant, 424
Flanary, Thomas, Jr , entitled to land-grant, 424
Flannary family build block-house, 131.
Flannary, James, killed by Indians, 153
Flannery, Daniel, entitled to land-grant, 425
Flannery, Elijah, entitled to land-grant, 424
Fletcher, Mary, notice, 303; marries James McRoberts, ib n
Flourisant, Mo , mention, 184, 356
Forbes, Gen John, captures Ft Duquesne, 65 , mention, 191 n.
Ford's [James] Ferry, mention, 207
Ford, Robert, mention, 373
Ford, Mrs Robert, notice, 373-4
Ford, Gov Thomas, birth, 373; education, 374, sketch, 375-7; mention, 289
Ford's "History of Illinois," reference, 376, ib n, 377
Forquer, Geo , birth, 373, education, 374, sketch, 374-5
Forsyth, Robert, imprisoned by British, 246, sketch, 247 n
Forsyth, Thomas, settler of 1809, 246; sketch, 247-52; mention, 247 n, 250, [died, St Louis, Oct 29, 1833]
Fort Adams, mention, 80
Fort Assumption, building of, 59
Fort Chambers, location, 405
Fort Chartres built, diagram of, 46; seat of government, ib ; injured by freshet, description, ib.; village adjacent to, 50; why built, 52; rebuilt, 62; courts at, 74; abandoned, 81; inundated, 113; population declining, 125, mention, 18, 22, 56, 57, 63, 74, 80, 115, 202, 288n, 329, 347
Fort Chenango, mention, 77
Fort Clark, logs cut for, 408, 409
Fort Creve Cœur, location, 36, mention, 32, 33, 34
Fort Cumberland, mention, 77
Fort Dearborn, mention, 247 n, 248 n.
Fort Deposit built, 200
Fort Detroit taken by English, 77
Fort Duquesne, founding site, capture and destruction, 65; evacuation, 191 n, mention, 291
Fort Frontenac, mention, 30, 31, 33, 34, 35, 36
Fort Gage, position and description, 81; capture, 87, mention, 221, 341.
Fort Green-Bay, mention, 77
Fort Hamilton, mention, 141, 198, 387 n
Fort Jefferson built, 129, 198, 199, now the Iron Banks, 124, mention, 339
Fort Johnston burned, 409

Fort Leavenworth, mention, 139 n, 362 n
Fort LeBœuf, mention, 77
Fort L'Huillei, mention, 43
Fort Ligonier, mention, 77, 155
Fort Mackinac taken by British, 77; by Indians, 78
Fort Madison burned, 409
Fort Malden, mention, 248
Fort Mason, mention, 408
Fort Massac (or Massacre) building, name, 53, called Fort Cherokee, 92, true origin of name, 191 n, depot for immigrants, 286, military road from to Kaskaskia, 281, repaired and garrisoned, 221; mention, 93, 94, 126, 131, 137, 236, 285
Fort Matagorda Bay destroyed by Indians, 52
Fort Miami, destroyed by Indians, 77
Fortress Monroe built, 309 n
Fort Natchez, destroyed by Indians, 52
Fort Necessity surrendered, 63
Fort Niagara, strongest fortification in Western country, 76
Fort Orleans building, location, destruction, 52
Fort Ouiatenon, or Weastown, mention, 77
Fort Pitt beseiged, 79, mention, 77
Fort Presque Isle captured by Indians, 78, mention, 77
Fort Prudhomme, occupied by British, 61; mention, 36, 37
Fort Recovery, mention, 276
Fort Russell, see Camp Russell
Fort Sackville built, 81; captured and surrendered by Americans, 99, 100; mention, 128, 341, see Vincennes, 102
Fort Sandusky, mention, 77
Fort Scott, mention, 263 n
Fort St Charles, mention, 248 n
Fort St Francis building, 59
Fort St Joseph, mention, 77
Fort St Louis, location, 34, mention, 36
Fort Ticonderoga, mention, 156
Fort Washington, location, 197, 277.
Fort Wayne, mention, 224
Fort Winnebago, mention, 248 n
Fountaine Creek, mention, 177, 259, 346.
Foutch, John, mention, 264 n
Foutch, Mahala, marries Joseph Pulsifer, descendants, 265 n
Foutch, Mary A , marries E R Alsbury, 265 n
Foutch, Rachael, mention, 264 n
Foutch, Susan, marries Wm Rhea, 264 n
Fox Indians, Western immigration of, 21; mention, 127, 150, 151
Fox River, mention, 26, 103
France, mention, 30, 37, 41, 73, 211, 419
Frankfort, Ky , mention, 205, 397 n, 406.
Franklin, George, settler about 1804, 356
Franklin, Benj., mention, 170, 293, 375

Franklin Co , representative, 387 n
Frazier, ——, settler about 1804, 356
Frazier (Fraser or Frazer), Lord [should be Lieut. Alex], mention, 80
Frazier, Major [should be Farmer], mention, 74
Frederick Co , Md , mention, 319, 323
French, settlements of in Illinois, 1730, 53-4, as pioneers, 61, 125-6, endeavor to retain supremacy in West, 62-5, emigrate from Illinois at cession, 74; those remaining confirmed in rights, 125-6, 350-1, 352; settlers, 211, 286; peculiarities, 297, their forts destroyed by Indians, 52, villages in Illinois described, 47, 168, immigration, 41-2, villages, decline of, 66, 125, farming and social life, 67-73, friendly to Americans, 89
French, Gov Augustus C , mention, 386 n
French-Canadians as voyagers, 108
French Licks, now Nashville, Tenn , 110
French Fur-Company, mention, 422
Frontenac, (Louis de Bande), Count de, governor-general of Canada, 30, 37
Fulton, John, mention, 352, 358

G.

Gaborit Island, mention, 232, 329
Gage, Gen Thomas, mention, 74
Gagnie Creek, mention, 364
Galbreath, see Gilbreath
Galena, called Fevre River, 309 n; mention, 21, 166
Gallaher, Philip, entitled to land-grant, 425
Gallatin County, salt springs, 109, established, 367; senators and representatives, 368, 392, 415, treasurer, 368 n settlements in, 390, county-seat, 392, 393, mention, 19, 79, 110, 368, 392, 415.
Gallipolis, mention, 287
Game before 1765, 73, about 1800, 169
Garretson, Samuel, killed by Indians, 154
Garretson (also written Garrison), James, early settler, 112, 113, 114, 115, shot at by Indians, 153, entitled to land-grant, 425; mention, 255
Garrison, Miss, marries John Murdoch, 149
Gaskill, David, marries Miss Sally McMahon, 197
Gaston, Alexander, settler about 1804, 356
Gatewood, William J (Jeff), settler at Shawneetown, 90
Gay, Picard du, mention, 33, see Auguel
Genet, Edmond Charles, French minister to U S , 220
Gentry Co , Mo , mention, 264 n, 265 n.
Georgia, invited to join in disunion measures, 219, settlers from, 413 n, 417; mention, 83, 121, 398

INDEX 437

Gerardine, Antoine, buys property in 1764, 129; mention, 74.
Gere, Miss L K, marries Benjamin J. West, Jr., 418 n
Germany, settlers from, 319, mention, 289 n.
Giard, Basil, resident of Prairie du Chien in 1812, 151
Gibault, Father Pierre, of Kaskaskia, 96, 97.
Gibralter, Ill, mention, 245.
Gibbons family, mention, 185
Gibbons, John, settler of Horse Prairie, 200; settles near Bellefontaine, 205; mention, 259, 270, 357.
Gibson [George], settler about 1804, 356.
Gilbreath family, mention, 398.
Gilham family, mention, 241.
Gilham, Clement, see James Gilham, 201.
Gilham, James, Sr., settler of 1797, 201; wife and two children (Clement and Samuel) captured by Kickapoos, 201, 241-4, mention, 202, 303, 357
Gilham, Mrs. [James] (Ann Barnett), captured by Indians, 242-4; obtains land-grant, 244.
Gilham, Samuel, see James Gilham, 201.
Gill, Charles, entitled to land-grant, 424, 425.
Gillespie, Joseph, recollections of Painted Rock, 27 n, notes on the Whiteside Family, 189 n, Hiram Arthur and Thos. Higgins, 381 n, mention, 289 n, [died, Edwardsville, Ill, Jan 7, 1885]
Gillum, ——, murderers of, 312.
Girard, see Giard
Girard's (Basil) River, mention, 151
Girty, Simon, sketch, 86, mention, 87.
Gist, Christopher, ag't of the Ohio Co., 62
Gladwyn, Maj Henry, baffles plans against Fort Detroit, 78-9.
Glasgow, mention, 300.
Going's [Wm.] Block-House, 405.
Going family, mention, 185.
Going, William, sketch, 181-2; settler about 1804, 357
Going, William, Jr., sketch, 182-4.
Golconda, Ill, mention, 281, 335, 357
Golden, ——, erects block-house, 132.
Goodner, Dr. Salem, mention, 379 n
"Goody Two Shoes," mention, 324
Gookins, Judge Samuel B., mention, 423.
Gordon, William W, mention, 248 n
Goshen Settlement, camp-meeting in, 267; location, name, 280; enlarged, 314; road to laid out in 1808, 392; mention, 260, 299, 315, 319, 354, 392.
Governors of Illinois, reference to, 327, 365, 368 n, 369 370 n, 375, 384, 400 n, 403, 413.
Grand-Pierre Creek, mention, 386
Grand-Point Creek, mention, 263 n.

Grand-Risseau Creek, mention, 131.
Grand Tower, mention, 138, 401.
Grammar, John, member of first territorial legislature, 368
Grant, Ulysses Simpson, mention, 415 n
Gratiot, Adèle, marries E. B Washburne, 309 n
Gratiot, Charles, Sr, sketch, 305-9, 419-23; descendants, 309-10, ib. n.
Gratiot, Charles, Jr, sketch, 309 n; mention, 309, 422
Gratiot, Chas Hempstead, mention, 309 n
Gratiot, David (sometimes called Henry), father of Chas. Gratiot, Sr, 419, ib. n
Gratiot, Col. Edward Hempstead, mention, 309 n.
Gratiot, Henry, mention, portrait, 309; sketch, ib n
Gratiot, Jean Pierre Bugnion, mention, 309 n.
Gratiot, Julie, marries John P. Cabanné, 420.
Gratiot, Marie (Bernard), mother of Chas. Gratiot, Sr, 419
Gratiot, Paul M, mention, 422, 423.
Gratiot's Grove, mention, 309 n.
Gravelly Creek, mention, 215, 360.
Gray, James, entitled to land-grant, 425.
Great Britain, mention, 65, 73, 116, 119, 121, 170, 220, 287, 300.
Great-Western R.R, mention, 388 n.
Green, Rev. Thomas, mention, 254 n
Green Bay, French name, Le Baie des Puants, 20, mention, 26, 28, 32, 245.
Greenbrier Co, Va., mention, 263 n, 264 n.
Green Co., Ill, organization, representative, 382; first sheriff, county-seat, 383; mention, 330, 384 n
Greene, Gen. Nathaniel, mention 156.
Greenup, William C., clerk of Illinois territorial legislature, 367.
Greenville, Ill., mention, 337 n, 378.
Greenville, treaty of, 84, 87, 200
Gregg, Jacob, settler of 1803, 357.
Greggs, Jesse, settler about 1804, 357.
Griffin, [Joseph?], settler near Bellefontaine, 185, 205.
Griffin family, mention, 357.
"Griffon," vessel, 31, 32.
Grigg [John] & Elliot [Hugh] mention, 254 n [Now J B Lippincott & Co.]
Griswold, Stanley, judge in Illinois Terr'y, Wabash District, 365, 371; notice, 402.
Groot family, mention, 314, 339
Grosvenor, John, settler of 1799, sketch, 184
Grundy, Felix, mention, 301 n
Guard, Seth, settler at salines, 390.
Gulf of Mexico, mention, 36, 219.
Gunn, John H, notes by, on Gen. A. C. Dodge and family, 138-9 n; John Todd and family, 143-4 n; refers to "Fergus'

438   PIONEER HISTORY OF ILLINOIS.

Historical Series," 175 n; origin of name Ft Massac, 191 n; C. R. Matheny and descendants, 261-2 n, Abner Jolliff and descendants, 263-5 n; Gov Bond and descendants, 327 n, Bradsby family, 336 7 n, Matthew Duncan and *Illinois Herald*, 366 n; Alexander Wilson and descendants, 368 n, Gov Edwards and descendants, 370 n; John Boucher and descendants, 379 n, referring to Reynolds' "My Own Times," 381 n, Thos Higgins, ib , Gov. Carlin and descendants, 384-5 n; Omelvany family, 385-6; Dr John Logan and descendants, 386-7 n, Alex M. Jenkins 388 n; Quick family, 399-400, James Lemen, Sr., and descendants, 411-2 n; Zadoc Casey and descendants, 413-4 n, Gen John A McClernand, 414-5 n; West family, 417-8 n; Kaskaskia land-grants, 424 5, Jacksonville, and John Taylor and Jas H Peck, 426.

H.

Hacker, George, mention, 389.
Hacker, John S, notice, 389.
Hagerstown, Md , mention, 248, 401 n.
Haggin, James, early lawyer, 360
Halfpenny, ——, early school-teacher, 152, mill owner, 177
Haliburton, ——, mention, 247 n
Hall's, Judge Jas , "Annals of the West," reference, 381 n
Halleck, Gen Henry Wager, mention, 415 n
Hamilton, Lady Anny, letter of, 225-6
Hamilton Co , representative, 413 n, mention, 278, 368 n
Hamilton, Gov. Henry, captures Vincennes, 99, 100; is captured, 101-6
Hampden Sydney College, mention, 276
Hamtramck, Col John Francis, of St Clair's expedition, 199.
Hamtramck, Mrs John Francis, marries Judge Jesse Burgess Thomas, Sr , 401 n
Hand, Gen Edward, mention, 91.
Hanging-Man Town, mention, 312.
Hanley, Samuel, entitled to land-grant,424
Hannibal of Carthage, reference, 75, 326
Hanniberry, Patrick, settler of 1801, 280
Hanson, Joseph, entitled to land-grant, 424
Hardin, Benjamin, of Ky , mention, 397
Hardin, Jeptha, settler in Shawneetown, 390. sketch, 397-8, descendants, ib n
Hardin, John, mention, 397 n, 398 n
Hardin, John J, sketch, 397-8 n, mention, 386 n, 397.
Hardin, Martin D, sketch, 398 n
Hardy Co , Va , mention, 235, 236, 259, 337, 358, 379 n.

Hargrave, Willis, captain in war of 1812, 406, 407.
Harmar, Gen. Josiah, his campaign against the Indians, 197-8, 216, his defeat, 276, 397 n; mention, 21
Harness, Leonard, entitled to land-grant, 424
Harniss, ——, settler of 1783, 143.
Harper's Ferry, mention, 348, 411 n.
Harpe [Micajah, The "Big"], murder of, 286
Harrington, Wm., Indian fighter, 186.
Harris, George, mention, 400 n.
Harris, John, entitled to land-grant, 424
Harris, Maj. Thomas L , mention, 415 n
Harrison, Albert B , member of congress from Missouri, mention, 372
Harrison, Benjamin (father of Wm. H), governor of Virginia, 276, thanks Gen. Clark, 130; mention, 120
Harrison County, mention, 426
Harrison, George, mention, 400 n
Harrison, Rev Thomas, sketch, 398-9
Harrison, William Henry, campaign of 1813, 34, elected to congress from Northwestern Territory, 157; takes possession of La., 229, sketch, 276-9; campaign of 1811, 391; convenes first Ind. legislature, 401 n, nominated for president, 402 n; attacks Indians at Tippecanoe, 404-5, mention, 228, 248 n, 264 n, 309 n, 358, 397.
Harrisonville, Ill , mention, 260, 261, 374
Harrod, Capt. William, mention, 92.
Harrodsburg, mention, 88
Harrods' [James] Station, 87.
Hartford, Conn., mention, 253 n.
Havana, Cuba, mention, 423
Hawesville, Ky , mention, 243.
Hay, Maj Jehu, gov of Upper Canada, 225; mention, 106.
Hay, John, sketch, 225-9; clerk of court, 365
Hay, Mrs John (Margaret Pouport), 227
Haynie, Gen Isham N , mention, 413 n.
Hays, Elizabeth, marries Laurent Pensoneau, 363 n
Hays, John, sketch, 223-5, settler of 1803, 335; sheriff, 365; entitled to land grant, 425, mention, 363 n, 377.
Heacock, Russel E., early lawyer, notice, 361.
Head, James, entitled to land-grant, 424
Heald's, Capt Nathan, company, 249.
Heard, Joseph, settler about 1804, 356.
Hebert, Edw , entitled to land-grant, 425
Heckewelder, Rev. John, missionary to Indians, mention, 18
Helm, Capt. Leonard, at capture of Kaskaskia, 93, commander at Vincennes, 98; surrenders Ft. Sackville, 99-100, intercepts British convoy, 107, ment'n, 105

INDEX. 439

Helm, Lieut Linai T , ransom, 250, mention, 249
Hempstead, Charles S , notice, 309 n
Hempstead, Edward, member of congress from Missouri Territory, 309 n
Hempstead, Stephen, mention, 309 n
Hempstead, Susan, marries Henry Gratiot, 309 n
Hempstead, William, mention, 309 n
Henderson [James?], settler of 1783, 143
Hendricks, Geo , entitled to land-grant, 424, 425
Hennepin, Louis, the explorer, 30, 31, 33, 34; mention, 39
Hennepin, Ill , name, 39
Henry, Alexander, British trader, 78
Henry's, James Dougherty, battalion of spies, Black-Hawk War, 384 n
Henry [Moses], soldier of American army, anecdote of, 100
Henry, Patrick, governor of Va , 143 n, conference as such with Gen Clark, 88, mention, 102, 120; mention, 420
Henry V , reference, 147.
Herd, see Heard.
Herkimer, N Y , mention, 302 n
Hewitt, ——, of Goshen Settlement, 357
Hickman, John, settler in Miss Bottom in 1806, 364
Hicks (or Hix), David, entitled to land-grant, 424
Hiel, Maria Catharine, marries Benjamin H West, 418 n
Higgins, Catharine M , marries Wm H Bradsby, 336
Higgins, Lucinda, mention, 337 n.
Higgins, Mary, marries John Bradsby, 336 n
Higgins, Richard, mention, 337
Higgins, Thomas, sketch, 378-81, duel and character, 381 n, mention, 341.
Hill, Adam, mention, 352
Hill, Nathaniel, mention, 357, 405
Hill's Ferry, mention, 408.
Hill's [Isaac] Fort, location, 405; mention, 378
Hillsborough, Ill , mention, 331
Hiltebrand, John, one of Gen Clark's soldiers, 339, mention, 215, entitled to land-grant, 424
Hix, Daniel [David ?], mention, 215
Holly, Horatio, mention, 301 n
Holmes, Joseph B , mention, 327 n
Holsclaw, Enoch, mention, 265 n
Homer, the poet, mention, 77
Hontan and Herseche, Armand Louis de Delondarce, Baron de la, untruthful (?) explorer, 43
Hook's, G W , company in Mexican War, 289 n
Hopkins, Gen Samuel, leads troops against Indians of Illinois, 407.

Hopkinsville, Ky , mention, 298
Horse Creek, mention, 157, 159, 162, 201.
Horse Prairie, early settlers and location, 200, 201, old name Washington, 184; mention, 181, 184, 185, 197, 205, 270, 349.
Horse-racing, 336, 345.
Horses and cattle, 51, 344
Howard County, Mo , mention, 426
Howard, John, mention, 407
Howard's, Gen and Gov Benjamin, expedition against Indians, 292-3, mention, 249, 320, 383, 408-9
Howard, Hon Tilghman A , mention, 373, [died 1844, buried at Rockville, Parke Co , Ind]
Howe, Wm , entitled to land-grant, 424
Hoyle, Edmund, mention, 350.
Hubbard, Adolphus Frederick, early settler of Shawneetown, 390
Huff, Michael, settler of about 1780, 137; killed by Indians, 138, 146, entitled to land-grant, 424
Huff, Mrs ——, killed by Indians, 256-7
Huff, Mrs Michael (widow Murdoch), killed by Indians, 138
Huff, Rebecca, marries Josiah Lemen, 412 n.
Huggins [Robert and David] family, mention, 352
Hughes, Thos , sketch, 125, one of Gen. Clark's soldiers, 339, entitled to land-grant, 424, 425, mention, 215
Huguenots, mention, 305, 419
Huitt, Rebecca, marries Thomas Carlin, 384 n
Hull, Daniel, settler of 1794, 208
Hull, Daniel, son of Nathaniel, death, 208
Hull, Nathaniel, erects block-house, 131, commands squad against Indians, 175, 176, sketch, 207-10, establishes ferry and opens road to Kaskaskia, 281, entitled to land-grant, 424
Hull, Sarah, marries Moses Lemen, 412 n
Hull's [Nathaniel] Landing, mention, 207, 281
Humphrey, Edward, early school-teacher, 358, 374; mention, 371
Humphries, Rev. Thomas, of S C , mention, 262
Hunt, Rev James, William Wirt's tutor, mention, 376.
Hunter, Gen. David, mention, 247 n, 248 n
Husking parties, 316

I.

Iberville, Pierre LeMoine d', explorations of, 42, 43, mention, 41
Iberville Bayou, mention, 80
Ill-in-i, meaning, 17.
Illinois under French, 46-73, under Brit-

ish government, 73, 79-82; under government of Va , 83-144, boundaries of county of, 98, county of organized, 107, 144, 157; under Northwestern T'y, 145; a part of Indiana T'y, 148, 276, what known as, 297, about 1800, 314, territory established, 344, Virginia's cession to U S of, 350-1, territorial organization, 365, 385, boundary extended, 394. Agricultural College, mention, 400n, American settlers in, 112-8, 125, 127, 130, 137-44, Indian depredations against, 1786-95, 152-4, their social life, 273-5, principally from Western and Southern States, 346; second child of American parents in, 412, attorney-generals of, mention, 361, 367, 370n, 375, bees in, 169-70; block-houses, 131-2, life in, 132-4; year of blood, 1789, 154, commerce about 1712, 44; cotton and tobacco in, 64, constitutional conventions, reference to, of 1818, 358, 390, 401 n, 413, of 1847, 370 n, 388, 418 n, currency about 1783, 108, disunion measure of 1786 in, 219, 221, earthquake of 1811, 399, early explorers of, 25-44; early races of cattle and horses, 51, early lawyers, 170, 370-2, early mills, 49, 116, 128, 129, 143, 146, 158, 162, 176-7, 192, 193, 210, 213 4, 346, 399t early orchards, 190, early physicians, 358-60, early school-masters, 152, 399n; early preachers, 256-73; unvisited by British during British sway, 81, exports, 60, 357, 401, fertility when first discovered, 24, 28, 29, fires on prairie, 231-2, first court, 74, fiist duel, 81-2; first high-school and seminary, 254 n, first camp-meeting and meeting-house, 267; first wool-carding mill, 289 n; first surveyor, 331, first newspaper, 366, first cotton-gin, 398; first railroad, 418; French-and-Indian war, peaceful condition of during, 65, French immigration, 41-2; declining of villages of, 66, 125, farming and social life of, 67-73, 275; friendly to Americans, 89, 86,000 pounds of flour furnished by one man in 1766, 82, font commissioner, mention, 417; game before 1765, 73; about 1800, 169, governors, reference to, 327, 365, 368 n, 369, 370 n, 375, 384, 400 n, 403, 413, horses, see under cattle, horse-racing, 345, 336, husking parties, 316, immigration after 1708 from South, 43; increasing after treaty of Greenville, 200, commences in earnest about 1800, 279, after 1815, 410; inhabited portion, 1803, 345, about 1810, 365; inhabitants change mode of life about 1800, 346; intoxicating drink little used, 111, iron but little used, 111; judges, mention, 190, 289 n, 302 n, 370, 372, 375, 386 n, 393, 396, 401, 414 n; see John Edgar, J. B. Barbeau, John de Moulin, judicial system, 73; see first court, improvement in the judicial system, 181, 370-1, 401, land claims allowed, 326, 350-1, 352; land offices of Eastern Ill., 372 n, land speculation, 209, 213, 229; legislation but little needed before 1790 in, 144, legislatures, territorial, 149, 293, 320, 335, 358, 367, 368; lieutenant-governors, mention, 293, 386 n, 388, ib. n, 413 n, 414, marshal of, 411 n; mechanical arts in pioneer days, 111; members of congress, reference, 289 n, 325, 326, 365, 387 n, 391, 396, 397 n, 411, 413 n, 415 n, military road in, 281, militia, 130, 190, 209-10, mining, 65, mormon war, reference, 376-7, see negro slaves; New England furnished few early settlers, 280, bitterness of political feeling, 173, population increasing about 1750, 64, in 1765, 74; in 1791, 130-1; in 1803, 346, products, 1800-12, 346; public system of 1837, 388 n, rangers of 1812, 337 n, 338, ib n; religion and morals prior to 1818, 253, undisturbed during first years of revolution, 83; see Salt Springs, want of schools in, 215; secretary of state, 374, 393, 410, characteristics of settlers, 44-5, its sickly condition, 315-6, social habits in, about 1800, 317-9, speaker of house, reference, 332, State penitentiary, 414 n; improved stock, 344, superintendent of instruction, 370 n, survey of northern boundary, 332; timber increasing in modern times, 54-6, happy times in 1732, 54-6; tornadoes or hurricanes, 347-8, traveling in 1797, 157, and in 1800, 298-9, treasurer of State, 417; U -S. district judge, 394, U.-S senator, reference, 289 n, 301 n, 372 n, 386 n, 387 n, 392, 401 n, 410; vegetation, 1800, 231, volunteer regiments of in war of rebellion, 18th Cav., 368 n, 62d Inf , 265 n; 84th Inf , 265 n, 110th Inf, 414 n, 111th Inf , 264 n, 265 n; 130th Inf , 262, 142d Inf , 418 n; war of revolution opens immigration, 111-2, independent expeditions during, 122-4; during war of 1812, 405-9; wheat raising introduced, 54, about 1800, 162, harvest, 202

Illinois-Central R R , early charters, 388 n, land-grant, 413 n

"Illinois in the 18th Century," reference, 426 n.

Illinois or Illini, Indian confederacy, 17, name, 17, 24, tribes composing confederacy, 18-9, territory inhabited by in 1673, 18, migrations, 22-3, fate, 23; annihilation, 79.

INDEX. 441

Illinois-and-Michigan Canal, advocated by Gov Bond, 327; mention, 302 n, 415, 417.
Illinois River, mention, 17, 18, 19, 20, 28, 33, 123, 157, 232, 247 n, 248, 249, 250, 252.
Illinoistown, first brick-house in, 363
Immigration, 41-2, 43, 111-2, 200, 279, 410
Indiana Territory established, 149, its boundaries, 276, territorial legislature, 290, 325, 332; mention of territory and state, 19, 101, 114, 145, 278, 365, revision of statutes of, reference, 171
Indians can not be civilized, 19; best policy toward, ib n; seek to terrify explorers, 26, can not be christianized, 42, friendly to French, 54, 61, French *vs* British treatment of, 75; hostile to Americans, 152-4, converted to christianity, 153, employed by whites to commit crimes, 285, depredations by, 1791, 175-6, 186 -9, before 1800, 193-7, 197-200, cease from hostilities, 409; see under Indians; outrages, 152-4, 249, 280, 285, 337 n, 340-1, 379 80, 404, two great races, 17-8, trade, how conducted, 234-5; social life, 282, religion, 283-5; tradition generally unreliable, 17, war in 1774, 83, war prosecuted for nineteen years, 84; war under Pontiac, 75-9
Iowa, mention, 109, 139 n, 172, 253 n, 264 n
Iowa Indians, locality, 21
Ireland, settlers from, 116, 162, 177, 298, 300, 361, 385 n, 386, 389, mention, 116, 127, 143 n, 246, 271, 300, 361, 413 n
Iron banks on Ohio settled, 339, mention, 125, 129, 139
Iroquois drive the Delawares west, 18; war with French, 34, 56; become friendly, 56, mention, 17.
Irvington, Ill , mention, 264 n
Island Grove, Ill., mention, 264 n.
Island No 22, mention, 131

J.

Jackson, Andrew, mention, 43, 156, 301 n, 326, 372, 384
Jackson Co , organization, name, 358, county clerk, 387 n, representatives and senators, ib , 388, mention, 48, 363 n, 388.
Jacksonburg, mention, 156.
Jacksonville, Ill , mention, 397 n, 398 n, 415 n
Jacksonville, St.Clair Co., Ill , advertisement in 1815 of lots for sale at, 426
James I , mention, 180
James, Gen Thomas, builder of mill, 177, 192

James, James A , anecdote of, 347-8
Janette, a supposed witch, 175.
Jarrot, an Indian, 212-3
Jarrot, Nicholas, sketch, 211-4
Jarrot, Mrs Nicholas (Marie C Barbeau), 214
Jarrot, Mrs Nicholas (Julia [St Gemme] Bauvais), 214-5
Jarrot, Col Vital, mention, 362 n
Jarvis, Franklin, settler of 1797, 205
Jay, John, mention, 120, 220
Jefferson College, mention, 336 n.
Jefferson County, Ill , representatives and senators, 413 n, 414 n, mention, 26 n, 264 n, 386
Jefferson, Thomas, mention, 91, 121, 180, 210, 300, 329, 356, 375, 423
Jenkins, Alex M , notice, 388; sketch, ib n, mention, 386 n, his company in Black-Hawk War, mention, 387 n
Jenkins, Elizabeth, marries Dr John Logan, 386 n.
Jersey County, Ill , mention, 385 n
Jerseyville, Ill , mention, 385
Jesuit missionaries, praise of, 25-6, mention, 49
Johnson, Col Richard M , mention, 86, 171, 172
Johnson Co , Ill , established, 367; senators and representatives, 368
Joliet, Louis, the discoverer, 25-8
Joliet, Ill , name, 39; mention, 300 n, 302 n, 414 n
Jolliff, Aaron, mention, 263 n
Jolliff, Rev. Abner, sketch, descendants, 263-5 n.
Jolliff, Abner (2d), and descendants, 263 n.
Jolliff, Abner (3d), mention, 263 n, 264 n
Jolliff, Elijah, and descendants, 264 n
Jolliff, Elijah, jr , mention, 264 n
Jolliff, Elizabeth (1st), marries Edward Russell, 263 n
Jolliff, Elizabeth (2d), marries James Willard, 264 n.
Jolliff, Elizabeth (3d), marries John Faulkner, 265 n; descendants, ib n
Jolliff, Jackson, mention, 264 n
Jolliff, Jacob, mention, 263 n
Jolliff, Col James, and descendants, 263-4 n.
Jolliff, James E , mention, 263 n.
Jolliff, Jehoida, marries Enoch Holsclaw, 265 n
Jolliff, Martha, marries Reece Williams, 263 n
Jolliff, Rachael, marries James Rhea, 264 n; descendants, ib n.
Jolliff, Randall, mention, 264 n
Jolliff, Reuben W , mention, 264 n
Jolliff, Richard, marries Elizabeth Taylor, 263 n, descendants, ib n, mention, 265 n.
Jolliff, William, mention, 264 n.

Jonesboro', first settler in, 389, county-seat of Union Co., ib., mention, 386
Jones County, Ia., mention, 379 n
Jones, Emsley, murders Reed, 304
Jones,' Fort, location, 405
Jones, Gabriel John, delegate to Virginia assembly, 88, killed by Indians, ib
Jones, George W., the U.S. senator, 172
Jones, John, entitled to land-grant, 424, 425
Jones, John Rice, first lawyer, sketch, 170-2; entitled to land-grant, 425, mention, 180, 221, 299
Jones, Michael, commissioner to examine land titles, 326, register of Kaskaskia land-office, 351, sketch, 352, early settler at Shawneetown, 390, 424, 425
Jones, Rice, death, 173-4
Jones, Rev. William, member of first territorial legislature, 368, entitled to land-grant, 425; notice, 270; mention, 336
Joplin, Mo., mention, 379 n
Joseph, mention, 289
Josephine, Empress, reference, 174
Jourdan, Francis, erects fort, 406
Jourdan, James, wounded by Indians, 406
Jourdan, Thomas, erects fort, 406
Journey, Fort, mention, 405
Journey's, Lieut. John, corps, and its encounter with Indians, 378-80
Journey, Nathaniel, captain of company in war of 1812, 406
Joutel, Henry, survivor of LaSalle's expedition, 37, commands soldiers in the expedition, 38, estimate of LaSalle, 39
Joy, Comfort, establishes fort, 335
Judy, Jacob, settler in Kaskaskia about 1783, 138, erects first water-mill, 176, 315, discovers bodies of McMahon family, 196, 1788 pioneer, 319, entitled to land-grant, 424, 425, mention, 357
Judy, Nancy, mention, 319
Judy, Samuel, Indian fighter, 186, 188, removal to Madison Co., 201, bravery, 320; sketch, 321-7, member first territorial legislature, 368, captain company of spies, 407, entitled to land-grant, 425, mention, 280, 319, 320
Jumonville [Coulon de], French officer, [also called Villiers de J.], 63

K.

Kane, Elias Kent, sketch, 410, mention, 372
Kankakee River, called the The-an-ke-ki, 32; mention, 247 n
Kannahwa salt-works, 110
Kansas, visited by French in search of mines, 43, mention, 265 n
Kansas River, mention, 265 n
Kaskaskia, established 1686, 40, missionaries and traders of, 41; growth about 1700, 41, flour and skins shipped from, 44, seat of British government in Ill., 46; Jesuit college in, 50, 54, metropolis of the West, 50; commerce, 51, sold in 1766, 82, captured by Americans, 93-6, inundated, 113, 114, immigrants, 115, importance, 116, American settlers, 1783, 138-9, settlers about 1783, 142-3, legislatures held at, 149, 320, largest town at West, 161, court held at, 180, county-seat Randolph County, 252, road to Fort Massac, 281; and to Vincennes, 293; land-office, mention, 326, 327, 351; constitutional convention held in, 332, gayety in 1810, 366; population, ib., capital of Illinois Territory, 367, mention, 18, 19, 46, 49, 66, 81, 87, 88, 91, 92, 93, 98, 101, 104, 107, 109, 112, 116, 117, 124, 125, 131, 138, 139, 144, 156, 157, 160, 162, 163, 164, 165, 167, 170, 172, 173, 174, 176, 185, 191, 207, 215, 218, 221, 245, 247, 249, 258, 269, 271, 272, 291, 294, 295, 296, 297, 299, 301, 303 n, 304, 306, 311, 313, 315, 319, 325, 326, 335, 339, 348, 349, 350, 352, 353, 358, 359, 360, 361, 362, 368, 385, 401 n, 410, 426
Kaskaskia Indians, location, 18; fate, 21, 22, 23, mention, 215, 304
Kaskaskia River, mention, 19, 113, 146, 181, 183, 184, 201, 215, 236, 311, 339, 356, 357, 392, 401, 408, 418
Kay, John, mention, 305, 419
Kay (John) & McCrae (David), mention, 305
Ke-kauk-kem-ke, Indian name for Peoria, 246
Kekionga, British trading-post on Maumee, 124
Kelly [Wm.], settler on Kaskaskia River, 1796, 215
Kennedy, Patrick, entitled to land-grant, 424
Kenton, Simon, sketch, 86-7, commanded detachment of Americans at Kaskaskia, 95
Kentucky, settlers from, 182, 184, 185, 191, 193, 202, 205, 264 n, 310, 333, 357, 358, 359, 360, 361, 364, 378, 379, 382, 392, 393, 395, 397, 410, 411, 414 n, mention, 83, 87, 88, 90, 91, 104, 106, 107, 130, 143 n, 172, 182, 184, 185, 192, 193, 197, 198, 202, 205, 216, 223, 238, 241, 259, 260, 269, 270, 319, 335, 343, 357, 367, 379 n, 386 n, 391, 393, 396, 411, 420
Kentucky River, mention, 217, 276
Keokuk, chief of Sac, sketch, 292-3
Keokuk, Ia., name, founding, 292
Kerlerec, Louis Billouart, Chevalier de, governor of La., 65

INDEX 443

Keys, Charles A., mention, 415 n.
Kickapoo Indians, locality, 20, 206, 244; enmity to whites, 21; mention, 80, 160, 168, 186, 201, 342, 363 n, 364.
Kidd, Robert, early settler, 112, 113, 114, 115; entitled to land-grant, 425, mention, 137, 255
Kiercereau, Pelagie, marries Pierre Chouteau, 421
Kierseran, see Kiercereau
Kincade (Kinkead), James, entitled to land-grant, 424
King, Rachael, marries Zadoc Casey, 413n.
Kingston on site of Fort Frontenac, 30.
Kinney, Andrew, mill owner, 192-3, mention, 320
Kinney, Joseph, settler of 1794, sketch, 190-2.
Kinney, Mary, marries Joseph Lemen, 412 n
Kinney, Sam'l, settler of Horse Prairie, 200
Kinney, William, incident when boy, 191, lieutenant-governor, ib , sketch, 333-5; mention, 412 n.
Kinney, Winder, settler of Horse Prairie, 200
Kinzie, Arthur M , mention, 248 n.
Kinzie, Eleanor L , mention, 248 n
Kinzie, Elizabeth, mention, 247 n
Kinzie, Ellen Marion, mention, 247 n.
Kinzie, George H , mention, 248 n
Kinzie, James, mention, 247 n.
Kinzie, John, and descendants, sketch, 247 n, mention, 247
Kinzie, John Harris, sketch, 248 n, mention, 247, ib. n
Kinzie, John Harris, Jr., mention, 248 n
Kinzie, Maria, mention, 247 n
Kinzie, Robert Allen, mention, 247 n
Kinzie, William, mention, 247 n
Kirkpatrick, Thomas, settler of Shawneetown, 390, mention, 315, 378
Kitchen, Charles, fights Indians, 407
Knox County, Ill., original boundaries. 157, representative, ib
Knox Co , Tenn , mention, 298, 312, 354
Knoxville, Tenn , mention, 311
Koerner, Gov Gustavus, mention, 289 n

L.

L'Abbe [Cahokia] Creek, mention, 426
LaBalme's [Col Moltin de] expedition to capture Detroit, 124
LaChappelle, see Chappelle
Laclede, Pierre Ligeuste, mention, 419
LaCompte, see LeCompt
LaCroix, Michael, settler of 1800, sketch, 350, born on Big Island, 355
LaFlamme, Md'lle, marriages to Sainte Ange (Pelate) in 1765, M LaCompt in 1780, and Thomas Brady, 168

LaPerouse's [Jean François de Galaup, Count de] expedition to Australia, 423.
LaSalle County, name, 39
LaSalle, Robert René Chevalier de, explorations, 29-38, death, 38, characteristics, 39, visits site of Peoria, 244, mention, 89, 304
La Trappe monks in Ill , 355-6
LaVossierre, Louis, of Peoria, tragic death of, 134-5
Lacy, Gen Edward, establishes ferry, 286
Lacy, John, settler of 1804, mention, 356, 357
Lafayette County, Wis , mention, 309 n
Lake Bigler, mention, 289 n
Lake Erie, 31
Lake Michigan, mention, 17, 31, 89, 122, 168, 394
Lake Ontario, 31
Lake Peoria, 149
Lake Superior, mention, 123, 124, 306
Lake of the Woods, 223
Lancaster County, Pa mention, 143 n.
Land system before 1800 a curse, 277-8
Lane, John, settler at Salines, 390
Laurel Hill, mention, 63
Lausanne, mention, 308, 419
Law courts, none among French, 73; first court, 1768, 74-5
Law, Judge John, mention, 423
Law, John, and his schemes, 46
Lawrenceburg, Ind., mention, 401 n
Lawyers of Illinois, early, 170, 370-2
Layola, see Loyola
LeBare des Puants, see Green Bay
LeCompt, Mad ——, sketch, 168-9, see Md'll LaFlamme.
LeCompt, Lizette, marries Louison Pensoneau, 362 n
LeCompte [Louis], 168
LeGallois de Beaujeu, see Beaujeau
LeMotte, Miss Sarah, marries Thomas Forsyth, 248, [died Nov. 21, 1829]
LePense, Antoine, mention, 249
LeVille a Maillet, old name for Peoria, 122
Lead-smelting in Ill., 48, first cupola furnace for, 171
Lebanon, Ill , mention, 197, 254 n, 267, 269, 336, ib. n
Lee County, Ill., 139 n
Lemen family, mention, 197, 207
Lemen, Ann, mention, 412 n
Lemen, Catharine, 412 n
Lemen, Hetty, mention, 412 n
Lemen, Rev James, sr , Indian fighter, 175, settler of 1786, 256, sketch, 271, notice, 411 n, 411-2; denounces slavery, 412 n; entitled to land-grant, 424, 425; mention, 196, 259, 266, 273, 357, 377.
Lemen, Mrs James, sr. (Catharine Ogle), 259.

Lemen, Rev James, jr., notice, 412 n, 413, mention, 273
Lemen, Rev Joseph, marries daughter of Joseph Kinney, sends wife to school, 191, notice, 412, mention, 266. 412 n
Lemen, Mrs Joseph (Mary Kinney), 191, 412 n
Lemen, Joseph B, mention, 412 n
Lemen, Rev Josiah, notice, 412 n
Lemen, Rev. Moses, notice, 412 n
Lemen, Robert, marshal under territorial government, 266, accident to, 271; teacher, 412
Lemen, William, notice, 412 n.
LeMoine, see Beinville, Iberville, Montigny
L-en-ni-L-en-ape Indians, 17
Leotot, ——, one of the assassinators of LaSalle, 39
Lesueur, Chas Alex, mention, 423
Levens, Henry, settler of 1797, sketch, 157-8, settles in Horse Prairie, 201; early miller, 315, entitled to land-grant, 425
Lewis (Merriweather) and Clark's (Wm) expedition visits Illinois, 356.
Lewis, Wm, entitled to land-grant, 425
Leyba, Francisco de, mention, 423
Lexington, Ky, mention, 143 n, 375.
Licking River, mention, 87
Lillard, Rev. Joseph, preacher of 1793, notice, 257-8, mention, 260, 269.
Limestone Creek, mention, 88
Lime-Stone, Ky, mention, 257.
Lincoln, Abraham, mention, 143 n, 370 n, 386 n, 415 n
Lincoln, Mrs Abraham, mention, 143 n
Lincoln County, Ky., mention, 256
Lincoln & Edmunds, mention, 254 n
Lincoln, Robert Todd, mention, 143 n
Linn, Capt. William, of Clark's expedition, 98
Litchfield, Conn, mention, 172, 253 n.
Little Muddy River, mention, 299
Little Prairie, mention, 348
Little Rock, mention, 264 n.
Little Village, mention, 256, see St. Phillipe
Little Wabash River, mention, 102, 364
Lively [John and Joseph] family, mention, 352
Liza, Emanuel, mention, 167, 208, 294
Loftus, Maj [Arthur], defeat of, 80
Loftus [Arthur] Heights or Ft Adams, 80
Logan County, Ky., mention, 391.
Logan [Tah-gah-jute], the Indian, murder of family, 83
Logan, Dr. John, notice, 386-7; sketch, ib n; descendants, 387 n
Logan, John Alexander, mention, 386 n, sketch, 387 n.
Logan, Stephen T., mention, 262 n.

Logan, William H, notice, 387 n
Logstown, Indian treaty of, 62
Loire des Ursins, Marc Antoine de la, secretary of Company of the West, 46
London, mention, 269, 305, 419, 420, 421.
Long Point, Ill, mention, 411.
Looking-Glass Prairie, mention, 326, 405
Lorton, Mr ——, mention, 357
Loubois, ——, appointed gov. of La, 54.
Louis XIV, reference to, 36, 209, 419
Louisiana, named in honor of king of France, 33; difficulty in colonizing, 44, territory, 309 n, see under St. Louis, purchase of, 356, mention, 47, 73, 110
Louisville, mention, 98, 170, 191, 218, 254 n, 342, 387 n, 393
Louisville and Evansville R R, mention, 368 n.
Low, Gen Fleming, mention, ? ⁻n
Low, Nicholas, mention, 247 n
Lower Rapids, mention, 292
Lower Sandusky, defence of, 403.
Loyola, Ignatius de, mention, 25.
Ludlow's Station, mention, 198
Lunceford (or Lunsford), George, settler of 1783, 143; one of Gen. Clark's soldiers, 339, entitled to land-grant, 424; mention, 201
Lusk, John T, builds taverns and runs ferry, 285, 286, settler of 1805, 357
Lusk's [James] Ferry, 110 miles to first house, 298, mention, 281, 285, 357
Luth, Sieur de, see Duluth
Luther, Martin, mention, 26
Lyle (or Lisle), Dr. John, early physician, notice, 359
Lyle, John, entitled to land-grant, 424.
Lynn, Dr. Lewis, death, 139 n
Lyon, Matthew, sketch, 328-9
Lyons, France, 287.

M.

McBride, William, mention, 352.
McCann, James, early miller, 315
McCarty, Capt. Richard ["English"], of Gen Clark's expedition, 102, notice, mill owner, 128; entitled to land-grant, 424
McClernand, John A, notice, 414-5; sketch, ib n, mention, 386 n.
McClernand (John A) & Keyes (Charles A.), mention, 415 n
McClure, Samuel, killed by Indians in 1786, 153.
McConnell, ——, married Mary Omelvany, 385 n
McCormick, John, entitled to land-grant, 424
McCrae, David, mention, 305, 419
McCrae, David, & Co (John Kay), mention, 305, 419.

INDEX   445

McDonald, Robert, mention, 352.
McDonough's "History of Randolph, Monroe, and Perry Counties," quoted, 366 n, 400 n
McDonough's "History of St. Clair Co.," quoted, 412 n
McDonough, Stace, of Randolph Co., 133; sketch, 216-9
McElmuny family builds block-house, 131.
McElmuny, John, Jr, entitled to land-grant, 424.
McFarland, David, of Ridge Prairie, mention, 288 n.
McHenry, William, captain of company in war of 1812, 406, 407.
McKee, Susan, marries Wm. Omelvany, 386 n
McKendree, Bp. Wm., builds first meeting-house and holds first camp-meeting, 267, mention, 268.
McKendree College, mention, 289 n, 336n, 400 n, 413 n, 414 n, 418 n.
McKillup, Mrs. Eleanor (Lytle), marries John Kinzie, 247 n
McLaughlin, Robert K., lawyer, notice, 410-1.
McLean, —— [McLain, Rev. David], attacked by Indians, 408.
McLean, John, settler of Shawneetown, 390; sketch, 391-2
McMahon, Robert, settler of 1794, sketch 193-7; settles at Horse Prairie, 200
McMahon, Mrs Robert, and her four children killed by Indians, Dec., 1795, 193-4.
McNabb, Alexander, entitled to land-grant, 425.
McNabb, Archibald, entitled to land-grant, 425.
McNabb, Edward, entitled to land-grant, 425.
McNair, Col. Alex, in Gen Howard's expedition, 408
McRae, see McCrae.
McRoberts, Elizabeth, mention, 302 n.
McRoberts, Frank H, mention, 302 n.
McRoberts, Judge James, settler of 1786, 256; sketch, 300-3; descendants, 300 n; entitled to land-grant, 425
McRoberts, James, Jr, mention, 300 n
McRoberts, Judge Josiah, sketch, 300 n; mention, 302; [died, Joliet, Ill., June 2, 1885.]
McRoberts, Josiah, Jr., 302 n.
McRoberts, Louise M, marries Edward C Aiken, 302 n.
McRoberts, Mary, marries Maj Zerses F. Trail, 300 n
McRoberts, Samuel, sketch, 301 n, 371-3, mention, 302 n, 374.
McRoberts, Thomas, 300 n.
Macarty Mactique, see MaKarty.

Macauley, Mr. ——, settler of 1809, mention, 364.
Mactique, Macarty, see MaKarty
Mackinac boats described, 234-5; mention, 26, 35, 36, 122, 168, 223, 245, 248 n, 306, 419, 420
Mackinac Indians, trading with, 233.
Mackinaw Creek, mention, 157.
Mackinaw River, mention, 20
Mackenzie, John, father of John Kinzie, 247 n
Mackenzie, Margaret, marries John Kinzie, 247 n
Macoupin Co., county-seat, 384.
Macoupin Creek, mention, 383, 407.
Mad River, Ohio, mention, 268.
Madagorda Bay, LaSalle lands at, and thus misses finding the mouth of the Mississippi River, 38.
Madison County, representatives and senators, 270, 320, 368, county commissioner, 321; judge, 329; salt manufacture in, 344; circuit-court clerk, 362; established, 367; its county-seat, 378; first court-house, ib.; sheriff, 416; treasurer, 418 n; mention, 110, 197, 239, 270, 280, 289 n, 321, 322, 336, 368, 383, 401, 417, 426.
Madison, James, mention, 367, 401 n
Madrid, Spain, mention, 139 n
Magill, Arthur, mention, 248 n.
Magill, Juliette A, mention, 248 n.
Maillet, Paulette, exploits, 122-3; selects new site for Peoria, 122, 246; mention, 126, 134, 135
Major, John, of S C., mention, 262
MaKarty, [Mactique, or Malartie, or Macartie], Chevalier, gov. of Illinois, 60.
Manscoe, see Mansker
Mansker, John, settler of Mississippi Bottom in 1806, 364
Manuel, hung for being witch, 175, ib. n.
Maple sugar manufactured, 395.
Marest, Rev. Gabriel, missionary at Kaskaskia, 41; life in Illinois, 42.
Margot Creek, mention, 59
Marietta, mention, 156
Marion County organized, 413; representative, 143 n; mention, 263, 264, 386 n.
Marion, Gen. Francis, mention, 413 n.
Marquette County, name, 39
Marquette, James (Jaques), the explorer, 25-9, death, 31
Marrs, Thos, entitled to land-grant, 424.
Marshall, John, chief-justice, mention, 84
Marshal, John, settler of Shawneetown, 390, entitled to land-grant, 424
Marshal, Rev William, mention, 269.
Martin, Charles, entitled to land-grant, 425
Mary River, mention, 304.
Maryland, settlers from, 113, 323, 341, 342, 348, 367, 401 n, 402, mention, 223.

Mascoutah, Ill , mention, 290, 363, 1b n, 399 n
Mascouten Indians, 80
Mason County, Ill , mention, 264 n
Mason's, Edward Gay. "Col. John Todd's Record Book," quoted, 175 n, 426 n
Mason, George, mention, 91.
Massac County, mention, 53.
Massac Trace, mention, 335
Massachusetts, population in 1774, 120; settlers from, 207, 330
Matheny, Charles E , notice, 261 n
Matheny, Charles R , sketch, 261-2, descendants, ib. n.
Matheny, Charles W , mention, 262 n.
Matheny, E Cook, mention, 262 n.
Matheny James H , notice, 262 n.
Matheny, L D , notice. 262 n
Matheny, Noah W , notice, 262 n.
Martinique, mention 174
Matteson, Gov. Joel A , mention, 302 n.
Mattox, Susan, marries James Rhea, 264 n
Maumee, Ohio, mention, 247.
Maumee River, mention, 77, 124, 197, 306
May, George, mention, 264 n.
Mayfield, James, entitled to land-grant, 424
Maysville, mention, 88.
Mears, William, early lawyer, sketch, 361, 372.
Membre, Zenobe, sent with dispatches to France, 37; missionary, 1690, 43
Memphis, Tenn., mention, 25
Ménard County, name, 294
Ménard, François, sketch, 294-7; mention, 291
Ménard, Hypolite, notice, 296; mention, 291, 294
Ménard, Pierre, marriage, 287; sketch, 291-4, in first territorial legislature, 368; mention, 289 n
Mengwe, name for Iroquois, 17, 18.
Mercier, François le, missionary, 1721, 51.
Merionthshire, Wales, mention, 170.
Merrimac, Mo., mention, 308.
Merrimac River, Ill., mention, 110, 347
Meroe District, Tenn , mention, 311.
Messenger, Charles, mention, 400 n
Messenger, John, teacher, 254, 273; sketch, 330-2; mention, 328, 333
Messenger's "Manual or Hand Book of Practical Surveying," reference of, 331
Methodists, churches and preachers, 207, 257, 260, 262, 263, 267, 268, 269, 390, 418 n.
Miami Indians, locality, 19; removal, 140; mention, 124, 198, 224
Miami River, mention, 198.
Michigan, name, 18, mention, 19, 141, 145, 402.
Middleton's Block-House, 405.
Middletown, Conn., mention, 248 n.

Miles, ——, mention, 186
Miles' Ferry, mention, 281, 286.
Miles, Rev Samuel J , visits Kaskaskia, 273.
Militia of St. Clair County, 189.
Milk sickness, 322-3
Miller, John, mention, 352
Miller, Maud, marries William Leman, 412 n
Miller, William, mention, 237, 313.
Mills, see under Illinois, early mills.
Mills, Benj , member of Illinois bar, 372.
Miwaukee, mention, 247 n
Mississippi Bluffs, mention, 110, 131, 210, 222, 280, 328, 348, 418
Mississippi Bottom, cultivated by French, 150; mention, 113, 304, 364, 403, 408.
Mississippi River, called Fish River, Indian name, Namæsisipu, 17; discovery by DeSoto, 25; by Marquette, ib ; called St Louis River, 33; outlets discovered, 36; called River Colbert, 37; rediscovered, named Malbouche and LaPalisade, 43; destruction by overflow, 46-50, 113-4, unvisited by British until 1765, 59, 60, 65-6; first Anglo-American settlement on, 80; navigation in 18th century, 108-9, free navigation of, 219, 220; voyaging on, 294-6, steam navigation on, 400 n; mention, 18, 21, 27, 33, 43, 47, 49, 57, 75, 80, 112, 122, 124, 125, 138, 146, 150, 157, 227, 232, 248, 266, 271, 273, 276, 293, 297, 304, 306, 307, 329, 347, 365, 385, 421, 426.
Mississippi Valley, extent and fertility, 28-9; exploration of, 33
Missouri lead-mines opened, 54; supreme court, reference, 171; first constitutional convention, 171; Roman Catholic religion established, 266, mention, 140, 141, 159, 229, 249, 268, 309 n, 348, 366 n, 386.
Missouri Compromise, introduced by Jesse B. Thomas, 402; reference, 401, 1b n
Missouri Gazette and Illinois Advertiser, reference, 366, 400 n; extracts from, 426.
Missouri Indians at war with Spaniards, 52-3.
Missouri River, called by Indians Peckitanoni, 27, its discovery, ib., Ft. Orleans erected on, 1724, 52, mention, 37, 123, 140, 362 n.
Mitchagamie Indians, 18, 22.
Mitchell family, mention, 237, 417.
Mitchell, Clark W., mention, 265 n.
Mitchell, Frances, marries Washington West, 418 n.
Mitchell, Louisa A , marries Benjamin J. West, Sr , 418 n
Mitchell, Mary, marries Tilghman H. West, 418 n.
Mitchell, Peter, notice, 337; mention, 336.

Mobile, French at, 42, 43; mention, 49, 51, 54, 56.
Mondovi, Sardinia, mention, 419
Monette's "History of the Valley of the Mississippi," quotation from, 191 n.
Monohon County, Ireland, 300.
Monongahela County, mention, 138
Monongahela River, mention, 63, 65, 236, 397 n.
Monongahela whisky, 202, 316.
Monroe Co., circuit judge, 301 n; representatives and senators, 312, 372, 374, 386 n, 400 n; clerk, 386 n; mention, 18, 47, 110, 113, 115, 131, 146, 149, 152, 175, 176, 177, 184, 255, 260, 261 n, 300, 300 n, 301 n, 312, 360, 371, 372, 374, 386 n, 400 n.
Montcalm, Gen Louis Joseph de St. Viran, Marquis de, mention, 246
Montgomery County, Ind, mention, 367, 418 n
Montgomery County, Pa, mention, 300
Montgomery, Capt and Maj. John, 92, 96, 98; settler of 1783, erects watermill, 143, visits Peoria about 1781, 245; one of Gen Clark's soldiers, 339, entitled to land-grant, 424; mention, 215.
Monticello, Ia, mention, 379 n.
Montreal, mention, 226, 227, 247, 419, 421
Montrenger, Creval du [Margry III, 90], LaSalle's nephew, assassinated, 38. See Moranget—erroneously printed
Moony, Mary, entitled to land-grant, 424
Moore family, mention, 197, 417
Moore, Andrew, and son killed by Indians, 406
Moore, James, early settler, 112, 113, 114; settler of 1781, 255; entitled to land-grant, 424, naturalization oath of, 426
Moore, Jas, jr, entitled to land-grant, 425
Moore, James Biggs, mill owner, 194, captain of company in war of 1812, 338 n, 353, 406
Moore, John, coroner, 365; entitled to land-grant, 425
Moore, John M lton, mention, 255
Moore, Col. Mi ton, mention, 300 n.
Moore, Risdon, notice, 417.
Moore, William, captain of company in Black-Hawk war, 337 n, entitled to land-grant, 425
Moore, W W, mention, 386 n
Moore's [Andrew] Prairie, mention, 406.
Moran, Miss M S., marries Thomas J. Casey, 414 n.
Moranget, nephew of LaSalle, assassinated, 38 See Montrenger
Moreau, ——, hung for being witch, 175, ib n
Moredock, see Murdoch.
Morehead, Senator James T., of Kentucky, mention, 372.

Morgan County, Ill, mention, 330.
Morgantown, mention, 236
Morris, Jemima, marries Joseph Chance, 270
Morris, Joseph, entitled to land-grant, 424.
Morris, Robert, mention, 276.
Morrison, Guy, sketch, 167.
Morrison, James, marries daughter of Francis Saucier, 287; mention, 166
Morrison, James, jr, mention, 166
Morrison, Jesse, sketch, 166-7, marries daughter of Francis Saucier, 287
Morrison, Robert, sketch, 165; represents Illinois in Indiana legislature, 293, mention, 299
Morrison, Mrs. Robert (Donaldson), sketch, 165-6.
Morrison, Samuel, sketch, 167.
Morrison, Samuel, jr, note on Senator Jesse Burgess Thomas, sr., 401 n
Morrison, William, sketch, 160-5; entitled to land-grant, 425; mention, 167.
Moscow, mention, 214.
Moulin, John de, judge of Illinois under Northwestern Territory, 180, 209-11
Mount Vernon, Ill, founding of, 413 n; mention, 265
Mount Vernon, Ohio, mention, 402 n.
Muddy River, mention, 321
Mun, de, see DeMun
Murdoch, Barney, mention, 146
Murdoch (or Moredock), Maj. John, enmity against Indians, 138, sketch, 146-50, major in Gen. Howard's expedition, 408, entitled to land-grant, 425, 290.
Murdoch (or Murdict), John, mention, 202, eccentricities of, 238-41
Murdoch (or Murdict), Mr ——, mention, 202, 238.
Murdoch (or Murdict), Mrs ——, widow, marries Geo. Blair, 202, 238
Murdoch, Mrs John (Garrison), 149
Murdoch, Widow (——), mother of John and Barney, killed by Indians, 138.
Murpheysboro, Ill, mention, 387 n
Murphy family, mention, 298
Murphy Settlement, mention, 299.
Murray, William, entitled to land-grant, 424, 425; mention, 260.
Music, Mr ——, of Mo., mention, 349.
Musick family, mention, 185.
Musick, Wm, settler about 1783, 142, 185.

N.

Namæsisipu, see Mississippi
Napoleon I. (Bonaparte), mention, 25, 39, 75, 214, 403, 423.
Nashville, Ill, mention, 336, 379 n
Nashville, Tenn, mention, 110, 114, 311.
Natchez, mention, 163.
Naturalization Record, earliest in Ill, 426.

448   PIONEER HISTORY OF ILLINOIS.

Nebuchadnezzar, mention, 63
Negro slaves introduced into Illinois in 1719, 47
Nelson County, Ky, mention, 259
Nelson, Elisha, entitled to land-grant, 425
Nelson, Lord Horatio, mention, 374
New Berlin, mention, 264 n, 265 n
Newby's, Col Edward W B, regiment in Mexican war, 289 n, 387 n
New Design, settled 1782, 146, settlers of 1797, 235-6, great mortality, 237, mention, 152, 157, 162, 181, 184, 190, 191, 192, 193, 195, 196, 200, 201, 205, 236, 255, 256, 257, 258, 259, 265, 270, 271, 315, 319, 328, 335, 337, 358, 359, 373, 379 n, 413
New-Englanders nicknamed "Bostonians," 92, 93
New Hampshire, population in 1774, 120
New Harmony, Ind, 423
New Jersey, population in 1774, 120; settlers from, 216, 399, mention, 155, 216, 399 n.
New Madrid, mention, 161
Newman [Joseph ?], settler about 1804, 356
New Minden, Ill, mention, 379 n.
New Orleans, laid out, 46, trade with Ill, 108, 346, 401, flat-boating to, 385 n, mention, 49, 51, 56, 57, 67, 107, 108, 110, 111, 127, 161, 162, 163, 211, 273, 296, 396, 423.
Newspaper, first in Illinois, 366
New York, population in 1774, 120; settlers from, 223, 410, mention, 110
New-York City, mention, 223, 247 n.
Niagara River once had its outlet into the Illinois River, 34, mention, 31
Niles, Col Nathaniel, mention, 189 n
Nine-Mile Creek, mention, 125, 215, 341
Nixon, Capt. ——, mention, 253 n
Noble, Henry, settler in 1804, 357
North America, mention, 113, 121.
North Bend, home of Gen Harrison, 278
North Carolina, population in 1774, 120, settlers from, 80, 339, 391, 416; mention, 80, 156, 185, 203, 267, 270, 338, 390, 398, 413 n, 416
Northwestern Territory, organized, 154-5, 156-7, legislature, 157, 343; courts organized, 179, 180-1 mention, 114, 117, 170, 350
Nowlen, Rev J, mention, 268

O

Oakland, Cal, mention, 386 n
Ogle family, mention, 197, 201, 260, 314
Ogle, Benjamin, shot by Indians, 153; Indian scout, 175; entitled to land-grant, 425, mention, 412 n
Ogle, Catharine, marries James Lemen, sr., 271.

Ogle, Joseph, sr, Indian scout, 175, first Methodist class-leader, 257, mention, 255, 260, 261, 271, entitled to land-grant, 425.
Oglesby, Dr Joseph [should be Ogle], 261.
Oglesby, Joshua, member first territorial legislature, 368
Oglesby, Richard J., U-S senator, 387, governor, 400; mention, 302
Oglesby, Wm, entitled to land-grant, 425
O'Hara family, mention, 207
O'Hara, Henry, entitled to land-grant, 424
Ohio, mention, 34, 87, 145, 273
Ohio Co, established, 61, mention, 63
Ohio River, unknown for many years, 27, explored, 53; called River of the Iroquois, ib, chief ferries across, 281, mention, 17, 19, 27, 43, 67, 79, 80, 86, 87, 112, 117, 125, 129, 143 n, 145, 157, 191, ib. n, 197, 207, 217, 218, 236, 243, 271, 276, 277, 280, 287, 300 n, 301, 319, 335, 343, 365, 385, 386, 405
Ohio salines, 110, 335, 364, 392
Omelvany, Constantine, notice, 386 n.
Omelvany, Edward, notice, 386 n.
Omelvany, Elizabeth, mention, 386 n.
Omelvany, George, mention, 386 n
Omelvany, Harvey K S, notice, 386 n
Omelvany, James M., notice, 386 n
Omelvany, John, notice, 385 n, descendants, 386 n
Omelvany, Margaret, marries Mr Wood, 386 n
Omelvany, Martha, mention, 386 n.
Omelvany, Mary, marries —— McConnell, 385 n, mention, 386 n
Omelvany, Nancy, marries W W Moore, 386 n
Omelvany, Patrick, mention, 385 n, 386 n
Omelvany, Samuel, notice, 385-6, ib n, 389
Omelvany, Susan, mention, 386 n
Omelvany, Wm, 385 n, descendants, 386 n
Omelvany, William W, notice, 386 n
Orange County, N C, mention, 339.
Ordinance of 1787, 154-5
Oregon County, Mo, mention, 264 n
Orr, William, printer of St Louis, 331
Orvis, E, mention, 264 n
Osage Indians, hostilities of, 160; mention, 43
Ottawa, Ill, mention, 418.
Ouiatenon, mention, 80, 98, 102, 198.
Ouisconsin, Portage of, 420
Owen, Hannah, mention, 143 n
Owen, Robert, mention, 423
Owen's Station, 184, 265

P.

Paget, see Pagi
Pagi, Prix, killed by Indians, 60; mention, 116.

INDEX. 449

Pagon, David, one of Gen. Clark's soldiers, 339; entitled to land-grant, 424, 425; mention, 340.
Paine, Sarah, marriage to John M. Peck, 253 n.
Painted Rock, discovery, 27; how it looked in 1823, ib n
Palatine land-office, 372 n.
Palmyra, ruins of, reference, 177.
Papin, Joseph M , mention, 421
Parke, Benjamin, mention, 401 n.
Paris, treaty of, 65, 119, 121, mention, 36, 47, 73.
Paris, Ky., mention, 403.
Parrish, W. H., circuit judge, 388 n.
Parsons, Sam'l Holden, U.-S. judge, 156.
Pate, John, mention, 265 n
Pate, Mathew, mention, 265 n
Patterson, Rev Josiah, mention, 268
Patoka, Ill., mention, 264 n
Pawnee Indians, mention, 43, 52.
Pecan, Kickapoo chief, 187, 188.
Peck, Asa, mention, 253 n.
Peck, Eli Payne, mention, 253 n.
Peck, Hannah F , mention, 253 n
Peck, Harvey T., mention, 253 n
Peck, James A., mention, 253 n
Peck, Jas. H., lawyer, of Peck & Taylor, (John), 426.
Peck, Rev. John Mason, letter to Gov. Reynolds, portrait, 254-5; sketch, ib n, 416; mention, 385.
Peck, John Q. A , mention, 253 n.
Peck, Martha, mention, 253 n
Peck, Mary Ann, mention, 253 n
Peck, Deacon Paul, mention, 253 n.
Peck, William E , mention, 253 n
Peck's "Guide for Emigrants," "Gazetteer of Illinois" (2d edition), "New Map of Illinois," reference to, 254 n
Pelate, see Saint Ange
Pendleton, Edward, mention, 120
Pennsylvania, population in 1774, 120; settlers from, 90, 138, 143, 158, 160, 165, 172, 269, 300, 360, 373, 410; mention, 79, 83, 86, 91, 95, 125, 155, 156, 157, 197, 276, 390.
Pensoneau, Augustine, mention, 290, 390.
Pensoneau, Augustine, jr., mention, 363 n.
Pensoneau, Bridget, marries Amable Tramble, 362 n
Pensoneau, Charles, mention, 363 n
Pensoneau, Edward, mention, 363 n
Pensoneau, Edward, jr., mention, 363 n.
Pensoneau, Etienne, marries Mad. Perry, 290 n; mention, 362, ib. n; notice, 363; lays out Jacksonville, St. Clair Co., and advertises land, 426.
Pensoneau, Felicite, marries Narcisse Pensoneau, 363 n; mention, 290 n.
Pensoneau, François (1), mention, 363 n.
Pensoneau, François (2), mention, 363 n.
Pensoneau, Laurent, notice, 363 n.
Pensoneau, Louis, and his descendants, 362-3 n; mention, 290 n.
Pensoneau, Louis F., mention, 290 n.
Pensoneau, Louis Perry mention, 362-3 n.
Pensoneau, Louisa, marries Trotier, 362 n
Pensoneau, Louison, and his descendants, 362-3; sketch, 364; mention, 290 n
Pensoneau, Marie, marries John Valentine, 362 n
Pensoneau, Narcisse, and descendants, 363 n.
Pensoneau, Paschal, notice, 363 n
Pensoneau, Wm Bissel, mention, 363 n.
Pequea, Pa , mention, 143 n.
Perry, Commodore Oliver Hazard, mention, 264 n
Perry, Adelaide, marries Adam W Snyder, 288 n
Perry, Harriet, marries Louis Pensoneau, 290 n, 362 n.
Perry, Jean Francis, settler of 1792, 287-91, judge, 209; mention, 362 n.
Perry, Mad Jean François, marries Augustine Pensoneau, 290 n, 363 n
Perryman, Dr. James L , mention, 337 n.
Peoria, established 1686, 40; supposed copper mines near, 48, founding of, 122; greatest trading-post in Mississippi Valley, 233; early history of, 244-6; oldest settlement in Illinois, 246; raid on by Thos. E. Craig, 251; campaign against, 382; expedition, 402; mention, 21, 34, 41, 127, 134, 213, 222, 239, 248, 249, 250, 251, 350, 362, 364, 377.
Peoria Indians, location, 18; killed Pontiac, 75; mention, 23.
Peoria Lake, encampment on, 408-9, mention, 32, 320, 354
Peters, John, entitled to land-grant, 424
Petersburg, Va., mention, 267.
Petosi, Mo., mention, 171.
Pettit [Jonathan], mention, 215.
Phelps, ——, settler of 1805, 336
Philadelphia, mention, 119, 121, 155, 160, 165, 170, 246, 254 n, 276, 287, 300, ib n, 361, 422.
Phillip, Capt. John, U.S.A., mention, 409.
Phillips, David, sketch, 338-9.
Physicians of Illinois, early, 358-60
Piankeshaw Indians, location, 19; mention, 98, 340
Picardy, mention, 47.
Pichawillany, British trading-post, destroyed, 62.
Pickett, see Piggott
Piggot's [James] Fort, mention, 342
Piggot, James, builds block-house, 131; settler about 1780, 137; settlers at Kaskaskia about 1783, 142, settler of 1781, 255, one of Gen. Clark's soldiers, 339; entitled to land-grant, 424

Piggot, Jonas, entitled to land-grant, 425
Piggot, Levi, entitled to land-grant, 425
Piggot, Wm., entitled to land-grant, 425.
Pike, Zebulon, as subaltern, U S A., 221
Pillars, James, settler of 1797, 125
Pincenneau, see Pensoneau.
Pine Bluff, A k., mention, 263 n, 264 n
Pinet [François or Pierre], Father, missionary at Cahokia, 41.
Pioneer, The, 2d paper of St. Clair Co., 254 n.
Pioneers, characteristics, 85; life in Illinois, 135-6
Pittsburg, Gen. Clark receives powder at, 88; three companies raised for the expedition, 91, treaty at, 155: mention, 50, 62, 63, 65, 91, 161, 162, 248 n, 319
Platin Creek, Mo., mention, 382.
Point a la Pierre, location, 362 n.
Polk, James Knox, 289 n.
Pollock, Oliver, agent for United States at New Orleans, 107.
Pont-au-Sable, Jean Baptiste, mention, 417
Pontiac, sketch, 75-9; death, 23, ability, ib
Pontotoc County, Miss., mention, 58.
Pope County, established, 367; representative, 390, name, 394, mention, 335, 385 n, 389, 390, 393
Pope, John, of Kentucky, mention, 394
Pope, Nathaniel, secretary of Illinois T'y and acting governor, 365; sketch, 393-5, mention, 273, 396
Porter, John, Indian scout, 175, 186
Posey, Thos., settler of Shawneetown, 390
Posey's, Alexander, brigade in Black-Hawk war, 414 n
Postlewait, John, bravery at battle of Tippecanoe, 163-4
Potomac, Va., mention, 286.
Pottawatomies, location, power, 19; at Au Sable, 250; mention, 168, 198, 224, 249, 250, 418.
Potts, Mr ——, mention, 286.
Poupart, Miss Margaret, marries John Hay, 227
Poure, Eugene, mention, 420.
Powers, Geo., entitled to land-grant, 425
Prairie flies, 395
Prairie Fort, mention, 263
Prairie du Chien, position, name, 150-1; settlers, 151-2 Indian trade at, 212, 233, captured by Brit'h, 1814, 409; mention, 161, 163, 211, 227, 248 n, 404, 420.
Prairie-du-Long Creek, 184, 194.
Prairie du Pont, location, 51; in 1763, 67; inundated, 114; founding of, 129, mill at, 287; mention, 89, 128, 290, 348, 355
Prairie du Rocher, settlement destruction, 50; inundated, 114; court held at, 180, 181; mention, 49, 138, 192, 196, 214, 295, 296, 368, 369.
Prairie-fires, 231-2.

Prairies, cause of, 231-2
Prairie Tamarawas, name, 206
Prairie Tammarais, see Twelve-Mile Prairie.
Pratte, Bernard, mention, 421.
Presbyterian churches and ministers, 166, 256, 272, 353.
Price, ——, killed by Indians, 404.
Primm, John, settler of 1803, sketch, 328.
Prince, ——, judge in Ky., mention, 298.
Prince-Edwards Co., Va., mention, 411.
Princeton, battle of, reference, 156.
Procter's [Gen. Henry A.] army of 1813, 36
Prophet, the (Tecumseh's brother), notice, 403
Pruit, Abraham, settler 1804, mention, 354
Pruit, Col. James, skirmish with Indians, 404, 409
Pruit, Solomon, early miller, 315.
Pulaski Co., representative, 414 n; mention, 419
Pulliam, John, settler near Bellefontaine, 182; sketch, 184.
Pulliam, Mary, marries James Lemen, jr., 412 n.
Pulliam, Robert, anecdote of, 349.
Pulsifer, Joseph, mention, 265 n
Pulsifer, Nevi, mention, 265 n.
Pulsifer, Nevo, mention, 265 n
Pursley, Mrs. ——, bravery, 381.
Pyle, Addison, mention, 336 n.

Q.

Quakers, mention, 386.
Quebec, mention, 25, 28, 30, 44, 52, 57, 155, 225, 247, ib n, 291, 347
Queenstown, Canada, mention, 221.
Quentine Creek, mention, 314, 315, 355.
Quentine Mound, rendezvous of Indians, 168.
Quentine Village, 355.
Quick, Aaron, notice, 399 n, 400 n.
Quick, Amy, marries Charles Messenger, 400 n.
Quick, Edwin, mention, 400 n
Quick, Isaac, sketch, 399-400 n
Quick, Lucretia, marries Geo. Allen, 400 n.
Quick, Mary, marries Cornelius Rettinghaus, 400 n
Quick, Moses, builds first flat-boat, 399-401; early miller, 400 n; sketch, ib.
Quick, Orlando T., mention, 400 n.
Quick, Rhoda, marries George Harrison, 400 n
Quick, Sarah, marries Henry Allyn, 400 n
Quick, Thomas, mention, 399 n, 400 n
Quincy land-office, 384, mention, 408.

R.

Raikes, Robert, mention, 136
Rain, Abraham, entitled to land-grant, 425

INDEX 451

Rains, Misses, marry two Mr Whitesides, 189, ib n
Rallings, Moses M , settler of Shawneetown, 390.
Rancé, Abbé Armand Jean le Bouthilier de, notice, 355–6
Randle, Rev Josiah, local preacher, 269
Randleman, Martin, mention, 313.
Randolph, Gov Beverly, county named for, 252
Randolph County, judge, 197, 300, organized, boundaries, 252; sheriff, 358, 411; settlements, 364; senators and representatives, 368, 410, mention, 48, 125, 128, 143, 181, 197, 261, 289 n, 293, 304, 327 n, 336, 341, 356, 360, 364, 367, 368, 385 n, 418
Randolph, Edmund, clerk of Virginia House, 99
Randolph, John, of Va , mention, 151
Randolph, Peyton, president Continental Congress, 119
Raper, Daniel, Indian scout, 175, entitled to land-grant, 425
Rasles, Sebastian, missionary, 42; murdered in Illinois, ib
Ratcliff, ——, settler about 1804, 357.
Ratcliff, Chance, settles at Horse Prairie, 200, 357
Rattan, Thomas, mention, 357
Rattan's Prairie, mention, 240, 270
Reading, Pa , mention, 289 n
Reagan, Mrs Reason, and six children killed by Indians, 409.
Ribourde, Gabriel de la, missionary, 43
Rector family, sketch, 353, 354
Rector, John, early lawyer, notice, 360
Rector, Nelson, bravery of, 353–4, early surveyor, 354
Rector, Stephen, notice, 353
Rector, Thomas, duel of, 354
Rector, Col Wm , early contractor, 331, notice, 353–4; mention, 407.
Reddick, ——, killed by Indians, 154
Red River, Tenn , notice, 223, 298
Red-Stone Fort, now Brownsville, Pa , mention, 138, 373
Reed, ——, see Emsley Jones, 304
Reed, Col John (of Jackson Co), mention, 74
Renault, Philip François, agent of French mining company, 47, his mechanics a great acquisition, 48, smelting of lead by, ib ; mention, 305
Rettinghous, Cornelius, mention, 400 n
Revolutionary war, begun and ended at West, 84; notice, 118–22, reference to, 145, 184, 203, 245.
Reynolds, Gov John, hatred of British, 67; reminiscence of Jarrot, 213; of a prairie fire, 232; commissioner of Rock Island treaty, 293; witnesses executions, 304, governor, appoints S Judy warden of State penitentiary, 322, a U -S ranger, 338; appointed Thomas Ford prosecuting-attorney, 375, writes of old courts, 378, a member of Judy's company of spies, 407, sergeant in Whiteside's company, 408, mention, 289 n, 370, 413 n
Reynolds' (John) "My Own Times," reference to, 381 n
Reynolds, Robert, father of John Reynolds, represents Illinois in Indiana Territorial Legislature, 293, settler of 1800; 298, sketch, 300; mention, 189
Reynolds, Robert, jr , marries daughter of Wm B Whitesides, 189 n
Reynolds, Thomas, member of Illinois bar, 372
Reynolds, Dr Wm L , early physician, sketch, 358–9.
Rhea, Eliza, marries Richard Rhea, 264 n
Rhea, Elizabeth, marries Geo. May, 264 n
Rhea, James, mention, 264 n
Rhea, James, jr , mention, 264 n
Rhea, Jehoida, marries Jno Foutch, 264 n; descendants, 264-5 n
Rhea, Richard, mention, 264 n
Rhea, Thos F , and descendants, 265 n; mention, 264 n
Rhea, William, mention, 264 n
Rhode Island, population, 1774, 120
Richland, Ill , mention, 269
Richland County, senators and representatives, 413 n
Richland Creek, location, 338 , Baptist church at, 412 n, mention, 184, 194, 400 n.
Richmond, Va , mention, 276.
Richview, Ill , mention, 263 n, 264 n, 379 n
Rider, Nancy Ann, marries John K Simpson, 269
Ridge Prairie, mention, 289 n, 314, 411 n, 412 n
Riggs, Rev Hosea, early preacher, sketch, 260, miller, 315; mention, 206
Right, Capt Toliver, killed by Indians, 487 See Wright
Riley, Daniel, miller, 50, 60
River Mary, mention, 364
Riverside, Ill , mention, 248
Riviere des Peres, mention, 306, 308
Roanoke, mention, 80
Robb, William, early miller, 214
Roberts, Wm., settler near Bellefontaine, 205
Robins, Chas., entitled to land-grant, 424
Robins, William, entitled to land-grant, 424, 425
Rocheblave, Philip François de Rastel, Chevalier de, lieut -gov [?] and commander at Fort Gage [Kaskaskia?], 92, captured, 95, 143 n, 144, sent a prisoner to Virginia, 96, mention, 85

452   PIONEER HISTORY OF ILLINOIS.

Rochelle, France, French fleet fitted out at, 37
Rochester, John Wilmot, Earl of, mention, 223
Rock Fort, mention, 32
Rock-House Creek, mention, 192, 330
Rock Island, treaty of, 293; engagements with Indians at, 353-4, 409, mention, 21, 292.
Rock-Island County, clerk, 362
Rock River, mention, 20, 95, 141, 192, 247 n
Rock Spring, location, 254 n, its seminary the first in the State, 254 n; mention, 253 n, 255, 331, 416
Rockville, Ia., mention, 253 n
Rocky Mountains, mention, 44, 105, 122, 161, 167, 208, 226
Rogers, Benj., entitled to land-grant, 425
Rogers, Capt John, of Clark's expedition, 102
Rogers, Mrs R., entit'd to land-grant, 425
Rogers, Maj. Robert, mention, 77
Roman Catholic churches, etc., 55, 164, 165, 215, 230, 266 See Catholic
Rose, Dr. James, settled at Kaskaskia in 1805, 359
Rotrou, I., Count of Perche, founder of LaTrappe Order, 355
Rountree, Allen, mention, 379 n
Rountree, Mary B., marries John Vincent Boucher 379 n.
Royal Highlanders, mention, 65, 74.
Runyon, Lucretia, marries Isaac Quick, 399 n
Rush, Dr. Benjamin, mention, 170, 290
Russell, Edward, mention, 263 n.
Russell, John, reference to, 27 n.
Russell, J K., mention, 263 n
Russell, Thomas, mention 263 n
Russell, William, in command at Fort Massac, 221, colonel of ten companies of rangers, 405, mention, 407
Russia, mention, 214
Rutherford County, N C., mention, 395.
Rutherford, Larkin (or Larken), early settler, 112, mention, 113, 115, 137, 255, 272, 412 n, entitled to land-grant, 424, 425
Rutland, Vt., mention, 264 n, 265 n
Rutledge, John, mention, 120
Ryan, Catharine, entitled to land-grant, 424, 425
Ryan, Josiah, Indian scout, 175; builds water-mill, 177; entitled to land-grant, 424, 425
Ryan's [Josiah] Creek, mention, 252

S.

Sac and Fox Indians, mention, 249, 252, 292, 293.
Sack, John, entitled to land-grant, 425
Sainte Ange, or Pelate, and wife, settlers at Chicago about 1765, 168
Saline River, mention, 19, 43
Salines, settlers at, 390.
Salt Creek, mention, 244
Salt River, Ky., mention, 257
Salt springs, early, of Illinois, 109-10
Sandusky, Ohio, mention, 86, 247 n
Sandwich, Canada, mention, 248 n.
Santa Fé, Spanish expedition from, 52.
San Francisco, mention, 289 n, 362 n
Sangamon County, organization, 261 n, county clerk, ib., 262 n, judge, 262 n, representatives ("Long Nine"), 370 n, mention, 244, 247 n, 264 n, 337 n, 374
Sangamon River, mention, 20, 186, 242, 407
San Jose, Cal., mention, 386 n
Sargeant, Winthrop, Gov. St Clair's secretary, 156
Sarpy & Co., John P., mention, 362 n
Saucier, Adelaide, marries Jean François Perry, 288, ib n
Saucier, Brigitte, 421
Saucier, Jean François, notice, 286, sons-in-law, 287
Saucier, Jean Bte., notice, 286, 287; mention, 288
Saucier, Margaret, marries Edward Pensoneau, 363 n
Saucier, Matthieu, notice, 287; mention, 363 n
Saugrain, Dr. Anthony F., of St Louis, inoculates for small-pox, 313
Sauk Indians, western immigration, 21; mention, 20, 127
Saunders, John, of Kaskaskia, guide of American army, 93.
Savage's Ferry, location, 251; mention, 245
Savannah, Ga., mention, 248 n.
Schneider, John Henry, of London, mention, 421
Schook, Samuel, early miller, 315, mention, 206
School-houses, early, 357-8
Scioto River, campaign to the, 83, 84; mention, 319
Scotland, settlers from, 152, 155, 260, 300
Scott, Gen Charles, expedition against Indians, 198, mention, 397 n
Scott County, Ky., mention, 385, 395
Scott, James, entitled to land-grant, 425
Scott, Wm., sketch, 205-7, mention, 377
Scott, Gen Winfield, commissioner for treaty at Rock Island, 293; mention, 291
Scripps, Rev John, mention, 268
Seely, Sam'l John, first American schoolmaster in Illinois, 152
Selkirk's [Thomas, Earl of] Settlement, mention, 223

INDEX. 453

Semple, James, private, in Black-Hawk War, 289 n, U.-S senator, 1b
Senat, Antoine, a monk, burnt to death by Indians, 58
Seneca Indians, 86
Senegal, M. ——, kills P Maillet, 123
Severns, Ebenezer, entitled to land-grant, 425.
Sevier, Ambrose H , U.-S. senator from Arkansas, 372
Seybold, Robert, one of Gen. Clark's soldiers, 339
Seybold family, mention, 314.
Shannon, William, trader of Ste Genevieve, 396, 397
Sharp, ——, Indian trader, 248.
Shawnee Indians, location, 19; mention, 84, 140, 198, 285
Shawneetown, visited by Col George Croghan, 79 ; ferry at, 368 n, name, early prominent settlers, 390, countyseat, 392, mention, 19, 218, 253 n, 273, 368, 387 n, 391, 397 n, 398, 414 n, 410
Shelby County, Ky , mention, 382
Sherman, Roger, mention, 120
Sherwood's horse-mill, 264 n
Shields, James, mention, 386 n.
Shiloh, mention, 267, 268
Shiloh College, mention, 387 n.
Shoal Creek, skirmish at, 186, 187, mention, 110, 270, 320, 404
Shoemaker, Catharine (Myers), mention, 302 n
Shoemaker, Gertrude Helmer, marries Judge Josiah McRoberts, 302 n
Shoemaker, Robert, mention, 302 n
Shook, Mrs. Margaret, widow, marries John Boucher, 379 n, mention, 336
Shook, Solomon, mention, 236 379 n
Short, Capt Jacob, settler near Bellefontaine, 205, company of rangers, mention, 338 n, 378 n, 406, member of first legislature, Illinois Territ'y, 368; builds first flat-boat, 399-401; mention, 377
Shuff, James, mention, 265 n
Shultz, Daniel, entitled to land-grant, 425
Shurtleff, Benjamin, gift to Shurtleff College, 254 n
Shurtleff [Benj] College, mention, 254 n
Silver Creek, name, 48, settlements, 336; block-house, 405; mention, 110, 174, 195, 270, 337, 364, 378
Simpson, Nancy Ann (Ryder), mention, 412 n
Simpson, Rev Gideon, mention, 270
Simpson, Rev. John K , sketch, 269- 70, entitled to land-grant, 424, 425
Singleton [Edward], of Tate & S , millers, mention, 346
Sink, Daniel, entitled to land grant, 425.
Sipp, ——, killed by Indians, 258

Six-Mile Prairie, early settlers, name, 280, mention, 315, 355, 357
Six Nations, hostile to British, 53.
Slab Spring, location, 114
Slavery agitation in Illinois, reference to, 254 n See Negroes.
Small-pox ravages, 1801, 312, inoculation for, 313
Smith, Ashford, marries Hannah F. Peck, 253 n, printer of Alton, 234 n
Smith, Christopher, entitled to landgrant, 425
Smith, Rev Daniel, visits Kaskaskia, 1814, 273
Smith, Daniel D , murdered by S H Winchester, 301 n
Smith, Elijah, entitled to land-grant, 424; mention, 215
Smith, Henry, entitled to land-grant, 424, mention, 215
Smith, Rev. James, sketch, 256-7; mention, 272
Smith, Nicholas, entitled to land-grant, 424, 425
Smith [Peter], settler in American Bottom, 1801, 357.
Smith, Peter (Dutch Pete), anecdote of, 258-9, entitled to land-grant, 424
Smith, Samuel G , marries Mary Ann Peck, 253 n
Smith, Maj William B , raises American troops for the frontier, 91
Snyder, Adam Wilson, sketch, 288-9 n mention, 363 n
Snyder, Frederick Adam, sketch, 289 n
Snyder, Dr. John Francis, 289 n.
Snyder, Hon Wm H , sketch, 289 n
Sorel, on the St Lawrence, mention, 155
Sougrin, see Saugrain.
South Carolina, population of, 1774, 120, settlers from, 241, 352, 398; mention, 156, 263, 264, 357, 386 n
South-Farms, Conn , mention, 253 n
Spain, jealous of French colonization of Illinois, 52, mention, 139 n, 220
Spaniards open Upper Louisiana to settlers, 297-8
Spanish country, all west of Mississippi, 281
Spanish Pond, Mo , mention, 266
Spottswood, Gov. Alexander, of Virginia, mention, 61
Sprigg, Judge Wm , 371, 402, mention, 365.
Springfield, Ill , mention, 143 n, 261, 336 n, 370 n, 404, 407, 415 n
Squires, Amos, settler at Six-Mile Prairie, 357
St Ange de Belle Rive, Louis, French governor of Illinois, 60, last French governor, 74; mention, 80 [Died Dec. 27, 1774, aged 73]

St. Anthony, mention, 33.
St Anthony's Falls, visited by Hennepin, 33, mention, 108, 123, 124.
St Charles, Mo , nicknamed *Petite Cote*, 82; mention, 166, 253 n, 254.
St. Charles County, Mo , 426
St. Clair, Gen Arthur, governor Northwest Territory, 117; visits Kaskaskia, organizes territorial government, 144, 179; sketch, 155-7; expedition against Indians, 198-9; defeat, ib , 216-7, 277; acquitted by court-martial, 199-200; unpopular, 276; mention, 21, 128, 228, 277
St. Clair, Arthur, jr., candidate for Congress from Northwest Territory, 157
St. Clair County, judges, 114, 209, 214, 228, 290, 329, 344, 359, 360, senators and representatives, 148, 149, 289 n, 332, 335, 344, 368, 417, organization, name, original boundaries, 157, judiciary organized, 179, 180; sheriffs, 224, 312, 343, 377; treasurer, 228, Tunkers colony in, 273; settlements, 364, county-seat, 377-8; mention, 18, 48, 114, 115, 128, 190, 197, 252, 253 n, 254 n, 260, 261, 270, 274, 331, 337 n, 356, 361, 367, 385, 399, ib. n, 400 n, 401 n, 412 n, 418, ib. n, 426.
St. Clair, Wm , clerk of St. Clair County Court, 157, 180
St Francis River, mention, 299
St François, Antoine, at Peoria, 1765, 246
St. Gemme, see Bauvais
Ste. Genevieve, started, 82; nicknamed *Misster*, ib , salines, 140; mention, 43, 110, 138 n, 139, 140, 161, 168, 173, 214, 259, 299, 396.
St Helena, mention, 75.
St Jean, Peter, mention, 407.
St Joseph, founded, 89; called Cow Pens, ib ; captured by Americans, 90, 122 3; expedition against, fitted out at St Louis, 126-7, mention, 245, 247 n, 248
St. Joseph River, mention, 32, 37
St Laurent, ——, commander of French company, 59
St. Lawrence River, mention, 155
St Louis, founded, 82, 308, 419, nicknamed "Pain Court," 82, expedition against, 123-4; land titles at, 165, see Zenoe Trudeau, 266; Louisiana transferred to the U. S at, 306 n, ferry, 363; university, 418, mention, 74, 80, 101, 110, 113, 114, 124, 138, 161, 171, 184, 188, 192, 205, 218, 221, 228, 229, 230, 232, 249, 250, 252, 253 n, 254 n, 265 n, 266, 272, 273, 280, 290 n, 306, 309, ib n, 327, 331, 333, 349, 354, 356, 362 n, 363 n, 366 n, 369, 373, 400 n, 415 n, 418, see memoir of C Gratiot, 419-23, 426
St. Louis County, mention, 382, 426.

St Louis and Northwestern Railroad, builders of, 368 n
St Mary's College, Mo., mention, 302 n.
St Peter's River, mention, 43, 227.
St. Philips, Ill., founded 1719, 47, population diminishing, 125, called "Little Village," 347; mention, 49, 288 n.
St Sulpice Mission, near Cahokia, 74; mention, 129, 287.
St. Vincent, mention, 350
Stafford, Va., mention, 328
Stanberry, Mo., mention, 329 n
Standlee, Joseph, entitled to land-grant, 424.
Stanley, Abraham, entitled to land-grant, 425.
Stark, Julia A., marries John Rhea, 264 n.
Starling, see Stirling
Starr [Henry], member of Illinois bar, 372
Starved Rock, tradition of, unknown to Indians, 34
Steagall, Moses, vengeance on, 286.
Steele, John, mention, 364
Stephenson, Col Benj., in Gen. Howard's expedition, 408; notice, 411, mention, 407.
Sterling, see Stirling.
Stillman, Gen. Joshua, battle with Indians, reference, 141.
Stillman, Jas., entitled to land-grant, 425
Stirling, Capt. (Sir) Thomas, first Briton to visit Upper Mississippi, 65-6, takes possession of Illinois for British Government, 74.
Stockton, Jas., settler 1804, mention, 354
Stokes family, mention, 386.
Stokes' Settlement, mention, 386
Stony Point, battle of, reference, 183
Stookey, Abraham, mention, 236.
Stookey, Daniel, mention, 236, 313.
Strasburg, mention, 288.
Street, Joseph M , settler of Shawneetown, 390
Stuart, Alexander, judge, 365, resident of Prairie du Rocher, 369
Stuart, Alonzo C., lawyer, notice, 410
Stuart (John Todd), Edwards (Benj S), & Brown (Christopher C), of Springfield, mention, 370 n.
Stuart, John Todd, mention, 143 n. [died, Springfield, Ill , Nov 28, 1885, aged 78 years, 18 days]
Stuart, Rev Robert, see Hannah Todd, 143 n.
Stubblefield, Thomas, mention, 357.
Sueur, M C le, exploration of, 43.
Sugar-cane, introduced into La , 64
Sugar Creek, mention, 195, 337 n.
Sugar-Creek Bottom, 409
Sugar Loaf, near Cahokia, 201
Sullivan, John, entitled to land grant, 424.
Sumner County, Tenn , mention, 413 n.

INDEX. 455

Sumpter, Gen Thomas, mention, 413 n.
Swanwick, Col. Frank, mention, 327 n
Switzerland, settlers from, 209, 305, 419
Sybold, Robert, of Kaskaskia, about 1783, 142-3; entitled to land-grant, 424, 425
Sycamore Creek, mention, 141
Symmes, Judge John Cleves, father-in-law of Gen Harrison, 277, mention, 156; judge of U.-S. court at Cahokia, 182.

T.

Tafia, drinking, 203, 316
Talbot, Benj., early miller, 315, member of first legislature, Illinois Terr'y, 368
Tallahatchie River, mention, 56
Tallyrand-[Périgord, Prince Charles Maurice de], mention, 403.
Talon, Jean, intendant of Canada, 25.
Tammarais, Indian location, 18, 19; tradition of, 206, mention, 50.
Taneytown, mention, 348
Tannahill, Jas, Belleville hotel-keeper, 378
Taumur de la Source, Dominic, missionary at Cahokia, 51
Tate [John], of T. & [Edward] Singleton, millers, mention, 346
Taylor, ——, settler in American Bottom, 1801, 357
Taylor, John, lawyer, of Peck (Jas H) & Taylor, 426.
Taylor, Meg, mention, 265 n
Taylor, Gen Zachary, expedition against British and Indians at Rock Island, 409, mention, 248 n.
Tecumseh, sketch, 403, and Gen Harrison, 404-5, mention, 76, 264 n.
Teel, Levi, one of Gen. Clark's soldiers, 339, anecdote of, 340-1; mention, 215
Tell, William, mention, 307
Tennessee, settlers from, 300, 354, 360, 418, singular condition of, 311, mention, 110, 114, 189 n, 197, 270, 311, 385, 413 n, 418 n
Tennessee River, 129, 311.
Terre Haute, Ind , mention, 244, 423
Teter, Abraham, settler of 1804, 336,
Teter, John, settler at Horse Prairie before 1810, 201, settler of 1797, 313; mention, 237
Teter, Solomon, mention, 336
Texas, mention, 21, 174, 236 n, 426
Thames, battle of, reference, 86
Theankeki, see Kankakee, 32
Theel (see Teel, Levi), entitled to land-grant, 424, 425
Thomas, Judge Jesse Burgess, sr , del to Congress, 365; judge, 261 n, 365, 371; resident of Prairie du Rocher, 369, notice, 401-2, sketch, ib n, builds first wool-carding mill in Illinois, 289 n, mention, 362

Thomas, John, of St. Clair, clerk of Ill. Terr'y council, 367, colonel, 289 n.
Thomas, Richard Symmes, mention, 401 n
Thompson [James and Archibald] family, mention, 352
Thompson, Charles, secretary of Continental Congress, 119
Thompson, John B. [P], settler about 1804, 356
Thompson, Rev Sam'l H , sketch, 268-9
Three-River Settlement, Canada, 363
Three Rivers, Canada, mention, 225.
Tiffin, Gov. Edward, surveyor-gen'l, 331.
Timon, Rev John D , mention, 302 n
Tindale, Robert, settler of Randolph Co., 1804, 356.
Tippecanoe, battle of, mention, 21
Todd, David, and descendants, 143-4 n
Todd, Edward, entitled to land-grant, 425; mention, 201
Todd, Hannah, marries Rev Rob't Stuart, mother of John Todd Stuart, 143 n
Todd (——) & Hay (John), mention, 224, 227
Todd, Rev. John, uncle of Col John Todd, 143 n.
Todd, Col. John, defeat, 88; commandant of Illinois, 98, 107, death, ib ; organizes government of Illinois, 143-4; see Edward G Mason, 175 n
Todd, Dr. John, brother of Mrs N. W Edwards and Mrs A Lincoln, his descendants, 143 n
Todd, Gen Levi, notice, 143 n.
Todd, Rob't S , and Illinois descendants, 143-4 n
Todd, Thomas, entitled to land-grant, 425, mention, 201
Todd, Wm , entitled to land-grant, 425
Tolin, Hester, marries Rob't Lemen, 411 n
Tolin, Mrs ——, sister of Joseph Ogle, mention, 258
Tom, Mr (Thomas Brady), 89.
Tombigbee River, mention, 56, 65
Tonnawanto Creek, mention, 31
Tonty (Tonti), Henry de, lieutenant of LaSalle's expedition, 30, in possession of Fort Creve-Cœur, 34, abandons it, 35; in command of Illinois country for 21 years, 39-40, mention, 31, 33, 36, 37, 41, 305
Towles, Judge Thomas, notice, 402.
Tradewater Creek, Ky , mention, 285, 286
Trail, Mrs Mary, mention, 300 n.
Trail, Mary Francis, marries Col Milton Moore, 300 n
Trail, Samuel, mention, 300 n
Trail, Maj Xerxes F., marries Mary McRoberts, 300 n.
Tramble, Amable, mention, 362 n
Tramble, François, mention, 362 n.
Tramble, Louis, mention, 362 n

Trammel, Philip, member of Illinois Territorial Legislature, 1812, 368, and 1814, 393; settler at Salines, 390
Transylvania University, 301 n, 302 n, 370 n, 372, 393, 397 n
Travis, Rev John, first circuit-preacher in Missouri, 267
Treaty of Greenville, mention, 200, 277.
Treaty of Madrid, mention, 220
Treaty of Portage de Sioux, 229
Trent's, Capt Wm., company surrenders to French, 63
Trinity River, LaSalle assassinated at, 39
Trotier, August, mention, 355
Trotier, Joseph, settles in Cahokia, 1775, 108, trades with New Orleans, ib ; mention, 362 n
Trotier, Mary, marries Vital Jariot, 362 n.
Trout, Jackson, mention, 265 n.
Troy, mention, 197
Troy, Ill., mention, 405
Trudeau, Zenoe [or Zenon], commandant at St Louis, anecdote of, 266
Tunaca, Indian, mention, 80
Turgion, Nicholas, mention, 355.
Turkey-Foot, Pottawatomie chief, 280
Turkey Hill, description, old name, 205, settlers, 206, settlement, 337, mention, 315
Turkey-Hill Scott, see Wm Scott
Turner, James, killed by Indians, 154
Tuttle, Dr Trueman, early physician, sketch, 359
Twelve-Mile Prairie, old name, 19
Twigtwees Indians, killing of, 62
Two Rivers, mention, 248
Tyler, President John, mention, 248 n.

U

Union County, representatives and senators, 387 n, 389, mention, 273, 386
Union Grove, Ill., mention, 269
Uniontown, Penn, mention, 373
United-States Biographical Dictionary, quotations from, 411-2 n.
United-States census, 1774, 120
United-States land-system, 145-6
United-States rangers of Illinois, services, 383, reference, 240, 416
University of Kentucky, mention, 387 n
Ursins, Marc Antoine de la Loire des, secretary of Company of the West, 46

V.

Valentine, Dennis, early miller, 355
Valentine, Geo, mill owner about 1798, 176, settler near Bellefontaine, 205.
Valentine, John, mention, 362 n
Valentine, Louisa, mention, 362 n.
Vallis, John, anecdote of, 342-3.

VanBuren-Harrison campaign, 279.
VanBuren, Martin, mention, 301.
Vance, John, manufacturer of salt, 110.
Vandalia, capital of Illinois, 384, mention, 370 n, 381, 411
Vanhoozer, [Abraham ?], mention, 357
Vanlavingham [Vanlandingham, Oliver C. ?], settler at Shawneetown, 390
VanMeter, John, murdered by Indians, 280, 314
VanSwearengen, Thos., bravery of, 163-4.
Varnum, Jas Mitchell, U.-S. judge, 156
Varnum, Sarah, marries Moses Lemen, 412 n
Vaundreuil-Cavagnal, Pierre François de Rigaud, Marquis de, governor of La., 59, leads expedition against the Chickasaws, 64-5, transferred to Canada, 65.
Vermilion County, Ill., mention, 110.
Vermont, mention, 329, 330
Vicksburg, Miss., siege of, reference, 415 n
Vigo, Col. François, sent to reconnoitre Fort Sackville, 101, sketch and portrait, 423, lived at Vincennes, 291, mention, 305, 307
Villiers, Neyon de, a French officer, captures Fort Necessity, 63.
Vincennes, Ind., first settlement, 53, name, 58; abandoned by Brit. troops, 97, under America, 98, recaptured, 100-6, disunion meeting at, 1786, 219, capital of Indiana Territory, 293, 401 n, land-office, 351, mention, 80, 81, 87, 88, 109, 124, 128, 139, 170, 171, 173, 244, 269, 281, 290, 291, 304, 325, 327, 343, 363 n, 364, 365, 385
Vincennes, Chevalier Jean Baptist Bissot, Sieur de, fame, 57; burnt to death by Indians, 58, gave name to town of Vincennes, Ind., ib., mention, 305.
Vincennes trace, 108, 263 n
Virginia, people called by Indians "Long Knives," 92, Virginia legislature creates county of Illinois, 98, without means to pay troops, 107, cedes to U. S. her public domain, 145; population, 1774, 120, settlers from, 235, 236, 238, 255, 259, 260, 264 n, 267, 271, 328, 329, 336, 337, 358, 368, 411 n, 412 n, 417, soldiers of, who settled in Illinois, 339, mention, 79, 83, 91, 102, 130, 143 n, 265 n, 269 n, 336 n, 368 n, 418 n, 420
Virginia, Ill., mention, 289 n
Voisin, ———, youth of sixteen, leads French on retreat, 58.
VonPhul, Henry, merchant of St Louis, mention, 334.

W.

Wabash County, representatives and senators, 413 n.

INDEX. 457

Wabash Indians, mention, 80, 98, 198, 219
Wabash River, mention, 19, 20, 27, 77, 80, 102, 124, 140, 199 216, 244, 293, 306, 327, 343, 364, 385
Waddle family, mention, 357
Waddle, Alexander, entitled to land-grant, 425
Waddle, David, settler of 1786, 256; entitled to land-grant, 425
Waddle, David, jr, tomahawked and scalped, recovered, 154
Waddle, Jesse, entitled to land-grant, 425
Wales, settlers from, 170
Walker, George E, sketch, 418
Walker, Rev Jesse, sketch, 267-8.
Wallace, Dr. ——, early physician, 359
Wallace, David (written Wallis), entitled to land-grant, 424
Wallace, Mrs Wm. S, mention, 143 n.
Wallis, see Wallace.
Walnut Hills, mention, 279
Walsh, Robert, of Philadelphia, publisher, 166
Walter's Ferry, Tenn., mention, 278
War, see Black-Hawk War
War of 1812, in Illinois, 405-9; reference to, 140, 141, 149, 163, 167, 190, 248-9, 264 n, 320, 353, 354, 361, 368 n, 378, 381, 382, 397 n, 403, 416; see Battles
War, Mexican, reference to, 263 n, 265 n, 289 n, 300 n, 328, 387 n, 397 n, see Battles
War of the Rebellion, reference, 139 n, 263 n, 264 n, 265 n, 379 n, 385 n, 387 n, 398 n, 414 n, 415 n, 418 n, see under Illinois Volunteers, see Battles
War of the Revolution, reference, 185, 199, 260, 276, 301, 328, 342, 373, 397 n, 413 n 417 n; see Battles
Ward, Ensign [Edward], mention, 63
Ward, Samuel, member of Continental Congress, mention, 120
Ware, George (written Wear), entitled to land-grant, 424, 425
Washburne, Elihu Benjamin, mention, 189 n, 309 n
Washburne, Mrs. E B (Adèle Gratiot), 309 n
Washington City, 181, 247 n, 279, 301 n, 373, 396
Washington County, Ill, mention, 164, 167, 263 n, 264 n, 265 n, 270, 336 n, 372, 379 n, 400 n
Washington Co., Ky, mention, 397 n
Washington Co, Mo, mention, 171, 426
Washington County of Northwestern Territory, mention, 156
Washington, George, sent to Logstown, 63, skirmish with French, surrenders Fort Necessity, ib; mention, 23, 83, 84, 120, 121, 155, 156, 203, 220, 271, 277, 291, 326, 328, 375, 417 n.

Washington, Ill., town of, laid out, 181, mention, 182, name changed to Horse-Prairie Town, 184
Washington, Pa, town of, mention, 300 n
Waterloo, Ill, proprietors of, 374, mention, 114, 131, 177, 255, 300 n, 320, 346, 373, 386 n, 400 n
Watts, James, entitled to land-grant, 424.
Watts, Rob't, entitled to land-grant, 425
Wayne, Gen Anthony, storming of Stony Point, 95, 183, treaty with Indians, 84, 153, 203, 206, successful campaign, 200, 218, mention, 21, 87, 95, 183, 277
Wayne County, representatives and senators, 413 n, mention, 336 n
Wear, George, see Ware
Weai, Hardy, entitled to land-grant, 425
Weastown, mention, 343
Weiser, Frederick, entitled to land-grant, 425.
Wells, Hayden, or Haydon, entitled to land-grant, 424, mention, 215
Wentworth, Hon John, mention, 301 n
Wesley, John, mention, 263.
West family, sketch, 417
West, Benjamin, mention, 417 n
West, Benjamin Hillary, notice, 418 n
West, Benjamin J, notice, 418 n
West, Benjamin J, jr., notice, 418 n
West, Edward M, notice, 418 n.
West, Emanuel J., clerk Madison-County court, 362
West Indies, mention, 47, 111.
West, Isaac, entitled to land-grant, 424
West, John, and his descendants, 417 n
Westmoreland Co., Penn, mention, 269
West Point, mention, 309 n
West (Edward M) & Puckett (Wm R), mention, 418 n
West Stockbridge, Mass, mention, 330
West, Tilghman Hillary, notice, 418 n
West, Washington, notice, 418 n
West, Washington, notice, 418 n.
Western Pioneer and Baptist Standard Bearer, reference to, 254 n
Wheeling, Va. mention, 255, 271.
Whetstone, ——, mention, 236
White County, name, 391
White, H C, jr, of Tenn, mention, 372
White, Isaac, U-S agent at Salines, 390; notice, 390-1
White, James, killed by Indians, 153
White, John, of Kentucky, speaker of U.-S. Congress, mention, 372.
White, Layton, entitled to land-grant, 425
White, Leonard, settler at Salines, 390
White River, Indiana, mention, 244
Whisky drinking, 346
Whistler, John, jr, mention, 247 n.
Whistler, Col William, mention, 248 n
Whitehead, Robert, settler about 1780, notice, 137

458   PIONEER HISTORY OF ILLINOIS.

Whiteside family and its connection, 185-6, mention, 314, 319, 404
Whiteside, Ann, mention, 412 n
Whiteside County, mention, 189 n
Whiteside, Davis, mention, 383
Whiteside, Rev. Jacob, mention, 268.
Whiteside, Joel, settler of Ridge Prairie, 1803, 314, wounded by Indian, 319-20.
Whiteside, John, Revolutionary soldier, 185, Indian scout, 186, entitled to land-grant, 425, mention 185, 190
Whiteside, John D , sketch, 417
Whiteside, Johnson J , lays out town of Washington, Ill., 181; Indian scout, 188
Whiteside, Michael, mention, 189 n
Whiteside, Robert, mention, 383
Whiteside, Sally, mention, 412 n
Whiteside, Sam'l, Indian scout, 186, 188, his company of rangers in War of 1812, 338 n, 406, bravery, 409, made first improvements on Ridge Prairie in 1803, 314
Whiteside [Wm.] Station, location, 255, mention, 131, 175, 176, 185, 187, 188, 190, 315, 320, 377, 417
Whiteside, Stephen, mention, 383.
Whiteside, Thos., killed by Indians, 188
Whiteside, Uel, wounded, 188, marriage, 189, marriage denied, ib. n.
Whiteside, Wm , sketch, 185-90, blooded stock, 344, mention, 416, 417.
Whiteside, William Bolin, marriage, 189; nickname, marriage denied, ib. n; major in Gen Howard's expedition, 408; sketch, 416; reference to his company of rangers, 337 n, 338, ib n, 378, 382, 406, mention, 357
Whiteside, Mrs. William Bolin (Arundel), mention, 189.
Whiteside, William F , entitled to land-grant, 425
Whiteside, William Lot, Indian scout, 186, 188, mention, 412 n
Whiteside, William Young, entitled to land-grant, 425
Whitney, Eli, cotton-gin inventor, mention, 64
Wiggins, ——, settler of 1801, 280
Wiggins' [Samuel] Ferry Landing, mention, 213
Wilcox, Lucinda, marries Thos. F. Rhea, 265 n
Wiley, James, entitled to land-grant, 424, 425
Wilkins, Col. [John], appoints judges for Illinois, 74
Wilkinson's, Gen Jas., expedition against Indians, 198, singular conduct of, 221.
Will, Conrad, manufacturer of salt, 110
Willard [Simon ?], settler about 1804, 356
Willard, Elizabeth, marries Jacob Jolliff, 263 n

Willard, James, mention, 264 n
Williams, Capt. John, commands forces at Kaskaskia, 98
Williams', Capt. Harrison, company in Black-Hawk War, 414 n
Williams, J. H , mention, 336 n
Williams, John, entitled to land-grant, 424
Williams, Reece, mention, 263 n
Williamsburg, N Y , mention, 247 n
Williamsburg, Va , mention, 91
Williamson County, Ill , representative, 387 n.
Wilson, Alexander, member of first Illinois Territorial Legislature, 368, sketch, descendants, ib. n.
Wilson, Maj. Bluford, solicitor of treasury, 368 n
Wilson, Caroline Gilbert, marries Arthur M. Kinzie, 248 n.
Wilson, Harrison, sketch, 368 n.
Wilson, Maj. Henry S., mention, 368 n.
Wilson, James, entitled to land-grant, 425
Wilson, Gen James Harrison, mention, 368 n
Wilson, John Andrew, mention, 368 n
Wilson, John Lush, mention, 248 n
Wilson, Marie E. (Whipple), mention, 248 n
Winchester, Solomon H , reference to trial, for murder of, 301 n
Windham, N Y , mention, 253 n
Windsor, see Wiser.
Winn, Thos , entitled to land-grant, 425
Winnebago Indians, French name for, locality, habits, no connection with other tribes, 20, mention, 212, 213, 251, 309
Winstanley's, Capt. John, company in Black Hawk War, mention, 288 n.
Wirt, William, mention, 367.
Wisconsin, mention, 19, 21, 138, 139, 141, 145, 259, 337 n
Wisconsin River, mention, 26, 28, 33, 150
Wiser, Peter, settler about 1806, 356.
Woddle, see Waddle
Wolcott, Dr Alexander, mention, 247 n
Wolf, Rev. George, notice, 390
Wolfe, Gen. James, mention, 155, 246.
Wood, ——, mention, 386 n.
Wood, Chas , entitled to land-grant, 425
Wood-River, colony, 354, 364, mention, 190, 405, 409.
Woodford Co , Ky., mention, 205
Worley, James, killed by Indians, 1789, 160
Worley, Joseph, settler of 1785, 255, entitled to land-grant, 424, 425
Wright, Capt. Toliver, killed by Indians, 407; see Right.
Wycoff, William, entitled to land-grant, 424
Wythe, Geo , mention, 91

Y.

Yankee Prairie, mention, 193
Yates, Richard, governor, mention, 385 n, 400 n; resignation as United-States senator, 387 n
Yazoo River, mention, 56
York District, S C, mention, 398
Yorktown, siege of, reference, 156, 300 n

Young, Rev Benjamin, anecdote of, 162; first circuit preacher in Illinois, 260-1
Young [François], killed by Indians, 408.

Z.

Zeisberger, Rev. David, missionary to Indians, 18
Zenobe, Father, see Membre

NOTE.—In the preparation of the foregoing index and notes, we acknowledge our indebtedness to HIRAM WILLIAMS BECKWITH, Danville, Ill.; FREDERIC LOUIS BILLON and OSCAR W COLLET of St Louis, Mo, LYMAN C DRAPER, Madison, Wis; the late Judge JOSEPH GILLESPIE, Edwardsville, Ill, JOHN HENRY GUNN, Springfield, Ill; W. D HIXON, Maysville, Ky, SAMUEL MORRISON, jr, Indianapolis, Ind, Dr JOHN FRANCIS SNYDER, Virginia, Ill; R M. STIMSON, Marietta, O; and to ALBERT DAVID HAGER, FREDERICK A. HUNT, Rev HENRY CLAY KINNEY, EDWARD GAY MASON, WM FREDERICK POOLE, Mrs. E B WASHBURNE, and JOHN WENTWORTH, Chicago.

G H F.

Chicago. Dec 10, 1886

BIBLIOLIFE

Old Books Deserve a New Life
www.bibliolife.com

Did you know that you can get most of our titles in our trademark **EasyScript**™ print format? **EasyScript**™ provides readers with a larger than average typeface, for a reading experience that's easier on the eyes.

Did you know that we have an ever-growing collection of books in many languages?

Order online:
www.bibliolife.com/store

Or to exclusively browse our **EasyScript**™ collection:
www.bibliogrande.com

At BiblioLife, we aim to make knowledge more accessible by making thousands of titles available to you – quickly and affordably.

Contact us:
BiblioLife
PO Box 21206
Charleston, SC 29413

Made in the USA
Charleston, SC
13 October 2010

1	**The Pioneer History of Illinois containing The Discov** 111767794X

Billing Address:
Returns Dept.
360 concord st suite 304
Charleston SC 29401 US

Shipping Address:
Christine A. Crawford
PO BOX 10
DYERSVILLE IA 52040-0010 US

Your Order of 10/13/2010 10:55:10 PM (Order ID 12372107)

Qty	Item

IN THIS SHIPMENT

OCT 2 0 2010

BookSurge
7290 Investment Drive B
North Charleston, SC 29418

1673